Praise for net books™

In bookstores now!

NetGames

NetGames is a guide to playing games online, finding opponents, learning strategies, and discovering tips and cheats. *NetGames* covers thousands of hot games, including AirWarrior, Cyberstrike, Doom, and Bolo.

ISBN 0-679-75592-6
US: 19.00/Canada:$25.50/UK: £17.49 Net

NetTrek

NetTrek charts the amazing world of *Star Trek* in Cyberspace. *NetTrek* includes more than 400 pages detailing Trek-related online forums, chat areas, newsgroups, mailing lists, Websites, sound and picture archives, plus episode guides for all the series.

ISBN 0-679-76186-1
US: $19.00/Canada: $25.50/UK: £17.49 Net

NetChat

NetChat describes more than a thousand places in Cyberspace where people meet to pursue romances, have netsex, or just chat the night away. *NetChat* covers sex spots, fan clubs, political talk, identity forums, gay life discussions, support groups, and ethnic bulletin boards.

ISBN 0-679-75814-3
US: $19.00/Canada: $25.50/UK: £17.49 Net

NetSports

NetSports is a guide to sports news, game and player stats, sports talk, team sites, and fan clubs in Cyberspace. *NetSports* covers more than 60 sports, from football, baseball, and basketball to rugby, frisbee, and paintball.

ISBN 0-679-76187-X
US: $19.00/Canada: $25.50/UK: £17.49 Net

NetMoney

NetMoney takes you into the world of cyberinvestments, taxes, banking, and budgeting. It is the first personal finance guide to the vast financial resources now available online, from buying a car to paying for college to getting the most out of Quicken.

ISBN 0-679-75808-9
US: $19.00/Canada: $25.50/UK: £17.49 Net

NetTech

NetTech is your guide to the tech speak, tech info, and tech support on the information highway. It also includes information on product news, user groups, and software resources. *NetTech* is geared to all platforms, product brands, and user levels.

ISBN 0-679-76054-7
US: $19.00/Canada: $25.50/UK: £17.49 Net

NetGuide—2nd Edition

NetGuide—The Second Edition is the only guide that covers the Internet, America Online, Prodigy, and CompuServe, plus Usenet, the Web, gophers, FTP sites, mailing lists, and chat channels. At more than 800 pages, *NetGuide II* is the most comprehensive guide in Cyberspace.

ISBN 0-679-76456-9
US: $27.95/Canada: $39.00/UK: £25.99 Net

NetMusic

NetMusic describes the new world of online music, from rock to techno to jazz to opera. Find chat groups, discographies, and photos of your favorite artists, plus concert information, fan clubs, and hundreds of sound clips. *NetMusic* is your guide to the sound of music in Cyberspace.

ISBN 0-679-76385-6
US: $19.00/Canada: $25.50/UK: £17.49 Net

Coming soon!

Fodor's NetTravel

Fodor's *NetTravel*—from Fodor's and the creators of *NetGuide* and the Net Books Series—tells you how to find the best online travel sites. Find your way to brilliant travelogues and wonderful travel secrets—plus subway maps, restaurant and hotel guides, movie listings, and train schedules.

ISBN 0-679-77033-X
US: $19.00/Canada: $25.50/UK: £17.49 Net

NetGames 2

NetGames 2 is the all-new, updated addition of the original bestseller. It contains more than 4,000 games, including Doom, Marathon, Heretic, and Myst, a special guide to MUDs, MUSHes, and MOOs, plus demos, tips, and free upgrades!

ISBN 0-679-77034-8
US: $22.00/Canada: $30.00/UK: £20.49 Net

NetMarketing

NetMarketing is the first book that spells out strategies for how corporate marketers and mom-and-pop businesses can use the Net to powerful advantage. It includes hundreds of successful Websites, a primer for getting started, and a directory of more than 1,000 marketing sites.

ISBN 0-679-77031-3
US: $22.00/Canada: $30.00/UK: £20.49 Net

Now Net Books Pocket Guides!

NetJobs

NetJobs tells you how to take advantage of the Iway to land the job you've always wanted. It includes the email addresses of over 1,000 companies, special tips for '96 college grads, and a complete directory of online classifieds, help wanted, and job notice boards.

ISBN 0-697-77032-1
US: $12.95/Canada: $17.95/UK: £11.99 Net

NetTaxes '96

NetTaxes '96 tells you how to file your tax returns electronically and get an instant refund! Find out where to get forms online (for offline filing too!), where to get questions answered online, and where to get tax-savings tips online.

ISBN 0-679-77035-6
US: $12.95/Canada: $17.50/UK: £11.99 Net

NetVote

NetVote is a handbook for following the '96 Presidential Campaign online. *NetVote* takes the user to all the places where the political pros and the media elite hangout. It gives the user access to the same news sources that the news media uses. In fact, with *NetVote* you can be your own political reporter, lobbyist, consultant, and voice of reason (or nut case). Which party does the NetGeneration align itself with? We'll let you know which cover sells best.

ISBN 0-679-77028-3
US: $12.95 paper/Canada: $17.50/UK: £11.99 Net

Instant

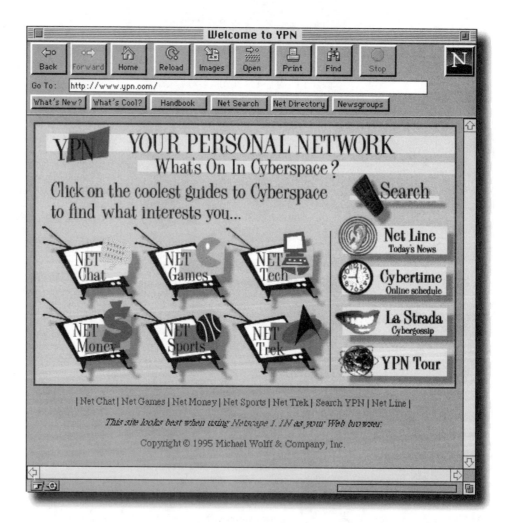

Visit our Web guide at

Updates.

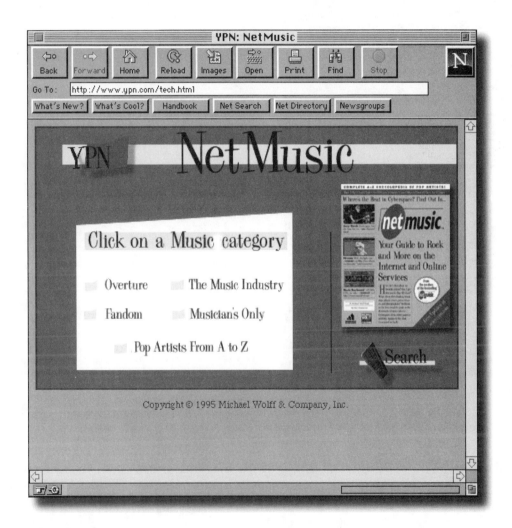

http://www.ypn.com/

Your Complete Guide
to Rock and More on the
Internet and
Online Services

A Michael Wolff Book

By Ben Greenman

For free updates visit our Website at http://www.ypn.com/

RANDOM HOUSE
ELECTRONIC PUBLISHING

MICHAEL
WOLFF
& COMPANY
PUBLISHING

New York

The Net Books Series is a co-publishing venture of Michael Wolff & Company, Inc., 1633 Broadway, 27th Floor, New York, NY 10019, and Random House Electronic Publishing, a division of Random House, Inc., 201 East 50th Street, New York, NY 10022.

NetMusic has been wholly created and produced by Michael Wolff & Company, Inc. *NetGames*, *NetChat*, *NetMoney*, *NetTech*, *NetTrek*, *NetSports*, NetHead, NetSpeak, and CyberPower are trademarks of Michael Wolff & Company, Inc. All design and production has been done by means of desktop-publishing technology. The text is set in the typefaces Garamond, customized Futura, Zapf Dingbats, Franklin Gothic, and Pike.

Published simultaneously in the U.S. by Random House, NY, and Michael Wolff & Company, Inc., and in Canada by Random House of Canada, Ltd.

0 9 8 7 6 5 4 3 2 1

ISBN 0-679-76385-6

Trademarks

New York   Toronto   London   Sydney   Auckland

A Michael Wolff Book

Michael Wolff
President and Editor in Chief

Kelly Maloni
Executive Editor

Ben Greenman
Managing Editor

Jeff Hearn
Art Director

Senior Writer: Kristin Miller

Associate Editor: Mary Goodwin

Assistant Editor: Cathryn Majkowski

Editorial Administrator: Shaun Witten

Editorial Assistants: Deborah Cohn, Donna M. Spivey

Assistant Art Director: Eric Hoffsten

Production Assistants: Rob Hardin, Linda Pattie

Copy Editors: Jonathan Gregg, Jill Rappaport, Elizabeth Upp

Contributing Writers: Richard Gehr, Joshua Greenman

Vice President, Marketing: Jay Sears

Online Director: Jonathan Bellack

Technical Assistant: Patrick Vanderhorst

Web Illustrator: Cynthia Dauzier

Special thanks:

Random House Electronic Publishing—Charles Levine, Tracy Smith, Tom Willshire,
Terry Chisholm, Patricia Damm,
Jennifer Dowling

Alison Anthoine

Peter Ginsberg at Curtis Brown Ltd.

And, as always, Aggy Aed

The editors of *NetMusic* can be reached at Michael Wolff & Company, Inc., 1633 Broadway, 27th Floor, New York, NY 10019, or by voice call at 212-841-1572, fax at 212-841-1539, or email at editors@ypn.com.

Contents

Part 4. Genres

Part 5. The Music Industry

Part 6. Musicians Only

Contents

Appendices

FAQ

"Frequently Asked Questions" about the Net and NetMusic

1. What is the Net, anyway?

The Net is the electronic medium spawned by the millions of computers networked together throughout the world. Also known as Cyberspace, the information highway, the IWay, or the Infobahn, the Net comprises four types of networks—the Internet, a global, noncommercial system with more than 30 million computers communicating through it; the commercial online services, such as America Online, Prodigy, CompuServe, and eWorld; the discussion groups known as Usenet that traverse the Internet; and the thousands of regional and local bulletin board services (BBSs). More and more, the Internet unites all the diverse locations and formats that make up the Net.

2. What can music fans do on the Net?

You can join a fan club, trade tapes, find rides to concerts, and publish transcriptions of your favorite lyrics. You can publicize your band. You can download sound clips of new song releases. You can read concert and album reviews. You can exchange thoughts and song interpretations with other fans or even email your favorite artists. You can search through databases of music trivia and discographies. You can research almost any artist imaginable, from Otis Redding to Henry Rollins to Bonnie Raitt to The

Rolling Stones. You can collect high-quality images of celebrity musicians (and thousands of unknown artists). You can read the world's most famous music magazines or the newest underground music e-zines. You can scan the charts, get tour schedules, and learn how to play the drums. You can lose yourself in a new medium and a new world.

3. I'm game. What do I need to get started?

A computer and a modem, and a few tricks to find your way around.

4. Can you help me decide what computer and modem I'll need?

If you've bought a computer fairly recently, it's likely that it came with everything you need. But let's assume you have only a bare-bones PC. In that case you'll also need to get a modem, which will allow your computer to communicate over the phone. So-called 14.4 modems, which transfer data at speeds up to 14,400 bits per second (bps), are standard. You should be able to get one for less than $100. But 28,800 bps modems are fast replacing them. Next, you need a communications program to control the modem. This software will probably come free with your modem, your PC, or—if you're going to sign up somewhere—your online service. Otherwise, you can

---

ONLINE SERVICES

America Online:
- 800-827-6364 (voice)
- Monthly fee: $9.95
- Free monthly hours: 5
- Hourly fee: $2.95

CompuServe:
- 800-848-8199 (voice)
- Monthly fees: $9.95 (standard), $24.94 (value)
- Free monthly hours: 5 (standard); 20 (value)
- Hourly fee: $2.95 for baud rates up to 14,400 (standard); $1.95 (value)
- Email: 70006.101@compuserve.com

eWORLD:
- 800-775-4556 (voice)
- Monthly fee: $8.95
- Free monthly hours: 4
- Hourly rates: $2.95
- Email: askeac@eworld.com

Prodigy:
- 800-PRODIGY (voice)
- Basic Plan: $9.95/month includes 5 hours of access; $2.95 each additional hour
- Value Plan: $14.95/month includes unlimited core time plus 5 hours of access to plus services (Internet and chat); $2.95 each additional hour
- 30/30 Plan: $29.95/month includes 30 hours of access; $2.95 each additional hour

buy it off the shelf for under $25 or get a friend to download it from the Net. Finally, you'll want a telephone line (or maybe even two if you plan on tying up the line a couple of hours per day). And if that's still not good enough, you can contact your local telephone utility to arrange for installation of an ISDN line, which allows data to be transmitted at even higher speeds. It's not as expensive as you'd think.

5. What kind of account should I get?

Y ou'll definitely want to be able to get email; certainly want wide access to the Internet; and probably want membership on at least one online service.

Here are some of your access choices:

Email Gateway

This is the most basic access you can get. It lets you send and receive messages to and from anyone, anywhere, anytime on the Net. Email is quickly becoming a standard way to communicate with friends and colleagues. (Yesterday: "What's your phone number?" Today: "What's your email address?") Email gateways are often available via work, school, or the online services listed here.

Online Services

Priciest but often easiest, these services have a wealth of options for the cyber-traveler. Commercial services are cyber city-states. The large ones have more "residents" (members) than most U.S. cities—enough users, in other words, to support lively discussions among their membership, and enough resources to make a visit worthwhile. They generally require their own special start-up software, which you can buy at any local computer store or by calling the numbers listed in this book. (Hint: Look for the frequent starter-kit giveaways.) AOL, CompuServe, and Prodigy all provide access to many of Usenet's more than 10,000 newsgroups, and through email you can subscribe to any Internet mailing lists. Fairly recently, the three most popular commercial services—America Online, CompuServe, and Prodigy—took a large step toward the Internet by offering full access to the World Wide Web (WWW); America Online is even incorporating links to Websites in its own forums. The cyberwalls are tumbling and the easy-to-use online services are making the Internet accessible to millions of technophobes.

Internet Providers

There are a growing number of full-service Internet providers (which means they offer email, Usenet, FTP, IRC, telnet, gopher, and WWW access). In practical terms, the Internet enables you to read the online version of *Rolling Stone*, attend a live conference with U2 or Michael Jackson, argue with Courtney Love on Nirvana newgroups, search a database of lyrics, and shop at Tower Records. A dial-up SLIP (serial line Internet protocol) or PPP (point-to-point protocol) account is the most fun you can have through a modem. It is a special service offered by most Internet providers that gets you significantly faster access and the ability to use point-and-click programs for Windows, Macintosh, and other platforms.

BBSs

BBSs range from mom-and-pop, hobbyist computer bulletin boards to large professional services. What the small ones lack in size they often make up for in affordability and homeyness. In fact, many users prefer these scenic roads over the info highway. Many of the large BBSs are as rich and diverse as the commercial services. BBSs are easy to get started with, and if you find one with Internet access or an email gateway, you'll get the best of local color and global reach. You can locate local BBSs through the Usenet discussion groups alt.bbs.lists and comp.bbs.misc, the BBS forums of the commercial services, and regional and national BBS lists kept in the file libraries of many BBSs. See the BBS list in the back of the book for more information. Once you've found a local BBS, contact the sysop (system operator) to inquire about the echoes (or conferences) you want. These are the BBS world's equivalent of Usenet newsgroups. With echoes, you're talking not only to the people on your particular BBS, but also to everyone else on a BBS that carries the echo (in other words, a universe of millions). Even if the discussion of your choice is not on their board yet, many sysops are glad to add an echo that a paying customer has requested. Many, if not most, local BBSs now offer Internet email, as well as live chat, file libraries, and some quirky database, program, or directory unique to their little corner of Cyberspace.

Direct Network Connection
Look, Ma Bell: no phone lines! The direct network connection is the fast track of college students, computer scientists, and a growing number of employees of high-tech businesses. It puts the user right on the Net, bypassing the phone connections. In other words, it's a damned sight faster.

6. By the way, exactly how do I send email?

With email, you can write to anyone on a commercial service, Internet site, or Internet-linked BBS, as well as to those people connected to the Net via email gateways, SLIPs, and direct-network connections.

Email addresses have a universal syntax called an Internet address. An Internet address is broken down into four parts: the user's name (e.g., mary), the @ symbol, the computer and/or company name, and what kind of Internet address it is: **net** for network, **com** for a commercial enterprise—as with Your Personal Network (ypn.com) and America Online (aol.com)—**edu** for educational institutions, **gov** for government sites, **mil** for military facilities, and **org** for nonprofit and other private organizations. For instance, the associate editor of this company, who is never, ever mistaken for her twin sister, would be mary@ypn.com.

7. What about the Web?

The World Wide Web is a hypertext-based information structure that now dominates Internet navigation. The Web is like a house where every room has doors to every other room—or, perhaps more accurately, like the interconnections in the human brain. Words, icons, and pictures on a page link to other pages that reside on the same machine or on a computer anywhere in the world. You have only to click on the appropriate word or phrase or image—the Web does the rest. With invisible navigation, you can jump from a live chat session with other Prince fans to an archive of Beatles photos to a list of Aretha Franklin's accomplishments. All the while you've FTPed, telnetted, gophered, and linked without a thought to case-sensitive Unix commands or addresses.

Your dial-up Internet provider undoubtedly offers programs to access the Web. Lynx and WWW are pretty much the standard offerings for text-only Web browsing. Usually you choose them by typing **lynx** and **www** and then **<return>**. What you'll get is a "page" with some of the text highlighted. These are the links. Choose a link, hit the return key, and you're off.

If you know exactly where you want to go on the Net and don't want to wade through Net directories and indexes, you can type a Web page's address, known as a URL (uniform resource locator), many of which you'll find in this book. The URL for The Rock and Roll Hall of Fame Website, for example, is **http://www.rockhall.com**. On some Web browsers, such as the current version of Netscape, "http://" is not required. In our example, you could type **www.rockhall.com**.

8. What about graphical Web browsers? What are these things?

With the emergence of new and sophisticated software like Netscape (http://www.netscape.com), the Web is starting to look the way it was envisioned to—pictures, icons, and appetizing layouts. Some commercial services, most notably America Online and Prodigy, have even developed customized Web browsers for their subscribers; if you subscribe to one of these services, head to the Internet forum for instructions on how to get this software and how to get on the Web. Web browsers are more than just presentation tools. Most of them allow Netsurfers to see all kinds of Net sites through a single interface. Want to read newsgroups? Need to send email?

Interested in participating in real-time chat? You can do it all with your browser. And many Internet providers, including Prodigy, allow subscribers to build their own Web pages.

9. And these newsgroups?

T he most widely read bulletin boards are a group of some 10,000-plus "newsgroups" on the Internet, collectively known as Usenet. Usenet newsgroups travel the Internet, collecting thousands of messages a day from whoever wants to "post" to them. More than anything, the newsgroups are the collective, if sometimes Babel-like, voice of the Net—everything is discussed here. And we mean *everything*. Was Kurt Cobain murderered? Is hip-hop subversive? Who's playing at the Blue Note in Greenwich Village on Saturday? While delivered over the Internet, Usenet newsgroups are not technically part of the Internet. In order to read a newsgroup, you need to go where it is stored. Smaller BBSs that have news feeds sometimes store only a couple dozen newsgroups, while most Internet providers and online services offer thousands. (If there's a group missing that you really want, ask your Internet provider to add the newsgroup back to the subscription list.)

The messages in a newsgroup, called "posts," are listed and numbered chronologically—in other words, in the order in which they were posted. Usenet is not distributed from one central location, which means that a posted message does not appear everywhere instantly. The speed of distribution partly depends on how often providers pick up and post Usenet messages. For a message to appear in every corner of the Net, you'll generally have to wait overnight.

You can scan a list of messages before deciding to read a particular message. If someone posts a message that prompts responses, the original and all follow-up messages are called a thread. The subject line of subsequent posts in the thread refers to the subject of the original. For example, if you were to post a message with the subject "That Batman song is bewitching" in alt.music.seal, all responses would read "Re: That Batman song is bewitching." In practice, however, topics wander off in many directions.

Popular newsgroups generate hundreds of messages daily. To cut back on repetitive questions, newsgroup members often compile extensive lists of answers to frequently asked questions (FAQs). Many FAQs have grown so large and so comprehensive that they are valuable resources in their own right, informal encyclopedias (complete with hypertext links) dedicated to the newsgroup's topic. This is especially true in the music world; there are hundreds of FAQs devoted to specific artists and styles of music.

10. Mailing lists?

Mailing lists are like newsgroups, except that they are distributed by Internet email. The fact that messages show up in your mailbox tends to make the discussion group more intimate, as does the proactive act of subscribing. Mailing lists are often more focused, and they're less vulnerable to irreverent and irrelevant contributions. As a result, they are an incredible resource for the online music fan—if you're looking for a fan community and Usenet newsgroups don't suit your tastes (too big! too inclusive!), make a beeline for the world of mailing lists.

To subscribe to a mailing list, send an email to the mailing list's subscription address. Often you will need to include very specific information, which you will find in this book. To unsubscribe, send another message to that same address. If the mailing list is of the listserv, listproc, or majordomo variety, you can usually unsubscribe by sending the command **unsubscribe <listname>** or **signoff <listname>** in the message body. If the mailing list instructs you to write a request to subscribe ("Dear list owner, please subscribe me to…"), you will probably need to write a request to unsubscribe.

Once you have subscribed, messages are almost always sent to a different address than the subscription address. Most lists will send you the address when you subscribe. If not, send another message to the subscription address and ask the owner.

11. And telnet, FTP, gopher? Can you spell it out?

Telnet:

When you telnet, you're logging on to another computer somewhere else on the Internet. You then have access to the programs running on the remote computer. If the site is running a library catalog, you can search the catalog. If it's running a BBS, you can chat with others logged on. Telnet addresses are listed as URLs, in the form **telnet://domain.name:port number.** A port number is not always required, but when listed it must be used.

FTP:

FTP (file transfer protocol) is a method of copying a file from another Internet-connected computer to your own. Hundreds of computers on the Internet allow "anonymous FTP." In other words, you don't need a unique password to access them. Just type "anonymous" at the user prompt and type your email address at the password prompt. The range of material available is extraordinary—from lyrics to images to sound clips to videos! Since the advent of Web browsers, Netsurfers can transfer files without using a separate FTP program. In this book, FTP addresses are listed as URLs, in the form **ftp://domain.name/directory/filename.txt.** And passwords aren't required with Web browsers.

Gopher:

A gopher is a program that turns Internet addresses into menu options. Gophers can perform many Internet functions, including telnetting and downloading files. Gopher addresses throughout this book are listed as URLs, with all necessary steps chained together as pieces of a URL.

12. So, how does the book work?

If you know what kind of information or entertainment you need, turn to the *NetMusic* index, where every subject and site in the book is listed alphabetically. Of course, you can browse *NetMusic* at your leisure—the book is divided into six sections:

- Overture
- Fandom
- Artist Guide
- Genres
- The Music Industry
- Musicians Only

Overture collects general music resources, including reference works, magazines, charts, radio stations, and stores. **Fandom** focuses on the relationship between artists and audiences, with lists of tour dates, archives of lyrics, information on rock memorabilia, and a special section devoted to bootleg and tape-trading culture. The **Artist Guide** sits at the core of the book, collecting thousands of sites devoted to hundreds of pop artists in every sub-genre imaginable—from classic rock stars like The Doors and The Who to new blood like Bush and Alanis Morissette. Artists with especially large online fan bases are awarded special Spotlight sections that detail the resources and excerpt fan discussion. **Genres** moves through the various styles that make up modern popular music, from rock to punk to soul to reggae to New Age to hip-hop to opera. **The Music Industry** reviews the business of music-making, with resources pertaining to managers, agents, studios, and even a large section on record labels. **Musicians Only** demonstrates how the Net can be instrumental in helping musicians learn their craft, buy and sell their equipment, and talk to other guitarists, pianists, and violinists.

All entries in *NetMusic* have a name, description, and address. The site name appears first in boldface. If the entry is a mailing list, "(ml)" immediately follows; if a newsgroup, "(ng)."

After the description, complete address information is provided. A red check mark (✓) identifies the name of the network—Internet, Usenet, or a commercial service provider. When you see an arrow (→), this means that you have another step ahead of you, such as typing a command, searching for a file, subscribing to a mailing list, typing a Web address (also known as a URL, or Uniform Resource Locator). Additional check marks indicate that the site is accessible through other networks; an ellipsis indicates another address on the same network; and more arrows mean more steps.

If the item is a Website, FTP site, telnet, or gopher, it will be displayed in the form of a URL to type on the command line of your Web browser. If the item is a mailing list, the address will be an email address followed by instructions on how to subscribe (remember—the address given is usually the subscription address; in order to post to the mailing list, you will use another address that will be emailed to you upon subscribing). An entry that includes an FTP, telnet, or gopher address will provide a log-in sequence.

In a commercial service address, the name of the commercial service is followed by the site's keyword (also called "go word" or "jump word"). Additional steps are listed where necessary.

IRC addresses indicate what you must type to get to the channel you want once you've connected to the IRC program.

Entries about newsgroups are always followed by the names of the newsgroups.

In addition, there are a few special terms used in addresses. **Info** indicates a supplementary informational address. **Archives** is used to mark collections of past postings for newsgroups and mailings lists. And **FAQ** designates the location of a "frequently asked questions" file for a newsgroup.

13. I love music, but what if I want to branch out and investigate other topics?

Try *NetGames*, *NetChat*, *NetMoney*, *NetTrek*, *NetSports*, *NetTech*, and the second edition of the best-selling *NetGuide*. And keep an eye out for *NetTaxes* and *NetTravel*—they're coming soon.

Part 1

Overture

First notes

Taking a first step into the wealth of music resources online is a little like taking a first

step onto the surface of the moon—you need to forget everything you know, everything you are, because the near-total transformation of your mind, body, and spirit will leave you unrecognizable to yourself. On second thought, maybe it's nothing like that. But it's still pretty amazing. From gigantic resources like the **All Music Guide Forum** and the **Internet Underground Music Archive** to online chat corners (America Online's **Center Stage**, **The CompuServe Auditorium**, Prodigy's **Music 1 BB**, and Usenet's **rec. music.misc**), the Net is filled with places to learn about artists, take notes on musical styles, study musical history, and talk to other fans about the albums that changed your life.

IUMA, the Internet Underground Music Archive—from http://www.iuma.com/

On the Net

Across the board

All Music Guide Forum Sponsored by the creators of the *All Music Guide*, a reference guide with information on thousands of musicians, this forum is one more area for fans to discuss their favorite musicians and musical styles. Unlike the usual gossip and zealous ravings of music fans, this discussion is more information-oriented ("Please ID this song—Who's the artist who sang 'The Ballad of Lucy Jordan?'" "What years did Otis Redding record?"). ✓**COMPUSERVE**→*go* amgpop

Fan Club Forum Music fans flock to this forum to discuss, investigate, and gossip about their musical idols. They come to report Elvis sightings, to speculate about Cobain death plots, to describe getting Elton John's autograph, to review an Annie Lennox concert, and to discuss the Janet-Michael duo, among other things. Sections are set up for fans of Queen, Aerosmith, Rick Springfield, Barry Manilow, Elton John, Madonna, Live, Pearl Jam, Chicago, and several other artists and groups. (If your favorite group doesn't have its own section, just hang around for a while and holler a lot—section topics are not fixed in stone.) And in the libraries, fans can download Chris Isaak tour dates, a biography of Jimi Hendrix, a Madonna screen saver, Barry Manilow sound clips, an FAQ about Queen, and other musical artifacts. ✓**COMPUSERVE**→*go* fanclub

Internet Underground Music Archive One of the most impressive sites in Cyberspace, IUMA creates Web pages for a number of labels, from the tiny (Blue Goat) to the humongous (Warner Bros.), as well as designing home pages for individual bands and housing a number of e-zines. You'll have to register, but, once you do, you'll be privy to a cornucopia of popular music resources. Divided into four sections—Bands, Record Labels, Publications, and What's Brewin'—the Bands section is by far the biggest, with Web pages for more than 600 independent artists. Visitors can either use the search field to locate a specific band or choose a genre—say, rhythm and blues—and browse. Band (or individual artist) pages include audio clips, pictures, profiles, and a section for comments and reviews. The Record Labels section includes more than 20 labels that use the Web pages to announce new releases, publicize artist tour dates, link to their artists' Web pages, and even sell from their catalogs. And when you need to take a break from the hype and self-promotion of the band and record label pages, head for the music e-zines resident on IUMA. The half-dozen or so publications available offer critical reviews, interviews, music news, and a lot of attitude. To stay on top of musical events at IUMA and elsewhere on the Net, check in regularly to the What's Brewin' section. If you're still overwhelmed, take the guided tour. And take it without shame—this place is really that big! ✓ **INTERNET**→*url* http://www.iuma.com/

Music & Bands Buried in the middle of the Entertainment Drive Forum, the Music & Bands topic is home to a small group of fans who come to weigh in on the musical issues of the day. Has Courtney Love ever been photographed topless? Has Mariah Carey had her ears pierced? Has Weezer vocalist/guitarist Rivers Cuomo been accepted to Harvard University? ✓ **COMPUSERVE**→*go* eforum→Messages *and* Libraries→Music & Bands

Music/Arts Forum For the most general music chat and resources on CompuServe, visit the Music/Arts Forum, where posts range from the rumor of a Lou Reed/Neil Young collaboration ("The Needle and the Monotone?") to an announcement of a Jelly Roll Morton tribute album to an analy-

sis of Bach's cantatas. The board is divided into dozens of discussion and library sections, including The Blues, Opera, Dance, Religious Music, Classical Music, and Pop/Rock. Pick up Nirvana pictures, Beethoven sound clips, and artist FAQs in the libraries. ✓ **COMPUSERVE**→*go* musicarts

MusicBase Links to labels like Deconstruction, MCA, and Polydor as well as some spectacular Websites for assorted bands such as Radiohead, the Beastie Boys, and Live. ✓ **INTERNET**→*url* http://www.elmail.co.uk/music/

rec.music.info (ng) A central repository for the music FAQs, music announcements, and general-interest music lists such as the Internet Music Wantlists or the list of music mailing lists. ✓ **USENET**→rec.music.info

Rock Web Interactive No, this is not another long list of links to music sites on the Net. Sponsored by Silicon Forest Media, it's more like a mini-magazine, with features on music festivals, interviews with activist musicians, a regular

music critic and gossip (House of Boo), an area to discuss music (From the Hip Chat), and a section for music-related videos and illustrations (Artists). But the real attraction is the Bands section. Like a page out of a high-school yearbook, the section opens with little pictures of a dozen or so bands tagged with mini-descriptions (Tantrums— "We're not exactly the happy-go-lucky Carpenters or even Sonny and Cher from hell"). Click on the band name for a bio, a calendar of performances, album advertisements, merchandise for sale, information on sending the band email or joining a mailing list, and other features depending upon what the band makes available. These are the bands to watch, we're told; keep checking in to see how they're doing and what other bands are up and coming. ✓ **INTERNET**→*url* http://www.rockweb.com/rwi/

Rolling Stone Forum *Rolling Stone* magazine sponsors a forum with discussion areas on hip-hop, country, R&B, rock and roll, alternative, and metal—but keep in mind that alternative rules the

Music from the old country—http://www.elmail.co.uk/music/

board the way that *Beavis & Butt-head* rule the minds of our nation's youth. Fans post reviews of the concerts they went to last night, discuss the annual Lollapalooza festival (anyone else agree that Sonic Youth blew everyone away at this year's tour?), and speculate about upcoming tours and albums. They also seek the truth. In the pursuit of musical truths, for instance, Peggy declares KISS a "bad as hell" band. Jeff takes offense. Enter Mike, who tries to broker peace: "I'm assuming that when she said they were Bad, she meant that to say that she liked them, as in they are good." While band and genre debates garner the most messages here, the Rolling Stone Forum also features discussions on Gonzo journalism, e-zines, tickets, and national affairs. You can interact with the *Rolling Stone* editors—just post a message or comment on the Ask the Editor board. The library isn't humongous, but it carries photos (including dozens of *Rolling Stone* covers), sound clips, music newsletters, and more. ✓ **COMPUSERVE**→*go* rsforum

The Vibe Former MTV veejay Adam Curry left the network to register mtv.com, which became Metaverse after a flap with his former employer. Metaverse serves as the Internet headquarters for several high-profile events, some musical (the Grammy awards) and some not (the NFL Draft), and it also has a number of more specific rock resources; grouped in its Vibe section, they range from music reviews to celebrity interviews to columns. Metaverse comes to the Web world courtesy of a number of corporate sponsors, including Sprint, Reebok, Scotch, Zima, and NEC. ✓ **INTERNET**→*url* http://meta-verse.com/vibe

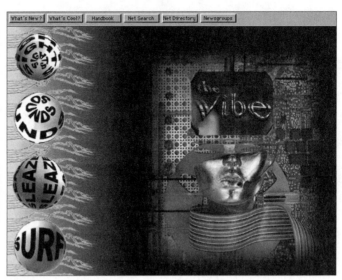

Adam Curry's sweet revenge—from http://metaverse.com/vibe

Chat

Center Stage More than 35,000 AOL members at once can attend Center Stage events (5,000 in each of seven auditoriums), and, since the forum hosts the biggest names in show biz, the music industry, or politics, its auditoriums fill to capacity. On any given evening, a supermodel might be chatting with AOLers in one auditorium while a senator fields questions in another, and a star athlete in another. And, like Carnegie Hall in New York or Hammersmith Odeon in London, Center Stage consistently draws big-name guests: Mick Jagger, Ice-T, Cheap Trick, the Doors (excepting, of course, deceased Lizard King Jim Morrison), Billy Joel, and many, many more. Visit the huge archives for transcripts of past events and publicity photos of the guest stars. ✓ **AMERICA ONLINE**→ *keyword* centerstage

The CompuServe Auditorium Imagine full-length, live concerts on the Net. You can't get tickets to these yet, but you can go to the CompuServe Auditorium with thousands of other CompuServe members to interview famous bands and musical artists. Events are scheduled regularly. ✓ **COMPUSERVE**→*go* auditorium

Music 1 BB Prodigy has about two million subscribers, all of whom seem to hang out on this message board talking about alternative rock, dance music, oldies, the Grateful Dead, grunge, metal, R&B, techno, and other popular music. While most pop genres have their own topics on the Music 1 BB, the lion's share of activity occurs in the four topics dedicated to artists and bands (Alternative Rock A-K, Alternative Rock L-Z, Rock Music A-K, and Rock Music L-Z). In these areas, mini-fan clubs have sprouted up with loyal members checking in regularly to discuss their favorite artists—from Aerosmith to Frank Zappa. And artists and bands actually visit the board; Prodigy invites them (post your requests in the Guest Wish List topic), opens up a topic for

them, and lets Prodigy members ask them questions. The board also has topics reserved for chart news, concert tour information, music biz news, and tape trading. ✓**PRODIGY**→*jump* music 1 bb

Music 2 BB Fans of musical genres that fall outside the scope of pop convene to chat about jazz, a capella, folk, classical, contemporary Christian, reggae, gospel, world music, and more. From the serious ("Are Dylan's live performances any good anymore?") to the less-than-serious ("Okay, everybody, let's hear it—what do you all think of B. B. King's new commercial for blue M&M's?"), Prodigy members chat about all things musical. ✓**PRODIGY**→*jump* music 2 bb

Prodigy Chat Prodigy's live chat area revived the dying online service. Members were given an area in which to hold live meetings, flirt with each other, and attend major events with big-name stars. How big? Ever hear of a certain pop singer named Michael Jackson? Check the calendar for a schedule of upcoming events. But you don't need a star to take advantage of the area; click "Prodigy Chat" and then select "Music" for a selection of rooms in several musical genres. ✓**PRODIGY**→*jump* chat

rec.music.misc (ng) Mack's announcing a new music Web page, Jack's objecting to a review he read in rec.music.reviews, dozens of people are participating in a discussion about song titles with female names ("Gloria," "Michelle," "Lucy in the Sky With Diamonds," "Peggy Sue," "Good Golly Miss Molly," "Mustang Sally," "Martha My Dear"…), Ned's announcing the creation of a mailing list for Suede fans, radio stations are posting their playlists, and polling companies are posting music charts. You've entered the chaotic world of rec.music.misc. Anything music goes. ✓**USENET**→ rec.music.misc

Facts & info

Music FAQs The Rolling Stones have an FAQ. R.E.M. has an FAQ. Billy Joel has an FAQ. Industrial music has an FAQ. The acronym stands for frequently asked questions. But, in many cases, an FAQ becomes more than a list of questions and answers. It grows to include near-comprehensive coverage of a subject. Music FAQs often include background information about artists, contact info for studios, guides to other online resources, explanations of lyrics, discographies, and more. FAQs are conveniently archived together at these sites. If the artist or musical topic you're looking for doesn't have an FAQ at these sites, it doesn't mean there isn't one. Just keep looking. ✓**INTERNET** …→*url* http://www.cis.ohio-state.edu:80/text/faq/usenet/music/top.html… →*url* http://american.recordings.com/WWWoM/ubl/faq_list.shtml

Rockmine Archives You can shop here for music and memorabilia, but if you're not in a spending mood, don't be scared away— you don't have to buy anything to enjoy this site. Instead of scanning the Beatles Memorabilia Set Sale List, you could read a transcript of a 1984 interview with the Doors; instead of shopping for rare vinyl, CDs, and cassettes, you could read one of several articles on the Rolling Stones or take a rock trivia quiz. And when you've had your fill of music information, you can learn how to become a genuine Scottish Laird (as in Lord). No, really. ✓**INTERNET**→*url* http://www.wintermute.co.uk/rockmine/

"Well, it now looks like a single standard has been agreed upon for the next generation CDs, the so-called (if Toshiba gets its way) 'High Density Discs.' These can hold around 4 Gb (with compression), compared to the 660 Mb that the current standard-conforming CD holds. I'm wondering what this means for future music issues. Even without compression, the new discs can hold about 4x what todays discs can. This means you can put around 280 minutes of music on one disc--the equivalent of most 4CD boxed sets, or an old-style 7 record set (think: Beethoven's nine symphonies on one CD)."

"Or the record companies can start packaging videos in with the album (for those lucky enough to be able to afford the new generation compact disc/laserdisc players): Consumers still only get one disc; Record companies have an excuse to charge more for it."

-from **rec.music.misc**

Music indexes

You read about one great music site in a fanzine. A friend tells you about another. Then

you find a third, and a fourth, and a fifth. There's so much music information in the online world, in fact, that someone should write a book. (Hmm…now there's an idea.) But until someone does, the only way to catalog old sites and keep abreast of new ones is to pay close attention to Websites like the **Web Wide World of Music**, commercial service resources like AOL's **A Tribute to Rock and Roll**, and vital documents like the **List of Music Mailing Lists**.

Scream shot—screen shot from America Online's Tribute to Rock and Roll

Across the board

Addicted to Sounds Most indexes divide their sites neatly into categories like bands, lyrics, commercial sites, etc. Not this one. This index isn't even big or comprehensive. Instead, it's an interesting collection of sites grouped into categories like "Links to Good Musicians" (musicians who have done benefit concerts) and single listings that range from the Rock and Roll Hall of Fame to the Band Name Server. ✓ **INTERNET**→ *url* http://www.mindspring.com/~labrams/a2sound.htm

Andy's Music Links A small collection of 50 or so links to music sites. So, who's Andy? ✓ **INTERNET**→ *url* http://oss.cit.cornell.edu/Andy/links/musiclinks.html

A Tribute to Rock and Roll The tribute is more of a souped-up index to America Online's music resources than a site with original content. It pulls together music resources from across AOL, including some that have been created specifically for the tribute. FedEx, for instance, has developed a series of guides to the "top rock and roll cities" with dining, lodging, shopping, sightseeing, and night life information for each city. The only question is whether the extras that you probably wouldn't be able to get to from other parts of the service (the Name That Tune Contest, the live NTN Rock and Roll Trivia, the FedEx travel guides, etc.) are worth the time to download the hundreds of new graphics for the site. Probably not. ✓ **AMERICA ONLINE**→*keyword* rock and roll

BLAM The Big List of Artists and Music isn't huge, but it is big. It's

an index to online music resources with links to sites for bands, audio clips, lyrics, newsgroups, and musical types (e.g., reggae, gothic, industrial). What's listed and what's not appears arbitrary: the Bob Dylan FAQ is listed; the James Taylor FAQ is not. With the exception of the band sites, all links feature a brief description. ✓ **INTERNET**→*url* http://www.primenet.com/~virogen/blam!.html

The English Server Music Pages A collection of music sites divided into categories such as criticism, theory, performance, composition, and journals. Although this is slightly more highbrow in tone than the other indexes, we expect that many of the same music resources that are indexed on other sites will eventually find their way here. ✓ **INTERNET**→ *url* http://english-www.hss.cmu.edu/music/

Ever Expanding Web Music Listing Like most music indexes, this one begins with links to several generic sites, and then proceeds to a band-specific section. Ever expanding, the site also includes links to mailing list home pages, music reviews, record-label sites, regional music sites (radio stations, local garage bands, etc), radio playlists, e-zines, and other publications. Special attention is given to electronic music here, with entire sections devoted to digitized music on the Net, and ambient/techno/trance/rave Websites. **/INTERNET**→*url* http://woof.music.columbia.edu/~hauben/music-index.html

Global Electronic Music Marketplace Music fans have needs. They need albums, CDs, videos, and other music memorabilia. And they'll pay to get these items, although discounts are always welcome. If they're online, they also expect sound clips, pictures, reviews, discographies, artist Web pages, fan discussion groups, and other Internet music resources. At GEMM, one search generates listings for both types of needs. A search for Neil Young, for instance, retrieves several dozen merchandise and online listings, including a used *Harvest* LP for only $5 and the Neil Young mailing list, which you can click and join. The site can also be searched for Internet resources only. **/INTERNET**→*url* http://192.215.9.13/Flirt/GEMM/gemm2.html

The Hub An annotated list of music resources online. The list is divided into musical genres, record labels, magazines and news, and other music services. **/INTERNET**→*url* http://www.cris.com/~Schankmn/hub.html

Iceblink's Music Page The au-thor of this Web page (that's Iceblink to you) likes to listen to "beautiful female vocals" and his Web page is an index to sites for many of his favorites, including the Cocteau Twins, Colder than Death, the Rose Chronicles, Lush, Aneli Drecker, the Sundays, and the Cranberries. Along with links to several other groups, the page also links to an index of industrial music sites. **/INTERNET**→*url* http://www.suba.com/~iceblink/music.html

Internet Music Resource Guide A small, disorganized collection of links to music sites. Each link is annotated with a brief description, however, and a "hot site of the week" is a standard feature. **/INTERNET**→*url* http://www.teleport.com/~celinec/music.shtml

Kramer's Korner—Music Kramer (not the one from Seinfeld, not the one from Bongwater) likes hard rock, and so his page links to artists like Queensrÿche, Van Halen, Alice in Chains, Nirvana, and Pearl Jam. But for those with different tastes, Kramer also links to several of the biggest music indexes on the Web—from the Ultimate Band List to the Musical Web Connections—and also features links to guitar resources and online music stores. **/INTERNET**→*url* http://mars.superlink.net/user/jkramer/music.html

The LEO MUSIC Archive This archive in Germany carries charts, lyrics, MIDI utilities, photos of artists and bands, archives about the Woodstock festivals, and links to other sites. **/INTERNET**→*url* http://www.leo.org/archiv/music/music_e.html

Library of Musical Links This elegant site breaks music resources down into Websites, FTP sites, mailing lists, gophers, newsgroups, and image libraries. And, yes, you can search it by subject as well. It's certainly not the largest music index on the Net, but its collection of Websites and newsgroups rivals the big boys'. And, ahh, the simplicity. One drawback: The image library, with only a few dozen images, is something of a disappointment. **/INTERNET**→*url* http://www.scf.usc.edu/~jrush/music/index.html

List of Music Mailing Lists More intimate than most newsgroups and more social than Web pages, mailing lists are the Net's closest thing to a fan club. Members of mailing lists share rumors and concert information, speculate

The Big List of Artists and Music—http://www.primenet.com/-viro gen/blam!.html

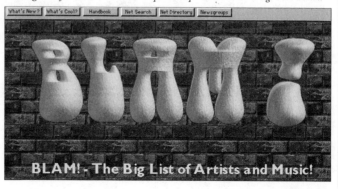

Music Indexes Overture

Library of Musical Links—http://www-scf.usc.edu/~jrush/music/index.html

about the meaning of lyrics or the release date on a band's next album, psychoanalyze favorite musicians, and become friends with other list members based on their musical interests. There are hundreds of Internet mailing lists about artists and musical genres, and the maintainer of the List of Music Mailing Lists regularly verifies the addresses of these lists and offers complete subscription info for fans trying to join them. With hundreds of band lists, dozens of genre lists, and a list for virtually every musical instrument (bagpipes, even). This site will provide every music lover with his or her own special form of satisfaction. ✓ **INTERNET** ...→*url* http://server. berkeley.edu/~ayukawa/lomml. html ...→*url* ftp://ftp.uwp.edu/ pub/music/misc/mail.lists.music

The Mammoth Music Meta-List Maintained by *Vibe* magazine's online editors, the index is easy to navigate. Just choose a subject—lyrics, reviews, music festivals, radio stations, or Irish music—and the server will return links to sites. With the exception of the artist listings, which are sketchy, the rest of the index offers an amazing number of resources. ✓ **INTERNET**→*url* http://www.path finder.com/vibe/mmm/music. html

Music Part of the World Wide Web Virtual Library, this music index is large but also random. Some of the links are annotated with brief descriptions; most are not. The index breaks down into classical music, programs and instruments, artists, big catalogs (general resources), FTP archives, and "other interesting links" (record companies, university music departments, radio stations, etc.). ✓ **INTERNET**→*url* http://syy. oulu.fi/music.html

The Music AXIS Page An elegant index of music sites with brief annotations, Music AXIS is divided into four sections—research resources that include other indexes, reference guides, and genre-specific sites, such as rock pages; music newsgroups sorted by name, category, and artist; a mammoth A-to-Z guide to band home pages; and more than a dozen online record stores. ✓ **INTERNET**→*url* http://www.tiac.net/users/mpao lini/music.html

Music Free for All Although now part of another index (the Web Wide World of Music), this site was one of the original music indexes on the Web. Although normally disorganization thwarts an index, it can be offset by a playful presiding spirit, and that's the case here. It's like a college ride board with announcements for Websites tacked up—"#250 How about an R.E.M. page?" or "#251 Creamed corn? No thanks. How about the Beastie Boys Home Page?" View the list either with images or without. ✓ **INTERNET**→*url* http://american.recordings.com/ WWWoM/mfree/mfree.html

Music Hall Music Hall doesn't look very impressive, but don't be deceived—CompuServe's offerings include Rolling Stone Online, the All-Music Guide, several music forums with message boards for fan discussions, music stores, MIDI forums, and much more. ✓ **COMPUSERVE**→*go* music

Music Ready Reference Not as comprehensive as it could be, but a good starting-off point. The directory lists five or six links under each heading: categories include general, instruments, audio systems, classical, country, folk, jazz, rock/popular, and world music. ✓ **INTERNET**→*url* http://ipl.sils.umich. edu/ref/RR/ENT/Music-rr.html

Music Resources on the Internet The package shouldn't be everything, but in this case the wrappings are so bad that the site suffers significantly. This large index to music sites isn't illustrated with graphics, but it doesn't really need them. There isn't much annotation, but that's not essential. The organization, however, is baffling. Hundreds of sites are organized into divisions such as Academic Sites with Music Related Information (the Jazz Improvisation Page is listed here), User Maintained Music Information (the Dutch Jazz Music Page is listed here), Geographically Local Sites (U.K's Alternative Music Scene page is listed here), etc. In a world where dogs were classified as Mammals, cats as Slightly Cuter Mammals, and frogs as Animals That Aren't Mammals But Sometimes Steal Food From Mammals' Food Dishes, this might make sense. In this world, it doesn't. ✓**INTERNET**→ *url* http://www.music.indiana.edu/misc/music_resources.html

MusicLand "If music be the food of love, then play on..." So you want to find music on the Internet? It's there, man. It's everywhere. This Web page leads off with comments and critiques of music sites and finishes with a mid-size index of sites, most of which are band pages. ✓**INTERNET**→ *url* http://www.cs.umd.edu/~lgas/music/

MusicSpace AOL's impressive lineup of music companies and media make this one of the hottest music hangouts in Cyberspace. Browse through this month's *Spin* magazine, read the entertainment section of the *New York Times*, download goodies from Warner Brothers and Virgin Records, and shop at Tower Records. Music fans gossip and exchange news in forums run by MTV and ABC, forums dedicated to rock, and even forums exclusively created for Grateful Dead fans. You can also use MusicSpace to get news and record reviews, download pictures and sound clips, and even locate a nearby concert. And while MusicSpace seems to have more than enough music content to keep fans happy, AOL has also built in a directory to Websites on the In-

Web World Wide of Music—from http://american.recordings.com/wwwof music/

ternet. One day soon, MusicSpace might even supplant this book; for now, though, it's the second best music resource in the world. ✓**AMERICA ONLINE**→*keyword* music

NerdWorld Music It's not pretty or comprehensive (pop music had listings for only three Web pages when we checked), but it's a good resource to begin your search for online music sites. Leading off with a list of the biggest and best music sites on the Net, NerdWorld then organizes sites into categories such as Music Reviews, Blues Music, and Classical Music. ✓**INTERNET**→*url* http://www.tiac.net/users/dstein/nw60.html

The Newbie's Guide to Music Divided by musical genre, this selection of links to music sites is designed for Netters who are just beginning to explore music in Cyberspace. ✓**INTERNET**→*url* http://ug.cs.dal.ca:3400/music.html

Randomness An illustrated index of random music Websites that includes the Beastie Boys Home Page, the Frank Sinatra Home Page, and Hip-Hop Lyrics. ✓**INTERNET**→*url* http://www.cs.ucdavis.edu/~swanston/kdvs/current/common/random.html

Web Wide World of Music

With thousands of music sites on the Internet, there are never enough ways to organize them. At least that's the philosophy of this fabulous Website, which breaks sites down into e-zines, charts, discussion forums, directories, band pages, lyric servers, and more. And each breakdown comes with its own series of options. Do you want a complete listing of bands? A listing of bands in a specific genre? A listing of bands with FAQs? However you decide to browse, don't miss the site's Ultimate Band List—one of the best places in Cyberspace for band information. The Web Wide World of Music also lets visitors vote on sites they like and don't like and sponsors live chat sessions with musicians. Check the calendar for events. While the site is designed for ease of navigation, you may get lost here on purpose. It's just that good. ✓**INTERNET**→*url* http://american.recordings.com/wwwof music/

Yahoo's Music Index The index of indexes, the ultimate listing, the only list of music sites you'll ever need...No, it's not an online introduction for James Brown; it's an honest assessment of the power of Yahoo's music listings. ✓**INTERNET**→*url* http://www.yahoo.com/Entertainment/Music/

Music library

What band notched a string of Top 100 hits in the seventies, all the while handicapped-

by a lead vocalist with a devastating drug problem? What seminal rock singer once showed up at the mansion owned by another seminal rock singer, waving a gun and saying "You tell him to come out here and we'll see who's king"? What blues guitarist switched to piano after two of his fingers were shot off in a bar fight? Curious? Sure you are. They may tell you that music is about emotion, but it's also all about facts—anecdotes, statistics, names, and dates. Match artist and art at the **WWW Music Database**; read up on stars and songs at the **All-Music Guide**; probe your tests at **The Similarities Engine**; and then find out where the long road ends at **The Death of Rock 'n' Roll.**

Covering a lot of ground—from http://www.hollywood.com/rocknroll/

On the Net

Across the board

Ron Smith Oldies Calendar
Ron posts a weekly calendar with events from rock-and-roll history marking each day—Elvis sails for West Germany while in the Army in 1958, Paul McCartney is busted for growing pot on his Scottish farm in 1972, George Michael looks in the mirror in 1987 and says to himself "I am so wonderful and talented…but I need a shave." All in an average week… ✓ **INTERNET**→*url* http://www.interaccess.com/users/ronsmith/cal.htm

Who was Born or Died Today? Check the calendar for the names of artists who were born or who died on this date in years past. If you can get beyond the spelling mistakes and the gaps in information, it's a fun site. ✓ **INTERNET**→*url* http://www.leo.org/archiv/music/birthday/

Databases

CD Search You remember Dr. Sardonicus from your parents' record collection, but for the life of you, you can't remember which group recorded the album, and the irritation of forgetting is scratching at the surface of your high. With the magic of the Web, you don't have to remember. Just visit CD Search, enter key words, select categories, and the search engine will retrieve all relevant titles. It's Spirit, in case you were wondering, and it's the *12 Dreams of Dr. Sardonicus.* Now don't you feel better? ✓ **INTERNET**→*url* http://www.btg.com/~cknudsen/query.html

WWW Music Database More than 5,700 albums by more than 2,000 artists; each listing includes catalog numbers, tracks, total playing time, comments, and pertinent Web links. While coverage is spotty, this is one of the best organized databases, and one that allows fans to move quickly from discographies to fan pages. And if your favorite album isn't listed, you can submit a listing with an easy-to-use form. ✓INTERNET→*url* http://www.gcms.com/~burnett/MDB/

Dictionaries

The All-Music Guide Music Dictionary The exploration of musical terminology at this site is broad and thorough, covering technical explanations (de capo to dynamics), general knowledge (Nashville to note), instrument definition (zheng to zither) and more. One warning about this dictionary: broad terms such as "punk rock" get the same aphoristic definition as simple terms like "guitar" and genre-specific terms like "loft jazz." Consequently, you should use this list to define particular terms, not for an overview of genre terminology. ✓INTERNET→*url* http://cdnow.com/

Discographies

An Index of Rock Music Discographies on the World Wide Web An alphabetical listing of links to artist discographies. Some of the discographies are merely plain text listings, while others are more elaborate (click an album cover for a list of songs). Large but not comprehensive. ✓INTERNET→*url* http://www.teleport.com/~xeres/discog.shtml

Wiretap Music Library A sizeable music resource, with discographies for dozens of artists difficult to find elsewhere—John Zorn, Einstürzende Neubaten, Meat Beat Manifesto, Shonen Knife, and more—label discographies, and a large collection of liner notes, FAQs, and rock texts (Kurt Cobain's suicide note, for in-

stance). ✓INTERNET→*url* gopher://wiretap.spies.com/11/Library/Music

Encyclopedias

All-Music Guide In addition to a list of this week's most popular albums and singles, this site offers access to one of the largest music databases in the world, let alone the online world. With hundreds of thousands of albums listed, and thousands of artists catalogued in genres ranging from rock to pop to punk to funk to hip-hop to reggae to classical to jazz to soundtracks to vocals to experimental music, this is a stellar resource, and one that no music fan should ignore. Try to find an artist that's been overlooked—it may take a while. The Website is a discussion forum and informational site for the guide; entries are linked to band descriptions in the CDNow! database. ✓COMPUSERVE→*go* allmusic ✓INTERNET→*url* http://cdnow.com/

Compton's Encyclopedia Information on Rock 'N' Roll *Compton's Encyclopedia* contains a variety of entries on rock stars, musical styles, and events, and it's collected and re-catalogued here. ✓AMERICA ONLINE→*keyword* compton rocks

Entertainment Encyclopedia Who said encyclopedias were dull? This gold mine of entertainment information includes a list of music celebrity horoscopes (Sly Stone was a Pisces; what more information do you need?), a Beatles tour history, Grammy award-winners, and an A-Z listing of pop and rock musicians that includes the release dates for all albums and singles. ✓COMPUSERVE→*go* hhl-249

Gibraltar Encyclopedia of

Progressive Rock and Related Music What is progressive rock? According to the Gibraltar Encyclopedia, everything from ambient to art rock to classical to progressive, from the Canterbury sound to Euro-rock to space fusion. This generous and gigantic reference work includes capsule biographies for hundreds of artists, along with cross-references, and, while the tone is sometimes too informal for those who don't know the genre well, the authors don't skimp on judgment. ✓INTERNET→*url* http://www.cogsci.ed.ac.uk/~philkime/gepr.html

History

The Death of Rock 'n' Roll In addition to excerpting chapters from Jeff Pike's book-length list of dead rock stars—not only Elvis, Lennon, and Cobain, but everyone from Duane Allman to Danny Whitten to Hillel Slovak—this site lists hundreds of dead rock stars, along with date of death, age at time of death, and cause of death. The documents are inventively cross-referenced; Tommy Bolin is listed under both "Heroin" and "Guitar Heroes." Hey hey, my my, rock and roll may never die—but all its practitioners eventually will, and they'll be added to this necrology. ✓INTERNET→*url* http://weber.u.washington.edu/~jlks/pike/DeathRR.html

The History of Rock 'n' Roll Based on the 10-hour Time-Life television series that aired in March of 1995, the sites feature interviews, sound clips, video clips, and pictures of rock legends like Bono, Quincy Jones, Aerosmith, and Little Richard. Listen to a clip of Gladys Knight as she recalls the first time she heard the Beatles. Get a photo of Stevie Wonder. Read Pete Townshend's tale of his confrontation with Jimi Hendrix. The site is more than an advertisement for the series; it's a rock and roll history resource in its own right. ✓**INTERNET**→*url* http://www.hollywood.com/rocknroll/ ✓**AMERICA ONLINE**→*keyword* music →EXTRA→Rock and Roll

Rock-and-Roll Hall of Fame

When Roger Daltrey sang, "Hope I die before I get old," he may have been having a premonition of the Rock and Roll Hall of Fame, the Cleveland-based institution that finally got off the ground with a bang-up concert on September 2, 1995. What is the museum's mission? To preserve the unique cultural heritage of rock and roll—or, if you side with the detractors, to embalm the most vital and spontaneous art form the world has ever known. Should three-minute pure pop singles be placed in the Louvre? Probably not, but that's exactly what's in the Rock and Roll Hall of Fame's Museum—along with dead rock star memorabilia such as Buddy Holly's high school diploma, Jimi Hendrix's handwritten lyrics for "Purple Haze," Big Joe Turner's passport, and Keith Moon's report card. The Rock and Roll Hall of Fame also includes a list of the top 500 songs of all time and a rock archive overseen by the *Cleveland Plain Dealer* that manages to misspell two out of every three names it mentions (Julio Inglesias? Donna Summers? Sheesh). ✓**INTERNET**→*url* http://www.rockhall.com

Lists

Hype! One-Hit Wonder Compilation

A list of artists who made it big on the charts with one hit and were never heard from again. The artist's name, the hit, and his or her fate (when known) are listed. Remember Kim

Carnes's "Bette Davis Eyes," Bonnie Tyler's "Total Eclipse of the Heart," Sugarloaf's "Green Eyed Lady," Patrick Swayze's "She's Like the Wind." They're all here as one-hit wonders. The site links to another page for Near One-Hit Wonders—ever wonder what happened to the Captain & Tenille? Get your Darryl Dragon here. ✓**INTERNET**→*url* http://www.hype.com/nostalgia/onehit/onehitin.html

Recommendations

HOMR Music Recommendation Service Before you buy an album or take an artist into your heart, you can consult with other Netters. HOMR, also known as the Helpful Online Music Recommendation Service, has a community of subscribers who rate albums and pool musical expertise. Members can check in with HOMR to see what others think of artists and albums or they can track their own tastes based on the albums they've rated. ✓**INTERNET**→*url* http://rg.media.mit.edu/ringo/ringo.html

The Similarities Engine It's bound to happen sooner or later. The CD that you just can't listen to often enough, that fits your every mood, is going to become boring. You will need something different. But not too different. Turn to The Similarities Engine— the self-proclaimed "best toy on the Web" to find more customized ear suits. Here's how it works: Simply fill out a Web form and submit the names of five artists and recordings with which you're currently obssessed. Within a couple of days, maybe sooner, you'll be emailed a list of other similar artists and music to try. It's worth a shot. ✓**INTERNET**→*url* http://www.webcom.com/~se/

Trivia

Name That Tune An old game goes high-tech. Download 10 sound clips each week from this site, identify as many as you can, and submit your answers via a Web form. You can submit answers as many times as you want, and only your highest scores are kept. Last week's answers, a ranking of players, and an all-time players' list are maintained. ✓**INTERNET**→ *url* http://www.omg.unb.ca/~glenn/nameThatTune.html

Name That Tune Contest Download the tunes (one file for Mac, one for Windows) each day, choose the "Enter to Win Icon," and fill out the online form with the names of the 10 songs you think are on the sound clip. ✓**AMERICA ONLINE**→*keyword* rock and roll→MORE→Name That Tune Contest

Rock-N-Roll Trivia NTN runs an interactive roll-and-roll trivia contest on America Online. Fifteen questions flash by during each trivia session and members compete against other music fans in the room. ✓**AMERICA ONLINE**→ *keyword* rock and roll→MORE→ NTN Rock Trivia

Tower Trivia Contests "What TWO bands have replaced bassist/vocalist Randy Meisner with Timothy B. Schmit?" Everyday at noon EST, Tower Records posts a trivia question. AOL members have until the following day at noon to answer (Poco and the Eagles, in this instance). If more than one person answers correctly, a winner will be chosen by lottery. And the lucky winner will win a CD sampler. Here's the catch: You can only win once per month! ✓**AMERICA ONLINE**→*keyword* tower →Door #2→Tower Trivia Contests

Charts, polls & awards

Billboard rules the roost, of course, but there are plenty of other polls and charts

out there that track popular singles and albums. Want to know who's rocketing up the **Cash Box Charts** or MTV's **Chart Attack**? Find out for yourself. If you'd rather kneel at the altar of **Billboard's Top 100 Albums**, you can do that, too. And if you're tired of playing cultural xenophobe, stop waving the flag and look at **Korean Top 10 Singles** and the **Dutch Top 40**.

The Hitlist—http://www.cas.american.edu/~todd/hitlist.html

On the Net

Across the board

Charts/News How many singles from Michael Jackson's *HIStory* set will go to Number One? Will Prince ever have another top 10 single? How about Bob Dylan? Prodigy members post their own personal music charts, poll each other about favorite musical genres (pop albums, R&B, dance, etc.), and discuss the Billboard charts. ✓**PRODIGY**→*jump* music 1 bb→Choose a Topic→Charts/News

The Hitlist: Music Charts Home Page The Hitlist should be on everyone's hotlist. The site has managed to compile radio charts and playlists from radio stations nationwide, international charts (The Official Norwegian Singles Chart, Dutch Dance Singles), personal charts regularly posted on dozens of Websites (Andy's Top 15, Steve's Top 10, etc.), and national charts like Rick

Dees' Weekly Top 40 and Casey Kasem's Top 40. The site also sponsors its own chart—The Daily Internet Top 20 Hitlist. How does it work? Each day, or at least fairly regularly, a "music charts freak," the guy who runs this site, calculates the top 20 hits based on more than 60 radio playlists, personal music charts, and other music charts published on the Internet. The names of artists making the Top 20 are then linked to the artist home pages. But The Hitlist: Music Charts Home Page lets you do more than cast a vote for your favorite singles of the week. You can also compete against other music enthusiasts. The Hitlist, the granddaddy of all chart resources on the Net, pits Netter against Netter in a race to see who is best at picking the songs that will rise to the top of the charts. The contest is called Hitpicks. Just send in your picks every week and the site will keep track of how many of them make the top 10 of The Daily Internet Top 20 Hitlist and how

far ahead you picked them. After a few weeks of picks, you will be eligible to be crowned HitQueen or HitKing. And, yes, there's another chart here tracking the best hitpickers. ✓**INTERNET**→*url* http://www.cas.american.edu/~todd/hitlist.html

U.S.

Billboard's Top 100 Albums This weekly chart lists *Billboard*'s Top 100 albums. For each album, the chart tracks the current position on the chart, the positon last week, the position it peaked at, and the number of weeks it's been on the chart. Albums with Websites are linked. ✓**INTERNET**→*url* http://web3.starwave.com/show biz/numbers/

Billboard's Top 40 Singles This weekly chart lists *Billboard*'s Top 40 singles. For each single, the chart tracks the current position on the chart, the position last week, the position it peaked at, and the number of weeks it's been on the chart. ✓**INTERNET**→*url* http://web3.starwave.com/show biz/numbers/

Casey's Top 40 "Dear Casey, I am a high-school student in Alexandria, Virginia. I moved here after my sophomore year, and instantly made friends with the girl who lived next door. Her name was Susan. For months, Susan and I were inseparable—we went to the mall together, we helped each other with homework, we shared clothes and even boys (well, if you can call our chemistry teacher a boy). And then, one day, I came home from band practice and saw a bright light hovering over Susan's house and heard a noise that was more like the sound of Jesus screaming than anything I had ever heard. I passed out, and when I woke up I was in my own bed, my parents standing over me, a cool washcloth on my forehead. They said that Susan had been taken by aliens. I loved her, and now I miss her, and I want to go to whatever planet she's on so that we can shop for shoes again. I can even get cheaper shoes now, because I'm blind from the bright light and can't match colors anymore. Casey, could you please play 'I'm So Sad That You Got Taken By Aliens, Because You Were My Friend' for Susan. Signed, Julie. Well, Julie, this song goes out to Susan, wherever she is." While this site doesn't actually include Long Distance Dedications, it does list this week's Top 40 chart, and includes links to archives of past charts. ✓**INTERNET**→*url* http:// www.magi.com/~menardd/kcla test.htm

Cash Box Charts Links to *Cash Box*'s charts of the Top 100 Pop Albums, Top 100 Pop Singles, Top 100 Country Singles, Top 75

R&B Albums, Top 100 Urban Singles, and Top 25 Rap Singles. If you didn't already know, Cash Box publishes one of the leading entertainment industry trade papers in the country. The online version is available at this site, with features, reviews, news, and, of course, the charts. (Hint: Head to the bottom of the table of contents to find links to the charts.) ✓**INTERNET**→ *url* http://www.silence.net/table cnt.htm

ThE ChaRTs SoundScan calculates and charts weekly over-the-counter record sales in a variety of categories: Hard Music Albums, Independent Releases, and Alternative Albums. Foundations magazine, an industry news source about hard and alternative music, publishes its own charts for hard music albums and singles based on radio play. Each of these charts is available at this site. ✓**INTERNET**→ *url* http://www.webb.com/con crete/charts.html

Chicago's Top Songs The top songs from Chicago this week in the sounds of the fifties, sixties, and seventies. ✓**INTERNET**→ *url* http://www.interaccess.com/ users/ronsmith/no1.htm

Gavin Home Page Gavin publishes a respected weekly print trade magazine with charts, music industry news, and interviews. Excerpts from the publications and the charts are online at this Website. Based on playlists for more than 1300 radio stations, Gavin's music charts come in twelve categories: top 40, rap, urban, A/C (adult contemporary), country, Americana (alternative country), adult alternative (smooth jazz), A3 (album adult alternative), jazz, alternative, college, and Gavin Rocks (based on playlists for college and commercial hard

rock/metal stations). ✓**INTERNET**→ *url* http://www.iuma.com/gavin/ issues/current/inside.html

MTV's Chart Attack Features weekly versions of Tower Records' Top 50 Albums and the *College Music Journal's* Radio Top 50. ✓**AMERICA ONLINE**→*keyword* mtv→ music→Music Matters→CHART ATTACK

Rick Dees' Weekly Top 40 A simple Top 40. Every week Rick Dees counts down the nation's top 40 hits on his syndicated radio show. The number-one hit and the thirty-nine runners-up are listed here. ✓**INTERNET**→*url* http://www. themix.com/ top40.html

Top 30 Albums RockNet's listing of the top 30 CDs and albums in the U.S. ✓**AMERICA ONLINE**→ *keyword* rocknet→Reviews/Charts/ Concertline→Top 30 Albums

Top 30 Singles RockNet's listing of the top 30 singles in the U.S. ✓**AMERICA ONLINE**→*keyword* rock net→Reviews/Charts/Concertline →Top 30 Singles

International

Australian Music Report Weekly charts of Australia's top 10 singles and albums, and several other categories (dance, alternative single, alternative album, hard rock/heavy metal album, country music album, music video, airplay additions, and even the No. 1 Single Five Years Ago). ✓**INTERNET**→ *url* http://www. aussiemusic.com. au/amr/amrchart.html

Bavarian Top 15 An archive of the year's weekly Top 15 chart in Bavaria. ✓**INTERNET**→*url* http:// oberon.informatik.uni-wuerz burg.de/~heuler/topsi/br3top15. html

British Top 40 An annotated list of the 40 most popular records sold in Britain this week. ✓ **INTER-NET**→*url* http://www.glas.apc. org/~yook/ukchart.html

Dutch Top 40 (Rabo) An unofficial page devoted to the Dutch Top 40 singles chart. Updated infrequently. ✓ **INTERNET**→*url* http:// www.sci.kun.nl/thalia/funpage/ top40/top40_en.html

European Top 20 Chart (ml) The weekly European chart, direct from MTV Europe. ✓ **INTERNET**→ *url* eu20-request@a3.xs4all.nl ✍ *Type in message body:* subscribe eu20 <your email address>

Finnish Top 40 Although the list is in Finnish, names like Michael Jackson, Red Hot Chili Peppers, and Alanis Morissette look the same in any language. ✓ **INTERNET**→ *url* http://www.radiomafia.yle. fi/radiomafia/lista.html

Korean Top 10 Singles Seoul music—the top 10 singles in Korea this week. Note: you'll see nothing but ASCII gibberish unless you have the proper font. ✓ **IN-TERNET**→*url* http://www.iworld. net/Entertainment/Gayo/

Latvian Airplay Top 20 The top 20 songs currently playing on Latvian radio; while most of them are English-language versions, you'll find the occasional Saule or Pamatinstinkts record. ✓ **INTER-NET**→*url* http://www.lanet.lv/ news/airplay/new.html

Norwegian Top 10 Singles Chart position, last week's position, and the number of weeks that singles have made the Norwegian Top 10. ✓ **INTERNET**→*url* http://www.cs.uit.no/~toman/ single.html

Internet

rec.music.misc Top Albums Polls And the winner is.... Every December music fans on the Internet vote for their favorite albums of the year. A tradition since 1988 (when *The Travelling Wilburys—Volume 1* took first place), this survey resembles the *Village Voice*'s famous Pazz & Jop poll, except that the voting is done not by paid critics, but by ordinary Netsurfers. Netters cast their ballots for their favorite albums on the rec.music.misc and alt.roc-n-roll newsgroups, and the top 50 albums are posted at the beginning of the new year. If you've missed the vote for this year, you can browse the archives. ✓ **INTER-NET**→*url* http://pscinfo.psc.edu/ ~geigel/Poll_Results/poll_intro. html

Top Hits Online What started as a way for music fans on Prodigy to chart their current favorites has since expanded to include charting info for FidoNet and Internet fans. Each week Netters on all three networks vote for their favorite 15 singles, and a chart listing the top 15 vote-getters is then posted on Prodigy and the Website and sent to members on the mailing list. The voting week ends on Saturday. Charts from weeks past are also archived on the site. ✓ **INTERNET** ...→*email* hits-request@ webcom.com ✍ *Write a request* ...→ hits@webcom.com ✍ *Send in your vote* ...→*url* http://www.web-com. com/~dtobias/hits/ ✓ **PRODI-GY**→ *jump* charts 1bb→Charts/ News→ Top Hitsonline

Indexes

The Chart Index So what are the British listening to? The site carries four official music charts for the UK, including singles, al-

bums, R&B, and dance. Each chart takes a slightly different form. On the Singles chart, listings tagged with an "i" icon include commentary from reviewer James Masterson while the albums chart often includes links to Web pages for the album and the R&B chart links to U.S. R&B charts. ✓ **INTERNET**→*url* http://www.dot music.com/MWcharts.html

ChartAttack A page of music charts from across the world—VH-1 Charts in Germany, FM stations in Canada, and Top 20s lists in Israel and Sweden. ✓ **INTERNET**→*url* http://www.edu. isy.liu.se/~d93andwa/stuff/html/ chart.html

Charts A list of links to European music charts. ✓ **INTERNET**→*url* http://www.si.hhs.nl/~v942317/ um.html

Charts Galore Links to music charts from all over the world—mostly European charts (France, Germany, and Britain), but also Japan, Australia, Canada, and the United States. ✓ **INTERNET**→*url* http://www. dsv.su.se/~mats-bjo/chart.html

Dance Charts Worldwide Montreal's Top 20, the Swedish Dance Chart, the Brazilian Charts, the Asian DJ Coalition Top 40, the German Dance Chart, and several other dance charts are accessible from this site. ✓ **INTERNET**→ *url* http://www.oden.se/~bjorn/ charts.html

Music Charts A menu of *Billboard* music charts including charts for country, R&B, jazz, rap, dance, pop, adult contemporary, European, modern rock, and top concert grossers. ✓ **PRODIGY**→*jump* music charts

Charts, Polls & Awards **Overture**

And the Grammy goes to—http://metaverse.com/grammy

Awards

The 37th Annual Grammy Awards The NARAS (the National Academy of Recording Arts & Sciences) has its finger on the pulse of the mainstream nation. Millions of viewers worldwide tune in to find out which superstars sold the most albums, er, I mean were deemed the most accomplished, talented musicians in their genres. Predicting winners can be complicated, especially when it comes to the enigmatic Best New Artist category—Tiffany? Milli Vannilli? And Whitney Houston, and later Paula Abdul, two years in a row (how's that possible?). The site links to sound and video clips of the winners, album info and bios, archives citing all the winners back to the first show in 1958, and more. ✓INTERNET→*url* http://metaverse.com/grammy/

Awards Keep tabs on the winners and losers in the entertainment world. Prodigy not only reports on the nominees and winners for the Grammys, the American Music Awards, and the Tonys, but it also runs polls on upcoming award ceremonies—e.g., the MTV Video Awards. Photos and sound clips are also sometimes featured. ✓PRODIGY→*jump* awards

MTV's 95 VMA Main Menu As the wet-eyed anime poster-child says: yummm! Links to bios and images for the lucky few—Weezer, T.L.C., and the Jacksons cleaned up. Presenters and a few losers are immortalized with JPEG images in the archives. If you want multimedia material from the Video Music Awards of the past, browse AOL's MTV Online. ✓INTERNET→*url* http://mtv.com/vma/vmamain.html

TNN Music City News Country Music Awards '95 Sponsored by The Nashville Network, the Country Music Awards are the country answer to the People's Choice Awards. This site is currently under constuction, with only a handful of links. ✓INTERNET→*url* http://www.hcc.cc.fl.us/services/staff/dawn/tnnaward.htm

Tony Awards For one night every year, the proles are given a fleeting glimpse of the music legends, the new stars, and the magic that is The Theater. This site gives you all kinds of information on the nominated plays, including cast and crew, synopsis, playbills, reviews, and the other awards. ✓INTERNET→*url* http://artsnet.heinz.cmu.edu/OnBroadway/tony_index.html

OTHER AWARDS

1995 Grawemeyer Award in Music Composition ✓INTERNET→ *url* http://www.louisville.edu/groups/library-www/music/speccoll/adams.html

1995 San Diego Music Awards ✓INTERNET→*url* http://orpheus.ucsd.edu/sdam/awards/

America's Christian Music Awards ✓INTERNET→*url* http://www.ipc.uni-tuebingen.de/art/amg-archive/hyper-94-Sep/0284.html

Austin Chronicle 1994-95 Music Awards ✓INTERNET→*url* http://www.auschron.com/top10.html

BAMMIES Bay area Music Awards. ✓INTERNET→*url* http://sweb.srmc.com/bammies

CMW Online: Awards Canada's Juno Awards. ✓INTERNET→*url* http://www.cmw.com/CMW/awards.html

Contemporary A Cappella Recording Awards ✓INTERNET→ *url* http://lemur.Stanford.EDU/~jbaxter/acd/CARA/

East Coast Music Awards—The Winners ✓INTERNET→*url* http://www.chatsubo.com/ecma/winners/winners.html

Sweden Dance Music Awards ✓INTERNET→*url* http://www.oden.se/~bjorn/sdma.html

Record stores

Downloading free sound clips is great, sure, but when it comes right down to it there's

nothing quite as satisfying as buying records. It's hard to substitute a file transfer for the unequivocal pleasure of feeling the heft of a CD in your hands, removing the shrink-wrap, slicing through the dog bones (that's the butterfly-shaped hologram seal, in case you haven't been to the record store since the days of the long-box), and depositing the disc on your very own player. Cue track one—aren't you getting goosebumps just thinking about it? On-line, shop at megastores (**CDNow!**, **Tower Records**) or ministores (**A B CD**, **Big Bro Records Cyberspace**). And if you're uncertain where to shop, read **Online Music Stores: A Review**, where veteran Netconsumers help newbies navigate the Sargasso of online catalogs, shipping and handling fees, and weeks allowed for delivery.

No broken dreams on this boulevard—from http://www.musicblvd.com

On the Net

Across the board

A B CD New and used CDs, and a searchable CD catalog. Selection is spotty. Frequent customers receive an account number for easy ordering. ✓**INTERNET**→*url* http://

www.iea.com/~abcds/

Allegro Corporations The nation's largest distributor of classical music has a Website, from which they sell jazz, world music, and spoken-word recordings. ✓**INTERNET**→*url* http://www.teleport. com/~allegro/

Big Bro Records Cyberstore European dance music and music-related items. ✓**INTERNET**→*url* http://www.cyber.nl/bigbro/

BMG Music Service Choose from more than 450 selections and start building your record collection today! Pick four CDs free when you join, buy one CD at the regular store price within the next year, and then get these additional free CDs. BMG just wants to please: They promise you'll receive your introductory selection within ten days. After visiting this site, you'll think that BMG stands for "Big Music Giveaway." ✓**COMPUSERVE**→*go* cd

Borders Bookshop Online Order books, music, and books about music. A clickable map of real-world Borders stores is also here. ✓**INTERNET**→*url* http://www. borders.com/borders/

Cassette House Blank cassettes, DATs, and more resources for musicians and songwriters. ✓**INTERNET** →*url* http://www.edge.net:80/ch/

CD Banzai Search a catalog of more than 100,000 domestic CDs and more than 35,000 imports in various genres, and then order them online. ✓**INTERNET**→*url* http://www.lainet. com/~cdbanzai/

CD Land Order online, search a database with the Bullet Express shopping service, and learn about the Bay Area rock scene (venues and studios). ✓**INTERNET**→*url* http://www.cdland.com/cdland/

CD World The self-proclaimed "largest music discount store on the Net," CD World offers a catalog of more than 100,000 CDs and music videos. Shop the catalog by hot list, record title, or artist, and then order online. ✓**INTERNET**→*url* http://www.cdworld. com

CDNow! One of the best online resources for music lovers, CD-Now! is now not only a fully operational record store (with cheap prices, too!), but a gateway to the superlative All-Music Guide, an online resource that offers information and ratings for thousands of albums by hundreds of artists in every genre imaginable. ✓**INTERNET**→*url* http://www.cdnow. com/

Columbia House If you were ever an adolescent with a hunger for new music and a shortage of cash, then you're probably familiar with Columbia House, that mass-market music remanufacturing outfit that sells CDs at prices so low it's almost like giving them away. Now, Columbia House is on CompuServe, offering 10 CDs free when you join—and you only need to buy six more selections in the next three years at regular club prices. If the prospect of getting something for nothing thrills you as much as it did when you were 15 years old, sign right up. ✓**COMPUSERVE**→*go* freecd

EMusic More than 100,000 artists in a wide variety of genres, searchable by song, year, album, and artist name. EMusic also includes special spotlight sections for new releases and top sellers. ✓**INTERNET**→*url* http://www.emusic. com/

The Good Vibe Zone Reggae, soul, jazz, house, jungle, and other releases—mostly on vinyl, but some available on CD. ✓**INTERNET**→*url* http://www. easynet.co.uk/ goodvibe/index.htm

CDNow!'s home page—from http://www.cdnow.com

1? Music/Media More than 100,000 records, not only by established independents, but by unsigned artists as well. ✓**INTERNET**→*url* http://www.icw.com/cd/ imm1.html

Music Boulevard After logging in you can listen to, shop for, and buy from Music Boulevard's catalog of more than 145,000 titles covering a number of genres. ✓**INTERNET**→*url* http://www.musicblvd. com

Music Connection More than 75,000 CDs in a variety of genres, along with a search engine. ✓**INTERNET**→*url* http://www.inetbiz. com/music/

The Music Express A list of selected CDs and an order form that lets you select from more than 20,000 rock, jazz, and classical albums. ✓**INTERNET**→*url* http:// branch.com/cdexpress/index.html

Newbury Comics An online version of the Boston-area alternative music store. ✓**INTERNET**→*url* http://www.newbury.com/

Noteworthy Records If Henry James had ever recorded a rap album, it might have gone something like this: "It had all gone so fast and with such unexpected violence that after the moment of confrontation Rogers turned to his left and spoke to the woman in the black hat—who was also the woman in the red coat—with a poise that bordered on stillness, moving his hands slowly so as not to upset those at the dinner who still remained. 'Step off,' he said. 'This shit is wack.'" And if Henry James had ever recorded a rap album, it might have been sold at Noteworthy Music, an online CD store with a large selection of releases in various genres. ✓**INTERNET**→*url* http://www.netmarket.com/ noteworthy/bin/main

Off the Shelf With more than 100,000 CDs in stock, this online record store has no search function, but you can email an inquiry regarding availability. ✓**INTERNET**→*url* http://empire.na.com/ots/ otshp.html

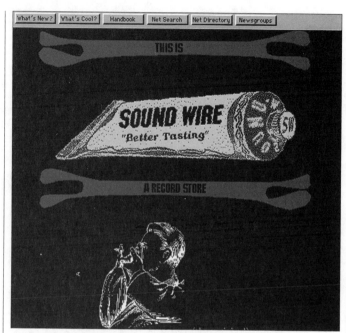

| What's New? | What's Cool? | Handbook | Net Search | Net Directory | Newsgroups |

Sound Wire: A Record Store—from http://soundwire.com/

Pentagon CDs A flashy online record store with wonderful graphics but a rather narrow selection. ✓**INTERNET**→*url* http://www. butterfly.net/pentagon/w

Planet Music Domestic and import releases (almost 150,000 total)—but there's no complete list, so you'll have to email to see if your selection is available. ✓**INTERNET**→*url* http://www.execpc.com/ planet/

PolyEster An Australian email-order store that carries CDs and cassettes in a variety of genres. ✓**INTERNET**→*url* http://www. glasswings.com.au/PolyEster/index.html

Soundwire At a site decorated with nineteenth-century catalog sketches—toothpaste tubes, tight corsets, and the like—this record store carries plenty of vinyl, and includes sound samples, reviews, and purchasing recommendations. ✓**INTERNET**→*url* http://soundwire. com/

That's Entertainment Records Show tunes, show tunes, show tunes! Musicals and collections from this online CD store. ✓**INTERNET**→*url* http://www.dircon. co.uk/ter/

Time Warp Records A large collection of used records, both for sale and for auction. Not for everyone, but if you're looking for a perfect copy of Kim Carnes's *Mistaken Identity* (that's the one with "Bette Davis Eyes" or Clarence Carter's *Touch of Blues*, look no further. ✓**INTERNET** →*url* http://www.vintage.com/ record/

Tower Records Tower Records' Website doesn't allow you to purchase albums online (it lists a toll-free number, 1-800-ASK-TOWER), but Tower on America Online lets you fill a virtual shopping cart with musical goodies, charge them to a credit card, and have them delivered to your home. Both sites showcase a huge online catalog, which is divided into Boxed Sets, Children's Music, Classical, Comedy, Country, Jazz, Soundtracks, Vocals, and Rock/Pop/Hip-Hop. Each category features new albums and old favorites, and prices are competitive with other online stores. Perhaps most importantly, the Tower sites make it fun to browse. ✓**INTERNET** →*url* http://www.shopping2000. com/shopping 2000/tower/aol. tower ✓**AMERICA ONLINE**→*keyword* tower

V2...Archief CDs, LPs, cassettes, books, and video from a Dutch store. ✓**INTERNET**→*url* http://www. vpro.nl/www/arteria/V2onW3/ Archief/ARPage.html

Classifieds

CD, Tapes, Vinyl Classifieds Hundreds of recordings by various artists—from Mannheim Steamroller to Sting to Pearl Jam—are on sale here. Listings give record title, artist, price in U.S. dollars, and the country/state of seller/buyer. The classifieds section also provides information on placing an ad here. ✓**EWORLD**→*go* marketplace →classifieds→CDs, Tapes, Vinyl

Reviews

Online Music Stores: A Review Reviews of major online music stores in Q&A format. The reviews are written by actual shoppers, and even links to all the stores under review, so you can check them out yourself. ✓**INTERNET**→*url* http://www.rpi.edu/~ sellsp/music/reviewhome.html

The music press

The great rock critics—Greil Marcus, Lester Bangs, Greg Tate—are almost as exciting

to behold as the great rock performers, and even a novice wordsmith can be elevated to Andean heights of eloquence by the passions of fandom. A bad album isn't just bad—it betrays everything that rock music has ever been, and everything that rock music will ever be. And a good album isn't just good—it explodes like a volcano, showering the ash of inspiration all over the corrupt Pompeii of traditional rock. Online, rock journalism ranges from the canonical (**Rolling Stone Online, Spin**) to the eccentric (scores of e-zines, including **Dirty Linen, Joey Joey, HYPE Electrazine**, and **Addicted to Noise**). Interested in local scenes? Want to read reviews? Start clicking.

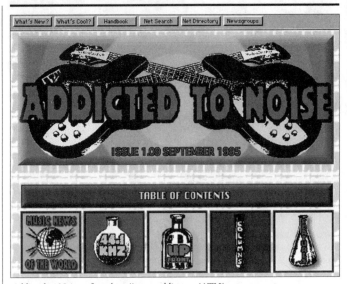

Addicted to Noise—from http://www.addict.com/ATN/

Amateur reviews

Al's Review Archive Al Crawford, an average music fan with a penchant for writing about and rating albums and singles, has written hundreds of reviews and posted them online. This is an archive of his reviews, organized by artist (Nine Inch Nails, the Human League, and the Thompson Twins, to name but a few). ✓**INTERNET**→*url* http://www.dcs.ed.ac.

uk/students/pg/awrc/review/

CapSoul Reviews UnPulped Written and designed by a group of New Yorkers, this mini-mag reviews music performances and new releases (mostly punk). Occasionally, they get sidetracked, though, and write about comic artists, Coney Island, and other things that interest them. Lots and lots of pictures. ✓**INTERNET**→*url* http://www.inch.com/~skeever/

Dens Traffic Jam College student Dennis Narcisco posts short reviews of the CDs (mostly R&B and hip-hop) that he listens to in his car. Not updated very often. ✓**INTERNET**→*url* http://neuromancer. hacks.arizona.edu/~dens/TrafficJam.html

Everyone's a Critic Carries announcements about music jour-

nalism awards and conferences, and reviews of e-zines, albums, concerts, and books. ✓**EWORLD**→*go* mu→Everyone's a Critic

Green Mountain Music Review A monthly review of records. Each month about a dozen albums—indie to hard rock—are reviewed. ✓**INTERNET**→ *url* http://www.insignia.com/people/j/laropage.htm

Internet Music Review Service (IMRS) Record companies and artists send in copies of their recordings, and writers from IMRS review them. Music reviews are archived by artist name. Each review includes artist info, date of review, label contact info, links to related Net sites, and a 150+ word review. The site also links to other music sites. ✓**INTERNET**→*url* http://www.monsterbit.com/IMRS/

Mike Wasson's Record Reviews Short—very short—reviews of new pop albums. Wasson, who also moderates rec.music.reviews, covers artists ranging from Madonna to Bubblegum Crisis. ✓INTERNET→*url* http://www.io.com/user/wasson/records.html

Music CD Review Rate the CDs (on a scale of 0 to 15) on this week's Billboard Top 15 list. The site keeps track of how other Netters voted, even breaking down ratings by gender. ✓INTERNET→*url* http://www.batech.com/cgi-bin/showcd

Quick Fix Music Reviews Using a rating system of one to five stars and a twenty-five-words-or-less review style, Swag Valance reviews live performances and recordings by artists in the alternative rock genre—a genre he calls "guitar-oriented 'college radio fodder.'" ✓INTERNET→*url* http://www-leland.stanford.edu/~witness/qfmrl/qfmrl.html

Ram's Music Page "I listen to all sorts of music ranging from ABBA to ZZ Top. I love self-indulgent music the most. My favourite groups are Pink Floyd, Primus, and Deep Purple. Ian Gillan is my favourite singer and Ritchie Blackmore happens to be my favourite guitarist." With that intro, Ram Samudrala links to the concert and album reviews he's written (of a 1994 Billy Joel concert, he writes, "The concert sucked big time!! Billy Joel is a decent singer, but his live show put me to sleep."), CD lists, bootleg lists, and other music info. ✓INTERNET→*url* http://www.ram.org/music/music.html

rec.music.reviews (ng) If you're looking for music recommendations, follow this newsgroup for a

The first edition of Bombast—from http://www.mw3.com/bombast

while. Several regulars (and occasionally someone new) post reviews of concerts, albums, and even music books. The newsgroup is moderated and accepts only reviews—no discussion allowed! Discussions about reviews are posted to rec.music.misc. ✓USENET→rec.music.reviews *FAQ:* ✓INTERNET→*url* http://www.access.digex.net/~awrc/rmr/index.html

Recent Recording Reviews Reviews of new recordings of world music. Anyone can submit a review. ✓INTERNET→*url* http://www.hear.com/rw/reviews.html

Shopping 2000: Music Reviews What are the critics saying? Shopping 2000 lists new albums, briefly summarizes for each album the views of music critics nationwide, and rates the album with a one-to-four-star scale. Many of the reviews focus on the career of the artist rather than album being reviewed. ✓INTERNET→*url* http://shopping2000.com/shopping2000/1musrev.html

TOTAL: Substance Short, smart album reviews illustrated with a few audio clips. ✓INTERNET→*url* http://www.totalny.com/sb/sb.html

The Unknown Reviewers Home Page The Unknown Reviewers have written about dozens of well-known artists and bands, including AC/DC (a 1991 concert), Meat Loaf (a 1993 concert), and Reba McEntire (a 1995 concert). The reviews aren't polished or professional, but they're entertaining first-person accounts about "last night's" concert, usually concerts held in the University of Chicago vicinity, where the reviewers attend school. The reviewers also run the Dear Dudes advice column and answer questions like, "My brother is in a band, and well, let's just say that the band really sucks. How do I tell him without hurting his feelings?" Answer: "First off we're the ones who decide whether a band sucks or not!

But, anyway, if you feel you must, maybe the easiest way would be to try to get Union Board to book them so that we could review them." Cool, dude. ✓**INTERNET**→ *url* http://www.iit.edu/~thedudes/

The War Against Silence Commited to winning the war, but not by any means necessary (the battles should be won with good music, not just loud music), this site reviews and recommends new music—from Laurie Anderson to John Waite. Reviews average about 350 words. ✓**INTERNET**→ *url* http://metaverse.com/vibe/twas/twasiss.html

E-zines

10 THINGS fanzine A punk 'zine based in Washington State. ✓**INTERNET**→ *url* http://weber.u.washington.edu/ten/

Acoustic Musician As unplugged as you can be while still remaining on the Net. ✓**INTERNET**→ *url* http://www.netinterior.com/acoustic/

Addicted To Noise An excellent online music magazine that covers the cutting edge as well as venerable artists who haven't lost their currency. With news updates, profiles, interviews, and reviews, ATN is also one of the best-written rock mags around, with regular contributions from Dave Marsh and Greil Marcus. If they ever get connectivity in heaven, this is the e-zine Lester Bangs will write for. ✓**INTERNET**→ *url* http://www.addict.com/ATN/

AMP Magazine Coverage of modern rock and pop artists, the vast majority of whom are signed to MCA Records (the company

that oversees AMP). Coincidence? Probably not. ✓**INTERNET**→ *url* http://www.mca.com/mca_records/index.html

Beat Magazine Large Australian music e-zine updated every Wednesday evening (that's Australian time). Each issue includes dozens of album reviews, single reviews, concert reviews, video reviews, music charts, industry gossip, interviews, tour info, and local Australian music and entertainment info. ✓**INTERNET**→ *url* http://www.ozonline.com.au/beat/beat.htm

BMI MusicWorld Features on mainstream "alternative" rock artists such as the Cranberries and Counting Crows, along with industry news. ✓**INTERNET**→ *url* http://bmi.com/MusicWorld/MW1994/MWSU94/index.html

BOMBAST Features and reviews new music, links to interesting music Websites, and interviews with artists. ✓**INTERNET**→ *url* http://www.mw3.com/bombast/

Bunnyhop Magazine Excerpts from the print magazine of pop culture and music. ✓**INTERNET**→ *url* http://www.slip.net/~bunnyhop/'

Cash Box Online Along with Billboard, Cash Box is the music industry's leading source of chart information. Its electronic magazine includes music reviews, Website recommendations, music columns, and, of course, charts. ✓**INTERNET**→ *url* http://www.silence.net/CASHBOX.HTM

ConnXtion Magazine Typos riddle this interactive music magazine, which is devoted primarily to new, loud rock. ✓**INTERNET**→ *url* http://www.herts.ac.uk/~cs1ca/

Follow that rabbit—http://www.slip.net/~bunnyhop/

Bunnyhop Magazine is a twice-annual, print-based publication exploring the finer points of "alternative" music, pop culture, and other soft & fluffy things.

Consumable Online An eclectic 'zine whose contents range from Tom Petty tour dates to an interview with Queensryche's Michael Wilton. ✓INTERNET→*url* http://www.westnet.com/consumable/Consumable.html

Convulsion An in-your-face, not-what-you'd expect music e-zine originating in Scotland. Includes feature articles, interviews, reviews, rants, and intense graphics. ✓INTERNET→*url* http://www.southern.com/Convulsion/

Dead Angel A e-zine that walks the line between sadism and hedonism. ✓INTERNET→*url* http://www.eden.com/zines/deadangel/deadangel.html

Dirty Linen Carries the electronic version of this bimonthly folk, electronic folk, traditional, and world music magazine. Reviews, a gig guide, classified ads, letters to the editor, and features are included in each issue. ✓INTERNET→*url* http://kiwi.futuris.net/linen/

Electronic Urban Report (EUR) Subscribe here to receive free daily updates on the biggest stars in urban/black music, including Janet Jackson, TLC, Whitney Houston, The Artist Formerly Known As Prince, The Artist Who Formerly Possessed the Face of Michael Jackson, and more. ✓INTERNET→*url* http://www.trib.com/bbs/eur.html

EST Interviews, articles, and reviews of hardcore, hardbeat, and experimental noise music, including hundreds of cassette-only releases. ✓INTERNET→*url* http://www.

hyperreal.com/zines/est/

!*@# (Exclaim) Magazine Gaudy graphics and across-the-board coverage of contemporary pop culture. ✓INTERNET→*url* http://www.shmooze.net/pwcasual/exclaim/

F Magazine Hard music news, album and single reviews, video reviews, tour dates, interviews, and more. ✓INTERNET→*url* http://www.webb.com/concrete/foundm.html

Fizz Be Fizzy! Read Fizz! And read about punk and hardcore, which these days means bands like Cop Shoot Cop, Rancid, and more. Features include Petting Zoo, a guide to the pets of the stars. ✓INTERNET→*url* http://www.iuma.com/Fizz/

The Hard Music Zone A guide to who's touring, who's on the charts, who's been signed and who's still unsigned, what albums and videos are being released, music industry gossip, and all things music. ✓INTERNET→*url* http://www.webb.com/concrete/second.html

Hot Press Get an online preview and subscription information about one of Ireland's premier music magazines. ✓INTERNET→*url* http://www.iol.ie/hotpress/

HYPE Electrazine Three issues old and counting, this Webzine has sound clips, cartoons, and software for fans of Amerindie rock. ✓INTERNET→*url* http://www.phantom.com/~giant/hype.html

Internet Music World On-line

An e-zine reporting on music resources and technology on the Net. ✓INTERNET→*url* http://www.mw3.com/imw/

InterState 4 Digital Music Magazine A graphically rich magazine of music reviews. ✓INTERNET→*url* http://interstate4.ids.net/i4/

Joey Joey A fanzine dedicated to the Canadian East Coast music scene, which includes such bands as Sloan, Eric's Trip, Thrush Hermit, and Hardship Post ✓INTERNET→*url* http://dragon.acadiau.ca/~011000b/Joey1.html

Le Hit Parade Multimedia Newsletter *Le Hit Parade* promotes contemporary French and Francophone music throughout the U.S. Site contains subscription info. ✓INTERNET→*url* http://www.lhp.com/

LiSTeN Up MAGaZINE An online magazine based on real-audio technology. Get a real-audio player and listen to or contribute interviews, reviews, and profiles of pre-releases. ✓INTERNET→*url* http://

Get Fizzy with Fizz—http://www.iuma.com/Fizz/

plaza.interport.net/listenup/

London Calling Film, media, and music may share the spotlight in this U.K. online magazine, but it's music news that's the real star—interviews with Isaac Hayes and Kinky Friedman, promotional pages for record labels, and home pages for a variety of artists, as well as an archive of past features. ✓INTERNET→*url* http://www.demon.co.uk/london-calling/filmmus.html

Magical Blend Magazine Online Read online demos of this alternative culture and music e-zine for free, and then purchase access to back issues. ✓INTERNET→*url* http://www.eden.com/magical/main.html

MDI Magazine Reviews, interviews, features, and an extensive album listing divided by genre. ✓INTERNET→*url* http://www.u-net.com/mdi/

The Muse "Reflecting on the Creative Arts, Music, Cinema, Books, Dance and Theatre" is this monthly magazine's subtitle. Includes music reviews and music features, with regular sections devoted to jazz and techno. ✓INTER-NET→ *url* http://www.hyperlink.com/muse/

Muse Magazine A journal devoted to the role of women in music. Covers all genres. ✓INTERNET→ *url* http://www.val.net/Village Sounds/Muse/index.html

NoisePop Hip-hop, trip-hop, avant-funk, and other emerging genres. ✓INTERNET→*url* http://www.hooked.net:80/buzznet/beats/

OffBeat Magazine Music news and listings for Louisiana. ✓INTER-NET→ *url* http://www.neosoft.com/~offbeat/

The Plague The heavy metal print fanzine is now online with interviews, reviews, tour dates, and music news. ✓INTERNET→*url* http://www.efn.org/~dhinds/test.htm

RAD Cyberzine The oldest alternative music e-zine on the Net, *RAD* reviews CDs, recommends music Websites, and interviews artists (Circle Jerks and Elastica, for instance). ✓INTERNET→*url* http://www.intele.com:80/~rad/

Rock-It Comix Comics featuring rock artists (Metallica, Black Sabbath, Lita Ford, and others) as the main characters. ✓INTERNET→*url* http://www.nando.net/music/gm/Rockit/

Rockstar On Line The rock world through Italian eyes. ✓IN-TERNET→*url* http://www.videomusic.com/edicola/rockstar/rockhome.html

Salty and Delicious Western Australia's punk community. That's not a 'zine—this is a 'zine. ✓INTERNET→*url* http://multiline.com.au/~langham/chapter/salty.html

Seconds Magazine An online version of the alternative music 'zine. ✓INTERNET→*url* http://www.iuma.com/Seconds/

Sonic Verse Music Magazine

(ml) An email magazine with music reviews, interviews, trivia, and more, covering both major-label and "alternative" acts. ✓INTERNET→ *url* uicd@vm.marist.edu ✍ *Type in message body:* subscribe <your full name>

Sound Out An electronic magazine dedicated to contemporary classical music. ✓INTERNET→*url* http://www.tmn.com/0h/Community/juechi/soundout.html

Sour Grapes Magazine Devoted to Austin music—Jimmie Dale Gilmore and more. ✓INTER-NET→*url* http://www.eden.com/sourgrapes/sourgrapes.html

Spontaneous Combustion Web Zine White punks online. ✓INTERNET→*url* http://www.spontaneous.com/scol/

Spunkzine A slick Australian indie rock 'zine covering bands like Labradford, Palace Brothers, Flying Saucer Attack, and Guided by Voices, and labels like Xpressway and Flying Nun. ✓INTERNET→*url* http://www.usyd.edu.au/~mwoodman/spunk.html

Streetsound An e-zine for DJs. ✓INTERNET→*url* http://www.phantom.com/~street

Strobe Magazine West Coast music magazine. ✓INTERNET→*url* http://www.iuma.com/strobe/

Thora-Zine Tomorrow's rock and roll today. ✓INTERNET→*url* http://www.eden.com/zines/thora-zine.html

Topp 40 A Swedish music and entertainment magazine. ✓INTER-

NET→*url* http://www.everyday.se/kiosk/topp40/

TumYeto Digiverse: Earfood department News and gossip. ✓**INTERNET**→*url* http://www.tumyeto.com/tydu/music/earfood.htm

West Coast Music Review West Coast music magazine. ✓**INTERNET**→*url* http://www.cyberstore.ca/WCMR/

General entertainment

People Magazine Wondering whether there will be a Beatles reunion? Interested in who your favorite rock star is dating ? Head to People for feature stories and photographs, along with reviews and lots of celebrity news, both musical and nonmusical. Check out "The Insider" for the scoop on private rehearsals, celebrity reunions, and bands in conflict. ✓**COMPUSERVE**→*go* people ✓**INTERNET**→*url* http://www.pathfinder.com/people/

TimeOut Covering Europe and New York, *TimeOut's* online version offers calendars of art and entertainment events in Amsterdam, Berlin, London, Madrid, New York, Paris, and Prague, as well as dozens of articles on such topics as the bar scene in Paris, the theater in London, sightseeing in Prague, concerts in New York, and coffee shops in Amsterdam. ✓**INTERNET**→*url* http://www.timeout.co.uk/

Interviews

Celebrity Interviews Interviews with Soundgarden, Will Smith, Alice Cooper, the Beastie Boys, Megadeth, Branford Marsalis, and many other celebrities are available at this site. The interviews are part of Adam Cur-

The contents page from InterState 4—http://interstate4.ids.net/i4/

ry's Website, Vibe, and were written by the Vibe staff. ✓**INTERNET**→*url* http://metaverse.com/vibe/interviews/index.html

Rock Interviews Profiles of artists from across the rock spectrum, leaning toward bands about to break into the public eye (Kerboog, Bile, Machine Head, Korn, etc.). ✓**AMERICA ONLINE**→*keyword* rocklink→Rock Interviews

Magazines

ABC Rock & Road Imagine going on the road—not down Route 66—but to a different concert every night. Then, imagine that you and some friends keep a journal with enthusiastic and often very personal impressions of the shows you see. Hell, even when you don't see a show, you might enter some thoughts into the journal. Oh, you also keep set lists, sort of review the performances, and announce additional tour

dates when you know them. Maybe you also take photos of performers or pick up publicity shots. Or don't bother imagining, just drop by this forum where stream-of-consciousness rock and roll runs rampant. ✓**AMERICA ONLINE**→*keyword* rr

BigO Asia's "most respective rock magazine" has odd contents to go along with its odd subtitle—Western music served up for English-speaking Easterners. A recent cover story told the riches-to-emotional-rags story of Paula Abdul, and record reviews range from John Prine to Pavement. ✓**INTERNET**→*url* http://www.asia-online.com/bigo/

Grooves Online Time-Life Music puts out a CD each month with 16 selections from an assortment of established and up-and-coming artists deemed worthy of greater exposure by that media conglomerate (including artists not on the Time-Warner label). Accompanying the CD is a print mini-magazine known as *Grooves*, which includes features on the selected artists (from oldies like The Allman Brothers to new artists like Liz Phair) and short reviews. the Web edition of *Grooves* includes sound clips in the reviews. √**INTERNET**→*url* http://www. pathfinder. com/TL-Music/Grooves/index.html

Magazine News Dozens of music magazines listed, along with subscription information and masthead information. √**EWORLD**→ *go* mu→Everyone's a Critic →The Music Press→Magazine Newsstand

RoJaRo Not exactly a magazine, but a magazine database—a huge resource that bills itself, with customary modesty, as "a key to the contents of more than 250 music magazines from 20 different countries." With an archive stretching back to January 1992, RoJaRo (the name stands for Rock-Jazz-Roots, but the magazines also cover blues, country, gospel, soul, rap, metal, and more) not only lists and describes the magazines, but allows you to search the contents. Full-text articles are not available, but this is a wonderful bibliographic tool, capable of pulling citations both from glossy monthly magazines and the LA punk 'zine *Nipple Hardness Factor.* √**INTERNET** →*url* http://www.notam.uio.no/ rojaro/

Rolling Stone Online A lavish new area devoted to the venerable rock and pop music magazine. Read current articles, check out record reviews, and even download pictures from *Rolling Stone*'s classic rock archive. But be careful not to believe everything you read; in the photo forum, the magazine has incorrectly labeled Robbie Robertson "the leader of the 60s

rock group the Byrds." Hope we die before we get old. √**COMPUSERVE**→*go* rsonline

Spin Bob Guccione, Jr.'s music magazine was once a young upstart taking on *Rolling Stone*. More than ten years later, it's an older upstart, with a by now familiar mix of excellent coverage, self-indulgent reporting, and low-rent sensibility. AOL's *Spin* online includes daily rock news updates along with a generous helping of content from the print magazine. And the photo gallery has some beautiful images of the late, great Kurt Cobain. √**AMERICA ONLINE**→*keyword* spin

Stereo Review The audiophile's dream, *Stereo Review* listens to CDs not only for their creative content, but for their technical expertise. Learn all about new recording procedures, and whether the naked ear can detect any difference, and then get the latest on home stereo systems. Music isn't music if you can't hear it properly. √**AMERICA ONLINE**→*keyword* stereo

Vibe Though it's mostly about soul and hip-hop, *Vibe*—the urban-music magazine of the Time-Warner empire—covers movies, celebrities, sports, and more. While *Vibe*'s photos are beautiful and its attitude unimpeachable, the writing tends toward the slack with short pieces that don't get to the point and long pieces that dissolve in setup and self-indulgence. √**INTERNET**→*url* http://www. pathfinder.com/Vibe/

Music columns

CyberSleaze Who's on trial? Who's divorcing? Who's pregnant? Who's releasing a new album? Former MTV VJ Adam Curry writes this daily news (and gossip) col-

umn about the entertainment world, primarily the music world. √**INTERNET**→*url* http://metaverse. com/vibe/sleaze/00latest.html

Music Now! An excellent music column reporting on the gossip, news, and events in the music world. √**INTERNET**→*url* http://www. intermind.net/kedg/music.html

New releases

The B-Side of the Month Homepage The page features a selected B-side (a sound clip from the B-side of Tom Petty's "You Don't Know How It Feels," for instance), archives of other B-sides, and links to sound utilities and other music resources. √**INTERNET**→ *url* http://www.telepath.com/ simon/

MP Music Previews Maybe you read about an artist's new CD in *Rolling Stone*. And maybe the review was so-so, but you want to hear it for yourself. Head to MP Music Previews, which works with record labels and artists to feature previews of new releases. Music fans can view the cover, read a brief description of the CD, and hear audio clips from at least three songs. The site previews artists from several different musical styles, including rock, alternative, hip-hop/rap, R&B, jazz and blues, Christian, country, and collections. Still fairly new, the site gets an A for effort, but a C for coverage—there are still too many big new releases not featured here. As MP Music Previews expands its relationships with artists and labels, the new release that you're interested in hearing will have a better chance of actually being there. √**INTERNET**→*url* http://www. mpmusic.com/

New Discs Weekly lists of new

tum★yeto
Digiverse

Whoa and behold! It's the quantum reticulating pontoon community otherwise known as the TUM YETO DIGIVERSE! and stuff. Thought it wasn't, biatch? You may begin with this stupendous, mind-altering *INDEXGUIDETHINGAMAGIG.* Achoo! If you think we're joking think again, or better yet don't think at all. Let us do it for you. Now move forward into our galactic expanse of communicative preposterousness.

The "Tum Yeto Ghetto"—http://www.tumyeto.com/tydu/music/earfood.htm

releases. See what's hitting the record stores this week, check back into archives of past weeks, or look ahead to coming weeks. ✓**AMERICA ONLINE**→*keyword* critics→Music & Concerts→New Discs

New Releases (ml) A huge list of recent and upcoming CD releases in a variety of genres. The list tracks date of release, artist name, and CD title. Re-releases and greatest hits are marked. The list is published weekly and some of the sites carry archives of past lists. ✓**INTERNET** ...→*email* majordomo@cs.uwp.edu ✍ *Type in message body:* subscribe new-releases <your email address> ...→*url* http://www.dsi.unimi.it/Users/Students/barbieri/releases.html ...→*url* http://nabalu.flas.ufl.edu/kperkins/music/nre/newrele.htm ...→*url* http://www.cloud9.net/new-releases/ ...→*url* http://www.

cs.colorado.edu/~millert/new_releases.html

Rock 104 Upcoming Releases A season-by-season listing of upcoming rock album releases. ✓**INTERNET**→*url* http://www.jou.ufl.edu/about/stations/rock104/releases.htm

Warner/Reprise Upcoming Releases Warner posts announcements for all of its artists with upcoming releases. Sorted alphabetically, each announcement includes the release date and the names of the selections on the upcoming album. ✓**AMERICA ONLINE** →*keyword* warner→Upcoming Releases

Newswires & news

Entertainment Weekly's Music News Music news, reviews, features, and chart-toppers from the current issue of *Entertainment Weekly.* ✓**AMERICA ONLINE**→*keyword* music→Entertainment Weekly--Music

Music News Paul McCartney sings for Bosnia, Springsteen plans new album, Garcia dies of heart attack, James Taylor and Carly Simon team up at the Vineyard .... Click one of the headlines that rush through here to read a story straight off the Reuters newswire. AP photos can be browsed online. ✓**AMERICA ONLINE**→*keyword* entertainment news→Click Here for Categories:→Music

NY Times Music & Dance Straight from the pages of the *New York Times,* this area features a weekly schedule of musical events for New York City, reviews of performances and albums, directories of New York musical venues, and *New York Times* music photos. ✓**AMERICA ONLINE**→*keyword* times music

Random Notes For years, *Rolling Stone* has been tracking the movements of the rock elite with its Random Notes column. Has Springsteen jumped onstage with an up-and-coming talent? Have the members of Yes patched up their differences again? Updated daily, this column brings you the latest news from the world of pop music. ✓**COMPUSERVE**→*go* rsrandom

RockNet Rock News A Kiss wedding? Carlos Santana touring with Jeff Beck? Get all the rock news you need with this online wire service. The categories—news, gossip, and daily beat—are relatively arbitary; obituaries sometimes end up in gossip, and rumors in news. ✓**AMERICA ONLINE** ...→*keyword* rocklink→Rock News ...→*keyword* rocklink→Gossip

Professional reviews

Adam Curry's Music Reviews
Former MTV VJ Adam Curry didn't write these music reviews, but he has set aside space on his site for an archive of music reviews written for his Website, Vibe. Reviews are broken down into audio, video, concert, and convention categories. ✓**INTERNET**→*url* http://metaverse.com/vibe/reviews/index.html

Current Reviews An archive of short concerts and album reviews written by freelancers for the Syndicated review organization Critics Choice. Reviews have a one-to-four-star rating. ✓**AMERICA ONLINE**→*keyword* critics→Music & Concerts→Current Reviews

HotWired Soundz *HotWired* is one of the Net's most innovative and interesting magazines, mixing coverage of cyberculture with pop culture. Its music review section, aptly enough, mixes coverage of music Websites with new music releases. Reviews include links to artist home pages and sound clips from the songs described. ✓**INTERNET**→*url* http://www.hotwired.com/soundz/

MTV Reviews MTV posts its concert reviews in the "It's Alive!" folder and album reviews in the "Blather" folder. Fans can submit concert reviews for possible inclusion (the editors will choose) in the Field Notes folder. ✓**AMERICA ONLINE**→*keyword* mtv→Music Matters→REVIEWS

Music Reviews The full text of more than a hundred music reviews that were originally published in *Time*, *People*, *Vibe*, and *Entertainment Weekly* magazines. ✓**INTERNET**→*url* http://www.pathfinder.com/pathfinder/reviews/music.html

RockLink Reviews Eclectic and disorganized, this collection of rock reviews finds RockNet contributors weighing in on everything from the new Neil Young to the Canadian faux-Beatles foursome Klaatu. Concert reviews have no dates listed—you'll have to check the submission line. ✓**AMERICA ONLINE** ...→*keyword* rocklink→Reviews/Charts/ConcertLine ...→*keyword* rocklink→Album and CD Reviews

RockNet Reviews RockNet's writers review concerts and albums and archive them in folders for members of America Online to read. Interesting, huh? Actually, the reviews are pretty well written. See if you can figure out what bands were being reviewed with the leads that follow. First: "No, they didn't play any Nirvana. Did you really think they would?" That was easy. Next: "The band with the stupidest name and stupidest album titles puts on a helluva show." A little harder, maybe. In order of mention, the bands were the Foo Fighters and the Goo Goo Dolls. How'd ya do? ✓**AMERICA ONLINE**→*keyword* rocknet→Reviews/Charts/ConcertLine ✓**COMPUSERVE**→*go* rock→Libraries→Reviews

Urban Desires Music Reviews
Each issue of this hip, bimonthly "interactive magazine of metropolitan passions" includes music reviews and features. Reviews often have sound clips, images, and artist biographical info. *Urban Desires* is a magazine created by the same company that designed *Sports Illustrated* Online and *Vibe* Online. ✓**INTERNET**→*url* http://desires.com/1.5/Music/Docs/review.html

NOTES

Greil Marcus on Elastica:
"Like their market-niche peers, Elastica know how to preen. Like Veruca et al, they might have been designed for cover stories, even if all they have to sell is attitude--which is short of posture, which is short of stance, which is short of position, which is short of action, which is short of blood on the floor, which is to say short of Heavens to Betsy. The attitude Elastica and the others are selling is that the last thing on their minds is a good pop song, like Veruca Salt's 'Seether' cool, disdainful, hip, those high, high voices instantly catching your ear and then refusing to let go. Within days (if not hours) the performance has turned into an irritation that reveals its genius: this was a jingle before it was a song, and so effective a jingle that it's as if the number had already been licensed..."

-from **Addicted to Noise**

Broadcast media

Fifteen years ago, no one had heard of MTV. Today, it controls the audio. It controls

the video. It sends us *Beavis & Butt-head, The Real World, Singled Out,* and *Alternative Nation*. It makes stars of borderline no-talents like Dan Cortese and Pauly Shore, and makes pin-ups out of veejays like Kennedy and Idalis. It decides what music we listen to, and when we listen, and if we insist that this is not the case, we are insisting only because we cannot bear the thought of our own suggestibility. Capitulate at **MTV Online** and then analyze your capitulation on **alt.tv. mtv**. If you absolutely insist on steering clear of the network, consult the national guide to radio stations online—many of the stations' Websites link to charts, playlists, and local scene information.

A screen shot from MTV on America Online

On the Net

Television

alt.mtv-sucks (ng) Consider this a junk-mail newsgroup. Discussions are only tangentially related to music and almost never about MTV. ✓USENET→alt.mtv-sucks

alt.tv.mtv (ng) MTV, a network that has defined a generation (or so it's said over and over and over again), is a network of music videos, right. Not quite. The net-

work also produces *Beavis & Butt-head* (it's NOT just a cartoon), the *Real World, Singled Out,* and dozens of other non-musical programs. It also covers the news and elections, stages an annual awards shows, and even focuses on fashion. But what about the music? Newsgroup members seem more concerned with the politically-conservative-big-mouth-airhead-of-a-DJ Kennedy than videos. When is she going on vacation? Where are the shots of her topless? What could she possibly be talking about? So much for Kennedy. But what about the music? Well, MTV fans on this newsgroup spend a lot of time arguing about the balance, defending their favorite shows, and spewing venom at the corporate big-wigs at parent company, Viacom ("If you want to be a network of 'shows' then start up another network...if you want to be MTV, the way MTV is suppose to be, i.e. MUSIC Television, then get it together before we all

switch to *C-SPAN*.") But what about the music? Well, that's a pretty big topic of discussion here too. Come by and see. ✓USENET→alt.tv.mtv

Boycott MTV Boycott MTV? The idea is downright Unamerican. But it's so crazy that it just might work. ✓INTERNET→*url* http://www.moscow.com/home-pages/boycott@mtv.html

MTV Online Recently redesigned, MTV's online area on AOL now opens with a high-tech sphere that gives way to a Rube Goldbergian screen decorated with link options. Though this is an appealing site, its appeal is diminished considerably by the interminable loading times—as a result of the redesign, each screen needs many new pieces of artwork, and AOL's software locks out all other computer functions during download. Still, this is a comprehensive guide to MTV programming, both regular shows and special features, and also features daily music news updates, message boards for music fan discussions, concert and album reviews, and multimedia downloads (you can even download clips of heavy rotation videos). The Website has a similar look, but it doesn't have as much content—yet. ✓**AMERICA ONLINE**→*keyword* mtv ✓**INTERNET**→*url* http://www.mtv. com

MuchMusic Canada's only 24-hour Music Video Channel has its own forum on eWorld. Although somewhat empty (like the rest of Canada—er, eWorld) the forum carries programming info, bios of VJs, and a message board for viewer and general music fandom discussions. ✓**EWORLD**→*go* muchmusic

Music Television Chat about music videos and music television—and not just MTV. In fact, most of the regulars are country fans who enjoy discussing The Nashville Network. ✓**AMERICA ONLINE**→*keyword* etv→Messages *and* Libraries

rec.music.video (ng) Low-volume newsgroup with discussions about where to buy music videos, which local cable stations run videos, and what the best cable connections are. ✓**USENET**→rec. music.video

VH-1 Derland If you can navigate through all the German, VH-1 Derland site is a musical treasure trove. With music news, chat, a sound-clip gallery, reviews of CD-ROMs (with short QuickTime clips included), album charts, concert news, and even a page of utilities and programs to help you listen to and watch the clips you've downloaded, this site may make you wonder why VH-1 has been getting such a bad rap all these years. ✓**INTERNET**→*url* http://www. vh1.de/

Net networks

Internet Rockhouse With plans for multilingual versions (sorry, Africa and Asia—only European languages will be represented), Internet Rockhouse is aiming to be one of the premere online clearinghouses for musicians of all kinds. In addition to creating free home pages for professional musicians, the site organizes artists by genre. A new artist is featured each day, and sound clips are often available. While the other resources—booking contacts, gig guides, etc.—aren't in place, this promises to be an interesting site. ✓**INTERNET**→*url* http://www.rockhouse.com/

Troubadour Under continual redesign (they can't catch you if you keep moving), Troubadour (also known as TroubWorld) offers an Internet venue for unsigned musicians. Where else can you hear the alternative rappers Frontside, or the hard-rocking Lear-influenced Out Vile Jelly? Answer: nowhere. In addition to archiving sound clips, Troubadour includes a chat room, a photo archive, a music store, and—this is the exciting part—live CU-SEE ME concerts featuring nationally known acts such as Janis Ian, Material Issue, Vonda Shepherd, Brave Ulysses, and Everclear. ✓**INTERNET**→*url* http://www.iuma.com/Troubadour/

Virtual Radio Virtual Radio isn't exactly a radio station—it's more like an independent distributor that collects bands (signed and unsigned) and makes their songs available to interested fans on the Internet. More than 50 bands are represented, and each band has a dedicated page with a bio, images, and sound clips. Again, few of these bands are known to more than a few dozen people, but if you want to fill up on the latest by Sidesaddle or Wear-n-Tear, come here. ✓**INTERNET**→*url* http://www. microserve.net/vradio/

Radio

alt.radio.college (ng) College DJs swap playlists, exchange station Web-page addresses, and talk about music on this low-volume newsgroup. ✓**USENET**→alt.radio. college

Cool Radio Stations A state-by-state list of radio stations with very, very brief station descriptions. ✓**INTERNET**→*url* http://www. rain.org/~gary1580/radiost.htm

Radio Stations Extensive collections of links to radio stations with an Internet presence. Almost 700 stations are online. ✓**INTERNET** ...→*url* http://american.recordings.com/WWWoM/radio/radio. html ...→*url* http://web.mit.edu/afs/athena.mit.edu/user/w/m/wmbr/www/otherstations.html ...→*url* http://kzsu.stanford.edu/other-radio.html ...→*url* http://www.cs.ucdavis.edu/~swanston/kdvs/current/common/webradio. html

Rockline *Rockline*, the nationwide call-in radio show that allows fans to talk to their favorite rock stars, has been broadcasting for almost fifteen years. Come hell or high water, the show has brought rock news and opinions to the nation—as the press materials note, the show even broadcast on January 17, 1994, despite the fact that the studios were almost completely destroyed by the San Francisco earthquake. The busy AOL forum includes lists of upcoming Rockline guests, both on the radio and online, a catalog of memorabilia from the Rock Shop, and information about other shows (like Live from the Crazy Horse, an hour of the finest new country music). And there are some less serious features as well—RockThrobs, a file of rock-related supermodels (Estelle Halladay, Rachel Hunter) and image-obsessed rock stars; and Bite This, a collection of sound clips and .GIFs that includes a listener photo gallery. ✓**AMERICA ON-LINE**→*keyword* rockline

Wavelength Lists of radio stations for the major cities in the U.S. Brief descriptions of each station are included. ✓**AMERICA ON-LINE**→*keyword* mtv→music→Music Matters→Wavelength

Alaska

101.1 FM—MAGIC An adult contemporary station in Fairbanks, Alaska. The site offers profiles of its staff, a Top 20 list, announcements about upcoming concerts, a programming guide, and its own guide to artists online (particularly artists that the station plays). ✓**INTERNET**→ *url* http://www.polarnet.fnsb.ak.us/Users/COMCO/magic.htm

Arizona

101.5 FM—KZON An alternative rock station in Phoenix, Arizona. The site links to three other Arizona rock stations in Tucson (101.5 FM), Prescott (100.5 FM), and Flagstaff (106.3 FM). ✓**INTERNET**→*url* http://www.kzon.com/

106.3 FM—KEDJ Phoenix's hard rock station (The Edge). This site has programming schedules, local concert information, DJ profiles, and Deep Thoughts of the Day ("If you were a poor Indian with no weapons, and a bunch of con-

quistadors came up to you and asked where the gold was, I don't think it would be a good idea to say, 'I swallowed it. So sue me.'"). ✓**INTERNET**→*url* http://www.getnet.com:80/kedj/

93.3 FM—KDKB An Arizona rock station. This glossy Website advertises programming, announces local events and concerts, and lists contact information for several Phoenix, Scottsdale, and Tempe arenas and clubs. ✓**INTERNET**→*url* http://www.netwest.com/kdkb/

96.9 FM—K-HITS A Phoenix, Arizona, radio station that plays the music of the 1970s. Its Website has programming info, job listings, updates on its radio promotions, and even the names of the artists that the station plays (ZZ Top, Fleetwood Mac, Elton John, etc.). ✓**INTERNET**→*url* http://www.getnet.com:80/khits/

Arkansas

B 98.5 FM Website for Little Rock's pop music station. ✓**INTERNET**→*url* http://dragon.axs.net/b98.5/

California

102.1 FM—KDFC San Francisco's classical music station. The Website includes a programming schedule, station info, and links to other classical sites. ✓**INTERNET**→*url* http://www.tbo.com/kdfc/index.html

102.7 FM—KIIS Los Angeles Top 40 station with nationally known DJ Rick Dees. The Website merely advertises the station's promotional events. ✓**INTERNET**→ *url* http://www.gointeract.com/radio/kiis/kiishome.html

103.7 FM—KKSF San Francisco's jazz station. The Website has staff

Rockhouse in the house—from http://www.rockhouse.com/

and station information, concert announcements, playlists and charts, an electronic version of the station's newsletter, and more. ✓**INTERNET**→*url* http://www.tbo.com/kksf/index.html

103.7 FM—Rock Mix Home page for San Diego's rock radio station. ✓**INTERNET**→*url* http://www.electriciti.com:80/~danlopez/

104.7 FM and 530 AM—KBBK Home page for Christian rock station at Biola University in La Mirada, California. ✓**INTERNET**→*url* http://www.biola.edu/orgs/kbbk/index.html

104.7 FM—KSR Basic info about campus radio station at the University of Southern California. ✓**INTERNET**→*url* gopher://cwis.usc.edu/11/Campus_Life/KSCR

106.3 FM—KRAB An alternative rock station with live Internet broadcasts, local concert info, and announcements about station promotions. ✓**INTERNET**→*url* http://www.lightspeed.net/~krab/krab.htm

89.7FM—KFJC Campus radio station for Foothill College in Los Altos Hills, California. ✓**INTERNET**→*url* http://www.cygnus.com/misc/kfjc/

90.1 FM—KZSU Home page for Stanford University's radio station. ✓**INTERNET**→*url* http://kzsu.stanford.edu:80/index.html

90.3 FM—KUSF Home page for the University of San Francisco's radio station. ✓**INTERNET**→*url* http://www.usfca.edu/usf/kusf/

93.7 FM—KRXQ Sacramento's rock station. The Website has programming info and links to other

rock links. ✓**INTERNET**→*url* http://www.93rock.com

95.5 FM—KLOS Los Angeles rock station. Its glossy Website is primarily a tribute to its infamous DJs Mark and Brian. ✓**INTERNET**→*url* http://wavenet.com:80/~mandb/

98.5 FM—KOME Alternative rock station for the San Jose, California, area. The Website links to music news, the station's playlist, a list of new releases and CD reviews, a regularly featured bio of a musical artist, and a list of the station's favorite Websites. ✓**INTERNET**→*url* http://www.kome.com/

KDVS The Website for the radio station at the University of California at Davis includes seasonal programming guides, transcripts of station editorials, and a small index to music sites on the Internet. ✓**INTERNET**→*url* http://www.cs.ucdavis.edu/~swanston/kdvs/current/pg.html

Q-92 Monterey Bay's classic rock station. Get local concert info, a list of the 400 best classic rock tunes of all time, a weekly review of events in classic rock history, and a large selection of links to classic rock artists on the Web. ✓**INTERNET**→*url* http://www.q92.com/

Canada

107 FM—CHMA Campus radio station serving Mount Allison University in Canada. ✓**INTERNET**→*url* http://aci.mta.ca/TheUmbrella/CHMA/chmastart.html

93.1 FM—CKCU Website for the campus-based community radio station operating at Carleton University in Canada. ✓**INTERNET**→*url* http://www.carleton.ca/~jkirkham

/ckcu.html

93.9 FM—KOOL Radio programming, pictures of station DJs, and a small page of music links. ✓**INTERNET**→*url* http://www.worldlink.ca/koolcfra/kool.htm

Colorado

106.7 FM—KBPI Rock and heavy metal station in the Colorado Rockies. The Website is an enormous music resource with both station info and playlists as well as an A-to-Z guide to rock and metal resources on the Internet. ✓**INTERNET**→*url* http://www.rmii.com/kbpi/

Connecticut

88.1 FM—WESU Website for this radio station, which is run by community volunteers and Wesleyan University students. Based in Middletown, Connecticut, the station claims to be the oldest college station in the country. ✓**INTERNET**→*url* http://www.con.wesleyan.edu/groups/wesu/wesu.html

Florida

101.1 FM—WJRR A Miami alternative rock station. The Website has concert information, station news, and links to other music sites. ✓**INTERNET**→*url* http://oo.com/~wjrr/

99.9 FM—KISS Home page for this Florida country music station. Includes links to other country music sites. ✓**INTERNET**→*url* http://prod1.satelnet.org/wkis/index.html

Rock 104 If you're one of those people who listen as a radio station counts down the top 500 songs of the year, you can skip it this year. Rock 104, a north Florida station, puts its list online along with programming info, a list of the week's Top 10, DJ profiles, album reviews, and links to other music sites. And don't miss the page advertising the Seventies-at 7 radio show—it's filled with links to sites like the Unofficial Brady Bunch Homepage perpetuating seventies culture. ✓**INTERNET** →*url* http://www.jou.ufl.edu/about/stations/rock104/

Georgia

104.3 FM—WBBQ Home page for the Top 40 station in Augusta, Georgia. ✓**INTERNET**→*url* http://csra1.csra.net/wbbq/

93.9 FM—WGOR Oldies station in Augusta. The site links to other oldies sites. ✓**INTERNET**→*url* http://www.csra.net/coolfm

99.7 FM—99X An Atlanta alternative rock station. The Website carries a playlist, a guide to live music on the Internet, and links to other big music sites online. ✓**INTERNET**→*url* http://www.com/99x/front.html

Illinois

89.3FM—WNUR Run by students at Northwestern University in Chicago, this jazz station has assembled a good collection of links to jazz sites on the Internet. ✓**INTERNET**→*url* http://www.nwu.edu/WNUR/

93.1 FM—WXRT Progressive rock radio station in Chicago with links to concert info, staff bios, and its own directory of Internet band sites. ✓**INTERNET**→*url* http://www.wxrt.com/

Indiana

94.7 FM—Q95 Indianapolis rock station. The Website pro-

Welcome to the Troubadour—from http: //www.iuma.com/Troubadour/

motes station gimmicks (songs for cash), lists the Top 20 chart (with links to relevant artist home pages), and features staff bios and other station news. Oh, and you can even email the station a joke. ✓**INTERNET**→*url* http://www.iquest.net/Q95/

Kansas

90.7 FM—KJHK University of Kansas pop-rock station. Carries station info, programming schedules, and a playlist for the current week. ✓**INTERNET**→*url* http://www.cc.ukans.edu/~kjhknet/index.html

99 FM—KTLI Contemporary Christian music station in Wichita, Kansas. The site carries station news, announcements about local concerts and station contests, DJ profiles, sound clips from new releases, and a terrific list of links to Christian music and other Christian Websites. ✓**INTERNET**→*url* http://www.southwind.net:80/ktli/

Kentucky

102 FM—WLRS Home page for this Louisville, Kentucky, adult contemporary station. ✓**INTERNET**→

url http://iglou.com/mix102/

90.5 FM—WUOL Home page for the classical music station from the University of Louisville. ✓**INTERNET**→*url* http://iglou.com/wuol/

Louisiana

90.7 FM—WWOZ No-nonsense Website for New Orleans's award-winning radio station. The station plays "the sounds of New Orleans," which include jazz, rhythm & blues, Cajun, and Brazilian. ✓**INTERNET**→*url* http://www.gnofn.org/~wwoz/

Maine

90.5 FM—WMHB Operated by Colby College and community members from Waterville, Maine, the station offers a broad range of musical programming. The Website has pages for many of the station's shows. ✓**INTERNET**→*url* http://www.colby.edu/wmhb/

Massachusetts

100.7 FM—WZLX Boston's classic rock station is online with information about its promotions and contests, release dates for upcoming classic rock CDs, trivia, rock and roll history, links to other classic rock Web pages, and information on the station, its staff, and its sponsors. ✓ **INTERNET**→*url* http://www.wzlx.com/wzlx/index.html

101.7 FM—WFNX Home page for this alternative rock station in Boston. ✓ **INTERNET**→*url* http://www.wfnx.com/

102.5 FM—WCRB This Website for Boston's classical radio station offers info about the station, playlists, and even a glossary of classical music terms. ✓ **INTERNET**→*url* http://www.wcrb.com/wcrb/index.html

104.1 FM—WBCN Boston rock station. This Website offers a guide to entertainment in Boston (from concerts to the Celtics). ✓ **INTERNET**→*url* http://www.wbcn.com/

107.3 FM—WAAF Rock station for Boston. The site carries info about the Boston concert scene, the station's current playlist, and profiles of the station DJs. ✓ **INTERNET**→*url* http://www.tiac.net/waaf/home.html

88.1 FM—WMBR Home page for MIT's radio station. ✓ **INTERNET**→*url* http://web.mit.edu/afs/athena.mit.edu/user/w/m/wmbr/www/home.html

89.3 FM & 640 AM—WTBU A button-down site for Boston University's radio stations. ✓ **INTERNET**→*url* http://ivory.lm.com:80/~donnpat/wtbu.html

96.3 FM—WRZE Top 40 station in Hyannis and Nantucket. The Website carries a schedule of local concert and club performances, programming info, and local nightlife news. ✓ **INTERNET**→*url* http://www.ccsnet.com/wrze/

Michigan

94.5 FM —WKLQ A Grand Rapids rock station. The Website links to band pages, programming info, and even a page of absurd rumors. ✓ **INTERNET**→*url* http://www.wklq.com/klq/index.html

98.7 FM—WLZZ A Detroit alternative rock station. The Website announces upcoming music events, carries programming info and bios of station personnel, and even takes requests. ✓ **INTERNET**→*url* http://oeonline.com:80/~wllz/

EZ-15.7FM and WOOD AM 1300 An elaborate Website for these two Michigan radio stations. You can even dedicate a love song by email—pick up to three songs and include a short message. Doesn't it warm the cockles of your heart? (Did you even know you had cockles?) ✓ **INTERNET**→*url* http://www.woodradio.com/cgi-bin/var/wood/home.htm

Minnesota

93.1 FM—KXLP Southern Minnesota's classic and alternative rock station. The simple Website lists the programming lineup and links to home pages for several of the bands that the station frequently plays (Van Halen, Aerosmith, the Doors, etc.). ✓ **INTERNET**→*url* http://proradio.mankato.mn.us/kxlp/kxlp.html

Mississippi

93.5 FM—WHJT This Contemporary Christian music station operated at Mississippi College offers programming and staff info, but it also carries the Christian Top 40 list and Christian music concert info for Mississippi. ✓ **INTERNET**→*url* http://www.mc.edu/~alive935/

99.9 FM—WQNN A Columbus, Mississippi, station playing hits of the 1980s and 1990s. The Website links to music stores and artist home pages, and offers station info. ✓ **INTERNET**→*url* http://www.ebicom.net/Q99/

Missouri

104.3 FM—KBEQ It may very well be the "world's #1 country music station," but its Website is fairly simple (station news, a list of upcoming country concerts, and the top four country songs of the day). ✓ **INTERNET**→*url* http://falcon.cc.ukans.edu/~mills/q104.html

105.1 FM—KTOZ An alternative rock station in Springfield, Missouri. The Website offers a playlist, local concert schedules with ticket info, music news, and even the option to request songs. ✓ **INTERNET**→*url* http://www.woodtech.com/channelz/index.html

Montana

100.1 FM—KZOQ Rock station for Missoula. The Website offers staff info and links to interesting rock pages online. ✓ **INTERNET**→*url* http://www.montana.com/Z100/z100.htm

1340 FM—KYLT Home page for Missoula, Montana's oldies station. ✓ **INTERNET**→*url* http://www.montana.com/Z100/kylt.htm

Nebraska

102.7 FM—KFRX Top 40 station in Lincoln, Nebraska. ✓ **INTERNET**→

url http://www.lincnet.com/
lincnet/pages/kfrx.htm

92.1 FM—KEZO Rock station in
Omaha, Nebraska. Each of the
station's radio personalities contributes to the Website: Allison
Steele does music interviews, Marv
offers concert news and schedules,
Craig reports on rock news, and
more. ✓INTERNET→*url* http://www.
expanse.com:80/ads/z92/menu.
html

Nevada

103.5 FM —KEDG Known as
The Edge, this rock station in Las
Vegas has a Website with local
concert info, programming schedules, a regular music news column,
links to other music Websites, and
even sound clips of the DJs. ✓IN-
TERNET→*url* http://www.intermind.
net/kedg/

103.5 FM—KSNE Pop music station in Las Vegas. ✓INTERNET→*url*
http://www.vegas.com/sunny/
106.html

96.5 FM—KRZQ A less than impressive presence on the Web, this
site advertises Reno, Nevada's rock
station and links to a few other
music sites. ✓INTERNET→*url* http://
africa.connectus.com/~krzq/

New Jersey

100.1 FM—WJRZ Top 40 sta-
tion for the Jersey shore. ✓INTER-
NET→*url* http://www.injersey.com/
Clients/WJRZ/

New Mexico

88.7 FM—KTEK Home page for
New Mexico Tech's campus radio
station. ✓INTERNET→*url* http://nmt.
edu/~ktek/

Adult contemporary , Teutonic-style—http://www.vh1.de/

94ROCK—KZRR This rock and
roll radio station in Albuquerque,
New Mexico, has staff info, programming schedules, concert announcements, pages for local
bands, and playlists online. ✓IN-
TERNET→*url* http://www.swcp.
com:80/kzrr/

New York

102.7 FM—WNEW New York
City's premier alternative rock station has a pretty fab Website too.
Check out the monthly calendar
of local concerts (Jones Beach,
Madison Square Garden, Big
Birch, the Beacon Theater, and
several other big concert arenas),
send in a song request, and link to
hundreds of the best sites on the
Internet ✓INTERNET→*url* http://
www.wnew.com

89.1 FM and 810 AM—WNYU
New York University's rock station. ✓INTERNET→*url* http://www.
users.interport.net/~stoner3/wfuv.
html

90.7 FM—WFUV Pop music and
New York City—they go together
like radio stations and the Internet. ✓INTERNET→*url* http://www.
users.interport.net/~stoner3/wfuv.
html

93.1 FM—WNTQ Syracuse's Top
40 station maintains a Web page
with station information, a calendar of local events, links to other
music sites, and a playlist of their
most popular hits. ✓INTERNET→*url*
http://128.230.1.12/~dbgrandi/
ajur/snet/93q/

Ohio

100.7 FM—WMMS An alternative rock station in Cleveland,
Ohio. ✓INTERNET→*url* http://www.
concourse.com/wmms/w

Broadcast Media Overture

102.7 FM—WEBN A Cincinnati rock station. You can't get into this Website without passing a three-question rock and roll admissions test (if you fail, you can try again, but there will be new questions), but once you're in, you can listen to Real Audio programs, get local concert info and programming schedules, and more. ✓INTERNET→*url* http://www. webn.com/

107.9 FM—THE END Cleveland's modern rock station is online with DJ profiles, concert info, playlists, interviews with local bands, audio clips, musical advertisements, and even public service announcements. ✓INTERNET→*url* http:// www.americast.com:80/wenz/

92.5 FM—KISS Why's the damn Web page loading so slowly? Because you're downloading the sound of a kiss, that's why. Smooch! This radio station from Toledo, Ohio, features its playlists, programming info, and its own index to music sites on the Internet. Links to the home pages of artists that the station plays are also available! ✓INTERNET→*url* http://www. toledolink.com/kissfm/

92.9 FM—WGTZ A Dayton, Ohio, Top 40 station. Its Website has local concert info, the weather, and a Website of the week. ✓INTERNET→*url* http://www.erinet.com:80/wgtz/

97.7 FM—WOXY A rock station in Cincinnati, Ohio. Sounds awfully familiar... ✓INTERNET→*url* http://www.woxy97x.com/

Oregon

101.1FM—KUFO The Website for this Portland, Oregon, alternative radio station carries the station's playlist linked to short sound clips from the songs, a con-cert calendar, links to other music sites, and station info. ✓INTERNET →*url*http://www.europa.com/kufo

92.3 FM—KGON Classic rock station in Portland, Oregon. The Website carries Portland-area concert listings, links to classic rock artist home pages, and info about the station. ✓INTERNET→*url* http://www.teleport.com/~kgon/index.html

970 AM—KBBT An alternative rock station in Portland, Oregon. The site offers station and local concert info. ✓INTERNET→*url* http://www.europa.com/thebeat/

Pennsylvania

100.3 FM—Y100 An alternative rock station for Philadelphia. The Website offers profiles of the DJs, playlists, and even a list of the "300 coolest songs of the 80s." ✓INTERNET→*url* http://www.y100.com/

88.3FM—WCRT Home page for the Carnegie-Mellon University radio station in Pittsburgh, Pennsylvania. ✓INTERNET→*url* http://www.cs.cmu.edu/afs/andrew.cmu.edu/usr/wrct/www/home.html

Tennessee

103.3 FM—WKDF Nashville rock station. ✓INTERNET→*url* http://www.edge.net/kdf/

104.5 FM—WGFX Nashville oldies station. The Website links to Web pages for oldies artists and maintains its own rock history calendar. ✓INTERNET→*url* http://edge.edge.net/~arrow104/

106.5 FM—WSKZ Classic rock station in Chattanooga, Tennessee. ✓INTERNET→*url* http://www.chattanooga.net/RADIO/index.html

Texas

102.7 FM—KTFM Dance and R&B station in the San Antonio, Texas, area. ✓INTERNET→*url* http://www.txdirect.net:80/ktfm/

91.7 FM—KTRU Playlists, show schedules, staff lists, event announcements, and even its own quarterly magazine. All this and more at the Website for the Rice University radio station. ✓INTERNET →*url* http://www.rice.edu/projects/ktru/index.html

92.5 FM—KZPS Dallas's classic rock station. The Website has local classic rock concert info, programming announcements, and more. ✓INTERNET→*url* http://www.kzps.com/kzps/index1.html

93.7 FM—KLBJ Rock station in Austin, Texas. ✓INTERNET→*url* http://www.lbj.com/fm/fm.html

96.5 FM—KHMX Houston, Texas, station that features a mix of 1970s, 1980s, and 1990s music. The Website carries station info, a playlist, and contest details. ✓INTERNET→*url* http://www.khmx.com/default.htm

Q102 FM Check this Texas rock Website for programming schedules, lists of top songs and bands, tour info for favorite bands, local concert announcements, and station and staff info. ✓INTERNET→*url* http://www.pic.net/q102/index.html

Utah

96.1 FM—KXRK Salt Lake City alternative rock station. The Website features a playlist, station promotional info, and a local concert schedule. ✓INTERNET→*url* http://www.x96.com/x96

Your virtual radio station—http://www. microserve.net/vradio/

97.9 FM—KBZB Utah's smooth jazz radio station publishes local news and a Top 20 list of jazz songs on its Website. ✓**INTERNET**→*url* http://www.intele.net/breeze/index.html

Virginia

97.5 FM—WWWV Charlottesville's rock station. The Website has station and staff info, links to music sites, local concert announcements, and an area to send in a song request. ✓**INTERNET**→*url* http://grace.fwnet.com/~wwwv/wwwv.html

Washington

90.3 FM—KCMU Let's play a game. I'm thinking of something. It's politically correct. It plays a broad range of music, from reggae to blues. It broadcasts from Seattle, Washington. And it's online, with programming information and a series of music charts that the station creates. "Uh, what is KCMU?" That's right! ✓**INTERNET**→*url* http://www.kuow.washington.edu/kcmu.htm

94.1 FM—KMPS The Website for this country music station in Seattle, Washington, features album reviews by the station manager, the station's own country music chart, articles about and interviews with country singers, and programming info. ✓**INTERNET**→*url* http://fine.net:80/kmps/

94.9 FM—KUOW Just the facts, ma'am. A simple Website for a radio station at the University of Washington in Seattle. The site includes links to programming info and links to other radio-related sites. ✓**INTERNET**→*url* http://www. kuow.washington.edu/kuow.html

95.7 FM—KJR Step back into the 1970s with this Website. Sure, there are profiles of DJs and staff members of this Seattle, Washington, radio station, but there are also links to the Disco Web, 1970s T.V. Web pages, 1970s movie Web pages, and more. Get out your white suits. Fluff up your Afros. It's time. ✓**INTERNET**→*url* http://www.halcyon.com/normg/kjr_fm.htm

Part 2

Fandom

Lyrics

Rock fans love to hum tunes to their favorite songs, but they also like to obsess over

the words—to write them on their notebooks in high school, to send them in letters to friends in college, to subject them to puffed-up herme-neutics in grad school ("Picture Perfect: Photography in the Lyrics of Def Leppard, as Seen Through the Lens of Roland Barthes's *Camera Lucida*"). If you've ever spent hours reviewing *Exile on Main Street* just to figure out what the hell Mick Jagger is saying at the beginning of "Tumbling Dice" ("Women think I'm tasty"?), then you know how important it is to get the words right. Visit the **Internet Lyrics Server** and other sites—for better or for verse.

On the Net

Across the board

alt.music.lyrics (ng) You can talk about lyrics almost anywhere in the online music world, but this is one newsgroup that foregrounds its interest in the popular poem. Alt.music.lyrics is composed of two kinds of posts—lyrics requests and lyrics answers. And while you may sometimes be shocked by the ignorance of young fans ("I'm looking for the song which contains the lyrics, "little old lady got mutilated last night" and mentions Lon Chaney..."), there's always room for another expert,

Words, man. Just words.—http://www.ccs.neu.edu/home/skilmon/music/lyrics.html/

Jim. ✓**USENET**→alt.music.lyrics

Everyday Lyric You know the old adage about a lyric a day, or was that...? Whatever the adage, this site features lyrics to a different song every day (except Sunday). Today Tom Petty. Tomorrow Madonna. The day after, maybe Roky Erickson. If you're good. ✓**INTERNET**→*url* http://das-www. harvard.edu/users/students/Zheng _Wang/lyric.html

Grendel's Lyrics Archive An archive of lyrics organized by band name. Lyrics for Liz Phair, Silverchair, Queen, Sponge, Violent Femmes, XTC, and dozens of other artists are available. ✓**INTERNET**→ *url* http://www.seas.upenn.edu/~ avernon/lyrics.html

Internet Lyrics Server If you've ever struggled to remember a lyric, struggle no more. This site is the Mecca of forgetful rock fans, or those who can't quite wrap their

ears around the bent syllables of Sinead O'Connor, Phil Lynott, or Marc Bolan. And how about early Stipe? Geez, that guy murmured and murmured! For several years the University of Washington has maintained one of the largest lyrics collections on the Net. The site includes lyrics from hundreds of artists from ABBA to ZZ Top— Sheena Easton, Duke Ellington, Nirvana, Terence Trent D'Arby, Hootie & the Blowfish, Neil Young, Yaz, and anyone-else-you-can-think-of. Recently one of the site's mirrors (the Vivarin site) was outfitted with a powerful search engine that makes looking for lyrics absolutely laborless. Impress your friends with your vast knowledge of pop music—you don't even have to tell them that the Net sent you. ✓**INTERNET** ...→*url* http://vivarin.pc.cc.cmu.edu/lyrics. html ...→*url* ftp://mirrors.aol. com/pub/music/lyrics/ ...→*url* http://music.wit.com/mirrors/ music/lyrics/ ...→*url* ftp://ftp.

informatik.tu-muenchen.de/pub/rec/music/vocal/lyrics/uwp/

The Lyrics Page "Words, man. Just words." The site carries a random selection of lyrics for alternative rock bands—Smashing Pumpkins are here, but where's Nirvana? ✓INTERNET→url http://www.ccs.neu.edu/home/skilmon/music/lyrics.html/

The Music Page—Lyrics An A-to-Z listing of a small number of musical artists followed by the lyrics for some of their albums. ✓INTERNET→url http://gene.fwi.uva.nl/~ketel/Music/lyrics.html

Random 80's Lyrics "Karma karma karma karma karma chameleon, / You come and go, you come and go / Loving would be easy if your colours were like my dream / Red gold and green, red gold and green." The year is 1983 and Culture Club is playing on every pop station. Connect to the page for lyrics from a song from the 1980s. The song is randomly chosen. ✓INTERNET→url http://itg-pc1.acns.nwu.edu/cgi-bin/lyric

The Ultimate Band List Lyrics Organized by band name, this Web page indexes hundreds of sites with band and artist lyrics—from Harry Chapin to The Cure to Alanis Morrisette. ✓INTERNET→ url http://american.recordings.com/WWWoM/ubl/lyric_list.shtml

Folk

Digital Tradition Folk Song Server The server is a searchable database of lyrics for thousands of traditional songs. Search and retrieve lyrics to gems like "Dead Dog Scrumpy," and "The Man on the Flying Trampeze." ✓INTERNET→ url http://pubweb.parc.xerox.com/digitrad

Hard rock

HeadBang's Home Page An archive of hard rock lyrics organized by band name—Depeche Mode, Bad Company, Nirvana, Pearl Jam, and Sepultura are here, along with many more. ✓INTERNET→url http://www.stack.urc.tue.nl/~niels/

Hip-hop

The Hip-Hop Lyrics WWW Site "Power, equality / And we're out to get it / I know some of you ain't wid it / This party started right in 66 / With a pro-Black radical mix / Then at the hour of twelve / Some force cut the power / And emerged from hell / It was your so-called government..." So begins Public Enemy's "Party For Your Right to Fight." The full lyrics for this song, several other Public Enemy songs, and the songs of dozens of other rap singers are archived here. Who else? House of Pain, Ice Cube, Snoop Doggy Dogg, The Beastie Boys, Digital Underground, and many others. ✓INTERNET ...→url http://www.brad.ac.uk/~ctttaylo/lyrics.html ...→url http://library.uncc.edu/people/chris/lyrics

Miscellaneous

Internet Greek Song Database If you've been humming the melodies of Greek songs (maybe folk songs from your town's Greek festival or pop songs from Athenian radio), and you now want to stop humming and start singing, you'll need lyrics. You can get the lyrics here in both Greek and English characters. ✓INTERNET→url http://www.edu.uch.gr/Docs/songs/

Russian Club Songs Home page Lyrics to Russian songs in Cyrillic or transliterated Cyrillic. ✓INTERNET→url http://anxiety-closet.mit.edu:8001/activities/russian-club/catalog.html

Schoolhouse Rock Lyrics to those catchy educational lyrics that played on television in the 1970s: You know the ones: "I'm just a bill / Yes, I'm only a bill / And I'm sitting here on Capitol Hill / Well, it's a long, long journey / To the capital city / It's a long, long wait / While I'm sitting in committee / But I know I'll be a law someday... / At least I hope and pray that I will / But today I'm still just a bill." ✓INTERNET→url http://hera.life.uiuc.edu/rock.html

The Hip-Hop Lyrics WWW Site—from http://www.brad.ac.uk/~ctttaylo/lyrics.html

Sights & sounds

Want Peter Frampton above your bed? Need a huge picture of Prince astride a motor-

cycle, flowers strewn on the ground around him? Getting pictures of your favorite rock stars—whether you like Maria Muldaur or Teena Marie, Paul Weller or Urge Overkill—used to mean a special trip to the local record store, an afternoon spent looking through racks and racks of posters. Now, though, finding rock images is as easy as beginning a download. At sites like **NY Times Music Greats**, **University of Washington—Parkside Pictures**, and **Rock Photos**, you can feast your eyes on the history of rock. And then you can feast your ears by collecting sound clips from audio archives like **VibeLine**, the **SDSU Sound Archives**, and **Musicians on the Internet MOI**.

Spinal Tap—from eWorld's Everyone's a Critic Clips

On the Net

Multimedia

BITE THIS Rockline is a central area for rock chat, news, pictures, and sounds. The forum, which is based on the weekly radio shows *Rockline* and *Modern Rock Live*, offers a large selection of pictures and sound clips of artists like Nine Inch Nails, Hole, Metallica, Pearl Jam, Elton John, etc. Each of the two radio shows has its own library with photos of past guests

and its own library with sound clips. The Crazy Horse Saloon, a California club, also has its own library here with pictures and sound clips of country stars who have performed there. See the Utilities Library for a good selection of Mac and Windows utilities for listening to sound clips and viewing images. ✓**AMERICA ONLINE**→*keyword* rockline→BITE THIS

SpinOnline's Multimedia Laboratory With 10 years' worth of *Spin* magazine covers, publicity and concert shots of hundreds of musicians, sound clips of acts ranging from Live to Beck, and even utilities to hear and view your multimedia goodies, this is one of the best archives of sounds online. ✓**AMERICA ONLINE**→*keyword* spin→Multimedia Laboratory

Warner /Reprise Records Multimedia Library Video clips of R.E.M. on tour, an Elvis Costello publicity photo, a shot of the Goo Goo Dolls live, a Red Hot Chili Peppers' sound clip from "Shallow Be Thy Game,"

and more electronic music memorabilia from your friends at Warner/Reprise. ✓**AMERICA ONLINE**→*keyword* warner→Multimedia Library

Music pictures

Archive Photos Forum A huge library of quality stock photos, including images of Keith Richards, Buster Poindexter, Henry Rollins, Les Paul, Thelonious Monk, Tommy Dorsey, Metallica, Beverly Sills, Elvis (dozens and dozens of Elvis), Jimmy Buffett, and many more. ✓**COMPUSERVE**→*go* archives→Libraries→Music/Musicians

NY Times Music Greats Browse through a gallery of *New York Times* music photos (Madonna, Streisand, Joplin, Jagger, Bernstein, and many others) or download them to your computer. ✓**AMERICA ONLINE**→*keyword* times music→Photo Gallery: Music Greats

Reuter News Pictures Forum Download the same photos that appeared in newspaper entertainment sections across the country. This large archive of Reuters news photos includes many shots of musical performers (Lyle Lovett at the White House, Bob Dylan at the Rock Hall of Fame, Little Richard kissing Yoko Ono, David Bowie in concert, etc.) as well as other celebs. ✓**COMPUSERVE**→*go* reuters→Libraries Entertainment GIFs *and* Entertainment JPEGs

Robert Altman Communications Not the film director, not the BCCI bigwig, this Robert Altman is the San Francisco native who has spent the last 30 years recording the concert performances of rock, folk, and soul stars such as Mick Jagger, Jim Morrison, Tina Turner, Janis Joplin, Elton John, Phil Ochs, Aretha Franklin, Neil Young, Joan Baez, and Iggy Pop. Under each picture—some of which are hand-tinted—Altman has furnished links to related music sites online, and his online archive also includes portraits of nonmusical celebs such as porn star Seka and quarterback Joe Montana. ✓**INTERNET**→*url* http://www.cea.edu/robert/x.index.html

Rock Photos Rock photos—from Madonna to Prince to Tom Waits. ✓**EWORLD**→*go* me→Everyone's a Critic Clips

Rock & Road Photo Library Part of ABC's Rock & Road Forum, this large collection of photos includes James Brown and Aretha Franklin at the Rock and Roll Hall of Fame, publicity shots of Hootie & the Blowfish and Phish, concert shots of Bob Dylan, and much more. ✓**AMERICA ONLINE**→*keyword* rr→Load-In Library Photos

Rolling Stone Online Photo

Sheryl Crow—from eWorld's Everyone's a Critic Clips

Gallery An online gallery with photos from the current and back issues of *Rolling Stone* magazine. The gallery divides into photos of live performances, photos of celebs in the news that week (whether for birthdays, deaths, weddings, arrests, or other reasons), photos picked by the editors especially for the online site, and photos taken by famous *Rolling Stone* photographer Mark Seliger. Images change frequently. ✓**COMPUSERVE**→*go* rsonline→Photo Gallery

University of Washington-Parkside Pictures As mountains are to Mt. Everest, as bodies of water are to the grand Pacific, picture archives are to the University of Parkside. Take a deep breath, clear some space on your hard drive, and plunge in to this rich resource of music photos. In the "A" directory is the Aerosmith archive. Head to "E" for Brian Eno photos or shots of Melissa Etheridge. Nirvana, Nine Inch Nails, and New Order reside in the "N" directory. And did we mention that the other 23 letters have photos too? Images are primarily in JPEG format. ✓**INTERNET**→ ftp://mirrors.aol.com/pub/music/pictures/ ✓**INTERNET**→ *url* http://music.wit.com/mirrors/music/pictures/ ✓**INTERNET**→ ftp://ftp.uwp.edu/pub music/pictures

Docs & utilities

alt.binaries.pictures.utilities (ng) This newsgroup includes discussions about graphics viewers and utilities. The postings are mostly requests for information, and do not delve into technical jargon. If you're having trouble locating a graphics tool, it's worth your while to log on here. ✓**USENET**→alt.binaries.pictures.utlities

alt.graphics.pixutils (ng) A lightly visited newsgroup concerning image editors, file converters, and other graphics utilities. ✓**USENET**→alt.graphics.pixutils

The Graphic Utilities' Site & Version FAQ A guide to graphics programs for DOS, Windows, Macintosh, and X-Windows systems. The guide lists which programs are required for which file extensions and then links to sites where you can download the programs. ✓**INTERNET**→ *url* http://www.public.iastate.edu/~stark/gutil_sv.html

Graphics An excellent, detailed (perhaps even a bit too technical) hypertext guide to file formats ✓**INTERNET**→ *url* http://www.dcs.ed.ac.uk/%7Emxr/gfx/

Graphics File Formats FAQ A four-part FAQ describing file formats and graphics resources on the Internet. ✓**INTERNET** ...→*url* ftp://rtfm.mit.edu/pub/usenet/news.answers/graphics/fileformats-faq/ ...→*url* http://www.dcs.ed.ac.uk/%7Emxr/gfx/faqs/FileFormats.faq

Graphics Support Forum Frustrated that your decoder program won't turn that alphanumeric jumble into a topless picture of Courtney Love? Burning with indignation because your graphic-designer boyfriend won't explain the difference between .GIFs and JPEGs? This forum offers a message board for posting questions about viewing, downloading, converting, and printing graphics. The libraries offer a large selection of graphics utilities and viewers. ✓**COMPUSERVE** →*go* graphsup

Graphics Viewers, Editors, Utilities and Info One-stop shopping (except there are no charges) for graphics viewers and related utilities. Want a file explaining file formats? A .GIF viewer? A JPEG viewer? A program that converts JPEGs to .GIFs? A TIFF file program? A QuickTime to MPEG converter? A morphing program? Heavily oriented toward Windows and DOS systems, the site brings the most commonly used graphics programs together on one page. Links to pages with compression and audio utilities are also featured. ✓**INTERNET**→*url* http://www2.ncsu.edu/bae/ people/faculty/walker/hotlist/ graphics.html

Image Compression Information Simple explanations of image dimensions and compression formats such as JPEG and .GIF. While the text is written for users of the OTIS art gallery, the information is relevant to anyone looking for basic image-compression info. ✓**INTERNET**→*url* http:// sunsite.unc.edu/otis/notes/ otis-compression.html

JPEGView A small forum dedicated to the Macintosh graphics viewer that supports JPEGs, PICTs, and .GIFs. Ask questions on the message board or download the latest version of the viewer from the library. ✓**AMERICA ONLINE**→*keyword* jpegview

PEGView Page Every Mac user

Traci Lords—from eWorld's Everyone's a Critic Clips

should have a JPEG viewer. It's standard fare and this site includes three versions of the latest release of JPEGView—one that runs on standard Macs, another that runs native on PowerPCs, and another that runs on both. ✓**INTERNET**→*url* http://guru.med.cornell.edu/jpeg view.html

Viewer Resource Center This is a convenient file library on AOL containing programs and utilities for viewing graphics files and animations. You'll find decoders, translators, and viewers for practically every graphics file type, from JPEG to .GIF. The library is divided into Macintosh and Windows/DOS viewers, to make your search a little easier. A nice feature of this forum is the collection of information files explaining many graphics file issues. ✓**AMERICA ONLINE**→*keyword* viewers

Sounds

alt.binaries.sounds.midi (ng) UUencoded binary MIDI files (*.MID) of every musical genre are the focus of this newsgroup. Where else would you expect to

find discussions and examples of the work of Elton John, Mozart, Yanni, and Nine Inch Nails (to name but a few) in the same group? Open the files you are interested in, save them to your hard disk, and then decode them with a freeware program called uuDecode. ✓**USENET**→alt.binaries.sounds. midi

American Recordings Noises Audio clips of various American Recordings artists such as Jesus and Mary Chain, The Jayhawks, Johnny Cash, and Skinny Puppy. ✓**INTERNET**→*url* http://american. recordings.com/audio.html

Carl's Vaudeville & Ragtime Show Take a trip through Vaudeville's history. Begin with some background information about vaudeville in New York, browse the photo gallery for images of vaudeville stars, and then download sound clips of famous recordings, from Murray Hill's "Grandma's Mustard Plaster" to Arthur Collins & Byron Harlan's "Under the Anheuser Bush." ✓**INTERNET**→ *url* http://www.netrunner.net/~ phono/index.htm

Classical MIDI Archives Hundreds of files, from Barber to Wagner, are available for downloading, or (if your Web browser supports it) immediate online listening. If you are using Windows and find your browser lacking this feature, the authors have graciously provided Midi Gate, a Web browser helper application that automatically plays MIDI sequences. Yes, they have Rachmaninov's Third Concerto for the Piano. ✓**INTERNET** →*url* http://www.hk.net/~prs/ midi.html

Classical Music Auditorium Click on Beethoven's Ninth Symphony, Second movement or Johann-Sebastian Bach's IT3 to hear the sounds of classical music. Several other clips are also available. ✓**INTERNET**→*url* http://www.rutgers. edu/sounds/classical_music/bethvn90.au

Cuban Music Samples Excerpts of Cuban music, along with some translations of lyrics into English. ✓**INTERNET**→*url* http://itre.uncecs. edu/music/cuban-music.html

IAMfree Sound Features a rotating exhibition of aural composers with an avant-garde sensibility. Sometimes songs, sometimes spoken word 'n noize, usually interesting. ✓**INTERNET**→*url* http://www. artnet.org/iamfree/IAMFREE/html /sound.html

Internet Underground Music Archive Listen to sound-file snippets from your favorite unsigned band or link to a major label's home page for information on your favorite corporate artists. The site encourages bands to upload samples of their latest demos. Who knows? Maybe you'll be snapped up by Warner or Geffen. ✓**INTERNET**→ *url* http://www.iuma. com/

Jukebox Links to .AU files for Alice in Chains, Guns N' Roses, Jimi Hendrix, the Eagles, Led Zeppelin, Nine Inch Nails, Pearl Jam, the Red Hot Chili Peppers, Sepultura, Testament, and uh…Whitesnake. ✓**INTERNET**→*url* http://cc.lut.fi/~mega/jukebox. html

Macintosh Music & Sound Forum A Neil Young fan drops off a few dozen sound clips, including "Rockin' in the Free World," "Like a Hurricane," "Tonight's The Night," and other Young classics. A Tom Petty fan contributes clips from "Free Fallin'" and "Last

Brian Wilson—from eWorld's Everyone's a Critic Clips

Dance With Mary Jane." Motley Crüe, Dire Straights, Jethro Tull, the Beatles, and Meatloaf fans add sounds from their favorite songs. The Sound Samples library currently has four sections packed with music samples while the Songs library is packed with audio clips in .MOD format (both PCs and Macs can read this format). ✓**AMERICA ONLINE** …→*keyword* mms→Software Libraries Songs …→*keyword* mms→Software Libraries Sound Samples Music Samples*

Musicians on the Internet MOI The songs you can download here aren't being promoted with multi-million dollar advertising campaigns. Quite the opposite. The featured artists are unsigned bands promoting themselves by giving away sound clips on the Net. C'mon. Give 'em a try. ✓**INTERNET**→*url* http://www. escape.com/~rpisen/MOIhome. html

PC Music Forum Carries audio clips for rock, contemporary, and other musical genres. The selection is enormous and broad in coverage—The Pretenders, Elastica, U2, Springsteen, The Rolling Stones, and P.J. Harvey, for starters. The most recent additions

are at the top of the list. Although the clips are in the PC Forum, Mac users may also download and play them with the proper sound player. ✓**AMERICA ONLINE** …→*keyword* pcmusic→Browse Software Libraries Digitized Sounds WAV Sounds Music Clips …→*keyword* pcmusic→Browse Software Libraries Digitized Sounds VOC Sounds Music Clips

SDSU Sound Archive A large archive with links to clips from hundreds of popular songs. ✓**INTERNET**→*url* gopher://sounds.sdsu. edu:71/1

Songs An A-Z directory of musical artists. Visit the site for sound clips from the 10,000 Maniacs, Bob Marley, The Beach Boys, Depeche Mode, Sly & The Family Stone, Edie Brickell, Genesis, the Talking Heads, ZZ Top, and many more. All clips are in .au format. ✓**INTERNET**→ *url* http://peace.wit. com/ sounds/songs/

Songs Who do you want to try? Who haven't you heard yet? Santana? Tori Amos? Alice in Chains? The Black Crowes? Megadeth? The site has a large selction of sound clips from the world's most popular bands. Listen closely. Can you hear the strains of "Jeremy" coming from the Pearl Jam Directory? ✓**INTERNET**→*url* http://ftp. luth.se/ pub/sounds/songs/

Sony Music Clips Dozens of clips from Sony artists of all kinds, including Godflesh, The London Suede, Terence Trent D'Arby, Michael Jackson, Basia, and Esa-Pekka Salonen conducting Stravinsky's violin concerto with Cho-Liang Lin on violin. Clips appear in .WAV and .AU formats and are mono. ✓**INTERNET**→*url* http://www.music.sony.com/Music/SoundClips/index.html

Sound Bytes: The WWW TV Themes Home Page Hey, is that the theme from *Leave It to Beaver*? *Chicago Hope*? Or the "Coke is it!" commercial? This Website houses an amazing collection of several hundred clips of T.V. theme music. The clips are in .AU format and divided into several categories: comedy shows, daytime soaps, children's shows, network intros, commercials, etc. Sound players for Windows, DOS, Mac, and Unix systems are linked to the site. ✓**INTERNET**→*url* http://ai.eecs.umich.edu/people/kennyp/sounds.html

VibeLine Preview excerpts of songs from all the latest bands profiled in *Vibe* magazine—every artist reviewed is represented and sound clips are organized by issue. See why *Vibe* loves Massive Attack, Adina Howard, and others by downloading samples of their music. Consider it your very own online listening booth. ✓**INTERNET**→*url* http://www.pathfinder.com/vibe.html

Virtual Radio A great find for underground fans. You can download entire songs with broadcast quality from dozens of indie bands. ✓**INTERNET**→*url* http://www.microserve.net/vradio

Docs & utilities

General Audio Information This site connects to several popular .AU and .WAV sound players and sound-clip archives. ✓**INTERNET**→*url* http://www2.ncsu.edu/bae/people/faculty/walker/hotlist/audio.html

MMS Extras Not sure which sound player you need to listen to the sounds clips in the AOL libraries? Read through the information in this folder. It carries a list of frequently asked questions about sound files (file formats, the how's of downloading sounds from AOL, etc.) and, in the Information Center, there's an overview of playing and recording sounds on the Macintosh. ✓**AMERICA ONLINE**→*keyword* mms→Extras

PC Music & Sound Information Center A resource guide for PC users just beginning to experiment with sound on their computers. The Center defines commonly used terminology, explains how to play sound files and record sounds, describes different file types, and more. ✓**AMERICA ONLINE**→*keyword* pcmusic→Music & Sound InfoCenter

Real Audio Sometimes sounds can be so aggravating. They take hours to download, and then you have to move them through a sound player. Or at least you had to. Now, though, the waiting is over. With Real Audio, sounds play as they download—your computer merely creates a buffer file that it deletes after the entire sound is played. Download a Real Audio test version and link to pages with Real Audio sounds, from NPR's *Morning Edition* to college radio. ✓**INTERNET**→*url* http://www.realaudio.com

Sight and Sound Forum The forum has library sections with graphics and sound utilities for both the PC and the Macintosh. ✓**COMPUSERVE**→*go* ssform→Libraries

Sound and Music Part of the experience of music fandom online is downloading sound clips—clips from old songs, previews of upcoming songs, and clips from bands you've never heard of. In the past few years, formats for these clips have become fairly standard, most formats can be played on all computer platforms, including the Macintosh, Windows, DOS, and Unix systems. As easy as playing sounds on your computer has become, there are still questions (What sound players should I get? What do the different file formats mean? Where can I get sound players online?). This guide serves two functions: to explain computer sound formats and utilities and to link Netters to all the resources and programs (no exaggeration) they'll ever need to play these sounds. ✓**INTERNET**→*url* http://ac.dal.ca/~dong/music.htm

Vibe Online Helper Applications Frustrated that the sound clip of TLC you downloaded sounds like a '57 Chevy with a busted muffler? Get the proper software at this archive, which includes sound players for both the Mac and the IBM. ✓**INTERNET**→*url* http://www.pathfinder.com/vibe/soft/helpers.html

Videos

American Recordings Visuals Clips from music videos for artists on the American Recordings label. Artists include Jesus and Mary Chain, The Jayhawks, Johnny Cash, Julian Cope, and Skinny Puppy. ✓**INTERNET**→*url* http://american.recordings.com/video.html

MTV Heavy Rotation Video Clips "Hey, Butt-head." "What is it, Beavis?" "This archive is cool. They have, like, videos here and stuff." This online library collects clips from the most popular videos on MTV. When a video moves out of heavy rotation on the network, the clip heads to an online library designated for Former Heavyweight Champions. ✓**AMERICA ONLINE**→*keyword* mtv

Concerts & festivals

Every rock fan knows the ritual of going to a show. Spend an edgy day at work. Grab a

quick shower and throw on some comfortable clothes. Suffer through the long drive to the stadium, or a long subway ride to the club. Endure the lines—for admittance, for beer, for merchandise. Cheer when the band appears. Push up toward the mosh pit. Pull back to see the guys working the sound board. Yell for hits. Absorb new material. Leave satisfied, or disappointed, or wired, or exhausted. Save the ticket stub. Tell friends you were there. On the Net, concert resources range from national show listings (**Wilma Tour Directory, Musi-Cal**) to special features on festivals (**Mammoth List of Music Festivals**) to a huge site sponsored by noted monopoly—er, company—TicketMaster.

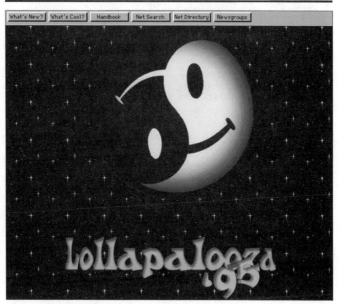

The yin and yang of Lollapalooza—http:// www. lollapalooza.com

National

Club Guide Listings of concerts nationwide. ✓**EWORLD**→*go* mu→ Club Guide

Concert Dates Large selection of concert tour schedules (date, venue, and city) alphabetized by performer. ✓**AMERICA ONLINE**→*keyword* critics→Music & Concerts→ Concert Dates

The Concert Hotwire A searchable database of concert information based on Pollstar's Route Book Database, a frequently updated resource of tour schedules for all musical genres. Search by city, venue, or artist. ✓**INTERNET**→ *url* http://www.pollstar.com/ pollstar/search.html

Metaverse Concert Information Concert information by artist, updated bi-weekly. ✓**INTERNET**→*url* http://metaverse.com/ vibe/concerts/index.html

Musi-Cal A worldwide listing of live musical performances that you can search by performer, city, venue, or event. Want to know where Neil Young is playing in upcoming months? Enter his name, designate "performer," and search.

Looking for something to do this Saturday night in your area? Search by city name (not just the big cities!), and listings for performances at local nightclubs, bars, colleges, and arenas are retrieved. Listings include dates, performer names, and contact numbers. Anyone can submit listings, and while the site is certainly not comprehensive, it's pretty amazing! ✓**INTERNET**→*url* http://www. calendar.com/concerts/

Music on TV (ml) A list with announcements and discussions of television musical events. ✓**INTERNET**→*email* amedrano@euclid. ucsd.edu ✍ *Type in message body:* subscribe mtvglist

Radio Concerts (ml) Advance notice of upcoming radio con-

Wilma, the tour directory—from http:// wilma.com/ index.html

certs. ✓**INTERNET**→*email* radio-concerts-request@cs.albany.edu ✍ *Type in message body:* subscribe

Wilma Tour Directory This huge index of concert and venue information links to city guides, tour schedules, and even concert reviews. Visitors can preview hundreds of cities for information about arenas, clubs, theaters, colleges, and coffeehouses. (New York City has more than 100 listings, while L.A. comes close to 200.) In many cases, venues have their own home pages (The Knitting Factory in New York City, for instance) and the Wilma Tour Directory links directly to these pages. While venues are only just beginning to trickle onto the Net, record labels have hit the Net like a deluge. Wilma links to many of these labels, most of which feature extensive concert tour information for their artists. Wilma also has a directory of artists who are currently on tour, and there are links to tour schedules and concert reviews. ✓**INTERNET**→*url* http://wilma.com/ index.html

Regional

102.7 WNEW Concert Calendar A monthly calendar of New York City concerts. The schedule covers performances at Jones Beach, Madison Square Garden, Big Birch, The Beacon Theater, and several other big concert venues. Check out this month's and next month's schedule. ✓**INTERNET**→*url* http://www.wnew. com/concerts/

107.9 END Concerts Concerts for Cleveland are listed by band and by place of performance. Each listing for a local band is linked to a page with band philosophy, member profiles, show dates, sound samples, and more. ✓**INTERNET**→*url* http://www.americast. com:80/WENZ/concerts/

96Rock: Upcoming Concerts Concert info for Tucson and Phoenix, Arizona. ✓**INTERNET**→*url* http://biz.rtd.com/klpx/concerts. html

Alive 93-5 Concert Connection Concert info for Christian music in the Mississippi area. ✓**INTERNET**→*url* http://www.mc.edu:80 /~alive935/concerts.html

Boston Concert Scene A list of this month's concert and club performances in the Boston area. ✓**INTERNET**→*url* http://www.tiac.net/ waaf/concert.html

Channel Z Concert Connection Not a B-52's site; concert schedules and ticket info for Missouri. ✓**INTERNET**→*url* http:// www.woodtech.com/channelz/ concert.html

Concert onLine Concert info for northern Florida. ✓**INTERNET**→*url* http://www.jou.ufl.edu/about/ stations/rock104/concert.htm

The Edge Rock concert info for Arizona. ✓**INTERNET**→*url* http:// www.getnet.com:80/kedj/concerts. html

Fox's Concert Page Concert info for Colorado with links to artist Websites. ✓**INTERNET**→*url* http://www.rmii.com/thefox/ concrt1f.html

Jersey Area Music Guide A guide to music in the New York City, Jersey City/Hoboken and New Jersey, and Philadelphia area. Still under construction. ✓**INTERNET**→*url* http://www.iuma.com/ JAMS/

KLQ's Concert Connection Concert info for Grand Rapids, Michigan. ✓**INTERNET**→*url* http:// www.wklq.com/klq/ concert.htm

KZZR Concert Update Concert

LOCAL EVENTS

The Colorado Music Festival ✓**INTERNET**→*url* http:// www.aescon.com/music/ cmf/index.htm

Glastonbury Festival ✓**INTERNET**→*url* http://www. crg.cs.nott.ac.uk/~nlc/glast/ glast.html

New Orleans Jazz & Heritage Festival ✓**INTERNET** ...→*url* http://www. neworleans.com/events.html ...→*url* http://www.wisdom. com/la/jfinfo.htm

Scandinavian Music Festivals ✓**INTERNET**→*url* http:// www.uio.no/~henrikb/uteliv/ konsert/festivaler/festivaler. html

South by Southwest (SXSW) ✓**INTERNET**→*url* http://monsterbit.com/sxsw. html

schedules for the Albuquerque, New Mexico, area. ✓**INTERNET**→*url* http://www.swcp.com:80/kzrr/concerts.htm

LA Club Listing Daily club listings for the Los Angeles area. ✓**INTERNET** ...→*url* http://www.primenet.com/~sk8boy/shows.html ...→*url* http://www.dnai.com/~lmcohen/lacd.html

The Q102 Concert Calendar Rock concert schedules for Texas. ✓**INTERNET**→*url* http://www.pic.net/media/q102/calendar.html

Quebec Sur Scene A directory of theaters and clubs in Quebec. ✓**INTERNET**→*url* http://www.clic.net/surscene/

Texas Country Concerts Covers country concerts in the Dallas–Forth Worth area, from fairs to major arenas. ✓**INTERNET**→*url* http://www.iadfw.net/kyng/concerts.html

Underground Network Concerts Rock concert information for Tennessee, New York, Massachusetts, and Arkansas. ✓**INTERNET**→*url* http://www.undernet.com/undernet/update.html

Z•93 Concert Information Concert info for the Dayton, Ohio, area. ✓**INTERNET**→*url* http://www.erinet.com:80/wgtz/concerts.html

International

The Ultimate Gig Guide A guide to upcoming band performances in the U.K. ✓**INTERNET**→*url* http://carlton.innotts.co.uk/~deejay/

Tickets

All American Inc. Concerts

TicketMaster's home page—http:// www.ticketmaster.com/

Links to concert information for several major artists on tour (surprisingly enough, all tours that All Americans, Inc., sells tickets for). You can't buy tickets online, but there's an 800 number available if you want to order. ✓**INTERNET**→*url* http://cybermart.com/american/concerts.html

Canadian TicketMaster Home Page TicketMaster has an entirely separate Canadian site with its own rock concert, country concert, and venue info databases. The site also has information about ticket centers in Canada and entertainment-oriented features such as the biographies of Canadian artists. ✓**INTERNET**→*url* http://www.ticketmaster.ca/

Ticket Trader The site functions as a guide to buying tickets for concerts, plays, and sporting events. It features seating charts for major venues, schedules for professional sports teams, and a guide to buying tickets nationwide. Click on "Tickets" for a list of sports teams, concert performances, or theater shows. Click on the event you're interested in (Diana Ross, Blues Traveler, Bon Jovi, etc.), for a tour schedule and numbers to call in each city for tickets. ✓**INTERNET**→*url* http://www.ticket-trader.com/trader.html

TicketMaster Online You want tickets to a Bob Dylan concert. Who you gonna call? TicketMaster. You want tickets to a Hootie & the Blowfish concert. Who you gonna call? TicketMaster. You want tickets to the Beastie Boys concert? Who you gonna call? TicketMaster. You want tickets to Pearl Jam concert? Well, maybe not (the Almighty TicketMaster and the Almighty Pearl Jam are not working well together lately). But can you buy tickets online? Not yet, but keep checking in, it can't be too far off. For now, though, TicketMaster offers a huge searchable database of concerts, sporting events, theater productions, and family events. It also features a list of the top 25 bands touring that week with links to city-by-city schedules, a guide to venues (search for events by venue), an incredible selection of entertainment features (interviews with entertainment-industry icons, previews of concerts and sporting events, etc.), and information about Ticketmaster promotions. ✓**INTERNET**→*url* http://www.ticketmaster.com/

TicketWeb Features a national service scheduled to be up in 1996 that will sell concert tickets online. ✓**INTERNET**→*url* http://www.ticketweb.com/

WebTix Colorado Concert and Events Schedules Four tickets for Jimmy Page in Chicago for sale. Three tickets for R.E.M.

in D.C. desperately wanted. Two tickets for Elton John in New York for sale. Deadheads with tickets for scheduled shows wondering what to do—the Grim Reaper offers no rain checks. It's a national classifieds board devoted to concert tickets and other events. The site also includes a monthly calendar of upcoming Colorado events. ✓**INTERNET**→*url* http://www.inetmkt.com/webtix/index.html

Venues & clubs

Concert Seating You're on the phone with TicketMaster trying to buy tickets for the concert of the decade. You can have any seat in the house (wake up!), but you're not sure what's good and what's not. Get a floor plan. This site carries floor plans for the Worcester Centrum, Foxboro stadium, Great Woods Stadium, Providence Civic Center, the Wang Center, the Or-

pheum Theater, and the Harbor Lights Center. ✓**INTERNET**→*url* http://www.wzlx.com/wzlx/seating.html

Music, Dance and Theater Directories It isn't hard to find music in the Big Apple, but here's a list of places to go looking. The site is a listing of venues in New York City, broken down into Blues & Folk, Classical & Opera, Dance, Jazz, Concert Halls, Rock & Pop, and Rock Clubs. ✓**AMERICA ONLINE**→*keyword* times music →Music, Dance & Theater Directories

Troubworld Who's played at the Troubador? Well, Miles Davis, Arlo Guthrie, Neil Diamond, Bruce Springsteen, Etta James, KISS, James Taylor, Jimmy Buffett, Motley Crüe, Sheryl Crow, and Pearl Jam, and that's just for starters. Visit its online site for a calendar of upcoming events, an archive of press clips and photos from past performances, a chat room, and links to Web pages for unsigned bands that the Troubadour recommends and sells CDs for. ✓**INTERNET**→*url* http://www.iuma.com/Troubadour/

Festivals

Lollapalooza Every summer, this site leaps to life, with coverage of the rock festival that has come to define alternative music in the nineties. ✓**INTERNET**→*url* http://www.lollapalooza.com

Mammoth List of Music Festivals A list of U.S. music festivals with links to festival home pages when available. The lists covers festivals ranging from Lollapalooza to the New Orleans Jazz and Heritage Festival. ✓**INTERNET**→*url* http://www.pathfinder.com/vibe/mmm/music_festivals.html

The searchable Musi-Cal—http://www.calendar.com/concerts/

Musi-Cal(tm) is the first online calendar that provides easy access to the most up-to-date worldwide live music information: concerts, festivals, gigs and other musical events. We place a premium on quality data. No weird pictures. No 200 kilobyte scanned album covers. No outdated listings. Just up-to-date music information. Musi-Cal is free to users and is supported by Automatrix and its sponsors.

Check out what's new...

Boots & taping

Artists release plenty of official records; in the case of performers like Bruce Spring-

steen and Guns N' Roses, they even release two records at once. But consumers are greedy. Enough is never enough. And that's why they go searching for bootlegs—both unauthorized recordings of live shows and collections of studio demos. In the past, tape trading occured mainly through newsletters and in the parking lots at Dead shows; the Net, with its ability to unite a worldwide community of fans, has enabled tape culture to proliferate wildly. Talk to other tapers at **alt.music.bootleg** and **TapeXchange**; peruse the **Internet Music Want-lists**; and then check out the bootleg selection for artists from the Beatles to Prince to (of course) the Dead.

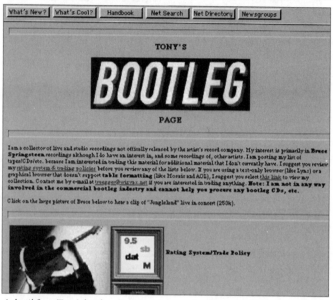

A detail from Tony's bootleg page—http://www.wizvax.net/truegger/tape-trades.html

On the Net

Across the board

alt.music.bootlegs (ng) This newsgroup is a classifieds section for cybertraders dealing in boots—Todd will trade any recording of the last Cranberries tour for anything in his current collection; Susan offers the Clash's *USA Live* and Bauhaus' *Rest in Peace* for just one copy of Alice Cooper's *Paracidal Slumbers*. Occasionally there's a short thread recommending

recording equipment, but mostly this is a newsgroup devoted to the glories of the barter system. ✓**USENET**→alt.music.bootlegs

Bootlegs/Concerts A virtual address book of bootleg traders in Cyberspace. Check in here to see who's got what to trade for what, especially if you're looking for Phish recordings—they seem to be the darlings of traders here. ✓**COM-PUSERVE**→*go* amgpop→Messages *and* Libraries→Bootlegs/Concerts

Live Music Recording Data-base A database for live-music trading enthusiasts that lists a variety of concert and studio boots. These recordings are for trading purposes only, of course; selling bootlegs is a violation of U.S. copyright law, after all. ✓**INTER-**

NET→*url* http://www.webcom.com/~joshbrow/boots.html

TapeXchange "Trying to provide an inexpensive mechanism for tape traders to list their tapes" is the motto of the Tape XChange, which does its best to prove that there is such a thing as a free lunch. With a list of traders, a database of available tapes by category, and an explanation of trading policy, this promises to be a valuable resource for the serious tape trader. ✓**INTERNET**→*url* http://joe.infotank.com/TapeXchange/

Equipment

alt.music.tape-culture (ng) Despite its promising name, this newsgroup is dominated by discussions of low vs. high speed dubbing and posts pushing demo tapes of Long Island garage bands. Tape-culture fans can use this group as a resting room from alt.music.bootlegs. ✓**USENET**→alt.music.tape-culture

Guide to Cassette Decks and Tape Trading How do you clean tape heads? How do you demagnetize them? Is Dolby preferred by concert tapers these days? How much does a good cassette deck cost? Can you buy tapes wholesale, or will the heat in your car melt cassettes? Get information on equipment, etiquette, and other topics vital to the survival of the tape trading economy in this great nation of ours. While this site focuses on the Grateful Dead—the Mecca of tape traders—the information will be useful for anyone who has ever shelled out $800 for a Nakamichi DR-2. ✓**INTERNET**→*url* http://www.cs.cmu.edu/~mleone/gdead/taping-guide/index.html

Etiquette

Tape Trading Etiquette Want to start tape trading but nervous about making a faux pas? Anxious that you may accidentally address a fellow bootlegger as "sir" rather than "dude"? Never fear. Tape Trading Etiquette is here. With sections on Arranging the Trade, Making the Tapes, Posting the Tapes, and Trading Videos, this document explains the ins and outs of getting unofficial studio and concert tapes. ✓**INTERNET**→*url* http://tamos.gmu.edu/~harlan/trading_etiquette.txt

Philosophy

The Free Music Philosophy The text of a manifesto describing why and how music should be available for free distribution with-

out concern for copyright and intellectual property. The document is aimed both at the concert taper and the distributer of sound clips on the Net. Will there be a revolution in aural property law? Probably not. But if there is, the Free Music Philosophers will be at the forefront of the movement. ✓**INTERNET**→*url* http://www.ram.org/ramblings/philosophy/fmp.html

Trader's pages

Colin's Bootleg List You can get recordings of literally hundreds of shows from Colin's soundfactory. He'll trade them for other recordings or for blank tapes, and he'll even send you the tape cases if you promise to do the same. Colin promises at least "B+" grade sound quality on his recordings of Blind Melon, Pearl Jam, Tori Amos, Alice in Chains, and Nirvana, among others. ✓**INTERNET**→*url* http://www.tc.cornell.edu/~cushing/boots.html#milla

Harlan's Collection of Illegitimate Recordings While Harlan specializes in Pink Floyd and They Might Be Giants, he also links to general tape-trader and RoIO resources online. ✓**INTERNET**→*url* http://tamos.gmu.edu/~harlan/roio.html

Tony's Tape Trading Page While Tony specializes in Bruce Springsteen, he also has information on R.E.M., U2, the Who, and other rockers, as well as links to other tape traders online. ✓**INTERNET**→*url* http://www.wizvax.net/truegger/tape-trades.html

Wantlists

Internet Music Wantlists I want *Alone At My Piano* by Kate Bush, and I'll pay $40. I want an unofficial David Bowie CD and

I'll pay $25. I want an early Arlo Guthrie LP and I'll pay $15. Netters looking for a specific music recording can post what they're looking for and how much they're willing to pay on either the Internet CD Wantlist or the Internet CD Vinyl Wantlist. The Wantlists are not exactly lists of "I want" messages—they're organized lists of music requests (name of recording, artist, email address, the bid, and date of request). Each week a third list noting just the changes to the masterlists is also available. Those adding requests to either of the lists are required to post their email addresses so that they can be contacted by anyone who has the music. ✓**INTERNET** …→*url* http://www.swcp.com/~lazlo/Wantlists.html …→*url* ftp://ftp.swcp.com/pub/users/lazlo/

Selected artists

Beatles Bootlegs—A Little Guide A different kind of Beatle boot is being discussed here! Diehard Beatles fans will appreciate these reviews of boots like BBC, Yellow Dog, Get Back, and Artifacts. Especially interesting is the review of The Quarrymen: The Dawn of Modern Rock, which revels in the fact that this bootleg contains a version of "I'll Follow the Sun," proving that Paul wrote the song all the way back in 1960. ✓**INTERNET**→*url* http://www.prairienet.org/~dauber/bootlegs.html

Dire Straits Bootleg List Dire Straits is very cool when it comes to bootlegs: its management company's newsletter even sports a classifieds section where fans can trade bootlegs! So don't feel guilty for checking out this list of CDs, cassettes, and LPs—chances are you already own all the official releases anyway! ✓**INTERNET**→*url* http://www.physics.sunysb.edu/

~gene/DS/FAQ/boot.html

Grateful Dead Taper's Corner
As anxious fans wonder if the Dead will tour after Jerry's death, the massive number of concert bootlegs available for the group will provide some consolation. There is so much interest in these recordings that the message board of the Dead Forum has devoted an entire section to them. Come here to post or read classifieds looking to sell or buy recordings. If you just want to show off your list of acquisitions, there's a Lists Only section where you can catalog your taped treasures. In the Equipment Flea Market File, you'll find all the equipment you need to tape shows (not the Dead's). If you buy anything through the Market, you can later check into the Taper's Tech topic for any help or advice you might need. Basically, if the subject is bootlegging and the Dead, this is the place to find out anything you want to know. ✓**AMERICA ONLINE**→*keyword* dead→Dead Messaging→Taper's Den

Green Day Bootlegs Known to Exist Listed in chronological order of their release, the bootlegs on this list include takes from concerts, old punk radio shows, and studio work. Click any song title on any track list for the full lyrics of the song (which could come in very handy in case of poor sound quality)! ✓**INTERNET**→*url* http://www.cs.caltech.edu/~adam/GREENDAY/MUSIC/boots.html

Lepplin Bootlegs This tiny portion of the Led Zeppelin FAQ offers a list of recommended bootlegs and some interesting stories about them. Here's one: "Robert Plant has often been known to autograph bootlegs, and all three members have from time to time requested copies of some

of the better known productions. And a Page fan reports meeting Page and giving him a copy of a 10-album Zeppelin bootleg set. Page said, 'Thanks,' and continued walking on, as rock stars usually do when fans hand them something. But when he saw that the gift was a bootleg, Page stopped, went back to the fan, and said, 'Thanks! This is great!'" ✓**INTERNET**→*url* http://www.cs.brown.edu/people/jsw/zeppelin/faq.html

Marillion & Fish Bootleg CD List Extensive reviews of bootleg recordings of the band. Each review lists the name of the CD, the label that released it, where the CD was recorded, the playing time, sound quality, and the songs. Cover art is also shown, where available. A total of 72 CDs are covered, including *Marillion Live in Liverpool* (1982), *Something Fishy Going On* (1989), and *Plenty of Fish in the Sea* (1989). ✓**INTERNET**→*url* http://www.let.ruu.nl/~jeroen/boots/

Nirvana Boot Guide Kurt died without leaving behind a tremendous amount of unreleased material, but he did leave some—and there are plenty of Nirvana concerts floating around out there. This Website lists of concert bootlegs (organized chronologically by date of the concert), demo recordings, and bootleg compilations, and also gives fans advice on how to obtain Kurt boots. (Hint: the Internet is a good place to start!) ✓**INTERNET**→*url* http://seds.lpl.arizona.edu/~smiley/nirvana/boot.html

Prince—The Conflict over Bootlegs This site addresses some very interesting questions regarding one of the most heavily-bootlegged artist of all time, in-

cluding "Do you think Prince does not want us to hear any material that he doesn't officially release?" and "How do bootlegs sneak out of the studio, and how do you think Prince feels about it?" If you have a conscience about pilfering The Paisley Park Vault, come here to assuage your guilt; otherwise, start surfing the Net with your eyes open for *Chocolate Box* or the *Royal Jewels* box set. ✓**INTERNET**→*url* http://morra.et.tudelft.nl/npn/living_room/best_of_list/views.on.boots.html

Rush CD Bootlegs Listing This list reviews boots from various Rush tours from 1974 to the present. The reviews include some little gems, like the fact that even the intermission music is indexed on the *Atmospheric* liner notes. ✓**INTERNET**→*url* http://syrinx.umd.edu/rush/HTML/bootlegs.html

U2 Bootlegs List A very well-researched effort to catalog all known U2 bootlegs. Organized alphabetically by title, this list names the manufacturer, total running time, track list, source, and sound quality for each release. The excellent annotations note exceptional CD graphics, liner notes, and any guest players. ✓**INTERNET**→*url* gopher://wiretap.spies.com/00/Library/Music/Disc/bootleg.u2

Zappa Bootlegs Frank Zappa disliked for-profit bootleggers so much, he launched the Beat the Boots series to re-issue bootleg recordings on a legitimate label. He thought trading was OK, though, so Frank smiles down from above on this annotated list of unofficial concert and studio recordings. ✓**INTERNET**→*url* http://www.catalog.com/mrm/zappa/html/faq8.html

Memorabilia

When rock stars die, fans descend on their belongings like vultures on carrion. John

Lennon's glasses, Jimi Hendrix's jacket, Kurt Cobain's driver's license—somehow, the fact that these objects have come in contact with strato-spheric talent invests them with importance far beyond their ordinary value. And this sort of capitalist necro-philia that doesn't even begin to scratch the surface of rock memorabilia. Old posters, records, shirts, and magazines have transfixed fans since the genre's beginnings, and the new versions of these same things continue to make money for merchandisers. Check out **ArtRock**, **rec.music.marketplace**, and more—and get your piece of the rock.

On the Net

Across the board

ArtRock This San Francisco based gallery specializes in rock posters, from Stanley Mouse's groovy renditions from the seventies to Frank Kozik's commemoration of Green Day's recent Seattle show. Click the Order Catalog button and have a list of their entire stock shipped directly to your door. ✓**INTERNET**→*url* http://www.shopping2000.com/shopping2000/artrock/

Beatles Memorabilia The bulk of the musical offerings listed here

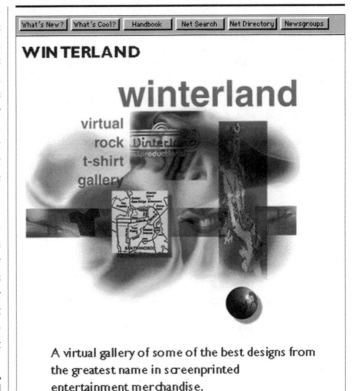

WINTERLAND

winterland

virtual rock t-shirt gallery

A virtual gallery of some of the best designs from the greatest name in screenprinted entertainment merchandise.

Winterland t-shirt gallery—from http://www.mca. com/winterland/index.html

is recording equipment stripped from John Lennon's Tittenhurst Park Studios (the one he was using at the time Imagine was recorded). A headphone control box is not an exciting item unless it happened to be owned by John Lennon! Read a list of the wares and then click on the email address listed here for further info. ✓**INTERNET**→*url* http://www.cityscape.co.uk/users/cp87/beatles.htm

Memorabilia News A set of News articles that will keep you

abreast of memorabilia auctions and their offerings. One recent feature focused on the Elvis auction in Las Vegas where his Formal Notice of Induction into the U.S. Army, his 1966 white Rolls Royce, and his Exxon gas card all went up on the block. ✓**EWORLD**→*go* The Music Universe →*Find:* Memorabilia

Music Memorabilia If you're looking for Beatles Christmas tree ornaments, 78-rpm records from the 1930s and 1940s, or a Coca-

BE A HIT !

SEND NOW AND GET WITH IT !

Available from ArtRock—http://www. shopping2000.com/shopping 2000/artrock/

Cola Rock Ola juke box, look no further than this site! Collectors of music memorabilia meet here to advertise and shop for these and other interesting pieces, including autographs, old instruments, and sheet music. This is also a good place to get advice on the authenticity of that antique Strat you bought at the last Sotheby's auction. (Danny advises, "There are 4 fourlegitimate Major dealers in the world who deal in Rock and Roll Memo. The rest are just guy's along for the ride, who spell John Lennon P-R-O-F-I-T.") ✓**COMPUSERVE**→*go* Collectors Forum→Music Collectibles

Music Screeners A promotional page that lists installation instructions, minimum system requirements, and functions of screensavers featuring a number of artists, including Michael Jackson, Cyndi Lauper, Indigo Girls, and Harry Connick, Jr. Look at the Where to Find Them section for retail stores that sell the savers. ✓**INTERNET**→*url* http://www.sony.com/Music/Screeners

rec.music.marketplace (ng) Don't miss out on the Pop Will Eat Itself paraphernalia auction in Detroit! Read this newsgroup faithfully, and you'll keep up on music memorabilia auctions, conventions, and sales nationwide. ✓**USENET**→rec.music.marketplace

Rock and Roll Collectibles and Memorabilia Choose from ephemera to do with any of over a hundred artists—from Prince to the Brady Bunch—including promo CDs, concert posters, stickers, press kits and books. The catalog is updated weekly. ✓**INTERNET**→*url* http://www.current.com/rockroll.html

Rockworld—All Music Cyber-Galleria It's hard to imagine—the sheet music for Billy Joel's "My Life" that you bought all those years ago is now actually worth money! So is a song book of Uriah Heep's *Wonderland* and a picture of the band Blue Cheer from circa 1968. If you feel you just can't make it without that autographed Motley Crue poster, you can phone or email your order or bid. ✓**INTERNET**→*url* http://www.sonnet.com/webworld/rockworld.htm

Winterland Productions T-Shirts Don't worry! Winterland doesn't sell Hendrix t-shirts splattered with Woodstock mud. They sell all-new, spanking clean shirts adorned with the images of artists like the Beatles, Led Zeppelin, Beastie Boys, and even Pantera! Winterland showcases their wares in the T-Shirt Gallery and provides ordering and shipping info. ✓**INTERNET**→*url* http://www.mca.com/winterland/index.html

Part 3

Artist Guide

Pop stars from A to Z

What is Popular Music?

Critics can talk all they want about genres, styles, and aesthetic gains, but fans know that popular music is about one thing and one things only—the artists.

What would the British Invasion have been without the Beatles? What would funk have been without Sly Stone? What would soul have been without Aretha Franklin? What would self-

important, anthemic rock have been without U2? Lyle Lovett, Joni Mitchell, James Brown, Nirvana, Tom Waits, Lenny Kravitz, Björk, Hank Williams, the Jesus & Mary Chain—these are the reasons that fans listen to popular music. And these are also the reasons fans flock to the Net; the online world is carpeted with fan pages and chat sites devoted to individual artists and bands.

Sites For All Tastes
Whether you're a seventies addict who sits in the attic and listens to old Black Oak Arkansas records or a nineties junkie who has prognostic dreams of Nirvana, you can't get away from the fact that artists make the music, not critics, not radio stations, not magazines or categories. The *NetMusic* Artist Guide catalogs the wealth of artist-related sites on the Internet and the online services.

Using The Guide
The Artist Guide seems simple—hundreds of individual performers and bands listed in simple alphabetical order. But there are a few wrinkles. First of all, there's the matter of artist chat sites. Chat about a particular artist varies little from site to site—CompuServe's users may have a slightly different perspective on the career of Bob Dylan than America Online's, but discussion on both services will focus on Dylan's albums, his concert tours, his historical importance, and his unruly hair. Consequently, we have decided to create a combined listing for all commercial-service chat message boards, and to describe these sites only briefly (usually with the unexciting, but entirely accurate, phrase "Message-based discussion"). Usenet newsgroups have received more detailed descriptions, not only because Usenet tends to generate the most interesting discussion, but also because of the powerful sense of community in newsgroups.

Why is Elvis Missing?
As you browse the Guide, you may notice that some of the biggest names in music history—the Beatles, the Stones, Dylan, Elvis—have entries, but no sites. Don't panic. Artists with large numbers of online sites have been pulled out of the main listings, and those performers have been awarded special Artist Spotlights. In addition, sites about artists in other genres—New Age, for instance, or classic soul—may also appear in the Genres section of *NetMusic* (pages 215-310).

Artist & Band Indexes

Library of Musical Links
✓**INTERNET**→*url* http://www-scf.usc.edu/~jrush/music/index.html

Mammoth Music Meta-List
✓**INTERNET**→*url* http://www.timeinc.com/vibe/mmm/music_artists.html

Music et al Archives ✓**INTERNET**→*url* http://www.webjammers.com/projects/bands.html

Music Land ✓**INTERNET**→*url* http://www.cs.umd.edu/~lgas/music/

On-Line Artists at IUMA
✓**INTERNET**→*url* http://www.iuma.com/IUMA-2.0/olas/genre/ALL_001.html

Rock and Roll Hall of Fame Inductees ✓**INTERNET**→*url* http://www.rockhall.com/induct

The Ultimate Band List
✓**INTERNET**→*url* http://american.recordings.com/WWWoM/ubl/ubl.shtml

Virtual Music Spotlight
✓**INTERNET**→*url* http://www4.ncsu.edu/unity/users/d/decox/WWW/TVMS.html

Yahoo ✓**INTERNET**→*url* http://www.yahoo.com/Entertainment/Music/Artists/

ABBA Artist Guide

ABBA

ABBA Although this site is little more than an ABBA songbook, with a full discography linked to lyrics, the Swedish hit machine's greatest songs are all here, from "Waterloo" to "Fernando" to "Dancing Queen." ✓**INTERNET**→*url* url http://phymat.bham.ac.uk/ABBA/

ABBA Chat Message-based discussion. ✓**AMERICA ONLINE**→*keyword* mmcb→Rock/Pop→Rock Artists A-L→ABBA

alt.music.abba One ABBA fan who went to see the Alicia Silverstone vehicle *Clueless* thought that the main character's mother looked like Agnetha Falskog. Another ABBA fan responds not with scorn, but with a similar admission: "Funny you should say that, 'cos a similar thing befell me quite a while back. It had nothing to do with any movie or anything, mind, but at the local college, the assistant French teacher (gone now) looked remarkably like the (1983-ish?) picture of Agnetha found on the back of *ABBA Gold*." When ABBAns aren't dreaming of a world where every man, woman, and child is a doppelgänger of an ABBA member, they're comparing notes on trips to Europe, nominating Best Songs of All Time, and letting their Swede emotions flow freely. ✓**INTERNET**→alt.music.abba

ABDUL, PAULA

Paula Abdul Chat Message-based discussion. ✓**AMERICA ONLINE**→*keyword* mmc→Rap/R&B →R&B/Soul→PAULA ABDUL

Paula Abdul Homepage Pic-

tures, fan club addresses, and links to related artists like Janet Jackson. ✓**INTERNET**→*url* http://www.xs4all.nl/~hammer1/paula_abdul.html

Paula Abdul List (ml) She's got a new album, and fans are head over heels in love with Paula again. Subscribe to this mailing list to find out why. ✓**INTERNET**→*email* amedrano@ucsd.edu ✍ *Type in subject line:* subscribe Paula Abdul list

The Paula Abdul Web "Those who know that I have this huge crush on Paula ask if I would ever leave my wife and children for her given the opportunity. Certainly not!" Though infidelity might not be an option, the author of this dense and impressive page gets close to Paula in every other way, with an FAQ, pictures, rumors, and a huge library of sound samples. ✓**INTERNET**→*url* http://www2.csn.net/~danzirin/paula.html

AC/DC

AC/DC Home Page A tribute in French to the bad boys of Australian hard rock. ✓**INTERNET**→*url* http://olympe.polytechnique.fr/~ramet/acdc/acdc.html

The AC/DC Homepage A brief introduction to the wealth of AC/DC resources online, along with lyrics for hundreds of songs. ✓**INTERNET**→*url* http://www.acsu.buffalo.edu/~house/acdc.html

alt.rock-n-roll.acdc (ng) Diehard AC/DC fans plug in here to suggest that their Aussie guitar heroes have never written a bad song ("Some of their lyrics are a tad weak—'Texas, yea Texas...we had some fun.' Shit that song was really weak up until the chorus. But they write the killer chorus pretty much every time"), that *Back in Black* may have been composed of leftover songs from the

Paula Abdul—from http://www2.csn.net/~danzirin/paula.html

Bon Scott days ("It sounds nothing like subsequent albums"), and that AC/DC could consolidate its fan base by recording an Unplugged set. ✓**USENET**→alt.rock-n-roll.acdc

Fusebox Sooner or later, every band gets a tribute album. AC/DC's is called *Fusebox*, and features such alternative hardcore heroes as Fur, Yothu Yindi, Suiciety, Rig, and Downtime, performing classic AC/DC songs. The Brisbane thug-hop trio Regurgitator earns the dubious privilege of covering "Back in Black." ✓**INTERNET**→*url* http://www.next.com.au/bmg/fusebox/menu.html

Live Wire Comprehensive, reverent, and crass enough to capture the essence of a band whose latest album is named *Ballbreaker*, this site offers a full list of albums, an FAQ, and a history of the band ("AC/DC was just getting worldwide popularity when tragedy struck on February 19, 1980. AC/DC's frontman, Bon Scott, was found dead in the back seat of a friend's car. In official AC/DC press releases it said that he died from natural causes, but he had been drinking quite heavily the night before and it is common knowledge now that Bon had died by passing out and choking on his own vomit"). And they say you can't dust for vomit. ✓**INTERNET**→ *url* http://www.sdstate.edu/~cc92/http/acdc.html

ADAMS, BRYAN

Bryan Adams Chat Message-based discussion. ✓**AMERICA ON-LINE**→*keyword* mmc→Rock/Pop→ Soft Rock/Pop/Oldies→Bryan Adams

The Bryan Adams Home Page Lyrics to Bryan's newest songs, press clips, guitar tabs, and images. ✓**INTERNET**→*url* http://www.glue.umd.edu/~xiaoqin/music/adams.html

Bryan Adams Home Page Illustrated with tiles of the microphone-bearing Adams taken from the cover of *Waking Up the Neighbors*, this site is the worldwide home of the Bryan Adams News Service, which furnishes reports on the Canadian rocker in German and English. ✓**INTERNET**→ *url* http://www.cadlab.de/~tichel/BryanAdams/bryan.htm

Bryan Adams Mailing List (ml) Everything Bryan Adams does, he does for you, and he does it in full view of this mailing list, which scrutinizes his career from "Cuts Like a Knife" to the present. ✓**INTERNET**→*email* jiinx@csra.net ✍ *Write a request*

AEROSMITH

Aerosmith Sony Music's official site, with press releases and a screen saver. ✓**INTERNET**→*url* http://www.music.sony.com/Music/ArtistInfo/Aerosmith.html

Aerosmith "Sex, drugs, & rock 'n' roll. Take out the drugs and

Bryan Adams Home Page—http://www.cadlab.de/- tichel/BryanAdams/bryan.htm

there's more room for the other two." This densely packed page is a bottomless pit of Aerosmith resources, from magazine articles to online surveys to FAQs to lyrics to guitar tabs. ✓**INTERNET**→*url* http://coos.dartmouth.edu/~joeh/

#aerosmith Liv, Alicia. Alicia, Liv. Chat about the possibilities as well as the band. ✓**INTERNET**→*irc* #aerosmith

Aerosmith and EFF Rock the Net Press materials and merchandising information from Aerosmith's December 1994 Virtual Tour, which let fans worldwide speak to the band on major online services. ✓**INTERNET** ...→ *url* http://www.eff.org/virtour.html ...→*url* http://www.aerosmith. com/aerosmith/

Aerosmith Chat Message-based discussion on a variety of topics, from the lead singer (that's Tyler) to the lead guitarist (that's Perry) to Aerosmith's resurgence in the 1990s. ✓**AMERICA ONLINE** ...→*keyword* mtv→Message Boards→Bands

That Do Suck→aerosmith ...→*keyword* mtv→Message Boards→Bands That Don't Suck→Joe Perry and Aerosmith ...→*keyword* rockline→Messages→KEEPING THE 70S' ALIVE→AEROSMITH ...→*keyword* rockline→Messages→KEEPING THE 70S' ALIVE→steven tyler ✓**COMPUSERVE**→*go* fanclub→Messages *and* Libraries→Aerosmith

Aerosmith Lyrics This site includes all the known poetry of Tyler and Perry and company, from "dream yourself a dream come true" to "I go crazy, crazy, baby I go crazy." ✓**INTERNET**→*url* http://lydia.bradley.edu:1971/aero/

Aerosmith Sights and Sounds Page Almost 100 images of the band—album covers, live shots, magazine photos—and more than a dozen sound samples. ✓**INTERNET** →*url* http://pandora.st.hmc.edu/Aerosmith/

alt.rock-n-roll.aerosmith (ng) There's some talk of music, from the band's hard-boogie 1970s origins to its current superstardom. But there's just as much conversation concerning merchandising and memorabilia—the winged logo, old magazine covers, etc. The lesson? What goes around comes around, and when it comes around, it's usually worth something to a sucker with the wrong idea about "history." ✓ **USENET**→ alt.rock-n-roll.aerosmith

A-HA

a-ha Fill out a Netsurfer survey, browse a list of albums, review the 1987 world tour, and learn more about one of Europe's most enduring ear-candy outfits. ✓ **INTERNET**→ *url* http://www.site.gmu.edu/~kkasmai/a-ha.html

a-ha A band history, an FAQ, a discography, and a list of solo projects by band members. ✓ **INTERNET**→*url* http://www.wwiv.com/a-ha/

a-ha list (ml) Discuss Morten, Pal, Magne, and other aspects of this Norwegian sensation. ✓ **INTER-NET**→*email* majordomo@ainet.com ✍ *Type in message body:* subscribe a-ha <your email address>

ALICE IN CHAINS

Alice in Chains Updated every few months, this page includes a discography, guitar tabs, and fan club info. ✓ **INTERNET**→*url* http://www.peak.org/~mikec/aic.html

Alice in Chains Chat Message-based discussion. ✓ **AMERICA ON-LINE**→ *keyword* mmc→Alternative Rock→Bands A-L→Alice in Chains!!!!

alt.music.aliceinchains (ng) Fans sell records, talk about the Mad Season side project, and speculate on whether the fall 1995 album will sound more like *Facelift* or *Jar of Flies.* ✓ **USENET**→

alt.music.aliceinchains

Angry Chair (Alice in Chains List) Discussion of Alice in Chains. ✓ **INTERNET**→*email* angrychr@halcyon.com ✍ *Type in subject line:* subscribe *Type in message body:* <your email address>

ALLMAN BROTHERS BAND

The Allman Brothers Commemorating the band's 1995 induction into the Rock and Roll Hall of Fame, this page includes a brief career biography and sound clips. ✓ **INTERNET**→*url* http://www.rockhall.com/induct/allmanbr.html

Allman Brothers Band Sony's official site, with tour info and press releases. ✓ **INTERNET**→*url* http://www.music.sony.com/Music/ArtistInfo/AllmanBrothersBand.html

Allman Brothers Band Keyed to the band's appearance at Woodstock in 1994, this page has a complete discography and videography. ✓ **INTERNET**→*url* http://metaverse.com/woodstock/artists/allmanbrothersband/index.html

Allman Brothers Chat Message-based discussion. ✓ **AMERICA ONLINE**→*keyword* mmc→Rock/Pop →Rock Artists A-L→The Allman Brothers Band

Allman Brothers Email Want to ask Gregg about his marriage to Cher? Want to find out whether new live shows will be released? Email the band at America Online. ✓ **INTERNET**→*email* allbroband @aol.com ✍ *Email with general correspondence*

Allman Brothers List (ml) A dedicated mailing list for discussing the venerable blues-rock ensemble. ✓ **INTERNET**→*email* listserv@netspace.org ✍ *Type in message body:* subscribe allman <your

NOTES

"Some time ago, I saw a cute leetle photo of Steve Tyler in a restaurant, wearing glasses and trying (in vain, I'd wager...) to decipher the meal of the day..."

"Well I'll be damned! I guess we'd all better burn our Aerosmith albums now. Gee, Mr. You've just opened my eyes. I have been fooled all this time. Steven Tyler wearing glasses? OH! THE HORROR!"

"So what if he wears glasses! You probably think he runs around with with all those scarves too! Well I've got news for YOU. Steven is one of the nicest people I've met. When he isn't touring, he wears t-shirts and jeans, glasses, goes to movies, the dentist, sits by his pool, and is a father to his two young children, etc. Maybe it is YOUR illusions that were shattered! I wonder if you'll be able to do backflips when you are in your forties."

—from alt.**rock-n-roll.aerosmith**

full name>

Allman Brothers Live Chat An hour-long Allman Brothers fan chat session in AOL's People Connection every Wednesday night at 8:30 p.m. EST. ✓**AMERICA ONLINE**→*keyword* people→list rooms→private rooms→abbchat

alt.fan.allman-brothers (ng) Quieter than Rose Hill Cemetery at midnight. Rose Hill is where Duane Allman is buried, in case you've been stuck in the attic listening to your old Yaz records—this newsgroup collects occasional posts about the band, including announcements of TV appearances and tour dates and information on related bands (the Grateful Dead, the Georgia Satellites). ✓**USENET**→alt.fan.allman-brothers

Hittin' the Web with the Allman Brothers Band An official Website still under construction, with plans for a complete band history, a huge concert database, reviews, and images. ✓**INTERNET**→*url* http://www.netspace.org:80/allmans/

ALPHAVILLE

Alphaville A discography, news, lyrics, and information on the band's mailing list. ✓**INTERNET**→*url* http://access.digex.net/~evatac/Alphaville.html

Alphaville List (ml) Discuss the latest releases (and old standbys) recorded by the German dance-pop band. ✓**INTERNET**→*email* blackwells@yvax.byu.edu ✍ *Type in message body:* subscribe alphaville

AMERICA

America A band bio, a discography, lyrics, and information about the America Express newsletter. ✓**INTERNET**→*url* http://www.pacificrim.net/~wahlgren/

America Chat Message-based discussion. ✓**AMERICA ONLINE** ...→*keyword* rockline→Messages→KEEPING THE 70S' ALIVE→AMERICA ...→*keyword* mmc→Rock/Pop→Rock Artists A-L→America:Beckley and Bunnell

AMERICAN MUSIC CLUB

American Music Club A promotional site for the band's LP *San Francisco* that includes track listings and a sound sample of "Wish the World Away." ✓**AMERICA ONLINE**→*keyword* http://www.iuma.com/Warner/html/American_Music_Club.html

AMC album cover—http://www.iuma.com/Warner/music/American_Music_Club/

American Music Club Message-based discussion. ✓**AMERICA ONLINE**→*keyword* mmc→Alternative Rock→Bands A-L→AMC

American Music Club A band bio, images, and press releases for the *San Francisco* LP. ✓**AMERICA ONLINE**→*keyword* warner→alternative→American Music Club

American Music Club List (ml) Talk about Mark Eitzel's literary, slightly depressive lyrics, or comment on AMC's ever-expanding sound. ✓**INTERNET**→*email* firefly@world.std.com ✍ *Write a request*

AMOS, TORI
See page 76.

ANDERSON, LAURIE

A Record of the Time Named for Anderson's most concise explanation of postmodern simulacra ("This is the time...This is a record of the time"), this article tracks the performance artist as she moves through her *Nerve Bible* Tour. ✓**INTERNET**→*url* http://www.demon.co.uk/london-calling/musfeat.html

HOMEpage OF THE BRAVE: Laurie Anderson An FAQ, a discography/filmography/bibliography, a collection of reviews, lyrics, tour dates, and a random quote generator that delivers pearls of Andersonian wisdom ("I was looking for you, but I couldn't find you...I couldn't find you"). ✓**INTERNET**→*url* http://www.c3.lanl.gov:8080/cgi/jimmyd/quoter?home

Laurie Anderson A transcript of a Halloween 1994 real-time chat conference in which the cool-voiced one explained her recent shift toward Luddite views, during the course of which Balzac, Pynchon, Lenin, Spalding Gray, and Peter Gabriel are mentioned. The site also includes biographical and discographical information. ✓**AMERICA ONLINE**→*keyword* warner→alternative→Laurie Anderson

Laurie Anderson Principal sponsor Voyager's promotional page for 1995's *Nerve Bible* Tour and the accompanying CD-ROM *Puppet Motel*. ✓**INTERNET**→*url* http://www.voyagerco.com/LA/VgerLa.HTML

(cont'd pg. 79) →

Tori Amos

Bounced from Baltimore's prestigious Peabody Conservatory for "improvising," Tori

Amos first broke onto the pop scene as the front-bimbo for the short-lived heavy-metal band Y Kant Tori Read. When the redhead resurfaced with the 1991 LP *Little Earthquakes*, it was as a sensitive singer-songwriter who drew on the introspective feminism of Kate Bush and Joni Mitchell without sacrificing her potent sexuality. Though her melodramatic vocals and overly pretty piano work sometimes forgo women's lib for women's Liberace, Amos has a fervent online following. Visit **Tori, The Tori Amos Homepage**, and **Welcome to the First International Church of Tori** to find out what fans are saying about Tori, her music, and her magic.

Tori with a cold-blooded friend—from http://www.cs.virginia.edu/~bcs9a/pics/

On the Net

Across the board

Gary's Tori Amos A link to the Tori newsgroup, subscription information about the Really Deep Thoughts mailing list, and links to images, lyrics, and other Tori sites online. ✓**INTERNET**→*url* http://web.cal.msu.edu/gary/tori.html

Precious Things Subtitled "a tribute to Tori Amos," this page reveals that the creator once had

his cassette collection stolen. Fascinating. In addition, the page contains information about Tori's music, her life, and her massive popularity online. ✓**INTERNET**→*url* http://www.gtlug.org/~rduncan/tori.html

Tori Lyrics, pictures, and even a link to songs by Sarah McLachlan. ✓**INTERNET**→*url* http://cadman.cit.buffalo.edu/~dalewis/toriamos.html

Tori Amos Pictures of Tori Amos in concert, with brief but accurate annotation ("pretty turquoise lighting"). ✓**INTERNET**→*url* http://www.mit.edu:8001/people/abbe/tori.html

Tori Amos Lots of pictures of Tori—because fans like to look at

Tori—along with lyrics to all her songs, including those recorded with the heavy-metal outfit Y Kant Tori Read. ✓**INTERNET**→*url* http://www.mit.edu:8001/people/jwb/Tori.html

Tori Amos Is Tori Amos the female Jerry Lewis? You'd think so after looking at this page, which collects a Tori Amos FAQ, a discography, lyrics, interviews, pictures, and sound clips. But the highlight of the site is the set of Amos parodies, which range from scatological takes on "Crucify" to a hilarious moron's version of "Silent All These Years": "So you found a girl who thinks really deep thoughts / What's so amazing about really deep thoughts / A tree fell in the woods and made a lot of noise / How's that thought for you? / My scream got lost in a paper cup / I wanna know where the hell has it gone? / I've got 25 bucks and a lighter do you think it's enough / To start a forest fire." ✓**INTERNET**→*url* http://olympe.polytechnique.fr/Tori/

Tori Amos "In real life I'm bone dry and when I play I'm a mango and in sex I'm starving to be a dripping mango." Okay, okay, Tori. We understand. You're deep or something. Just don't drip on the carpet. ✓**INTERNET**→*url* http://watt.seas.virginia.edu/~jds5s/music/tori/tori.html

The Tori Amos Homepage Pictures, a discography, various text files about Tori, and more. ✓**INTERNET**→*url* http://www.mit.edu:8001/people/nocturne/tori.html

Tickling the ebonies—from http://www. cs.virginia.edu/~bcs9a/pics/

Tori Amos Online "For those who are unaware, Tori Amos is quite potentially the most intriguing, socially relevant artist of our time. Amos speaks about issues that impact everyone, and she has earned the respect and admiration of fans around the world." Or at least one fan around the world. The page links to a full discography; a picture archive; Tori's abuse, rape, and incest hotline; and other home pages devoted to the most famous of Amoses. ✓**INTERNET**→ *url* http://www.ksu.edu/~tmservo/tori.html

The Tori Amos Thumbnail Picture Archive Hundreds of Tori photos that feature the artist in every imaginable pose, from every imaginable source, splashed on the Web page in miniature. ✓**INTERNET** → *url* http://www.csv.warwick.ac.uk/~psucj/tori.html

The Tori Amos WWW Tour Links to other sites pertaining to Tori and all things Toriffic. ✓**IN-TERNET**→ *url* http://gto.ncsa.uiuc.edu/khawkins/tori.html

Tori Story Tori Amos kissed this fan's cheek. Read about the events surrounding this transforming experience at this page. ✓**INTERNET** → *url* http://ayup.res.wpi.edu/~xine/tori.html

Welcome to the First International Church of Tori "I've got enough guilt to start my own religion," said Tori in an interview, and some poor sap took her seriously enough to found a faith based on red-headed confessional singer-songwriters who can dress demure or slinky depending on the seasons. "If you wish to become one of the chosen ones, then contact either Cardinal Gladish or Cardinal Murphy with your reason for despising Men, God, or both, and a small donation." ✓**INTERNET**→ *url* http://cctr.umkc.edu/user/cgladish/tori.html

Chat

Really Deep Thoughts (Tori Amos List) (ml) Share your really deep thoughts with other Tori Amos fans on this mailing list. ✓**INTERNET**→rdt-request@gradient.cis.upenn.edu ✍ *Type in message body:* subscribe rdt

rec.music.tori-amos (ng) Fans can't get enough of the racy red-headed savior of self-indulgent piano rock, and they're falling over themselves talking about concert appearances, new releases, and Tori's increasingly idiosyncratic smash-hit covers ("Smells Like Teen Spirit," "Losing My Religion," and the lubricious deconstruction of Led Zep's cock-rock classic "Whole Lotta Love"). ✓**USENET**→rec.music.tori-amos

Tori Amos Chat Talk about Tori's next album, her contributions to soundtracks (John Singleton's simple-minded social drama *Higher Learning* is mentioned frequently), and her seemingly end-less series of foolish and unselfconcious videos. ✓**AMERICA ONLINE** ...→*keyword* mmc→Alternative Rock→Bands A-L→Tori Amos ...→ *keyword* mtv→Message Boards →Bands That Don't Suck→Tori Amos ✓**EWORLD**→*go* eaz→Pump Up the Volume→Music Talk→Tori Amos is God?

Images

Rare Photos of Tori Amos Tori smiles at a rat. Tori shaves. Tori stares into a mirror and contemplates her own hair. Tori steps up to the microphone. And she does it all at this page, which posts video stills and other rare photos. ✓**INTERNET**→*url* http://uvacs.cs.virginia.edu/~bcs9a/tori.html

Tori Amos Image Archive A set of pictures of Tori, presented with very little annotation (which is too bad, because it would be nice to know how on Earth the author of this page managed to acquire a photograph of a birthday cake with frosting script that says "Happy Birthday, Tori"). ✓**INTERNET**→ *url* http://starry-night.mit.edu/tori/

Leg maintenance—http://www.cs. virginia.edu/~bcs9a/pics/

Tori Amos

"Joyous hello, Tori lovers! Am I welcome here? I love Tori too. She sings those things I never thought I could put into words. She makes the most rotten things seem tolerable, sometimes even pretty.

"She makes me so happy to be a human, because we get to experience all this heartbreak and anger and sorrow and we get to make these observations about people and things that somehow make the day seem beautiful. Tori is beautiful, in all kinds of ways. I'll be seeing you?"

—from **Tori Amos Chat** on AOL's Music Message Center

"Tori's not God. Tori Amos is my favorite singer and has a passion and beauty in her music that no other modern singer has reached, but she sure isn't God.

I know it was a joke, but anybody who has listened to her music knows that what she sings about is when the person you rely on (often God) fails you. It's silly to make her up to be a god. She's telling you to think for yourself. Do it."

—from **Tori Amos Chat** on eWorld's Pump up the Volume

"Tori claims to have met (the) Anastasia (or her ghost) a few years back and this song has a lot to do with that. Heaps has been written about it in the past--can't remember all the details--still it's one of my favourites for sure!"

—from **rec.music.tori-amos**

Laurie Anderson—Bright Red
A promotional site for the *Bright Red* LP. ✓**INTERNET**→*url* http://www.iuma.com/Warner/html/Anderson,_Laurie.html

Laurie Anderson Chat (ng) When you see L.A., don't think Los Angeles, think Laurie Anderson. And think die-hard fans swapping rumors about new projects, reviewing recent releases, and even celebrating Laurie's July 1995 appearance as the cover girl for Continental Airlines' in-flight magazine. ✓**USENET**→alt.fan.laurie-anderson

Laurie Anderson Info Sparse, like a dying lawn—only a few music samples and links to other sites. ✓**INTERNET**→*url* http://www.netpart.com/phil/laurie.html

THE AFGHAN WHIGS

The Afghan Whigs A discography from Sub Pop to Elektra, with occasional lyrics and sound files. ✓**INTERNET**→*url* http://ernie.bgsu.edu/~bfundak/afghan_whigs/

Congregation (ml) Greg Dulli and friends get their due on this mailing list, on which die-hard fans flip their Whigs. ✓**INTERNET**→*email* majordomo@iglou.com ✍ *Type in message body:* subscribe congregation <your email address>

B

B-52'S

B-52's Chat Message-based discussion. ✓**AMERICA ONLINE**→*keyword* mmc→Alternative Rock→Bands A-L →B-52's

The B-52's Fan Pages A discography, biography, pictures, quotes, and an explanation of the connec-

They came from Planet Claire—from http://www.dur.ac.uk/~d43e4d/b-52s.html

tion between the band and the Commodore Amiga computer. ✓**INTERNET**→*url* http://www.dur.ac.uk/~d43e4d/b-52s.html

Planet Claire (B-52's) Described as "a type of fanzine for the computer which promises to bring you a 'Hot Pants Explosion,'" this bright-purple page cuts right to the heart of B-52 fandom, with "an in-depth psychological analysis of the band" (actually just a history), cheesey images, and links to other pages. ✓**INTERNET**→*url* http://www.dur.ac.uk/~d43e4d/b-52s.html

BAD BRAINS

Bad Brains A promotional site for the LP *Rise*. ✓**INTERNET**→*url* http://www.music.sony.com/Music/ArtistInfo/BadBrains.html

Bad Brains Whatsup Should Bad Brains be numbered among contemporary artists "saved" by their religious beliefs? How angry

is H. R.? And what about the summer 1995 fracas in Lawrence, Kansas that may have "permanently ended the life of the greatest punk-jazz-fusion-hardcore-rasta-reggae-gospel outfit ever." These are your Bad Brains. These are your Bad Brains online. Any questions? ✓**INTERNET**→*url* http://www.computel.com/~whatsup/brains/

BAD RELIGION

Bad Religion Official Sony info for the *Stranger Than Fiction* LP. ✓**INTERNET**→*url* http://www.music.sony.com/Music/ArtistInfo/BadReligion.html

Bad Religion Chat Message-based discussion. ✓**AMERICA ONLINE**→*keyword* mmc→Alternative Rock→Bands A-L→Bad Religion

Bad Religion Homepage Loading times can try one's patience, but Bad Religion diehards should wait them out—this is an excellent page, with a full discog-

The Band Artist Guide

raphy, lyrics, pictures, guitar tabs, and a link to Epitaph Records. ✓INTERNET→*url* http://nebuleuse. enst-bretagne.fr/~lepoulti/BAD. RELIGION/

Bad Religion News Why did Mr. Brett quit? What songs does the band cover live? Post to the Web newsgroup. ✓INTERNET→*url* http://nebuleuse.enst-bretagne. fr/~lepoulti/BAD.RELIGION/ NEWS/

THE BAND

alt.music.the-band (ng) As with any band who recorded the bulk of its work before the advent of MTV, there's something of a comprehension gap over which younger listeners must vault. "My friend John swears that there's a new record of Dylan playing with the Band," says Steve, and it's left to an older and wiser Band fan to point out that Dylan and the Band haven't played together since 1976. Jill wants to rhapsodize about the harmonies on "The Rumor": "Not only is this a great song in itself, but it's almost eerie and spooky if you're in the right mood. There's a true sense of a partnership in three voices in this song. What makes it special is the separate roles throughout the verses, bound by that one ending line in the choruses where they tie into a harmony." In addition to discussion of Helm, Robertson, Danko, Hudson, and Manuel, there's plenty of talk about the group's musical associates—Van Morrison, Bob Dylan, and Neil Young, for example. ✓USENET→alt.music.the-band

The Band Any page that uses as a recurring icon a small version of The Band's Big Pink home in Woodstock—and, moreover, dubs it "Little Pink"—is bound to be a winner, and this page lives up to its high expectations, offering a

well written history of The Band, a discography, and new information on solo projects by ex-Band members. And that's in addition to the usual complement of lyrics, images, guitar tabs, and sound clips. ✓INTERNET→*url* http://www-ia.hiof.no/~janh/TheBand.html

The Band Commemorating The Band's 1994 induction into the Rock and Roll Hall of Fame, this page includes a brief career biography and sound clips. ✓INTERNET→ *url* http://www.rockhall.com/ induct/band.html

Band Chat Message-based discussion. ✓AMERICA ONLINE→*keyword* mmc→Rock/Pop →Classic Rock→The Band

BARENAKED LADIES

alt.music.barenaked-ladies (ng) Mostly devoted to tour dates—they're bare naked in Seattle! they're bare naked in Chautauqua!—this newsgroup occasionally addresses BNL's material. ✓USENET→alt.music.barenaked-ladies

Barenaked Ladies An official Warner Brothers site that includes a band bio, fan club information, and tour dates. ✓AMERICA ONLINE→*keyword* warner→Alternative→Barenaked Ladies

Barenaked Ladies Chat Message-based discussion. ✓AMERICA ONLINE→*keyword* mmc→Alternative Rock→Bands A-L→Barenaked Ladies

Gordon's Place (Barenaked Ladies) Basic information on these Canadian practitioners of cleverrock ("Be My Yoko Ono," "Brian Wilson," "Alternative Girlfriend"). ✓INTERNET→*url* http:// www.cs.mun.ca/~craig/bnl/ barenaked.html

 NOTES

"On December 30 and 31, 1971, The Band did special shows at The Academy of Music on 14th Street in New York (this venue is now the nightclub called The Palladium). These are the shows that resulted in the official Capitol release called Rock of Ages, a double live album. To that point, The Band in performance sought to reproduce exactly the sound of the records. For the shows at The Academy of Music, they decided to do something completely different. Allen Toussaint was commissioned to write horn parts, and five New York hornmen were recruited. The arrangements were richer, slower, roomier, and the net effect was to make the familiar new again. The liner notes to this CD, The Night They Drove Old Dixie Down, are accurate in a very cloying way: 'were culled,' it says. That is correct; these are the culls, the recordings that didn't make the cut."

-from **alt.music.the-band**

Where Barenaked Ladies Work And Play Bios for band members, tour dates, a discography, and more. ✓**INTERNET**→*url* http://yar.cs.wisc.edu/~gnat/bnl/

BASIA

Basia Press releases and sound clips from Sony Music. ✓**INTERNET**→*url* http://www.music.sony.com/Music/ArtistInfo/Basia.html

Basia Home Page Lyrics and dozens of pictures of the lovely Ms. Trzetrzelewska. ✓**INTERNET**→*url* http://www.cc.gatech.edu/ugrads/c/Ben.Combee/basia/

Basia List (ml) The queen of smooth jazz-pop likes to tour, play upscale theaters, and then retreat to the privacy of her home while her fans talk about her on this mailing list. Help make Basia's dream a reality. ✓**INTERNET**→*email* basia-request@jane.tiac.net ✍ *Type in message body:* subscribe basia

BAUHAUS

Bauhaus Discographies All the band's official releases. ✓**INTERNET** ...→*url* http://www.evo.org/html/group/bauhaus.html ...→*url* http://gothic.acs.csulb.edu:8080/~vamp/Gothic/Text/bauhaus-discog.html

THE BEACH BOYS

alt.music.beach-boys/rec.music.artists.beach-boys (ng) Bud wants to compile a list of artists who have referred to Brian Wilson overtly in their music (he has Tears for Fears and The Seventy Sevens, but not Barenaked Ladies or Terence Trent D'Arby). Marty wants to know about the rare Dylan/Brian collaboration, "The Spirit of Rock and Roll." And fans from all over have opinions about the band's best recordings. While the rec.music* group is more active than the alt.music*

The Beach Boys—from http://www.nando.net/music/gm/BeastieBoys/

group, many articles are cross-posted. ✓**USENET** ...→alt.music.beach-boys ...→ rec.music.artists.beach-boys

The Beach Boys Commemorating the band's 1988 induction into the Rock and Roll Hall of Fame, this page includes a brief career biography and sound clips. ✓**INTERNET**→*url* http://www.rockhall.com/induct/beachboy.html

Beach Boys Chat Message-based discussion. ✓**AMERICA ONLINE**→*keyword* mmc→Rock/Pop Rock→Artists A-L→The Beach Boys = Brian Wilson

Beach Boys List (ml) Imagine a world with a mailing list that allows you to discuss the ins and outs of the Beach Boys—Brian Wilson's demented genius, the band's commercial success, the voices in the firmament. Wouldn't it be nice? ✓**INTERNET**→*email* smile@smile.sbi.com ✍ *Write a request*

Heroes and Villians Online Affiliated with the Beach Boys mailing list, this Web page includes lyrics, links, and an FAQ about the band. ✓**INTERNET**→*url* http://www.iglou.com/scm/bb/hvo.html

BEASTIE BOYS

alt.music.beastie-boys (ng) When they were just obnoxious punk-rappers, the Beastie Boys couldn't get the time of day. Now that they're funk auteurs, critics' darlings, and mainstays of Manhattan's alternative-culture scene, they get all the time they want. Beastie newsgroup posts range from lyric analyses (Adrock is talking about golf, not cocaine!) to traders' price lists to musicological digs for the sources of samples. ✓**USENET**→alt.music.beastie-boys

Beastie Boys A beautiful and well maintained site with links to *Grand Royal* magazine, Grand Royal Records, and lots of information about the Beasties. ✓**INTERNET**→*url* http://www.nando.net/music/gm/BeastieBoys/

Beastie Boys Chat Message-based discussion. ✓**AMERICA ONLINE** ...→*keyword* mtv→Message Boards→Bands That Do Suck→BEASTIE BOYS ...→*keyword* mtv→Message Boards→Bands That Don't Suck→BEASTIE BOYS ...→ *keyword* mmc→Rap/R&B→Rap/hip-Hop/Funk→The Beastie Boys

Beastie Boys Screen Saver Check your heads at the door before downloading this wacky screen saver, which features the

Beasties in a number of computer-animated adventures reminiscent of the 1970s Jackson 5 cartoon. Plotless, profoundly surreal, and more fun than a barrel of monkeys. ✓**INTERNET**→*url* http://underground.net/Beastie/beastie.html

Brad's Boutique A list of sample sources for the Boys, covering all four of their LPs to date. ✓**INTERNET**→*url* http://www.csulb.edu/~bsb/BeastieBoys/

I'll Have Some Fries With Those Beastie Boys Links to other Beastie Boy sites, and reviews of the band's albums. ✓**INTERNET**→*url* http://www.hooked.net/users/clayton/links.html

THE BEATLES

See page 84.

BECK

alt.music.beck (ng) How old is Beck? Is his birthday in the summer? Is he still writing a journal for *Spin* magazine? Don't be a loser—read this newsgroup. ✓**USENET**→alt.music.beck

Beck A fan page that reviews Beck's career, noting that *One Foot in the Grave* reveals that Beck "is indeed a bodhisattva papa...a child preacher who reminds [you] that you can find truth in a convenience store." ✓**INTERNET**→ *url* http://www.cc.columbia.edu/~aeb23/beck.html

Beck Chat Message-based discussion. ✓**AMERICA ONLINE**→*keyword* mtv→Message Boards→Bands That Do Suck→Beck

BECK, JEFF

Jeff Beck Official Sony info for Beck's last few releases, including the instrumental effort *Frankie's House* and the Gene Vincent trib-

Jeff Beck—from http://sashimi.wwa.com/hammers/ pictures/jbeck.htm

ute *Crazy Legs*. ✓**INTERNET**→*url* http://www.music.sony.com/Music/ArtistInfo/JeffBeck.html

Jeff Beck A photo from *Musician* magazine of Beck in Surrey, England in 1989. ✓**INTERNET**→*url* http://sashimi.wwa.com/hammers/pictures/jbeck.htm

THE BEE GEES

The Bee Gees Pictures of Barry, Robin, and Maurice, along with an elaborate discography that includes cover art of all of the Bee Gees albums. ✓**INTERNET**→ *url* http://www.ncl.ac.uk/~n4017075/beegees.htm

Bee Gees Chat Message-based discussion. ✓**AMERICA ONLINE**→ *keyword* mmc→Rock/Pop Rock→Artists A-L→The Bee Gees

Bee Gees List (ml) They had their heyday in the late sixties, and their payday in the late seventies. Pay tribute to one of the most popular bands in music on this mailing list—if you like, you can even mourn the fact that little brother Andy Gibb has joined the big Shadowdance in the sky. ✓**IN-**

TERNET→*email* listproc@cc.umanitoba.ca ✍ *Type in message body:* subscribe Bee-Gees <your full name>

BEL CANTO

Bel Canto Home Page Lyrics, a discography, images, concert reviews, and more. ✓**INTERNET**→*url* http://math-www.uio.no/belcanto/

Bel Canto List (ml) Get the latest news on the Norwegian trio. ✓**INTERNET**→*email* dewy-fields-request@ifi.uio.no ✍ *Write a request*

BELLY

Belly An annotated discography of the band's 4AD releases. ✓**INTERNET**→*url* http://www.evo.org/html/group/belly.html

Belly Tour schedule, news, pictures, lyrics, interviews, reviews, and sound samples from Tanya Donnelly's pet project. ✓**INTERNET**→*url* http://www.evo.org/html/group/belly.html

Belly Chat Message-based discussion. ✓**AMERICA ONLINE**→*keyword* mtv→Bands That Don't Suck→Belly. Throwing Muses.Veruca Salt

BIG AUDIO DYNAMITE

Big Audio Dynamite Sony press releases for the *Higher Power* album, along with information on previous B.A.D. LPs. ✓**INTERNET**→*url* http://www.music.sony.com/Music/ArtistInfo/BigAudioDynamite.html

Big Audio Dynamite Chat Message-based discussion. ✓**AMERICA ONLINE**→*keyword* mmc→Alternative Rock→Bands A-L→The CLASH + Big Audio Dynamite

BIG BLACK

Big Black A discography, along with lyrics, pictures, and links to other home pages. ✓**INTERNET**→*url*

http://ucunix.san.uc.edu/~
hahnmt/big.black/BigBlack.html

Big Black / Rapeman / Shellac discography Steve Albini's
bands are the focus of this page, illustrated with a drawing from the
cover of *Songs about Fucking.* ✓**INTERNET**→*url* http://www.mcs.net/~
alester/html/bigblack.htm

BIG HEAD TODD

Big Head Todd and the Monsters Home Page News, notes,
tour dates, sound clips, images,
and video clips. ✓**INTERNET**→*url*
http://www.phoenix.net/USERS/
cbyrne/bhtmhome.html

Big Head Todd & The Monsters An official Warner Brothers
promotional site for the band's LP
Stratagem. ✓**AMERICA ONLINE**→*keyword* warner→Alternative→Big
Head Todd & The Monsters

BIG STAR

Big Star Home Page Guitar
chords, band information, and
links to other sites for power pop
bands, including Velvet Crush, the
Posies, and Teenage Fanclub. ✓**INTERNET**→*url* http://comp.uark.
edu/~cbray/bigstar/bigstar.html

BJORK

alt.music.bjork (ng) Though
she's from Iceland, Björk is hotter
than ever—her second solo LP,
Post, is netting her the best reviews
of her career. If you want to talk
Björk, you can join the two Icelandic music mailing lists, the
Björk newsgroup, or the Björk
IRC channel, where loyal
Björkians share their opinions on
everything from the album's
strongest songs to a news report
that Björk has won a court case
over authorship credit from songs
on her first album, *Debut.*
✓**USENET**→alt.music.bjork

*The self-love of Björk—from
http://www. bjork.co.uk/bjork/*

Bjork Interviews, merchandise,
pictures, links, and a discography.
✓**INTERNET**→*url* http://www.math.
uio.no/bjork/

Bjork Mostly links, along with a
set of pictures. ✓**INTERNET**→*url*
http://www.nvg.unit.no/~thomasr
/bjork.html

#bjork Live chat about Björk.
✓**INTERNET**→*irc* #bjork *Info:* ✓**INTERNET**→*url* http://131.188.190.
131/~mikel/bjorkIRC.html

Bjork Chat Message-based discussion. ✓**AMERICA ONLINE**→*keyword* mtv→Message Boards→Bands
That Don't Suck→bjork

Bjvrk, Broerk, Bjork!! Links to
other sites, a wealth of Björk
ASCII art, and a brief Icelandic
phrasebook ("just in case you run
into Björk on the street and would
like to impress her with your command of the language"). ✓**INTERNET**→*url* http://131.188.190.131/
~mikel/bjork.html

Blue-Eyed-Pop (ml) Has there

ever been an article written about
Björk that didn't use the word
"pixieish"? Probably not. But you
can read about the former Sugarcube and her Icelandic contemporaries all you want on this mailing
list. ✓**INTERNET**→*email* listserv@morgan. ucs.mun.ca ✍ *Type in message
body:* subscribe Blue-Eyed-Pop
<your full name>

WebSense Overseen by Björk
herself, or so the page claims, this
is the most elaborate Website devoted to the pixie-sized powerhouse. In addition to standard features—discography, biography,
lyrics, and images—this official
page includes an interactive guide
to the five senses, which casts
Björk as a sort of Web Virgil leading surfers to sensual sites across
the online world. ✓**INTERNET**→*url*
http://www.bjork.co.uk/bjork/

Won's Astro Bjork Page A
complete Björk discography, an
FAQ, and links to other sites devoted to the Icelandic sprite. ✓**INTERNET**→*url* http://www.ee.umn.
edu/groups/hkn/.bjork/bjork.html

THE BLACK CROWES

Black Crowes American Recording's home page for the band, with
a stylish photo collage, a band biography, and lyrics. ✓**INTERNET**→
url http://american.recordings.
com/American_Artists/Black_
Crowes/bcrowes_home.html

Black Crowes Frequently updat-

Black Crowes—http://american.recordings.com/American_Artists/Black_Crowes/bcrowes_home.html

*(cont'd
pg. 88)*
→

The Beatles

Meet the Beatles. These four chipper lads are from Liverpool—Liverpool, England—

and they're hoping to become pop stars. Will they? Well, only time will tell, but those industry insiders who have listened to the band's demos say that they sound promising. With a double-barreled songwriting attack—both Paul McCartney and John Lennon fancy themselves wordsmiths—and tight, ensemble playing (McCartney plays bass, Lennon rhythm guitar, and mates George Harrison and Ringo Starr pitch in on lead guitar and drums, respectively), the Beatles have talent to burn and their cute-boy image is sure to capture the hearts of fans everywhere. Help a new band get off the ground by visiting **Beatlemania, PEPPERLAND**, and **rec.music. beatles**. You may even want to hold their hands.

The Fab Four and their fab autographs—http://www.primenet.com/~dhaber/bpix/

On the Net

Across the board

Beatlemania This site probes the theory that character is place, conducting a virtual tour of Liverpool that stops at Eleanor Rigby's bench and reprints clips from local newspapers. (Real estate speculators will be thrilled to learn that Paul's childhood home is for sale!) ✓ **INTERNET**→*url* http://www.csc. liv.ac.uk/users/u2jww/tour/beatle

mania/beatlemania.html

The Beatles Lyrics, discographies, biographies, Beatles trivia, and info on the solo careers of all four lovable moptops. ✓ **INTERNET**→*url* http://www.eecis.udel.edu/ ~markowsk/beatles/

The Beatles The famous rejected *Yesterday and Today* cover—you know the one, with the four members of the Beatles surrounded by butchered baby dolls—is here, along with lyrics, a discography, and trivia. ✓ **INTERNET**→*url* http://turtle.ncsa. uiuc.edu/alan/beatles.html

The Beatles How many records did the Beatles release on labels other than EMI? You'll have to visit this German site to find out. Even if you're not interested in label trivia, you'll find plenty of Beatles-related information here, from fan club addresses to Beatles bootlegs (given the clever portmanteau name "Beatlegs"). And what do you get if you click the link titled "email addresses of the

Beatles"? A lament that none of the Fab Four are online. Hello, goodbye. ✓ **INTERNET**→*url* http:// cip2.e-technik.uni-erlangen.de: 8080/hyplan/gernhard/beatles. html

The Beatles A British Beatles site with a few nice images and standard links. ✓ **INTERNET**→*url* http:// sun1.bham.ac.uk/cca93054/ beatles/index.html

The Beatles "They call them The Beatles, / The Boys, The Fab Four, / The Lads from Liverpool, / But I call them John, Paul, George, and Ringo." A poem? A recently discovered promotional jingle for a Beatles children's show? Nope. It's the epigraph for this page, which collects lyrics for dozens of songs by the Beatles, John Lennon, Paul McCartney, George Harrison, Ringo Starr, and Julian Lennon. ✓ **INTERNET**→*url* http://www.umd.umich.edu/~ infinit/Beatles/

The Beatles Find out what songs

the Beatles recorded, when they recorded them, and what MacLen compositions they gave away to other artists. ✓ **INTERNET**→*url* http://www.cc.columbia.edu/~brennan/beatles.html

The Beatles Annotated links to other Beatles sites online, presented with a minimum of flash and a nice Pepperland glove graphic. ✓ **INTERNET**→*url* http://www.cs.rochester.edu:80/users/grads/jonas/beatles/beatles.html

The Beatles Commemorating the band's 1988 induction into the Rock-and-Roll Hall of Fame, this page includes a brief career biography and sound clips. ✓ **INTERNET**→ *url* http://www.rockhall.com/induct/beatles.html

Beatles A collection of Beatles links, illustrated by a thumbnail image of the *Sgt. Pepper's Lonely Hearts Club Band* cover. ✓ **INTERNET**→*url* http://gagme.wwa.com/~boba/beatles.html

The Beatles A Finnish Web page devoted to the Beatles, with cover photos, quotes, and a description of the band as "a popular rock and roll group." Roll over, Beethoven, and tell Nirvana the news. ✓ **INTERNET**→ *url*/http://lyyra.otol.fi/~simoaro/beatles.html

The controversial "butcher" cover—http://turtle.ncsa.uiuc.edu/alan/beatles/

Young, gifted, and puckish—from http://www.primenet.com/~dhaber/bpix/faces.gif

The Beatles Page A page devoted to the basics of Beatles collecting, including a discussion forum on the Fab Four, an offline list of fanzines and reference guides, and descriptions of pieces of Beatles memorabilia. ✓ **INTERNET**→*url* http://www.islandnet.com/~sclif-for/beatles/fabhome.htm

Internet Beatles Album A wealth of Fab Four info, including lyrics, discographies, bios, multimedia surprises, and more. ✓ **INTERNET**→*url* http://www.primenet.com/~dhaber/beatles.html

PEPPERLAND A Beatles photo archive—British album covers, American album covers, British EP covers, and year-by-year images of the band. ✓ **INTERNET**→*url* http://www.wam.umd.edu/~pepperlh/

The rec.music.beatles Home Page The official home of the rec.music.beatles FAQ, along with an archive of hundreds of past posts from the newsgroup and a large MPEG of noted cartoon intellectual Lisa Simpson in Pepperland. ✓ **INTERNET**→*url* http://kiwi.imgen.bcm.tmc.edu:8088/public/rmb.html

Backmasking

seltaeB ehT (Beatles) A site devoted to backward messages in the Beatles oeuvre, with sound clips (in Sun format) and trivia about various backmasked bits of dialogue. Did you know that at the end of "I'm So Tired," John's alleged backward obituary for Paul is actually a request for a waiter? I'll have the check, please. ✓ **INTERNET** →*url* http://www.cs.rochester.edu/users/grads/jonas/beatles/backwards.html

Books

Revolution in the Head An ad for Ian MacDonald's book about the Beatles and their inestimable contribution to sixties culture. ✓ **INTERNET**→*url* http://www.webcom.com/~beatlebk/

Chat

Beatles Chat Which Beatle had the best solo career? Which Beatle took the most drugs? Which Beatle played his instrument the best? When you listen to the Beatles, how can you tell the difference between John's songs and Paul's? Join these and other ongoing discus-

Spotlight: The Beatles **Artist Guide**

The Beatles, taken by Astrid Kirschner—from http://www.primenet.com/~dhaber/

sions about the most beloved band in the history of rock and roll on America Online and CompuServe's various Beatles message boards. **✓AMERICA ONLINE** ...→*keyword* rockline→Messages→KEEPING THE 70S' ALIVE→the beatles ...→*keyword* mmc→Rock/Pop→Rock Artists A-L→The Beatles & solo work **✓COMPUSERVE**→*go* oldies→Libraries *or* Bulletin Board→Beatles/British

rec.music.beatles (ng) Talk John. Talk Paul. Talk George. Talk Ringo. Talk Yoko. Talk Badfinger. Talk Elvis Costello. Talk George Martin. Talk Stu Sutcliffe. Talk *Backbeat*. Talk *The Hours and the Times*. And while you're there, ask about the rumors of a new Beatles song ("Free As a Bird") to accompany a documentary that will be televised in the United States sometime this fall. **✓USENET** →rec.music.beatles

Images

The Beatles Multimedia Art Exhibit This page collects a variety of Beatles art and photography, and then displays them in thumbnail- and full-size. **✓INTERNET**→*url* http://orathost.cfa.ilstu.edu/public/oratGallery/artsExhibits/kaufmanExhibit/home.html

George Harrison

George Harrison Lyrics, images, and more information on the shyest Beatle. **✓INTERNET**→*url* http://www.cs.mcgill.ca/~timelord/Harrison/George.html

John Lennon

John Lennon Who was John Lennon? Let the creator of this page explain: "John Lennon was an artist, poet, novelist, actor, peace provoker and, if that weren't enough, he also happened to be a pretty good musician, singer and songwriter." This Lennon Website contains a discography, images, sound clips, and some wonderful

movies, including one of John singing "Instant Karma" on *Top of the Pops*. **✓INTERNET**→*url* http://www.missouri.edu/~c588349/john-page.html

John Lennon

John Lennon The Beatles were inducted into the Rock-and-Roll Hall of Fame in 1988; six years later, John Lennon was inducted on his own. The page includes a brief career biography (ending with the December 8, 1980 assassination of Lennon by Mark David Chapman). **✓INTERNET**→*url* http://www.rockhall.com/induct/lennjohn.html

Paul McCartney

Paul McCartney Pictures of Paul, a list of bootlegs, a videography, and a complete list of singles and albums. Macca collectors will be thrilled to find information on rarities like the orchestral version of *Ram* (released under the pseudonym Percy Thrillington) and the 1993 dance album *Strawberries Oceans Ships Forest* (released under the pseudonym The Fireman). **✓INTERNET**→ *url* http://cip2.e-technik.uni-erlangen.de:8080/hyplan/gernhard/macca.html

A good day at the BBC—http://psy.ucsd.edu/~scott/beatles3.html

The Beatles

"Ringo actually was the one to quit the Beatles first!! True. But with a catch. He walked out for two weeks during the recording of The White Album. Why I don't know. Everyone begged him to forgive them and return..when he arrived back at the studio, there were flowers all over his drums.

"During this time, Paul was left to play the drums on Back In The U.S.S.R. True fact."

—from **Beatles Chat** on AOL's Rockline

"I just fell in love with the Beatles over Spring Break. Why hadn't I noticed them before? They're all I listen to now; my family is going crazy because I keep playing their music over and over again. My favorite song is 'Hey Jude.' Paul sings it and it just so happens that he is my favorite Beatle.

"It's a song he wrote for Julian Lennon when John and Cynthia were going through a divorce because John fell in love with Yoko (the bitch) and Julian naturally, felt sad and so Paul tried to cheer him up by writing it and he also spent a lot of time with Julian."

—from **Beatles Chat** on AOL's Rockline

"There are several reasons why I never ever believed the Beatles were behind the Paul Is Dead rumor. But here's one to think about: Sure they all denied it, but Lennon strongly denies it in the Rolling Stone interview from early 1971, you know, the Lennon Remembers/Primal/Working Class Hero interview, the most famous he ever did? It would seem very strange that a man who casually admits taking a thousand acid trips, being hooked on heroin, having touring members stage non-stop illegal orgies, and wanting to punch fellow Beatles is going to, in the same conversation, deny putting little hidden messages in albums."

—from **Beatles Chat** on AOL's Rockline

ed, this page includes a discography, lyrics, tour dates, articles, a song list, an FAQ, and fan club info. ✓**INTERNET**→*url* http://rock.net/fan-supported/black-crowes/

The Black Crowes Tour dates, lyrics to the *Hard to Handle* and *Southern Harmony and Musical Companion* LPs, and press releases for *Amorica*. ✓**AMERICA ONLINE**→*keyword* warner→Alternative→black crowes

---

Black Crowes Chat Message-based discussion. ✓**AMERICA ONLINE**→*keyword* mmc→Rock/Pop→General Rock →Black Crowes

BLACK, FRANK

Frank Black Link to Frank Black's record company, get an artist bio, consult lyrics, and learn more about the roly-poly ex-Pixie. ✓**INTERNET**→*url* http://rugmd0.chem.rug.nl/~pieter/frankblack/frankblack.html

---

Frank Black Pictures of Frank, lyrics from his songs, and even transcripts of interviews. ✓**INTERNET**→*url* http://www.stack.urc.tue.nl/~patrick/frank_black/index.html

---

Frank Black Discography A discography of Frank Black's 4AD work. ✓**INTERNET**→*url* http://www.evo.org/html/group/blackfrank.html

BLACK SABBATH

alt.music.ozzy (ng) If the names Warren DiMartini, Randy Rhoads, and Randy Castillo sound like baseball players of the late 1960s, then you should visit another newsgroup. Otherwise, join in as metalheads from around the world discuss Ozzy Osborne, Black Sabbath, and more. ✓**USENET**→alt.music.ozzy

Black Sabbath Sounds, lyrics, and pictures, including a huge image of the cover of *Cross Purposes*. ✓**INTERNET**→*url* http://www.eecs.nwu.edu/~autopsy/metal/black_sabbath.html

---

Black Sabbath Chat Message-based discussion. ✓**AMERICA ONLINE**→*keyword* mmc→Rock/Pop→Rock Artists A-L→Black Sabbath/Ozzy

---

Black Sabbath Home Page A collection of links that highlight the band's history, lyrics, guitar tabs, and images. ✓**INTERNET**→*url* http://www4.ncsu.edu/eos/users/j/jbmyers/www/BlackSabbath.html

---

Black Sabbath Tribute Album Album info for the Black Sabbath tribute album *Nativity in Black*, which features such bands as White Zombie, Fight, Metallica, Sepultura, Therapy? (with Ozzy Osborne), Megadeth, Biohazard, Corrosion of Conformity, Type O-Negative, and Godspeed. ✓**INTERNET**→*url* http://www.music.sony.com/Music/ArtistInfo/BlackSabbath.html

---

Rockit Comix Presents Black Sabbath An advertisement for the Rockit Black Sabbath issue, which tells the story of the "fathers of music so rockin, so ON that you would swear they sold their souls." ✓**INTERNET**→*url* http://www.nando.net/music/gm/Rockit/blacksab/

BLONDIE

Blondie List (ml) Blondie fans cluster to discuss the endless reissues of the band's material, as well as the mixed blessing of Deborah

Harry's solo career. ✓**INTERNET**→*email* lab@primenet.com ✍ *Write a request*

Deborah Harry Home Page The headquarters for the Deborah Harry/Blondie mailing list, this page includes lyrics, discographies, an FAQ, and more. ✓**INTERNET**→*url* http://www3.primenet.com/~lab/DHDeborahHarry.html

BLUES TRAVELER

alt.music.blues-traveler (ng) Is Blues Traveler the Grateful Dead of the 1990s? Is John Popper the Mama Cass of men? This newsgroup sometimes drifts into other H.O.R.D.E. band camps, especially Phish. ✓**USENET**→alt.music.blues-traveler

Blues Traveler A discography, lyrics, guitar tabs, and tour information. ✓**INTERNET**→*url* http://www.contrib.andrew.cmu.edu/usr/mr6d/blues.traveler.html

---

Blues Traveler Chat Message-based discussion. ✓**AMERICA ONLINE**→*keyword* mmc→Rock/Pop→General Rock →Blues Traveler

---

Blues Traveler List (ml) Run-around the hard-touring, smooth-sounding pop blues band with this mailing list. ✓**INTERNET**→*email* blues-traveler-request@cs.umd.edu ✍ *Write a request*

BLUR

alt.music.blur (ng) Less traffic than there was on the L.A. freeway during the O. J. chase, with just a few posts from fans looking for bootleg tapes or tour dates. ✓**USENET**→alt.music.blur

---

Blur A discography, lyrics, re-

views, and sound clips. ✓**INTERNET**→*url* http://lispstat.alcd. soton.ac.uk/~prbt/blur.html

BOLTON, MICHAEL

alt.fan.michael-bolton (ng) When you think Michael Bolton, you think hair, and Otis Redding covers, and chart success, and plagiarism suits, and crooning so intense it simply can't be heartfelt. If you think anything else, or want to hear what others think, drop by this newsgroup, which splits evenly between Bolton-lovers and Bolton-haters. ✓**USENET**→alt.fan. michael-bolton

---

Michael Bolton Album info for *The One Thing*, along with tour dates. ✓**INTERNET**→*url* http:// www.music.sony.com/Music/Artist Info/MichaelBolton.html

BON JOVI

Bon Jovi Mercury's official Bon Jovi page includes a biography of the band, a large photo gallery, video clips, and a sample from "Hey God," the first single from the summer 1995 release *These Days*. Email the band at bonjovi@polygram.com, to muse about anything from *Slippery When Wet* to what they do on the weekends. ✓**INTERNET**→*url* http:// www.polygram.com/bonjovi/ BonJovi.html

---

Bon Jovi Chat Message-based discussion. ✓**AMERICA ONLINE**→ *keyword* mmc→Rock/Pop→Hard Rock/Metal→Bon Jovi

BOWIE, DAVID

alt.fan.david-bowie (ng) Diehard Bowie fans are a troubled bunch. They love their idol, but they're not sure why he hasn't sold records since *Let's Dance*, and why he hasn't made a good record since his collaborations with Brian Eno. As a result, they tend to overvalue

Bowie's late 1980s and early 1990s work, especially the failed Brancasonics of Tin Machine. And if you really want to enrage the group, call Nine Inch Nails impresario and Outside tour co-headlines Trent Reznor "the Bowie of the nineties." ✓**USENET**→alt.fan.david-bowie

---

Bowie Tribute Twenty years ago, he was a gaunt and tortured figure who galvanized rock with a stiff mix of androgyny, nihilism, and personality crisis. Today, David Bowie is happily married to super-model Iman, and his music has lost much of its vitality. But that doesn't faze the author of this page, who pays tribute to the old Bowie with an animation, sound clips, and a brief essay. ✓**INTERNET** →*url* http://www. dcs. gla.ac.uk/ ~leonarca/music/bowie/

David Bowie Chat Message-based discussion. ✓**AMERICA ON-LINE**→*keyword* mmc→Rock/Pop→ Classic Rock→David Bowie

---

The David Bowie File Illustrated with a photo from *The Man Who Fell to Earth*, this site covers Bowie's music, films, life, and relentless image-making. ✓**INTERNET** →*url* http://liber.Stanford.EDU: 80/~torrie/Bowie/BowieFile.html

BOYZ II MEN

alt.music.boyz-2-men (ng) Talk about upcoming singles, tours, and Boyz II Men's appearance on Michael Jackson's *HIStory*. ✓**USENET**→alt.music.boyz-2-men

---

Boyz II Men Motown's promotional site for the group. ✓**INTERNET**→*url* http://www.musicbase. co.uk/music/motown/motobtm. html

---

Boyz II Men Polygram's official Boyz II Men site is little more

"David Bowie is indeed a marvellous man. I first got into his music when I was 15, and I found 'The Man Who sold the World' on an old tape. I used to be scared of that song, then I realised it was Ace. I love all the albums (before Lets Dance, then it gets a bit shady), but my absolute favourites are Hunky Dory and Low. My favourite Bowie songs are 'The Wild-Eyed Boy from Freecloud,' 'Life on Mars' and 'Time.' Is this interesting? I don't think it is, but I don't care. It's cool in 'Time' when Bowie goes 'Time--he flexes like a whore, falls Wanking to the floor,' because it's the only song I can think of that says "wanking", and he says it really well (if anyone knows of other recorded songs that say 'wanking,' please let me know.). And Bowie's eyes are dead smart. I wish I had eyes like that. Apparently he got punched in the eye when he was a nipper, resulting in much coolness."

-from **Bowie Tribute**

than an online press kit, with bios of the Boyz and a brief history of their career thus far. ✓**INTERNET**→ *url* http://www.polygram.com/ polygram/Boyz2Men.html

Boyz II Men If you manage to live through the interminable loading time, you'll find ample Boyz info here, including large reproductions of cover art, lyrics, sound clips, and links. ✓**INTERNET** →*url* http://pages.ripco.com: 8080/~pvranas/boyzIImen.html

Boyz II Men Chat Message-based discussion. ✓**AMERICA ON-LINE** ...→*keyword* mtv→Message Boards→Bands That Do Suck →BOYZ II MEN ...→*keyword* mtv→Message Boards→Bands That Don't Suck →BOYZ II MEN ...→ *keyword* mmc →Rap/R&B→R&B/ Soul→Boyz II Men

BRAGG, BILLY

Billy Bragg A short biography, a shorter FAQ, recent news of Billy, and updates on his new LP, slated for a winter 1996 release and tentatively titled *Reaching to the Converted*. While this page is sometimes sketchy, it maintains a huge list of related artists—everyone from Barenaked Ladies (they have toured with Billy) to Chumbawamba (they have sampled Billy) to Mott the Hoople (Billy has quoted them). ✓**INTERNET**→*url* http://noel.pd.org/~usul/billy-bragg. html

Billy Bragg Chat Message-based discussion. ✓**AMERICA ONLINE**→ *keyword* mmc→World Beat→Billy Bragg

Billy Bragg List (ml) Talk about pop and politics, and England's favorite pop populist. Rumor has it that Billy once lurked on his own mailing list using a false name. ✓**INTERNET**→*email* billy-bragg@

The Breeders—from http://www.nando.net/music/ gm/Breeders/

fish.com ✍ *Type in message body:* subscribe billy-bragg

Don't Try This At Home Lyrics to Bragg's excellent 1991 album, including the hit "Sexuality" and more introspective fare like "Accident Waiting to Happen" and "Everywhere." ✓**INTERNET**→ *url* http://www.ama.caltech.edu/~ phil/billybragg.html

BREEDERS

Breeders A discography, lyrics, sound clips, and a preview of the band's interview disk. ✓**INTERNET**→ *url* http://www.nando.net/music/ gm/Breeders/

The Breeders A discography of the group dating back to its 4AD days. ✓**INTERNET**→*url* http://www. evo.org/html/group/breeders.html

BUCKLEY, JEFF

Jeff Buckley Sony Music's official site traces Buckley's young career, from *Live at Sin-é* to *Grace*. ✓**INTERNET**→*url* http://www.music. sony.com/Music/ArtistInfo/ JeffBuckley.html

Jeff Buckley "What does Jeff Buckley sound like?" This question takes precedence at this fan Website, and the answers, culled from sources as diverse as Bob Mould and Rainier Maria Rilke, may surprise you. The page also includes a Jeff Buckley FAQ, transcriptions of interviews, sales fig-

ures, and photos. ✓**INTERNET**→*url* http://www.goodnet.com/~ gkelemen/jeffhome.html

Jeff Buckley Chat Message-based discussion. ✓**AMERICA ON-LINE**→*keyword* mtv→Message Boards→Bands That Do Suck→jeff buckley shouldn't be here

Jeff Buckley List (ml) Fans gush about Buckley's voice, and his young career. And Buckley himself sometimes shows up on the list to complain about Internet bootleggers ("Unfortunately, in this age of Internet, one can't avoid having one's dreck smeared all over the computer waves by curious Net-surfers"). ✓**INTERNET**→*email* buckley@mordor.com ✍ *Write a request*

BUFFETT, JIMMY

alt.fan.jimmy-buffett (ng) Newlyweds in Vegas are looking for an appropriate Jimmy Buffett quote to celebrate their impromptu nuptials. A Pennsylvania suburbanite wonders if Buffett has his own ice cream flavor. And parrotheads from across the country want to compare notes on shows, talk about new releases, and declare their Parrotheadedness proudly. ✓**USENET**→ alt.fan.jimmy-buffett

The Church of Buffett, Ortho-dox What is the apostasy of Margaritaville? How about the holy quotient of Marvin Gardens? Get cool pics and learn the tenets of the COB. ✓**INTERNET**→*url* http://www.homecom.com/mhall/cobo/

Jimmy Buffett Sure, you can get Buffett lyrics and images, but what else can you do? Read the *Coconut Modem*, AOL's Parrot Head e-zine, hook up to the Key West travel bureau, or get a recipe for that tasty Margarita Jell-O you slurped on St. Patty's Day. ✓**INTERNET**→*url* http://www.homecom. com/buffett/

Jimmy Buffett In the Parrot Survival Manual, fans can download the original recipe for a salty dog and reach out across the network looking for others who are wasting away in Margaritaville. Where else can an overweight underachiever with a penchant for mermaids be lauded as a role model? ✓**INTERNET**→*url* http://www. homecom.com/buffett/

Jimmy Buffett Chat Message-based discussion. ✓**AMERICA ON-LINE**→*keyword* mmc→Rock/Pop→ Rock Artists A-L→Buffett/Parrot Head Madness

Jimmy Buffett's Margaritaville Matriculate into Domino College, where Professor Buffett teaches Manatee Awareness and How to Drink Tequila From Your Favorite Body Part. And while you're waiting for your diploma, get lyrics, images, and a complete Jimmy Buffett discography. ✓**INTERNET**→*url* http://key-west.com/margaritaville/

Live Parrotheads Chat Discuss Jimmy Buffett and his music with other fans in a real-time chat room. ✓**PRODIGY**→*jump* chat→ Prodigy Chat→Select an Area: Music→Parrotheads

BUSH

Bush Chat Is Bush the Nirvana of England, or the Stone Temple Pilots of lowly Blighty? Get the lowdown on Transatlantic grunge in these message boards. ✓**AMERICA ONLINE** ...→*keyword* mtv→Message Boards→Bands That Do Suck→BUSH ...→*keyword* mmc→Rock/Pop→General Rock→Bush ...→*keyword* rockline→Messages→MODERN ROCK LIVE→Bush & Soundgarden

Bush Net Join the Bush leagues with this site, which includes a songbook, reviews, images, sound clips, and a discography (one album and counting). ✓**INTERNET**→*url* http://www.glue.umd.edu/~kgold/Bush/

BUSH, KATE

Cloudbusting—Kate Bush in Her Own Words An obsessive hypertextual collection of Kate Bush quotes culled from liner notes and interviews with the artist, her family, and associates. Learn about everything from Kate's early life ("Well, when I was about twelve, that sort of age, I was such a big fan of Elton John") to her dislike of airports ("Waiting for luggage at the terminal roundabouts is such a drag"). ✓**INTERNET**→*url* http://scott.cogsci. ed.ac.uk/~rjc/hyper_cloud/cloudbusting.html

Experiment IV (Kate Bush) An FAQ, a discography, and more on Kate Bush. ✓**INTERNET**→*url* http://www.aitec.edu.au/ExpIV/

Kate Bush Sony's official site, with information on the video collection *The Line, The Cross and The Curve*. ✓**INTERNET**→*url* http://www.music.sony.com/Music/ArtistInfo/KateBush.html

Kate Bush Chat Message-based

The Wit and Wisdom of Captain Beefheart:

"I'm lyrically less turbulent now. I'm like a woman because I have my periods, if you know what I mean. Every once in a while I get the cramps and do something far out. This album needs someplace to go, you know? So I sing with a definite woman in mind, not like those groups that have men on their mind."

" I live up at Eureka, among the big trees, and I tell you, those things are really saying something. You gotta work to hear what they're saying. They're great. But the eucalyptus is so far my favorite. They brought them over from Australia for lumber, but when they grew here they curved, and there was no way they could be used for lumber. I think maybe they threw a curve on the lumber companies. And I think that's heavy."

"I think nutrition is very important."

-from **HomePageReplica**

discussion. ✓**AMERICA ONLINE**→ *keyword* mmc→Alternative Rock→ Bands A-L→Kate Bush

Kate Bush Musical Extravaganza Sound samples from Kate's albums. ✓**INTERNET**→*url* http://actor.cs.vt.edu/~wentz/ index.html

Love Hounds (ml) Talk about Kate and her latest introspective masterpiece. ✓**INTERNET**→*email* love-hounds-request@uunet.uu.net ✍ *Write a request*

rec.music.gaffa (ng) Kate Bush hasn't had an album since *The Red Shoes*, but she's more than happy to lend her voice to Fruitopia to sell cutting-edge juice, and Ronald isn't that happy about it. "She can say it's not a sell-out, because there's a concept, and she can seem ethereal, but we should call it what it is, and that's a sellout." Adeline isn't so worried about Kate's artistic integrity—in fact, she just wants to talk about the similarities between the Rubberband Girl and Rush. Join this newsgroup, and join the sensual world. ✓**USENET**→rec.music.gaffa

BUTTHOLE SURFERS

alt.music.butthole.surfers (ng) Penis dissection? Sure. But that's not the only thing that BS fans are wont to talk about on their newsgroup, which also includes tour dates, rumors about Gibby Haynes's involvement with other artists (Daniel Johnston, in particular), and lists of other bands that sound like the Surfers (Killdozer gets top marks). ✓**USENET**→alt.music.butthole.surfers

Butthole Surfers A brief biography of the band, and precious little else. ✓**INTERNET**→*url* http:// www.peak.org/~zogwarg/ indices/bands/butt/main.html

Butthole Surfers Archive A small collection of Buttholy material, including sound clips, images, and a discography. ✓**INTERNET**→*url* http://kafka.southern.com:80/ Southern/band/BUTTL/

THE BYRDS

alt.music.byrds (ng) The Byrds haven't recorded as a group for more than 20 years, but that hasn't stopped their fans from flocking to the Net, where they speculate on the track order of the Byrds' boxed set, propose female duet partners for Roger McGuinn, and lament the passage of Wolfman Jack, who once co-hosted a radio special on which the Byrds appeared. ✓**USENET**→alt.music.byrds

The Byrds Commemorating the 1991 induction of the group into the Rock and Roll Hall of Fame, this page includes a brief career biography and sound clips. ✓**INTERNET**→*url* http://www.rockhall. com/induct/byrds.html

Byrds Chat Message-based discussion. ✓**AMERICA ONLINE**→*keyword* mmc→Rock/Pop→Rock Artists A-L→The Byrds/Roger McGuinn

Byrds List (ml) Lay down the newspaper, hang up the cuttlebone, and talk Byrds. ✓**INTERNET**→ *email* richruss@gate.net ✍ *Type in message body:* subscribe

C

CAPTAIN BEEFHEART

alt.fan.capt-beefheart (ng) Newcomers, mostly collegians, can't believe how odd the Captain is, and they're shocked that they missed him the first time through the cut-out bin. "This *Trout Mask Replica*," says one new convert, "it's…spectacular." Others are bet-

Captain Beefheart—from http://farcry. neurobio.pitt.edu/GIFs/CB/

ter versed in Van Vlietisms, and consequently more pragmatic about their interest in the Magic Band. "Looking," says one veteran, "for outtakes from *Doc at the Radar Station*. Will pay." When they're not marveling or haggling, Beefheart fans are talking about tribute albums, old concert posters, the theremin, and more. ✓**USENET**→alt.fan.capt-beefheart

HomePageReplica A list of Magic Band members, discographies, movies, MPEGs, and more. All in all, a giant Web resource devoted to the Captain. ✓**INTERNET**→ *url* http://www.rit.edu/~jcs1589/ hpr.html

Captain Beefheart Chat Message-based discussion. ✓**AMERICA ONLINE**→*keyword* mmc→Rock/ Pop→Classic Rock→Captain Beefheart

Captain Beefheart Pictures

Straight from the neurobiology department of the University of Pittsburgh—one of the lesser-known Beefheart enclaves in the U.S.—comes this collection of Beefheart cover photos. ✓**INTERNET** →*url* http://farcry.neurobio.pitt. edu/CB.html

CAREY, MARIAH

alt.music.mariah.carey (ng) Confess your love for the multi-octaved wife of Tommy Mottola—if you dare. ✓**USENET**→alt.music. mariah.carey

#Mariah Live chat about Mariah Carey—or is that Mrs. Sony? ✓**INTERNET**→*irc* #Mariah

Mariah Carey Link to other sites devoted to Carey. ✓**INTERNET**→ *url* http://biodec.wustl.edu:70/ 0h/audio/mariah

Mariah Carey Care to know about Mariah's *Vision Of Love*? No problem. Interested in downloading a discography, lyrics, or information on Danish fan clubs? It's all here. ✓**INTERNET**→*url* http:// www.southwind.net/~ksims/VOL. html

Mariah Carey Official Sony info on Mariah's *Merry Christmas* and *Music Box* albums. ✓**INTERNET** →*url* http://www.music.sony. com/ Music/ArtistInfo/MariahCarey.html

Mariah Carey Sound clips, pictures, album art, the Mariah Carey FAQ, and links to other Mariah Carey sites. ✓**INTERNET**→*url* http:// www.wi.leidenuniv.nl/~pverheij/ mariah.html

Mariah Carey Chat Message-based discussion. ✓**AMERICA ON-LINE**→*keyword* mmc→Rock/Pop→ Rock Artists A-L→Mariah Carey

Mariah Carey in Her Home-

Mariah Carey Website—from http:// www.wi.leidenuniv.nl/~pverheij/mariah.html

town Avid fans practice idol worship in Cyberspace, and nowhere more so than at this site, which proves that even huge superstars can keep in touch with their roots. ✓**INTERNET**→*url* http://www.cc.columbia.edu/~jes81/music/mariah.html

Thanksgiving Special Once Thanksgiving meant celebrating the bounty of the New World. Now it means celebrating Mariah Carey. Download dozens of pictures of the singer, and then think of her while you're biting into that big turkey drumstick. ✓**INTERNET**→ *url* http://www.d.umn.edu/~ clankow/mariah/mariah.html

Vision (ml) With the release of *Fantasy*, fans can moon over a whole new set of overproduced, over-sung compositions, while detractors must suffer through yet another multiplatinum season. Celebrate or commiserate on this mailing list. ✓**INTERNET**→*email* vision-request@biogopher.wustl.edu ✍ *Type in message body:* subscribe

CARPENTER, MARY

Mary Chapin Carpenter Sony Music's official site includes press releases and an interactive media

kit for *Stones in the Road*. ✓**INTERNET**→*url* http://www.music.sony. com/Music/ArtistInfo/MaryChapin Carpenter.html

Mary Chapin Carpenter Guitar tabs for dozens of songs, from "Passionate Kisses" to "Shut Up and Kiss Me" to "I Am a Town." ✓**INTERNET**→*url* http://www.umn. edu/nlhome/m161/schn0170/mcc/ index.html

CASH, JOHNNY

Johnny Cash Album covers, photos of the famous Folsom Prison concerts, lyrics, and links. ✓**INTERNET**→*url* http://american. recordings.com/American_Artists/ Johnny_Cash/cash_home.html

Johnny Cash Transcript of a recent speech given by the Man in Black at the SXSW Music and Media Conference in Austin, along with images and press releases. ✓**AMERICA ONLINE**→*keyword* warner→Alternative→Johnny Cash

CATHERINE WHEEL

Catherine Wheel WWW Home Page A discography, lyrics, tour information, and "the world famous Catherine Wheel mini-FAQ." ✓**INTERNET**→*url*

(cont'd pg. 98) →

Bob Dylan

When it comes to top-notch protest singers who become sixties icons and then betray

the liberal-pacifist alliance with a single act of electric-guitar defiance (remember Newport!), instead choosing to serve as a self-appointed national confessor, poet, and prophet, there's no one quite like Bob Dylan. After recording masterpieces like *Highway 61 Revisited* and *Blood on the Tracks*, Dylan has spent the last decade making inconsistent albums that alternate between the indifferent (*Under a Red Sky*) and the superb (*World Gone Wrong*), but his mystique remains intact. Dream **Bob Dylan's 115th Dream.** Learn more about how Dylan has mined the American landscape at the **Dylan Atlas.** And then revel in the songs that changed the century at **Bob Dylan Lyrics.**

The young Mr. Zimmerman in 1961—from http://bob.nbr.no/dok/gif/bobyoung.gif

On the Net

Across the board

Bob Dylan Dylan's official page, housed at Sony Music, contains standard PR material—press releases, tour dates, and discographies—along with links to unofficial sites and access to the electronic press kit for the Dylan CD-ROM *Highway 61 Interactive*. And don't forget to download the *Unplugged* video clips. ✓**INTERNET**→ *url* http://www.music.sony.com/ Music/ArtistInfo/BobDylan.html

Bob Dylan's 115th Dream While much of this site's content is standard—lyrics, images, a discography, and more—Bob Dylan's 115th Dream does include a reader's poll that lets Netsurfers vote for their favorite albums. ✓**INTERNET**→ *url* http://www.cen.uiuc.edu/~bdonalds/bob.html

Dylan Archive A full list of Dylan's public appearances and recordings, songs played on tour, and more. ✓**INTERNET**→ *url* ftp://ftp.netcom.com/pub/howells/dylan.html

Dylan FAQ What is a bootleg? Is *Renaldo and Clara* as awful as people say? When will Dylan record his new album? While this document doesn't in and of itself con- tain much information about Bob, it does have hints and tips for finding Dylan info elsewhere online. ✓**INTERNET**→ *url* http://www.cis.ohio-state.edu/hypertext/faq/usenet/music/dylan-faq/top.html

Dylan Stuff A huge picture of Bob from the *Real Live* cover and a selection of links. ✓**INTERNET**→ *url* http://www.agate.net/~dcraig/dylan.html

Expecting Rain A rich and varied Dylan site that includes a list of notable Dylan personages (the Bob Dylan Who's Who), a catalog of locations mentioned in Dylan songs (the Dylan Atlas), images from the "Jokerman" video, images of the artist, and more. ✓**INTERNET**→ *url* http://128.39.161.105/

Ragged Clown Little more than a collection of Dylan links, this page enables quick scanning of all Dylan-related resources online. ✓**INTERNET**→*url* http://www.ncl.ac. uk/~n328416/mate/

Bootlegs

Dylan Boots Having a hard time finding that mono mix of "I'll Keep It With Mine"? Hungry for the 1962 recordings done live for the *Billy Faier Show* in New York City? Review this list of bootlegs, and order them online if you're interested. ✓**INTERNET**→*url* http:// www.tecc.co.uk/magiccom/dylan. html

Tape Reviews Originally posted to rec.music.dylan, these reviews cover a wide range of unofficial Dylan releases, from the May 1961 Indian Neck Folk Festival to nineties shows in Melbourne, London, and Evanston, Illinois. Reviews are matter-of-fact, with introductory comments about sound quality and song selection and remarks on vocal technique—is Dylan relying on lung power, altering his phrasing, or just sleep-walking through the performance? The consensus— no one knows, and we're just pawns in his game. ✓**INTERNET**→*url* http://www.ncl. ac.uk/~n328416/mate/tapes.html

Chat

Bob Dylan Chat Jack wants to know why Dylan's voice is shot. Melissa insists it isn't—"it's just that he's got character, in a way that fans of trendy young bands can't understand." And Kai spreads a rumor that he says is all the rage at his high school, that Dylan "may do something like what Neil Young did with Pearl Jam, except that he'd be recording with the two surviving members

of Nirvana." Is it possible? Would Cobain fans be in an uproar? Would Dylan rise to prominence once more on the strength of a perverse grunge version of "It's Alright Ma (I'm Only Bleeding)"? Stay tuned. ✓**AMERICA ONLINE**→ *keyword* mmc→Rock/Pop→Rock Artists A-L→Bob Dylan

#dylan Live chat about Bob. ✓**INTERNET**→*irc* #dylan

Highway 61 (Bob Dylan List) (ml) This mailing list encourages discussion about any Dylan-related matter, from Bob's politics in the sixties to his blues albums in the nineties. ✓**INTERNET**→*email* list-serv@ ubvm.cc.buffalo.edu ✍ *Type in message body:* subscribe hwy61-l <your full name>

rec.music.dylan (ng) How does the online crowd feel about *Unplugged*? When will the second volume of *The Bootleg Series* be released? And what about the persistent rumor that Dylan has recorded an album of 14 Hebrew prayers? All the Dylan you can handle. ✓**USENET**→rec.music.dylan

Interpretation

Bob Dylan: Tangled Up In Jews "She was working in a topless place / and I stopped in for a beer / Just kept looking at the side of her face / Then I read my maftir." Did Dylan's seminal 1975 divorce album *Blood on the Tracks* originally begin with this tribute to Torah reading? Probably not. But Judaism has played an important role in the career of Mr. Zimmerman, from the Old Testament righteousness of his protest albums to the renunciation of the Hebrew faith during the great born-again phase (*Saved*, *Slow Train Coming*, and *Shot of Love*, in case you were on your way to the record store).

How to see the world like Bob—from http:// rosa.nbr.no/users/karlerik/gif/

Based on a *Washington Jewish Week* article of the same title, this site analyzes songs for Jewish content, includes a partial Hebrew translation of Dylan's "All Along the Watchtower" and a Jewish parody of "Tangled Up In Blue." ✓**INTERNET**→*url* http://www.well.com/ user/yudel/Dylan.html

Dylan Atlas When Dylan sings "I lived with them on Montague Street / In a basement down the stairs / There was music in the cafes at night / And revolution in the air," what Montague Street is he talking about? The one in Brooklyn, of course. And what other Dylan song mentions Brooklyn? Answer: "Joey," the ode to mobster Joey Gallo that begins "Born in Red Hook, Brooklyn in the year of who knows when / opened up his eyes to the tune of an accordion." Find out these and dozens more geographical facts at the Dylan Atlas, which catalogs place-names in Bob's work. ✓**INTERNET**→*url* http://128.39.161.105/ dok/atlas/atlas.html

Dylan Lyric Analysis Project Researched and written by

Giuseppe "Peppo" Valetto, this project submits Dylan's oeuvre to a computerized text analysis, and then draws some fairly obvious conclusions about his major periods. Protest songs tend to discuss war more than born-again songs, which tend to show a preference for words like "lord," "truth," and "salvation." Them computers sure are smart, huh? ✓**INTERNET**→*url* http://www.cs.columbia.edu/~gv/project_home.html

Leonard Cohen and Bob Dylan: Poetry and the Popular Song "The distance between the gleomannes gyd in Beowulf or 'Sumer is Icumen In' and the songs of Leonard Cohen or Bob Dylan may seem great, but it is one of time rather than aesthetics," writes the author of this paper, who goes on to analyze the personae adopted by Dylan and Cohen as lyricists in the sixties. The essay includes the observation that in "Subterranean Homesick Blues," Dylan "himself wants neither to chew gum nor please anyone." ✓**INTERNET**→*url* http://fy.chalmers.se/~jmo/LC3. html

Interviews

Bob Dylan Interviews and Press Conferences For more than 30 years, Dylan has been baf-

It's alright ma (he's only scowling)— http://rosa.nbr.no/users/karlerik/gif/

fling interviewers with his mix of homespun wisdom, contentious proclamations, surreal beat meanderings, and bald-faced lies. This page collects transcripts of interviews dating all the way back to 1961, when Dylan told CBS's Billy James that he "was in the carnival when I was about thirteen." Laugh as Dylan explains to Sydney Fields of the *New York Mirror* why he became a rambling man: "I didn't want to see the atomic bathrooms and electronic bedrooms and souped-up can-openers; I wanted to watch and feel the people and the dust and ditches and the fields and fences." Cry as he tells Philippe Adler of *L'Express* how he would handle the news that his son was taking drugs: "It depends on what kind of drug he was taking. You know. You can only talk, explain, people want to go through their own experiences themselves." Scratch your head as he holds forth on the role of art in the nineties: "Art to me doesn't mirror society. The very essence of art is subversive to society, and whatever society is putting out, art's got to do something else." Dylan fans will love this archive, but anyone with an interest in popular culture of the last forty years should consult it. ✓**INTERNET**→*url* http://www.ncl.ac.uk/~n246543/interviews.html

Lyrics

Bob Dylan Lyrics A rather scattershot collection of Dylan lyrics that includes a few highlights (such as Allen Ginsberg's liner notes to *Desire*). ✓**INTERNET**→*url* ftp://ftp.cs.pdx.edu/pub/dylan/lyrics

Bob Dylan Mondegreens What's a "mondegreen"? It's a fertile mishearing of a lyric. And how

many Dylan mondegreens are there? Dozens, from "Don't try No Doz" (actually, "Don't tie no bows," from "Subterranean Homesick Blues") to "My friend John, rigid bar door" (actually "My friend John, Brigitte Bardot," from "I Shall Be Free"). Lots of fun for the whole family, especially if the family happens to include a speech therapist. ✓**INTERNET**→*url* http://reality.sgi.com/employees/howells/lyrics/mondegreens.html

Dylan Lyrics Dozens of lyrics from Dylan albums, including *Oh Mercy* and *Good As I Been to You*. ✓**INTERNET**→*url* http://vivarin.pc.cc.cmu.edu/cgi-bin/ lyr.groups?dylan.bob

Software

The Bob Dylan Spotlight Primarily a promotional site for Dylan's *Highway 61 Interactive* CD-ROM, the site allows you to download sound and movie clips from various stages of his career. ✓**COMPUSERVE**→*go* dylan

Tours

Bob Dylan Tour Update Since the late eighties, Dylan has toured relentlessly, and this online service furnishes the latest Dylan tour dates, both confirmed and rumored. ✓**INTERNET**→*url* http://bob.nbr.no/dok/set/tour.html

Tim's Uncle Bob Adventure Tim went to see Bob Dylan in concert at RFK Stadium in Washington, D.C., and he committed his thrilling experience to print— electronically, that is. Read all about Bob's electric and acoustic competence, consult the set list, and even view pictures of His Grizzled Bobness. ✓**INTERNET**→*url* http://www.clark.net/pub/fervor/dylan.htm

Bob Dylan

"It was on a warm summer night at a beach called PIHA. I had just finished school for good and rushed away with a mate of mine for some surfing and goat-boating. However, in the warm night with our Black Heart Rum and Bolshevik Vodka, the only tape we could find was cassette 2 of Dylan's Masterpieces collection. Till this day we still don't know where it came from; we just found it under the back seat of my car. Anyway, we played it again and again (cause it was the only tape we had), and by the end of our little excursion we knew the words to half the songs on the tape.

"While we were there, we found a stray dog and named it Dylan in honour of our newfound hero. The dog's name was actually Toss (we found the owner later), but the experience of sitting around a camp-fire in the evening, playing cards and 'drinking white rum in a por-tugal bar' will remain with us forever."

—from **rec.music.dylan**

"Dylan is only a human being. Let him be that. Jesus didn't want to be an idol, and neither does a musician like Dylan. Get a life while chasing a fly."

—from **Bob Dylan Chat** on AOL's Music Message Center

"During the filming of the movie 'HELP,' The Beatles stayed completely stoned on weed. The lads also bragged of having smoked the herb in Buckingham Palace. Supposedly when Dylan heard of this exploit he remarked, 'maybe I shouldn't have turned them on,' then Dylan gave a wink. In recent years former Beatles band member Paul McCartney has been busted for trying to bring his stash into countries, such as Japan. Paul has admitted to enjoying hashish. Anyone with information on Dylan, The Beatles, and marijuana, please post here. Thanks."

—from **rec.music.dylan**

http://gdbdoc.gdb.org/~patty/CW/CW_home_page.html

Catherine Wheel WWW Home Page Discuss Catherine Wheel with other fans of the band. ✓**INTERNET**→*email* fruit-request@gdb.ord ✍ *Type in message body:* <your email address>

CAVE, NICK

Goodson (ml) Henry woke up from his dream, and he remembered that he was dreaming about this mailing list, on which the men and women of America share their secret fantasies about the deep voice and bottomless psyche of Nick Cave. ✓**INTERNET**→*email* goodson-request@ geog.leeds.ac.uk ✍ *Type in message body:* subscribe goodson

Nick Cave Here the moody lover man expounds what his creative work space looks like—metaphorically, mind you. ✓**INTERNET**→*url* http://www.mutelibtech.com/mute/cave/cave.htm

Nick Cave Page Excellent Nick Cave information, including a letter from the artist, reflections on Karen Carpenter, video clips, reviews, images, and guitar tabs. ✓**INTERNET**→*url* http://www.maths.monash.edu.au/people/brett/nick/nick.html

CHAPIN, HARRY

alt.music.harry-chapin (ng) Warm-hearted, sincere, and sometimes unabashedly sentimental, the Harry Chapin newsgroup is filled with fans willing to attest to the size of Harry's heart, or the purity of his motives, or the way his music walked the line between plaintive and mawkish. "Cat's in the Cradle" and "Taxi" get the most discussion, but Chapinites are also fond of testing other newsgroup participants by dropping the names of lesser known compositions. ✓**USENET**→alt.music.harry-chapin

Harry Chapin The cat's in the cradle, and the info's in the Web—much of it at this page, which contains lyrics, sound clips, a biography, guitar tabs, and more. ✓**INTERNET**→*url* http://www.fn.net/~jmayans/chapin/index.html

CHEAP TRICK

alt.music.cheap-trick (ng) How good is *Heaven Tonight*? How bad is *The Doctor*? Why was *Standing on the Edge* so maligned, especially in light of Robin's superb vocals on songs like "Tonight It's You" and "Cover Girl"? Will the band ever change its set list? And what's the origin of the name Bun E. Carlos, anyway? Get the latest news on the Rockford Four in this newsgroup. ✓**USENET**→alt.music.cheap-trick

Cheap Trick Official site for the *Woke Up with a Monster* LP. ✓**AMERICA ONLINE**→*keyword* warner→rock→Cheap Trick

Cheap Trick Chat Message-based discussion. ✓**AMERICA ONLINE**→*keyword* mmc→Rock/Pop→Hard Rock/Metal →Cheap Trick

THE CHURCH

The Church Join the Seance mailing list, download discographies, track the band's history, and get lyrics. ✓**INTERNET**→*url* http://www.cs.cmu.edu/afs/cs/user/vernon/www/church.html

The Church This unofficial Church homepage includes lyrics, a discography, and interviews. ✓**INTERNET**→*url* http://papillon.sd.monash.edu.au/~keith/church

Seance (ml) Spend your spare time in Church. ✓**INTERNET**→*email*

A few words from Nick Cave:

"I've been hammering away at this collection of murder ballads and it seems like we are going to be making a movie to accompany it at the end of the year, so that project probably won't see the light of day until early 1996. In Australia, The Bad Seeds recorded about eight new songs for this record, with titles like 'The Curse of Millhaven,' 'Henry Lee,' 'Where The Wild Roses Grow,' 'Crow Jane,' 'Lovely Creature,' 'King Kong Kitchee Kitchee Ki-Mi-O,' and a version of the Bob Dylan classic, 'Death Is Not The End,' but as its release date is so far in the future, I'm going to stop talking to people about that and get on with other stuff.

"Here's a groovy quote from Hannah Arendt. The sad truth is most evil is done by people who never make up their minds to be either good or evil."

-from **Nick Cave**

seance-info@thechurch.ebay. sun.com ✍ *Write a request*

CLAPTON, ERIC

Eric Clapton An interview with Clapton in which he considers his apotheosis in the sixties, his rocky solo career in the seventies, his pop success in the eighties, and his critical comeback in the nineties. ✓**AMERICA ONLINE**→*keyword* warner→rock→Eric Clapton

Eric Clapton Chat Message-based discussion. ✓**AMERICA ONLINE**→*keyword* mmc→Rock/Pop Rock→Artists A-L→Eric Clapton/ Cream/etc.

Eric Clapton—From the Cradle A sound clip of "Tore Down," along with track listings from Clapton's 1994 blues revival. ✓**INTERNET**→*url* http://www.iuma.com/ Warner/html/Clapton,_Eric.html

The Reason Why Sound samples from the entire span of Clapton's career, from the Yardbirds and the Bluesbreakers through Derek and the Dominoes and the solo years. ✓**INTERNET**→*url* http:// http.bsd.uchicago.edu/~d-hillman/ 46one/samples.html

Slowhand (ml) Talk about the venerable British blues guitarist. ✓**INTERNET**→ *email* slowhand-request@daacdev1.stx.com ✍ *Write a request*

THE CLASH

alt.music.clash (ng) Joe Strummer said that if he had his druthers he'd return to *London Calling* to edit the lyrics to "Hateful," and maybe even to delete "Four Horsemen" from the album. Fans debate whether or not "Should I Stay or Should I Go" masks homosexual content. And Big Audio Dynamite comes in for both admiration and derision.

✓**USENET**→alt.music.clash

The Clash Lyrics for the band's releases, and a single image. ✓**INTERNET**→*url* http://turnpike.net/ metro/punk/clash.htm

The Clash A discography and lyrics for the Only Band That Mattered. ✓**INTERNET**→*url* http:// www.idiscover.co.uk/paul/rob/ clash.html

Clash Chat Message-based discussion. ✓**AMERICA ONLINE**→*keyword* mmc→Alternative Rock→ Bands A-L→The CLASH + Big Audio Dynamite

COCKBURN, BRUCE

A Burning Light and All the Rest What's at this site? A novella-length biography of Bruce Cockburn. What else is at this site? Not much. ✓**INTERNET**→*url* http://www. cse.ogi.edu/~dhansen/html/ cockburn.html

Bruce Cockburn An official promotional site for the *Dart to the Heart* LP. ✓**INTERNET**→*url* http:// www.music.sony.com/Music/Artist Info/BruceCockburn.html

Bruce Cockburn Spiritualist,

moralist, and songwriter, Bruce Cockburn has one of the most perfervid followings in the world, and this site courts Cockburners with lyrics, images, and more. ✓**INTERNET**→*url* http://www.fish. com/music/bruce_cockburn.html

Humans (ml) We're all humans, of course, and many of us are humans who like to listen to Canadian singer-songwriter Bruce Cockburn. Good thing that this list exists, eh? ✓**INTERNET**→*email* major-domo@fish.com ✍ *Type in message body:* subscribe humans <your email address>

COCTEAU TWINS

Cocteau Twins General information on the band, including member bios, an image gallery, lyrics, and a form for sending email to the band. ✓**INTERNET**→*url* http:// grether.haas.berkeley.edu:8080/

Cocteau Twins Discography A discography of the band's work on 4AD. ✓**INTERNET**→*url* http://www. evo.org/html/group/cocteautwins. html

COHEN, LEONARD

alt.music.leonard-cohen (ng) Musings on Canada's gloomy bard

Cocteau Twins—from http:// grether.haas.berkeley.edu:8080/

Alice Cooper—from http://www.get net.com/alice/index.html

of angst and sexuality range from considerations of his own sexuality (is he gay?) to his songs (which are the best?) to his voice (what the hell happened to it?). ✓**USENET→** alt.music.leonard-cohen

Bird on a Wire With an opening quote from Cohen's excellent 1966 novel *Beautiful Losers* ("What is a saint? A saint is someone who has achieved a remote human possibility…"), this page achives the remote online possibility of collecting an eclectic set of Cohen links—a transcript of a BBC show, an interview with the *Jewish Book News*—as well as lyrics, guitar tabs, and images. ✓**INTERNET→** *url* http://ccat.sas. upenn.edu/cpage/Leonard_ Cohen/

Leonard Cohen Official Sony info on *The Future* LP. ✓**INTERNET→** *url* http://www.music.sony. com/Music/ArtistInfo/Leonard Cohen.html

Leonard Cohen A French site with lyrics and images. ✓**INTERNET→** *url* http://arctique.int-evry. fr/~cohen/lcohen/lcohetxt.html

COLE, LLOYD
Bad Vibes (ml) Make a commotion on this mailing list, which is devoted to the singing and songwriting of Lloyd Cole. ✓**INTERNET→** *email* majordomo@best.com ✍ *Type in message body:* subscribe badvibes-l <your email address>

Cole, Lloyd Lyrics, a discography, a bio, and images. ✓**INTERNET→** *url* http://www.best.com/~drumz/ Cole/

COLLECTIVE SOUL
Collective Soul Pictures, tour dates, and info. ✓**INTERNET→** *url* http://www.teleport.com/~ boerio/soul.html

Smashing Young Men Tour information, bios of band members, lyrics, images, and more. ✓**INTERNET→** *url* http://www.auburn. edu/~longmim/soul/soul.html

CONCRETE BLONDE
Concrete Blonde Chat Message-based discussion. ✓**AMERICA ONLINE→** *keyword* rockline→Messages→MODERN ROCK LIVE→ CONCRETE BLONDE

Little Conversations (ml) The band is no more, but Johnette Napolitano's powerful voice reverberates in the minds of adolescents everywhere. Discuss the band on this list. ✓**INTERNET→** *email* little-conversations-request@dover.cerf. net ✍ *Type in message body:* subscribe

COOPER, ALICE
Alice Cooper Download Dave McKean's art, which graced the cover of Cooper's last album, *The Last Temptation.* ✓**INTERNET→** *url* http://www.music.sony. com/Music/ArtistInfo/Alice-Cooper.html

Alice Cooper Autographed Photos How's this for a stocking stuffer—$35 for an autographed color picture of Alice and only $25 for a black-and-white autographed pic? Also available is a charming sound clip about the etiquette of biting the heads off chickens. ✓**INTERNET→** *url* http:// www. getnet.com/alice/ index.html

Alice Cooper Chat Message-based chat. ✓**AMERICA ONLINE→** *keyword* mmc→ Rock/Pop→ Classic Rock→Alice Cooper

Alice Cooper File A straightforward home page containing a library of Alice's albums, from *Love It to Death* to *Da Da*. Check out album covers and leave a friendly message about feeding your own Frankenstein. ✓**INTERNET→** *url* http://www.kajen.malmo.se/~ lare/cooperfile.html

COPE, JULIAN
Julian Cope A press release about the crazed British iconoclast, lyrics for the *Autogeddon* album, and more. ✓**AMERICA ONLINE→** *keyword* warner→Alternative→ Julian Cope

Soul Desert A list of St. Julian's albums, lyrics, articles, and set lists for past Radio 1 sessions. He's fried. ✓**INTERNET→** *url* http:// www. fsa.ulaval.ca/personnel/gaumondp/cope/ index.html

COSTELLO, ELVIS
alt.fan.elvis-costello (ng) Where are the Attractions? Who is in charge of Rykodisc's re-release program? Will Elvis ever record a duet with Tom

Waits? Enter the mind of rock's angry young man, who is well on the way to becoming a grumpy old man. ✓**USENET**→ alt.fan.elvis-costello

Elvis Costello The only site in town, with a complete list of albums, concerts, fan clubs, interviews, and a link to Rykodisc Customer Service. ✓**INTERNET**→*url* http:// east.isx.com/~schnitzi/ elvis.html

Elvis Costello Press releases and photos from the 1995 all-covers LP, *Kojak Varieties*. ✓**AMERICA ONLINE**→*keyword* warner→Alternative →Elvis Costello

Elvis Costello Chat Message-based chat about smart, sharp English rockers. ✓**AMERICA ONLINE**→*keyword* mmc→Alternative →Rock Bands A-L →Elvis Costello & Joe Jackson

Elvis Costello List (ml) Talk about Elvis Costello on this mailing list. ✓**INTERNET**→*email* majordomo@rain.org ✍ *Type in message body:* subscribe costello-l <your email address>

Red Shoes (ml) Talk about everything from *My Aim Is True* to the *Kojak Varieties*, and everything in between. ✓**INTERNET**→ *email* costello-request@en.com ✍ *Type in message body:* subscribe redshoes

#redshoes Live chat about Elvis. ✓**INTERNET**→*irc* #redshoes

COUNTING CROWS

alt.music.counting-crows (ng) Help tomorrow's music fans decide whether the Crows are Dylanesque, Van Morrisonesque, or might even have a shred of original inspiration. ✓**USENET**→alt. music.counting-crows

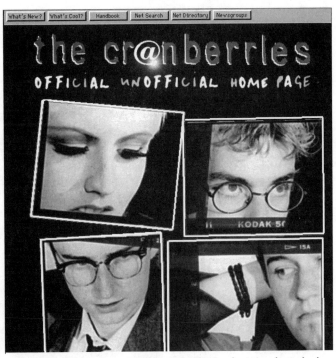

The Cranberries—http://www.nada.kth.se/~d90-fgi /Cranberries/cranberries.html

Counting Crows A band bio, a complete discography, tour dates, and an FAQ. ✓**INTERNET**→*url* http://sashimi.wwa.com/ hammers/crows/discog.htm

Counting Crows Chat Message-based discussion. ✓**AMERICA ONLINE** ...→*keyword* mtv→Message Boards→Bands That Do Suck→ Counting Crows ...→*keyword* mmc →Rock/Pop→Soft Rock/Pop/ Oldies→Counting Crows

Counting Crows List (ml) "Mr. Jones and me, we sometimes sit next to each other at the keyboard, and he tells me about the time when the world was free, and women had hair that swayed like coral, and a firm handshake was all the promise you needed, and I look at him the way that one brother looks at another and I just sing." Once you've gotten over the

fact that Counting Crows isn't exactly Cypress Hill, you'll have a wonderful time trading messages with other AOR fans on this mailing list. ✓**INTERNET**→*email* counting-crows-request@ariel.com ✍ *Type in message body:* subscribe counting-crows <your full name>

THE CRANBERRIES

The Cranberries Lyrics, discographies, guitar tabs, images, band news, sound files, tour dates, articles, and more. ✓**INTERNET**→*url* http://www.nada.kth.se/~d90-fgi /Cranberries/cranberries.html

The Cranberries Band bios, a Cranberries FAQ, and imagess. ✓**INTERNET**→*url* http://www.ama. caltech.edu/~phil/cranberries.html

Cranberries (ml) Are cranberries seasonal? Do they really prevent urinary tract infections? You

(cont'd pg. 108) →

The Grateful Dead

When Jerry Garcia died August 9, 1995, eight days after his 53rd birthday, the rock

world lost one of its gentlest spirits, and one of its most important figures. As the leader of the venerable hippie-rock band The Grateful Dead, Garcia did more than just write and perform songs—he created a subculture. But as any Deadhead knows, this is far too clinical and impersonal a description of what Garcia really accomplished, the way that he forged community despite the increasingly impersonal and commercial nature of rock music. Online Dead resources, which range from **Bobkirk's Deadhead Family** to **Dead Notes: Links From An Unbroken Chain** to **Skeleton Key: A Dictionary For Deadheads**, preserve Garcia's vision. Keep on truckin', Jerry. Rest in peace.

The Dead in the 1960s—http://www.mathcs.duq.edu/~wiegand/SYF/deadhead.html

Across the board

Bobkirk's Deadhead Family
Two generations of Bobkirks are certified Deadheads, and this page is basically a bio of the happy hippies and their equally blissed-out offspring. The site also features a collection of links to other fan pages and, of course, a number of electronic messages of mourning by Deadheads, young and old, from across the country. As the

Bobkirk family says, much peace and positive Netkarma to you and yours. ✓**INTERNET**→*url* http://www.primenet.com/~bobkirk/index.html

Dead Notes: Links from an Unbroken Chain A project whose goal is to create a Book of the Dead compiled solely from original material and comments from the Web. Send your comments, poems, scholarly writings, or what-have-yous to the authors electronically, or check out the sizable amount of material collected so far. One warning: If you still get teary over Jerry, bring the Kleenex, because much of this material is Garcia-memorial-oriented. ✓**INTERNET**→*url* http://www.netstreet.com/dead_notes.html

Dr. Beechwood's Grateful Dead Scrapbook This fan page

features a scrapbook with links to lyrics, interview clips, photos and a sound clip of the improv comedy skit "Calling Dr. Beechwood .." that the Dead performed in 1977. In addition, Dr. Beechwood's site includes an information file with links to memorial pages, an FAQ, sound clips, a newsgroup, and other Dead sites. ✓**INTERNET**→*url* http://www.mathcs.duq.edu/~wiegand/SYF/deadhead.html

Grateful Dead "This site rainbow spirals round and round / It trembles and explodes / It left a smoking crater of my mind." Links to an analog list, digital list, tape-deck specifications, show lists, images, a discography, and lyrics, as well as companion sites like nature images, comparable bands, an online art gallary, and an entire collection of cybercafés, cyberhouses, adventure worlds, and other virtual environments. ✓**INTERNET**→*url* http://shire.ncsa.uiuc.edu/Mike/

Grateful Dead A big, sweaty, generous page with links to an FAQ, tour dates, images, lyrics, set lists, sound clips, a tape tree, merchandise, articles and fiction, screen savers and icons, dozens of other Dead pages, and rumors (did anyone hear this crazy nonsense that something bad happened to Jerry?). ✓**INTERNET**→*url* http://www.cs.cmu.edu/~mleone/dead.html

Grateful Dead Almanac Browse back issues of the official Dead newsletter, which also incorporates the Grateful Dead Mercantile Company's catalog, offering more merchandise than all the head shops from here to eternity. ✓**INTERNET**→*url* http://www.well.com/Community/Grateful.Dead.Almanac/

Grateful Dead Forum Both touching tributes and snotty jokes made the rounds after Jerry Garcia passed on to that big Pollstar chart in the sky. "Q: What is the Grateful Dead without Jerry Garcia? A: Uh…what was the question, man?" And some of them got their debut on America Online's Grateful Dead Forum. The Grateful Dead Forum used to include tour dates and set lists; without Garcia, this is no longer an issue. So what does the forum have instead? Information for tape traders, images of the band, Deadhead diaries, and tributes to the late leader. ✓**AMERICA ONLINE**→*keyword* dead

Louisville Dead Page This site is really beautiful, man. It encompasses the music and the culture, with links to dozens of other Dead pages and resources—including

Jerry Garcia, smiling—http://www.mathcs.duq.edu/~wiegand/SYF/deadhead.html

articles, almanacs, tributes, lyrics and the like, and one of the surprisingly scarce Net collections of non–Rex Foundation "kindpages" (sites for charitable foundations and programs). ✓**INTERNET**→*url* http://wl.iglou.com/hippie/hippie1.html

Chat

Dead Chat (ng) The Grateful Dead has one of the most active online fan communities in the world—even without Jerry Garcia's bearish, bearded presence on the Earth. Come here to see what Deadheads are like online; you'll feel like you've finally found a home. ✓**USENET**→ rec.music.gdead

DeadHeads (ml) Talk about the Dead, even though the Dead are no more. ✓**INTERNET**→*email* DeadHeads-Request@gdead.berkeley.edu ✍ *Write a request*

Grateful Dead A huge area on eWorld devoted to the Dead and their fans. Visit the Vault, the Dead library. Read Grateful Dead news. Link to newsgroups and mailing lists. And then swim through the Phish bowl, a section

of the forum devoted to the junior Dead circuit. Live chat, tape listings, and rules for tapers used to dominate the discussion, which is now dominated by the seemingly endless series of tributes to the Dead's dead leader, the late Mr. Garcia. ✓**EWORLD**→*go* eaz→Pump Up The Volume→Music Talk→Grateful Dead

Grateful Dead Chat Message-based discussion. ✓**AMERICA ONLINE** …→*keyword* rockline→Messages→KEEPING THE 70s ALIVE→Jerry Garcia …→*keyword* mtv→Message Boards→Bands That Don't Suck→The Grateful Dead ✓**COMPUSERVE**→*go* rsforum→Messages and Libraries→Jerry Garcia …→*go* fanclub→Messages and Libraries→Grateful Dead …→*go* rocknet→Messages and Libraries→The Dead

Grateful Dead on the Web The Whole Earth 'Lectronic Link (WELL), the Bay Area's premier online service, has a wealth of Grateful Dead resources, with individual forums devoted to taping, trading, set lists, and studio recordings. This page serves as the WWW home for the WELL's Dead conferences, and offers conference annotation to help fans keep on truckin' in style. ✓**INTERNET**→*url* http://www.well.com/conf/gd.html

High Volume (ml) In-depth discussion of the Grateful Dead. ✓**INTERNET**→*email* Dead-Flames-Request@gdead.berkeley.edu ✍ *Type in message body:* subscribe deadflames

Live Deadheads Chat Jerry's not live anymore, but the chat on the Prodigy Dead area is. ✓**PRODIGY**→*jump* chat→Prodigy Chat→ Select an Area:→Music→DEAD Heads

Deadheads

The Deadhead Home Page Index A fan's delight—a hotlinked list of the hundreds of home pages of self-declared Deadheads. This page has such a sense of community, it may even make you want to write a little jingle ("Website at night / Deadhead's delight / Website in morning / Jerry's dead, and we're rhyming"). ✓**INTERNET**→*url* http://www.shore.net/~aiko/dead_html/index.html

Dictionary

Skeleton Key: A Dictionary for Deadheads The first definition of the word "deadhead" was reported in 1576, as a synonym for "caput mortuum," which is "the residuum remaining after the distillation or sublimation of any substance, 'good for nothing but to be flung away, all vertue being extracted.'" Since then, the *Oxford English Dictionary* has given the word's meaning as "a person admitted without payment to a theatrical performance, a public conveyance, etc.," "a non-combatant accompa-

nying a fighting force," "a train, freight car, truck, etc., carrying no passengers or freight," "a person who contributes nothing to an enterprise, activity, etc.; an unenterprising person," and "a faded flower head." So who needs some definitive, official ESTABLISHMENT dictionary? Everything you ever need to learn is in the Skeleton Key, which features links to expla-nations of Deadhead terms,

from "American Beauty" to "The Zone." Unfortunately, this is only a handful of sample entries, so if you want thoroughness, buy the book. ✓**INTERNET**→*url* http://www.bdd.com/newrl/bddnewrl.cgi/07-01-95/skel

Lyrics

The Annotated Grateful Dead Lyrics Created by David Dodd, an assistant professor at the University of Colorado, this site includes full discographies for the Dead and individual members, a bibliography of Dead-related materials, and thematic essays. What kind of thematic essays? "Light and Dark in the Lyrics of Robert

Hunter." "The Fractals of Familiarity and Innovation: Robert Hunter and the Grateful Dead Concert Experience." "Grateful Goose: Nursery Rhymes in the Dead's Lyrics." And then there are the annotated lyrics themselves, which attempt to explain every place name and literary reference in the band's oeuvre. The Dead should be grateful to Dodd. ✓**INTERNET**→*url* http://www.uccs.edu/~ddodd/gdhome.html

Tours

Tix Mix: The Grateful Dead Miracle Ticket Exchange This page will serve as a fabulous memorial. People scan their tickets and email them to the site, and they are added to the collection of ticket graphics, cataloged by date all the way back to '65. The collection is small now, and they're scrounging for back-date tickets, so every Nethead with the means should hop on this bus. ✓**INTERNET**→*url* http://www. well.com/user/plantone/tixmix/tixmix.htm

The Tour Before August 1995, you could have quit your job, given your suits away to charity, taken the kids out of school, sold the house, and traveled the golden road pushing fimo beads and hash brownies. Now that Jerry's gone, the Information Highway is a great road for Deadheads to travel, a way to keep linked with the family. *The Tour*, a fanzine, looks as good as it tastes, with news, images, Bryan's guide to North American cities, Dead links, archives, Garcia tributes, and links to other neat stuff on the Net. ✓**INTERNET**→*url* http://www.bcpub.com/phpl.cgi?contents.html

Grateful Dead

"You cook screen shavings in the bong soup? What a waste of a delicacy! The shavings (yes, they do have a slight tar taste) should be served sprinkled on sushi, or over the best vanilla ice cream you can buy.

"Watch for kitchen sneaks who will try to stick their fingers into your supply and savor the shavings straight. By the way, do you add the leavings from shroom tea to your bong soup, like my grandma used to do?

"P.S. Screen SAVINGS are best saved in a lead jar and sprinkled on Christmas cookies."

—from **Grateful Dead Chat** on CompuServe's Rocknet

"Anyone who picked up the Jerry Garcia memorial issue of Rolling Stone may have noticed the picture of a Jerry Garcia stamp from the Republic of Central Africa. Well, I got information on how to obtain this stamp and others a few days ago. I just called the number and they STILL HAVE some left. These are real collectors items and are very rare."

—from **Grateful Dead Chat** on CompuServe's Rocknet

"Hi there. The first time I ever laid eyes on Jerry I believed in Santa Claus. And he could be ornery at times, but that was just his body talkin', not his soul, because I never ever met a kinder man in the whole world. Everybody's askin' the big question, and love is the answer. And I'll always believe in Santa Claus."

—from **Grateful Dead Chat** on CompuServe's Rocknet

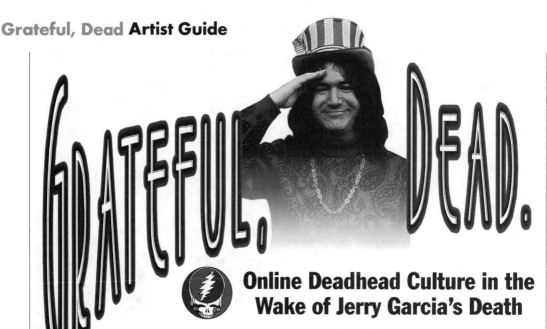

GRATEFUL. DEAD.

Online Deadhead Culture in the Wake of Jerry Garcia's Death

The Grateful Dead were always as much about community as music. So when Jerry Garcia died more or less unexpectedly of a heart attack in the early morning hours of August 9, 1995, the band's diverse fellowship of fans drew together to deal with the seven stages of grief in collective, if typically anarchic, fashion. Garcia wakes were held in major cities; Deadheads wept openly in Golden Gate Park and Central Park. And they also wept on the Net. True to the longtime affinity between Grateful Dead fans and infoculture, online Deadheads immediately flocked to Cyberspace to confirm and deal with the sad news. On The WELL, the Bay Area conferencing system that blossomed in the late 1980s thanks largely to its healthy population of Deadhead users, the news of Garcia's death caused a slowdown when unusually high numbers of members attempted to log on simultaneously. Usenet's rec.music.grateful-dead was likewise awash with posts—and the Usenet community even permitted the creation of 157 dummy newsgroups whose titles formed a giant banner reading "Jerry Garcia."

As word of Garcia's passing sank in, large and small sites devoted to the crafty guitarist mushroomed across the Web. In addition to the heartfelt and bittersweet memories of fans—who contributed to such sites as "Goodbye Jerry" or "Tributes to Jerry From WELL Deadheads"— Garcia was remembered in personal testimonies by Dead-affiliated writers, artists, and musicians, including Dead iconographer Stanley Mouse and frequent Garcia collaborater David Grisman. And Silicon Forest media even posted a cyber-condolence form that let Netsurfers send direct email to the members of the Dead and Garcia's survivors.

Garcia pages large and small, private and public, rejuvenated the Dead's presence in Cyberspace, with Mark Leone's Dedicated page spearheading the online wake. Corporate entities such as Time-Warner, *Wired* magazine, *Rolling Stone*, the *San Francisco Chronicle* and *Examiner*, and even the online entertainment publication *Mr. Showbiz*, jumped on the wagon. More personal, idiosyncratic expressions of grief included Dead lyricist and longtime friend Robert Hunter's funeral elegy, Garcia assistant Steve Brown's moving QuickTime tribute to other prematurely deceased '60s rockers, and Jerry Melloy's QuickTake photos of Haight/Ashbury shrines to Garcia.

It's been said that the Dead represent the same values as the Net—community, experimentation, radical democracy, even a healthy capitalism built on the back of the cycle in which counterculture becomes commodity becomes counterculture. Who knows. It's always been a long, strange trip. And in the end, the Net set the stage for a deeply emotional tribute to the first computer generation's quintessential musical figure. Not fade away, indeed.

In Memoriam

Dedicated ✓INTERNET→http://www.cs.edu/~mleone/gdead/dedicated.html

Jerry Garcia 1942-1995 ✓COMPUSERVE→garcia

Garcia: A Craftsman ✓INTERNET→http://levity.willow.com/digaland/garcia.html

Goodbye Jerry—from his fans ✓INTERNET→http://www.human.com/jerrymail/

In Memorium—Jerry Garcia ✓INTERNET→http://www.inetdirect.net/ghake/

In Memory of Jerry Garcia ✓INTERNET→http://www.apexsc.com/vb/garcia.html

Information about Jerry ✓INTERNET→http://www.well.com/user/gail/gd.html

Jerry Garcia 1942-1995 ✓INTERNET→http://199.170.0.53/garcia/condolences.html

Jerry Garcia ✓INTERNET→http://www.addict.com/ATN/Music_News_Of_The_World/

Jerry Garcia ✓INTERNET→http://www.pathfinder.com/people/jerry/

Jerry Garcia ✓INTERNET→http://www.rockweb.com/rwi/jerry-tribute/

Jerry Garcia ✓INTERNET→http://www.sfgate.com/garcia/

Jerry Garcia ✓INTERNET→http://www.sjmercury.com/garchome.htm

Jerry Garcia Haight Street Shrines ✓INTERNET→http://www.sirius.com/~jmelloy/jerry.html

Jerry Garcia Memorial ✓INTERNET→http://www.io.com/~ezra/dead.html

Jerry Garcia Memorial [JaguNET] ✓INTERNET→http://www.jagunet.com/ideal/garcia/

Jerry Garcia Memorial [Kevin Bieker] ✓INTERNET→http://www.primenet.com/~kbieker/jerry.html

Jerry Garcia Memorial [The Count] ✓INTERNET→http://www.primenet.com/~wrc/garcia/dead.html

Jerry Garcia Memorial Chat Room ✓INTERNET→http://www.rockweb.com/x/nph-jerry-chat

Jerry Garcia Remembered ✓INTERNET→http://techweb.cmp.com/techweb/net/netnow/jerry.htm

won't find any of that material here, because this mailing list is devoted to the Irish folk-rock group. But for fans of Dolores O'Riordan and company, there's plenty of information. ✓**INTERNET**→*email* majordomo@ocf.berkeley.edu ✍ *Type in message body:* subscribe cranberry-saw-us <your email address>

Cranberries Chat Message-based discussion. ✓**AMERICA ONLINE**→*keyword* mmc→Alternative Rock→Bands A-L→Cranberries

THE CRANES

Cranes Chat Message-based discussion. ✓**AMERICA ONLINE**→*keyword* mmc→Alternative Rock→Bands A-L→Cranes

Cranes List (ml) Stop whooping and start chatting on this Cranes mailing list. ✓**INTERNET**→*email* listserv@busop.cit.wayne.edu ✍ *Type in message body:* subscribe cranes <your full name>

CRASH TEST DUMMIES

alt.music.ct-dummies (ng) Talk about the deep-voiced folksters. ✓**USENET**→alt.music.ct-dummies

Crash Test Dummies Chat Message-based discussion. ✓**AMERICA ONLINE**→*keyword* mmc→Alternative Rock →Bands A-L →Crash Test Dummies

CROSBY, STILLS & NASH

Crosby, Stills, Nash, and Young Chat Message-based discussion. ✓**AMERICA ONLINE**→*keyword* mmc→Rock/Pop→Rock Artists A-L→Crosby, Stills, Nash (& Young)

Lee Shore (ml) With Neil Young, CSN was one of the most important folk-rock groups of the 'sixties. Without Neil Young, CSN was a trio of geezers. Or so say some of the subscribers to Lee

The Cure's unkempt leader—from http://www.acpub.duke.edu/~spawn/album.html

Shore. Get the latest on Steven Stills (who still plays), Graham Nash (who works with computers), and David Crosby (who has a new liver). ✓**INTERNET**→*email* majordomo@blender.digital.com.au ✍ *Type in message body:* subscribe leeshore <your email address>

CROW, SHERYL

Sheryl Crow Homepage An incredibly elaborate site for an artist who has only had a single solo release, this page links to a discography (again, only one album), a biography, quotes, lyrics, guitar tabs, images, movies, sounds, the Sheryl Crow FAQ, tour information, and even links to the pages of artists who have influenced Sheryl (like the Rolling Stones?!). ✓**INTERNET**→*url* http://www.csh.rit.edu/~cyke/sheryl/sheryl2.html

Sheryl Crow Page A British site devoted to Sheryl Crow, with lyrics, guitar tabs, images, and more. ✓**INTERNET**→*url* http://www.csh.rit.edu/~cyke/sheryl/sheryl2.html

CROWDED HOUSE

Crowded House Wondering what happened to the mournful

pop Kiwis? They're here, along with lyrics, pictures, sound clips, and more. ✓**INTERNET**→*url* http://www.bath.ac.uk/~ma4adas/crowded_house_home.html

Crowded House Interested in praying at the temple of the low men? Bow down at this Website, which includes lyrics, images, a band bio, and more. ✓**INTERNET**→*url* http://www.slnsw.gov.au/ausmusic/c/crowded-house/crowded-house-i.html

Crowded House Chat Message-based discussion. ✓**AMERICA ONLINE**→*keyword* mmc→Rock/Pop→General Rock→Crowded House/Split Enz

Crowded House List (ml) Come back to the five and dime, Neil Finn, Neil Finn. And when you do, bring more of those lovely songs, sung in your piercing Lennon-like voice. Okay? ✓**INTERNET**→*email* listproc@listproc.wsu.edu ✍ *Type in message body:* subscribe ch-digest <your full name>

THE CULT

The Cult Tour dates, discographies (legitimate and bootleg both), news, images, and lyrics for

Ian Astbury's Zeppelinish outfit. ✓**INTERNET**→*url* http://qb.island.net/~jtaylor/

The Cult A band bio, press releases, and a video clip of "Coming Down." ✓**AMERICA ONLINE**→*keyword* warner→alternative→The Cult ✓**INTERNET**→*url* http://www.iuma.com/Warner/html/Cult,_The.html

THE CURE

alt.fan.the.cure (ng) Very light traffic on this newsgroup, which includes as many spams and crossposts as actual messages about the band. ✓**USENET**→alt.fan.the.cure

Babble (ml) Keep up with the Smith on this mailing list. ✓**INTERNET**→*email* babble-request@anthrax.ecst.csuchico.edu ✍ *Type in message body:* subscribe

The Cure "Why can't I be you?" You can hear this identity crisis any time by downloading sound clips from this site. Also some really cool pictures from *Disintegration* and a few other Cure-like posters. ✓**INTERNET**→*url* http://www.best.com/~depemode/as-2.htm

The Cure This site features a charming explication of "Why the Cure is my favorite band" from a cheerful nihilist. What else is here? Lots of praise for *Disintegration*, images, lyrics, and even a prophecy: "The Cure are going to end up the Grateful Dead of the post-punk 1980s." ✓**INTERNET**→*url* http://www.itp.tsoa.nyu.edu/~student/brendonm/cure.html

Cure Lyrics How exactly does milk shake all over the windows and the doors? Or was it milk-shakes in the corridors? Find out from this site, which reprints lyrics to dozens of Cure songs. ✓**INTERNET**→*url* http://www.acpub.duke.

edu/~spawn/album.html

Cure Chat Message-based discussion. ✓**AMERICA ONLINE**→*keyword* mmc→Alternative Rock→Bands A-L→The Cure!!!

Cure Info Do you find existential crisis to be aptly expressed in Robert Smith's silhouette from *Boys Don't Cry*? You can download that image and ponder exactly what ontological quandary has got ol' Edward Scissorhands's goat. The page also includes lyrics, interviews, discographies, and links to other Cure sites. ✓**INTERNET**→*url* http://silver.ucs.indiana.edu/~ncosgray/home.html

The Cure's Big Drink Featured here is a transcript of a hearing in London where The Cure's members were sued for verbally abusing one of their friends. A Mr. Lol Tolhurst accompanied the band on the Orient Express in 1986, drank too much, and was later ridiculed for overdoing it. Mr Tolhurst says, "As a result of the continuous abuse and criticism, I became very ill and lost over a stone in weight." Hey buddy—if you're not part of the problem, you're not part of the cure. ✓**INTERNET**→*url* http://www.dnx.com/vamp/Gothic/Text/cure-interview.html

CURVE

Curve News, interviews, merchandise to trade, images, lyrics, pictures, and more. ✓**INTERNET**→*url* http://www.stack.urc.tue.nl/~conrad/curve/

Curve Mailing List (ml) Talk about the band, now defunct, or read old messages at the Web archive. ✓**INTERNET**→*email* curve-request@stack.urc.tue.nl ✍ *Type in message body:* subscribe *Info:* ✓**INTERNET**→*url* http://gonk.doit.wisc.edu/curve/

"Fellow Clash City Rockers:

I offer the coinage 'Strummerism' as being those shouted phrases and utterances that Joe Strummer has had a history of throwing out, in between the 'legitimate' lyrics of Clash songs. Often, I find these improvisations to be as essential a part of the song as the lyrics themselves. Some of the classics that I can think of:

'Fill 'er up, Jacko' ('Janie Jones')

'It's pretty baaaaaaad!' (same song)

'You're my gee-tar he-RO!' ('Complete Control')

'Look out for rules and regulations.' ("Remote Control")

'Blood claat!' (or *whatever* the hell he's saying at the very end of 'Last Gang in Town')

'Are you positively ab-so-lu-te-ly?' ('Car Jamming')"

-from **alt.music.clash**

D

D'ARBY, TERENCE TRENT

Terence Trent D'Arby Michael Jackson has his online *HIStory* museum, so it was only a matter of time before the humility-impaired Terence Trent D'Arby convinced Sony Records to give him something similar. TTD's online Monasteryo offers tour information, a biography, a discography, video and audio clips from the 1995 LP *Vibrator*, and plenty of images of the Beautiful One himself. ✓**INTERNET**→*url* http://www.music.sony.com/Music/ArtistInfo/TTD/index.html

TTD Chat Message-based discussion. ✓**AMERICA ONLINE**→*keyword* mmc→Rap/R&B→R&B/Soul→Terence Trent D'Arby

DANZIG

alt.music.danzig (ng) Danzig is so cool. He could kick your ass. He could kick mine. He knows Jeet Kune Do. But he wouldn't kick anyone's ass without a good reason—or, as Satanists would have it, a damned good reason. Talk about Glenn's muscles, his evil thoughts, and the topless women in his video. ✓**USENET**→alt.music.danzig

#Danzig Among hardcore Satanists, Glenn Danzig is something of a traitor, but to the rest of us, he's just a barrel-chested guy who can write a decent pop hook and chooses to trump up his act with Mephisophelean glee. Talk Glenn here. ✓**INTERNET**→*irc* #Danzig

Danzig Press releases, an artist bio, and more—including a transcript of a live-chat session with Glenn Danzig in which he discusses everything from sexual innuendo to Misfits politics to new music. ✓**AMERICA ONLINE**→*keyword* warner→rock→Danzig

Danzig Chat Message-based discussion. ✓**AMERICA ONLINE**→*keyword* mmc→Rock/Pop→Hard Rock/Metal→Danzig

DEAD CAN DANCE

alt.music.enigma-dcd-etc (ng) A light-traffic newsgroup devoted to the music of Dead Can Dance. ✓**USENET**→alt.music.enigma-dcd-etc

Dead Can Dance A band bio, lyrics, images, and a discography. ✓**INTERNET**→*url* http://dixson.slnsw.gov.au/ausmusic/d/dead-can-dance-i.html

Dead Can Dance An extensive DCD page with info on all albums and guest musicians, as well as spotlight features on anchor musicians Lisa Gerrard and Brendan Perry. ✓**INTERNET**→*url* http://www.evo.org/html/group/deadcandance.html

Dead Can Dance Artist bios, lyrics, and a full discography. ✓**INTERNET**→*url* http://www.nets.com/dcd

Dead Can Dance Lyrics, images, artist bios, and several disclaimers that suggest that this is a page with a complex. ✓**INTERNET**→*url* http://csclub.uwaterloo.ca/u/sfwhite/dcd.html

Dead Can Dance An official Warner Brothers site that includes a brief band biography and press releases. ✓**AMERICA ONLINE**→*keyword* warner→Alternative→Dead Can Dance

Dead Can Dance Chat Message-based chat. ✓**AMERICA**

Deep Purple—from http://www.tecc.co.uk/public/purple/Purple.html

ONLINE→*keyword* mmc→Alternative Rock→Bands A-L→Dead Can Dance

DEAD KENNEDYS

alt.fan.jello-biafra (ng) Once you've gotten over the fact that there's a human being walking the planet with the name "Jello" on his driver's license, you'll have loads of fun participating in this newsgroup, which treats all matters Dead and all matters Kennedy. ✓**USENET**→alt.fan.jello-biafra

Dead Kennedys Chat Message-based discussion. ✓**AMERICA ONLINE**→*keyword* mmc→Alternative Rock→Bands A-L→Dead Kennedys/Alt.Tentacles

DEEP PURPLE

alt.music.deep-purple (ng) Get the latest news on Deep Purple, whether it's a concert in Japan, racism in lyrics, or Richie Blakemore's mustache. ✓**USENET**→alt.music.deep-purple

Deep Purple "Can we have everything louder than everything else?" That's a question better left to philosophers; the rest of us can content ourselves with this Deep Purple page, which includes a bootleg discography and info about anyone remotely related to the Deep Purple family—Tommy Bolin, Ritchie Blakemore, Robin Trower, Steve Morse, and Nicky Simper, for starters. ✓**INTERNET**→ *url* http://www.tecc.co.uk/public/purple/Purple.html

Deep Purple Chat Message-based chat. ✓**AMERICA ONLINE**→ *keyword* mmc→Rock/Pop→Rock Artists A-L→Deep Purple

DEF LEPPARD

Def Leppard "The other day, Jackie [Phil Collin's wife] was walking down the street. Then 2 kids came to her. One of them asked her, 'What's the title of the new album gonna be?' Jackie answered, 'Adrenalize.' Then the other kids said, 'Cool! Adrian and Alice!!' This is the type of humor that keeps DL fans in stitches. This site is under construction and for the moment provides only a bootleg discography and anecdotes like the one above. ✓**INTERNET**→*url* http://www.lrc.edu/www/users/yutaka/deflep.html

Def Leppard Lyrics, pics and a discography, as well as reprints from the e-zine Cybersleaze. What's been up lately for the Leppards? Rick Allen got arrested for spousal abuse. Joe Elliot clocked a fellow soccer fan. So much for new and noteworthy. If you're easily bored by stories of pugnacious rock stars, link to other sites, including LepNet. ✓**INTERNET**→*url* http://www.princeton.edu/~nieder/defleppard/def.html

Def Leppard A huge site with sections devoted to news, fans, guitar tabs, and something called Funny Gize. Satisfy all your Def Leppard needs, and help the

Enjoy the silence—from http://www.best.com/~depemode/as-5a.htm

homeless children of America at the time (actually, the part about the homeless children is a lie, but there's no shortage of Def Lep info). ✓**INTERNET**→*url* http://www.xs4all.nl/~eldritch/leppard.html

Def Leppard Chat Message-based chat. ✓**AMERICA ONLINE**→ *keyword* mmc→Rock/Pop→Rock Artists A-L→Def Leppard

LepNet (Def Leppard List) (ml) The premier source for information on Def Leppard. ✓**INTERNET**→*email* lepnet-request@cs.niu.edu ✍ *Type in message body:* subscribe lepnet

DENVER, JOHN

alt.fan.john-denver (ng) Once he was one of the biggest stars of the seventies, a country-pop sensation with hits like "Grandma's Feather Bed," "Country Roads," "Rocky Mountain High," and more. Now he's a dependable touring act who occasionally records new material. Fans love talking about Denver, new and old. ✓**USENET**→alt.fan.john-denver

Rocky Mountain High List (ml) A Website and mailing list devoted to the John Denver fan club. ✓**INTERNET**→*email* emily@sky.net ✍ *Write a request Info:*

✓**INTERNET**→*url* http://www.sky.net/~emily/

DEPECHE MODE

Bong (Depeche Mode List) (ml) Chat about DM with other Depeche-heads. ✓**INTERNET**→*email* bong-request@fletch.earthlink.net ✍ *Type in message body:* subscribe bong

Depeche Mode They might be playing real instruments nowadays, but their lyrics still have adolescent appeal. Download some lovely sound clips from heart-warming DM faves, view images of the boys, and consider this: Humiliation is easier to take if it's set to a throbbing beat. ✓**INTERNET**→*url* http://www.best.com/~depemode/as-5a.htm

Depeche Mode "The summer of my freshman year I met this girl named Sue Ann, and she listened to them..." Once Sue Ann's friend turned to Depeche Mode, he never turned back, and today he wants to share the story of his devotion with the world, along with an incomplete discography. ✓**INTERNET**→*url* http://www.itp.tsoa.nyu.edu/~student/brendonm/depech.html

Depeche Mode What happened to Dave Gahan, and why was he at

Devo Artist Guide

Cedars-Sinai? (Rumor had it that he had tried to kill himself.) What are Alan Wilder's reasons for leaving the band? ("Whilst I believe that the calibre of our musical output has improved, the quality of our association has deteriorated to the point where I no longer feel that the end justifies the means.") Catch up on the latest episodes of As Depeche Mode Turns at this site, which functions as a sort of DM news service. ✓**INTERNET**→*url* http://www.mutelibtech.com/mute /dm/dm.htm

Depeche Mode Are you a fan of the new DM? Check out the art work from *Songs of Faith* and link to other sites for DM addicts. Also available are quality pictures of the troublesome group. ✓**INTERNET**→ *url* http://www.cis.ufl.edu/~sag/ dm/

Depeche Mode Chat Message-based chat. ✓**AMERICA ONLINE**→ *keyword* mmc→Alternative Rock→ Bands A-L →Depeche Mode

DM Something of a support group for DM fans, this page provides cover art, a reader's page, discographies, and even links to other synthpop pages. ✓**INTERNET**→*url* http://www.coma.sbg.ac.at/~ salchegg/DM/

DEVO

alt.fan.devo (ng) Jack wants to know if other Devo fans recognize that the Ohio band influenced Weird Al Yankovic. Peter wants to plug the Church of SubGenius. And Todd wants to explore the links between Devo and surf music. Whip it here. ✓**USENET**→ alt.fan.devo

Devo Lyrics and links. ✓**INTERNET** →*url* http://rampages.onramp. net/~rick/devo.html

Devo Chat Message-based discussion. ✓**AMERICA ONLINE**→*keyword* mmc→Alternative Rock→ Bands A-L→D E V O

MuteWeb Q: Are we not Website? A: We are Devo Website, and we have news, the Devo FAQ, an image gallery, articles, a discography, samples, a bootleg archive, and an archive of posts from alt.fan.devo. ✓**INTERNET**→*url* http://www.nvg.unit.no/~optimus/ devo/index.html

DIAMOND, NEIL

Neil Diamond Official Sony information on various albums, including *Up on the Roof—Songs from the Brill Building*, *Live in America*, and *The Christmas Album II*. ✓**INTERNET**→*url* http:// www.music.sony.com/Music/ ArtistInfo/NeilDiamond.html

Neil Diamond Chat Message-based chat. ✓**AMERICA ONLINE**→ *keyword* mmc→Rock/Pop→Rock Artists A-L→Neil Diamond

DIFRANCO, ANI

Ani DiFranco Ani DiFranco has two capital letters in her last name,

and maybe in elementary school she grew bitter writing the big D and the big F while all the other kids got away with a single capital and then lots of little letters. Maybe that's why Ani has decided to ditch capitals entirely for her statement of purpose: "i speak without reservation from what i know and who i am. i do so with the understanding that all people should have the right to offer their voice to the chorus whether the result is harmony or dissonance." Ponder whether this is a metaphor or not while you consult the other Ani resources, which include articles, interviews, quotes, a bio, lyrics, and guitar tablatures. ✓**IN-TERNET**→ *url* http://www.cc. columbia.edu/~marg/ani/

Ani DiFranco Funny that such an anti-establishment lyricist would allow herself to be called "Her Greatness" and "The Goddess." But if you're a Fan o' Ani, you can download great, goddesslike pictures taken at a concert in Keene, N.H., read her lyrics, and even consult a quote page that lets DiFrancophiles sharpen their wisdom teeth with help from such

Devo—from ftp://ftp.nvg.unit.no/pub/devo/pictures/

great thinkers as Lord Byron, Mel Brooks, Aristophanes, and Ani herself. ✓**INTERNET**→*url* http://www.catalog.com/chaos/ani.htm

Ani DiFranco Chat Message-based chat. ✓**AMERICA ONLINE**→*keyword* mmc→Rock/Pop→Soft Rock/Pop/Oldies→aNi DiFraNcO

DIRE STRAITS

Dire Straits Home Page Bootlegs, band information, and links. ✓**INTERNET**→*url* http://www-iwi.unisg.ch/~tgygax/ds/index.html

Dire Straits Home Page A band history, a discography, lyrics, and images. One warning: While much of the material at this site appears both in French and English, some has not yet been translated and appears only in the original French. *Vive les Dire Straits!* ✓**INTERNET**→*url* http://autan.enst.fr/~boute/ADireStraits.html

Mark Knopfler A page devoted to the soundtrack work of the Dire Straits frontman. ✓**AMERICA ONLINE**→*keyword* warner→rock→Mark Knopfler

DIS-N-DAT

Dis-N-Dat See these bumpin' homegirls party in a QuickTime video, listen to sound clips, and get album info here. ✓**INTERNET**→*url* http://www.sony.com/Music/ArtistInfo/DisNDat.html

DOLBY, THOMAS

Dolby, Thomas He's worked with artists from Lene Lovich to George Clinton, and along the way managed to carve out a niche as a progressive funkster. Get blinded with science at this Website, which includes a discography, a biography, lyrics, and images. ✓**INTERNET**→*url* http://www.kspace.com/KM/spot.sys/Dolby/

Jim Morrison—from from http://www.aleph.it/andre/doors/The_Doors.html

pages/home.html

Thomas Dolby Includes a live chat transcript featuring Dolby, a collection of press releases, and an artist bio. ✓**AMERICA ONLINE**→*keyword* warner→alternative→Thomas Dolby

THE DOORS

alt.music.the-doors (ng) Why was Jim Morrison the poet laureate of the Overdose Generation? Did Oliver Stone's movie do him an injustice? Flick your tongue at the memory of the Lizard King. ✓**USENET**→alt.music.the-doors

The Doors A page honoring the shaman and rock poet James Douglas Morrison, featuring a large selection of his poetry online. In addition to standard Doors stuff like a discography and an FAQ, the page includes a cyberinterview with the remaining Doors members, Robby Krieger, Ray Manzarek, and John Densmore. Densmore, by the way, is making a sizable amount of money touring college campuses and holding lec-

tures that are little more than extended answers to a single question: "What was Jim really like?" ✓**INTERNET**→*url* http://www.helsinki.fi/~palotie/Doors.html

The Doors Welcome to the Morrison Motel. You can click on the windows to access Rocktropolis, American Prayer info, and even chat channels where you can discuss the Lizard King. ✓**INTERNET**→*url* http://underground.net/Rocktropolis/Doors/

Doors Chat Message-based chat. ✓**AMERICA ONLINE**→*keyword* mmc→Rock/Pop→Classic Rock→The Doors

The Doors Home Page Lyrics, pictures, a bootleg discography, and the Doors FAQ. ✓**INTERNET**→*url* http://www.vis.colostate.edu/~user1209/doors/

DREAM THEATER

Dream Theater Articles attesting to Dream Theater's musicianship, lyrics, an FAQ and links to interactive stuff, and even a program for bootleg indexing for PCs. ✓**INTERNET**→*url* http://b62772.student.cwru.edu/~bill/music/dt/dt.html

Dream Theater Some pictures, but mostly links to other Dream Theater home pages. Consider the "inner battle between our innate human nature and the imposition of religious morality upon it." Decide whether DT practices Christian rock or punk nihilism. And then browse the band bios, mailing list archives, and admiring technical articles. ✓**INTERNET**→*url* http://www.cs.brandeis.edu/~mikeb/dt.html

Dream Theater What becomes a prog metal legend most? Find out at this site, which also includes a discography, a link to the Ystejam mailing list, and a transcript of an IRC interview session with Mike Portnoy and John Pertrucci. ✓**INTERNET**→*url* http://cs.muohio.edu/~mjones/music/dt/dt.html

Dream Theater Been looking for the lyrics to "When Dream and Day Unite"? If you couldn't find them on the other half-dozen Websites devoted to DT, never fear—they're here, along with Ytsejam stickers for all your, er, smooth surfaces. ✓**INTERNET**→*url* http://www.dreamt.org/

Dream Theater An assortment of files for Dream Theatergoers, including lyrics and images. ✓**INTERNET**→*url* ftp://ftp.netcom.com/pub/dr/drkhoe/www/dt.html

Dream Theater Chat Message-based chat. ✓**AMERICA ONLINE**→*keyword* mmc→Rock/Pop→Hard Rock/Metal→Dream Theater

Ytsejam (ml) It's "majesty" spelled backward; forward, it's a mailing list devoted to Dream

Theater. ✓**INTERNET**→*email* ytsejam-request@arastar.com ✍ *Type in message body:* subscribe ytsejam <your full name>

DURAN DURAN

Duran Duran Featuring medical motif—because The Medicine CD, a collection of B-sides, outtakes, and demos, has just become available—this page includes information on all Duran personnel, in addition to a special page devoted to the as-yet-untitled solo album by John Taylor (with the easy email link, you can send him title suggestions). ✓**INTERNET**→*url* http://freedom.ncsa.uiuc.edu/~smarch/durantest.html

Duran Duran Chat Message-based discussion. ✓**AMERICA ONLINE** ...→*keyword* mmc→Alternative Rock→Bands A-L→Duran Duran Lives ...→*keyword* rockline→Messages→MODERN ROCK LIVE→Duran Duran

The Duranie Connection Subtitled "For Duranies by Duranies," this site features articles and gossip about the band's comeback, recording practices, and even sexual proclivities. Get updates on the squabble between L.A.'s KROQ radio station and Duran Duran—reportedly, KROQ's mischievous DJs instructed Michael the Maintenance Man, a frequent guest to the show, to shout into a bullhorn "Duran Duran Sucks!" before a large group of fans waiting for tickets to the House of Blues show. Of course, Duran Duran objected—and the rest was history. ✓**INTERNET**→*url* http://www.chapman.edu/students/mathur/duran.html

Tiger (ml) Duran Duran is trendier than ever now that they're retro heroes, and you can ride the coattails of their resurgence here.

✓**INTERNET**→*email* tiger-request@ acca.nmsu.edu ✍ *Type in message body:* subscribe tiger-list

DYLAN, BOB

See page 94.

E

THE EAGLES

Eagles Guitar Tabs "Lyin' Eyes," "Desperado," "Already Gone," and more. ✓**INTERNET**→*url* ftp://ftp.nevada.edu/pub/guitar/ e/eagles/

Eagles: Hell Freezes Over Anchored by an annotated discography that traces the career of the California hit makers from "Take it Easy" to "I Can't Tell You Why" (the latter, it is rumored, is an explanation of the band's massive popularity), this page also contains information on the solo careers of the Eagles, sound clips, concert reviews, and a special picture of Henley, Frey, and company with Travis Tritt taken during the recording of *Common Thread*, country music's tribute to Eagles. ✓**INTERNET**→*url* http://www.coc. powell-river.bc.ca/eagles/eagles. html

The Last Resort "I couldn't wait until it was over, to get away from them"—Don Henley, 1990. "Everybody in the back of their minds knew how wonderful it would be to play together again"—Don Felder, 1994. Call it the tale of two Dons; the Eagles, after swearing never to share a stage again, reunited; if they can only shut out the critical derision, maybe they'll find a way to enjoy the millions they're raking in as a result of the comeback tour and happily pull in a fortune. If you're in the mood for that peaceful, easy

Elastica—from http://www.actwin.com/lineup/

feeling, then drop by this page, which furnishes lyrics for songs like "The Long Run," "Seven Bridges Road," and "Hotel California" (as if you didn't know them already), images, and links to pages devoted to the solo careers of the individual members of the band (even "singer"/"actor" Glenn Frey). ✓**INTERNET**→*url* http://www.metropolis.nl/~ annetted/eagles.html

ECHO & THE BUNNYMEN

Echo and the Bunnymen Ian and Will have formed a band named Electrafixion, and they've released an EP titled *Zephyr*. Is this the second coming of Echo and the Bunnymen? Find out by reading the review posted on this page, which also includes a number of press clips about the original Bunnymen, a picture gallery, and more. ✓**INTERNET**→*url* http://www. netaxs.com/~jgreshes/echo.html

Seven Seas (Echo and the Bunnymen List) (ml) The echo fades, but the fans live on. Share your thoughts with them on this mailing list. ✓**INTERNET**→*email* seven-seas-request@webcom.com ✍ *Type in message body:* subscribe

EINSTÜRZENDE NEUBATEN

Einstürzende Neubaten Don't

be half a man. Devise some strategies against boredom by visiting this EN home page, which includes a discography, pictures, and recent news—including the revelation that the band will perform a version of Faust and release an album of new material sometime in early 1996. ✓**INTERNET**→*url* http://www.uib.no/People/ henrik/neubauten/

Einstürzende Neubaten Home Page Does this Berlin outfit create music, or some ungodly noise that could best be described as "a symphony for angry carpenters"? Decide for yourself by consulting this site, which includes band news, a discography, photos, and special unreleased material available only on the Web. ✓**INTERNET**→*url* http://www.is.in-berlin.de/Culture/EN/

ELASTICA

Elastica The official Geffen site is anchored by a giant photo of Justine Frischmann, and includes a bio, sound clips, video information, and tour dates. ✓**INTERNET**→ *url* http://www.geffen.com/ elastica/

Elastica Chat Is Elastica just recycling an old New Wave formula, or are they the best power-

(cont'd pg. 119) →

Michael Jackson

He's been called a freak, a pedophile, and an anti-Semite, but at Michael Jackson's

altitude those epithets, like much else, seem like arrows shot at the feet of a giant by tiny, envious people. A superstar before he hit puberty, a megastar ever since, the King of Pop has redefined the rules of celebrity, rewritten every known sales figure for popular music, and resculpted his own image in the process. His 1995 greatest-hits collection, *HIStory*, generated unprecented hype, and then delivered on that hype, sending its second single, "You Are Not Alone," to the top of Billboard's pop singles chart—the first time this had occurred in the 37-year history of the chart. Stare awestruck at the Michael Jackson sites online, and then get domestic with the **Lisa Marie Home Page**.

The King of Pop, in a pensive moment—http://www.fred.net/mjj/

On the Net

Across the board

Australia's Michael Jackson Homepage "Michael Jackson, who has given his entire life to the music industry, has performed for millions and millions of fans throughout his 30-odd years in the music industry." Thirty-odd years? You're not kidding. This page celebrates the release of Michael Jackson's *HIStory* LP and collects a number of MJ resources,

including a review of *Dangerous*, tour pictures from *Dangerous*, and a transcript of Michael's interview with Oprah Winfrey. ✓**INTERNET**→ *url* http://www.monash.edu.au/ ccst7/rdt2110/fchi2/WWW/mj/ mjdan.html

Michael Jackson—Club Don't Scream If you're one of those nonplussed by Michael Jackson's smash single "Scream," you no longer have to confine your carping to a small circle of friends and confidants. Just email the owner of this page, and he will add your name to the ever-growing list of detractors. ✓**INTERNET**→*url* http:// www.wineasy.se/nygren/e-scream. htm

Michael Jackson Fan Club Lyrics for *HIStory*, updated sales figures, news of upcoming videos, and the latest gossip about Michael. Avoid the best-selling artist in pop history at your own peril. ✓**INTERNET** ...→*url* http:// www.fred.net/mjj/ ...→*email* mj@ fred.net ✎ *Type in subject line:* subscribe

Michael Jackson—HIStory Continues Gossip and straight information on the biggest pop superstar in the history of the world, including frequent reports that track the movement through Europe of a set of 30-foot statues commissioned to celebrate the release of the *HIStory* greatest-hits package. ✓**INTERNET**→*url* http://

The Moonwalker himself—http://www. en.com/ users/brown-mt/ShawnBrown/

www.primenet.com/~listen/

Michael Jackson: King of Pop
Read descriptions of all of Michael Jackson's albums, view his history as a pop artist on the charts (here's a hint: He's done well), and link to sites devoted to his musical collaborators, friends, and family. ✓**IN-TERNET**→*url* http://quasar.fastlane. net/homepages/rodshep/

Michael Jackson Spotlight Area Michael will personally welcome you to the site—just download the sound clip to hear his dulcet tones. He'll also sing for you: Check out clips for "Earth Song," "You Are Not Alone," and "HIStory." Sponsored by Sony Music, this site offers a cornucopia of multimedia files, including a high-tech screen saver, a Quick-Time movie clip, transcripts of a Jackson interview, and several images (Michael visiting a child in the hospital, cover artwork from *HIStory*, a publicity shot, etc.). ✓**COMPUSERVE**→*go* michael

Michael Jackson-HIStory Museum The ultimate in hubris—a site that looks like the Crown Jewels room in the Tower of London

but is in fact devoted to a single pop album. You'll need to become a subscription member of the HIStory Museum, but, once you do, you'll be able to spend hours clicking through Michael Jackson's musical past, and downloading audio, video, and text. ✓**INTERNET**→ *url* http://www.music.sony.com/ Music/ArtistInfo/MichaelJack son/main.html

Chart history

Michael Jackson Singles In 1970, "I Want You Back" went to #1 on the pop chart. "Ben," the story of the undying love between a boy and a rat, peaked at #4 on the R&B chart (but went all the way to the top on the pop chart). And each of Michael's solo albums since *Thriller* has spawned seven top-ten singles. Michael Jackson has said in published interviews that his proudest achievement is his success with the mass market, and this page shows that he has plenty to be proud of. ✓**INTERNET**→ *url* http://quasar.fastlane.net/ homepages/rodshep/chart.htm

Chat

Michael Jackson Chat Message-based discussion on the King of Pop and the ruler of all things platinum. ✓**AMERICA ONLINE** ...→*keyword* mtv→Message Boards →Bands That Do Suck→Michael Jackson ...→*keyword* aol mmc →Rap/R&B→R&B/Soul→Michael Jackson ✓**COMPUSERVE**→*go* rsforum → Messages *and* Libraries→ Michael Jackson ...→*go* fanclub→ Libraries *or* Messages→Michael Jackson

Michael Jackson Simulchat Michael Jackson touched down on the Planet Earth on August 17, 1995 to chat with CompuServe subscribers. What did he talk

about? Well, superheroes, for starters. When a Netsurfer asked the King of Pop which caped crusader he would most like to be, Michael responded, "Morph from X-Men. He can become anything. He is very mysterious, and he can even teleport. He can become all things. That is exciting to me. He is not as popular as the others, but that makes him exciting!" Michael also talks about the sales figures for *HIStory*, about Tchaikovsky, and about his favorite songs ("Got to Be There," "Heal the World," and "Ben"). ✓**PRODIGY**→*jump* chat→transcripts →*Search by date:* 08/18/95

Wives

The Lisa Marie Home Page In the summer of 1995, a St. Louis lawyer shocked the world—or at least the tabloid-TV-watching world—by filing an impersonation suit on behalf of a European woman who claimed that she, and not the woman who married Michael Jackson, was the actual Lisa Marie Presley. This page collects news reports, interviews, and even scientific analyses of facial structure that purport to back the claim. ✓**INTERNET**→*url* http://www. docs.uu.se/~y89hbo/presley/lisa. html

Michael with stripe on pants and hands on face—from http://www.fred.net/mjj/

Michael Jackson

"I'm fed up with the MJ hype too. I'm tired of the King of Pop references. I acknowledge his talents as a songwriter, singer, and dancer, but one does not become the King of Pop by completing one album every four years. Prince completes four albums worth of material every year and the press and the majority of the public consider him a has been."

—from **Michael Jackson Chat** on AOL's Music Message Center

"The only member in Michael's family to refute MJ's claim concerning his skin disorder was LaToya who is a pathological liar! If you are interested in vitiligo and discoid lupus it would be best for you and others who don't know about such diseases to go to the library and read!!!"

—from **Michael Jackson Chat** on AOL's Music Message Center

"In Oprah's interview you said that you wanted to raise a family someday. Do you plan to do so?"

"Yes that is my dream. I want children. I want my own. I want to adopt them. I love the idea of having my own family. I want to touch the entire world. I think we should reach out and touch everyone."

—from **Michael Jackson Simulchat** on CompuServe

pop/pop-punk since the Buzz-cocks? See whether the British sensation can make good for more than one album in a row. ✓**AMERICA ONLINE**→*keyword* mtv→Message Boards→Bands That Don't Suck→ELASTICA

The Elastica Connection A timeline of the band's history, an FAQ, a bio, a discography, lyrics, images, sound clips, concert dates, and links to related sites. ✓**INTERNET**→*url* http://www.actwin.com/lineup/

Stutter (Elastica List) (ml) Talk about Elastica on this mailing list. ✓**INTERNET**→*email* stutter-request@webcom.com ✍ *Type in message body:* subscribe

ELECTRIC LIGHT ORCHESTRA

alt.music.elo (ng) When Jeff Lynne went to join the Traveling Wilburys, was he elevated by his association with Tom Petty, Bob Dylan, Roy Orbison, and George Harrison, or did he drag them down into his overproduced, chart-topping world? And which ELO song contained the stilted couplet "Walking on a wave's chicane / staring as she called my name"? These are only two of the many questions that the august members of alt.music.elo can't get out of their heads. ✓**USENET**→alt.music.elo

Electric Light Orchestra Chat Message-based discussion. ✓**AMERICA ONLINE**→*keyword* mmc→Rock/Pop→Classic Rock→The E.L.O. Family

Electric Light Orchestra Home Page In addition to relatively standard ELO info—lyrics, a discography, images, and bios of members past and present (God help us all)—this page includes a detailed interpretation of the back-

masking on the ELO LP *Secret Messages*. Pass the mighty waterfall—it's what Jeff Lynne wants you to do. ✓**INTERNET**→*url* http://rampages.onramp.net/~myersrj/elo.html

Electric Light Orchestra List (ml) ELO fans are calling America, and America is answering them on this mailing list. ✓**INTERNET**→*email* elo-list-request@andrew.cme.edu ✍ *Type in message body:* subscribe

ENGLISH BEAT

English Beat English Beat is an abiding love of the author of this page; while he has "outgrown [his] parka, creepers, buzz cut, and scooter...THE BEAT GOES ON." How? With a history of the legendary ska band, placed in pop context; a discography for the Beat and related bands (General Public, Fine Young Cannibals); and roughly a dozen sound samples. ✓**INTERNET**→*url* http://www.best.com/~sirlou/ukbeat.html

ENO, BRIAN

alt.music.brian-eno (ng) Eno works with Bowie. Eno works with Cale. Eno works with Byrne. Eno works with Siberry. Eno works with U2. In fact, Eno works with just about everyone who has alternative credentials. Does that make him a music-industry whore or an important contributor to the sonic landscape of the nineties? Help the other members of this newsgroup decide. ✓**USENET**→alt.music.brian-eno

Brian Eno List (ml) Talk about Brian Eno's ambient projects, his collaborations with other artists, and his Roxy Music past. ✓**INTERNET**→ *email* eno-l-request@noc.pue.udlap.mx ✍ *Write a request*

Unofficial EnoWeb Sexy pic-

tures of Roxy-era Eno, distinguished photos of the older, balder, less made-up Eno, news about the BEEP (Brian Eno Electronic Portfolio) CD-ROM, a career chronology, and a 1974 article by the pre-Pretenders Chrissie Hynde that details Eno's love affair with pornography ("Mexican pornography is an interesting island of thought because they seem to be heavily into excretory functions") ✓**INTERNET**→*url* http://www.nwu.edu/music/eno/

ENYA

alt.music.enya/alt.fan.enya (ng) Post on Clannad, talk about the lush beauty of Enya's vocal arrangements, and fight off those skeptics who dismiss Enya as anesthetic for the brain. ✓**USENET**...→alt.fan.enya ...→ alt.music.enya

Enya List (ml) Enya's music will wash over your body like a lukewarm shower, and you should let it. Why? So you can share your experiences with the other members of this mailing list. ✓**INTERNET**→*email* majordomo@cs.colorado.edu ✍ *Type in message body:* subscribe enya <your email address>

ERASURE

Erasure List (ml) Devoted to the works of Vincent Clarke, including Yaz, Erasure, and Assembly. ✓**INTERNET**→*email* majordomo@tcp.com ✍ *Type in message body:* subscribe vincent-clarke <your email address>

ERICKSON, ROKY

Roky Erickson It's not rock music—it's Roky music! This page is devoted to the former lead singer of the 13th Floor Elevators and sometime mental patient, and includes a bio, lyrics, and links. ✓**INTERNET**→*url* http://www.hyperweb.com/roky/roky.html

ESTEFAN, GLORIA

Conga (ml) There are still Gloria lovers who want to talk about Gloria's near-fatal bus accident of more than a few years ago. Thankfully, they're not in the majority, and the rest of the Estefan fans content themselves with speculating on the Miami Sound Machinist's recent trip to Cuba, her upcoming albums, and her growing family. ✓**INTERNET**→*email* conga-request@tango.rahul.net ✍ *Write a request*

Gloria Estefan Chat Message-based discussion. ✓**AMERICA ON-LINE**→*keyword* mmc→World Beat→Gloria Estefan

ETHERIDGE, MELISSA

Melissa Etheridge Chat Message-based discussion. ✓**AMERICA ONLINE**→*keyword* mmc→Rock/Pop→Rock Artists A-L→Melissa Etheridge ✓**COMPUSERVE**→*go* fanclub→Messages *and* Libraries→Melissa Etheridge

Melissa Etheridge List (ml) So you go to her window, and you chin up on the sill, and when you look in, you don't see anything. There's no altar to Bruce Springsteen. There's no asylum bed on which Juliette Lewis can overact. There's not even a single guitar. So let yourself down, but easy. Walk home with your head in your hands. Think about why fans believe the things they believe. Tell yourself over and over again, "Kansas is a dream, a dream, a dream." And then submit your thoughts to this mailing list. ✓**INTERNET**→*email* etheridge-request@cnd.mcgill.ca ✍ *Write a request*

EXTREME

Extreme They're hard! They're soft! They're more than just the blurring of a simple dichotomy! Extremists can find a discography,

lyrics, a band bio, and lots of great pictures of the versatile rockers at this Website. ✓**INTERNET**→*url* http://www.eecs.nwu.edu/~dbleplay/extreme.html

Extreme Chat Message-based discussion. ✓**AMERICA ONLINE**→*keyword* mmc→Rock/Pop→Hard Rock/Metal Extreme

F

FABULOUS THUNDERBIRDS

The Fabulous Thunderbirds If you're tough enough for this Website, you'll be rewarded with a brief band bio, lyrics, a discography, and links to related blues-rock sites. ✓**INTERNET**→*url* http://www.quadralay.com/www/Austin/AustinMusic/TBirds/TBirds.html

FAITH NO MORE

Caca Volante (ml) Is it true that lead singer Mike Patton isn't exactly potty-trained, and that he uses the stage as a toilet between concerts? Discuss Faith No More (and Patton's other band, Mr. Bungle) on this mailing list, which handles all topics from the scatological to the musicological. The Website contains band lineups, discographies and album reviews, articles, concert and merchandise info, and links to other FNM sites. ✓**INTERNET**→*email* majordomo@tower.techwood.org ✍ *Type in message body:* subscribe cv <your email address> *Info:* ✓**INTERNET**→*url* http://www.preferred.com/~andy/cv.html

The European Faith No More Page Song and album polls in which Faith No More fans pick their favorites, discographies, lyrics, bios, import and concert info, a picture archive, song samples, and comments from fans. ✓**INTERNET**→*url* http://www.ping.

"I have no idea about Faith No More's concerts because they NEVER came to TURKEY!!!There are lots of fans waiting for them.If one of the member of the band is reading this PLEASE DON'T FORGET YOUR FANS IN TURKEY"

"The Real Thing, FNM's first with M. Patton, was great. it introduced us to that maniac. Angel Dust was much more experimental, but more disjointed (not a bad thing though). The new one is pretty cool, with a wide range. After reading reviews and reactions, i am suprised, which shows you people don't know shit (esp. Rolling Stone) But the best album is the second--even though Chuck sang (Patton has the better voice) who can deny those rockin' fuckin' songs? Groundbreaking funk-punk-riff-groove-crank-shit man!!"

"Mike Patton is the sexiest man in the universe."

—from **The European Faith No More Page**

be/~ping0104/faithnm.html

Faith No More Images, Quick-Time videos, band quotes, a bio, and a brief review of the band's tumultuous career. ✓**INTERNET**→*url* http://www.RepriseRec.com/FaithNoMore

Faith No More Chat Message-based chat. ✓**AMERICA ONLINE**→ *keyword* mtv→Message Boards→ Bands That Don't Suck→FAITH NO MORE

FARRELL, PERRY

alt.music.janes-addctn (ng) Amid spam posts about naked photos of MTV's Idalis and expositions of the lyrics of "3 Days" (Perry and Casey had a lover whom they enjoyed for three days, in a haze of heroin and skin), this low-traffic group ponders the musical past, present, and future of Perry Farrell. ✓**USENET**→alt.music. janes-addctn

Jane's Addiction Band lineups, sound clips, and information about Perry Farrell's first stab at immortality. ✓**INTERNET**→*url* http://raptor.swarthmore.edu/jahall/dox/JA.html

Jane's Addiction List Jane's Addiction, Porno for Pyros, and whatever group Perry Farrell forms next are the order of the day on this list. ✓**INTERNET**→*email* janes-addiction-request@ms.uky.edu ✍ *Write a request*

Porno For Pyros Band lineups, sound clips, and information about Perry Farrell's second stab at immortality. ✓**INTERNET**→*url* http://raptor.swarthmore.edu/jahall/dox/JA.html

FARRIS, DIONNE

Dionne Farris Sony's official site contains press info on *Wild Seed*,

The Nicks Fix—from http://www.iadfw.net/jkinney/index.htm

Wild Flower. ✓**INTERNET**→*url* http://www.music.sony.com/Music/ArtistInfo/DionneFarris.html

FIG DISH

Fig Dish Bios of Blake Smith and company, and a description of the Chicago band that makes the rather outlandish claim that "Fig Dish is to pop music what the Sex Pistols were to punk." ✓**INTERNET**→ *url* http://www.mcs.com/~bliss/starchild/rock/fig.html

FISHBONE

Fishbone Devoted to the poetry and thought of Fishbone's Angelo Moore, who won't comment on a rumor that John Cusack introduced Woody Allen to Fishbone's music, won't stand for rumors that Fishbone uses drugs, and won't go gently into the bright light of fame. ("Well, I don't feel like we have fame. We have some amount of fame, but most of all we have respect. That's what Fishbone has in the underground. We still have yet to get over that and reach out to the masses. Then we'll get their respect. And once we get their respect and understanding, THEN we'll get the fame. Michael Jack-

son's got fame. Who else—David Bowie's got fame. Mike Tyson's got fame. O.J.'s got fame. Even though it's an ugly fame.") ✓**INTER-NET**→*url* http://www.xensei.com/users/zug/maddvibe/mainmenu.html

Fishbone Message-based discussion. ✓**AMERICA ONLINE**→*keyword* mmc→Rap/R&B→Rap/hip-Hop/Funk→FISHBONE

FLEETWOOD MAC

alt.music.fleetwood-mac (ng) Stevie Nicks posted a message to a newsgroup objecting to a personal attack against her, and fans here want to talk about it. Founding member Peter Green died in August 1995, and fans want to talk about that. And they also want to talk about Lindsey Buckingham, Christine McVie, and Mick Fleetwood. Join them in discussions of the personnel changes, shifts in fortune, and musical metamorphoses that have marked the long history of this venerable British band. ✓**USENET**→alt.music.fleetwood-mac

Fleetwood Mac Chat Message-based chat. ✓**AMERICA ONLINE** ...→*keyword* mmc→Rock/Pop→ Classic Rock→Lindsey Buckingham ...→*keyword* mmc→Rock/Pop →Classic Rock→Fleetwood Mac ...→*keyword* mmc→Rock/Pop →Classic Rock→Stevie Nicks- Rock Priestess

The Nicks Fix (Stevie Nicks) The queen of gypsy chic, Stevie Nicks also has a long career as a bankable solo artist, and this page includes news, a discography, an alphabetical listing of all of Stevie's songs, fan club info, images, and concert sets. ✓**INTERNET**→*url* http://www.iadfw.net/jkinney/index.htm

Out of the Cradle Lindsey Buckingham shepherded Fleetwood Mac from blues-rock to pop superstardom, along the way earning a reputation as the Brian Wilson of the 1970s. This page is devoted to his solo career, which has met with more indifference than acclaim. ✓**INTERNET**→*url* http://www.eskimo.com/~cradle/

The Penguin Everything you always wanted to know about Fleetwood Mac, from the band's labyrinthine history to lyrics from *Tusk.* ✓**INTERNET**→*url* http://www.temple.edu/~madelson/index.htm

FOGELBERG, DAN

Dan Fogelberg Official promotional site for the *River of Souls* LP. ✓**INTERNET**→*url* http://www.music.sony.com/Music/ArtistInfo/DanFogelberg.html

Fogelberglist (ml) Dan Fogelberg has a long career as a singer-songwriter, and over the years he's accumulated millions of fans, many of whom talk to each other over this newsgroup. ✓**INTERNET**→*email* ai411@yfn.ysu.edu ✍ *Write a request*

FOO FIGHTERS

Foo Fighters Web Site This site is dedicated to Foo Fighters, Nirvana drummer Dave Grohl's new band. It features a Foo bio, Foo images, Foo lyrics, Foo concert reviews, and Foo sound samples. ✓**INTERNET**→*url* http://www.muohio.edu/~carmance/foo.html

FORBERT, STEVE

Steve Forbert Lyrics, discography, and images of Little Stevie Orbit, who has persisted long enough to become an elder statesman of folk rock. Be careful, though: Blink once and it may be gone. ✓**INTERNET**→*url* http://dip1.ee.uct.ac.za/music/steve_forbert.html

FORDHAM, JULIA

Falling Forward (ml) Find out more about the music, the personal life, and the visual style of the porcelain singer Julia Fordham. ✓**INTERNET**→*email* maillist@banana.demon.co.uk ✍ *Type in message body:* signon ff

Julia Fordham Discography, lyrics, interview/press releases, song parodies of Fordham's songs with feline lyrics ("We felines, feeling discontent, have hurt our souls and our heads / We've all made ourselves prisoners in this, our latest small-time war / The human with the feeding dish has decided to dismiss / My hunted paws; I shall resist, but inside I want to desist"), a photo gallery, FAQ, and links to both the Falling Forward mailing list and other artists of interest to Fordham's legion of fans. ✓**INTERNET**→*url* http://www.comp. vuw. ac.nz/~ecto phil/jules

G

GABRIEL, PETER

alt.music.peter-gabriel (ng) Where would you draw the line between old-school Peter Gabriel and new-school Peter Gabriel? If you ignore the obvious jokes—put the line right after his seminal double album *Takes a Nation of Millions to Hold Us Back*—you can participate in the textured discussion on alt.music.peter-gabriel, which compares early-period and late-period singing styles ("In the early days he sang with a raw, uninhibited passion, almost shouting the high notes at the maximum volume possible. In the later years, he has obviously learned to tame his vocals. He now sings with a softer, more 'gravly' quality that puts me to sleep"), lyrical concerns, and even hairstyles. ✓**USENET**→alt.music.peter-gabriel

And Through The Wire Various discographies, lyrics, links, and information for Gabriel traders and collectors. ✓**INTERNET**→*url* http://www.cs.clemson.edu/~junderw/pg.html

The Box (ml) Peter Gabriel doesn't record music all that often anymore, but when he does, his efforts are met with thunderous acclaim from fans of his experimental pop. Find out why. ✓**INTERNET**→ *email* 100070.157@ compuserve.com ✍ *Write a request*

My Secret World Images, lyrics, and links to newsgroups and Websites. ✓**INTERNET**→*url* http://www.wam.umd.edu/~bubba/peter.html

Peter Gabriel Geffen's official Gabriel site lauds the artist as "a longtime groundbreaker in rock" and hawks his Secret World Live concert. ✓**INTERNET**→*url* http://geffen.com/gabriel.html

Peter Gabriel A biography and discography. ✓**INTERNET**→*url* http://www.brad.ac.uk/~agcatchp/pg/gabriel.html

Peter Gabriel A "completely unofficial" Website pertaining to Peter Gabriel, with an FAQ, a discography, lyrics, pictures, sound samples, and more. ✓**INTERNET**→*url* http://www.cosy.sbg.ac.at/rec/Gabriel/

Peter Gabriel List (ml) Talk about Genesis's charismatic ex-leader (he once dressed as a flower for an entire concert), and speculate on whether his solo career will continue to break musical boundaries and employ high-tech musical inventions. ✓**INTERNET**→*email* majordomo@ufsia.ac.be ✍ *Type in message body:* subscribe gabriel <your email address>

Peter Gabriel Songs A list of songs, sorted by albums. ✓**INTERNET**→*url* http://www.nwu.edu/music/gabriel/songbook/

GALAXIE 500

Galaxie 500 Like all Galaxie 500 sites, this page seems to load as slowly as the band plays. But once it's all there, you'll have access to lyrics, images, sound clips, and more information on Galaxie 500 and related bands (especially Luna). ✓**INTERNET**→*url* http://uptown.turnpike.net/~AndyA/galaxie.html

Galaxie 500 Lyrics, images, a

discography, and links to related sites. ✓**INTERNET**→*url* http://sable.ox.ac.uk/~ba93013/Galaxie_500.html

GARCIA, JERRY

See page 102.

GENESIS

alt.music.genesis (ng) Is the past of progressive rock also the future of progressive rock? Put your two cents in at this newsgroup, which talks about everything from Peter Gabriel-era Genesis to *Abacab* to *Invisible Touch*. ✓**USENET**→alt.music.genesis

The Dance (Genesis) Not only links to other Genesis sites, but also substantial amounts of resident content, including pages for each individual member (Phil Collins, Tony Banks, Mike Rutherford), lyrics, an FAQ, and fan club info. ✓**INTERNET**→*url* http://www.brad.ac.uk/~agcatchp/gen_home.html

Genesis Discography A ludicrously extensive collection of video/discographies, bios, publications and organizations featuring everyone ever connected to the band, including material pertaining to all of the band member's solo endeavours. ✓**INTERNET**→*url* http://owl.rhic.bnl.gov:70/0h/satogata/Genesis/Discog/toc

Paperlate Genesis has evolved from an art-rock ensemble to an arena-rock staple, although now the group seems to be little more than an occasional meeting ground for Phil Collins and Mike Rutherford, where they can shake hands, share a beer, talk about solo projects, and record a few number-one hits. Discuss the band on this mailing list. ✓**INTERNET**→*email* paperlate-request@ansto.gov.au ✍ *Type in message body:* paperlate

GERMANO, LISA

Lisa Germano A full discography of Lisa Germano's 4AD work. ✓**INTERNET**→*url* http://www.evo.org/html/group/germanolisa.html

Sycophant (ml) Lisa Germano hasn't always had a happy love life, and her disappointments have informed her dark and bitterly funny body of work, which includes not only her work as a violinist for John Cougar Mellencamp, but also her own career. ✓**INTERNET**→*email* sycophant-request@webcom.com ✍ *Type in message body:* subscribe

GIBSON, DEBBIE

alt.fan.debbie.gibson (ng) Debbie used to be a little girl who listened to Billy Joel and Elton John. Now she's all grown up, and she listens to Billy Joel and Elton John. Just kidding—last summer, she told *Spin* magazine she was banging her head to the rough punk of the Circle Jerks. Find out why Debbie's pop tunes have survived longer than those of other pop teens like Tiffany and New Kids on the Block. ✓**USENET**→alt.fan.debbie.gibson

Between the Lines Share the latest news and gossip with other Debbie Gibson fans. ✓**INTERNET**→*email* btl@btl.org ✍ *Type in message body:* subscribe btl

Debbie Gibson Only in your dreams could you hope for a better Debbie Gibson site. Links to discographies, fan clubs and other fan pages, newsletters, events and promotional tour information, an archive, an FAQ, a newsgroup, and even a Gibson MOO, so fans can chat in real time. ✓**INTERNET**→*url* http://nova.decio.nd.edu/nrgup/

(cont'd pg. 127) →

Madonna

When future anthropologists unearth the American 1980s, only a few individuals will

stand head and shoulders above other cultural icons. Arnold Schwartzenegger. Michael Jordan. Ronald Reagan. Michael Jackson. And, of course, Madonna. Possessed of sex appeal, talent, and a professional savvy so unimpeachable that it seems like a force of nature, Madonna rose to prominence behind a seemingly endless series of canny dance-pop hits ("Borderline," "Like a Virgin," "Material Girl," "Express Yourself," and on and on and on), and then, against all odds, began to grow as an artist, releasing the sublime *Bedtime Stories* in 1994. Learn all about Miss Ciccone and her charms at the **Madonna FAQ, GIRLS,** and **alt.fan.madonna.**

On the Net

Across the board

Madonna Crypto-Catholic boy toy. Glam diva. Art-house whore. You've come a long way, baby. The queen of dance-pop has endured by passing through fashion after fashion, absorbing without being absorbed, and it's anyone's guess what she'll do next. Front a reggae band? Start a duo with Courtney Love? Visit this home page for a lesson in deep image, and come

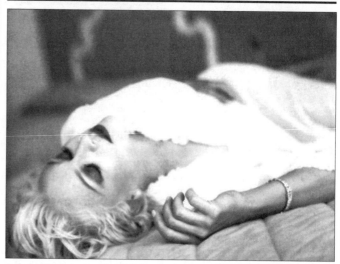

In bed with Madonna—from http://www.clark.net/pub/wmcbrine/

away Madonnafied. ✓**INTERNET→** *url* http://www.buffnet.net/~steve 772/maddy.html

Madonna "Surely whoever speaks to me in the right voice, him or her I shall follow..." Who would have guessed? That's Walt Whitman's creaky old voice Madonna is following these days, singing the body electric. So what if her lofty thoughts are left over from her first ballet class, when the bite of her leotard into her leg produced a galvanic mixture of pleasure and pain that was to reappear years later as a discourse of sacrifice in her art? At least she was paying attention. Download Madonna multimedia, visit the Madonna research library, peruse scholarly articles on the Material Girl ("Ceci n'est pas Madonna: Post-Reagan/Pre-Fascist Bodies and Feminist Disruptions"), check her performance on the pop

charts, and (of course) get pictures that find the hitmaker in various stages of undress. ✓**INTERNET→** http://www.st.nepean.uws.edu.au/ ~ppoulos/madonna/

Madonna—Bedtime Stories Warner Bros.'s official site for the *Bedtime Stories* LP, which netted Madonna some of the best reviews of her career. ✓**INTERNET→** *url* http://www.iuma.com/Warner/ html/Madonna.html

Madonna FAQ Is the mole real? Does she have any kids? Does somebody in Austin really have a sample of her pubic hair? They don't teach this kind of stuff in elementary school, and it's a damned shame—how can we expect our kids to survive the close of the century if they don't know their Madonna trivia from bottom to top? ✓**INTERNET→** *url* http:// www.mit.edu:8001/afs/athena.mit.

edu/user/j/w/jwb/Public/Music/Madonna/madonna.FAQ

The Madonna Home Page A playful Madonna home page, with a discography, top chart positions of Madonna songs, the Madonna FAQ, the Top Ten signs that David Letterman is Obsessed with Madonna ("Favorite Book: The Braille Version of *Sex*"), and a full version of the *Truth or Dare* script (originally titled *In Bed With Madonna*). ✓**INTERNET**→*url* http://www.mit.edu:8001/people/jwb/Madonna.html

Oh, Try to Be Like a Virgin "Madonna's biography! Madonna's newsgroup! Madonna's On-line Magazine! Madonna's lyrics! Madonna's sounds! Madonna's images!" And absolutely nothing on Madonna's attempts to have a child! ✓**INTERNET**→*url* http://www.cfn.cs.dal.ca/~ah190/madonna.html

Chat

alt.fan.madonna (ng) Is Madonna adopting kids? What new acts have signed to Maverick? Which videos show the Material Girl at her sexiest? And why is the only visible penis in the *Sex* book uncircumcised? ✓**USENET**→alt.fan.madonna

Madonna Chat Confer, consult, and commiserate with other fans of the Material Girl. ✓**COMPUSERVE**→*go* fanclub→Messages *and* Libraries→Madonna

Madonna List (ml) Express yourself on this mailing list. "Once you put your hand in the flame / You can never be the same / There's a certain satisfaction / In a little bit of pain." Discuss the merits of this statement, bringing in the work of authors such as

Sacher-Masoch and St. Augustine. ✓**INTERNET**→ *email* madonna-request@umich.edu ✍ *Write a request*

Images

GIRLS A number of pictures of Madonna, none of which find her dressed as a Civil War soldier. ✓**INTERNET**→*url* http://www2.labri.u-bordeaux.fr/~paries/Image/GIRLS.html

Strike a Pose Madonna's fame is founded on her canny manipulation of image, and this site shows why, with dozens of pictures from the Material Girl's career, most of them fairly recent and most of them fairly uncontroversial. ✓**INTERNET**→*url* http://www.mit.edu:8001/people/jwb/madpics.html/

Lyrics

Index for Madonna Song Lyrics She's been naked, she's been married, she's been in *A League of Their Own*. But she's never been shy about writing songs that express her feelings and explore the boundaries of religion and gender while simultaneously dominating the pop charts. Get the lyrics to all those infectious hits here, from "Borderline" and "Lucky Star" all the way up to "Secret." ✓**INTERNET**→*url* http://www.cs.rpi.edu/~zalewskk/madonna_lyrics/HomePage.html

Madonna: always in vogue—from http://www.clark.net/pub/wmcbrine/Madonna/

Madonna

"Madonna was set on meeting some of the most powerful people in the music industry. One of the people that she wanted to meet was the artist Prince. She finally met him backstage at the American Music Awards. She later said what she remembered most about him was how tiny he was, and the smell of his lilac perfume that he was wearing, along with the purple outfit."

—from **Madonna Chat** on Compuserve's Fanclub Forum

"I've been reading on the Madonna Mailing List that Madonna might have a guest appearance on Friends. Apparently Matt LeBlanc who stars on Friends said that there was a good chance that Madonna will play his sister or lover. If Madonna plays his sister it could lead to an ongoing role if the logistics can be worked out. I hope they can, Friends is one of my favorite shows. I'd like to see her play his sister so she can come back for more shows.

"I think it would be great to see Madonna appear on a sitcom. It would be even better to see her on a Roseanne episode. Now that would be a real rage. Is Sandra Bernhard still on that show? If so that could pose a problem."

—from **alt.fan.madonna**

"I've just seen Showgirls and something is puzzling me. The movie is about dancing girls, dancing boys, the dancing scene, striking poses, glamour…things that are right up Madonna's alley. So why isn't there any connection between the movie and Madonna?"

—from **alt.fan.madonna**

GOLDEN PALOMINOS

Golden Palominos When you're talking Golden Palominos, you're talking rotating membership, which is why it's vital to have a guide to the ever-changing personnel. Get the lowdown on Anton Fier, Bill Laswell, and company (Stipe! Straw! More!) and link to other pages. ✓ **INTERNET**→*url* http://ux1.cso.uiuc.edu/~apasulka /gopals/

GOO GOO DOLLS

Goo Goo Dolls Good timey, hard-rocking, and less lazy than they sound, the Goo Goo Dolls have always been replacements for the Replacements, an honorific if ever there was one. This page contains information on all the band's LPs, from Goo Goo Dolls (with its loopy Prince cover) to Superstar Carwash (with "We Are the Normal") and beyond. ✓ **INTERNET**→*url* http://www.rpi.edu/~velks/ GOOGOODOLLS.html

GORKA, JOHN

John Gorka For a folk artist, John Gorka is unusually versed in the ways of the online world, and the Website for this Dennis Miller lookalike contains sound samples, tour info, a biography, and a discography, as well as a toll-free number for ordering. ✓ **INTERNET**→ *url* http://www.windham.com/ ourmusic/artist_pages/gorka. empty.byartist.html

GRANT, AMY

alt.music.amy-grant (ng) Only Al Green has had more success than Amy at bringing God into pop music, and Al doesn't look like Andie McDowell. Get the latest news and gossip on Amy—why her fans stay seated during concerts, whether or not her crossover is harming her gospel base, and whether she will ever exploit her sexiness more overtly. ✓ **USENET**→

Goo Goo Dolls—from http://www.rpi.edu/~velks/GOOGOODOLLS.html

alt.music.amy-grant

Amy Response Team (ml) God is in the details, they say, and that's certainly the case for fans of this fresh-faced pop-gospel star. ✓ **INTERNET**→*email* art-request@ipc. uni-tuebingen.de ✍ *Type in subject line:* subscribe

GRATEFUL DEAD

See page 102.

GREAT WHITE

Psycho City Hard rock with wit and charm went out with the seventies, right? Don't tell Great White. This page includes a discography, lyrics, and images from the career of the modern-day cross between Mott The Hoople and Dokken. ✓ **INTERNET**→*url* http://www.usa.net/~shortdog/ great_white/great.html

GREEN DAY

alt.music.green-day (ng) What old band most resembles Green Day? The Who? The Seeds? The Buzzcocks? That Petrol Emotion? Cast your vote in this newsgroup, and while you're at it, try to make some quasi-critical point about the way rhythm and noise interact in Green Day's work. ✓ **USENET**→

alt.music.green-day

alt.music.green-day.sucks (ng) How do you become a pop music villain? Release an album with peppy harmonies that splits the difference between pop and punk, tour relentlessly, and refuse to swallow more than a small dose of the critical medicine prescribed to you. That's what Green Day has done, and, as a result of their self-possession, Billy Joe and company have made as many enemies as fans. ✓ **USENET**→alt.music.green-day. sucks

Green Day Everything you ever wanted to know about the golden boys of punk-pop. Includes links to discographies, bios, fan clubs, newsletters, music polls, media archives, an FAQ, and even links to dozens of other fans' personal email addresses. ✓ **INTERNET**→*url* http://www.cs.caltech.edu/~adam /greenday.html

Green Day Chat Message-based discussion. ✓ **AMERICA ONLINE**→ *keyword* mmc→Alternative Rock→ Bands A-L→Green Day ✓ **EWORLD**→ *go* eaz→Pump Up the Volume→ Music Talk →Green Day-Kick ass or Ass Kiss ✓ **AMERICA ONLINE**→*key-*

word mtv→Message Boards→Bands That Do Suck →Greenday blows!!

#greenday Admiration for the mainstream punk band. Remember Woodstock? They don't (they weren't even born), but they were on hand for the 25th Anniversary travesty. Share your thoughts and feelings here. ✓**INTERNET**→*irc* #greenday

GRIFFITH, NANCI

Nanci Griffith (ml) She has the voice of a little girl, but the career of a full-fledged adult, and the fans to prove it. ✓**INTERNET**→*email* majordomo@world.std.com ✍ *Type in message body:* subscribe nanci <your email address>

Nanci Griffith Chat Message-based discussion. ✓**AMERICA ON-LINE**→*keyword* mmc→Rock/Pop→ Soft Rock/Pop/Oldies→Nanci Griffith

GUIDED BY VOICES

Guided By Voices Is GBV poised on the brink of superstardom, or will the band crack under the pressures of hi-fi recording? Be at the Website when the future unfolds—you'll also get tour updates, lyrics, album covers, bootleg information, an interview with the band, and more. ✓**INTERNET**→*url* http://www-dev.lexis-nexis.com/~mikesell/gbv/

Guided By Voices A discography that tracks the band's output from its earliest independent releases to the major-label releases of the last few years. ✓**INTERNET**→*url* http://www.liii.com/~mcpart/guided2.htm

---

Guided By Voices Email Contact the band's manager directly. ✓**INTERNET**→*email* abbo666@aol.com ✍ *Email with general correspondence*

HotFreaks Lyrics, images, links, and more. ✓**INTERNET**→*url* http://www.netaxs.com/~jsalmon/gbv/hotfreaks.html

---

Postal Blowfish An electronic newsletter devoted to Guided by Voices that furnishes tour dates and gossip. ✓**INTERNET**→*url* http://www.netaxs.com/~jsalmon/gbv/pblowfish/pblowfish.html

GUNS N' ROSES

alt.rock-n-roll.metal.gnr (ng) We all know that Axl Rose is an anagram for Oral Sex, but we don't all know that some fans believe passionately that the band has sucked since *Use Your Illusion,* while others want to talk about the way that country music has influenced the group's music. And keep up to date on the myriad solo projects spinning out of G n' R. ✓**USENET**→alt.rock-n-roll.metal.gnr

Dust N Bones We all know that Dust N Bones is an anagram for Guns N' Roses, right? Ha! It's a trick! You probably don't even know what an anagram

is, do you? Don't worry, though. It doesn't really matter. In Guns N' Roses Land, spelling hardly counts—all you need is an attitude, some Stones-style riffs, and enough lyrical misogyny and homophobia to go around. Link from this page to the newsgroup, mailing list and G n' R Homepage. ✓**INTERNET**→*url* http://www.teleport.com/~boerio/gnr/dust-n-bones.html

---

Guns N' Roses How many Gunners bootlegs are there? According to this page, dozens and dozens, ranging from *No Refrain* to *.44 Calibre Horticulture.* Get track listings and the band's provenance here. ✓**INTERNET**→*url* gopher://wiretap.spies.com/00/Library/Music/Disc/bootleg.gnr

---

Guns N' Roses (ml) Guns n' Roses may have broken up. Fans aren't sure. Executives at Geffen Records aren't sure. The band members aren't sure. The only person who's sure, in fact, is a young man who lives outside of Normal, Illinois, and he spends most of his day perched atop a pole, a single eagle feather clutched in his hands, the words to "Paradise City" spilling from his lips like blood from a wound. You can't speak to this young man, and he won't post to this mailing list. But other G N' R fans will. ✓**INTERNET**→*email* majordomo@teleport.com ✍ *Type in message body:* subscribe gnr <your email address>

Guns N' Roses Message-based discussion. ✓**AMERICA ONLINE** ...→*keyword* mtv→Message Boards→Bands That Don't Suck→GN'R ...→*keyword* mmc→Rock/Pop→Rock Artists A-L→Guns'n'Roses

---

Guns N' Roses Home Page

Welcome to the jungle. There are enough links to get lost in, including discographies, lyrics, tour and Geffen news, song listings, guitar tabs, interviews and an FAQ, as well as info on Slash's solo projects and Axl's charitable stirrings (he sponsored an auction to support the Save the Earth Foundation). ✓**INTERNET**→*url* http://www.teleport.com/~boerio/gnr-home.html

Interview with Slash So, Slash, how do you explain your top hat, your curls, and the post-coital cigarette everpresent on your lip? Get the answers to this and other questions posed to the G n' R guitar god here. ✓**INTERNET**→*url* http://www.vpro.nl/www/vpro-digitaal/loladamusica-map/slash-interview

Slash Profile An interview with Slash that finds the guitarist on the road with Slash's Snakepit. Contains the riveting admission that Slash "likes driving around in people's cars." ✓**INTERNET**→*url* http://euphony.com/euphony/articles/33/Slash/Slash-CI.html

Slash's Snakepit A fan page devoted to the side-project founded by Guns n' Roses' lead guitarist that includes an interview with Slash, pictures, and more. ✓**INTERNET**→*url* http://www.teleport.com/~boerio/slash/

Slash's Snakepit Geffen Records' official site for *Beggars & Hangers-On*, the debut LP from Slash's Snakepit. ✓**INTERNET**→*url* http://geffen.com/slash/

GWAR

GWAR Learn about the albums, the lyrics, and the madness of Beavis and Butt-head's favorite shock-dinosaur band, which persists in "inadvertently killing off the human race by having sex with

apes." ✓**INTERNET**→*url* http://www.iuma.com/GWAR

GWAR For all fans of foam rubber and bodily fluids, this site gives a bio and band lineup, as well as links to audio files, other fan pages, catalogs, newsgroups, and info about films and comic books in the making. ✓**INTERNET**→*url* http://www.brad.ac.uk/~dparson/hypertext/music/bands/gwar.html

The GWAR Page Of course, you realize this means GWAR. Link to videographies and discographies, tour dates, reviews, images, guitar tabs, an FAQ, and even something entirely surreal—a link to the campaign to save convicted cop-killer Mumia Abu-Jamal. Who would have guessed psychotic, sex-crazed, homicidal aliens would be politically aware? ✓**INTERNET**→*url* http://www.-ti.informatik.uni-tuebingen.de/~graf/Gwar.html

HARVEY, PJ

PJ Harvey The official Polygram site for the queen of nineties gyno-rock, featuring a complete bio. ✓**INTERNET**→*url* http://www.polygram.com/polygram/PJBio.html

PJ Harvey She wants to bring you her love. She's your jolie-laide glamour queen. She has digested punk, blues, and industrial, and regurgitated a whole new thing. And now she's the subject of a comprehensive discography, an FAQ, a lyrics file, a picture archive, and a collection of guitar tabs. ✓**INTERNET**→*url* http://www.louisville.edu/~jadour01/pjh/

PJ Harvey List (ml) What will

"Jimi is buried in Greenwood Cemetary, which is in Renton WA, just south of Seattle. From downtown Seattle, take I-5 South to I-90 east. This will bring you accross Lake Washington via the 'floating bridge.' Take I-90 South and get off at the Sunset Blvd. (in Renton) exit. At the end of the offramp, turn right (you are now headed back northward). At the first set of lights is NE 3rd St. Turn right onto NE 3rd St. and follow it up a steep hill. After levelling out at the top of the hill, follow the road for about 1 m. Greenwood Cemetery is on the right. Jimi's grave is in the back left located near a sundial and couple of marble benches. This is indeed a public cemetery, so you will be most welcome to visit. Wax rubbings or charcoal rubbings are done at this site all the time, mainly because Jimi's gravestone is flat in the ground (it's not a headstone like you might expect)."

-from **alt.fan.jimi-hendrix**

happen to PJ now that she has fired her band, hooked up with Flood, and put a song on the *Batman Forever* soundtrack? Find out by chatting with the other members of this mailing list. ✓**INTERNET**→*email* majordomo@ homer.louisville.edu ✍ *Type in message body:* subscribe pjh <your email address>

HAWKINS, SOPHIE

alt.music.sophie-hawkins (ng) You wouldn't think that Sophie B. Hawkins would merit her own newsgroup. Maybe that's why almost no one posts here. ✓**USENET**→alt.music.sophie-hawkins

Sophie B. Hawkins Official Sony information for *Whaler*, the latest release from this pansexual siren. ✓**INTERNET**→*url* http://www. music.sony.com/Music/ArtistInfo/ SophieBHawkins.html

Whaler (ml) Talk about *Whales* and *Tongues & Tales* with other Sophie B. Hawkins fans. ✓**INTERNET**→ *email* whaler-request@idyramp. iquest.net ✍ *Write a request*

HENDRIX, JIMI

alt.fan.jimi-hendrix/alt.music.jimi.hendrix (ng) What do Hendrix fans discuss? Comparisons with Santana. Early recordings. Guitar tabs. Weigh in on the once and future king of the electric guitar. And if you get flamed, remember to employ this poised response—"Hey, baby, let me stand next to your fire." ✓**USENET** ...→alt.fan.jimi-hendrix ...→alt. music.jimi.hendrix

Electric Ladyland Links to bios, history, discographies, charts, lyrics, poetry, photo gallery, mailing lists, and other fan pages, as well as a quote archive, where other luminaries wax poetic about the Van Gogh of guitar. ✓**INTERNET**→

Jimi Hendrix—from http://www.univ-pau.fr/~minfo002/Jimi/

url http://www.univ-pau.fr/~ minfo002/Jimi/

Hey Joe (ml) "Hey Joe, where you going with that email account of yours?" "Going to flame my old lady—I caught her having cybersex with another man." Talk Jimi with like-minded individuals. ✓**INTERNET**→*email* hey-joe-request@ms. uky.edu Write a request

Jimi Hendrix Hendrix images, lyrics, guitar tabs, and more. ✓**INTERNET**→ *url* http://www.i-site. com/~artists/Jimi_Hendrix/

Jimi Hendrix Chat Message-based discussion. ✓**AMERICA ONLINE**→*keyword* mmc→Rock/Pop→ Rock Artists A-L→Jimi Hendrix

Limited Edition Hendrix As fans know, Hendrix himself was a limited edition, and when he checked out of the library of life in 1970, the world lost a visionary noisemaker. This site advertises Jimi Hendrix prints created by Mark Stutzman, who also drew the Elvis Stamp—and this Spanish Capitalist Magic can be yours for only $300. If prints aren't your speed, never fear—there are more

Hendrix items on the way. ✓**INTERNET**→*url* http://www.proxy.com/ hendrix/

Room Full of Mirrors: The Official Jimi Hendrix Home Page The ultimate Jimi Hendrix Experience, this page links to dozens of bios, discographies, photo and film archives, academic essays, a virtual museum, an astrological profile of the deceased guitar god, and even sites describing the beneficiaries of the Jimi Hendrix Foundation. Doesn't it just blow your mind? ✓**INTERNET**→*url* http://wavenet.com/~jhendrix/

HIMMELMAN, PETER

Daf Gematria (Peter Himmelman) Based out of the Center for Jewish life at Princeton University, this site includes links to lyrics, discographies, and other pages concerning Himmelman, Judaism, and what they mean to each other. ✓**INTERNET**→*url* http://cville-srv. wam.umd.edu/~mikesch/ himmelman.html

Peter Himmelman Official Sony info for the *Skin* LP. ✓**INTERNET**→*url* http://www.music.sony. com/Music/ArtistInfo/Peter Himmelman.html

Synesthesia (Peter Himmelman) A discography, links, lyrics, traders' classifieds, interviews, images, tour info, and more. ✓**INTERNET**→*url* http://www.cs.clemson. edu/~junderw/music/ph/

HITCHCOCK, ROBYN

A Gallery of Robyn Hitchcock Photo gallery featuring perfomances at Glastonbury '86 and the London club known only as "The Forum." ✓**INTERNET**→*url* http:// www.cogs.susx.ac.uk/ users/andyh/music/robyn_gallery. htmlw

A Robyn Hitchcock Page Got a thing for Queen Elvis? Your obscure, stream-of-consciousness dreams are answered. Links to the Mrs. Wafflehead page, discographies, interviews, liner notes, lyrics, and a photo archive dedicated to this truly strange man are here. ✓ **INTERNET**→*url* http://0/uvacs. cs.virginia.edu/~mad5c/fegmaniax/ index.html

fegMANIAX! (ml) Robyn Hitchcock mailing list. ✓ **INTERNET**→*email* fegmaniax-request@.rutgers.edu ✍ *Type in message body:* subscribe fegmaniax

Mrs. Wafflehead Information and merchandise for Robyn Hitchcock and friends. ✓ **INTERNET** →*url* http://remus.rutgers.edu/~ woj/wafflehead.html

Positive Vibrations A Robyn Hitchcock fanzine that's less weird than Robyn himself. Not so difficult to imagine, huh? ✓ **INTERNET**→ *url* http://remus.rutgers.edu/~ woj/pv.html

HOLE

alt.fan.courtney-love (ng) Courtney's hotter than Kurt, hotter than hell, hotter even than Hole, and so is her newsgroup, which ranges from deconstructionist analyses of Ms. Love's sexuality to laments about the fate of the Bean. ✓ **USENET**→alt.fan.courtney-love

Courtney Love FAQ (Hole) Why is Courtney such a problem? Was she shooting up during her pregnancy? Did she love Kurt? Why Evan Dando? Turn tragedy into trivia by digesting this three-part FAQ. ✓ **INTERNET**→*url* http:// www.mordor.com/rcmaric/clfaq. html

Hole Geffen's official site for Hole, the band led by the premier bitch goddess widow of the nineties. ✓ **INTERNET**→*url* http:// geffen.com/hole.html

Hole Photos of the band, along with a discography. ✓ **INTERNET**→ *url* http://seds.lpl.arizona.edu/~ smiley/hole/hole.html

Hole Get a sample from "Miss World," then make your bed, then lie in it, then make your bed, then die in it. ✓ **INTERNET**→*url* http:// www.iuma.com/IUMA/band_html /Hole.html

Hole Chat Message-based discussion. ✓ **AMERICA ONLINE** ...→*keyword* mmc→Alternative Rock→ Bands A-L→HOLE ...→*keyword* mtv→Message Boards→Bands That Don't Suck→HOLE AND COURTNEY ...→*keyword* rockline→Messages→MODERN ROCK LIVE →HOLE should be buried

HOTHOUSE FLOWERS

Hothouse Flowers Hothouse Flowers only recorded a few albums, but they live on in the hearts, minds, and souls of Celtic rock fans. Get song lists and more for *People*, *Home*, and *Songs From the Rain*. ✓ **INTERNET**→*url* http:// celtic.stanford.edu/pub/artists/ Hothouse.Flowers.discog

Hothouse Flowers List (ml) A discussion of the Hothouse Flowers' music and related things. ✓ **INTERNET**→*email* yaboss@cc.bellcore. com ✍ *Type in message body:* subscribe <your email address>

HOOTIE & THE BLOWFISH

Artist Biography—Hootie and the Blowfish Bio and tour dates. ✓ **INTERNET**→*url* http://www. walnutcreek.com/wca/bio/hootie. html

Hootie and the Blowfish Tour dates, lyrics, guitar tabs, photos, discography and lineup for the folk-rock, vocals-driven garage band, Hootie and the Blowfish ✓ **INTERNET**→*url* http://weber.u. washington.edu/~jnorton/hootie. html

Hootie and the Blowfish Message-based discussion. ✓ **AMERICA ONLINE** ...→*keyword* mtv→Message

Courtney Love's Hole—from http://seds.lpl.arizona.edu/~smiley/hole/hole.html

(cont'd pg. 135) →

Metallica

The 1983 release of Metallica's *Kill 'Em All* restructured the face of heavy metal music;

Metallica took the lumbering riffs and daffy pseudo-intellectualism of late-seventies hard rock and snapped its neck with malicious efficiency. In albums like *Master of Puppets* and *And Justice For All*, the band elevated thrash to a new level, and 1991's *Metallica*, which focused the group's overpowering sonics on shorter songs, made superstars of the group. Metallica fans (an elite group that includes MTV's Beavis) can bang their heads as they surf from **Jaymz' Unofficial Metallica Page**, **Luke Chang's Metallica Page**, and **alt.rock-n-roll. metallica**. And if you want to see your metal heroes rendered two-dimensionally, head to **Rockit Comics Presents Metallica.**

Our heroes—http://www.galcit.caltech.edu/~aure/metallica/metallica.html

On the Net

Across the board

Jaymz' Unofficial Metallica Page All the Metallica pages have lyrics ("Deafening / Painstaking / Reckoning / This Vertigo it Doth Bring"—oh James, oh Lars, how our hearts beat!), but how many of them have a transcript of a chat session with Kirk from America Online? This one does. And you can even get a sound clip of the new Metallica song "2 by 4," al-

though it probably won't be new by the time the book appears in bookstores, and the thrill of novelty will be dulled significantly. ✓**INTERNET**→*url* http://ezinfo.ucs. indiana.edu/~lwagers/metallica/

Luke Chang's Metallica Page Brief reviews of Metallica albums, and sound samples of entire songs from *Master of Puppets*. Load "Welcome Home (Sanitarium)" and use it as your computer's shut down sound. Your office mates will love you forever. ✓**INTERNET**→ *url* http://www.princeton.edu/~ lychang/metallica.html

Metallica An official record company page for Metallica that includes a band bio, a discography, images, sound and video clips, an account of the goings-on at the Molson Ice Polar Beach Party in Tuktoyuktuk, Canada, and interesting facts about the concert set *Live Shit: Binge & Purge* (the album includes "a genuine Metallica snakepit pass, a 'Scary Guy' stencil, and the unique 'flight-case' packaging"). ✓**INTERNET**→*url* http://www.pathfinder.com/

elektra/artists/metallica/metallica. html

Metallica Metallica brainbangers have been trying for years to tell the world that there's more to metal than big hair and spandex. If you can decipher the lyrics, you'll find intelligence, emotion and—dare we say—poetry. Then again, sometimes you just want to slam till comprehension gets knocked out your head. This site

Immortalized in comics—http://www. nando.net/music/gm/Rockit/metallica/

James Hetfield and his guitar—from http://www.galcit.caltech.edu/~aure/metallica/

features a brief (and recently tragic) band history, a band line up, images, a discography, and links to lyrics, sound clips, and other Metallica sites. √**INTERNET**→ *url* http://freeabel.geom.umn.edu:8000/metallica/metallica.html

Metallica Discography An extensive discography including all bootlegs and picture discs in addition to industry albums. √**INTERNET**→*url* gopher://wiretap.spies.com/00/Library/Music/Disc/metallica.dis

Metallica Home Page This page begins by reminding everyone in America why Metallica is popular—"Yes, this is Beavis's favorite band"—and then goes on to justify the adulation of that cute little blond miscreant, furnishing guitar tabs for all Metallica releases and links to related pages. √**INTERNET**→*url* http://www.eecs.ukans.edu/~chyong/metallica/kill.html

The NEW Metallica Home Page A simple, well-produced page with links to sound clips, lyrics, and lots of images. √**INTERNET**→*url* http://www.galcit.caltech.edu/~aure/metallica/metallica.html

Rockit Comics Presents Metallica "Better than a color

picture biography of the Marquis de Sade, it's got more stretch than a Richard Simmons video, and it's the Real Story (not some phoney Warrant crap-ass cherry-pie junker)." Metallica's bio-comic illustrates the history of the band up to and including the death of bassist Cliff Burton. Check out the Rock-it Comix link for other metal gods that went through the three-tone press. Warrant fans, if any actually exist, should look elsewhere. √**INTERNET**→*url* http://www.nando.net/music/gm/Rockit/metallica/

Chat

alt.rock-n-roll.metallica (ng) How do the members of Metallica feel about Dave Mustaine? Do

they like him better than they like Axl Rose? And how should Metallica fans who have been with the band since the beginning feel about the fact that the band's eponymous album created millions of new fans who understand nothing about the Metallican ethos? Share your hopes, fears, and frustrations with other Metallica fans here. √**USENET**→alt.rock-n-roll.metallica

Metallica (ml) Talk about Metallica on this mailing list. √**INTERNET**→*email* metallica-request@thinkage.on.ca ✍ *Write a request*

#metallica Lively discussion of the influential guitar band. √**INTERNET**→*irc* #metallica

Metallica Chat Message-based discussion. √**AMERICA ONLINE** ...→*keyword* mtv→Message Boards →Bands That Don't Suck→Metallica ...→*keyword* mmc→Rock/Pop→Rock Artists M-Z→Metallica

Merchandise

Cherry Lane Guitar tabs, songbooks, and fakebooks of Metallica's songs. √**INTERNET**→*url* http://www.cherrylane.com/METALLIC.HTM

The good old days—from http://www.galcit.caltech.edu/~aure/metallica

Metallica

"Jason gave me the pick he had used because I was the most energetic. After the show, I got pictures and autographs from ALL the guys. I talked to Bob Rock. James and Bob were impressed I knew all the lyrics. Bob's son was there. Here's a bit of trivia. That kid who said those lines in Sandman was Bob's son! He's a lot bigger now. Looks just like Bob. We talked about how bluesy the new album sounded and how heavy it was. I talked with Kirk about the AOL thing. He asked me what my name was. Then he said 'Whoa, that's you.' It kinda made me feel special."

—from **Metallica Chat** on AOL's Music Message Center

"To the fan who saw the reheasal:

Wow!! You definately are the envy of all of us Metallica fans!! I would have really liked to have seen a rehearsal.....oh well!! Thanks for the report though, it really helped!! Now I don't feel so Metallica deprived."

—from **Metallica Chat** on AOL's Music Message Center

"On August 13th my boyfriend and i went and saw Soul Asylum.(They were good!) any way we were in front, All I can say is that 'body surfing'(is that what is called?) sucks, I got kicked in the head twice and soon was helping the guy next to me pull them down , let them fall and kick them as hard as i could. We were also shoved ect. I'm not complaining cause i knew the risks!

"This is relavant to Metallica fans because when i saw Metallica last time there were more people there than at the Soul Asylum concert. And the other concert goers (at Metallica) were polite! No 'body surfing' no pushing, etc. JUST ONE BIG HAPPY PARTY!!! thanks to all in Des Moines IA on June 25, 1994."

—from **Metallica Chat** on AOL's Music Message Center

Indigo Girls' Swamp Ophelia—*http://www.music.sony.com/Music/Images/*

Boards→Bands That Do Suck→ Hootie and the Blowfish ...→*keyword* mmc→Rock/Pop→General Rock→Hootie & The Blowfish

Hootie and the Blowfish Home Page Links to the band lineup, tour and TV performance news, discographies, lyrics, bios, reviews, articles, merchandise and CD purchase info, and other fan pages. ✓**INTERNET**→*url* http://www.stcloud.msus.edu/~pullit01/music/hootie/hootie.html

South Carolina Hootie Homepage South Carolina's favorite sons are featured on this site, which includes sound clips for hits and rare tracks, a band lineup, tour dates, and a lovely holiday snapshot of the guys wishing their fans well. ✓**INTERNET**→*url* http://s9000.furman.edu/~oneal/hootie/yahoo.html

HUSKER DU

Husker Du Need a picture of Bob Mould taken in the Sideburns Era? Want the lyrics to *Zen Arcade*? You can get them here, along with a full discography. ✓**INTERNET**→*url* http://turnpike.net/metro/punk/hd.htm

Husker Du/Bob Mould/Sugar Minneapolis exported Prince, and then it exported this powerful

post-punk band, which recorded such terse masterpieces as *Land Speed Record, Zen Arcade, Flip Your Wig, Warehouse: Songs and Stories*, and *New Day Rising*. Get lyrics, images, and even a list of song cross-references so that you can keep track of what material Bob Mould's performing these days. ✓**INTERNET**→*url* http://math.montana.edu/~sanford/sugar.html

INDIGO GIRLS

alt.music.indigo-girls (ng) The Indigo Girls have their detractors, sure, and many of them are on this newsgroup, mocking Amy and Emily for their political correctness, criticizing the lyrics for opacity, and even questioning the playing of the duo. But the Indigo Girls also have their supporters, and many of them are here too, fawning over the folk pair. ✓**USENET**→alt.music.indigo-girls

Indigo Girls Find out all about the queens of folk-rock, and maybe, just maybe, you'll learn something about yourself. Interviews and photos from the Newport Folk Festival, press releases, discography and bios, album info for *Rites of Passage* and *Swamp Ophelia*, and, eventually, a music screener. ✓**INTERNET**→*url* http://www.music.sony.com/Music/ArtistInfo/IndigoGirls.html

Indigo Girls Chords Links to guitar charts and tabulature for Emily and Amy's introspective compositions. ✓**INTERNET**→*url* http://www.umn.edu/nlhome/m161/schn0170/ig/index.html

Indigo Girls List (ml) Talk about Emily and Amy—from their first acoustic demos to *Jesus Christ Su-*

"Dark thundering rain, cold wind blew in my face,
hey boy, don't dream your life, live your dream,
I saw into her sparkling eyes, you know what I mean,
you're so sweet Janet, is this world the right place

Janet laughed saying give it a try,
she's so cute and full of power,
I thought about her words for several hours,
first sunshine bright-end up the sky."

"Miss Janet, you make the world a better place / With your soft, kind words and your beautiful face
You're the kind of person I love to dream about / Your voice throws out words I have to listen to / Your love and happiness puts my mind in a trance
I'm knocked off my feet everytime I see you dance / From your Number One Fan, from world to the moon / I love you, Janet, and I hope I see you soon"

-from **Dreamworld Janet**

perstar: A Resurrection. ✓**INTERNET**→*email* listserv@geko.com.au ✍ *Type in message body:* subscribe indigo-girls <your full name>

Lifeblood Articles, lyrics, set lists, and guitar tabs to help put you in a mood Indigo. ✓**INTERNET**→*url* http://www.hidwater.com/lifeblood/ig.html

INXS

alt.music.inxs (ng) Australia's reigning rock superstars are a little bit on the outs with the alternative-music crowd, but they may still make a comeback on the strength of Michael Hutchence's charismatic vocals and matinee-idol presence. Get the one thing at this newsgroup. ✓**USENET**→alt.music.inxs

INXS List (ml) A discussion of INXS, Australia's late-eighties superstars. ✓**INTERNET**→*email* inxs-list-request@iastate.edu ✍ *Write a request*

INXS Mailing List WWW Page While this site lacks Kick, it does furnish links to spartan but serviceable FAQ, bio, and FTP sites. ✓**INTERNET**→*url* http://www.public.iastate.edu/~jlbraddy/inxs.html

INXS Song Archive Hallucinate, desegregate, then meditate on this collection of sound clips, now liberate, liberate, liberate... ✓**INTERNET**→*url* http://ftp.luth.se/pub/sounds/songs/inxs/

IRON MAIDEN

alt.rock-n-roll.metal.iron-maiden (ng) Axl Rose is dead from overdose! Not really, but that joke post seems to pop up on every heavy-metal newsgroup. On this one, Axl only gets a slight mention, and the rest is all Maiden—set lists for Japanese concerts,

collectors' information, and news of Bruce Dickinson's solo career. ✓**USENET**→alt.rock-n-roll.metal.iron-maiden

Iron Maiden Information Network Up the Irons! Links to album info, history, various band lineups, a video/discography, a family tree, cover references, and the location of the Derek Riggs Insignia. ✓**INTERNET**→*url* http://www.rpi.edu/~wallr/IronMaiden.html

Iron Maiden Page Bang your head to this. This page contains pics and a spot of news, links to album cover JPEG's and reviews, as well as Bruce Dickinson Pages, merchandise, sound clips, musician searches, and email addresses of fellow metal heads. ✓**INTERNET**→*url* http://www.cs.tufts.edu/~stratton/maiden/maiden.html

JACKSON, JANET

Dreamworld Janet If she was your girlfriend, the things she'd do

to you. But she's not, so you'll have to satisfy yourself with this garish Website, which includes album information, still photos from videos, lyrics, and more. ✓**INTERNET**→*url* http://www.wiso.uni-erlangen.de/~wgtauman/janet_dreamworld.html

Janet News, links, tour info, sound samples, softcore photos, and more information on Michael's little sister and the sexiest Jackson superstar. ✓**INTERNET**→*url* http://www.mit.edu:8001/people/agoyo1/janet.html

Janet DIGITAL List (ml) An electronic fan club for Miss Jackson that includes links to other sites and instructions for subscribing to the mailing list. ✓**INTERNET**→*email* list@xs4.all ✍ *Type in message body:* subscribe Janet <your email address>

Janet Jackson With a headline that reads "Janet Jackson—Under Heavy Construction!" (isn't that Michael?), this page delivers more than it promises, with a wealth of lyrics, sound samples, pictures, and more. ✓**INTERNET**→*url* http://

Janet Jackson fan Website—from http://www.mit.edu:8001/people/agoyo1/janet.html

www.wiso.uni-erlangen.de/~
wgtauman/janet_dreamworld.html

JACKSON, JOE

The Joe Jackson Archive Look sharp with this home page, which links to a mailing list, a bio, images, news, video / discographies, video and sound clips, film scores, sheet music, tour info, radio and TV appearences, articles, a chart history, awards, trivia, and a huge list of band members past and present. ✓**INTERNET**→*url* http://www.cryst. bbk.ac.uk/~ubcg5ab/JJ/joe.html

Steppin' Out Link to other Joe Jackson sites, or stay here and check out the images of Mr. Night and Day himself. ✓**INTERNET**→*url* http://www.megatoon.com/~chris/JJ/

JACKSON, LUCIOUS

Lucious Jackson Chock full of *Natural Ingredients* and other goodies, this LJ site contains links to an Internet interview, audio clips, album info, and a Quick-Time video of the band's SNL performance. ✓**INTERNET**→*url* http://www.nando.net/music/gm/Grand Royal/Bands/LusciousJackson/

JACKSON, MICHAEL

See page 116.

JAM & SPOON

Jam & Spoon Album, tour info, and sound clips of this popular Euro techno/dance duo. ✓**INTERNET**→*url* http://www.sony.com/Music/ArtistInfo/JamAndSpoon_TripomaticFairytales.html

JAMIROQUAI

Jamiroquai While this site contains album and tour info, it's most noteworthy for the labyrinthine Jamiroquai cyberhouse—a place called J's Joint, where you can move around seven virtual rooms viewing photos,

Joe Jackson—from http://www.megatoon.com/~chris/JJ/

movies and videos; listening to music, talking to people; reading articles; contacting charities; and MOOing with other Jamiroquai fans. While much of this stuff is connected to Jamiroquai only in spirit, the site is worth a visit even for people who've never heard of the band. ✓**INTERNET**→*url* http://www.music.sony.com/Music/ArtistInfo/Jamiroquai.html

JEFFERSON AIRPLANE

Jefferson Airplane List (ml) Jefferson Airplane sat at the center of the San Francisco psychedelic rock revolution in the late sixties, and then they began to change, to branch out, to experience other forms of being. What forms? Jefferson Starship, Hot Tuna, Starship, and even solo recordings by Slick, Kantner, Balin, Kaukonen, Thomas, and Chaquico are all fair game here—although there's no lamenting the passage of the "White Rabbit" era or taking cheap shots at the "We Built This City" era. ✓**INTERNET**→*email* listserv@netspace.org ✍ *Type in message body:* subscribe 2400fulton <your full name>

JESUS AND MARY CHAIN

Jesus and Mary Chain With links to email, cover pics, a news group, and a photo gallery, this

site features a bio and a promo for JMC's new album—*Stoned & Dethroned*, which is described as a "lilting, largely acoustic-based recording of seventeen new songs." The Jesus and Mary Chain mellowing out? The times, they are a-changin'. ✓**INTERNET**→*url* http://american.recordings.com/American_Artists/Jesus_And_Mary _Chain/jamc_home.html

JESUS JONES

Jesus Jones Right here, right now, you can get links to news and info, lyrics, images, a discography, samples, and email. There's no other place fans want to be. ✓**INTERNET**→*url* http://www.cs.rmit. edu.au/~jbl/jesus.jones/

Jesus Jones List (ml) Get the latest on this British band, right here, right now (is there another catch phrase associated with the group?). ✓**INTERNET**→*email* magazine@cs.rmit.edu.au ✍ *Type in message body:* subscribe <your email address>

JETHRO TULL

alt.music.jethro-tull (ng) Ian Anderson still has his flute greased after almost 30 years, and fans are still receptive. Get thick as a brick by speaking to other Tull fans, many of whom love to compare the band to artists such as Roy Harper, Led Zeppelin, and The Dead. ✓**USENET**→alt.music.jethro-tull

Jethro Tull WWW Server Links to email addresses a discography, lyrics, an FAQ, digest archives, sources, site stats, a mailing list, the newsgroup, and the Progressive Rock Home Page. ✓**INTERNET**→*url* http://remus.rutgers. edu/JethroTull/

The St. Cleve Chronicle (ml) Is the flute a phallic symbol? Was Aqualung really Diane Sawyer? Tell all (and Tull all) here. ✓**INTERNET**→*email* JTull-Request@remus.rutgers.edu ✍ *Write a request*

JOEL, BILLY

alt.music.billy-joel (ng) Will he ever tour with Elton John again? Will he ever get the respect he so richly deserves? And why does one fan keep screaming about a song called "In the Middle of the Night" when it's clear that he is referring to "River of Dreams"? ✓**USENET**→alt.music.billy-joel

Attila A page devoted to Billy Joel's late sixties heavy-metal duo Atilla, which was responsible for such lumbering tracks as "California Flash," "Wonder Woman," and "Brain Invasion." ✓**INTERNET**→*url* http://www.contrib.andrew.cmu.edu/usr/al49/attila.html

Billy Joel Official Sony info for the *River of Dreams* album. ✓**INTERNET**→*url* http://www.music.sony.com/Music/ArtistInfo/BillyJoel.html

Billy Joel Pictures, sound files, MIDI files, QuickTime movies, and links to other pages. ✓**INTERNET**→*url* http://www.rpi.edu/~goodsd/bj/billy.html

Billy Joel A large image-mapped discography, with links to images

Elton John & Billy Joel—from http://www.rpi.edu/~goodsd/BJ/billy.html

of album covers. ✓**INTERNET**→*url* http://smith-gregm.eigenmann.indiana.edu/BillyJoel.html

Billy Joel Chat Message-based discussion. ✓**AMERICA ONLINE**→*keyword* mmc→Rock/Pop→Rock Artists A-L→Billy Joel

Billy Joel Fan Page Born in the summer of 1995, this page includes album info, a photo gallery, an audio gallery, and links to other enthusiasms of the page's architect, including the Philadelphia Flyers. ✓**INTERNET**→*url* http://www.lehigh.edu/~dat3/bj.html

Billy Joel FAQ A complete list of questions and answers about the Piano Man, including a history of his career, a discography, and trivia about song lyrics. ✓**INTERNET**→*url* http://www.cs.umd.edu/users/mike/billy-joel.faq.html

Billy Joel Info Pages Album info, bootleg info, a full interactive discography for downloading, and links to other BJ sites. ✓**INTERNET**→*url* http://yallara.cs.rmit.EDU.AU/~s9407312/billy.html

Billy Joel List (ml) Follow this Piano Man's latest adventures with this mailing list. ✓**INTERNET**→*email* oel-request@chaos.taylored.com ✍ *Type in message body:* subscribe <your email address>

Glass Houses (Billy Joel) From Japan, a site that goes head over heels for Billy, with a catalog of live performances, trivia, and lists of lyric changes in concert (from "I don't know why I go to extremes" to "I don't know why I go for ice cream," and more). ✓**INTERNET**→*url* http://www.mt.cs.keio.ac.jp/person/shio/BJ/bj.html

The River of Dreams A page

devoted to "the greatest music artist of all time," with precious little information other than links. ✓**INTERNET**→*url* http://futures. wharton.upenn.edu:80/~pietra25/ billy.html

Welcome Billy Joel Fans Album info, concert dates, the Billy Joel FAQ, and links to other sites. ✓**INTERNET**→*url* http://www.sic. com/billy-joel/

JOHN, ELTON

The 22nd Row (ml) While this page is primarily an electronic circular for the Elton John mailing list, it also includes information about the Elton John AIDS foundation, a discography, tour info, publications and organizations, a daily news digest, and even a list of the 27 books written about Elton and/or lyricist Bernie Taupin—none of them, incidentally, were written by Julia Phillips. ✓**INTERNET**→*email* the-22nd-row-request@uiuc.edu ✍ *Type in subject line:* subscribe *Info:* ✓**INTERNET**→ *url* http://itchy.hrfs.uiuc.edu/elton. html

alt.fan.elton-john (ng) Other artists come and go, but Elton keeps getting bigger, and since *The Lion King*, he's the proud owner of the most recognizable voice on the planet. Can you feel the love tonight? If not, you'd better go see your physician. Talk to other EJ fans about the history of Reginald Dwight, complain about the opaque lyrics of Bernie Taupin, and confess that it's damned near impossible to get songs like "I Guess That's Why They Call It the Blues" and "Sad Songs (Say So Much)" out of your head. ✓**USENET**→alt.fan.elton-john

Artist Biography: Elton John Yet another site from the Hardee's Walnut Creek Amphitheater, fea-

turing a bio, fact sheet, and tour info on Reginald Kenneth Dwight. Yes, that is his real name. ✓**INTERNET**→*url* http://www.walnut creek.com/wca/bio/elton.html

Elton John Chat Message-based discussion. ✓**AMERICA ONLINE**→ *keyword* mmc→Rock/Pop→Rock Artists A-L→Elton John ✓**COMPUSERVE**→*go* fanclub→Messages *and* Libraries→Elton John

Elton John, Made in England Links to sound clips and movies created specifically for this site, a discography, awards, a photo archive, and quizzes. This site is part of the larger, not-so-crypto-consumerist Visa Gold Masterpage. ✓**INTERNET**→*url* http:// www2.editelchi.com:80/eltonjohn/ webzine/

Visa Gold Presents Elton John—Mainstage Don't leave home without this page. No, wait, that's the American Express card, another credit corporation that has forever soiled rock and pop music by encroaching upon the purity of the notes, the soul of the sound. Down with commerce! Up with rebellion! Long live rock! Okay, that should sift out all the idealists—if you're still left, you know that rock music has been corrupt from the first, that payola and sponsorship is as much a part of the genre as shaking hips and snaky beats. This page strengthens the marriage by linking to tour dates, trivia, the Webzine *Made In England*, and lots of great stuff you can purchase with a Visa Card, including tickets, limited edition CDs, and other general merchandise. ✓**INTERNET**→*url* http://www. visa. com/eltonjohn/mainstage/

JOY DIVISION

Joy Division Feeling chipper? Upend your smile with a visit to

"Consider this: In 1994 alone, Elton's 'Can You Feel The Love Tonight' won him a Grammy Award in the Best Male Pop Vocal division. It was just one in a string of honors accorded his collaborative work with Tim Rice for the Lion King. Overall, the soundtrack netted him five Grammy nominations, three Oscar nominations in the Best Song Category (for 'Can You Feel The Love Tonight,' 'Circle of Life,' 'Hakuna Matata'), and a Golden Globe Award for 'Can You Feel The Love Tonight.' It was yet another astounding record-breaker for the singer: It made 1994 the 25th consecutive year that an Elton John single was nestled high in the Top 40.

"The album was Billboard's Number One soundtrack of 1994 and has sold over seven million copies in the U.S. alone. Finally, if all this wasn't enough, Elton was inducted into the Rock n' Roll Hall of Fame."

—from Artist Biography: Elton John

(cont'd pg. 144) →

Nirvana

For twentysomethings and members of Generation X, the Day the Music Died is more

than a line in a crappy old Don Henley song, or whoever that "American Pie" guy is anyway. The Day the Music Died was April 8, 1994, the Friday that Kurt Cobain's body was found in his Seattle home, a fatal shotgun wound in the head, a driver's license left behind for purposes of identification. Cobain was survived by his wife, Courtney Love, his daughter, Frances Bean, and a back catalog of pile-driving pop-punk songs that rearranged the face of American music in the nineties. Visit **Nirvana** for basic information on the band; talk about Kurt, Chris, and Dave at **alt.music.nirvana**; and then spook yourself by reading **Kurt Cobain's Suicide Note.**

Rock and roll wreckage—http://www2.ecst.csuchico.edu/~jedi/Images/

Across the board

A Nirvana Home Page Some people looked at Nirvana and saw death, despair, and irresistible guitar riffs. Mr. Smiley looked at Nirvana and saw a prime opportunity for a Website, a place where Cobain, Novoselic, and Grohl could be enshrined in the pantheon of alternative rock at the same time that Nirvanamaniacs got their fandom fix. Complete

with a bootleg reference guide, a discography, a band history, a song list, and news, this is one of the best Websites for band fans who loved Cobain and Co. before (or after) the hand of fate came down. ✓**INTERNET**→*url* http://seds.lpl. arizona.edu/~smiley/nirvana/ home.html

More Done!! A database of Nirvana bootlegs, the Nirvana FAQ, a list of recording sessions, a concert

chronology, an equipment FAQ, guitar tabs, complete information on the *Fecal Matter* demo, and even a brief review of Dave Grohl's solo album (no, no, not the Foo Fighters, but a cassette-only release from his D.C. days). ✓**INTERNET**→ *url* http://www.america.net:80/ ~greg/nirvana.html

Nirvana A promotional site for Nirvana's *Unplugged* LP and the *Live! Tonight! Sold Out!* video. ✓**IN-**

A tender moment—http://www.dsu. edu/projects/nirvana/gif/

TERNET→*url* http://geffen.com/nirv. html

Nirvana With the lights out, you're more popular, as this page—subtitled "The Life and Times of a Modern Rock Hero"—attests. While the narrative of Cobain's short life sometimes has the feel of a children's book ("All he wanted to be was in the background with his sound. Kurt Cobain did not want the spotlight. It was the spotlight that did him in."), this is an honest and affecting tribute to Cobain, illustrated with some beautiful artwork. ✓**INTERNET**→*url* http://thoth.stetson. edu/music/cobain/Kurt.html

Nirvana Swedish Nirvana fans cried the day Kurt died, too, and some of them ran right off and put up sites. This one includes a special feature on the *Unplugged* album, a Nirvana rumors page, discographies, guitar tabs, and links. ✓**INTERNET**→*url* http://www. ludd.luth.se/nirvana/

Nirvana Web Archive A complete list of Nirvana compositions, as well as images, a discography,

and a summary of the events just before and after the click-boom-hush death of Kurt Cobain. ✓**IN-TERNET**→*url* http://www.ludd.luth. se/misc/nirvana/

Verse Chorus Verse—The Nirvana Home Page Kurt explains the band's sound ("all in all, we sound like the Knack and the Bay City Rollers being molested by Black Flag and Black Sabbath"), and the page's author links to the Nirvana FAQ, a full discography, a concert chronology, a description of Kurt's equipment (his musical equipment, sickos!), a list of Nirvana covers and tributes, a full lyric list, interviews, Usenet posts, sound clips, and images. ✓**INTER-NET**→*url* http://www2.ecst.csu chico.edu/~jedi/nirvana.html

Chat

alt.music.nirvana (ng) Screw you Kurt Cobain! Kurt is a genius! Kurt is a coward and sucks for being dead! Don't expect subtlety on this newsgroup; do expect pseudo-intellectual discussions of the place of power chords in Nirvana and updates on the Foo Fighters. ✓**USENET**→alt.music.nirvana

Nirvana Chat Message-based discussion. ✓**AMERICA ONLINE** ...→*keyword* mmc→Alternative Rock→Bands M-Z →Nirvana/Kurt Cobain ...→*keyword* mtv→Message Boards→Bands That Do Suck→NIRVANA ...→*keyword* mtv→Message Boards→Bands That Don't Suck→NIRVANA ✓**EWORLD**→ *go* eaz →Pump Up the Volume→Music Talk→NIRVANA Unplugged ✓**COMPUSERVE**→*go* fanclub→Messages *and* Libraries→Nirvana

Territorial Pissings—The Nirvana Mailing List (ml) The Nirvana mailing list is still going strong, despite the fact that its fa-

vorite subject has passed on to the great beyond. Visit the Web page for a brief history of the list and some caveats for posters ("It is for bootleg traders; it is not for conspiracy theories regarding Kurt's untimely death"). ✓**INTERNET**→ *email* nirvlist-request@nyx.cs.du.edu ✐ *Type in subject line:* subscribe *Info:* ✓**INTERNET**→*url* http://www. ludd.luth.se/misc/nirvana/misc/ mailing. html

Death

Kurt Cobain Investigation One of the oddest sites on the Net, this page presents a welter of evidence assembled by a California private investigator named Tom Grant, who suggests that Kurt Cobain's death was not a suicide. Weaving a tangled web of intrigue that fingers Courtney Love—implicating her not only in Cobain's death but also in the "apparent suicide" of Hole bassist Kristen Pfaff—the Kurt Cobain Investigation files are filled with transcripts, recollections, and eyewitness re-

He does *have a gun—from http://www. dsu.edu/projects/nirvana/gif/*

Better never than late?—from http://www2.ecst.csuchico.edu/~jedi/Images/

ports that support Grant's theory, written in a wide-eyed deadpan that toes the line between deep conspiracy and cultural comedy. And if you aren't transfixed by Grant's paranoia, slather his embattled-crusader rhetoric all over yourself until you are: "The world of secrecy is a dangerous place to live, especially when your mind holds information that could help convict a killer. I've placed my life in danger here in order to bring about justice and put an end to what may turn out to be more

than just one killing." ✓ **INTERNET**→ *url* http://www.muohio.edu/~carmance/kurt.html

Kurt Cobain's Suicide Note
After a less-than-sympathetic introduction ("I am printing this to show how much of a narcissistic, self-pitying guy KC was"), this document reprints Kurt's suicide note, from the teenage-angst-has-paid-off-well-but-now-I'm-bored-and-old opening ("I haven't felt excitement in listening to as well as creating music") to the odd

sign-off ("peace, love, and empathy"). If only Kurt's letter was as interesting as his songs. ✓ **INTERNET** → *url* gopher://wiretap.spies.com:70/00/Library/Music/Misc/cobain.not

Interpretation

Nirvana Kurt Cobain mumbled and slurred his lyrics, and sometimes the clotting of his words was so thick, his enunciation so poor, that it was nearly impossible to distill any meaning from the mess. That's why this Website's Nirvana Song Interpretations are so welcome. "Negative Creep" is a self-portrait of a misanthropic stoner. "Floyd the Barber" uses the old *Andy Griffith Show* character to draw some profoundly pessimistic conclusions about humanity. And "Swap Meet" is actually about swap meets. Learn all about Nirvana, even Kurt's pre-band years, here. ✓ **INTERNET**→ *url* http://mellers1.psych.berkeley.edu/~phil/nirvana.html

Lyrics

The Complete Nirvana Song List Dozens of Nirvana songs, from "Aneurysm" to "Verse Chorus Verse." Here's a quick quiz: "Find my nest of salt." That's right—"All Apologies." Amaze your friends with your talents for deciphering the mumbled suicidal prophecies of Kurt Cobain. ✓ **INTERNET**→*url* http://seds.lpl.arizona.edu/~smiley/nirvana/songs.html

Nirvana Lyrics Still not sure what Kurt's saying in "Smells Like Teen Spirit"? Check out this list of songs from every official release, as well as a handful of loose compositions culled from compilations and B-sides. ✓ **INTERNET**→*url* http://www .ludd.luth.se/misc/nirvana/lyrics/ lyrics.html

Nirvana

"I say Courtney did it. There are just too many interesting connections between his suicide and Courtney's career. She has always been the money-hungry one, and her Live Thru This album came out right after all the publicity of the death occurred. She had the gun destroyed, she had the note, and she knew that he was in Seattle when she told the private investigator that she didn't know where he was. What do y'all think?"

"If you couldn't see the signs of suicide in him then I think you need to listen to some of the songs."

—from **alt.music.nirvana**

"I've been lurking awhile and noticed no one has talked about Kurt's stomach problems. Supposedly this was one of the main reasons for his suicide. Before the flames start about his stom-ach problems being part of his addic-tion, I know first person that they probably were not. Six months ago I developed severe stomach pains and they have yet to leave me. I can't eat anything but bland food and sometimes not even that. I rarely sleep. I'm on seven different pills and they barely help. Yes, I thought of suicide and I even thought of using drugs but I decided I wasn't going to go out like that. My doctor who BTW is young and into Nirvana thinks Kurt probably had similar pain as myself."

—from **alt.music.nirvana**

"Do you remember that book called 'The Bible'? Well in part it told the story of someone who had a point to make, and then moved on. Well, in my way I believe that Kurt was Jesus. When he creat-ed Grunge, he gathered HIS 'disciples,' and through his music told his fables. I believe that he was warning us, and then was persucuted for it. Whether he died or was murdered is no matter (until it is known for sure!), but he is now gone and we shouldn't forget what he told us. Peace, Love, Empathy…"

—from **Nirvana Chat** on CompuServe's Fanclub Forum

this Joy Division page containing links to an FAQ, trivia, a band line-up, discographies, videos and films, and a band career history. A tidbit to get you started—the band's name comes from a banned novel about sadomasochism in concentration camps. Have a nice day. ✓**INTERNET**→*url* http://csclub. uwaterloo.ca/u/sfwhite/joyd.html

Joy Division An FAQ and discography for the moody English band. ✓**INTERNET**→*url* http:// www.dnx.com/vamp/Gothic/Text /jd-faq-discog.html

KELLY, PAUL

Other Pople's Houses (Paul Kelly List) (ml) Want to talk Paul? Join this small (less than 80 people) mailing list. ✓**INTERNET**→ *email* majordomo@ox-in.socs.uts. edu.au ✍ *Type in message body:* subscribe oph <your email address>

Paul Kelly Miami-born, Australian-raised, and world-renowned, Kelly has written some of the most impressive albums of the last few years, and this page celebrates his talent with a biography, discography, lyrics, guitar tabs, articles, images, and reviews. ✓**INTERNET** → *url* http://www.st. nepean.uws.edu.au/~ezsigri/pk/ pk.html

KERSHAW, NIK

Nik Kershaw A biography, discography, lyrics, and details on the Nik mailing list. ✓**INTERNET**→ *url* http://www.st.nepean.uws.edu. au/~ezsigri/nik/nik.html

Nik Kershaw List (ml) Nik's been charting in Britain for more than a decade now, and while he is

not as well known stateside, his fans are loyal to Nik and his New Wave and Eurosoul leanings. ✓**INTERNET**→*email* majordomo@fox-in.socs.uts.edu.au ✍ *Type in message body:* subscribe <your email address>

KILLING JOKE

Killing Joke There's a man watching video, remember, and the bomb keeps on ticking. He doesn't know why, but he's just cattle for the slaughter. Is it all coming back to you now? Get more information on Killing Joke, from lyrics to a band bio to a discography, at this site. ✓**INTERNET** →*url* http://coos.dartmouth.edu/~ dupras/kj/kj.html

KING, CAROLE

Carole King Promotional info and a wealth of sound clips taken from Carole's *In Concert* album, which features performances by special guests such as David Crosby, Graham Nash, and G N' R guitar-god Slash. Carole sings such hits as "It's Too Late," "You've Got a Friend," "Smackwater Jack," and "I Feel The Earth Move," but doesn't answer all-important questions like this one: If Graham Nash and Slash formed a band, what would they call it, and would they ask Johnny Cash and Sarah Dash to come along for the ride? ✓**INTERNET**→*url* http://www.iuma. com/GMO/html/King,_Carole. html

KING CRIMSON

CrimsOnline This is an odd site that links to other KC sites, screen savers, random music loops that become background computer noises, interviews, information on the Robert Fripp box, and an "amphorism quote generator." Just what you've always wanted. ✓**INTERNET**→*url* http://www.rockslide. com/crimson/

Elephant Talk The quote at the top of this newsletter reads, "King Crimson: prog-rock pond scum set to bum you out." Amazingly, it's a fan page—and all at once, you're thrust into the love-hate flux that is integral to the Crimson experience. Enter the Court of the Crimson King by linking to photo and journal archives, a newsletter, mail-order catalog, FAQ, newsgroup, reviews, sound clips, press and articles, discographies, and a collection of fan's email addresses. ✓**INTERNET**→*url* http://www.cs. man.ac.uk/aig/staff/toby/ elephant-talk.html

KING'S X

King's X News, a mailing list archive, images, and links to other King's X sites. ✓**INTERNET**→*url* http://mars.superlink.net/user/ jkramer/kingsx.html

King's X Get a discography, a videography, and more information on the Texas power trio. ✓**INTERNET**→*url* http://ewi.ewi.org/~ rroberts/kingsx/kingsx.html

King's X Message-based discussion. ✓**AMERICA ONLINE**→*keyword* mmc→Rock/Pop→Rock Artists A-L→King's X ✓**COMPUSERVE**→*go* fanclub→Messages *and* Libraries→ King's X

The Unofficially Cool King's X Home Page News, a discography, lyrics, articles, images, guitar tabs, merchandise, a fan club, mailing list subscription information, and newsletter archives. ✓**INTERNET**→*url* http://www.willamette. edu/~gsweeten/music/kingsx.html

THE KINKS

Kinks List (ml) Did Jimmy Page really play all the guitar on the early Kinks records? Is it true that Ray Davies once grabbed Dave Davies by the throat, spun him around, kicked him on the back of the pants, derriere-area, and snarled "Cain and Abel were lovers compared to us, you simpering no-talent straw-for-brains!"? Talk about the long-lived British pastoral rockers on this mailing list. ✓**INTERNET**→*email* otten@quark. umd.edu ✍ *Type in subject line:* subscribe

KISS

The KISS Army Information Server Does their legendary status come from the music, the showmanship, or the fact that they've been the number one last-minute Halloween costume 15 years running? This site includes links to an FAQ, gopher servers, Kisstory, discographies, images, merchandise, a mailing list, and 10 other Kiss pages. ✓**INTERNET**→ *url* http://www.wku.edu/www/ kiss.html

Kiss otaku You wanted the best! You got the best! The hottest band in the world! Kiss! And now you've got the Kiss Website, with links to a band history, tour dates, an FAQ, and more. Want some Kiss trivia? Gene Simmons has lived with Shannon Tweed for 11 years, and they have two beautiful children. Want more Kiss trivia? You can't have it—not unless you visit this page. ✓**INTERNET**→*url* http:// www.interaccess.com/users/ mikeb/kissotaku.html

KISS This Bigger than Eric's hair, sharper than Gene's tongue, this site includes links to lyrics, cover art, bios, fan clubs, mailing lists, a gopher server, an FAQ, discographies, images, sound/song archives, articles, guitar tabs, a mailbag, polls, convention info, catalogs, and other Kiss online sites. If you want to rock and roll all Net, this is the perfect place. ✓**INTERNET**→*url* http://www.galcit.

caltech.edu/~aure/strwys.html

KLF

K Foundation Info about KLF and affiliated bands, including the "K Cera Cera" single. ✓**INTERNET**→ *url* http://www.brad.ac.uk/~ alradtke/kf01.html

KLF Mainpage Samples, sound clips, lyrics, an FAQ, and the script to the movie version of *The White Room.* ✓**INTERNET**→*url* http://www.edu.isy.liu.se/~ d91johol/KLF/

Transcentral (ml) Dance music isn't just dance music anymore. It's trance music, magic music, punk music with happy feet. And it's KLF. Talk to other fans of the band here. ✓**INTERNET**→*email* majordomo@xmission.com ✍ *Type in message body:* subscribe klf <your email address>

KRAFTWERK

Kraftwerk There are few groups in the world that merit a Website more than Kraftwerk—the stern German progenitors of synthetic avant-pop. From this page, you can link to discographies, lyrics, images,

audio files, interviews and articles, mailing list subscription information, a Kraftwerk FAQ, reviews, concert info, and a family tree. ✓**INTERNET**→*url* http://www. cs.umu.se/tsdf/KRAFTWERK/

Kraftwerk Links to lyrics, and little more. ✓**INTERNET**→*url* http://www.sara.nl/Rick.Jansen/ Kraftwerk/kraftwerk-e.html

Cyndi Lauper—from http:// www. sni.be/en/goodies/cyndi/welcome.htm

Kraftwerk List (ml) Talk about Kraftwerk. ✓**INTERNET**→*email* kraftwerk-request@cs.uwp.edu ✍ *Write a request*

KRAVITZ, LENNY

Lenny Kravitz Discography First he *Let Love Rule.* Then he listened to what his *Mama Said.* Then, seized by a sudden paranoia, he asked *Are You Gonna Go My Way.* And then he stopped worrying and went to the *Circus.* Get a complete list of the songs recorded by the dreadlocked savior of retro pop. ✓**INTERNET**→*url* ftp://net.bio.net/pub/misc/music/ kravitz.lenny

L

LAUPER, CYNDI

Cyndi Lauper A sexy picture of Cyndi, plus complete discographies (singles and albums), covers by other artists, lyrics, and a brief biography. ✓**INTERNET**→*url* http:// www.sni.be/en/goodies/cyndi/ welcome.htm

Cyndi Lauper Albums, singles, lyrics, videos, films, and fan club

Led Zeppelin **Artist Guide**

information. ✓**INTERNET**→*url* http://www.clark.net/pub/ wmcbrine/html/cyndi.html

Cyndi Lauper List (ml) Talk about Cyndi Lauper—the voice, the bubbly persona, the faltering career. ✓**INTERNET**→*email* shebop-request@law.emory.edu ✍ *Write a request*

LED ZEPPELIN

alt.music.led-zeppelin (ng) When a band has been around for more than 20 years, sold millions and millions of albums, and made record numbers of backstage groupies happy (cf. Funkadelic's "No Head No Backstage Pass"), there's precious little left to say about them. But Led Zep fans keep trying—fretting over the legitimacy of the Page/Plant reunion tour, speculating about "Stairway" lyrics, and assuring newcomers that John Bonham didn't die in vain. As with many classic rock groups, from week to week, there's not much variation—in other words, the posts remain the same. ✓**USENET**→alt.music.led-zeppelin

Jimmy Page and Robert Plant—No Quarter Photos, sound samples, bios, interviews, and road dispatches related to the Plant/ Page reunion tour. ✓**INTERNET**→*url* http://mosaic.echonyc.com/unled/

Led Zeppelin Links to other sites, articles onsite, and even the Kashmir true-type font. ✓**INTERNET** →*url* http://www.dnaco.net/~ buckeye/lz.html

Led Zeppelin Guitar tabs, a Zep FAQ, digitized songs, and pictures. ✓**INTERNET**→*url* http:// uvacs.cs.virginia.edu/~jsw2y/ zeppelin/zeppelin.html

Led Zeppelin A French site with Zep information in pun-laden cat-

Robert Plant and Jimmy Page —from http://www.jbrowne.com/Zeppelin

egories, including Good News Bad News (band gossip), How Many More Records (a discography), and When the Memory Breaks (lyrics). ✓**INTERNET**→*url* http:// uvacs.cs.virginia.edu/~jsw2y/ zeppelin/zeppelin.html

Led Zeppelin The complete source for all things Zep, including an FAQ, lyrics, discographies, pics, digitized songs, addresses of other Zed-Heads, a mailing list, a French Zepplin page, info on Page and Plant's 1995 tour, and guitar tabs so a whole new generation of 14-year-olds can play the opening riff of "Black Dog" until the ears of the entire world bleed. ✓**INTERNET**→*url* http://www.cs.brown. edu/people/jsw/zeppelin

Led Zeppelin Archive Images, lyrics, and the Zep FAQ. ✓**INTERNET**→*url* http://www.jbrowne. com/Zeppelin/zeppelin.html

Led Zeppelin Chat Message-based discussion. ✓**AMERICA ON-LINE** ...→*keyword* mtv→Message Boards→Bands That Do Suck→Led Zeppelin ...→*keyword* mmc→Rock/ Pop→Rock Artists A-L→Led Zeppelin

Led Zeppelin List (ml) When the levee breaks, you'll want to be here, trading rumors and gossip with other Led Zep fans. ✓**INTERNET**→*email* listserv@cornell.edu ✍ *Type in message body:* subscribe zeppelin-l <your full name>

Proximity Get the Led out (couldn't see that one coming, eh?). *Proximity*, an offline collectors journal, is the "definitive publication for the serious Zepplin collector." Enough said. ✓**INTERNET**→*url* http://www.dnaco.net/ ~buckeye/prox/

LETTERS TO CLEO

Letters to Cleo List (ml) A mailing list devoted to the power-pop band and purveyors of cuteness. ✓**INTERNET**→*email* cleo@world.std. com ✍ *Write a request*

LEVEL 42

Level 42 List (ml) What have they done since "Something About You"? About as much as they did before—a series of inoffensive jazz-pop albums, with a little funk thrown in for flavor. ✓**INTERNET**→*email* level42-request@ enterprise.bih.harvard.edu ✍ *Write a request*

LIVE

alt.music.live.the.band (ng) Was *Throwing Copper* really a record-company concoction? Are anthems still possible in rock music? Will the band survive through another album, even if the album is named *Live: Guns N' Roses*? ✓**USENET**→*alt.music.live.the.band*

Iris (ml) Talk about Live with other live fans. ✓**INTERNET**→*email* list serv@core-dump.async.vt.edu ✉ *Type in message body:* subscribe live <your full name>

Live Chat Message-based chat. ✓**AMERICA ONLINE** ...→*keyword* mmc→Alternative Rock→Bands A-L→Live ...→*keyword* mtv→Message Boards→Bands That Don't Suck→Live

Living Colour Nothin in the attic 'cept some *Stain* info. ✓**INTERNET**→*url* http://www.music.sony.com/Music/ArtistInfo/LivingColour.html

Straight Outta York (ml) Live chat. ✓**INTERNET**→*email* live-request@mediafive.yyz.com ✉ *Write a request*

LIVING COLOUR

Glamour Boys Elvis is dead, and so is Living Colour, but fans can reminisce at this page, which contains links to sound clips, a discography, and half a dozen other Living Colour sites. ✓**INTERNET**→*url* http://server.uwindsor.ca:8000/~caira/livingcolour.html

Living Colour Images, lyrics, album art, and a brief band bio, as well as a dedicated news service that keeps fans up to date on the activities of ex-LC members (Vernon Reid has a new band, and Corey Glover is a VH-1 DJ). ✓**INTERNET**→*url* http://www.teleport.com/~quick/living_colour.html

LONDON SUEDE

The London Suede When they were just plain Suede, they were Britain's bright boys—"audacious, mysterious, perverse, sexy, ironic, hilarious, cocky, melodramatic, and downright mesmerising." One tiny lawsuit and an extra word later, and Suedemania is no more. But Brett and the boys are still swinging (both ways) at this site, which contains links to Dog Man Star info, press releases, sound clips, bios, and a discography. ✓**INTERNET**→*url* http://www.music.sony.com/Music/ArtistInfo/TheLondon Suede.html

LOUD FAMILY

Aerodeliria (ml) Remember the Game Theory? If you answered "no," welcome to the club. If you answered "yes," welcome to the mailing list. ✓**INTERNET**→*email* loud-fans-request@primenet.com ✉ *Type in message body:* subscribe

The Loud Family Audio excerpt of "Spot the Setup," from *Plants and Birds and Rocks and Things,* and other Loud Family information. ✓**INTERNET**→*url* http://www.eden.com/music/loudfam.html

The Loud Family Links to news, band and record info, Loud Family/Game Theory interviews, and other Loud Family Web sites. ✓**INTERNET**→*url* http://www.primenet.com/~dsacks/

The Loud Family HomePage Some say Scott Miller is "the most criminally unknown songwriter/performer/all-around Rock Genius in America today." If you agree, check out this site, which contains news, interviews, reviews, discographies, liner notes and press, a list of Scott's favorite things, images, album info, soundclips, an FAQ, and other Loud Family and/or Game Theory pages. ✓**INTERNET**→

Lyle Lovett—http://www.curb.com/ HTML/ CurbWeb/ArtistsForum/Artists/

url http://www.charm.net/~trow/

LOVETT, LYLE

Lyle Lovett A very big, very flattering picture of Lyle. What more could you possibly want? Eat your heart out, Julia—the rest of us have got him now. ✓**INTERNET**→*url* http://www.curb.com/HTML/Curb Web/ArtistsForum/Artists/Lyle Lovett/lyle.html

LUSH

Lush Links to info on every ethereal lick of music ever to come out of their brightly colored heads. ✓**INTERNET**→*url* http://www.evo.org/html/group/lush.html

Reality's Lush Homepage Lush, certainly the most prolific of the slew of shoegazer bands to emerge from England in the wake of My Bloody Valentine, is featured on this page, which contains links to a band description and history, interviews and news, discographies, a photo gallery, lyrics, and more. ✓**INTERNET**→*url* http://mugwump.ucsd.edu/bkeeley/play-stuff/lush/lush.html

MADONNA

See page 124.

M PEOPLE

M People They've been movin' on up the U.K. and U.S. charts ever since *Elegant Slumming* was released; QuickTime videos of singles and album info are available here. ✓**INTERNET**→*url* http://www.music.sony.com/Music/ArtistInfo/MPeople.html

MALMSTEEN, YNGWIE

alt.music.yngwie-malmsteen (ng) Can Swedes rock out? Can they change the face of slashing rock guitar forever? And is Yngwie Malmsteen really an anagram for Jimi Hendrix? Get the answers to all these questions in Yngwieland. ✓**USENET**→ alt.music.yngwie-malmsteen

The Unofficial Yngwie Page For Players Aimed at musicians, this site features links to news, tabulature, a photo gallery, bio, technical data, and other sites dedicated to the Swedish guitar legend. ✓**INTERNET**→*url* http://dolphin.upenn.edu/~bdp/yngwie/yngwie.htm

Yngwie Malmsteen "If ye be a true Malmsteen warrior and possessed of Viking valor, click any of the magic portals below with your runestaff and it shall be opened to you. Many paths lie beyond..." Valhalla for Yngwie fans, this site features links to tour info, an FAQ, a bio, fanclub information, a discography, a band line-up, sound clips, feedback, and a photo gallery. ✓**INTERNET**→*url* http://pd.net/yngwie/

MANILOW, BARRY

alt.fan.barry-manilow (ng) With hundreds upon hundreds of messages, this very busy newsgroup confirms forever that middle-of-the-road songsmiths and crooners like Barry Manilow become huge stars despite the absence of any creative spark. In fact, the Manilow cult is so huge that the newsgroup contains almost 100 messages debunking the rumor that Manilow himself may be online, and fans also start gigantic threads about recent recordings, ongoing concerts, and more. ✓**USENET**→alt.fan.barry-manilow

Barry Manilow Chat Message-based chat. ✓**AMERICA ONLINE**→*keyword* mmc→Rock/Pop→Rock Artists M-Z→Barry Manilow ✓**COMPUSERVE**→*go* fanclub→Messages *and* Libraries→Barry Manilow

The Lunatic Fringe of American FM While this site isn't exactly about Barry Manilow, it does contain one insult directed at fans of the seventies pop crooner—"To proceed into this hallowed haven on the information super-highway, you must prove yourself worthy. You must possess the proper knowledge and attitude. Barry Manilow fans, move along to the Estate and Funeral Planning site now." ✓**INTERNET**→*url* http://www.webn.com/

MANSON, MARILYN

Marilyn Manson The South Florida shock-rock terrorists have their own Web page, which includes lyrics, images, a discography, and more. ✓**INTERNET**→*url* http://www-home.calumet.yorku.ca/kmaling/www/mm/MM.html

Marilyn Manson Chat Message-based chat. ✓**AMERICA ONLINE** ...→*keyword* mmc→Alternative Rock→Bands M-Z→MaRilYN ManSoN ...→*keyword* mtv→Message Boards→Bands That Do Suck→Marilyn Manson ...→*keyword* mtv→Message Boards→Bands That Don't Suck→Marilyn Manson

MARILLION

alt.music.marillion (ng) Hey—there's a new Fish single! Exciting, huh? And how about this new female back-up singer, or the similarities between Marillion and Rush, or the bootleg CDs that have been making the rounds in college towns across the English-speaking world? Get the latest Fishy information here. ✓**USENET**→alt.music.marillion

The FishNet Links to interviews, news, tour info, gig reviews, a discography, sound clips, company addresses, company merchandise, pictures, a crossword, the Dick Brothers Record Company, and other interesting sites. ✓**INTERNET**→*url* http://www.livjm.ac.uk/fish/

Freaks (ml) Marillion's fans—including loyal followers of lead singer Fish—cluster on this mailing list to trade information about upcoming projects and past recordings. ✓**INTERNET**→*email* freaks-request@arastar.com ✍ *Type in message body:* subscribe freaks <your full name>

Marillion and Fish Bootlegs A list of bootlegs to assist tape traders in assembling the most impressive Marillion collection possible. ✓**INTERNET**→*url* http://www.let.ruu.nl/~jeroen/boots/

Marillion & Fish WWW Server Contains links to an FAQ, lyrics, images, articles, discography, and Websites of other prog-rock staples. ✓**INTERNET**→*url* http://www.cnam.fr/Marillion/

Nados Finnish Marillion and Fish Fan Network Marilliona- dos and Afishionados will love this impressive Finnish fanpage, which features links to bios, news, archives (discographies, interviews etc...), an anagram game, mer- chandise info, the scoop on *Afraid of Sunlight*, and endless opportuni- ties for Fish-Fins puns. ✓**INTERNET** →*url* http://www.tf.hut.fi/Nados/ index_n.html

The Warm Web Circles Maril- lions of links to everything even vaugely concerning Fish and Mar- illion, including album info, video /discographies, bios and histories, FAQs, other fan pages, and dozens of other sites dealing with progres- sive rock. ✓**INTERNET**→*url* http:// www.xs4all.nl/~egavic/WWC/

MARLEY, BOB

Bob Marley Pictures, lyrics, and sound clips that will satisfy casual fans of Bob Marley and devoted Rasta men alike. ✓**INTERNET**→ *url* http://www.missouri.edu/~ c643267/marley.html

Bob Marley Songs of Free- dom Feel the Rastaman vibration with this site, which pays tribute to the father of mass-market reg- gae and offers lyrics, a discogra- phy, a Marley bio, and pictures. Get up, get down, get up, stand up, get Jah, and chase those crazy baldheads out of town. ✓**INTERNET** →*url* http://student-www.uchicago. edu/users/djrivera/marley.html

Happy Birthday to Bob Mar- ley Had Bob Marley not been taken from the world early by lymphoma, he would have turned 50 on Februrary 6, 1995, and this site celebrates what might have been with some pretty scary-look- ing Rasta pictures and a scrapbook that surveys the history of Bob. The page is edited by Yvette/

Bob Marley Homepage—from http://www.missouri.edu/~c643267/marley.html

Ivette, Bob's Tuff Gong partner and the mother of Makeda Jahnes- ta Marley, and includes links to other reggae sites. ✓**INTERNET**→*url* http://www.netaxs.com/~aaron/ Marley/Marley.html

MATTHEWS, DAVE

Dave Matthews Band For those fans not irritated by the re- cent mainstream success of the Dave Matthews Band, this page links to history, bios, an FAQ, tour info, lyrics, chords, sound clips, polls, merchandise, and oth- er fan pages. Those fans who are irritated by the band's break- through will have to stew in their own juices. ✓**INTERNET**→*url* http:// liberty.uc.wlu.edu/~ajacob/dmb/

Dave Matthews Band Splashy page with links to merchandise, tour info, sound clips, bios, and news. ✓**INTERNET**→*url* http://www. dmband.com/

MAZZY STAR

alt.music.mazzy-star Discuss Hope Sandoval's recent appear- ance with the Jesus and Mary Chain, the heavenly quality of her voice, and more. ✓**INTERNET**→*url* alt.music.mazzy-star

Mazzy Star Lyrics, links, and photos. ✓**INTERNET**→*url* http:// www.acs.appstate.edu/~kj7341/ mazzy.html

MCKEE, MARIA

Little Diva (ml) She has a power- house voice, a country-rock pedi- gree, and impeccable credentials selecting songs. What else could you want? Well, fans maybe—and Maria McKee has hundreds of them flocking to this mailing list to discuss Lone Justice, solo pro- jects, guest appearances on the al- bums of other artists, covers, col- laborations with the likes of Richard Thompson, and more. And remember: You can't pull the wool over this little lamb's eyes. ✓**INTERNET**→*email* mckeefan@ kbourbeau.Kenmoto1.sai.com ✍ *Write a request*

MCLACHLAN, SARAH

alt.music.s-mclachlan (ng) Sarah has her own mailing list, a song in the new movie *The Broth- ers McMullen*, and a long tradition of collaborating with other West Coast Canadians such as Mae Moore, Barney Bentall, Gord Downie, Jane Siberry, and Holly Cole. Is Sarah the best of the bunch? Make your case in this newsgroup. ✓**USENET**→alt.music. s-mclachlan

Fumbling Toward Ecstasy (ml) What's ecstasy? A state of pure pleasure. Where is it? Near Sarah McLachlan's heavenly voice. How can you get there? For starters, you can subscribe to this mailing list. ✓**INTERNET**→*email*

(cont'd pg. 153) →

Pearl Jam

Nirvana may have triggered the Seattle revolution, but Pearl Jam kicked it into over-drive. A muscular band led by the melodramatic vocals and charismatic sulking of Eddie Vedder, Pearl Jam released a pair of fine, anthemic albums (*Ten* and *Vs.*) before falling off slightly with the spotty LP *Vitalogy*. Still, fans continued to buy Pearl Jam's records and flock to its concerts, and a much-publicized feud with Ticketmaster only increased the band's anti-establishment cachet. Get the low-down on the biggest band of the nineties by visiting **Garden of Stone, Hunger Strike,** and **Webology**; find out what Eddie's singing in concert at the **Pearl Jam Songbook**; and get the latest news, notes, and gossip by reading the PJ e-zine **RE-LEASE.**

On the Net

Across the board

Garden of Stone Eddie Vedder may get all the ink these days, but this page is named for Pearl Jam guitarist Stone Gossard. Resources on the page cover everything from studio recordings to live dates to guitar tabs. Keep track of fact and fiction with a rumors page that disseminates upcoming tour date info and debunks bunk. And if you were thinking about going to

Five in a Jam—http://www-personal. engin.umich.edu/~galvin/pictures/

a concert, but couldn't as a result of anti-trust crusade, be sure to download a JPEG image of the special beetle logo that appears on all non-Ticketmaster tickets. ✓**IN-TERNET**→*url* http://www.skypoint. com/members/calebl/gos.html

Hunger Strike Band bios, tour dates, lyrics, links, images, and more. ✓**INTERNET**→*url* http://vinny. csd.mu.edu/~cygnus/pj.html

Official Unofficial Pearl Jam Home Page Jam fans can check in on their favorite band at this site, which has a high-gloss front end but a shortage of actual information—just an interactive discography and guitar tabs. ✓**IN-TERNET**→*url* http://155.247.175.52/ pj/pj.html

Pearl Jam Dominated by news of the canceled tour, this deep resource also includes guitar tabs, images, a link to the Pearl Jam FAQ, and the fascinating tidbit that "Pry To" (from *Vitalogy*) includes a backmasked cry of "Pete Townshend, oh you saved my life." ✓**INTERNET**→*url* http://www.

engin.umich.edu/~galvin/pearl jam.html

Pearl Jam An interesting collection of eclectic links, including a page about Pearl Jam bootlegs, digitized sound clips of entire songs, and more. ✓**INTERNET**→*url* http://www.engin.umich.edu/~ros enblm/PearlJR.html

Pearl Jam A bio, a discography, news about the band, and more. ✓**INTERNET**→*url* http://pages.prod igy.com/NY/music_man2/pj.html

Web Pollution Decorated with the covers of all three PJ LPs, this page includes the Pearl Jam FAQ and links to other pages. ✓**INTER-NET**→*url* http://www.blkbox. com/~clark15/pearljam.htm

Webology Cleverly titled, this page is another fairly standard PJ site, with a few special features—

A new perspective on Eddie—http:// www-personal.engin.umich.edu/

band members' birthdays and a reprint of *Spin* magazine's Eddie Vedder interview. ✓**INTERNET**→*url* http://www.usmcs.maine.edu/ ~laferrie/music/pj/pj.html

Chat

alt.music.pearl-jam (ng) When Pearl Jam canceled its American tour in the summer of 1995, fans went nuts trying to explain the actions of their fave alternative rock demigods. Between impassioned attacks ("Eddie, if this somehow gets back to you, GO TO HELL!!!!!!!!!!!!!!!!!!! You said you were doing this for your fans. If you do schedule another tour, I know I won't get tickets. Hopefully nobody will.") and defenses ("I think you need to get one thing straight. EDDIE VEDDER DOES NOT HAVE TO DO A GODDAMN THING FOR YOUR ASS!! Why don't you grow up and stop whining. Everything isn't about you.") of Vedder & Co., fans can hardly find time to talk about *Mirror Ball.* And don't even try to suggest that PJ is just a 1990's version of the Doors, all insufferable posing and faux countercultural cachet. ✓**USENET**→alt. music.pearl-jam

Oceans (ml) Discuss Eddie and the boys. ✓**INTERNET**→*email* majordomo@tamos.gmu.edu ✍ *Type in message body:* subscribe oceans <your email address>

Pearl Jam Chat If you want to talk about Pearl Jam on the online services, you're in luck—with four separate message boards on America Online devoted to the band, and a PJ fan club on CompuServe, there's no shortage of forums in which you can speculate on the future of the group, comment on Eddie Vedder's recent marriage, or wonder aloud what classic-rock

Acoustic Pearls—from http://www.blkbox.com/~clark15/

geezer the band will collaborate with next. ✓**AMERICA ONLINE** ...→*keyword* mmc→Alternative Rock→Bands M-Z→Pearl Jam ...→*keyword* mtv→ Message Boards→Bands That Do Suck→Pearl Jam ...→*keyword* mtv→ Message Boards→Bands That Do Suck→Pearl Jammy Jam ...→*keyword* rockline→Messages→MODERN ROCK LIVE→Pearl Jam ✓**COMPUSERVE**→*go* fanclub→Messages *and* Libraries→Pearl Jam

Lyrics

Pearl Jam Songbook Lyrics to every single song Pearl Jam has ever recorded or performed—which means that you not only get Eddie Vedder's smells-like-teen-angst ravings ("At home, drawing pictures of mountain tops, with him on top / Lemon yellow sun, arms raised in a V / The dead lay in pools of maroon below"), but also Otis Redding's "Dock of the Bay," The Who's "My Generation," The Doors' "Light My Fire," Tom Petty's "I Won't Back Down," and Neil Young's touching "F*@!ing Up." ✓**INTERNET**→*url* http://www.eng.uc.edu/~broush/ songbook.html

Publications

RELEASE The international

fanzine for Pearl Jam aficionados, *Release* includes show reviews, bootleg updates, news of side projects, and more. The *Release* Website includes selections from issues and links to related sites. ✓**INTERNET**→*url* http://tam2000.tamu. edu/~m0w9907/release/release. html

Tape trading

Pearl Jam Traders' Page Casual fans need not apply. This page is for collectors only—those Vedder addicts who want to get their hands on "Sonic Reducer," "Stupid Mop," or Eddie's cover of "Baba O'Reilly," or the select few who start shaking every time they hear the phrase "Red Rocks." Meet other collectors, describe what you have and what you want, and even talk about other, lesser bands. ✓**INTERNET**→*url* http:// www.ualberta.ca/~jkeehn/pjtrade. html

Yuletide

Christmas Card An Eddie Vedder holiday card mailed by the editors of *Release*, the electronic Pearl Jam fanzine. ✓**INTERNET**→*url* http://tam2000.tamu.edu/~m0w9 907/release/pictures/ED-XMAS.JPG

Pearl Jam

"Hi everybody! I've been a huge PJ fan for about 3 years now, and since I don't live in the center of things (I'm in Finland), it's kind of hard to get any current info on the band outside of the Internet. I have a few questions for those who have maybe seen the band play live and/or follow the band closely. How is Eddie doing? A stupid question, but it made me so sad to see him looking like shit a year or so back. In the 1993 MTV Video Music Awards he looked fat, tired and bloated, and I heard stories of his heavy drinking. I know he's been doing better lately, but when I heard that he was pretty drunk again in one of their more recent shows, I was thinking 'not again.' Pearl Jam rules, even near the Arctic Circle."

—from **alt.music.pearl-jam**

"I don't want to sound like some retro activist freak, but I think the whole TicketMaster issue is worth a little more time. I was thinking of starting some sort of writing campaign that might renew action or interest or..well I don't know what really. What I do know is exactly what and who TicketMaster charges per show."

—from **Pearl Jam Chat** on CompuServe's Fanclub Forum

"A study just out reports that listening to Pearl Jam will make you depressed and irritated! The study says that listening to PJ increases feelings of 'anger and tension.'"

"Where did you see this? If you had said it was a study about how people felt after they discovered who was in the Presidential race, I could understand it."

"Suspiciously, the source of the study is a label producing music that soothes you, i.e., ambient."

—from **Pearl Jam Chat** on CompuServe's Fanclub Forum

listserv@yoyo.cc.monash.edu.au ✍
Type in message body: subscribe
fumbling-towards-ecstasy <your full
name>

Sarah McLachlan News, tour
dates, and links to other sites online. ✓**INTERNET**→*url* http://www.
tyrell.net/~vettek/sarah.html

Sarah McLachlan Mailing list
information, a bio of Sarah and
her band, reviews, lyrics, and
more. ✓**INTERNET**→*url* http://www.
webcom.com/~donh/sarah/

Sarah McLachlan Hypothesis:
Sarah McLachlan has an obscene
number of sites devoted to her
music. Evidence for: There are indeed a large number of sites devoted to her music. Evidence against:
The quality of her voice and her
songs and her performance merit
this depth of coverage. Decide for
yourself at this site, which offers
concert information, a discography, images, and more. ✓**INTERNET**
→*url* http://www.css.itd.umich.
edu/~hubt/sarah/

Sarah McLachlan Everything
you would ever want to know
about the Canadian thrush, including newsletters, tour dates,
catalogs, sound bits, and even a
transcript of a real-time chat session. ✓**INTERNET**→*url* http://watt.
seas.virginia.edu/~jds5s/music/
sarah/sarah.html

Sarah McLachlan Home Page
A promotional page for Sarah
McLachlan that celebrates the release of her *Fumbling Toward Ec-
stacy* LP. ✓**INTERNET**→*url* http://
www.nettwerk.com/sarpg.html

MEGADETH

Megadeth This page focuses on
the latest release, *Youthanasia*—a
children's album of sorts, which is
decorated with an image of babies

hanging upside down on a laundry
wire. The page also promises a
Hidden Treasures page for anxious
Megadeth enthusiasts. ✓**INTERNET**→
url http://www.webb.com/
concrete/mg.html

Megadeth A broad and deep
Megadeth page with everything
from lyrics to images to email addresses for individual members.
✓**INTERNET**→*url* http://www.brad.
ac.uk/~irpurdie/MusicPage/
megadeth.html

Megadeth A virtual city exists
on the Net. Inhabitants: you. Reason for living: Megadeth. At this
Website, get a map to help guide
you through hotspots like The
MegaDiner and other info links.
✓**INTERNET**→*url* http://phymat.
bham.ac.uk/PetticDW/music/
megadeth/megadeth.html

Megadeth, Arizona Welcome

to Megadeth, Arizona, where you
can have your Horrorscope read,
receive up-to-date info on the
group, and get lyrics and images
connected to the LP *Youthanasia*
✓**INTERNET**→*url* http://under
ground.net/Megadeth/megadeth.
html

Megadeth Page This page presents the standard slew of
Megadeth resources, along with
anarchy symbols for effect. ✓**IN-
TERNET**→*url* http://www.dorsai.
org/~jkeis/megadeth.html

MELLENCAMP, JOHN

Human Wheels (ml) When Jesus left Birmingham, he went
somewhere with email, and he began to post to this mailing list,
where he could share his thoughts
about Jack, Diane, the pink houses, authority, pop singers, Jackie
Brown, and getting a leg up. ✓**IN-
TERNET**→*email* da2x+request@

Sarah McLachlan—from http://www.css.itd.umich.edu/~hubt/sarah/pictures.html

andrew.cmu.edu ✍ *Write a request*

Human Wheels: The John Mellencamp Digest Archives of the electronic digest devoted to the recordings of John Cougar Mellencamp. ✓**INTERNET**→*url* http://www.cs.cmu.edu/afs/andrew/usr/da2x/mosaic/digestarchive.html

John Cougar Mellencamp An annotated discography for the roots-rocker otherwise known as the Man With the Changing Name, along with a transcript of an interview and tour information. ✓**INTERNET**→*url* http://www.cs.cmu.edu/afs/andrew/usr/da2x/mosaic/mellencamp.html

METALLICA

See page 132.

MIDNIGHT OIL

Oil Base—Midnight Oil Information Guide Dance while beds are burning, and you'll still retain your shiny conscience with Midnight Oil. Explore the best in Aussie protest-rock with this long collection of links to history, bios, discographies, lyrics, show registers, FAQs, other sites, and email addresses. ✓**INTERNET**→*url* http://cunnin.res.wpi.edu/oilbase/

Powderworks (ml) Talk to other fans of the resolutely political Australian band. ✓**INTERNET**→*email* majordomo@cs.colorado.edu ✍ *Type in message body:* subscribe powderworks <your email address>

MINISTRY

The Unofficial Ministry Home Page Jesus built Al's hotrod, and a fan with comparable omniscience has created a site with links to reviews, guitar tabs, a discography, graphics, sound clips, and more. ✓**INTERNET**→*url* http://pulsar.cs.wku.edu/~gizzard/ministry.html

MOBY

Moby In the world of Christian, environmentalist, vegan, techno performers, there's really only one choice: Moby. From this site, you can email the dance sensation and link to other outstanding Moby pages. ✓**INTERNET**→*url* http://copper.ucs.indiana.edu/~jwmurer/moby.html

Moby On this page Moby philosophizes about the ghettoization of our world. "I think people's identities are often too bound up with external things, in external constructs." Help the techno-savior liberate us from our shackles and expand our horizons. ✓**INTERNET**→*url* http://www.mutelibtech.com/mute/moby/moby.htm

MONKEES

alt.music.monkees (ng) If you were going to form a band from scratch, an appealing pop-music concoction to nab the kids, what would you do? You'd consider the example of the Monkees, probably. Talk about the music, the songwriters, and even the rumor that Michael Nesmith's mother invented Liquid Paper. ✓**USENET**→ alt.music.monkees

Monkees List (ml) Who's your favorite Monkee? Nesmith? Tork? Jones? Or the other guy? Compare notes with other Monkees fans here. ✓**INTERNET**→*email* majordomo@primenet.com ✍ *Type in message body:* subscribe monkees <your email address>

MOODY BLUES

Moody Blues Do nights in white satin still sound good to you? Check out this nostalgic page, which includes pictures, a discography, music info, and a mailing list. ✓**INTERNET**→*url* http://www.ids.net/~lrobbins/moodys.html

NOTES

"For those who haven't seen Falling From Grace I highly recommend it. If you like John and his music then you should like the movie.

"As he mentioned in a radio interview, if your favorite type of film is Terminator type movies, you should probably skip FFG. The acting isn't anything great. John Prine and Larry Crane struggle. JM holds his own. But the directing is subtle and provacative. The sites of rural Indiana are just right. It's basically a bunch of people sitting around and talking. But it's moving stuff. As John said, 'it feels like a folk song.'

"FYI, the film made Gene Siskel's top 10 list for 1992 and Roger Ebert's top 20 list. And, as much as John denies it, the movie has autobiographical tones all the way through. Als anybody have info on how that retrospective is coming?"

—from **Human Wheels: The John Mellencamp Digest**

Moody Blues The best and the brightest of the MB home pages. Learn their story, see their pictures, and read their diary. ✓**INTERNET**→ *url* http://www.imsa.edu/~locutus/moody-blues.html

Moody Blues Friendly Radio Stations This is, well, a comprehensive list of radio stations that do or ever might play "Go Now." ✓**INTERNET**→*url* http://www.otb.com/users/stefanb/default.htm

Moody Blues List (ml) Once upon a time, in your wildest dreams, you fantasized about a mailing list that would allow you to discuss the Moody Blues. Now the dream has become reality. Isn't life everything you hoped it would be? ✓**INTERNET**→*email* lost-chords-request@mit.edu ✍ *Write a request*

Van Morrison page—from http://www.harbour.sfu.ca/~hayward/van/van.html

MORISSETTE, ALANIS

Alanis Morissette A standard home page devoted to the very young, very vituperative pop songwriter, with photos, info about the album *Jagged Little Pill*, and a bio. No boot heel will ever be on this young woman's neck. ✓**INTERNET**→*url* http://www.RepriseRec.com/Alanis

Alanis Morissette Where did this long-haired beauty begin her career? Well, here's a hint: if Alanis had not made the move to pop stardom she would have felt obliged to empty a bucket of green goo on your head. Why? Because Alanis was formerly a regular on the Ottawan TV show *You Can't Do That on Television*, which was carried here in the States by Nickelodeon. ✓**INTERNET**→*url* http://charlotte.acns.nwu.edu/charm/html/alanis/

Alanis Morissette If you've seen Alanis Morissette on television, you know that she spares no ex-

pense in personal energy, volume, or dedication in delivering the goods onstage. This site also delivers the goods, with a bio, pictures, and tour dates. ✓**INTERNET**→*url* http://www.plu.edu/~feskencj/alanis.html

Alanis Morissette Lyrics and guitar tabs for *Jagged Little Pill*. ✓**INTERNET**→*url* http://www.umich.edu/~lpmz/pill.html

Alanis Morissette If you loved "You Oughta Know," then confess on "You Oughta Chat," the Web newsgroup for admirers of Alanis. You can also enter a nifty Alanis contest brought to you by The Slime Society (Alanis' former employers) and win the now-platinum CD *Jagged Little Pill*. ✓**INTERNET**→*url* http://cctr.umkc.edu/user/rbarrow/alanis.html

alt.music.alanis (ng) "Was anyone else as impressed as me with Alanis Morissette's performance the other night?" Apparently so, because more than a dozen Alanis fans flocked to the newsgroup to congratulate the 21-year-old Canadian sensation on her scorching rendition of "You Oughta Know." And even the detractors have some friendly advice: "Well, if Alanis has got Flea playing for her on the recorded version, then she needs to figure out what to do

for her permanent band. She just can't keep picking people out of thin air every time she goes to perform live." ✓**USENET**→alt.music.alanis

MORRISON, VAN

Days Like This A song list and sound clips from Van's latest work, the 1995 LP that contains songs such as "Ancient Highway," "Raincheck," "Russian Roulette," and "Melancholia." ✓**INTERNET**→*url* http://www.polygram.com/polygram/inrb695/vanmorrison.html

Van Morrison Maybe you never made love in the green grass, but Van Morrison did, and then he sang about it, with a rough-and-tumble voice that eclipsed other blue-eyed-soul Brits. The workingman's legend, Morrison has spent the last 30 years exploring the carnal, the spiritual, and the musical, and this page offers discographies, lyrics, and a sound sample from his latest album *Days Like This*. ✓**INTERNET**→*url* http://www.harbour.sfu.ca/~hayward/van/van.html

Van Morrison Digest On what Van album was there an allusion to Arthur Rimbaud? How about a reference to William Blake? Search the poorly categorized archives to find out, and then tell all your

Morrissey **Artist Guide**

friends that T. S. Eliot joined the ministry, joined the ministry, joined the ministry. ✓**INTERNET→** *url* http://www.fish.com/music/van_morrison/digest_archives

Van Movies So what's your pleasure? Hal Hartley's Trust, Ren & Stimpy's Powdered Toast Man, or a video clip of Van Morrison? The Morrison collection consists of a clip from *The Last Waltz* and a recent David Letterman Show performance with Sinead O'Connor. ✓**INTERNET →** *url* http://www.itec.sfsu.edu/jeff/movies/lettervan.mov

MORRISSEY

Cemetry Gates Don't forget the songs that made you cry, and the songs that saved your life. Go straightaway to this fanbloodytastic Morrisey/Smiths page with lovely graphics and links to news, interviews/articles, images, sound clips, fanzines, tour info and reviews; an email list, merchandise, and the Moz Web, which hooks you up to dozens of other raving fan pages. ✓**INTERNET→** *url* http://www.public.iastate.edu/~krajewsk/

Morrissey Internet Digest Link to a digest of posts from the online *Morrissey* magazine. ✓**INTERNET→** *url* http://copper.ucs.indiana.edu/~jstefani/

Sing Your Life His parents gave him "Irish defiance, Northern humility, implacable benevolence, not bad looks"; his fans gave him this rather pitiful fanzine page the only redeeming feature of which is a collection of links to better sites. ✓**INTERNET→** *url* http://www.primenet.com/~sylzine/

MOTLEY CRUE

alt.rock-n-roll.metal.motley-crue Vince Neil sucks, but he's still the only member of Motley

Morrissey—from http:// www.public.iastate.edu/~krajewsk/

Crue that anyone wants to talk about. Kickstart your argument here. ✓**INTERNET→** *url* alt.rock-n-roll.metal.motley-crue

MOTT THE HOOPLE

Mott List (ml) Mott's dead. But former leader Ian Hunter moved on to record "Once Bitten, Twice Shy," which may still be the best rock-and-roll song ever written, and to this day Hunter continues to record, most recently with a bunch of rough-and-tumble Norwegian musicians. Reminisce about the glory days of Mott ("Whizz Kid," "The Ballad of Mott the Hoople," even "The Journey"), Hunter's own stellar solo career ("Life After Death," "Ships," "Just Another Night," "Cleveland Rocks," and the sublime "The Outsider"), and collaborators such as Mick Jones and the late Mick Ronson. ✓**INTERNET→** *email* hunter-mott-request@dfw.net ✍ *Type in message body:* subscribe hunter-mott

MY BLOODY VALENTINE

My Bloody Mailing List (ml) Talk about the band and its dreampop compatriots (The Boo

Radleys, Slowdive, Chapterhouse, Lilys, Pale Saints, Swirlies, Lush, Catherine Wheel, Ride and more). ✓**INTERNET→***email* majordomo@sunshine.io.com ✍ *Type in message body:* subscribe mbv <your email address> *Archives:* ✓**INTERNET→***url* ftp://sunshine.io.com/pub/culture/mbv/archives

My Bloody Valentine Shoegazer bands come and go, but they all owe a drone of feedback to My Bloody Valentine. This site features news and rumors, press info, an FAQ, a discography, lyrics, articles, images, sound and video clips, and mailing lists. ✓**INTERNET→***url* http://desire. com/~eolcott/

My Bloody Valentine A comprehensive My Bloody Valentine site with news and rumors, press releases, the MBV FAQ, a discography, lyrics, articles, images, sound and video clips, and information about the band's mailing list. ✓**INTERNET→** *url* http://mbv.com/

My Bloody Valentine A long gushy ode-type bio, links to interviews, a discography, and other MBV sites. ✓**INTERNET→** *url* http://www.itp.tsoa.nyu.edu/~student/brendonm/mbv1.html

N

NEGATIVLAND

Word From Our Sponsors Don't run screaming. Media terrorists are your friends. Order *Over the Edge* shows, read articles about copyright infringment and certain Irish superstars who shall remain nameless, and build a teletour box. Hours of fun for the whole family! ✓**INTERNET→** *url* http://sunsite.unc.edu/id/negativland/

NEW KIDS ON THE BLOCK

NKOTB Chat Message-based discussion. ✓**AMERICA ONLINE** ...→ *keyword* mtv→Message Boards →Bands That Do Suck→NKOTB ...→*keyword* mmc→Rap/R&B→ R&B/Soul→NKOTB!!! ...→*keyword* mmc→Rock/Pop→Soft Rock/Pop/ Oldies →NKOTB/Solo

NKOTB List (ml) Did the Wahlbergs breed their children to be musical geniuses? Are they musical geniuses? Praise the New Kids or bury them on this mailing list. ✓**INTERNET**→*email* subscribe@ nkotb.com ✍ *Write a request*

NEW ORDER

Ceremony (ml) New Order fans don't stand on ceremony, but they do write to Ceremony, and they share information about New Order and associated bands. ✓**INTERNET**→ *email* ceremony-request@ niagara.edu ✍ *Write a request*

New Order Lyrics, a band bio, images of band members, and more. ✓**INTERNET**→*url* http://deniz. tamu.edu/neworder/

New Order FTP Server "Up, down, turn around / Please don't let me hit the ground / Tonight I think I'll walk alone / I'll find my soul as I go home." For angst and confusion partnered with a snappy beat and rhymes quick enough to impress Johnny Mercer, there was no band quite like New Order. The FTP site includes lyrics as well as more information about the band. ✓**INTERNET**→*url* ftp://fac-tory.niagara. edu/pub/Factory/

NEWTON-JOHN, OLIVIA

Olivia Newton-John Chat Message-based discussion. ✓**AMERICA ONLINE**→*keyword* mmc→Rock/ Pop→Soft Rock/Pop/Oldies → Olivia Newton-John

Olivia Newton-John List (ml) If you're hopelessly devoted to Olivia, you're not alone. Share your love with other fans. ✓**INTERNET**→*email* onj-request@anima. demon.co.uk ✍ *Type in message body:* subscribe soulkiss <your full name>

NINE INCH NAILS

alt.music.nin (ng) Trent Reznor is Nine Inch Nails, and Nine Inch Nails is one of the most popular groups on Usenet, with more than 2,000 messages posted by fans who think that the world is a frightening place that must be frightened back. Between posts about the Reznor-Bowie tour, speculations on the freedom at the end of the downward spiral, and sound clips of songs, NIN fans offer their own version of cruel-world lyrics: "I am twisted inside a castle of pain. Torn from the inside out. Bleed from a world that despises those that do not understand. Fuck those who hate Trent, they should be shot and hung." ✓**USENET**→ alt.music.nin

alt.music.nin.creative (ng) What constitutes a creative discussion about Nine Inch Nails? Well, it's any discussion that concentrates on the spark of inspiration at the core of Trent Reznor's music. Is Trent a musical genius? "Whatever. i wish you were dead. i hate you. It doesn't matter if he's a musical genius or not. The music is awesome and i will continue to enjoy till i die. Jerry Garcia (RIP-Rot In Pieces) is not musical genius yet legions of people followed him around for over 25 years (not that they remember any of it). Shut up." ✓**USENET**→alt.music.nin. creative

alt.music.nin.d (ng) General discussion about Nine Inch Nails and related bands—Bowie, Marilyn Manson, and more. ✓**USENET**→ alt.music.nin.d

Nine Inch Nails To be so loved you must also be hated. The home page for the industrial art band is full of links to other turbulent sites including some interesting anti-NIN pages. In one posting, Trent is likened to David Koresh (although no Koresh songs are provided to allow listeners to draw their own conclusions). ✓**INTERNET** →*url* http://www.fsl.orst.edu/ rogues/rosero/nin/ninlist.htm

Nine Inch Nails Chat Message-based discussion. ✓**AMERICA ONLINE** ...→*keyword* mmc→Alternative Rock→Bands M-Z→Nine Inch Nails ...→*keyword* mtv→Message Boards→Bands That Do Suck→NIN SUCKS ...→*keyword* mtv→Message

Trent Reznor—from http://www. scri.fsu.edu/~patters/nin.html

(cont'd pg. 161) →

Pink Floyd

From the first Pink Floyd hit, 1967's "See Emily Play," it was clear that this was a

different sort of British rock band. Psychedelic rock came into full flower with the Floyd; led by songwriter Syd Barrett, the band created album-length aural experiences awash in trippy lyrics and electronic effects. Barrett soon succumbed to psychological disability, but the band—behind bassist Roger Waters—rolled on, recording a pair of masterpieces (*Dark Side of the Moon* and *The Wall*) before dissolving in 1983. In the late eighties, guitarist David Gilmour revived the name, and Pink Floyd returned to commercial, if not critical, prominence. Visit **Dark Side of the Net**, **Echoes**, and **Dolly Rocker**, and remember—all in all, we're just another brick in the wall.

The Floyd in the late 1960s—http://helser07.res.iastate.edu/floyd/pics/floyd5two.jpg

On the Net

Across the board

Dark Side of the Net *Dark Side of the Moon* has spent something like four million weeks on the Billboard Hot 200 chart, and that's because Pink Floyd fans breed new Pink Floyd fans at an alarming rate. At this page, you can learn about the ins and outs of Floyddom with a discography, images, parodies of lyrics, and interpretations of selected songs. ✓ **INTERNET**

→*url* http://whirligig.ecs.soton.ac.uk/~rps92/floyd/floyd.html

Midwest Pink Floyd Archive Trippy graphics wallpaper this page, which includes discographies for the band and all noteworthy solo members. ✓ **INTERNET**→*url* http://cereal.me.iastate.edu/floyd/floyd.html

Pink Floyd Links to other Floyd pages, along with an FAQ and complete lyrics. ✓ **INTERNET**→*url* http://www.princeton.edu/~mwwest/pink.html

Pink Floyd A complete list of albums, links to lyrics and images, and some old photos of the band.

✓ **INTERNET**→*url* http://www.smartdocs.com/~migre.v/floyd/index.html

Pink Floyd With more than 100,000 hits, this is one of the most popular Floyd pages in Cyberspace, and there's a good reason for it—the resources are excellent, ranging from discographies to lyrics, to sound clips, to MPEG movie sequences recorded from *The Wall.* ✓ **INTERNET**→*url* http://humper.student.princeton.edu/floyd/

Pink Floyd Official information on the band's recent live LP (*P.U.L.S.E.*, which comes complete with a blinking LED light)

and most recent studio effort (*The Division Bell*), including a press release about the multimedia event celebrating the release of *P.U.L.S.E.* ✓**INTERNET**→*url* http://www.music.sony.com/Music/Artist Info/PinkFloyd.html

Bootlegs

Pink Floyd RoIO Home Page
A clearinghouse for Floyd bootlegs (a.k.a RoIOs, or Records of Illegitimate / Indeterminate Origin) which can be sorted by name, date, and number of accesses. Need a copy of a mid-eighties concert from Amsterdam? Interested in Syd Barrett studio demos? Come here and start searching. ✓**INTERNET**→*url* http://www.infor matik.uni-oldenburg.de/~herwig/

Chat

alt.music.pink-floyd (ng) Over the course of its existence, Pink Floyd has evolved more than mankind itself. Charles Darwin would have had a field day with this band. Every tour stops at the Galapagos. The band has changed quite a bit. Do you get the point? Fans on this newsgroup do. In fact, much of the discussion centers on different versions of Floyd—How would Roger Waters have handled *The Division Bell*? Would Syd Barrett have known what to do with *The Final Cut*? What if David Gilmour had written most of the material for *Piper At the Gates of Dawn*? Seminal psychedelia or lazy arena rock? You make the call. ✓**USENET**→alt.music.pink-floyd

Echoes (Pink Floyd List) (ml) Talk about Pink Floyd with other fans of the band here.→echoserv@ fawnya.tcs.com ✓**INTERNET**→*email* ✍ *Type in message body:* add echoes

#floyd Wish you were here? You can be. Think Pink with other Floyd fans, from the Barrett era to the Gilmour days. ✓**INTERNET**→*irc* #floyd

Pink Floyd Chat Message-based discussion. ✓**AMERICA ONLINE** ...→*keyword* rockline→Messages→ KEEPING THE 70S' ALIVE→Pink Floyd present and past ...→*keyword* mmc→Rock/Pop→Rock Artists M-Z→Pink Floyd & Solo Careers

Tour

Pink Floyd Tour Info Locations and set lists for 1994 and 1995 concerts, along with upcoming tour dates. ✓**INTERNET**→*url* ftp://ftp.twi.tudelft.nl/pub/music

Roger Waters

Roger Waters Chat (ng) James announces that Roger Waters has signed to tour with the band again. Joel is skeptical: "Makes me think of the pre-tour hype that was going on a few months before the Floyd were to go on tour last with *The Division Cut*. My local radio station broadcast the news that it was official...that management had worked everything out and that Roger Waters was to appear on *The Division Bell* as well as to go on the last tour...I know this gave me a little impetus to run out and get my tickets, but was he there? No, because it was all hype, no foundation of fact." And other fans continue to insist that Floyd without Waters is like scab baseball. ✓**USENET**→alt.music.roger-waters

Roger Waters Discography Like Pete Townshend, Roger Waters is always thinking. He's a rocker, sure, but he's also a conceptual architect, the kind of guy who wants ideas with his guitar

riffs. *Radio K.A.O.S.*, for example, was a rock opera of sorts, a grandly imagined sequence of ballads and mid-tempo rockers like *The Wall*. Was it successful? Well, not by critical or commercial standards, but maybe Waters got some satisfaction out of the project. Check on all his LPs and singles here. ✓**INTERNET**→*url* ftp://net.bio.netpub/misc/music/waters.roger

Syd Barrett

Dolly Rocker Dedicated to the legend of fragile rocker Roger Keith "Syd" Barrett, this page includes a brief biography of Syd, lyrics, images, and articles. Revel in the powerful naiveté of Syd's lyrics. ("Waving my arms in the air / love, my love, got no care / no care, no, no, pressing my feet to the ground / stand up right where you stand / call to you and what do you do / laying back in a chair?") Read quotes from Roger Waters about Syd, his friend and mentor. ("We've had problems with our equipment and we can't get the P.A. to work because we play extremely loudly. It's a pity because Syd writes great lyrics and nobody ever hears them. The human voice can't compete with Fender Telecasters and double drum kits.") See images of Pink Floyd's founder. And then lament the frangibility of man. ✓**INTERNET** →*url* http://www.reed.edu/~mhamilto/syd/syd.html

The Dolly Rocker himself—http://www.reed.edu/~mhamilto/syd/syd.html

Pink Floyd

"I was first exposed to Floyd at age negative one month, when my mother climbed over fences eight months pregnant to see 'em at Olympic Stadium in Montreal. That was July 6, 1977. Roger has said in interviews that this concert helped inspire him to write The Wall. I am proud to have been there, if you can't tell. Now, as an eighteen-year-old college freshman, I must say that early exposure influenced me into becoming the huge PF fan I am today. I managed to catch them last year out of the womb, once again with my mom."

—from **alt.music.pink-floyd**

"In the song 'Don't Leave Me Now,' in THE WALL, there are two lines that especially disturb me. These are, 'I need you, Babe / To put through the shredder / In front of my friends' and 'When you know how I need you / To beat to a pulp on a Saturday night.' Whereas the rest of the album depicts Pink as an otherwise decent man victimized by society and the 'silent reproaches' it instills within him. However, when it comes to Pink's relationship with his wife, he is (or seems to be) shown to be a cruelly abusive husband who beats his wife and mocks her in public. Does anybody wish to comment on this part of Pink's personality?"

—from **alt.music.pink-floyd**

"Dave may be one of the greatest guitar players ever and truly the heart of this band, but Roger was without a doubt the soul of Pink Floyd. Rog was the John Lennon of this band. Dave has the ability to take the mind into a dreamland, Roger injected venomous amounts of reality into this dreamland and gave the dream a purpose. Many a time in my past I was saved from a bad acid trip by this band whose god-like combination of words and music was nothing short of inspirational."

—from **Pink Floyd Chat** on AOL's Rockline

Boards→Bands That Don't Suck→ nine inch nails ...→*keyword* rockline→Messages→MODERN ROCK LIVE→NINE INCH NAILS ✓**EWORLD**→*go* eaz→Pump Up The Volume→Music Talk→n i n e i n c h n a i l s

Nine Inch Nails Imports The human condition is decadent, depraved, and depressing. But it sure makes for great pop music. Check out the NIN music that's been released in other nations. ✓**INTERNET** →*url* http://www.csh.rit.edu/~ jerry/NIN_RI/welcome.html

This Broken Machine Links to dozens of sites that will please even the most hard-core NINnies. ✓**INTERNET**→*url* http://www.shu.edu/~ brenycan/twiggy/twignin.htm

Unofficial Nine Inch Nails Trent is the voice inside your head, the lover in your bed, the sex that you provide, the hate you try to hide. He takes you where you want to go, and this site, one of the best on the Net, gives you all you need to know. Links to images, sound clips, an amazing photo archive, lyrics, a discography, an FAQ, guitar tabs, interviews/reviews, other fan pages, stats, and Usenet news. ✓**INTERNET**→*url* http://www.scri.fsu.edu/~ patters/nin.html

NIRVANA
See page 140.

NITZER EBB
Nitzer Ebb Cathryn is a bonafide Ebbhead. Deborah saw her first show recently and is now a fullfledged industrial vixen. Feel the Nitzer vibe flow through you at this site, which includes images, lyrics, and discographies. ✓**INTERNET**→*url* http://140.175.5.92/nitzer. htm

OASIS
Oasis Does Oasis have the talent to become one of the biggest bands in the world? Definitely. Maybe. Find out more at this official Sony music site. ✓**INTERNET**→ *url* http:// www.music.sony.com/ Music/ArtistInfo/Oasis.html

Oasis Lyrics, images, sound clips, a band bio, a discography, and more. ✓**INTERNET**→*url* http://www. cts.com/browse/ginger/

THE ORB
Cumulonimbus (ml) Talk about the Orb with other Orbheads. ✓**INTERNET**→*email* majordomo@ xmission.com ✎ *Type in message body:* subscribe orb <your email address>

Orb Lots of info here about Captain Paterson and the location of the Mothership during the Earthcycle 95. Check out updates on the Oxbow Lakes file and other interplanetary happenings. ✓**INTERNET**→*url* http://hyperlink.com/ orb/

Orb Learn all about the greatest reconstructive surgeon in the galaxy of house music. Find screensavers, mailing lists, and articles about the collaborative works of the Orb. ✓**INTERNET**→*url* http://www.hyperreal.com:80/ music/artists/orb/www/

Orb Capt. Paterson's latest creation, *Orbus Terrarum*, "offers fantastic visions for the non-pedestrian traveller." There is an adequate amount of Web space devoted to this band, which seems unable to stick with a single metaphor. Perhaps that's the way of the future.

✓**INTERNET**→*url* http://www. undergrad.math.uwaterloo.ca/~ trobbs/techno/groups/orb.html

ORCHESTRAL MANEUVERS

OMD Is Paul Humphreys really working on the new album? Will Universal ever be released? Bite your nails with the rest of us as we wait to see what OMD can do without John Hughes. ✓**INTERNET**→ *url* http://www-leland.stanford. edu/~kikhoon/OMD/

OMD Flashy unofficial home page with a discography, photos, lyrics, and embarrassingly poor sound clips from *Tesla Girls.* ✓**INTERNET**→ *url* http://www.sas.upenn.edu/~ plevin/omdpage/omdpage.html

OMD List (ml) Gimme an O! Gimme an M! Gimme a D! Gimme a mailing list! Gimme a large online fan base! ✓**INTERNET**→ *email* omd-request@cs.uwp.edu ✍ *Write a request*

PANTERA

Pantera A Vulgar Display of Pantera, with links to a discography, lyrics, images, and even issues of the Pantera digest. ✓**INTERNET**→*url* http://gwis2.circ.gwu. edu/~pantera/music/Pantera/

Rock-It Comix Presents Pantera Learn to live with your mistakes, harness the power of noise, and then enjoy this Rock-It comic book, which traces the rise of Pantera. ✓**INTERNET**→*url* http://www. nando.net/music/gm/Rockit/ pantera/

PARKER, GRAHAM

Graham Parker List (ml) "Out in the jungle there's a war going down / You end up feeding on the friends you found." Since "Heat Treatment," Graham Parker hasn't gotten any more optimistic, but he has gotten more prolific, releasing a series of excellent albums that show how an Angry Young Man can mature productively. If you're skeptical, listen to the beautiful "Disney's America" from the 1995 release *12 Haunted Episodes.* When you're done crying, subscribe to this mailing list. No one should be without their Parker. ✓**INTERNET**→ *email* majordomo@ primenet.com ✍ *Type in message body:* subscribe graham-parker <your email address>

PARLIAMENT-FUNKADELIC

Parliament-Funkadelic Say goodby to Sir Nose D'Voidoffunk at this Web page, which features a P-FAQ, a full P-Funk discography, and vintage pictures that approach maximumisness. ✓**INTERNET**→*url* http://www.acpub.duke.edu/~ eja/pfunk.html

Parliament-Funkadelic Chat Message-based discussion. ✓**AMER-ICA ONLINE**→*keyword* mmc→Rap/ R&B→Rap/hip-Hop/Funk→P-Funk, Bernie, Bootsy, Maceo

rec.music.funky (ng) While the bands discussed on this newsgroup are varied (Spearhead, Patra, Dag, Groove Collective) all roads lead back to the triple pillar of American funk—Sly and the Family Stone, James Brown, and the P-Funk Empire. And because Sly is lost in limbo and JB is greatly diminished, most of the vital chat is P-Chat. Talk about Bootsy all the way live in Boston. Talk about Baby P-Funk. Talk about the Trey Lewd. If there's a part of you that's afflicted, just lay that part on the keyboard. Remember—funk not only moves, it can remove. Dig? ✓**USENET**→rec.music.funky

PAVEMENT

Pavement MTV's Beavis has berated Pavement for not trying, for lounging around in the college-aristocrat post while other bands attack their songs with ferocity and passion. Beavis may have a point, but that doesn't stop America's youth from lapping up Pavement like a cat laps up milk. This page collects Pavement sound clips, images, rumors, and more. ✓**INTERNET**→*url* http://weber.u. washington.edu/~mookie/ pavement.cgi

Pavement Chat Message-based chat. ✓**AMERICA ONLINE** ...→*keyword* mmc→Alternative Rock→ Bands M-Z→Pavement ...→*keyword* mtv→Message Boards→Bands That Don't Suck→PAVEMENT

Pavement Mailing List (ml) Contribute your concert experiences, help decipher the lyrics to a song, or just speak from within the Pavement aura. ✓**INTERNET**→ *email* pavement-request@uts.edu.au ✍ *Type in message body:* subscribe

PEARL JAM

See page 150.

PET SHOP BOYS

Introspective (ml) Talk about the Pet Shop Boys—the songs, the fashions, the synthesizers—on this mailing list. ✓**INTERNET**→*email* majordomo@tcp.com ✍ *Type in message body:* subscribe introspective <your email address>

Mats Bjorkman's Pet Shop Boys Lyrics, images, links, and more, all wrapped up in characteristically interesting packaging. ✓**INTERNET**→*url* http://www.dsv. su.se/~mats-bjo/psb.html

Music for Boys An album-by-album lyrics resource with audio clips and concert info. ✓**INTERNET**→

url http://www.airworld.com/psb/

Music for Boys and Girls A complete discography, biography, and FAQ, presented in a text-heavy, quickly loading format. ✓ **INTERNET**→*url* http://homepage. seas.upenn.edu/~hcheng/psb.html

PETTY, TOM

Not-So-Official Tom Petty Page Not so official and not so great, this page is mostly a collection of links to other Petty sites, although it also includes a discography and lyrics from the Heartbreakers' albums. ✓ **INTERNET**→*url* http://eclipse.bgsu.edu/~doug/ petty.html

Tom Petty A thorough bio on Tom and the Heartbreakers that includes a press release for *Wildflowers* and fall 1995 tour dates. ✓ **AMERICA ONLINE**→*keyword* warner→rock

Tom Petty Chat Message-based discussion. ✓ **AMERICA ONLINE**→ *keyword* mmc→Rock/Pop→Rock Artists M-Z→Tom Petty

Tom Petty Home Page Learn how to play the long-faced man's songs on guitar, explore his lyrics, and scan a list of other Petty devotees. ✓ **INTERNET**→*url* http://www. ugcs.caltech.edu/~hedlund/tom_ petty/enhanced.shtml

Unofficial Tom Petty Home Page He's been making good music for a long time and will be for a long time to come. Like a reed in the wind—flexible, yet rooted, in touch with his origins but not afraid to reach for the sky... What were we talking about? Oh, yes, Tom Petty. This page reviews the career of the grizzled Gator, furnishing tour dates, album info, a discography, lyrics, images, guitar tabs, and links to other pages.

✓ **INTERNET**→*url* http://www.ugcs. caltech.edu/~hedlund/tom_petty/ enhanced.shtml

PHAIR, LIZ

alt.fan.liz-phair (ng) Mostly a clearing house for Liz photos, this newsgroup also includes speculation on Liz's next album, criticisms of her performance style, and analyses of her lyrics. ✓ **USENET**→alt.fan.liz-phair

Little Guyville Pictures, guitar tabs, and a discography. The next time you wake up alarmed, and almost immediately feel sorry, come here—it may set your mind at ease. ✓ **INTERNET**→*url* http://www. is.co.za/andras/music/lp/

Liz Phair Chat Message-based discussion. ✓ **AMERICA ONLINE**→ *keyword* mmc→Alternative Rock→ Bands M-Z→Liz Phair

Liz Phair Homepage Lyrics, a discography, rumors, tour dates, and plenty of pictures of Ms. Liz. ✓ **INTERNET**→*url* http://txfs1.hfb.se/ people/mlu/MusicPage/LizPhair

Liz Phair List (ml) If you're standing six-foot-one, or thinking about it, come to this mailing list. ✓ **INTERNET**→*email* listproc@ phantom.com ✍ *Write a request*

Ross Jeffcoat's Liz Phair Site An attractive, openly celebratory collection of lyrics, reviews, and guitar tabs for Phair phans. ✓ **INTERNET**→*url* http://www.armory. com/~fisheye/lpml.html

Stratford-on-Guy Links to all the other Phair sites around the world, lyrics, and a picture of the sweet high-school girl who turned into a cynical rocker. ✓ **INTERNET**→ *url* http://www.math.macalstr. edu/~awalker/phair/liz.html

Liz Phair—from http://www.armory. com/~fisheye/lpml.html

PHILLIPS, SAM

Home Page A bare-bones on-ramp to the Sam Phillips mailing list. ✓ **INTERNET**→*url* http://boris. qub.ac.uk/tony/sam/intro.html

Sam Phillips List (ml) Did you know that Sam is married to T-Bone Burnette? Did you know that Sam appeared in *Die Hard 3: With a Vengeance*? Try to describe the indescribable wow on this mailing list. ✓ **INTERNET**→*email* p9490086@qub.ac.uk ✍ *Type in message body:* subscribe sam

PHISH

Dan's Concert Review Site Although the archive of reviews of Phish's 1990s shows is complete, someone must have been doing some heavy recreational pharmeceuticals when it came to the 1980s reviews. Why? It's just a list of years with no information. Some kind of head game, man. ✓ **INTERNET**→*url* http:// tbone. biol. sc.edu/~dan/review/phishrev.html

The Hole in the Web Phish Phorum Links to bootleg trading and screen-savers, as well as other Phish/Dead pages. ✓ **INTERNET**→ *url* http://cinti.cent.com/dfessel/ phish.html

The Pixies Artist Guide

The International House of ZZZYX A very strange, raving egomaniac who calls himself ZZZYX (probably to annoy his folks) has created a page entirely dedicated to...himself! He also happens to listen to Phish and the Dead. If you want to fuel this guy's narcissism and check out some set lists and stats, visit his International House. ✓**INTERNET**→*url* http://www.eskimo.com/~zzyzx/

Into the Ozone with Phish Phish-heads should hang in shame. It took the Net e-zine *Addicted to Noise* to build the best site for the band, one that consists of an in-depth article on the kings of concert-driven cult bands, interviews, links to discographies, images, sound clips, and more. ✓**INTERNET**→*url* http:// www.addict.com/ATN/issues/ 1.07/Features/Phish/

Live Phish Chat Nestled in America Online's Grateful Dead forum is this live chat room, which lets Phish-heads share their concert experiences, recreational pharmaceutical knowledge, and universal vibe. ✓**AMERICA ONLINE**→*keyword* dead→The Phish Bowl

Lukas's Phish Page Like most Phish ponds, this is primarily a place to trade tapes of shows. ✓**INTERNET**→*url* http://www.cs.oberlin. edu/students/karlsson/music/ phish/phish.html

Phish With multicolored graphics that put most Web pages to shame, this page includes information on Phish tours and more. ✓**INTERNET**→*url* http://cec.wustl. edu/~hewins/music/phish.html

Phish Chat Message-based discussion for the band that proves that fan loyalty is everything, and critical legitimacy nothing.

✓**EWORLD**→*go* eaz→Pump Up The Volume →Music Talk→Phish

Phish.Net (ml) Subscribe to the Phish mailing list, and see what information about experimental rock you can reel in. ✓**INTERNET**→ *email* phish-info-request@phish.net ✉ *Type in message body:* subscribe

Phish Net Home Page A strong site featuring links to chords, lyrics, a tour schedule, article archives, memorabilia and merchandise, an FAQ, images, info on making tapes, reviews, and help for Phish and Internet Newbies. ✓**INTERNET**→*url* http://www. netspace.org/phish/

rec.music.phish (ng) Jerry Garcia's death cast a pall over the entire Dead-related world, and the Phish newsgroup went ashen for a moment, too. "I mean, what if Page or John got sick, and what if the band had to stop playing, and what if there was no more music anywhere." Hey—one day it may happen. But until then, Phish Phans can continue to trade information on tour dates, taping conferences, and more. Bend your mind—it doesn't do much for you as long as it stays straight. ✓**USENET** →rec.music.phish

Sunflower Studios Tape Covers Yet another Phish site dedicated to links to other sites, which feature links to other sites, which feature links to other sites, and so on. And they say pot suppresses motivation. ✓**INTERNET**→*url* http:// www.tiac.net/users/jezmund

Zim's "Rare Tape" Server Phish heads compare the size of their bootleg catches and offer them up for trade. In more ways than one, the band is doing its best to label itself the Grateful Dead of the virtual age. ✓**INTERNET**→*url* http://www.svs. com/users/zim/phishstuff.html

PINK FLOYD
See page 158.

THE PIXIES

Home Page A fully wired, comprehensive discography of the mid-late 1980s band led by Frank Black and Kim Deal. Discover how they helped to define today's contemporary alternative scene and made some music in the process. ✓**INTERNET**→*url* http:// www.evo.org/html/group/pixies. html

Pixies WWW Page Photos, lyrics, and interviews with the

Phish fan page—from http://cec.wustl. edu/~hewins/music/phish.html

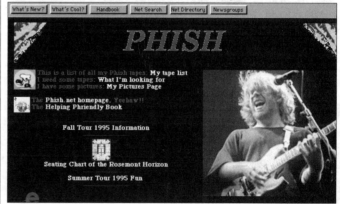

band. ✓**INTERNET**→*url* http://www.stack.urc.tue.nl/~patrick/pixies/index.html

Tommy's Pixies Page A brief band history culled from music magazines, and links to other sites. ✓**INTERNET**→*url* http://www.peak.org/~zogwarg/indices/bands/pixies/main.html

POGUES

Unofficial Home Page You can't move beer over the Internet. So what is the next best thing? Images and lyrics of former Pogue leader Shane McGowan. This site details the pre- and post-Mc-Gowan eras, with an emphasis on the band's Celtic roots. ✓**INTERNET**→*url* http://crow.acns.nwu.edu:8082/kultur/pogues/

POI DOG PONDERING

Poi Dog Page Everything the Dog dragged in, including clips from Poi's alter-ego band, Palm Fabric Orchestra. ✓**INTERNET**→*url* http://charlotte.acns.nwu.edu/charm/html/poi/

Poi-Pounders (ml) Ponder the Poi Dog with other fans of the band on this mailing list. ✓**INTERNET**→ *email* poi-pounders-request@presto.ig.com ✍ *Write a request*

THE POLICE

alt.music.the.police (ng) Not much traffic on this newsgroup, but what there is focuses on the release of the Police box set, the solo careers of band members, and more. ✓**USENET**→alt.music.the.police

Police The Police took over the world in the early eighties, and no one protested. In fact, fans were thankful. This site contains links to lyrics, discographies, tour dates, tabs, press, audio samples, and fan pages for Stu Copeland and Andy

The Police—from http://violet.berkeley.edu:8080/

Summers. Hmm…aren't they forgetting someone there? ✓**INTERNET**→*url* http://www.dsi.unimi.it/mow/police/

The Police A page full of audio samples, press releases, and (old) tour dates. ✓**INTERNET**→*url* http://www.dsi.unimi.it/mow/police/

Police Chat Message-based discussion. ✓**AMERICA ONLINE***keyword*→Rock/Pop →Rock Artists M-Z →Police & Solo

The Police List (ml) Sting, Sting, Sting, Sting, Sting. Were there other guys in the band? ✓**INTERNET**→*email* majordomo@mission.com ✍ *Type in message body:* subscribe police <your email address>

The Police WWW Home Page Nine out of ten English speaking people over the age of 18 could sing you every single the Police ever released, from plastic reggae to solid pop. Links to bios, rare images, sound clips, lyrics, polls, and all the solo stuff, with lots of Sting pages. They're meaningless and all that's true. ✓**INTERNET**→*url* http://violet.berkeley.edu:8080/

POP, IGGY

alt.music.iggy-pop (ng) They say Pop will eat itself. If that's true, it will be the only thing Iggy Pop has eaten in a month. Get the latest straight dope on the real King of Pop. Is it true he's working with Bowie again? What about the rumors of a collaboration with the surviving members of Nirvana? Is Courtney Love the female Iggy? Answer these questions, compare favorite recordings (*Raw Power* and *Fun House* are way out in front, but *Brick By Brick* doesn't do so badly), and generally genuflect to the Popster. ✓**USENET**→alt.music.iggy-pop

POP WILL EAT ITSELF

alt.music.pop-eat-itself (ng) The dance of the mad bastards continues on this newsgroup, which collects fan posts on tape trades, samples, and more. ✓**USENET**→alt.music.pop-eat-itself

Pop Will Eat Itself List (ml) Discuss Pop Will Eat Itself on this mailing list. ✓**INTERNET**→*email* majordomo@concorde.com ✍ *Type in message body:* subscribe pewination <your email address>

PWEI Nation Merchandise,

(cont'd pg. 170) →

Elvis Presley

You may remember him as a fat buffoon in a 30-pound jumpsuit, but to those in the

know, Elvis Presley is one of the giants of modern music—a vocalist whose ability to bring rhythm-and-blues styles into the mainstream touched off the rock-and-roll revolution, a cultural figure without whom there would have been no Beatles, no Bob Dylan, no Led Zeppelin (and certainly no Dread Zeppelin). In the years following his 1977 death by overdose, Elvis has become a tabloid joke, and the slide from "Suspicious Minds" to inquiring minds has both created a new fan base for the King and forced old fans to justify their love. Start at the **Elvis Home Page**. Take a tour of **Graceland**. And then consult **The Inventory of the Estate of Elvis A. Presley.**

Because we can't show the real Elvis—http://bradley.bradley.edu/~elvis/whatever.html

On the Net

Across the board

Elvis Mojo Nixon once sang, "Elvis is everywhere / Elvis is everything / Elvis is everybody / Elvis is still the king." Decide for yourself after perusing this moving tribute, which includes a dramatic monologue written for Elvis's still-born twin brother Jesse Garon, an essay on "the only mythological figure of our time," and other links. ✓ **INTERNET**→*url* http://www. xs4all.nl/~rragas/elvis.html

Elvis Home Page (ml) Shut down now and again by Graceland legal representatives, this page still has a wealth of Elvis resources, and the absence of sound clips and images will only bother you once you've digested the Elvis gossip (he's going to come out of hiding!), the Last Will and Testament of Elvis A. Presley, Elvis Internet sightings, Elvis souvenir collections, Elvis pen pals, and even Elvis downloadable software (Tiny Elvis for Windows is especially hilarious). ✓ **INTERNET** ...→*email* pelvis@princeton.edu ✍ *Write a request* ...→*url* http://www.princeton.edu/~pelvis/

Elvis Presley Commemorating Elvis's 1986 induction into the Rock-and-Roll Hall of Fame, this page includes a brief artist biography and sound clips. ✓ **INTERNET**→*url* http://www.rockhall.com/induct/preselvi.html

Graceland An annotated photo tour of Graceland that moves from Elvis's glass "EP" sculpture, to his car collection, to his grave. ✓ **INTERNET**→*url* http://www-swiss.ai.mit.edu/summer94/graceland.html

The Inventory of the Estate of Elvis A. Presley What a bargain! For only $7.95, you can order a copy of the inventory of Elvis's estate—a vital historical document that lists the King's property assets, financial assets, security transactions, artist royalty rights, personal possessions, and more. This page is an advertisement for the inventory, and little more, although it does contain a nice sketch of Elvis. ✓ **INTERNET**→*url* http://www.aksi.net/rjay/

PElvis: Princeton for Elvis (ml) Princeton may be for Elvis, but that raises a much knottier question—who's against him? Yale? Mount Holyoke? Rhodes College in Memphis? Dedicated to "spreading the magic of the King," this student group runs a mailing list and oversees a Website, which is composed mostly of links. ✓**INTERNET**→*email* pelvis@princeton.edu Write a request

Virtual Voyager—In Search of Elvis Are you one of those well-meaning kooks who stays up late on the phone trying to convince friends that Elvis isn't really dead, that he's just waiting in the wings until the world is ready to hear him sing once more? If so, you'll love this site, featuring a multi-part essay from the online version of the *Houston Chronicle* that seeks out the bits and pieces of Elvis that haunt the American ethos. Elvis appears in a vision. Elvis hovers over Graceland. Elvis inspires the lawyers who manage his estate to consider licensing the Elvis name for a renaming of the constellation Orion. In addition to these essays, the site includes an Elvis trivia quiz, an Elvis schedule of activities, a library of Elvis sounds, Elvis software, and a vari-

Again, not the King—http://rampages. onramp.net/~leary/dave.html

ety of Elvis-related articles that originally appeared in the Chronicle, including "Elvis lives in hearts of immigrant family," "Keeping guard on Elvis," and "Elvis as religious icon." ✓**INTERNET**→*url* http://www.chron.com/voyager/elvis/

Astrology

Elvis Presley's Astrological and Psychological Profile Get yourself a handful of hunka hunka burning insights at this site, which offers a reading of the King based on his astrological chart and psychological profile. What kind of reading? "1935 started cold in East Tupelo, Mississippi, one of the coldest, bitterest winters anyone could remember, and not just because of the weather. These were hard times, the lean years of the Great Depression. The whole world was hungry. Christmas had just passed two weeks before, and all over the world people were dreaming of better times ahead. This was especially so in the little town of Tupelo. Even in the best of times, there wasn't much money to be had there. But that January, in the deep of winter, a baby was born in Tupelo, a baby who could change the world forever." It was all in the stars from the beginning—Elvis's meteoric rise, his difficult celebrity, his early death. This Website lets you download an excerpt from the profile, prepared by Lifestyles International Astrological Foundation, and order the full *Elvis Presley's Astrological and Psychological Magazine* for only $6. "Elvis was an immensely complicated man. As you will see, the stars predicted that too." ✓**INTERNET**→*url* http://oeonline.com/~lifeintl/mag.html

Chat

alt.elvis.sighting (ng) The next

A full menu of King things—http://sunsite.unc.edu/elvis/elvishom.html

time you see Elvis, jot down the time and the place, take a Polariod (if possible), and tell other fans. Maybe someone saw him at the exact same time somewhere else. It happens, you know. ✓**USENET**→alt.elvis.sighting

Elvis Chat (ng) Sometimes obsessive, sometimes reverent, but never boring, the Elvis cult is alive and well and living on the Internet. Need to unload some old 45s? Convinced that the rock revivalists Orion are Elvis in disguise? Desperate to share your latest Elvis-themed novel ("Call me Elvis")? Don't be a stranger in your own town. ✓**USENET** ...→alt.elvis.king ...→ alt.fan.elvis-presley

Elvis Presley Chat Message-based discussion. ✓**COMPUSERVE** ...→*go* oldies→Messages *and* Libraries→Elvis/Male Singers ...→*go* rsforum→Messages *and* Libraries →Elvis, Etc. ...→*go* fanclub→Messages *and* Libraries→Elvis Presley

Churches

The First Presleyterian Church of Elvis the Divine "Welcome to the only religion that will matter in the next millennium," proclaims this page, which attempts to "bring the word of Elvis to the entire planet." With a millennarian bent, the page insists that the Second Coming of the King will occur between Christmas 1999 and January 8, 2000. The Presleyterian church does their part to help true believers prepare for that hallowed moment when "all good Presleyterians will receive their very own pink Cadillac which they will drive to that great Graceland beyond the sky, where Elvis will greet [them] with a big, sweaty hug and say 'Let's eat.'" ✓**INTERNET**→*url* http://pages. prodigy.com/NJ/zvqj45a/zvqj 45a.html

Conferences

The First International Conference on Elvis Presley Held in Oxford, Mississippi in August 1995, the First Annual International Conference on Elvis Presley sought to explore the different parts of the King's musical oeuvre, with seminars on Country Elvis, Rockabilly Elvis, the Blues Elvis, the Gospel Elvis, Elvis and Black Rhythm, Elvis as Outsider Artist, Elvis as Sign System, and Elvis as Dead Guy. The conference also included a Memphis Elvis tour, with stops at Sun Studios and Graceland. While there are no papers reported on "The Semiotics of Pizza, Pharmaceuticals, and Toilets: Elvis's Death Recontextualized," this seminar takes its King as seriously as pre-revolutionary France. Learn about the program and the participants, and give yourself ten good reasons to start saving for next year's big event. ✓**INTERNET**→ *url* http://imp.cssc.olemiss.edu/ elvis.html

Impersonators

Library of Elvis Sounds Elvis didn't really say "My daugher married who?" but you can download a clip of him speaking these very words. How? With this easy-to-use archive of Elvis sounds, with voice impersonations by a Houston Elvis fan. Hear Elvis on nutrition ("Hey, man, pass me one of those jelly doughnuts"), footwear ("You can step on my blue suede shoes anytime you want, baby"), and immortality ("Hey, baby, I'll be back"). ✓**INTERNET**→*url* http:// www.chron.com/voyager/elvis/ sounds/1005.au

Postage

Elvis Stamps Did you know that Elvis was slightly overweight? Did you know that he almost slept with Cybill Shepherd? Of course you did. But you may not know that the King's bejeweled jumpsuits weighed more than 30 pounds, or that he loved to snack on burnt bacon and lemon meringue pie. If you're intrigued by even the most minute details about the King, get yourself a copy of *99 Little Known Facts About Elvis Presley*, which is free when you order $10 worth of Elvis Presley stamps from Antigua and Barbuda. ✓**INTERNET**→*url* http://www.kiosk.net/elvis/efacts. html

Software

Elvis in the Machine Tiny Elvis talks about your computer from within your computer (Windows only). The Elvis Detector sets off an alarm whenever Elvis is near an open application (Windows only). And the Elvis Decoder Ring encodes email so that only Elvis can read it (Macs only). Elvis never used a home computer, but it was no fault of his own. Help right history. ✓**INTERNET**→*url* http://sunsite.unc. edu/elvis/download.html

"Why Elvis? Really, the man is dead. There are many other artists-ALIVE, I might add, who are more talented than Elvis ever dreamed of being.

"Todd Rundgren was in town on the 8th and 9th. Your paper, I seems, did not review the performance.

"Shame on you for being totally reactionary (the focus on Elvis) to sophomoric public sentiment while ignoring the exciting new things that an artist like Todd is doing with music, computers and computer graphics.

"I know intelligent people who bought your paper every day, looking for a review on the Rundgren concert and other articles related to his Interactive Music efforts. Other cities' newspapers covered his shows.

"Please, no more Elvis. I want to move forward in life, maybe others do too."

—from **Virtual Voyager: In Search of Elvis**

Elvis Presley

"Bob: Don't forget to email Elvis at Graceland at the following addresses:

graceland@icomm.com
or elvis@icomm.com

Also, call your mother."

−from **alt.elvis.king**

"He was called the 'King of Rock and Roll,' a title which disturbed him. When a fan presented him with a gold crown and said, 'This is for you, you're the King, he gently corrected her. 'No honey,' he said. 'Christ is the King. I'm just a singer.' Elvis never lost his faith in God. And he was troubled that some might have believed he was anything more than human. He never intended for anyone to adore him. He made very human choices. He aged. Perhaps it was frightening, as much for his critics as for himself: if Elvis Presley reached middle age, then we all must be losing part of our youth."

−from **Elvis Chat** on Compuserve's Fanclub Forum

lyrics, and transcripts of interviews with the band. ✓**INTERNET**→*url* http://kzsu.stanford.edu/uwi/pwei/pwei.html

PWEI Nation There are a lot of sites out there for Pop Will Eat It-self; what else would you expect from techno-freaks? But this is the only site a Poppie fan will ever need, with links to sound clips, lyrics, a discography, graphics, im-ages, an FAQ, tour info, news, merchandise, reviews, interviews, mailing lists, chat, and more. A rave in Cyberspace. ✓**INTERNET**→ *url* http://www.musicbase. co.uk/music/pwei/

PWEI Nation Neat little icons help you find your way at this site, which contains sound clips, im-ages, and more. ✓**INTERNET**→*url* http://www.hallucinet.com/uwi/pwei/pwei.html

PORTISHEAD

Portishead An excellent page de-voted to the kings of trip-hop, with photographs, MPEG and QuickTime movies, and a series of nested pages featuring musical treats and colorful annotation ("if Cypress Hill were into Fellini, if Ice-T were to score the sequel to *Taxi Driver* rather than to star in it"). ✓**INTERNET**→*url* http://www.godiscs.co.uk/godiscs/porthead.html

The Unofficial Portishead Site Links to news, tour info, a discog-raphy, lyrics, images, bios, reviews, and other fan pages. ✓**INTERNET**→ *url* http://gladstone.uoregon.edu/~jbunik/portishead.html

THE POSIES

Dear 23 (ml) Punk-pop rarely had as much punk or pop as the Posies, the Seattle band that made loud noise and irresistible melodies a way of life long before

the Pixies appeared. Catch up with other fans of the band here. ✓**IN-TERNET**→*email* dear23-request@seanet.com ✍ *Write a request*

The Dear 23 Home Page Read all about power pop, and bask in the glow of an excellent essay on Seattle music by Posie Ken Stringfellow. ✓**INTERNET**→*url* http://www.seanet.com/litlnemo/dear23.html

PRESLEY, ELVIS
See page 166.

THE PRETENDERS

A Tribute to Chrissie Hynde For all those who wish they could be Hynde, a straightforward discography with some links to other areas of interest. ✓**INTERNET**→ *url* http://thored.tft.tele.no/Music/Pretenders/Pretenders.html

Pretenders Press releases, images, and Chrissie Hynde's "Advice to Chick Rockers," which urges women to disregard the male hege-mony but "Shave [their] legs, for chrissakes!" ✓**AMERICA ONLINE**→ *keyword* warner→rock→Pretenders

PRIMAL SCREAM

Primal Scream A promotional site for Scream's latest album, *Give Out, But Don't Give Up.* ✓**INTERNET** →*url* http://www.music.sony.com/Music/ArtistInfo/PrimalScream.html

Primal Scream The interactive press kit and links to Websites. ✓**AMERICA ONLINE**→*keyword* warn-er→alternative→Primal Scream

Primal Scream Chat Message-based discussion. ✓**AMERICA ON-LINE**→*keyword* mmc→Alternative Rock →Bands M-Z→Primal Scream

PRIMUS

alt.music.primus (ng) An Ari-zona fan has recorded versions of

"Seattle's musical explosion onto the mainstream was responsible for/coin-cidental with punk-influenced music reaching great num-bers of people for the first time, the effects of which have been severely appar-ent. Some forms of behavior that would have been unknown to the average person suddenly became hip things to do. House-wives took heroin. Men-on-the-street became men-in-the-mosh-pit. This led to a flux of inexperi-enced citizens flock-ing to enjoy punk rock for the first time, without really understanding it. The media abetted the changes. Some gross infractions: a Subaru commercial that com-pares an automobile to punk rock (favor-ably, I might add); another that implied that purchase of their product would aid in a fashion makeover into 'that grunge thing'; and the inclusion of hun-dreds of flannel-encrusted teenage models."

—from **Dear 23 Home Page**

Primus songs using Teddy Ruxpin, the talking teddy bear doll. Geez, those guys are weird. Join the geeky, lots-o-chops, mostly male world of Primus fans on this newsgroup, who spends much of their time talking about Les's oddness and reveling in how much the band sucks. √USENET→alt.music. primus

The Cheesy Homepage Evereager Primus likes to talk about disgestion and so, apparently, do Primus fans. Contains lyrics, pictures, and "miscellaneous debris." √INTERNET→*url* http://www.music. sony.com/Music/ArtistInfo/ PrimalScream.html

Los Bastardos Created "in a fit of insane boredom," featuring interviews and articles alongside its catalog of general discographic information. √INTERNET→*url* http:// www.csua.berkeley.edu/ ~savage/primus/primus.html

Primus Chat Message-based discussion. √AMERICA ONLINE ...→ *keyword* mtv→Message Boards→ Bands That Do Suck→Primus ...→ *keyword* mmc→Rock/Pop→General Rock→Primus

PRINCE
See page 174.

QUEEN

alt.music.queen (ng) Roger woke up with a funny feeling, and now he wants to share it with the world: "I've always felt that John had more influence than usual on the *Hotspace* album. I have no evidence to back this up, it could be completely untrue. It's just the feel of the album. Can't explain it really." A Queen fan with the handle

Nonetheless objects to rumors that Queen will reform with George Michael as lead singer: "Freddie Mercury was so much a distinct personality and the creator of a great deal of the Queen music, that he is not to be 'replaced.' They would need to change the name of the band...after all, Freddie named it." And Ricky has noticed a strange similarity between the incidental music on the *X-Files* and the B-side to "A Kind of Magic," "A Dozen Red Roses for My Darling." √USENET→alt.music. queen

QMS (ml) Fans are still mourning the passage of Freddie Mercury, and some are still flogging away at the Freddie Mercury memorial concert, in which aging British rock stars demonstrated that dignity is just another word for nothing left to sing. When they're not lamenting the fact that Freddie's dead, Queen fans are nominating other bands for pop royalty, wondering about the vexed status of homosexual rock stars, and fantasizing about a band reunion. √INTERNET→*email* majordomo@stat.lsa. umich.edu ✍ *Type in message body:* subscribe qms <your email address>

Queen at the BBC A promotional page, including a couple of music clips, for an upcoming Queen album featuring "the last recorded vocals and music" by Freddie Mercury. √INTERNET→*url* http://www.polygram.com/ polygram/Queen.html

Queen Chat Message-based discussion. √AMERICA ONLINE→*keyword* mmc→Rock/Pop Rock→Artists M-Z →Queen √COMPUSERVE→*go* fanclub→Messages *and* Libraries→ Queen

Queen Page Photos and a

discography of the late, great, reigning purveyors of power rock. √INTERNET→*url* http://lilly.ping. de/~af/Queen/

QUEENSRYCHE

Promised Web Lyrics, interviews, and links, including access to *Screaming in Digital* digest. √INTERNET→*url* http://www. usmcs.maine.edu/~laferrie/ music/qr/qr.html

Queensrÿche They've come a long way from their Mob days. Now the band that won the MTV Viewer's Choice Award produces some of the best guitar metal around. This page offers a discography, an FAQ, and more band information. √INTERNET→*url* http:// www.cs.cmu.edu/afs/cs/user/ nkramer/ryche/ryche.html

Queensrÿche FTP Server The maximum number of users for this site is three in the afternoon and five in the evening. Call in the morning and cross your fingers. If you happen to get through, you'll find a wealth of Queensrÿchian files, including lyrics, sound clips, and more. √INTERNET→*url* ftp://arginine.umdnj.edu/pub/ queensryche

Queensrÿche Homepage "Machines have no conscience. Punch Punch Punch!" In addition to computer jokes, this site offers every scrap of prose ever written that pertains to Queensrÿche, including interviews, email addresses, tour news, interviews, reviews, transcripts, discographies, new album info, a CD-ROM preview, and backstage secrets (rumor has it that Scott has to pick all the blue M&M's out of the bowl in the green room). √INTERNET→*url* http://www.mcs.net/~ryche/

rec.music.artists.queensryche

(ng) Talk about Queensrÿche with other fans, who aren't above letting the conversation drift toward other progressive metal bands. ✓**USENET**→rec.music.artists.queensryche

Screaming in Digital (ml) Find out all about Queensrÿche with this electronic fanzine. The Website contains links to archived issues, guidelines for submissions, Net-related interviews, and other information on this electronic Q-zine. ✓**INTERNET**→*email* qryche@ios.com ✍ *Write a request Info:* ✓**INTERNET**→*url* http://www.ios.com/~qryche/

R

RADIOHEAD

W.A.S.T.E. A discography might not seem to be a valuable resource when the band in question has a total of two albums, but this site's got one. Radiohead's music may be ambivalent, but nothing says their fans have to be that way too. ✓**INTERNET**→*url* http://www.musicbase.co.uk/music/radiohead/

RAGE AGAINST MACHINE

Homepage Torn between music and politics? This is the place for you! With Che Guevara staring into the distance, check out all the Rage in activist music. Plus, before jumping to another link, don't forget to free Leonard Peltier. ✓**INTERNET**→*url* http://www.engin.umich.edu/~aklink/Rage/rageout.html

Rage Against the Machine A promotional site for the band's debut album. ✓**INTERNET**→*url* http://www.music.sony.com/Music/ArtistInfo/RageAgainstTheMachine.html

Rage Against the Machine

Homepage Done in forest green—and with a picture of Che Guevara to boot—this page offers Rage fans a wealth of resources on their favorite uncompromisingly political band. Pictures? Discography? Reviews? Even more information on why Leonard Peltier should be freed? It's all here. ✓**INTERNET**→*url* http://www.engin.umich.edu/~aklink/Rage/rageout.html

RAITT, BONNIE

Bonnie Raitt Primarily a promotional site for Bonnie's *Longing in Their Hearts* LP, this site also includes an electronic press kit for downloading. ✓**INTERNET**→*url* http://www.nando.net/music/gm/BonnieRaitt/

RAMONES

Ramones Chat Message-based discussion. ✓**AMERICA ONLINE**→*keyword* mmc→Alternative Rock→Bands M-Z →The Ramones

Rockaway Beach Although the band has broken up—ending things with an album entitled *Adios, Amigos* and an album cover full of dinosaurs—they do have a lead singer who looks an awful lot like Howard Stern, and they did appear on the *Simpsons* once. Links, fan club info, and a discography are featured. ✓**INTERNET**→*url* http://www.albany.edu/~orrin/ramones.html

RED HOT CHILI PEPPERS

Red Hot Chili Peppers Downloadable album cover art, as well as video clips of the "Warped" single and a file called Kmart Photo Shoot containing low-cost shots of the band members covering their private parts with jumbo crayons and teddy bears. ✓**AMERICA ONLINE**→*keyword* warner→Alternative→Red Hot Chili Peppers

Lou Reed—from http://charlotte.acns.nwu.edu/charm/html/lou/

REED, LOU

Lou Reed's Web Home "In Berlin, by the Web, you were four feet ten inches tall..." News, lyrics, images, interviews, and more resources on the former Velvet Underground leader and vibrantly monotonous solo artist. ✓**INTERNET**→*url* http://charlotte.acns.nwu.edu/charm/html/lou/

R.E.M.

See page 186.

THE REPLACEMENTS

The Skyway (ml) The Replacements only have a single mailing list for online fans, and it's a damned shame, because any band that recorded *Hootenanny, Tim, Let it Be, Pleased to Meet Me, Don't Tell a Soul,* and *All Shook Down* deserves much, much more. Children by the millions sing for Paul Westerberg and company, and some of them are here, talking about Westerberg's solo career, Bash and Pop, Chris Mars's solo projects, and more. ✓**INTERNET**→*email* lists@phoenix.creighton.edu ✍ *Type in message body:* subscribe skyway-l

THE ROLLING STONES
See page 194.

ROLLINS, HENRY

Henry Rollins' Stuff The most outspoken hard rocker since Mozart (who was also a liar), Rollins has generated a mini-industry. He acts, he speaks, he writes, and he rocks. √**INTERNET**→ *url* http://www.st.nepean.uws.edu.au/~alf/rollins/

Official Rollins Home Page Comments by Rollins on some of his most recent projects. √**INTERNET**→*url* http://www.two1361.com/rband/rollins.html

ROXETTE

Dan Kroll's Roxette Home Page Most certainly the only place in the universe where, among other things, you can take part in "Interactive Roxette Song Wars." Don't worry: they're not battles to the death. √**INTERNET**→ *url* http://turnpike.net/metro/DanKroll/roxette.html

International Roxette Fan Club "The world's favorite" Roxette club insures possible members that the organization is non-profit. Thank god—we wouldn't want anyone to profit from crassly commercial music, would we? √**INTERNET**→*url* http://www.wirehub.nl/~introxfc/

Roxette The shrewd Swedish band is preparing for their new album due to be released in October. "Don't Bore Us, Get To The Chorus" is sure to please fans around the globe, and this site furnishes sound clips, images, and some pictures of the band scantily clad. √**INTERNET**→*url* http://www.ccsf.caltech.edu/~dmz/roxette/

Roxette List (ml) Are they the new ABBA or the new a-ha? Talk

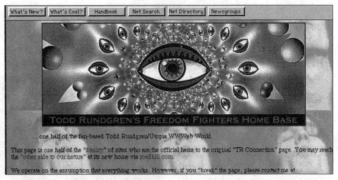

Todd Rundgren's Freedom Fighters —http://www.iglou.com/scm/cgi-bin/todd.pl

to other Roxette fans here. √**INTER-NET**→*email* owner-roxette@eiunix.tuwien.ac.at ✍ *Write a request*

Roxette Page An open invitation to join the Roxette Joyride, with fan club information, lyrics, images, and more. √**INTERNET**→*url* http://turnpike.net/metro/DanKroll/roxette.html

ROXY MUSIC

Avalon (ml) Why is Roxy Music not hailed as one of the greatest bands in the history of rock and roll? One fan suggests it's because they weren't one of the greatest: "*Avalon* is a wonderful album, very mysterious and romantic, and the early art-rock stuff really pushes my buttons, but there's not a very good case for arguing that Roxy Music was as important as David Bowie or Lou Reed, even with the achievements of its solo members." Other fans concur and dissent on this mailing list. √**IN-TERNET**→*email* avalon-request@webcom.com ✍ *Type in message body:* subscribe

Madness in my Soul—The Brian Ferry and Roxy Music Homepage Pictures, concert reviews, and interviews with the music makers. √**INTERNET**→*url* http://www.scp.caltech.edu/~bryan/roxy/

RUNDGREN, TODD

alt.music.todd-rundgren (ng) Todd still has loyal fans who think that *Something/Anything* is the best pop album ever recorded, and they're not about to let a little thing like a 25-year drought in creative inspiration get them down. Talk about Todd's recent multimedia projects. Recall the Nazz. And then conduct a psycholanalytic reading of the lyrics for "Piss Aaron." √**USENET**→alt.music.todd-rundgren

The Difference with Todd Rundgren Summaries, etc. of each installment of a Rundgren-hosted alternative music show. √**INTERNET**→ *url* http://www.roadkill.com/cgi-roger/difference

The Todd Rundgren Connection Vote in the "Todd is Godd" poll, read the TR quote of the day, and brush up on your Rundgren trivia. √**INTERNET**→*url* http://www.roadkill.com/todd/trconn

Todd Rundgren List (ml) Talk Todd. √**INTERNET**→*email* awizard-request@ planning.EBay.Sun.COM ✍ *Write a request*

Todd Rundgren's Freedom Fighters Home Base Another part of the integrated TR-i world, this page offers Rundgren fans so-

(cont'd pg. 178) →

Prince/

At first merely a one-man soul/funk/pop/rock wrecking crew, Prince quickly became
one of the few true artists of popular music. In albums like *1999*, *Purple Rain*, and *Sign 'O' The Times*, the diminutive multi-instrumentalist demonstrated an obsession with such heady topics as libido and Armageddon, but never forgot to wed his idiosyncratic lyrical concerns to nearly perfect pop melodies. But geniuses can be temperamental, and when Prince decided not to release the ultrafunky *Black Album* in 1988, it seemed to trigger a new phase of self-indulgence that culminated in a 1993 decision to change his name to an unpronouceable symbol. Did fans follow? Check out **The Love Experience**, the **New Power Network**, and **Prince Chat** to find out.

On the Net

Across the board

The Artist Formerly Known as Prince When Warner Brothers finally announced that it would be releasing ♀'s *Gold Experience*, visitors of this page chuckled into their purple collars. Why? Because they already had the lyrics. Tippy, tippy, tin, my friend, shall we begin? If so, maybe we should begin with the transcripts of live chat sessions, fan club information, im-

ages, sound clips, and gossip. ✓ **INTERNET**→*url* http://www.inetdirect. net/hammer/prince.html

Come Official information for the 1994 Warner release *Come*, which allegedly marked the death of the Artist Known As Prince. The page includes a bio, a discography, and a sound sample from

the single "Letitgo." ✓ **INTERNET**→ *url* http://www.iuma.com/War ner/html/Prince.html

The Love Experience His name is Prince (or is that ♀?), and he is funky, and he is also well-represented on the Net, as this list of links proves. ✓ **INTERNET**→*url* http://www.cs.uwm.edu/public/ap

His name was Prince, and he is funky—from ftp://morra.et.tudelft.nl/pub/prince/jpg/

A symbol, but of what?—from ftp://morra.et.tudelft.nl/pub/

rild/prince.html

N.P.G. Experience "We may as well face it, no matter where we were, what we did and what we thought, as we reflect on the past 15 years, there is a six letter word that doesn't name a human being as much as it defines a sub-genre of our culture. For where else could there be so many layers of art assembled so cohesively while retaining a singular identity and influence but under the heading—PRINCE." It's hard to follow an introduction like that, but this Website manages, offering a lavishly annotated Prince discography, sound clips, and images. ✓**INTERNET**→*url* http://orathost.cfa.ilstu.edu/public/oratGallery/artsExhibits/coatsExhibit/home.html

New Power Network A worldwide center for all things Princely (or Formerly-Known-As-Princely), including news briefs, music for downloading (including bootlegs), and an interactive chat area. ✓**INTERNET**→*url* http://morra.et.tudelft.nl/npn/

Prince A discography and links to other Prince sites. ✓**INTERNET**→*url* http://www.winternet.com/~char

bone/prince.html

Prince FAQ Why exactly did Prince change his name to an unpronounceable symbol? The fans who maintain this FAQ have a half-dozen theories, which range from cynical to soft-headed. What are they? Okay, okay. Stop asking. (1) It's a ploy to get lots of media attention. (2) It's a genuine artistic / spiritual rebirth. (3) It's an attempt to find a loophole in his contract with Warner Brothers. (4) There's no good reason; he's finally gone overboard with ego and insensitivity to others, all in the name of art. (5) A symbolic name is one that better fits his personality. (6) The name change is an attempt to avoid death. When they're not negotiating the onomastics of Minneapolis funk, this FAQ offers Prince fans a wealth of information about the puny purple polymath. ✓**INTERNET**→*url* http://huizen.dds.nl/~nmarrale/ampfaq.html

Prince FTP Site Lyrics, images, sound clips, interview transcripts, and more. ✓**INTERNET**→*url* ftp://morra.et.tudelft.nl/pub/prince

Prince Lyrics Is "Sister" really about incest? In what song does Prince express his desire for a 24K relationship? And how long will it take to search for the purple banana? Find out for yourself by perusing this collection of Prince lyrics. ✓**INTERNET**→*url* ftp://math.montana.edu/pub/carlson/pltt

Princely Page Prince fans know this information like the backs of their own hands. A comprehensive Prince discography just for you, along with links. ✓**INTERNET**→*url* http://huizen.dds.nl/~nmarrale/tafkap.html

Sampled Prince Songs A gen-

erous assortment of unreleased and live tracks, including "Proud Mary," "Hallucination Rain," and "M. D. Is Alive." ✓**INTERNET**→*url* http://www710.univ-lyon1.fr/~burzlaff/songs.html

Articles

Prince An interview with Prince from *Vibe*'s August 1994 issue. ✓**INTERNET**→*url* http://www.pathfinder.com/vibe/archive/august94/docs/TAFKAP1.html

Bootlegs

Many Prince Bootlegs An incredibly complete list of Prince bootlegs, studio and live. ✓**INTERNET**→*url* http://www.unik.no/~mariush/bootlegs.html

Maxine's List of Boots While it's not limited to Prince recordings, this list is dominated by them—everything from tour recordings to studio leaks. ✓**INTERNET**→*url* http://bat710.univ-lyon1.fr/%7Eburzlaff/resume.html

Prince in Boots A fan's list of unofficial Prince recordings. ✓**IN-**

U Got the Look—from ftp://morra.et.tudelft.nl/pub/prince/

The NPG, with its fearless leader—from ftp://morra.et.tudelft.nl/pub/prince/

TERNET→*url* http://www.cs.vu.
nl:80/~lberg/my_boots.html

Prince Swap List Need to trade
Prince bootlegs and rarities? Going
crazy trying to assemble a complete home version of *Crystal Ball*?
Come to this page, which advertises a national tape-trading network.
✓INTERNET→*url* http://www.mtsu.
edu/~spth0001/

Chat

alt.music.prince (ng) This
Artist-Formerly-Known-As nonsense has infected the entire Prince
fan world. Now, ♀-maniacs leap
into terminological fury at the
drop a hat; responding to a poster
who has misspelled the name of
the NPG drummer, a newsgroup
regular snarls "his name is
MichAEl Bland. Notice that it's A
before E. I mean, this isn't one of
those picky typo deals; this is the
guy's name (and mine too for that

matter) for cryin' out loud…Mis-
spelling someone's name is just
kind of personal." Oh, yeah—the
group sometimes talks about new
music, and Prince's Warner Bros.
contract, and past hits. ✓USENET→
alt.music.prince

#Prince Chat about the artist formerly known as hitmaker. ✓INTER-
NET→*irc* #Prince

Prince Chat Message-based dis-
cussion about Prince and all relat-
ed artists—the Family, T. C. Ellis,
Jill Jones, Tevin Campbell, the
Time, and even Taja Sevelle.
✓AMERICA ONLINE→*keyword* mmc→
Rap/R&B→R&B/Soul→PRINCE
✓EWORLD→*go* eaz→Pump Up The
Volume→Music Talk→PRINCE

Prince List (ml) Discuss the artist
formerly known as Prince and currently known as ♀, and why he
might be the artist known as
Prince once more. ✓INTERNET→

email prince-request@icpsr.umich.edu
✍ *Write a request*

Prince List What's worse—the title song to *Graffiti Bridge* or the title song to *Diamonds and Pearls*?
Send a subtle message of "Shut up
already, damn"—or anything else
that's on your mind— on this
mailing list for Prince fans . ✓IN-
TERNET→*email* prince@morra.et.
tudelft.nl ✍ *Write a request*

Fonts

Prince Fonts True-type fonts for
the IBM and Macintosh that let
you work the keyboard like ♀
works his guitar. ✓INTERNET→*url*
ftp://morra.et.tudelft.nl/pub/princ
e/true.type.fonts/fonts.read.me

Lyrics

The DTT Experience Everyone
knows that ♀ never sleeps, that he
eats only bee pollen and drinks
only Nehi, and that he records 40
to 50 songs each week that never
see the light of day. But not everyone has access to this huge list of
lyrics for unreleased ♀ songs,
from "Be My Mirror" to "Moon-
beam Levels." Highly recommended. ✓INTERNET→*url* http://www.
cs.odu. edu/~daniel/daniel.html

Prince Lyrics A comprehensive
list of lyrics for all official Prince
and ♀ releases. ✓INTERNET …
→*url* ftp://morra.et.tudelft.nl/
pub/prince/lyrics …→*url* ftp://
math.montana.edu/pub/carlson/
pltt/Lyrics/

Merchandise

**New Power Generation
Store** Order music and other
products from Prince's Minneapo-
lis-based store. ✓INTERNET→*email*
NewPwrGen@aol.com ✍ *Email
with general correspondence*

Prince

"Ok, folks. My two-year relationship has just ended. Therefore, it has become necessary for me to sell several items of our joint collection, which includes a 12"x12" paperback from the 80's about Prince. It was signed on the inside cover backstage at a concert (the book includes a letter of authenticity detailing the events of that night). He signed it 'Prince' (this was during the Under A Cherry Moon Tour) and 'Love God' and then added a couple of flowers to it. Minimum bid for this item is $50. Please contact me if you're interested. Authenticity is guaranteed."

—from **alt.music.prince**

"I, too, am disheartened by the fact that Prince seems to shout MF and nigga in his concerts all the time, so it seems. Sure, he's cursed before. But before, he said it for a purpose instead of just to say it. It wasn't as plentiful and it didn't sound forced. He says this is a spiritual revolution. This is not like the Lovesexy revolution, I'll tell you that. Is there at least one 'spiritual' song on The Gold Experience? Prince used to have at least one on every album."

—from **alt.music.prince**

"Prince has managed to create some incredibly catchy, (if not great) music within the past 17 or 18 years. So what if he hasn't created a 'When Doves Cry' in several years. I seriously doubt we'll see him creating pseudo Broadway crap like 'Can you feel the Love Tonight' like Elton. He keeps creating music. This seems to be his first and foremost ambition in life. When you make hundreds of hours of music each year, some is destined to be less than great. So what. It certainly is better than much of what is out there."

—From **Prince Chat** on AOL's Music Message Center

lace that there are other people in the world who are equally obsessed with the man and his aura. ✓**INTERNET**→*url* http://www.iglou.com/scm/cgi-bin/todd.pl

RUPAUL

RuPaul "Don't let your mouth write a check your ass can't cash." "Don't let the smooth taste fool ya." A list of don'ts from the hurricane on high heels, along with sound and movie clips from Ru-Performances. ✓**INTERNET**→*url* http://copper.ucs.indiana.edu/~jfleming/rupaul.html

RuPaul's House of Love "Flawless, fierce attitude. Disposable razors. Shaving gel. Body lotion. Full coverage pancake makeup in light, medium, and dark. Translucent loose powder, plus a compact for your purse. Makeup sponges that don't crumble. Tucking panties. Panty hose. Corset. Push-up bra. Gym socks rolled up tight (for breasts). High-heeled shoes. Hotpants. Mini-dress. Gloves." Bill Clinton's Christmas wish list? No, it's RuPaul's checklist for Drag Queens, just one of the many entertaining features at this Website. You better link. ✓**INTERNET**→*url* http://www.cyber-dyne.com/~tprebble/rupaul/index.html

RUSH

alt.music.rush (ng) Songs matter. But chops matter more. Is Rush the Who of Canada or the Yes of the nineties? And is it true that they're preparing a series of songs in the vein of *Tom Sawyer* that pay tribute to other heroes of American literature? Find out at this newsgroup. ✓**USENET**→alt.music.rush

Fly by Night's Rush Page Download MIDI arrangements and fill out a crossword puzzle (1. Down? "Rush." 2. Across? "Rush"

4. Across? "*Limelight.*"). ✓**INTERNET**→*url* http://www.exit109.com/~jgeoff/rush.html

The National Midnight Star The next time you want to rave about Neil Peart's drumming, don't hold back. Join this mailing list and sing Neil's praises as loud as you can. Some things are too important for restraint. ✓**INTERNET**→*email* rush-request@syrinx.umd.edu ✍ *Write a request*

#p/g! Concert reports on the aging, cynical Canadian rockers. ✓**INTERNET**→*url* http://ewi.ewi.org/~rroberts/pg/

Rush Chat Message-based discussion. ✓**AMERICA ONLINE**→*keyword* mmc→Rock/Pop→Rock Artists M-Z →Rush ✓**EWORLD**→*go* eaz→Pump Up the Volume →Music Talk→RUSH

Wilderness of Mirrors A discography, articles on the band, and more. ✓**INTERNET**→*url* http://silver.ucs.indiana.edu/~scebell/music/rush/rush2.html

Zim's "Rare Tape" Server A forum for investigating and exchanging bootlegs. ✓**INTERNET**→*url* http://www.svs.com/users/zim/rushstuff.html

RUSTED ROOT

Rusted Root Powerful lyrics, rich vocals, and primal rythym make Rusted Root rising stars in the world of indie-rock. This page offers links to album info, video clips, screen savers, tour dates, and images. ✓**INTERNET**→*url* http://www.polygram.com/polygram/Rusted.html

Rusted Root Links to archives, lyrics, a fanzine, tour dates, sound clips, images, and more. ✓**INTERNET**→*url* http://www.starg.com/rust.html

NOTES

"I had the rare and unbelievable experience of singing onstage with Todd! I missed his show in Jackson-ville but caught the one in Orlando. At one point, Todd said,'Oh no, he's back; some guy who keeps yelling for "The Wheel (Another Live)."' He then said that if the guy yelled it again, Todd would have him come up onstage and sing it. Later in the show there was a lull so I yelled it out. Todd asked that I be brought onstage. Another guy from the audience was sent up also. Todd started playing the riff from the song, and the other guy froze. He asked Todd if he could sing,'Can We Still Be Friends' but Todd said this was the song we were doing. The other guy was taken off the stage and I started singing. Even though I've sung profesionally for about fifteen years, my legs were like jello. I started forgetting words and Todd started 'feeding' them to me."

-from The Todd Rundgren Connection

S

SADE

Sade Information on Sade, her music, and her life. ✓INTERNET→ *url* http://www.diku.dk/~terra/sade/

Sade An official Sony site, with information about Sade's albums *Love Deluxe* and *The Best of Sade*, an artist bio, and QuickTime video clips. ✓INTERNET→*url* http://www.music.sony.com/Music/ArtistInfo/Sade.html

Sade's Temple Sound clips and complete lyrics for Sade's oeuvre. ✓INTERNET→*url* http://gwis2.circ.gwu.edu/~merlin/sade/sade.html

SANTANA

Rock-It Comix Presents Santana How did a young dishwasher rise through the rock ranks to become one of the greatest space-blues guitarists of this or any other century? Follow Carlos Santana's career, or buy Santana-related merchandise. ✓INTERNET→*url* http://www.music.sony.com/Music/ArtistInfo/Sade.html

SCORPIONS

Scorpions This page will rock you like a hurricane, dude. Link to news, an FAQ, articles, reviews, interviews, a discography, a history, a world-tour book, fan club info, images, mailing list, guitar tabs, lyrics, and 'other fan pages. ✓INTERNET→*url* http://www.indirect.com/user/ggmorton/scorpion.html

Scorpions Album covers, a song list, and special Scorpions animation. ✓INTERNET→*url* http://weber.u.washington.edu/~mforney/scorpions.html

Sebadoh by waffle house—from http://joemama.mit.edu/sebadoh/pics/black-white/

SEAL

alt.music.seal Without *Batman Forever*, would Seal have vanished into oblivion? Probably not. But at least one fan of the gigantic English mood-rocker is thankful for the exposure. "I can't tell you how happy it makes me when I hear Seal on the radio, and the song comes near its chorus. It's so much better than that U2 song." Keep track of Seal's ever-changing hairstyle, his mysticism, and his over-produced, ballad-laden albums. ✓USENET→alt.music.seal

Clueless Inkorporated (Seal) Song clips, documents related to Seal, and lyrics. ✓INTERNET→*url* http://www.xmission.com/~eheintz/CIStandard/Seal/

Future Love Paradise (Seal) News, images, a Seal FAQ, a discography, concert info, tran-scrips of online conferences, a Seal screensaver, and links. Very comprehensive, detailed, and well-designed, this page earns the Seal of Approval (and maybe even the approval of Seal). ✓INTERNET→*url* http://minerva.cis.yale.edu/~ariedels/seal.html

SEBADOH

Sebadoh A Sebadoh FAQ, a discography, tour dates, band pictures, lyrics, and an archive of the band's mailing list. ✓INTERNET→*url* http://joemama.mit.edu/sebadoh/

Sebadoh Archive Lou Barlow left Dinosaur, Jr., never to return. The band he formed after parting ways with J. Mascis, Sebadoh, remains one of the great enigmas of Amerindie rock—a band capable of hopping from genre to genre with nary a thought of inconsistency. Get Sebadoh sound clips, images, lyrics, and more. ✓ **INTER-NET**→*url* ftp://ftp.std.com/pub/sebadoh/sebadoh.html

Sebadoh Discography A list of all the band's singles, albums, and even split singles. ✓ **INTERNET**→*url* http://www.subpop.com/bios/seb-disc.htm

SEPULTURA

Infected Voice (ml) Brazilian death metal is in good hands these days. Find out why on the Sepultura mailing list. ✓ **INTERNET**→*email* sepultura@cougar.vut.edu.au ✍ *Type in subject line:* ADD ME *Type in message body:* <your email address>

Sepultura Official Sony information for the *Chaos A.D.* album. ✓ **INTERNET**→*url* http://www.music.sony.com/Music/ArtistInfo/Sepultura.html

Sepultura Bios of band members, a discography, and information on how to subscribe to the Brazilian metal band's fan club. ✓ **INTERNET**→*url* http://www.d.umn.edu/~nbradley/sepultura.html

Sepultura A full discography, images, and even a list of bootlegs. ✓ **INTERNET**→*url* http://www.lut.fi/~moro/sepu.html

SEX PISTOLS

Never Mind the Bollocks Here's the Sex Pistols Web Page It's Monday morning, you're dragging, and all you want to do is hear Johnny Rotten snarl "I'm not an animal, an animal, an animal." Well, you've certainly come to the right place. The Sex Pistols Website includes lyrics for "Anarchy in the UK," "Bodies," "God Save the Queen," "I Wanna Be Me," and "No Feelings," clips from interviews, biographies, and a set of links. As pick-me-ups go, it's better than a cup of coffee and

an Egg McMuffin. ✓ **INTERNET**→*url* http://www.yab.com:80/~stumbras/sex-pistols/

Sid Vicious Did you know that Sid's real name was John Ritchie? Did you know that he was sort of a moron? Get the lowdown on the Sex Pistols' bass player and homicidal junkie. ✓ **INTERNET**→*url* http://weber.u.washington.edu/~jlks/pike/svicio.html

SHAMEN

alt.music.shamen (ng) The Shamen have changed tremendously over the years, moving from rock to funk to spacey dance music. In fact, only Colin Angus remains from the original line-up. But fans remain loyal, the same way they do to baseball teams whose entire rosters change. On the newsgroup, fans are talking about solo projects, band projects,

and more. ✓ **USENET**→alt.music.shamen

Nementon A well-rounded primer on the band, written in British with English subtitles, that features images of the band, sells merchandise, and sometimes even offers Shamen singles for download in advance of their record store release. ✓ **INTERNET**→*url* http://www.demon.co.uk/drci/shamen/nemeton.html

SHONEN KNIFE

alt.music.shonen-knife (ng) Japanese women's fashion values cuteness above all. Short skirts. Hello Kitty t-shirts. Hair done up in pigtails. And, of course, a Shonen Knife album in the tape deck. Behind stilted English lyrics and power-pop guitars, Shonen Knife became an underground sensation in the late eighties, and went over-

Cuts like a Shonen Knife—from http://www.netropolis.net/shonen/knife/shrine.htm

Frank Sinatra—from http://www.io. org/~buff/sinatra.html

ground when bands like Nirvana and Sonic Youth confessed their addiction to the princesses of Japanese bubblegum. Find out about new releases, concert tours, and collaborations on this newsgroup. ✓**USENET**→alt.music.shonen-knife

Ikko-O Ikko-O Comic artist John MacLeod is obsessed with Shonen Knife, and through the powers of his devotion has managed to create a sizable, attractive site with practically no original material at all! Links to lots of other Shonen Knife and comparable chick-punk pages. ✓**INTERNET**→*url* http://www.cs.ubc.ca/spider/ forsey/Mouser/shonen.knife.html

Shrine to Shonen Knife Album covers, color pictures, and links. ✓**INTERNET**→*url* http://www. netropolis.net/shonen/knife/shrine. htm

The Unofficial Shonen Knife Page Princesses of plastic punk, Shonen Knife are a veritable cult phenomenon. Their fans vow to spread the word worldwide. This

site has links to images, bios, cover art, and more. ✓**INTERNET**→*url* http://152.42.32.64/Alumni/ AnAntonelli/Shonen/Shonen.html

SIMON AND GARFUNKEL

alt.music.paul-simon (ng) Is Paul really working on a Broadway music with Derek Walcott? Why can't he seem to record an album more frequently than once every five years? Is Mother and Child Reunion really the name of a Chinese egg-and-chicken dish? ✓**USENET**→alt.music.paul-simon

Simon and Garfunkel Guitar tabs, a complete discography, lyrics, album photos, bootlegs, and links to related sites. ✓**INTERNET**→ *url* http://www.dur.ac.uk/~ d213ga/

Simon and Garfunkel Commemorating the duo's 1990 induction into the Rock and Roll Hall of Fame, this page includes a brief biography and sound clips. ✓**INTERNET**→*url* http://www.rockhall. com/induct/garfsimo.html

Simon and Garfunkel/Paul Simon With guitar tabs, lavish annotations, and even some live sound clips for a handful of songs, this page is a fitting tribute to one of the most influential and enduring duos in the history of pop music. And if you only know Paul Simon through his solo work, you'll have hours of fun getting Art Garfunkled. ✓**INTERNET**→*url* http:// fy.chalmers.se/~jmo/acoustic. guitar.song.collection.html#S&G

SIMPLE MINDS

New Gold Dream (ml) She's a river, and this is a mailing list. Any questions? ✓**INTERNET**→*email* new-gold-dream-request@dfw.net ✍ *Type in subject line:* subscribe

Simple Minds Yes, they're still

alive and kicking, and no, no one has forgotten about them. This page offers links to video- and discographies, promos, song index and lyrics, articles, an FAQ, merchandise, graphics, books, and a mailing list. ✓**INTERNET**→*url* http://matahari.cv.com/people/ Simon.Cornwell/simple_minds/

SINATRA, FRANK

Frank Sinatra Dean, Sammy, Joey, Peter, Shirley, and Jerry come alive on this page, which brings the spirit of the Rat Pack into the online Era. ✓**INTERNET**→*url* http:// www.interport.net/~sinatra/

Frank Sinatra Mailing List (ml) Talk all about Frank—his enduring appeal, his weakened condition, and his cultural significance. ✓**INTERNET**→*email* listserv@ vm.temple.edu ✍ *Type in message body:* subscribe sinatra <your full name>

Ring-a-Ding Ding! Long before he was Bono's doubles partner, Frank Sinatra was one of the seminal vocalists of the twentieth century, a monumental figure in popular music who was Elvis before Elvis, Dylan before Dylan, and Bowie before Bowie. The Howard Cosell quote that stands as epigraph to this page explains Frank's appeal ("Frank Sinatra, who has the phrasing, who has the control, who understands the composers, who knows what losing means as so many have, who made the great comeback, who stands still, eternally, on top of the entertainment world. Ladies and gentlemen, from here on in it's Frank Sinatra!"), and the page also includes information on the Frank Sinatra mailing list, a transcript of Bono's tribute speech from the 1994 Grammies, a Sinatra FAQ, a discography, a filmography, concert reviews, press clips, images, and even a list of rock songs alluding to Sinatra (from Cracker's "Teen Angst" to The Pogues "Fairy Tale of New York"). And if your Sinatra obsession runs to extreme lengths, you can even link to a *Playboy* pictorial featuring Frank's daughter Nancy. ✓**INTERNET**→*url* http://www.io.org/~buff/sinatra.html

SIOUXSIE & THE BANSHEES

Siouxsie and the Banshees Lyrics, a discography, and biographical information. ✓**INTERNET**→*url* http://www.dnx.com/vamp/Siouxsie/

Siouxsie and the Banshees Chat Message-based discussion. ✓**AMERICA ONLINE** ...→*keyword* rockline→MODERN ROCK LIVE→SIOUXSIE & THE BANSHEES!!! ...→*keyword* mmc→World Beat→SIOUXSIE AND THE BANSHEES

Siouxsie and The Banshees List (ml) Share your thoughts—they're fairly bleak, huh?—with other Siouxsie and the Banshees fans. ✓**INTERNET**→*email* listserv@brownvm.brown.edu ✍ *Type in message body:* subscribe satb-l <your full name>

SISTERS OF MERCY

Sisters of Mercy Concert info, a discography, and other resources for fans of this band named after a Leonard Cohen song, which was probably named after something else. ✓**INTERNET**→*url* http://www.cm.cf.ac.uk/Sisters.Of.Mercy/

Sisters of Mercy Sound Clip Heaven Short clips of some regularly unavailable Sisters' tracks. ✓**INTERNET**→*url* http://www.sjca.edu/~bodyelec/bodyelec.html

SKINNY PUPPY

Skinny Puppy Comprehensive info, including rumors about the band. ✓**INTERNET**→*url* http://www.cling.gu.se/~cl3polof/SP.html

Skinny Puppy Biographical information, interviews, and more. ✓**INTERNET**→*url* http://jupiter.pt.hk-r.se/student/pi92mos/skinny.puppy.html

Smothered Hope (ml) A mailing list for fans of the venerable industrial outfit. ✓**INTERNET**→*email* smothered-hope-request@mrfrostie.ecst.csuchico.edu ✍ *Type in subject line:* subscribe

SLOWDIVE

Slowdive Info on soundtrack projects, recordings in progress, and concert news. ✓**INTERNET**→*url* http://www.musicbase.co.uk/music/creation/slowdive/

Slowdive An article on the band, complete with discography. ✓**INTERNET**→*url* http://www.itp.tsoa.nyu.edu/~student/brendonm/slowdive.html

SLY & THE FAMILY STONE

Sly and the Family Stone Commemorating Sly and the Family Stone's 1993 induction into the Rock and Roll Hall of Fame, this page includes an essay about the band and sound clips. ✓**INTERNET**→*url* http://www.rockhall.com/induct/slyfam.html

Sly and the Family Stone Reviews of Sly's albums, from *A Whole New Thing* to *High on You*. ✓**INTERNET**→*url* http://homebrew.geo.arizona.edu/sly.html

The Sly Stone Homepage A discography, sound samples, rumors, images of Sly, Larry Graham, and other band members, and an archive of articles. ✓**INTERNET**→*url* http://www.columbia.edu/~jhd10/funkpub/family.html

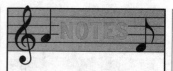

"As many folks are aware, Sly has kept an incredibly low profile the last few years. The last releases of new, original material from Sly were a song with Earth Wind and Fire on their 1990 LP Heritage, and a song on the 1990 Bill Laswell-produced album by Maceo Parker.

"The last album to bear his name as artist was the 1994 CD Precious Stone: In the Studio with Sly Stone, but features no material that appears to have been recorded after 1970. The last time he appeared in the same room with members of the Family Stone was at their 1993 induction into the Rock and Roll Hall of Fame. Now rumors are flying about a new release from Sly on Avenue Records. Fans have written saying they have heard new material from Sly, even citing names of songs, such as 'Sleeping Pill' and 'Coming Back for More.'

—from **The Sly Stone Homepage**

The smashing Smashing Pumpkins—from http://www.wpi.edu:8080/~joev/sp/

SMASHING PUMPKINS

alt.music.smash-pumpkins (ng) What is the image on the front of the *Pisces Iscariot* cover? Is it a glass of milk being poured or someone with their hand around the arm of a shirtless little boy? Is there a bird in the background, in front of the half-opened mini-blinds, and is that bird a parrot? These are only a few of the Holmesian questions pursued doggedly by Smashing Pumpkins fans, who also love to submit guitar tabs, talk about tour dates, and compare the Pumpkins with other bands. ✓USENET→alt.music.smash-pumpkins

Smashing Pumpkins Although this page isn't frequently updated, it is still a smashing addition to the roster of Pumpkins pages online, with lyrics, images, guitar tabs, and more. ✓INTERNET→*url* http://www.muohio.edu/~carmance/sp.html

Smashing Pumpkins Images, lyrics, a discography, and more. ✓INTERNET→*url* http://www.wpi.edu:8080/~joev/sp/

Smashing Pumpkins Pumpkins screen savers dispute the myth that it's better to burn out than to fade away. Pumpkins guitar tabs reveal that Billy Corgan is making a noise that most people can't make. And articles about the band suggest that a Siamese dream is a rare psychological phenomenon in which two people share the same nocturnal narrative. ✓INTERNET→*url* http:// acmex.gatech.edu:8001/~ss128/sp_index.html

Smashing Pumpkins Page A few photos—album covers, video covers, and illustrations from magazine features—and not much else. ✓INTERNET→*url* http://www.deakin.edu.au/~benmo/smashing.html

Smashing Pumpkins Software A version of the popular tile-matching game GunShy customized for Pumpkins users, the Smashing Pumpkins font, screensavers, and more. ✓INTERNET→*url* http://www.muohio.edu/~carmance/sp/SPSOFTWARE.HTML

SMITHEREENS

Smithereens Chat Message-based discussion. ✓AMERICA ONLINE→*keyword* mmc→Rock/Pop→Classic Rock→The Smithereens

Smithereens List (ml) Climb to the top of the pops, and when you get there, talk to the others there about the British-Invasion-Goes-American craftsmanship of the Smithereens. ✓INTERNET→*email* Smithereens-request@hookup.net ✍ *Write a request*

THE SMITHS

alt.music.smiths (ng) Jean is building a case that Morrissey has achieved more as a solo artist than he ever did as lead singer of The Smiths, and she's using *Your Arsenal* as Exhibit A: "If you listen to 'We Hate it When Our Friends Become Successful,' you can tell that he's more confident as a singer, angrier as a lyricist, and that he's better able to push his band toward crescendos." Unfortunately, no one on this newsgroup really wants to argue with Jean, maybe because they're too busy accusing one another of latent homosexuality. "Have you seen the album covers?" asks Bob. "They are homoerotic. If you like them, you're gay. No question." Bill returns fire: "You wouldn't know homoerotic if it put you in nipple clamps, stomped you with army boots, and fisted you fifteen ways to Christmas." Hey, how about that Morrissey? ✓USENET→alt.music.smiths

Bigmouth (ml) As long as angst-ridden adolescents with chips on their shoulders and a powerful ambivalence about their own sexuality roam the earth, The Smiths will be popular. And as long as The Smiths are popular, this mailing list will be in existence, providing a friendly discussion forum for Morrissey and Smiths fans. ✓INTERNET→*email* majordomo@langmuir.EECS.Berkeley.EDU ✍ *Type in message body:* subscribe bigmouth <your email address>

Cemetery Gates News, pictures, music, and merchandise on The Smiths and Morrissey, everyone's favorite but his own. ✓**INTERNET**→*url* http://www.public.iastate.edu/~krajewsk/

Smiths Chat Message-based discussion. ✓**AMERICA ONLINE**→*keyword* mmc→Alternative Rock →Bands M-Z→The Smiths & Morrissey

SONIC YOUTH

alt.music.sonic-youth (ng) GIFs of Kim, reviews of Thurston's solo album, critiques of the politics of new SY fans, and Beach Boys covers are all fair game. Not much in-depth analysis of Sonic Youth's place in the alternative rock scene, though, or what it means to be a college band whose members are in their forties. ✓**USENET**→alt.music.sonic-youth

Sonic Youth One lousy picture. They look bored, too. ✓**INTERNET**→

url http://www.iuma.com/IUMA/band_html/Sonic_Youth.html

Sonic Youth Sonic Youth was making cool music before the meaningless label "alternative" was a glint in the eye of a marketing major. Get instant art-pop credibility at this site, which gives you tour info, graphics, sound clips, a list of the band's favorite albums, and links to other fan pages. ✓**INTERNET**→*url* http://theory.stanford.edu/people/donald/sonic/sonic_index.html

Sonic Youth This graph-chic site has tons of info on all the albums divided between *The Underground Years* and *The Corporate Wave.* ✓**INTERNET**→*url* http://geffen.com/sonic.html

Sonic Youth "We played out of tune, because we couldn't afford guitars that would stay in tune." And the rest was legend. Bios, a band history, images, and a discography of the band that broke punk. ✓**INTERNET**→*url* http://www.itp.tsoa.nyu.edu/~student/brendonm/sonic.htm

Sonic Youth Index An entertaining and idiosyncratic collection of SY information, including current tour dates, graphics and sounds, and the band members' all-time favorite albums. What bends the ear of a legendary alternative rock band? Well, Thurston likes punk forbears like Television, the Velvet Underground, the Stooges, Richard Hell and the Voidoids, and the Ramones. Kim favors an eclectic mix that includes everything from Billie Holiday to the Rolling Stones to Funkadelic. Lee has poppier tastes, giving the nod to Joni Mitchell, Elvis Costello, and Madonna. And Steve returns to mainstream male alternative rock, listing Tom Waits, Neil Young, Nick Cave, and Captain Beefheart. And that's the Sonic truth. ✓**INTERNET**→*url* http://moon.st.rim.or.jp:1969/band/sonicyouth/

SOUL ASYLUM

Soul Asylum Do you have *Time's Incinerator*? How about *And The Horse You Rode In On*? Or did you jump on the Soul Asylum bandwagon for *Grave Dancers Union*? This page will help you decide by offering Soul biography, Soul discography, Soul photography, and more. ✓**INTERNET** →*url* http://www.crown.net/~wirtes/sa/soulasylum.html

Soul Asylum Sony's official site for the band includes tour info, photos, and press releases on *Grave Dancers Union* and *Let Your Dim Light Shine.* ✓**INTERNET**→*url* http://www.music.sony.com/Music/ArtistInfo/SoulAsylum.html

Soul Asylum Chat Message-based discussion. ✓**AMERICA ONLINE** ...→*keyword* mtv→Message Boards→Bands That Do Suck→Soul Asylum rules ...→*keyword* mmc→Rock/Pop→General Rock→Soul Asylum

Sonic Youth—from http://moon.st.rim.or.jp:1969/band/sonicyouth/sygrf.html

SOUNDGARDEN

alt.music.soundgarden (ng) Chris Cornell doesn't like Michael Jackson. In fact, in a recent interview with the British music press, Cornell launched an obscenity-filled tirade against the King of Pop: "That f***ing guy makes me wanna puke! Sending a statue of himself on tour! What the f*** is that all about? What a f***ing jerk. He's got way, way, way too much f***ing money. "You know how much his piece of shit record is selling for? Fifty f***ing bucks! "You know what I hope? I hope he's buggering Lisa Marie. That's what I f***ing hope. And I'll bet you he is f***ing buggering her too. Shit, that asshole. Elvis must be rolling in his grave. F***er!" Soundgarden fans are split on their idol's loss of self-control, with some supporting his vitriol ("Michael Jackson is a total toss. And Chris Cornell is about a hundred times better than Michael Jackson would ever even dream of being") and others defending MJ ("Why can't Soundgarden and Michael Jackson just stay in their separate corners. It's not as though they're competing directly for market share or anything"). In addition to reviewing the Cornell-Jackson bout, fans of the Northwest's answer to Led Zep talk about concerts, bootlegs, and sound-alike bands like Brother Cane. ✓**USENET**→alt.music.soundgarden

Soundgarden A nicely designed guide to the habits and hobbies of the daddies of grunge. ✓**INTERNET**→ *url* http://web.mit.edu/afs/ athena/user/s/a/saperl/www/ somms/soundgarden.html

Soundgarden Chat Message-based discussion. ✓**AMERICA ONLINE** ...→*keyword* mmc→Alternative Rock→Bands M-Z→Soundgarden ...→*keyword* rockline→MODERN

ROCK LIVE→Bush & Soundgarden

SOUTHSIDE JOHNNY

Southside Johnny Homepage An introduction to the band, upcoming tour dates included. ✓**INTERNET**→*url* http://pease1. sr.unh.edu/1/southside/

Southside Johnny Mailing List (ml) The best Springsteeen albums of the eighties may not have been recorded by Springsteen, at least as far as fans of Southside Johnny and the Asbury Jukes are concerned. Talk to other Hearts of Stone here. ✓**INTERNET**→ *email* southside-request@ici.net ✍ *Type in subject line:* subscribe *Type in message body:* <your email address>

SPIN DOCTORS

Spin Doctors Sony's official site includes information for *Turn It*

Upside Down and *Homebelly Groove*, along with a wealth of sound and video clips. ✓**INTERNET** →*url* http://www.music.sony.com/ Music/ArtistInfo/SpinDoctors.html

The Spin Doctors' House Prescription: boogie. The band's official site brings insights and good tidings directly from the doctors. ✓**INTERNET**→*url* http://levity. willow.com/spindoctors/index.html

Spin Doctors List (ml) If you thought "Cleopatra's Cat" was an underrated masterpiece, then this is the mailing list for you. ✓**INTERNET**→*email* spins-request@world. std.com ✍ *Write a request*

SPINAL TAP

alt.fan.spinal-tap (ng) Hello, Cleveland! Everyone wants the longest possible version of Spinal

This is Spinal Tap—from http://rhino.harvard.edu/elwin/SpinalTap/home.html

(cont'd pg. 190) →

R.E.M.

If you had dared compare R.E.M. with the Beatles ten years ago, you would have been
laughed out of Liverpool. But today the parallels seem almost self-evident. What other bands have lasted for so long as a unit without sacrificing even an iota of their artistic independence? Behind the poetic lyrics of Michael Stipe—even when they were unintelligible, they were poetry, dammit!—the rest of the band has ranged over the whole of American rock, and this delicate balance (Stipecult on the one hand, compelling rock music on the other) has served R.E.M. well. Find out what's up next for Athens' finest at **Take a Break Surfer 8, Yaurs,** and **alt.music.rem.** Decipher Stipe at **R.E.M. Lyrics.** And then boost Mike Mills's ego by visiting **OICM3H.**

A little night swimming—from http://www.halcyon.com/rem/gif/

On the Net

Across the board

R.E.M. How did a modest Georgia rock quartet become the band most likely to capture the zeitgeist of nineties America? Pick up some clues at this Website, which includes a full list of R.E.M. albums, tour dates, reports on Bill Berry's aneurysm, and a special promotional page for the Automatic Box. ✓**INTERNET**→*url* http://www.wfu.edu/~david/rem/

R.E.M. "R.E.M. is part lies, part heart, part truth, and part garbage," said Peter Buck, although he tactfully neglected to mention which part of the band is garbage. This page contains guitar tabs, lyrics, a list of boots and tapes, and even bass tablature. ✓**INTERNET**→*url* http://www.gtlug.org/~dgoodman/rem.html

R.E.M. AOL's site is sponsored by Warner Records, which uses R.E.M. as a testing ground for multimedia press kits and other innovative variations on publicity staples. ✓**AMERICA ONLINE**→*keyword* warner→Alternative→R.E.M.

R.E.M. Home Page A biography, lyrics, chords, reviews of al-

Stipe and friends—from http://sashimi. wwa.com/hammers/pictures/

bums and tours, and links. ✓**IN-TERNET**→*url* http://www.eeng. dcu.ie/~rohanlon/rem.htm

R.E.M.—Monster Warner's official site for the *Monster* album, which links to a track list and press release. ✓**INTERNET**→*url* http://www.iuma.com/Warner/ html/R.E.M..html

R.E.M. Stuff A bootleg show list, images of the band, and a link to the tour-review database. ✓**INTER-NET**→*url* http://www.cs.oberlin. edu:80/students/spostel/remstuff. html

Take a Break Surfer 8 With a name taken from R.E.M.'s most puzzling, disorganized, and rewarding album—that's *Fables of the Reconstruction*, and it's fact, not opinion—this page contains lyrics, a discography, and images of the band, along with fancy graphics. ✓**INTERNET**→*url* http://www. powertech.no/~baarde/rem.htm

Talk About the Passion Everything you always wanted to know about R.E.M. and weren't particu-larly afraid to ask, including lyrics, chords, images, sound clips, bios, and a collection of R.E.M. FAQs. ✓**INTERNET**→*url* http://www.s-gimb.lj.edus.si/peter/rem/rem.html

UK R.E.M. Page Brits like R.E.M. as well, and they share concern for Bill Berry's health, an interest in Michael Stipe's visage, and a penchant for collecting articles, chords, images, and sound clips. ✓**INTERNET**→*url* http://http2. brunel.ac.uk:8080/~cs94smp/rem page.htm

Yaurs The cover photo of *Monster* graces this page, which also includes band .GIFs, sound clips, excerpts from videos, and even an FAQ which attempts to wade through the obscurity of the song's meanings. ✓**INTERNET**→*url* http:// miso.wwa.com:80/~liko/

Boots

R.E.M. Rare Tape Server A comprehensive resource for the R.E.M. tape collector, with a bootleg discography, a message board for would-be traders, and an explanation of the page's trading policy. ✓**INTERNET**→*url* http://www. svs.com/users/zim/remstuff.html

R.E.M. Recordings Available A list of R.E.M. bootlegs, along with the email addresses of the tape owners. ✓**INTERNET**→*url* http://www.webcom.com/~josh brow/remboot.html

Chat

alt.music.rem/rec.music.rem (ng) The *Monster* world tour was all the rage in the summer of 1995, and fans have lots of tapes to trade, news about set lists, and updates on the condition of Bill Berry (he looks fine) and Mike Mills (he's getting around just fine, thanks). In addition, Net R.E.M. fans like to try to trump each others' liberalism and advertise their own fan clubs. And there are even the occasional detractors ("Michael Stipe is a terrible singer and I'm not afraid to say it!"). ✓**USENET** ...→alt.music.rem ...→rec. music.rem

R.E.M. Chat Message-based discussion that proves that the Athens foursome has become one

At The Rat in Boston in the mid-eighties—from http://www.halcyon.com/rem/gif/

Skinny attention-hog Michael Stipe—http://www.halcyon.com/rem/gif/

of the most popular—and consequently one of the most inessential—bands on the planet. ✓**AMERICA ONLINE** ...→*keyword* mmc→Alternative Rock→Bands M-Z→R.E.M. Fanclub ...→*keyword* mtv→Message Boards→Bands That Do Suck→R.E.M. ✓**EWORLD**→*go* eaz →Pump Up the Volume→Music Talk→R.E.M. ✓**AMERICA ONLINE**→*keyword* mtv→Message Boards→Bands That Don't Suck→R.E.M. tour ✓**COMPUSERVE**→*go* fanclub .→Messages *and* Libraries→R.E.M.

Lyrics and chords

R.E.M. Chord Archive Guitar tabs and bass tabs for all of R.E.M.'s officially released songs. ✓**INTERNET**→*url* http://comp.uark. edu/~cbray/rem/rem.html

R.E.M. Lyrics Lyrics from all the band's albums, including early, unreleased material and outtakes that have turned up on soundtracks and compilation albums. ✓**INTERNET**→*url* http://www.sys.uea.ac. uk/~u9333975/rem_lyrics.html

Pictures

R.E.M. An extensive picture archive of Stipe, Buck, Berry, Mills, and friends, along with lyrics to all R.E.M. songs and links to related pages. ✓**INTERNET**→*url* http://www.bath.ac.uk/~ma4pwb /rem/home.htm

R.E.M. Pictures Pictures of the band, most of them dominated by skinny attention-hog Michael Stipe. Stipe looking like a leprechaun. Stipe looking like a Buddha. Stipe remembering Andy Kaufman. Stipe losing his religion. And all the while, three other guys hanging in the background, thinking quietly about the next indelible melody they can write to extend Stipe's conspicuous celebrity. Hardly seems fair, don't you think? ✓**INTERNET**→*url* http://sashimi. wwa.com/hammers/pictures/rem. htm

Tours

Monster Tour Reviews Culled from rec.music.rem posts, these reviews of the *Monster* tour furnish set lists and impressions, including accounts of between-song chatter. ✓**INTERNET**→*url* http://fas-www. harvard.edu/~jsage/remenu.html

Unofficial R.E.M. Tour Page Dates and reviews of the illness-plagued 1995 tour (which fans have dubbed The Aneurysm Tour, the Scalpel Tour, or the Monster Medical Bill Tour). ✓**INTERNET**→*url* http://www.gla.ac.uk/Clubs/Web Soc/members/9402198d/rem/ index.html

Mike Mills

OICM3H Some people liked John. Some people liked Paul. Some people liked George. And some people liked Ringo (but not many). The same goes for R.E.M., whose glamour twins (Stipe and Buck) draw most of the ink while the battery (Mills and Berry) languishes in obscurity. And that's why the world needs more organizations like OICM3H, the Organization Intended to Catapult Mike Mills into Musical History. Will it work? Not unless you and all your friends join up. The page also includes pictures of Mills, essays on his bass technique, and links to more R.E.M. sites. ✓**INTERNET**→*url* http://www.csua. berkeley.edu/~briank/

Stipe, bald, with a clever t-shirt—from http://www.powertech.no/~baarde/files/

R.E.M.

"So I'm at our high school dance Friday night and the teachers informed us after one song that moshing or slam dancing as they called it, was no longer allowed. In fact, jumping up and down was no longer allowed. They eventually got fed up with us and declared that alternative music was not allowed. Fine. So I went to the DJs to suggest some songs—rock and roll, I thought—and I was told that REM was alternative music. Where the heck is the line? They played dance music the rest of the night, just annoying the heck out of us. But I really don't understand when REM, the Hip, U2, etc., etc., etc., all became alternative. Help a poor, ignorant teenager learn. Teach me the ways of sorting songs."

—from **rec.music.rem**

"Bill Berry is my mom's cousin, and since I am the world's most devoted REManiac, I got backstage passes… I had met Bill twice before, but hadn't met the other guys or even been to a concert…Bill and I talked about the tour and how concerned the family was for him. He told me that he could have died, which I knew, but it was so much scarier to hear it from Bill himself. Suddenly I saw Michael emerging from behind the fence. He was wearing a cap, shades, yellow t-shirt, linen shorts, and flipflops. A group of women (grrrrr…they were horrible) were being introduced to him and they giggled for awhile. When the women dispersed, I introduced myself. He said he liked my necklace!… Though I was quite calm, everything I planned to discuss with Michael escaped me at the moment. By the time I met with my other friends in 9th row, center, I was shaking and crying!"

—from **R.E.M. Chat** on CompuServe's Fanclub Forum

"Sometimes I call him 'Michael Stipe' and other times I call him simply 'Michael' or 'Stipe.' At times I get the urge to call him 'Stipey.' I usually call him 'God.'"

—from **R.E.M. Chat** on America Online's Music Message Center

Tap, which is either the three-hour laserdisc version or the four-hour videocassette bootleg circulating through fan communities. So what is that, 50 hours? When fans aren't looking to collect Tap, they're comparing jokes—and there are hundreds of them, from "Oh, we've got a bigger dressing room than the puppets? Oh, that's refreshing" to "If you keep folding it, it keeps breaking." ✓**USENET**→ alt.fan.spinal-tap

Smell the Glove Adorned with a picture of the alternate *Smell the Glove* album cover—"there is something about this, that's that's so black, it's like, 'How much more black could this be?'"—this page links to the Tap FAQ, complete credits for the film, and even the full Spinal Tap script. ✓**INTER-NET**→*url* http://www.cs.rochester. edu/u/ferguson/spinal-tap/

Spinal Tap Home Page An informative Tap guide, with quotes, lyrics, images, and more. How much of it is true? Follow the philosophy of David St. Hubbins: "I believe virtually everything I read, and I think that is what makes me more of a selective human than someone who doesn't believe anything." ✓**INTERNET**→*url* http:// rhino.harvard.edu/elwin/ SpinalTap/home.html

Spinal Tap Script Relive the magic, the drama, and the tears with these hypertext and text versions of the script. And remember, "You don't do heavy metal in doubly." ✓**INTERNET** ...→*url* http:// ulke.hiMolde.no/~sveini/overvw.ht ml ...→*url* http://ulke.hiMolde. no/~sveini/wholescript.txt

Tappus Norwegicus A Scandinavian Tap site that includes lyrics, images, video information, and the complete movie script. ✓**INTER-**

NET→*url* http://ulke.hiMolde.no/~ sveini/menu.html

SPRINGSTEEN, BRUCE

Asbury Park Discographies, images, and the like, but bring your passport and your Scandinavian accent: the site is based in Sweden. ✓**INTERNET**→*url* http://www. everyday.se/~coc/engmats.html

#bruce Chat about the Boss and rumors of upcoming projects. ✓**INTERNET**→*irc* #bruce

Bruce Springsteen A vast collection of Springsteen rumors, essays, and informational files. ✓**IN-TERNET**→*url* http://e-street.eastlib. ufl.edu/bruce.html

Bruce Springsteen Chat Message-based discussion. ✓**AMERICA ONLINE**→*keyword* mmc→Rock/ Pop→Rock Artists M-Z→Bruce Springsteen ✓**EWORLD**→*go* eaz→ Pump Up The Volume→Music Talk→Springsteen

Bruce Springsteen Home Page A scan of the *Bruce Springsteen Greatest Hits* CD, along with lyrics and tour information. ✓**IN-TERNET**→*url* http://www.stpt. usf.edu/~greek/bruce.html

Bruce Springsteen Photos A trio of concert pictures, accompanied by brief essays. ✓**INTERNET**→ *url* http://sashimi.wwa.com/ hammers/pictures/bruce.htm

The First Unofficial Dutch Springsteen Home Page Just think of the excitement in the air at the unveiling of the First Unofficial Dutch Springsteen Home Page. The fine citizens of Dutchland—or wherever it is that the Dutch live—probably couldn't contain themselves. They probably spilled their beers in joy, maybe getting a kangaroo or koala bear

wet in the process. Oh, the joy in Dutchland is too much to even contemplate—thousands of men, women, and children in funny hats and shoes, arms locked, faces beaming, lips moving to the strains of "Darlington County." Get audio and MIDI files here in addition to more standard Bruce fare. ✓**INTERNET**→*url* http://huizen. dds.nl/~tgwb/

Lars Petter's Bruce Home Page Links to other sites and bootleg info on the Boss. ✓**INTER-NET**→*url* http://www.vestnett. no/~zuma/bruce.html

Lucky Town Information about the Lucky Town mailing list, chords, pictures, the Springsteen FAQ, a discography, lyrics, and more. All in all, one of the most comprehensive Springsteen pages in Cyberspace. ✓**INTERNET**→*url* http://www.mcs.net/~kvk/ luckytown.html

Lucky Town (ml) Talk about early Bruce, late Bruce, Julianne-era Bruce, Patti-era Bruce, and more. ✓**INTERNET**→*email* luckytown-request@netcom.com ✍ *Type in message body:* subscribe luckytown

rec.music.artists.springsteen (ng) Is Patti Scialfa just another rock wife who is riding the coat tails of her ultratalented husband? Steve doesn't think so. He offers a five-point white paper on why Patti's debut LP, *Rumble Doll*, is one of the best rock releases of the last five years, and even defends Patti for libidinal reasons. "Patti adds sexual energy. Some female posters have noted an extremely sexual experience at Springsteen concerts (bordering on orgasmic), and focused on Bruce. They have pitied us poor heterosexual males for missing this component of Springsteen concerts. (While Miami

Hot Rod—from http://www.iii.net/ users/bourbeau/rodfoto.html

Steve acts sexy, he just doesn't do it for me.) I find Patti attractive—after all, she is a Red-Headed Woman, and a Jersey Girl. Patti provides me with a catalyst for me to enjoy the Springsteen sexual energy. For a good example of Patti adding sexual energy to a song watch the 'Tougher Than The Rest' video." Speculate on new Springsteen recordings, trade old live bootlegs, marvel at the duet between Bruce and Dylan at the opening ceremonies for the Rock-and-Roll Hall of Fame, and act as Bossy as you want. ✓**USENET**→rec. music.artists.springsteen

STEELY DAN

Steely Dan List (ml) Talk about Walter, Donald, and their considerable jazz-pop achievements. ✓**INTERNET**→*email* steely-dan-request@ uiuc.edu ✍ *Type in message body:* subscribe

Steely Dan's Steely Fans A network for online fans that offers lyrics, images, band bios, tour information, and more. ✓**INTERNET**→ *url* http://itchy.hrfs.uiuc.edu/ dandom.html

Under the Banyan Trees An adequate site for the best non-band in the world. Links to Fagen

and Becker's lyrics, images and sound clips, FAQ, and maybe someday some touring info—although the next time these guys tour humans will be living on Mars, or underwater, or under a Democratic Congress. ✓**INTERNET**→ *url* http://www.seanet.com/Users/ stalfnzo/steeldan.html

STEWART, ROD

Rod Stewart Commemorating Rod's 1994 induction into the Rock and Roll Hall of Fame, this page includes a brief career biography and sound clips. ✓**INTERNET**→ *url* http://www.rockhall.com/ induct/stewrod.html

Rod Stewart/Storyteller Frequently Asked Questions about Rod, a discography, a photo album, and more. ✓**INTERNET**→*url* http://www.iii.net/users/bourbeau /story.html

Storyteller (ml) On Rod's very first albums, he interpreted the songs of others with sensitivity, power, and humor. Under the guidance of a young producer named Lou Reizner, he stood poised to become the next folk-rock superstar. Talk about the beginnings of Rod's career (as well as what's happened since) here. ✓**INTERNET**→*url* rodfans@kbourbeau. kenmoto1.sai.com

STING

Fields of Gold Links to lyrics, discography, bio history, guitar/ bass tabs, sound clips, tour info, lots of beautiful images, fanclubs, FAQs, and other Sting/Police sites. Every little thing he does is magic. ✓**INTERNET**→*url* http://www.rrz. uni-koeln.de/wiso-fak/ wisostat-sem/autoren/sting/index.html

The Soul Pages Poetry, proselytizing, and pretention abound, and Sting fans wouldn't have it

any other way. If you can maneuver your way around the ex-cop's spiky haircut, you can find your way to lyrics, a discography, images, sound clips, newsgroup chat, and more. ✓**INTERNET**→*url* http:// indy6.cpedu.rug.nl:8084/sting.html

Sting Work the black seam by visiting this page, which includes lyrics, a discography, images, and more. ✓**INTERNET**→*url* http:// morpheus.resnet.cornell.edu/sting/ sting.htm

Sting A damned impressive site with medieval icons that link to merchandise, sound-clip interviews, a book of illustrated lyrics, tour and new release information, and a preview of a new Sting CD-ROM. As Mr. Sumner himself says, "if you want egomania, bad taste and general insanity, you've come to the right place." ✓**INTERNET**→*url* http://underground. net/Rocktropolis/Sting/

STONE ROSES

alt.music.stone-roses (ng) A disorganized group, with an uncomfortable mix of Stone Roses faithful and clueless newbies. But nestled among the basic-information posts and secret handshakes, there is a decent amount of information about upcoming projects and concert dates. ✓**USENET**→ alt.music.stone-roses

The Stone Roses A history of the band, a complete discography, lyrics, pictures, articles, guitar tabs, merchandise, tour notes, and more. ✓**INTERNET**→*url* http://www. umr.edu/~mquinn/music/stone.r oses/sr001.html

The Stone Roses A discography, lyrics, album covers, rumors, and more. ✓**INTERNET**→*url* http://www. best.com/~thompson/roses/

Stone Temple Pilots **Artist Guide**

Stone Roses Chat Message-based discussion. ✓**AMERICA ON-LINE**→*keyword* mmc→Alternative Rock→Bands M-Z→STONE ROS-ES!!

Stone Roses List (ml) Get the first word on the second coming here. ✓**INTERNET**→*email* majordomo@best.com ✍ *Type in message body:* subscribe roses-list <your email address>

The Stone Roses Page With options for either graphical browsers or lynx users, this page includes a wealth of information about the band—a bio, a discography, guitar tabs, pictures, lyrics, and links. ✓**INTERNET**→*url* http://www.cm.cf.ac.uk/User/J.R.Candy/roses.html

The World of The Stone Roses The Official Geffen site for the band, with a discography, a bio, and samples from "Love Spreads," "Ten Storey Love Song," and "Driving South." ✓**INTERNET**→*url* http://geffen.com/sroses.html

STONE TEMPLE PILOTS
alt.music.stone-temple (ng)

Weiland got busted, got sent to a rehab center, and now he's out, working on a side project for the Magnificent Bastards. So where does that leave Stone Temple Pilots? Subscribers to this newsgroup aren't too sure, and the uncertainty is giving them a bad case of the jitters. And then there's the issue of the off-topic posts, which range from impromptu reviews of Windows 95 to complaints about the gender ratio of the group. Well, all this shifting and slipping has got one STP fan in a funk, and he's not afraid to tell the world about it: "Okay, being a HUGE STP fan, I found out about this section here, for STP Fans. Great, yeah, but what the f*** is the deal with some of this crap i'm reading? Windows '95? 'Is their, like, uh, any women out there, cuz i'm like, uh, ya know...' Give me a friggin break. This is about the STONE TEMPLE PILOTS, which RULE! ...I understand that it was a year ago *Purple* came out, and I can wait a while for a new album because I am sure that they need some rest, I just want a confirmation that everything is okay, and that their will be a new album

someday. I also read a message by someone saying STP's worst song is 'Pretty Penny.' Well I don't agree. I think their worst song is... well, sorry, but they don't have a bad song. I guess that's why I think they rule. But back to the problems STP seems to be having. I think that if all us STP fans get together here and support them, I think that alone can help the future of the band just by showing them we do support them." Love—it's a wonderful thing. ✓**USENET**→alt.music.stone-temple

Stone Temple Pilots Links to album info, images, and more. ✓**INTERNET**→*url* http://thoth.stetson.edu/music/pilots/index.html

Stone Temple Pilots Chat Message-based discussion. ✓**AMERICA ONLINE**→*keyword* mmc→Alternative Rock→Bands M-Z→Stone Temple Pilots

Stone Temple Pilots—Rock N' Roll BABY!!! They outlived their "rip-off of Pearl-Jam" phase, and are now heavy hitters in the world of call-us-pop-and-we'll-punch-you alternarock. This site features links to bios, album info, articles, images, and even STP FTP sites. ✓**INTERNET**→*url* http://gpu.srv.ualberta.ca/~vchan/stp.html

STYX
Styx List (ml) These days, Dennis De Young is well into a second career as a lead singer in rock operas, particularly *Joseph and the Amazing Technicolor Dreamcoat.* What are the other members of Styx doing? Probably reading the mailing list, dreaming of past glory, and feeling the big tears slide down their faces to the tune of "Renegade." ✓**INTERNET**→*email* majordomo@world.std.com ✍ *Type in message body:* subscribe styx <your email address>

Stone Temple Pilots—from http://gpu.srv.ualberta.ca/~vchan/pictures.html

Bob Mould of Sugar—http://math. montana.edu/~sanford/sugar.html

SUGAR

Sugar Fans of Bob Mould will flip their wigs for this extensive site, which features links to interviews, an FAQ, images, sound clips, lyrics, discographies, tabs, liner notes, album covers, and links to other fan pages. ✓**INTERNET**→*url* http://math.montana.edu/~sanford/sugar.html

Sugar Goodies Bob Mould may not be the most optimistic rocker on the planet, but he may be one of the most consistently excellent. Get more Sugar in your diet by visiting this site, which includes lyrics, a discography, images, and more. ✓**INTERNET**→*url* http://futon.sfsu.edu/~cbrooks/Bob.html

Sugar List (ml) Borrow a cup of Sugar from your cyberneighbors on this mailing list. ✓**INTERNET**→*email* majordomo@csua.berkeley, edu ✍ *Type in message body:* subscribe sugar <your email address>

SUNDAYS, THE

Sundays Chat Message-based discussion. ✓**EWORLD**→*go* eaz→ Pump Up The Volume→Music Talk→ The SUNDAYS

Sundays List (ml) Someone once said that every day is Sunday, and the diehard fans who subscribe to this mailing list turn that aphorism into a truth so bright it could blind a man at 50 paces. ✓**INTERNET**→*url* arithmetic-request@ uclink.berkeley.edu ✍ *Type in message body:* subscribe

SWEET, MATTHEW

Inside (ml) Go Inside today's premier purveyor of power-pop, and try to find out why you're sick of yourself. ✓**INTERNET**→*url* matthew-sweet-request@acca.nmsu.edu ✍ *Type in message body:* subscribe <your email address>

Matthew Sweet Virtually unreadable as a result of the tessellated *Altered Beast* logos behind the type, this page includes song lyrics and links. ✓**INTERNET**→*url* http://comp.uark.edu/~cbray/sweet/sweet.html

The Matthew Sweet Mini-Page Why mini? Well, it's more a self-image problem than anything—this page has plenty of photos, an FAQ, and a complete discography. ✓**INTERNET**→*url* http://gellersen.valpo.edu/~pmilliga/delirium/sweet/sweet.html

SuPeRdEfOrMeD (Matthew Sweet) If your ex-girlfriend used to sing you to sleep with "Someone to Pull the Trigger," and you miss her, and you fear that you'll never meet someone like her—kind eyes, talent, the scent of tea roses, and a laugh that comes to you like wind over a wheatfield—then you should drown your sorrows at this site, which contains a Matthew Sweet FAQ, tour dates, a discography, lyrics, articles, and more. ✓**INTERNET**→*url* http://www.xnet.com/~wakemich/msweet.shtml

T

TALKING HEADS

David Byrne The full text of an interview with Byrne and Jonathan Demme in which the former head Head quotes a little Gertrude Stein. The site also includes information on his recent albums and videos. ✓**AMERICA ON-LINE**→*keyword* warner→alternative →David Byrne

Talking Heads Follow David Byrne, Tina Weymouth, Chris Frantz, and Jerry Harrison from tiny New York pit-clubs to superstardom, all the while retaining innovation and integrity. This site features links to images, sound clips, interviews, video/discographies, and more. ✓**INTERNET**→*url* http://www.bart.nl/~francey/th.html

Talking Heads Avant-pop at its very best, the Talking Heads blazed through the college music

Matthew Sweet—http://gellersen.valpo.edu/~pmilliga/delirium/sweet/sweet.html

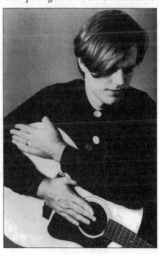

(cont'd pg. 197) →

The Rolling Stones

From the earliest days of the British Invasion, when they brought a new kind of strut

to blues, soul, and rock and roll, the Rolling Stones were the darker, crueler, riskier, and sexier counterparts of the Beatles. Mick Jagger (rhymes with swagger) pouted his oversized lips; Keith Richards (rhymes with heroin) spun out riff after riff; and bassist Bill Wyman and drummer Charlie Watts kept idiosyncratic time on classics such as "Satisfaction" and "Jumping Jack Flash." The band's raw power only increased with the addition of guitarist Mick Taylor, who helped propel albums like *Exile on Main Street* into the rock pantheon. Today, the Stones are more a corporation than a band (Gimme Tax Shelter?), but try telling that to the fans at **Completely Stoned** and other sites.

The Rolling Stones now!—http://camel.conncoll.edu/ccother/sf.folder/exile/exile.html

On the Net

Across the board

Completely Stoned Adorned with spiky tongue icons, this page offers pictures, sounds, band information, tour dates, and a link to the Rolling Stones newsgroup. You can always get what you want. ✓**INTERNET**→*url* http://www.leo.org/~tromsdor/stones.html

Exile on Main Street The author of this page wasn't even aware of the Stones' music until he heard *Steel Wheels* in 1989. But in the six years since then, he's grown up, memorized quotes from Mick and Keith, bought a few more albums—in fact, become a veritable Stones addict. With an essay on the Stones' career that links to dozens of hypertext lyrics, this page offers a good introduction to the band's music, as well as pages on the main band members and a list of Stones bootlegs. ✓**INTERNET**→ *url* http://camel.conncoll.edu/ccother/sf.folder/exile/exile.html

My Humble Rolling Stones Page Created after the release of the Grammy-winning *Voodoo Lounge* LP, this page includes lyrics, links, images, a band bio, and more. ✓**INTERNET**→*url* http://www.cen.uiuc.edu/~mc9279/stones.html

The Rolling Stones Commemorating the band's 1989 induction into the Rock and Roll Hall of Fame, this page includes a brief biography and sound clips. ✓**INTERNET**→*url* http://www.rockhall.com/induct/rollings.html

Rolling Stones FAQ Who is Nanker Phelps? Who are the Glimmer Twins? How many times have the Stones been arrested? How many times have they been married? Will the band break up? Are they going to tour? Do you think this is the last time, really? And how old are they, anyway? Get the Stones questions and the Stones answers here. ✓**INTERNET**→*url* http://www.cis.ohio-state.edu/hypertext/faq/usenet/music/rollingstones-faq/top.html

Rolling Stones Live at the Max Promotional materials for the video release of the giant-format Stones concert movie. Does the videocassette format, designed as it is for home screens, destroy the point of IMAX? Probably. But this is the Stones, damnit! The Stones! ✓**INTERNET**→*url* http://www.polygram.com/polygram/StoneVid.html

Rolling Stones Web Site The Stones have their own site. That's power. Too bad it's not more substantial—the cheesy fan fiction, the overblown cyber-events, and the shortage of actual information make this the electronic equivalent of a nineties Stones LP. ✓**INTERNET**→*url* http://www.stones.com/

Undercover A daily digest of Stones news, cross-posted to the alt.rock-n-roll.stones newsgroup, that lets you get sick of Mick on a regular basis. The Website includes information on tour dates, upcoming projects, and more. ✓**INTERNET**→ *email* undercover-request @tempest.cis.uoguelph.ca ✍ *Write a request Info:* ✓**INTERNET** →*url* http://cvi.hahnemann.edu/undercover

Chat

alt.rock-n-roll.stones (ng) We all know Mick and Keith and Bill and Charlie, but what about the other Stones? When was Brian in the band? Is it really true that he was murdered by pool repairmen? How long did Mick Taylor stick around, and why were the albums the band made with him so good? How can Ron Wood expect us to take him seriously when he insists on being a cut-rate Keith? Why wasn't Ry Cooder given full membership into the band? And why are the solo albums being recorded these days worlds better than the band product? ✓**USENET**→ alt.rock-n-roll.stones

Rolling Stones Chat Message-based discussion. ✓**AMERICA ONLINE**→ *keyword* mmc→Rock/Pop Rock→Artists M-Z→The Rolling Stones

Mick Taylor

Mick Taylor/Rolling Stones Websource Mick Taylor stares at you in blue, red, and yellow from this dedicatory Website, which opens with perhaps the only poem ever written in tribute to the Stones guitarist: "The yellow labels spun around, the little red tongue wagged out / Mick Taylor played the blues, and our world has never been the same / seems like 100 Years Ago, but he's still playing / track him down, give him a listen / The Vibrato still Cries." With an annotated Stones/Taylor discography—that's *Let It Bleed, Get Your Ya-Ya's Out, Sticky Fingers, Exile on Main Street, Goat's Head Soup,* and *It's Only Rock and Roll (And I Like It),* in case you thought that the Stones started rolling with *Voodoo Lounge*—information on how to order a limted-edition release of Mick's recent live LP *Coasting Home,* and even a live chat link, this page lets Stones fans tap into the bluesiest incarnation of the band. ✓**INTERNET**→*url* http://www.webcom.com/~garnet/m_taylor/

Exile on Main Street—*http://camel.conncoll.edu/ccother/sf.folder/exile/eoms/*

Rolling Stones

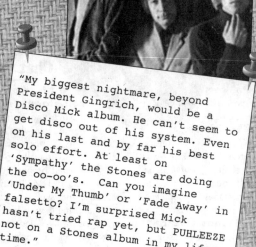

"I believe one of Keith's best songwriting efforts of the last five or so years is the song 'Tanquery' off of Johnny Johnson's album Johnie Be Bad. If someone can listen to that song and not enjoy it, they are as good as dead. The song is that good. I was thinking that I would like to see the Stones re-work one of their old songs for the live/new studio album. Something like Eric Clapton did with 'Layla' on the Unplugged CD. How about 'Start Me Up' in a reggae mode like it was first written and recorded?"

—from **Rolling Stones Chat** on America Online's Music Message Center

"My biggest nightmare, beyond President Gingrich, would be a Disco Mick album. He can't seem to get disco out of his system. Even on his last and by far his best solo effort. At least on 'Sympathy' the Stones are doing the oo-oo's. Can you imagine 'Under My Thumb' or 'Fade Away' in falsetto? I'm surprised Mick hasn't tried rap yet, but PUHLEEZE not on a Stones album in my lifetime."

—from **Rolling Stones Chat** on America Online's Music Message Center

"The woman that I will soon marry is Beatle crazy, she even goes over to Liverpool every other year. I wish I could make her understand that the Stones are far better then the Beatles ever wished they could be. This is not to say that the Beatles were not a good band, because they were. But let's face it while the Beatles were playing 'I Want to Hold Your Hand,' The Stones were playing 'Let's Spend the Night Together.'"

—from **alt.rock-n-roll.stones**

Talking Heads—from http://www.bart.nl/~francey/th.html

scene of the late seventies and early eighties, only to break up just as their music got its second wind. This site features links to a Heads FAQ, articles, surveys, a discography, polls, images, FTP sites, mailing lists, and more. ✓**INTERNET**→*url* http://penguin.cc.ukans.edu/Heads/Talking_Heads.html

Talking Heads List (ml) David Byrne has a solo career, and the other Heads continue to perform with their occasional side projects (Casual Gods, Tom Tom Club). Get the latest on the RISD sensations by subscribing to this mailing list. ✓**INTERNET**→*email* listproc@ukanaix.cc.ukans.edu ✍ *Type in message body:* subscribe talking-heads <your full name>

TAYLOR, JAMES

alt.music.james-taylor (ng) Talk about JT, plus talk about JT-related topics—Martha's Vineyard, Carly Simon, and traffic jams. ✓**USENET**→alt.music.james-taylor

James Taylor Official Sony information for the *Best of James Taylor* LP. ✓**INTERNET**→*url* http://www.music.sony.com/Music/ArtistInfo/JamesTaylor.html

James Taylor Chat Message-based discussion. ✓**AMERICA ONLINE**→*keyword* mmc→Rock/Pop→

Rock Artists M-Z→James Taylor

James Taylor Online James' perfect melding of soothing guitar and throw-yourself-off-a-bridge lyrics will leave you smiling through your tears. This fan page has lyrics, tabs, articles, discographies, sound clips, an FAQ, email, and links to sites devoted to other folk-rock stalwarts. ✓**INTERNET**→*url* http://www.shore.net/~jrisberg/JT.html

TEARS FOR FEARS

Tears for Fears Chat Message-based discussion. ✓**AMERICA ONLINE**→*keyword* mmc→Alternative Rock→Bands M-Z→Tears For Fears

Tears for Fears List Did "Everybody Wants to Rule the World" nick part of its melody from the Beach Boys' *Pet Sounds*? Will Tears for Fears ever regain the popularity they had when they were sitting in the Big Chair? Compare notes with other TfF fans. ✓**INTERNET**→*email* tears4-fears-request@ms.uky.edu ✍ *Write a request*

10,000 MANIACS

10,000 Maniacs List (ml) Natalie Merchant has gone solo, which means that the Maniacs are no more. But they live on in the hearts and souls of college women everywhere, and their finest musical moments—from "Candy Everybody Wants" to the now-deleted "Peace Train"—are frequently revived as topics of discussion on this mailing list. ✓**INTERNET**→*email* majordomo@egr.uri.edu ✍ *Type in message body:* subscribe 10k_maniacs <your email address>

10,000 Maniacs/N.Merchant Chat Message-based discussion. ✓**AMERICA ONLINE**→*keyword* mmc→Alternative Rock→Bands M-Z→10,000 Maniacs/N.Merchant

THE THE

The The Chat Message-based discussion. ✓**AMERICA ONLINE**→*keyword* mmc→Alternative Rock→Bands M-Z→The The

The The List (ml) Matt Johnson is all The The there is, and these days he's talking about a series of concept albums devoted to the finest songwriters in the history of popular music. He's already recorded a Hank Williams tribute, and rumor has it that there may be albums on the way toasting Noel Coward, Brian Wilson, and Julian Cope. ✓**INTERNET**→*email* thethexxx@aol.com ✍ *Write a request*

THEY MIGHT BE GIANTS

alt.music.tmbg (ng) Ana Ng doesn't post, but lots of other TMBG fans do, arguing about "Istanbul (Not Constantinople)," Flansburgh, Linnell, and any other Johns who happen to wander into the line of fire. The crowd is collegiate, literate, and borderline obsessive-compulsive. ✓**USENET**→alt.music.tmbg

Discography A complete list of singles and album releases for They Might Be Giants. ✓**INTERNET**→*url* ftp://net.bio.net/pub/misc/music/they.might.be.giants

The Might Be Giants List (ml) Talk about John. Then talk about John. Then talk about John and John. It gets easier, doesn't it? ✓**INTERNET**→*email* majordomo@super.org ✍ *Write a request*

They Might Be Giants News, a discography, links, and even a dial-a-song online service that includes the rare recording "Mario" ("In this rare spoken word recording the shadowy figure known only as Mario tells his version of the story behind the Giants' phenomenal success"). ✓**INTERNET**→*url* http://www.dnai.com/~obo/tmbg/

They Might Be Giants Chat Message-based discussion. ✓**AMERICA ONLINE** ...→*keyword* mmc→Alternative Rock→Bands M-Z →They Might Be Giants! ...→*keyword* mtv→Message Boards→Bands That Do Suck→They Might Be Giants

They Might Be Giants FAQ What are he two members of They Might Be Giants wearing on their heads in the "Don't Let's Start" video? Rolled up carpets, of course. What is the backwards message at the end of "Hide Away, Folk Family"? It's nonsense, forward or backward. What is "Purple Toupee" all about? It's a surreal deconstruction of the events of the sixties. And answers to dozens more TMBG questions. ✓**INTERNET** →*url* http://www.bio.net/music/TMBG-FAQ.html

They Might Be Giants Internet Directory Learn to tell the difference between the two Johns. Learn which John sings which song. Communicate with other tape traders. Link to the They Might Be Giants FAQ. And more. ✓**INTERNET**→*url* http://isolde.clarku.edu/TMBG/tmbg

THOMPSON, RICHARD

Henry the Human Fly Caught in the Web A Web page devoted to the folk-rock guitarist, with an extensive career biography, lyrics, a list of Thompson songs recorded by others, an image gallery, and more. Remember: you can't surf the Net if you don't know how. . ✓**INTERNET**→*url* http://www.mel.dit.csiro.au/~sfy/RT/Welcome.html

Richard Thompson List: Doom and Gloom on the Net (ml) Talk about Richard, both with Linda and without, and check out guitar tabs for a handful of songs, including "Al Bowlly's In Heaven," "I Want To See The Bright Lights Tonight," "I Misunderstood," and "Pharaoh." ✓**INTERNET**→*email* listserver@listserver.njit.edu ✍ *Type in message body:* subscribe r-thompson

Richard Thompson Page A brief discography and a selection of images from the Ben & Jerry's 1991 folk festival. ✓**INTERNET**→*url* http://csbh.gbn.net/~dkrebs/thompson.html

THOMPSON TWINS

Thompson Twins List (ml) Talk about the Thompson Twins, now disbanded, and Babble, the new band created by Tom Bailey and Alannah Currie. ✓**INTERNET**→*email* blackwst@uvsc.edu ✍ *Type in message body:* subscribe Thompson Twins

Thompson Twins/Babble A chronology of the Thompson Twins from their Chesterfield Grammar School days (that's all the way back in 1977) to the disbanding of the Twins and the reformation as Babble. ✓**INTERNET**→*url* http://www.empath.on.ca/~jdean/ttwins.html

THROWING MUSES

Throwing Muses A promotional site devoted to the band's LP *University* that also contains a band biography and a wealth of images. ✓**INTERNET**→*url* http://repriserec.com/Reprise_HTML_Pages/ThrowingMuses

Throwing Muses A full discography, images, guitar tabs, lyrics, and more. ✓**INTERNET**→*url* http://debra.rau.ac.za/Music/Throwing_Muses/

TLC

alt.fan.tlc (ng) Are any of the women in TLC gay? T-Boz says

Richard Thompson—http://www.mel.dit.csiro.au/~sfy/RT/PG-Cropredy.html

she isn't, and if she says she isn't, then she must not be. What motive would there be for a pop star to lie about her sexuality? When fans aren't speculating on TLC's bedroom activities, they're discussing the group's music, and wondering whether the trio will be able to sustain their popularity (à la En Vogue) or whether they will fade into the background (à la the Bangles). ✓**USENET**→alt.fan.tlc

alt.music.tlc (ng) The next time you decide to go chasing waterfalls, take a moment to consider the wisdom of your actions. In a waterfall, you may not be able to hear the smooth harmonies and rough hip-hop beats of TLC. In a waterfall, you may not be able to discuss the band's obvious Prince influence. And in a waterfall, you may not be able to light a match, which would greatly hamper your ability to burn down the home of Atlanta Falcons wide-receiver Andre Rison. ✓**USENET**→alt.music.tlc

TLC Chat Message-based discussion. ✓**AMERICA ONLINE** ...→*keyword* mtv→Message Boards→Bands That Do Suck→TLC ...→*keyword* mmc→Rap/R&B→R&B/Soul→TLC ...→*keyword* mmc→Rap/R&B→Rap/hip-Hop/Funk→TLC

TLC—Past, Present, and Future An electronic transcript of TLC's MTV special "Past, Present, and Future," this page contains information on the band's history, music, and nicknames. ✓**INTERNET**→*url* http:// www.wku.edu/~pier-ccm/misc/tlc_ppf.html

TOAD THE WET SPROCKET

A Page of Toad Stuff Dean, Randy, Todd, and Glen continue to record quality rock and roll, which is why it's nice to have a page that lists their albums, records their tour dates, offers tour reviews, and collects guitar tabs and band pictures. ✓**INTERNET**→*url* http://a54.cc.umist.ac.uk/~rootbeer/toad.html

Toad Lyrics, guitar tabs, an image gallery, information on the Toad mailing list, and more. ✓**INTERNET**→*url* http://www. prairienet. org/arts/listen/toad.html

Toad the Wet Sprocket Sony Music's official page for Toad includes a band bio and information on recent releases. ✓**INTERNET**→*url* http://www.sony.com/Music/Artistinfo/Toad/

Toad the Wet Sprocket Mailing List (ml) Talk Toad with other Toadies on this mailing list. ✓**INTERNET**→*email* listproc@sprocket. silverplatter.com ✍ *Type in message body:* subscribe toad <your full name>

TOOL

alt.music.tool (ng) Has there been a Maynard this famous since Maynard Ferguson? Probably not.

But Maynard James Keenan, the lead singer of Tool, is no popular jazz instrumentalist. He probes the dark places, and fans want to follow him there. "This is one band that lives by its talents and not its hype," insists one listener. "He practices something called Lachrymology, which is like the primal scream therapy John Lennon did on *Plastic Ono Band*. He's getting out his sadness and his anger, and he's a better person for it." Pry open the Toolbox here. ✓**USENET**→alt.music.tool

Cell Block's Tribute to Tool Images of the band, sound clips, and more. ✓**INTERNET**→*url* http://www. cs.utexas.edu/users/jwetzler/tool. htm

Tool A full discography, band news, guitar tabs, band bios, a large archive of articles, and lyrics.

✓**INTERNET**→*url* http://www.rpi. edu/~pier1/tool/

Tool List (ml) Tool talk is the order of the day on this mailing list. ✓**INTERNET**→*email* tool-request@ visix.com ✍ *Type in message body:* subscribe tool-list <your full name>

Tool Talk Message-based discussion. ✓**EWORLD**→*go* eaz→Pump Up The Volume→Music Talk→TOOL

THE TRAGICALLY HIP

alt.music.tragically-hip (ng) Huge in Canada, where they play R.E.M. to the Barenaked Ladies' They Might Be Giants, the Tragically Hip are a gigantic success. Here in the United States, they are still cult favorites. But thanks to the magic of the Internet, south-of-the-border fans can talk about the Hip with Canadians in the know. What songs do Hipsters

Canadian faves the Tragically Hip—http://www.cimtegration.com/tth/band5.htm

Urge Overkill—from http://sashimi. wwa.com/hammers/pictures/

like? "Nautical Disaster." What songs do they hate? "Cemetery Sideroad." What else do they like to talk about? Get thee to the newsgroup, and find out. ✓USE-NET→alt.music.tragically-hip

Hip Page Tour dates, unreleased lyrics, images, a newsletter, and links to other Tragically Hip sites across the Net. ✓INTERNET→*url* http://ugweb.cs.ualberta.ca/~petruk/hip.html

Tragically Hip Interviews, images, articles, lyrics, and more. ✓INTERNET→*url* http://www.cs.mun.ca/~scottmh/th/tragically.html

The Tragically Hip Band bios, concert dates, photos, and more. ✓INTERNET→*url* http://www.tuns.ca/~pyleck/hip.html

The Tragically Hip Selected Canadian Band of the Year, the Tragically Hip have long been a cult favorite among Americans in the know. Get pictures, news, a band FAQ, and more. ✓INTERNET→*url* http://gpu.srv.ualberta.ca/~

karmstro/the_hip.html

Tragically Hip Tour dates, information on on how to buy TH merchandise, and more. ✓INTER-NET→*url* http://www.teleport.com/~mattw/hip0.htmlalt.music.tragically-hip

Tragically Hip List (ml) A mailing list devoted to the Western Canadian rock band. ✓INTERNET→*email* listmanager@hookup.net ✍ *Type in message body:* subscribe tragically-hip <your full name>

TWO UNLIMITED

Two Unlimited Fans of this Dutch techno/rap duo will find news, discography and lyrics, tour info, and music video reviews as well as photos. There are links to other techno pages from here. ✓INTERNET→*url* http://www.acy.digex.net/~delaney

TYPE O NEGATIVE

alt.music.type-o-negative (ng) Type O Negative rose from the ashes of Carnivore, and now the eclectic hardcore band has developed quite a following of its own. Talk to other Type O Pessimists on this newsgroup, which covers everything from tour dates to rumors of new records to general updates on the death metal scene. ✓USENET→alt.music.type-o-negative

Type O Negative This graphics-intensive site concentrates on the LP *Bloody Kisses*—offering sound samples, lyrics, and more—and describes Type O Negative and frontman Peter Steele in prose that could only be described as purple: "At once freed from the constraints of their past and determined to cross all barriers that lie ahead, Steele's heathen world view continues to seek its most willful assertion. Where others will only

allude and proffer cowardly deceptions, Type O Negative unflinchingly reveals the truth, free of all sugary sentiments and pleasantries. Do you dare to look it squarely in the face, even if it means seeing a reflection of yourself?" The site also includes excerpts from Steele's July pictorial in *Playgirl.* ✓INTERNET→*url* http://lx1.benp.wau.nl/people/jgkoops/typeo.html

U

U2
See page 204.

UNCLE TUPELO

Uncle Tupelo Ken, Jeff, Jay and Max— four guys any college girl brought up on Sylvia Plath and Marlboro cigarettes would love to date. The folk-rock group has since disbanded, but echoes of their love-sick riffs can be heard in the music of splinter-group Wilco and other cute country-rock bands. ✓INTERNET→*url* http://www4.ncsu.edu/eos/users/s/sdhouse/Mosaic/uncle-tupelo.html

URGE OVERKILL

Mood Control (ml) Satisfy your Urges on this mailing list. ✓INTER-NET→*email* listserv@psyche.dircon.co.uk ✍ *Type in message body:* subscribe mood-control <your full name>

The Urge-o-Fonic Hyperbook Have you ever seen a *Playboy* magazine from 1968? No? Then how about Uma Thurman sporting the sexiest trench coat of the year? If you're not hip to the Barclords, then you wouldn't understand. The Chicago-based (but L.A.-intoxicated) band has the slickest look and grindingest guitars around. Check out Urge's new CD and get some retrolicious pictures of Nash and the boys. ✓**INTERNET**→ *url* http://www.mcs.net/~alester/ urge/uo-home.htm

V

VAN HALEN

alt.music.van-halen (ng) Once upon a time, Van Halen was the darling of American rock, a California foursome that played loud, fast, and fun. Then David Lee Roth and his cadre of advisors decided that the band was dragging the charismatic lead singer down, and that a bigger, better solo career might be waiting on the other side of a breakup. Enter Sammy Hagar, the former frontman of Montrose and a successful, if limited, solo performer, and exit the band's loyal fans. More than a decade later, Van Halen is still one of rock music's institutions, and David Lee Roth is a two-bit solo artist whose pitiful attempts at comebacks pop like soap bubbles against the thorny and unforgiving tree of the record-buying public. Check in on Van Halen's fans, and see if they have forgiven ol' David Lee yet. ✓**USENET**→alt.music. van-halen

alt.music.van-halen.sammy-sucks (ng) See Sammy sing. See Sammy sing about red. See Sammy sing about a three-lock box. See Sammy join Van Halen. See Sammy's popularity soar. See Sammy's detractors and enemies stare gape-mouthed at the platinum records. ✓**USENET**→alt.music.van-halen.sammy-sucks

David Lee Roth He's not in Van Halen anymore, much to his abiding sorrow, but David Lee Roth continues to release hard-rock albums that include precious little

of his legendary wit and charisma. This site includes a DLR bio and a press release for solo album *Your Dirty Little Mouth*. ✓**AMERICA ONLINE**→*keyword* warner→Rock→ David Lee Roth

Official Van Halen Entering this Van Halen Universe may turn out to be the most Zen experience you've had all day. This page is dominated by the new album *Balance*, the word "balance," the concept of balance, and every idea anybody has ever had about it. Why? Because the new, philosophical Van Halen likes to speculate on the way that ideas shape our lives, right now, and then they like to package up their speculations and sell them to corporate clients. ✓**INTERNET**→*url* http://vanhalen. warnerrcrds.com/Balance

Van Halen What do the members of Van Halen feel about balance? Find out at this site, which furnishes a conceptual interview that accompanied the release of the band's *Balance* LP. ✓**AMERICA ONLINE**→*keyword* warner→rock→ Van Halen

Van Halen Eddie's got a gun; in fact, the police found it on him. Isn't a guitar enough these days, or do rock stars feel so afraid of the outside world that they have to pack heat as well? This page contains a wide variety of resources about the band, circa *Balance*. ✓**INTERNET**→*url* http://www.acm. ndsu.nodak.edu/~cdubuque/ music/rock/van_halen/

Van Halen Get some great pictures of the band and remember what they were like before Sammy Hagar came to town. ✓**INTERNET**→ *url* http://weber.u.washington. edu/~jnorton/james.html

Van Halen The architect of this

home page is dedicated to providing Van Halen fans with their daily fix of information about Eddie and his crew. So far, there are only links to other Van Halen pages and a link to an online VH newsletter, *Round Sound*. ✓**INTERNET**→ *url* http://carroll1.cc.edu/~rhiggins/vh.html

Van Halen Pleasure Dome A full discography, an essay on the history of the band, a picture gallery, and an inexplicable link to the Kathy Ireland picture gallery. ✓**INTERNET**→*url* http://www1. usa1.com/~kb5150/vh.html

VAUGHAN, STEVIE RAY

Pay to Play with Stevie Ray After wrapping up a jam with Eric Clapton and Robert Cray, Vaughan's life came to an end in a helicopter crash. Are rock stars really more apt to die in a ground-bound steel coffin? Just a theory, but it sure seems that way. Visit this straightforward page, which allows for no equivocation—when it came to blazing blues-rock, Stevie was the greatest. ✓**INTERNET**→ *url* http://www.dmu.ac.uk/~ iah/srv

Stevie Ray Vaughan This official record company site hardly does justice to the best blues guitarist of the past two decades. Accolades will get you nowhere. ✓**INTERNET**→*url* http://www.music. sony.com/Music/ArtistInfo/Stevie RayVaughan.html

VEGA, SUZANNE

Suzanna Vega After Joni Mitchell and before Sinead, Suzanne Vega was the premier folksinger/child advocate of her time. Vega, a believer in social issues, is currently working on a book for Amnesty International titled *Childhood Lost*. She will also work collaboratively with Phillip

Velvet Underground **Artist Guide**

Nico and Lou Reed in the '60s—http://charlotte.acns.nwu.edu/charm/html/lou/

Glass on an upcoming movie and has had the pleasure of recording one of her favorite Leonard Cohen songs for a tribute album. Maybe being literate, conscientious, and kind will get you everything—and even if it only gets you a Website like this one, a comprehensive resource named one of the top ten rock sites by America Online, it is reward enough. ✓**INTERNET**→*url* http://www.meer.net/vega/

Undertow Talk to Marlene on the Web, and also to other Suzanne Vega fans on this mailing list. ✓**INTERNET**→*email* undertow-request@law.emory.edu ✍ *Write a request*

VELVET UNDERGROUND

Cafe Bizarre (Velvet Underground) Banana icons, a VU meter...this must be the Velvet Underground home page. A discography, images of the band, bios of the members (Doug Yule, please phone home) and VU miscellany.

✓**INTERNET**→*url* http://www.infi.net/~aland/vu/

Velvet Underground Chat Message-based discussion. ✓**AMERICA ONLINE**→*keyword* mmc→Alternative Rock→Bands M-Z→Velvet Underground / Lou Reed

VERUCA SALT

Louise Post Home Page This page bemoaning Louise's lack of exposure is eight sentences long. Ironic, no? ✓**INTERNET**→*url* http://www.pb.net/usrwww/w_despair/louise.htm

Veruca Salt All hail Veruca Salt. This site includes links to the tour schedule, concert and set lists, an FAQ, discography, articles, interviews, rumors, a VS cover story from *Addicted to Noise*, and other fan pages. ✓**INTERNET**→*url* http://www.interaccess.com/users/cheeks/Music/VerucaSalt.html

Veruca Salt Album info and a

collection of sound clips from the band named after the bad egg of *Charlie and the Chocolate Factory*. ✓**INTERNET**→*url* http://geffen.com/veruca.html

Veruca Salt Courtney may have the kinder-whore look down, but if you're looking for little-girl voices to go with your abuse/revenge lyrics, look no further than Veruca Salt. Links to abum info, images, sound clips, lyrics, discography, and other fan pages. ✓**INTERNET**→*url* http://www.gordian.com/users/daniel/veruca/

Veruca Salt Chat Message-based discussion. ✓**AMERICA ONLINE** ...→*keyword* mtv→Message Boards →Bands That Don't Suck→Belly. Throwing Muses.Veruca Salt ...→*keyword* mmc→Rock/Pop→General Rock→Veruca Salt

VIOLENT FEMMES

Violent Femmes Gordon Gano isn't the most powerful rock star in the world, but he's a consistently interesting songwriter who has steered his band, the Violent Femmes, through a number of incarnations. Get Femmes lyrics, images, sound clips, and more at this Website. ✓**INTERNET**→*url* http://ds1.gl.umbc.edu/~mmerry2/femmes.html

W

WAITS, TOM

alt.music.tom-waits (ng) While Waits is an artist with a narrowly defined audience, his newsgroup seems to veer off-topic frequently, with numerous posts on recording technology, vegetables, and apocalypse (this last message cross-posted to newsgroups for The Band, The Police, and The Doors). But many fans get right down to business, asking after *Bone Machine* outtakes, spreading rumors that Waits has throat cancer, and trying to keep a step ahead of Waits's experimental whims. ✓**USENET**→alt. music.tom-waits

Rain Dogs (ml) Are you gravel-voiced? Do you sometimes believe that you belong to another time? Have you recorded some songs in which you sound like a grizzled blues singer, and others in which you sound like Edith Piaf? Are you an American original? "Sane, sane, they're all insane / Fireman's blind, the conductor's lame / Cincinnati jacket and a sad luck dame / Hanging out the window with a bucket full of rain." Clap hands here. ✓**INTERNET**→*email* listserv@ucsd.edu ✍ *Type in message body:* subscribe raindogs <your full name>

WEEN

alt.music.ween (ng) "Which one's Dean and which one's Gene? Are those their real names?" "No, you simp. It's like Don Was and David Was. They were Was (Not Was), but neither of them was Was. And this Ween thing is the same. They're like, pseudonyms or something." Talk about the band, the music, and the legend on this newsgroup. ✓**USENET**→alt.music. ween

Ween Buenos tardes, amigo. Links to articles and press, and a discography with point-n-click access to lyrics, samples, liner notes, and more. It's trip music so good, you won't be able to pull yourself away. ✓**INTERNET**→*url* http://icg. pobox.com/Sarc/Ween/

Ween Chat Message-based discussion. ✓**AMERICA ONLINE**→*keyword* mtv→Message Boards→Bands That Don't Suck→WEEN

Tom Waits for no one—downloaded from eWorld's Music Universe

Ween List (ml) Weenies and other fans of experimental pop flock to this mailing list. ✓**INTERNET**→ *email* knvo@maristb.marist.edu ✍ *Write a request*

WeenWeb Lyrics, images, a band bio, a discography, and more. ✓**INTERNET**→*url* http:// www.nando.net/music/gm/Grand Royal/Bands/Ween/

WEEZER

Weezer If you look just like Buddy Holly, visit this site, which includes links to a bio, images, and a few sound clips. ✓**INTERNET**→ *url* http://geffen.com/weezer.html

Weezer A picture of Weezer. Bowl cuts for everyone! ✓**INTERNET** →*url* http://www.iuma.com/ IUMA/band_html/Weezer.html

Weezer Chat Message-based

chat. ✓**AMERICA ONLINE** ...→*keyword* mtv→Message Boards→Bands That Do Suck→Weezer ...→*keyword* mtv→Message Boards→Bands That Don't Suck→Weezer ...→*keyword* rockline→Message Boards→ MODERN ROCK LIVE→Weezer

WELLER, PAUL

Paul Weller A promotional site devoted to Weller's *Stanley Road* LP. ✓**INTERNET**→*url* http://www. godiscs.co.uk/godiscs/pweller.html

Paul Weller Gopher/WWW Archives Lyrics, guitar tabs, images, and the Paul Weller FAQ. ✓**INTERNET**→*url* http://biogopher. wustl. edu:70/1/audio/weller

Paul Weller List (ml) Paul Weller got out of the Jam, and now his peppy pastoral pop can help you get out of a jam. *Wild Wood*? *Stanley Road*? They're both *(cont'd pg. 207)* →

U2

Maybe you don't like U2. Maybe you think that Bono is a bozo, a self-important gasbag

whose stilted sermons on political injustice were the worst thing about the mid-eighties. Maybe you think that the Edge is a limited guitarist whose trademark stacatto shimmer is a gimmick that should have been discarded after a single song. Maybe you don't even know the names of the other two guys. If so, you'd be in the minority. The Irish foursome with the spy-plane name has spent the last decade securing its position as one of the most popular bands in rock history, and that popularity comes over to the online world. Visit **The Edge's U2 Directory**. See what other fans have to say at **The Zooropean**. And then get your Irish up at **alt.music.u2** and **alt.fan.u2**.

The jolly lads in Dublin—http://www2.ecst.csuchico.edu/~edge/u2/images/

On the Net

Across the board

The Edge's U2 Directory Still haven't found what you're looking for? Come to this page, which has more than five dozen links to home pages, discographies, bios, lyrics, sound clips, images, articles, interviews, newsletters, magazines, concert info, fanzines like Zooropea and Propoganda, guitar tabs, information services and an entirely separate collection of cyberpunk pages. ✓**INTERNET**→*url* http://argos.uniandes.edu.co/~l-arcini/

Mania Mansion—Home of U2 Collectormania Magazine *Collectormania* has been around since 1987, and according to The Edge, it's "great fun for a fan...well researched, very good. Very professional in every way." The words just glow, don't they? Browse some back issues if you dare; the lesson of the early issues, apparently, is that Dutch reporters can make anything sound boring. Better to check out the June '95 interview with *X-press* in which the band reveals they are working on two new albums simultaneously, one with low-energy, high-output impresario Brian Eno, and the other a new U2 album with "no whining" and a *Blade Runner* attitude. The Website is pretty slick, with links to concert documentary footage, sound clips, books and more. ✓**INTERNET**→*url* http://www.xs4all.nl/~pj/cm-index.html

U2 Archive Links to various and sundry tidbits of information organized into sections for bootlegs, albums, singles, and videos. ✓**INTERNET**→*url* http://www.iaehv.nl/users/jinx/u2/u2.htm

U2 Jukebox Links to sound and videoclips, mostly from the earlier jeans-and-muscle shirts, protest-rock, stage-stomping days. ✓**INTERNET**→*url* http://www.med.virginia.edu/~njz7p/

U2 WWW Home Page In the late seventies, four Dublin teens started a garage band that let them forget about their cares, even their bad skin and bad haircuts, and just play their music, man. Two name changes, 10 albums, and 15 years later, all four of those boys are men with lovely skin, fashionable coifs, and international pop stardom. At this site—which links to bios, a discography, lyrics, articles, images, FAQ and more—you can follow U2's evolution, from the raw growing pains and rain-soaked love songs of *Boy* to the tidal enormity of *The Joshua Tree*, from the anguished political anthems of *War* to the cyberpop cynikitsch of *Zooropa*. √**INTERNET** →*url* http://www2.ecst.csuchico. edu/~edge/u2.html

The Zooropean A couple of years ago during a band interview, Bono began, inexplicably, to strip in the middle of a diner. The interviewer asked him why, and The Edge replied on his behalf, suggesting that Bono was prone to disrobing "because he's an egomaniacal, sex-crazed rock god!" Some fans are still wondering what happened to those nice Irish lads. Well, here's the thing. The new U2 is all about irony. Irony, irony, irony. By the late eighties, the band's down-to-earth thing had become a persona in itself. So the members of U2 decided to throw themselves to the other end of the spectrum, embrace everything they were expected to loathe, and become obnoxious, ostentatious, cyberpunk-media-whore-cartoon SUPERSTARS! If you don't like their brave new sound, you're entitled to your opinion, but if you want to whine about the flash and attitude, remember that the members of U2 are laughing at themselves, and at your righteous indignation, all the way to the bank. Irony, see, irony. By the way, this homepage contains back issues of the *Zooropean* fanzine, images, soundclips, and more. √**INTERNET** →*url* http://www.luna.nl/~u2zoo rop/home.htm

Chat

alt.music.u2/alt.fan.u2 (ng) What are the risks of relentless innovation? Is U2 innovating or just pretending? Is Bono trying to turn himself into a cross between John

Bullet the blue sky—from http://www2.ecst.csuchico.edu/~edge/u2/images/

Lennon and Wayne Newton? And why wasn't the *Batman Forever* theme song ("Hold Me, Thrill Me, Kiss Me, Kill Me") offered to the James Bond producers. Could it be because the band's pro-Irish politics would clash with Bond's true-to-the-crown company-man image? Share your thoughts on Bono and the boys here. √**USENET** ...→alt.music.u2 ... →alt.fan.u2

U2 Chat Message-based discussion. √**AMERICA ONLINE** ...→*keyword* mmc→Alternative Rock→ Bands M-Z→U2 Anyone? ...→*keyword* rockline→Messages→MODERN ROCK LIVE→U2

Wire (ml) With or without you, the participants of this mailing list will discuss their Irish heroes. √**INTERNET**→*email* u2-list-request@ ms.uky.edu ✍ *Write a request*

Contest

U2 Guess the Lyric of the Week A Web contest for diehard U2 fans, with a great prize. No,

not money. Better than that. The winner one week gets to publish the following week's page. Talk about a trip through your wires. √**INTERNET**→*url* http://www.crl. com/~stheo/

FAQ

U2 FAQ Did you know that U2 was the name for a model of U.S. spy plane used after WWII? The plane was not supposed to be detectable by radar, but it was, and a U2 piloted by Francis Gary Powers was shot down four days before Bono was born. Coincidence? Doubtful. This FAQ includes basic information on the band, traces Bono's evolution from earnest working-class hero to hyperironic entertainer, and even describes friends and influences of the band, such as filmmaker Wim Wenders, beat William S. Burroughs, and the king of cyberfiction William Gibson. √**INTERNET**→ *url* http://www2.ecst.csuchico. edu/~edge/u2/faq/u2faq1.html

Spotlight: U2 Artist Guide

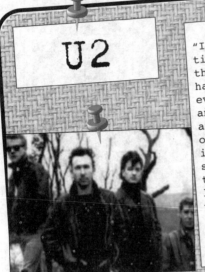

"I agree with you all. U2 has the most emotional songs I have ever heard. I think that 'So Cruel' and 'All I Want is You' have got to be two of the greatest U2 songs ever. 'Tomorrow,' 'Drowning Man,' 'One,' and 'With or Without You' and the other two are U2's truest love songs. These are the only songs that have ever made me cry, and it's becuase Bono is truely the most poetic songwriter out there, and he's got a band that can bring out the emotion of his lyrics. I can feel those songs when I hear them. That's what music really is."

—from **alt.fan.u2**

"I think Bill Gates made a bad choice when he decided to pay the Stones $12 million for the rights to play 'Start Me Up' for the Windows 95 commercials…if he really thought about it and really wanted to poke fun at the MAC Operating System (and Microsoft, for that matter) he should have used U2's 'Even Better Than the Real Thing,' since it's obvious that WIN 95 is a blatant rip off of the MAC."

—from **alt.fan.u2**

"Bono sometimes introduced 'Exit' as 'a song about a religious man who became a very dangerous man—this is a story about the hands of love.' I don't know whether to interpret this song as being about suicide or murder, but the lyrics bear a frightening resemblance to the Robert Mitchum movie Night of the Hunter which came out in 1955. If Bono had this movie, and specifically the Mitchum character, in mind when he wrote the song, then I would venture to say that it's about murder instead of suicide."

—from **alt.fan.u2**

Ween—from http://www.nando.net/ music/gm/GrandRoyal/Bands

on the map at this mailing list. ✓INTERNET→*url* kosmos-request@ mit.edu ✍ *Write a request*

WHITE ZOMBIE

Astro Creep 2000 A press release for the band's *Astro-Creep: 2000* LP, along with a transcript of a live interview. ✓INTERNET→*url* http://www.webb.com/concrete/ wz.html

Planet Zombie Selected by teen tastemakers Beavis and Butt-head as one of the coolest bands on the planet, White Zombie persists in loud and atmospheric metal. Visit Planet Zombie—Geffen's official site for the band—for a band bio. a discography, and a stirring quote from Pablo Picasso ("the chief enemy of creativity is good taste"). ✓INTERNET→*url* http://www.geffen. com/planetzombie/

White Zombie A graphics- and sound-intensive site devoted to the band's *Sexorcisto* and *Astro-Creep* LPs. ✓INTERNET→*url* http://www. your.net/~kbacon/WhiteZombie/

White Zombie Chat Message-based discussion. ✓AMERICA ON-LINE→*keyword* mtv→Message

Boards→Bands That Don't Suck→ WHITE ZOMBIE

THE WHO

alt.fan.whos.tommy (ng) What would happen if a deaf, dumb, and blind kid who sure played a mean pinball got himself online? He'd probably end up subscribing to a newsgroup like this one, a monomaniacal community devoted to discussing performances of Pete Towwnshend's seminal rock opera and its more recent Broadway incarnation. ✓USENET→alt.fan.whos.tommy

alt.music.who (ng) Between arguments over best albums and comparisons between members' solo careers (never mind that arguing the relative merits of Townshend vs. Daltrey is like suggesting that Alfred Hitchcock might have known a bit more about craft than Chris Columbus), diehard Whoists review classic albums, trade lyrics, and wonder about future projects. ✓INTERNET→*url* http://www.interport.net/ ~scottj/who/Lifehouse.html

The Hypertext Who Billed as "a multimedia guide to the best rock and roll band in the world," this site is a solid if unspectacular discography, with images of band members, album covers, and more. ✓INTERNET→*url* http://www. eden.com/~thewho/

The Lifehouse/Maximum R&B (The Who) A complete discography, interviews, lyrics, and some wonderful images, including an airborne Pete Townshend strumming a Les Paul that seems blissfully unaware of its impending destruction. ✓INTERNET→*url* http://www.interport.net/~scottj/ who/Lifehouse.html

The Who Images of the band up-

loaded by MCA Records. ✓AMERICA ONLINE→*keyword* rock→The Who

The Who Commemorating the band's 1990 induction into the Rock and Roll Hall of Fame, this page includes a brief biography and sound clips. ✓INTERNET→*url* http://www.rockhall.com/induct/ who.html

Who Bootleg List A list of vinyl and compact disc bootlegs. ✓INTERNET→*url* http://www.xmission. com/~legalize/who-boots.html

Who List (ml) Have information about the powerful purveyors of Maximum R&B emailed directly to you. ✓INTERNET→*email* majordo-mo@cisco.com ✍ *Type in message body:* subscribe thewho <your email address>

WIDESPREAD PANIC

Widespread Panic Oriented toward tape traders, this page includes tour dates, set lists, and links. ✓INTERNET→*url* http:// www.cs.utexas.edu/users/bright/ music/spreadsh/spreadsh.html

Widespread Panic A discography, lyrics, images, and more. ✓INTERNET→*url* http://www.netspace. org/Widespread/

WSP Home Page Tour dates, merchandise, and extensive coverage of WSP's live shows, including QuickTime movies of the events. ✓INTERNET→*url* http://iweb.www. com/wsp/index.html

WILLIAMS, LUCINDA

Lucinda Williams Guitar Chords Chords and tabs from *Lucinda Williams, Sweet Old World,* and more. ✓INTERNET→*url* http://www.umn.edu/nlhome/ m161/schn0170/lw/index.html

WOLFGANG PRESS

The Wolfgang Press A discography of the band's 4AD releases. ✓**INTERNET**→*url* http://www.evo.org/html/group/wolfgangpress.html

WONDER, STEVIE

Stevie Wonder A promotional site for the 1995 LP *Conversation Peace* that includes a press release for the album. ✓**INTERNET**→*url* http://www.polygram.com/polygram/Stevie.html

WONDER STUFF

Wonder Stuff List Talk about the Wonder Stuff on this mailing list. ✓**INTERNET**→*url* malasky@ecn.purdue.edu ✍ *Write a request*

The Wonder Stuff Page The Wonder Stuff is no more, but this Website continues nonetheless, including a discography, images, press releases, and information on the pair of bands that rose from the rubble—Vent and WeKnowWhereYouLive. ✓**INTERNET**→ *url* http://cernan.ecn.purdue.edu/~malasky/

The late Wonder Stuff—from http://cernan.ecn.purdue.edu/~malasky/pics.html

WU TANG CLAN

Wu Tang Clan Chat Go the way of the Shao-Lin sword, and you're on your own. Go the way of the Wu Tang sword, and you'll find plenty to talk about with other fans of this Philly rap posse, which has recorded one excellent LP and spawned a handful of successful solo careers (Method Man and Dirty Ol' Bastard). ✓**AMERICA ONLINE** ...→*keyword* mtv→Message Boards→Bands That Don't Suck→Da Wu-Tang Clan ...→*keyword* mmc→Rap/R&B→Rap/hip-Hop/Funk→Wu Tang Clan

X

The Unheard Music Fifteen years ago, X marked the spot for Billy Zoom, John Doe, Exene Cervenka, and D. J. Bonebrake; these days, X is back and better than ever, with a rejuvenated Doe and Cervenka pooling the wisdom of their solo careers, a new release (*Unclogged*), and even another

John Doe side project. Was X the new Doors, or the West Coast Pistols? Get the answers, as well as images, a discography, and sound clips here. ✓**INTERNET**→*url* http://www.cyberg8t.com/gene/

XTC

beatown A gallery of XTC cover photos, along with information about the band. ✓**INTERNET**→*url* http://www.charm.net/~duke/xtc/beatown.html

Chalkhills (ml) Chat about XTC. The Website contains images, lyrics, and more. ✓**INTERNET**→*email* chalkhills-request@presto.ig.com ✍ *Write a request Info:* ✓**INTERNET**→ *url* http://www.bio.net/chalkhills/ html/chalkhills.html

XTC Chat Message-based discussion about the venerable British pop trio. ✓**AMERICA ONLINE**→*keyword* mmc→Alternative Rock→Bands M-Z →X T C

XTC Discography A long list of XTC's songs and albums, lavishly annotated and frequently updated. ✓**INTERNET**→*url* gopher://wiretap.spies.com/00/Library/Music/Disc/xtc.dis

XYMOX

Clan of Xymox A discography of the band's albums from its 4AD years. ✓**INTERNET**→*url* http://www.evo.org/html/group/clanofxymox.html

Clan of Xymox A discography, news, a band history, and lyrics. ✓**INTERNET**→*url* http://mcmuse.mc.maricopa.edu/~xymox/xymox.html

The Clan of Xymox FTP Server Images, sound clips, a discography, and more. ✓**INTERNET**→*url* ftp://ftp.sunet.se/pub/music/lyrics/c/clan.of.xymox

Y

YANKOVIC, WEIRD AL

alt.music.weird-al (ng) What is Weird Al's religious background? Which songs of his are specific parodies and which are genre parodies? Is Weird Al the UNAbomber? Serious (and not so serious) questions about the modern-day Spike Jones. ✓**USENET** ...→alt.music.weird-al ...→ alt.fan.weird-al

Weird Al FAQ A complete discography (from "My Bologna" to "Living in the Fridge"), a videography (who can forget his commanding leading-man presence in *UHF* or his touching cameo in *The Naked Gun?*), and a partial guide to the places mentioned in "Biggest Ball of Twine in Minnesota." ✓**INTERNET**→*url* http://www.cs.umd.edu/~mike/weird-al.faq.html

Weird Al Yankovic A special preview sound clip from Weird Al's new album, along with concert sounds, links, and more. ✓**INTERNET**→*url* http://www.smartlink.net/~director/weird-al.html

Weird Al Yankovic Pictures, sounds, lyrics, and links that allow you a rare glimpse into the world of Weird Al. ✓**INTERNET**→*url* http://er7.rutgers.edu:2200/~dprossi/

Weird Al Yankovic A list of Al's band members, set lists for Al's tour, and more. ✓**INTERNET**→*url* http://www.smartlink.net/~producer/weirdal/areyou.html

Weird Al Yankovic A British site devoted to the Weird one himself, with set lists, lyrics, images,

and more. ✓**INTERNET**→*url* http://cr1.see.plym.ac.uk/dfsmith/index.html

The Weird Al Yankovic Web Page Illustrated with a picture of Gumby playing the guitar (and the little green guy is really shredding the six-string), this page includes pictures, interviews, sound clips, current news, and links about the only artist who benefits from staying six months behind all pop-music trends. ✓**INTERNET**→*url* http://www.xnet.com/~gumby/

YES

alt.music.yes (ng) How many fans have said "yes" to Yes? Thousands, and all of them seem to be on this newsgroup, falling over themselves as they hurry to remark upon the reunion of the progressive (read: flatulent) seventies rock band. Along with the new Yesmen—those who came aboard the bandwagon after the *90125* album, which featured such hits as "Leave It" and "Owner of a Lonely Heart"—the stalwarts discuss such Yes-related bands as Anderson, Bruford, Wakeman, Howe and Asia, compare tour notes, and take every kind of affirmative action imaginable. ✓**USENET**→alt.music.yes

Jon Anderson An official Windham Hill promotional site for the instrumental album *Deseo*, recorded by the Yes vocalist and international music visionary. ✓**INTERNET**→*url* http://www.windham.com/ourmusic/artist_pages/anderson.empty.byartist.html

Notes From the Edge (ml) Chat about Yes. The Web page includes information about the Notes from the Edge mailing list, as well as a considerable amount of native content—gossip, collector's news, and updates on the

Forever (Neil) Young—from http://www.dsi.unimi.it/Users/Students

band's rumored reunion. ✓**INTERNET**→*email* nfte@sol.cms.uncwil.edu ✍ *Write a request Info:* ✓**INTERNET**→*url* http://www.wilmington.net/yes/

Yes With lyrics, images, and cover art, this is one Website that can't say no. ✓**INTERNET**→*url* http://www.cen.uiuc.edu/~ea10735/yes.html

YOUNG, NEIL

Country Home "Neil Young has not a style; he is a style," proclaims this home page, which is long on love for the revered rocker but short on resources—just a few album covers and reviews. ✓**INTERNET**→*url* http://www.dsi.unimi.it/Users/Students/pasquar/Neil_Young

Hyperrust An excellent and comprehensive site, including a full list of Neil's official releases, appearances Neil has made on other artists' records, tour data, tape trees, bootlegs, guitar tabs, interviews, tributes, links, and even a lengthy but loving consideration of the question "How tall is Neil?" (based on eyewitness reports, he fluctuates wildly between four inches and "really tall"). ✓**INTERNET**→*url* http://www.uta.fi/~trkisa/ hyperrust.html

Neil Young A wealth of material—press releases, downloadable sound clips, and images—on the godfather of grunge. ✓**AMERICA ONLINE**→*keyword* warner→rock→ Neil Young

Neil Young Commemorating the singer-songwriter's 1995 induction into the Rock and Roll Hall of Fame, this page includes a brief biography and sound clips. ✓**INTERNET**→*url* http://www.rockhall.com/ induct/younneil.html

Neil Young An official site for Neil's 1994 album *Sleeps With Angels.* ✓**INTERNET**→*url* http:// www.iuma.com/Warner/html/ Young,_Neil.html

Neil Young and Pearl Jam An official record company site for the 1995 album *Mirror Ball* that includes a Quicktime video for the single "Downtown." ✓**INTERNET**→*url* http://www.RepriseRec.com/ NeilYoung

Neil Young Chat Message-based discussion. ✓**EWORLD**→*go* eaz→ Pump Up The Volume→Music Talk→ Neil Young

rec.music.neil-young (ng) Neil's star has been rising since the release of *Freedom*, and new fans love to fight over which nineties album is his best. *Ragged Glory? Harvest Moon? Mirror Ball?* But the newsgroup is also home to Neil purists, old-time diehards who refuse to listen to anything recorded after *Harvest*, even that noisy *Rust* thing. All in all, this is a wonderfully uncritical group, full

of the same *joie de vivre* that characterizes Neil's music. ✓**USENET**→rec.music.neil-young

Rust (ml) Rust never sleeps, and neither do Neil Young's fans. Come to this mailing list to see what they talk about during their wakeful hours. ✓**INTERNET**→*email* majordomo@fish.com ✍ *Type in message body:* subscribe rust <your email address>

Z

ZAPPA, FRANK
See page 211.

ZEVON, WARREN
Warren Zevon Home Page Lyrics, images, an annotated discography, an extremely short exclusive-for-Web interview that Warren granted to the creator of the page, and even a low-resolution scan of a Lee Ho Fook's menu (if you don't know what it is, don't even bother asking). Come here for the latest on the Mutineer.

✓**INTERNET**→ *url* http://sushi.st.usm. edu/~hamorris/zevon.html

ZORN, JOHN
John Zorn Discography As John Zorn fans know, the avant-garde saxophonist and composer has worked steadily over the past 15 years, contributing to soundtracks, movies, and more. This document lists all of Zorn's recordings, and annotates them so that fans can keep track of sidemen and collaborators. ✓**INTERNET**→*url* http://www.nwu.edu/WNUR/jazz /artists/zorn.john/discog.html

ZZ TOP
The Little Ol' Web Page From Texas An annotated discography that takes Top fans from the band's 1970 debut through 1994's *One Foot in the Blues.* Press releases, reviews, and pictures of the bearded ones (Billy Gibbons, Dusty Hill, and the clean-shaven Frank Beard) are also available. Velcro flies preferred. ✓**INTERNET**→ *url* http://www.cen.uiuc.edu/ ~pz3900/zztop.html

Grooming fugitives ZZ Top—from http://www.cen. uiuc.edu/~pz3900/zztop.html

Frank Zappa

Accomplished? You bet. Hilarious? No question. Dead? Absolutely. But even from the

grave, Frank Zappa remains one of the great cult rockers. As a composer, Zappa created some of the most important music of the last decades. As a songwriter, he skewered middle-class sanctimony with a scatological glee. And as a bandleader, he showed an unerring talent for selecting virtuoso players. Though pop success eluded Zappa—only his novelty songs, such as "Don't Eat the Yellow Snow," and "Valley Girl," were hits—prolificacy did not, and his December 1993 death robbed the world of a rare thing, a working artist. Get Zapped at **The Black Page**, **Hometown Sausage Jamboree**, and **St. Alphonso's Pancake**. And don't get no jism on the sofa.

Milk, cookies, and a smiling Zappa—from http://fileroom.aaup.uic.edu/FileRoom/

On the Net

Across the board

The Black Page "Ram it, ram it, ram it up your poop chute." Take that, *Godspell*, your time has passed. Now it's time for Zappa, one of the greatest satirical musicians of the universe and a whiz at supplying the American record-buying public with experimental sound collages, extended guitar solos, and scatological ballads from his back catalog. Too bad he's dead—rest in whatever you call peace, Frank. This page is brought to you by the Utility Muffin Research Kitchen (the Non-Association for the Preservance of Zappathought) and provides links to other Zappa sites, discographies, and FAQs. ✓**INTERNET**→*url* http://www.catalog.com/mrm/zappa.html

The Fabuloustrous Chocolate Chip Zappa Page Dozens of Zappa reviews, penned by the author of the page or culled from other sources, as well as links to Zappa pages elsewhere on the Net. ✓**INTERNET**→*url* http://alf2.tcd.ie/~djennis/Zappa.html

Frank Zappa Commemorating the artist's posthumous 1995 induction into the Rock-and-Roll Hall of Fame, this page includes a brief biography and sound clips. ✓**INTERNET**→*url* http://www.rockhall.com/induct/zappfran.html

Frank Zappa, American Composer and Musician When Tipper Gore attacked Zappa's lyrics for their sexual suggestiveness, Frank shot back, "I wrote a song about dental floss, but did anyone's teeth get cleaner?" Here is a no-nonsense page about the musician's accomplishments and philosophy, focusing on his tangles with censors. ✓**INTERNET**→*url* http://fileroom.aaup.uic.edu/File Room/documents/Cases/392 zappa.html

Frank Zappa Discography A full list of Zappa albums, along with song lists and generous annotation. ✓**INTERNET**→*url* http:// www.caos.kun.nl/zappa/

Hometown Sausage Jamboree Because he was, well, a little nuts, Frank Zappa frequently included backward messages in his songs, or recorded voices at different speeds so as to make them virtually incomprehensible. Find out what he's saying on that old record by downloading sounds that have been corrected for backwardness and speed and prepared for the human ear. ✓**INTERNET**→*url* http:// www.netaxs.com/~yirm/sausage/ sausage.html

My Guitar Wants to Kill Your Mama "I am gross and perverted / I'm obsessed and deranged / I've existed for years / But very little has changed / I am the tool of the Government / And industry, too / For I am destined to rule / And regulate you / Have you guessed me yet? / I'm the slime oozin' out / From your TV set." Is it the theme song to a kiddie show broadcast from the deepest reaches of Cynicland? Nope—it's a Zappa song, which amounts to much the same thing. Many years ago, a wise man with a weird beard insisted that the media was akin to hog cholera; today, the relationship between electronic systems of information delivery and braindrain dominates our lives. Think about this issue while you visit this page, which includes basic information about Zappa and links to related sites. ✓**INTERNET**→*url* http://204.96. 208.2/personal/student/edie/ music/zappa.htm

Pound for a Brown Link to other Zappa sites, read an interview with Steve Vai that remembers Frank, and get lyrics and more. ✓**INTERNET**→*url* http:// ireland.iol.ie/~arsenic/pound.html

St. Alphonso's Pancake Run by a student at the University of Amsterdam, this site includes Zappa news (he's still dead, although there's something odd happening with his wife), a complete discography, a Zappa FAQ, interviews, articles, and more. ✓**INTERNET**→*url* http://www.fwi.uva.nl/~heederik/ zappa/

Astrology

Asteroid Zappafrank Asteroid Zappafrank, a rather salty bit of spacejunk, was named in honor of Frank Zappa in July 1994 and passed close to Zappa's putative birthplace, the Earth, in March 1995. Learn about the asteroid, Zappa, and more. ✓**INTERNET**→*url* ftp://ftp.catalog.com/mrm/zappa /html/asteroid.html

Chat

alt.fan.frank-zappa (ng) Zappa would have hated the debate over Internet censorship. "Does humor belong in society?" he might have asked. But he's dead. So his fans are asking these kinds of questions for him, reflecting on the political and musical achievements of the Great Barking Pumpkin. ✓**USENET**→alt.fan.frank-zappa

Frank Zappa Chat Message-based discussion. ✓**AMERICA ON-LINE**→*keyword* mmc→Rock/Pop→ Rock Artists M-Z→Frank Zappa & MothersInvention

Obits & tributes

Frank Zappa Obituary Am-

bassador of Trade and Tourism for the Czech Republic, nemesis of the PRMC, visionary lyricist, dadaist musician, and nightmarish name-giver—Frank Zappa was all things to a very small group of people. This site reviews his career, wringing quite a bit of pathos from the life of a man who once wrote a rock opera in which the protagonist sang "Fuck me, you ugly son of a bitch" to a creature that looked like a piggy-bank covered with marital aids. A tribute page for a lotus-eater. ✓**INTERNET**→ *url* http://www.ward.com/obit/ zappa.htm

Tribute to Frank Zappa Coverage of major albums in Zappa's oeuvre (rock mostly), along with generous annotation. ✓**INTERNET**→ *url* http://www.cs.tufts.edu/ ~stratton/zappa/zappa.html

The Zappa Image Archive Presented on a background that looks like red silk, this page pays tribute to the late, great musician with a series of pictures that range from baby photos to album art to portraits taken in the years just previous to his December 1993 death from cancer. ✓**INTERNET**→*url* http://abominable.winternet.com/ ~zappa/zappa.html

Quotes

Zappa Quote of the Day At a concert at Mount Holyoke College in the 1970s, Zappa once boasted that he could "gross out anyone in [the] room." He was right, no doubt. Get the wit and wisdom of Zappa, from "Jazz isn't dead—it just smells funny" to "never try to get your pecker sucked in France." Touching and inspirational. ✓**INTERNET**→*url* http://204.96.208.2/personal/ student/edie/music/zappa.htm

Zappa

"Zappa was pretty safe in his use of the electric guitar, because he was dealing with a mature technology. When he got into sequenced electronic stuff... forget it. Once sampling became financially feasible, FZ dove right in, but the technology never existed to actually replace an acoustic instrument with a sampled counterpart. I wish the guy had lived a few years longer, because technology is advancing at a ridiculous pace. Not to mention the amusement potential of the 1996 presidential race. I miss Frank."

—from **alt.fan.frank-zappa**

"I had the good fortune to meet Frank at a book-signing for The Real FZ Book in 1988 in NYC. Having been a big fan since '69, I was quite flustered and all I came up with was something like this… 'Hi Frank, my name is John and this is really a thrill meeting you…I've been a big fan for about 20 years.' As he shook my hand (in a vigourous circular motion) he looked me straight between my beady little eyes and said something like, 'Well now I know who one of my biggest fans is…some guy named John.'"

—from **Frank Zappa Chat** on America Online's Music Message Center

"I'm getting married on January 6 and I'm trying to think of some good music to play at the reception. As a Zappa fan, I'd like to have a lot of his music played. Any suggestions?"

"How about 'Fine Girl,' 'Any Kinda Pain,' 'Stolen Moments' and as the big finale—'Don't you ever wash that thing?' I can't wait to see the video. Congratualations."

—from **alt.fan.frank-zappa**

Part 4

Genres

Rock & pop

Of all the genres in modern culture, pop music is perhaps the vaguest. What's pop?

A better question might be "what isn't pop?" Any genre that includes Olivia Newton-John and Nirvana—not to mention Petula Clark and Pearl Jam, the Beatles and the Beastie Boys, Henry Rollins and the Rolling Stones—isn't terribly exclusive; those rock fans wishing to pin down exactly what it is that thrills their ears might want to start at **alt.rock-n-roll, MP Music Rock Previews,** and **Rocktropolis.** More directed fans should check out the recources devoted to specific genres, from **The Acid Jazz Server** to **Dreampop-L,** from **Classic Rock/Oldies** to **Obscure Progressive Rock.** Absorb all the genres. That way, the next time the lead singer of your favorite band yells "Are you ready to rock?" you'll have some idea what he's talking about.

A rock and roll fantasy theme park—from http://rocktropolis.com/

On the Net

General rock & pop

Allmusic Mailing List (ml) As its name suggests, the Allmusic list handles all types of music—hippie funk, hip-hop, world music, guitar rock, atonal classical, avant-jazz, and more. But the lion's share of discussion on this mailing list is devoted to rock music. So if you have an idea about rock—that cable TV, and particularly MTV, has made the visual as important as the aural in modern music; that rap has productively infected other genres—share it here. ✓**INTERNET**→ *email* listserv@american.edu ✍ *Type in message body:* subscribe all-music <your full name>

alt.music.uk (ng) Everyone here is convinced that her favorite British pop band is the best—Sheila thinks it's Suede; Karen is sure it's Oasis; Paula knows that Blur is absolutely the bloody best in the world. You don't have to live across the pond to have an opinion, though, and if you want to add your tuppence to the debate, come to this newsgroup. ✓**USENET**→alt.music.uk

alt.rock-n-roll (ng) Sometimes this newsgroup seems like a welter of proper names that's as difficult to decode as a foreign language—Tom Waits, Jellyfish, Saga, Buzzcocks. But to the initiated, it's a wonderfully diverse community of rock fans coming together under one roof to make a joyous noise about the noise that makes them joyful. To explore specific rock genres, check out the other newsgroups in the hierarchy, which include alt.rock-n-roll.classic and

alt.rock-n-roll.oldies, both of which specialize in music that used to rouse the youth to lascivious acts but today just fills up the space between radio ads. ✓**USE-NET**→alt.rock-n-roll

List of Music Mailing Lists This massive master list of mailing lists will tell you how to meet other Bryan Ferry and Beastie Boys fans in Cyberspace. Come here to get contact info for hundreds of rock- and pop-oriented mailing lists. ✓**INTERNET**→*url* http://server.berke ley.edu/~ayukawa/lomml.html

MP Music Rock Previews Artists like Bruce Hornsby, Foo Fighters, Jimmy Buffett, and even Peter Frampton showcase their newest releases at this site; each preview features a short introduction, an album cover. Pic, the release date, and three to four sound clips. ✓**INTERNET**→*url* http://www. mpmusic.com/rock/rock.htm

#music An all-purpose music IRC channel with an informational home page. Talk about the new Joni Mitchell album, wonder aloud what has happened to silence as a compositional tool, or try to predict upcoming trends in classical music. Keep in mind, though, that most of the chat centers on the popular song, on guitar-bass-drums rock and roll. Why? Because that's what the market will bear. ✓**INTERNET**→*irc* #music *Info:* ✓**INTERNET**→*url* http:// www.onramp.net/redshift/index. html

Music Talk Though most of the folders in eWorld's Music Talk area have fewer messages than Blood, Sweat, and Tears had members, a few topics have begun to attract large numbers of music fans. Let's Talk Rock and Let's Talk Jazz draw a few messages each day,

and popular Gen X bands like Phish and Nine Inch Nails benefit from a steady flow of discussion. And if these topics don't tickle your fancy, read up on the alternative music scene, punk, concerts, blues, guitar gods, and dozens of specific artists, from Green Day to Prince to Pearl Jam to Liz Phair. ✓**EWORLD**→*go* eaz→Pump Up The Volume→Music Talk

Musical Listservs A quick list of music-oriented mailing lists, including rock lists like Rock-L and Soco-L (the Southern Rock Music List). ✓**INTERNET**→*url* http://www. clark.net/pub/listserv/lsmus1.html

NetHead Rock NetHead picks a rock site of the day, carries a schedule of live chat with rock celebrities on the Internet and the online services, links to several of the big music Websites, picks the best Websites for a specific rock topic (e.g., the best R.E.M. sites), and compiles a list of rock quotes. ✓**INTERNET**→*url* http://www.xmis sion.com/~verve/rock/

Rock List (ml) A scholarly discussion of current popular rock music. ✓**INTERNET**→*email* listserv@ kentvm.kent.edu ✍ *Type in message body:* subscribe rocklist <your full name>

Rock Music Want to know if Duran Duran is releasing a new album any time soon (it might take them a while to push something out after the strenuous cover-song-filled *Thank You*)? Can you hardly restrain yourself from telling other rock fans that you just got a tattoo of the Aerosmith logo on your...well, you know. Or do you just want to wish the Edge a happy birthday on his special day (which is August 8)? Then visit these message boards, where discussion of just about anything to do with rock music is welcomed with open arms (that's Journey, right?). Vist here, and you'll be on your way to rock and roll chat heaven. ✓**PRODIGY** ...→*jump* music 1 bb→ Choose a Topic→Rock Music (A-K) ...→*jump* music 1 bb→ Choose a Topic→Music (L-Z)

Rock & Roll and Pop Music

Message-based discussion of a diverse group of artists, including Green Day, Bob Seger, and Selena. Anything that could be remotely classified as rock and roll is fit for discussion at this site, which explains why the Peter Cetera Fan Club has a very strong presence here, posting its events schedule and news briefs. Thank you for sharing that information with us, Mrs. Cetera. ✓**COMPUSERVE**→*go* amgpop→Message *and* Library→ rock&roll/pop

RockNet Forum RockNet's generic rock boards are the perfect place for rock fans of all stripes to speak out on their favorite topics. Are you glad Kurt is dead? Is anyone from Los Angeles? Are you pissed at Pearl Jam? Vent, dude! RockNet also has narrower topics for discussing the Moody Blues, Racer Records, and WJRR Orlando, and the libraries contain hundreds of documents, sound clips, and pictures for bands ranging from the Grateful Dead to your neighbor's garage project. ✓**COMPUSERVE**→*go* rocknet

Rocktropolis Proclaiming itself "a Rock 'n' Roll fantasy theme park, a surreal city landscape inhabited by some of pop culture's greatest musicians and cult heroes plus its new pretenders," this Website takes you on a journey through a rock cybercity. And the trip's a blast. Littered with quotes from rock superstars and set up like an actual city, you can enter

Psychedelic Psyberspace—from http://www.cfn.cs.dal.ca/~af678/cyberspace.html

areas with concert info, search for sheet music, visit sites for unsigned bands, head to the Morrison Hotel (for info about Jim Morrison and sound clips from *An American Prayer*), read this week's episode of the Rocktropolis comics, travel to a live chat room for rock music discussions, and much more. You could explore here for hours and hours without seeing everything—and even if you did see everything, you wouldn't exhaust Rocktropolis, because it keeps changing. ✓**INTERNET** →*url* http://rocktropolis.com/

Rolling Stone Rock & Roll Chat Given the name of the famous magazine that sponsors this chat site, it's strange just how few fans come here to talk about the music. After a brief flurry of messages about the opening of Cleveland's Rock and Roll Hall of Fame (looking for a video of the opening? looking for a program? etc.), the board has quieted down, offer-

ing news briefs on artists like Rush and Lenny Kravitz and precious little else. ✓**COMPUSERVE**→*go* rsforum→Message *and* Library→Rock and Roll

Acid jazz

The Acid Jazz Server Everything you ever wanted to know about acid jazz, provided for you by acid jazz fan Erik Boralv. What has Boralv given to the world? An essay defining the genre, examples of bands with a low jazz pH (Guru, Lisa Stansfield, etc.), and lists of mailing lists, magazines, clubs, and record labels are here for the curious. ✓**INTERNET**→*url* http://www.cmd.uu.se/AcidJazz/

Acid-Jazz (ml) What is acid jazz? No one really knows, but it's not Michael Jackson, and it's not R.E.M., and it's usually a subgenre of alternative hip-hop that emphasizes benign spirituality. Talk about it here. ✓**INTERNET**→*email*

listserv@ucsd.edu ✍ *Type in message body:* subscribe acid-jazz <your full name> *Info:* ✓**INTERNET**→ *url* http://www.cmd.uu.se/Acid Jazz/Mail.html

Alternative & indie

alt.music.alternative.female
(ng) Adjectives describing the music here run the gamut from "bubble-gummy" to "killer" to "yuck." But what can you expect when the discussion is trained on artists as diverse as Shampoo, L7, Hole, Shonen Knife, Jennifer Trynin, and Joan Jett? Don't expect any PC rules to be observed—there's lots of band bashing that turns into woman bashing very quickly, especially when it comes to the reigning queen of female alternative music, Courtney Love. ✓**USENET**→alt.music.alternative.female

alt.music.independent (ng) Regional rock bands have a hard time breaking through to a national market—they can slave away at the same bar year after year, playing the same songs to an anonymous mass of college students, and still they can't crack the consciousness of the mass market. This newsgroup, devoted to independent labels and unsigned bands, is as Balkanized as you'd imagine it would be—fans of North Carolina alternative rockers probably aren't so interested in the threads about Minnesota shoegazers, and most of the band names will be meaningless to all but the omniscient. But the fragmentation feels like democracy, like energy—in short, like rock and roll. ✓**USENET**→alt.music.independent

Alternative Rock Who likes Weezer? How about Radiohead, Soundgarden, Pearl Jam, Foo Fighters, Nine Inch Nails, Blue,

Tripping Daisy, The Cranberries, Rusted Root, Blues Traveler, or any of the other chart-topping alternative-music acts discussed here? Dennis wants to know more about Bush. Byron can't decide who will have a more lasting impact on the pop landscape, Nirvana or Hole. And a fervent Green Day fan announces the track listing for the new album, only to be greeted with the sneers of a detractor: "Let me tell you about these songs. They will sound exactly the same as all of their other music. They don't have much talent." Come here for message-based talk with an alternative slant. ✓**COMPUSERVE**→*go* amgpop→Messages and Libraries→Alternative Rock

Alternative Rock If you can name that alternative tune in five words or less, you'll enjoy the Lyrics Quiz section of this board, where the music of artists like Kate Bush, Ben Lee, and the Mighty Mighty Mighty Mighty

(stop us!) Bosstones are dissected word-by-word. But that's just one feature of the enormous board—there's also room to debate which alternative band is the best ever (Superchunk is nominated frequently) and to discuss topical subjects like censorship in music (Kat said on the subject, "You can't void ideas and creativity just cuz some stupid kids are doing bad things. That's not the music's fault—that's the stupid kids!"). Well said, Kat. ✓**PRODIGY** …→ *jump* music 1 bb →Choose a Topic→Alternative Rock (A-K) …→*jump* music 1 bb→Choose a Topic→Alternative Rock (L-Z)

#altmusic Alternative rock in all its glory is discussed here, along with all the other parts of life that confound, infuriate, and excite those preoccupied with alternative rock—the young and the restless. Talk love. Talk drink. Talk drugs. Talk all night if you want to. ✓**INTERNET**→ *irc* #altmusic

A Dreampop page—http://www.itp.tsoa.nyu.edu/~student/brendonm/intrinfo.html

What's New? | What's Cool? | Handbook | Net Search | Net Directory | Newsgroups

A NOT-SO-RANDOM COLLECTION OF BANDS

All pages have about 16-70K of thumbnail images.

Yes, yes, I know not everyone has a 28.8 modem or T1...*sigh*

● The Cure

● Sonic Youth

● Paul Westerberg (The Replacements)

● Ride

● The House of Love

● Kitchens of Distinction

● Bob Mould (Sugar, Husker Du)

● My Bloody Valentine

● Slowdive

● Paul Weller (not my page; I'm working on one)

Live Alternative Chat The conversation here is mainly of the serve-and-volley variety—it doesn't get too far beyond, "Nirvana sucks!" and "So do you!" Still, this is definitely a good place to toss around names like Silverchair, Skaters, R.E.M., and Love Spit Love. Tennis anyone? ✓**PRODIGY**→*jump* chat→Prodigy Chat→Select an Area: →Music →Alternative

Live Indie Chat Wait! Don't get on that airplane! You don't have to fly to Tampa Bay to hear news and info about their local bands, like Pee Shy. And you don't have to fight through the smog-filled, slippery-floor rock and roll bars of New York City to get the latest on Manhattan indie faves such as God is My Co-pilot. You can engage in indie chat at this site and save yourself some time and travel expenses. ✓**PRODIGY**→*jump* chat→ Prodigy Chat→Select an Area: → Music →Indie

MP Music Alternative Previews This site features half a dozen new albums each month. Every album listed is accompanied by a small caption, two short sound clips, and one three-minute album preview. The albums are generally *Alternative Nation* fare (maybe a couple are *120 Minutes*) as opposed to real underground/ indie works—a typical month's collection will consist of college favorites like Björk and Big Audio Dynamite as well as never-heard-of-'em-but-soon-to-have-a-buzz-clip artists like Hum and Joan Osbourne. ✓**INTERNET**→*url* http:// www.mpmusic.com/altern/altern. htm

Rolling Stone Alternative Rock There is plenty of heated back-and-forth at this site about what makes a band truly alternative. Everyone has an opinion, and no firm criteria are ever established, but in the crossfire of the debate, you'll learn a lot from the message board and library here about bands like Silverchair, the Ramones, and Smashing Pumpkins. ✓**COMPUSERVE**→*go* rsforum→ Messages *and* Libraries→Library Alternative

UK Indie Music (ml) What is indie music? Who knows. What is British indie music? Who knows, old chap. It's not just independent labels anymore; this mailing list addresses almost any alternative band from the land that gave us Bush, Marc Bolan, The Sex Pistols, and a pumping piano rocker by the name of Elton John. ✓**INTERNET**→*email* stasia@mit.edu ✍ *Type in message body:* subscribe interactive

Classic rock & oldies

alt.rock-n-roll.classic (ng) At this newsgroup, you'll find messages on a variety of classic-rock topics, like Dan's recent open invitation for chat about the Eagles. And Bill wants to know if anyone remembers the album on which Melanie covered "Wild Horses" ("Does anyone know which one it was and where I can get it?"). Discuss the founding fathers (and mothers) of rock. ✓**USENET**→ alt.rock-n-roll.classic

alt.rock-n-roll.oldies (ng) Stay up all night with this musical version of *American Graffiti*. This newsgroup gives oldies fans a place to ask "Does anyone remember The Penguins?" and "Did I just imagine it, or did a group called Cornbread & Jerry really exist?" ✓**USENET**→alt.rock-n-roll.oldies

American Oldies Diner Hang out in the malt shop talking about the sock hop and staring at all the bobby soxers. Drop a nickel in the jukebox and listen for the rave-up sounds of Gene Vincent. And then talk all you want about Elvis, rockabilly, surf, the Beatles, vintage labels, and oldies from the 1950s, 1960s, and 1970s. Whether your tastes run toward Dick Dale or the Hollies, this is the place for you. ✓**COMPUSERVE**→ *go* oldies

Classic Rock Chat Exchange news and trivia about the cornerstones of classic rock with other fans. Mentions of the Beatles, Doors, and Yardbirds are more common here than fringes on a hippie's vest. Speaking of which, can you identify the rock star who wrote the lyrics "I thought I saw her flaxen hair in Jackson, Mississippi / But it was just some aging hippie / With feathers on his vest / I didn't see you were leaving me / But now I see I should have guessed"? If not, don't feel stupid. come here. Someone will know. ✓**PRODIGY**→*jump* music bb1 →Choose a Topic→Classic Music

Classical Rock/Oldies The good old boys are drinking whisky and rye. Mrs. Robinson is eyeing young Benjamin Braddock. And the Doors are breaking on through to the other side. While this message board doesn't have much activity, it does treat the concerns of fans of music passed. ✓**COMPUSERVE**→*go* amgpop→Messages *and* Libraries →Classic Rock/ Oldies

Golden Rock and Oldies The music of Elvis Presley, Gene Vincent, Ricky Nelson, Bobby Rydell, and others lives on and prospers through the fan-driven discussions on this board. ✓**PRODIGY**→*jump* music 1bb→Choose a Topic→Golden Rock/Oldies

Live Classic Rock Chat Doo wah, diddy, do you want to talk about the classics of rock and roll? Come here to chat about the oldies-but-goodies. ✓**PRODIGY**→ *jump* chat→Prodigy Chat→Select an Area:→Music→Classic Rock

Oldies OnLine Profiles, email addresses, audio clips, and booking information for many of the great performers of the 1950s and 1960s. Greats like Lou Christie, Chubby Checker (listen to a clip of him singing "The Twist"). The Mamas & the Papas, and the Turtles are all featured here. ✓**INTERNET** →*url* http://www.digimark.net/ oldies

The Routes of American Music With an essay based on a Kennedy Center series about the roots of American popular music, this site takes you on a musical road trip through the blues, country, and folk territory surrounding modern rock. A. P. Carter, Robert Johnson, and Robert Cray, among others, make appearances. ✓**INTERNET**→*url* http://artsedge.kennedy-center.org/KC-OpenHouse95.html

Vocal/EasyListening The names dropped here verge on the music-for-your-grandma genre. Messages about Sinatra and Nat King Cole are common. If this alarms you, go elsewhere. If not, enjoy. ✓**COMPUSERVE**→*go* amgpop →Messages *and* Libraries→Vocal/ EasyListening

Dreampop

Dreampop The editors of this e-zine believe that there "is a difference between Muzak and music that takes you to a higher plane." So they fended off a lot of "shoegazer" flames and established this site, which includes discographies (of Lush, Verve, and The Orb, among others), in-depth looks at specific works—including Hüsker Dü's not-exactly-dream-pop masterpiece *Zen Arcade*—and even a message board for dreamy discussion. ✓**INTERNET**→*url* http:// www.itp.tsoa.nyu.edu/~student/ brendonm/intrinfo.html

Dreampop-L (ml) What has a wash of guitars and flies? Dream-pop, of course, that affectless rock genre pioneered by My Bloody Valentine and popularized by bands such as Lush, Slowdive, Ride, Cocteau Twins, the Swans, and more. Dream a little dream-pop here. ✓**INTERNET**→*email* listserv@netcom.com ✍ *Type in message body:* subscribe Dreampop-L <your full name>

Progressive

alt.music.progressive (ng) Besides getting some good conversation about Smashing Pumpkins, Love Revolution, and the Blue Man Group, you'll also get some good advice about listening to them, like this note from Marc: "If you're in a band, or go to see lots of bands, do yourself a favor. WEAR EARPLUGS! I've had two ear surgeries, the last one to repair my damaged hearing, so I'm speaking from experience. Being 80 percent deaf in one ear is not cool, I've been there." Hey, man, thanks for the advice. You, like, saved my life or something. ✓**USENET**→alt.music.progressive

Obscure Progressive Rock (ml) You won't find any big-name bands here—as the helpful title suggests, this mailing list is strictly for news, reviews, and discussion of the music of smaller progressive acts like Anglagard, Ozric Tentacles, and Gong. ✓**INTERNET**→*email* gib@mailhost.tcs.tulane.edu ✍ *Write a request*

NOTES

"Just curious as to who you think has declined the most. You know, a band/ artist that started off great, but has now faded away and turned crappy."

"My nomination: Genesis. I loved their early stuff (I still maintain that Foxtrot is one of the best albums ever). But their latest offerings have paled in comparison… When I was at the latest Genesis concert, their early songs rocked much more than the soft Phil Collins 'Miami Vice' stuff. I thought as a drummer, he would make the songs rocking. I guess not."

"Although I am without question the most devoted Fleetwood Mac fan I know, the Fleetwood Mac of today is not the diverse group of songwriters and styles it once was… it now sounds like a bad reproduction of the way it used to be. For me, FM lives on.. the way they used to be.

—from **alt.rock-n-roll.classic**

Progressive Music (ml A German-language list for discussion of concert dates, record reviews, and background information on top-drawer progressive bands like Yes, Genesis, and King Crimson. ✓IN-**TERNET**→*email* prog-request@ darktow.gun.de ✍ *Write a request*

Progressive Rock Musicians Network (ml) Prog maestros assemble here to keep up with new albums, tours, and other news. ✓**INTERNET**→*email* progmaestros-request@arastar.com ✍ *Type in message body:* subscribe progmaestros <your full name>

rec.music.progressive (ng) Have any new anecdotes about the New Anekdoten? Want to talk about that Fisticuffs concert with Netters who saw the same show in a different town? You can discuss those topics at this newsgroup, but you can also engage in a never-ending thread that pits Yes against Genesis ("Who sucks worse now?") and a discussion of which Rush album "really was the worst." This newsgroup specializes in progressive rock with a slight backwards glance. ✓**USENET**→rec.music. progressive

Psychedelic

alt.music.psychedelic (ng) Conversation is infrequent here; most of the posts are in-depth reviews of recordings like Bevis Frond's *It Just Is* and Electric Orange's eponymous debut. There are also a few looking-for-this-psych-record-and-this-psych-record for-sale notices. ✓**USENET**→ alt.music.psychedelic

Psychedelic Psyberspace Links to canonical psychedelic bands, including Pink Floyd and the Beatles, as well as more mind-bending links. ✓**INTERNET**→*url*

http://www.cfn.cs.dal.ca/~af678/ cyberspace.html

Rockabilly

alt.music.rockabilly (ng) Grease down your ducktail, put on your poodle skirt, and head on down to this newsgroup for discussion of oldtimers like Glen Glenn and Sammy Gowens and newcomers like Southern Culture on the Skids and Simon and the Barsinisters. ✓**USENET**→alt.music. rockabilly

Rockabilly Mailing List (ml) Dick Dale made those kids in Brisbane rockabilly their little hearts out, even though it was pouring rain during the entire outdoor event. You see, it was his first tour Down Under, and he didn't want to let those little kangaroo-loving rockabilly fans down. Read a full account of his show, as well as reviews, news clippings, and biographies of other artists (like Big Sandy and even rockabilly-style Elvis) on this mailing list. ✓**INTER-NET**→*email* listserv@u-strasbg.fr ✍ *Type in message body:* subscribe rockabill<your full name> *Archives:* ✓**INTERNET**→*url* http://www.u-stras-bg.fr: 80/~kohler/mailing_list/ archives/

Synth-pop

alt.music.synthpop (ng) Jennifer asks, "I need help with a lyric from New Order's "Perfect Kiss." The line goes like this..'Tonight I should've stayed at home/playing with my...' I can't figure out if the last word is 'precious' or 'pleasures.' I'm sure someone out there knows the answer!" There were twelve responses stating that the missing lyric is "pleasure zone" and one response asserting that it is "precious cone." Get your Q-tips out, clean your ears, listen to

the song, and post your opinion about this and any other issue that has to do with synthpop rock. ✓**USENET**→alt.music.synthpop

Synth-Pop Mailing List (ml) For discussion of the second British Invasion. ✓**INTERNET**→*email* perfect-beat-request@acca. nmsu.edu ✍ *Write a request*

Other genres

AOR Music (ml) Do you love the classic rock of the 1960s, the art rock or the 1970s, or the concept rock of the 1980s? Of course you do. But keep quiet, especially around critics. They'll mock you. Only other fans will understand. ✓**INTERNET**→*email* thecompany@ aol.com ✍ *Write a request*

Live Industial/Gothic Chat Turn down the stereo and tune into some industrial and gothic chat here. ✓**PRODIGY**→*jump* chat→ Prodigy Chat→Select an Area:→ Music→Industial/Gothic

Southern Rock List (ml) Just what kinds of bands can be fairly categorized as Southern rock? Well, they usually play a mix of blues, funk, and straight-ahead rock and roll—like the Allman Brothers, for instance, or the Black Crowes. But don't take our word for it. Drive South to this mailing list and find out. ✓**INTERNET**→ *email* listserv@ubvm.cc.buffalo.edu ✍ *Type in message body:* subscribe soco-l <your full name>

Tyranny Corps What features grace the pale pages of this gothic e-zine? Concert and band reviews, divided into sections titled "Seen Them Live" or "Heard Them Dead," along with a healthy dose of gothic literature and culture. ✓**INTERNET**→*url* http://tyranny. com/tyranny/corps1/contents.html

Punk

When pop music stalled in the mid-seventies, it was punk that came to offer a jump

start. Snarling, sneering, and seething, early punks like the Sex Pistols, X-Ray Specs, and the Germs seized disco and arena rock by the collar and shook them until their fat chins trembled with fear. Since then, the punk aesthetic has captivated generation after generation of aimless adolescents; whether alternative luminaries like Sonic Youth or Hüsker Dü, grunge-punk superstars like Nirvana, or hardcore purists like Fugazi, punk outfits have given the lie to Johnny Rotten's proclamation of "No future." Start exploring online punk with **Flexbook**, **Godwalker**, and **Punkrock**. Mount a tour with the **Deterrent Tour Manual**. And go international with **Portugese Punx**.

Original punk rocker Sid Vicious—from http://www.yab.com/-stumbras/sex-pistols/

On the Net

Across the board

Flexbook What was the first Social Distortion record? How many albums did X record? This huge discography covers the North American punk scene, from its late-seventies beginnings to its early-nineties explosion with bands like the Pixies, Nirvana, and Green Day. √**INTERNET** ...→*url* ftp://ftp.uwp.edu/pub/music/lists/flex/ ...→*url* ftp://mirrors.aol. com/pub/music/lists/flex/

Godwalker A list of punk zines and e-zines, lyrics to punk songs, articles, and more. √**INTERNET**→*url* http:// web.cps.msu.edu/~walker-ma/index_text.html

Happy Farm—The Punk Rock Old Folks' Home Today, the "b" stands for baboon. Tomorrow, it might be boil, or bellwether, or breast. And Happy Farm contains information on punk rock's "Golden Age," which the page designer sets at 1980 to 1988. Subhuman? The Misfits? Bad Religion? Link and learn. √**INTERNET**→ *url* http://www.well.com/user/btanaka/pr.html

Hendrik's Basement Punk Homepage Links, a picture of Hendrik, and the Toothpick punk fanzine. √**INTERNET**→*url* http:// eduserv.rug.ac.be/~hdacquin/

Net Punk's Marvelous Page An impressively designed and still-evolving page that includes information on a variety of punk bands. Sounds pretty generic, huh? Well, if it's specificity you want, how about this poem, "Artless Motives," by someone using the name Chuck Brown: "Yah. punk sucks, these scenes cool, your town sucks, he's / so hardcore, she eats meat, he likes rap shut up / who cares about social crap-fuck it all rancid suck dick / jello and rollins are in details sex pistols were always a joke–gg allin wasn't cool cause he ate shit let's start / let's start caring about all people / no i'm not a hippy / i like to get stoned to many hippies in eugene i hate the cherry poppin

Fugazi: punk integrity personified—http://utkvx1.utk.edu/~anutron/fugazi.html

daddies / who cares / shits gonna happen soon / martial in eugene right now / i'm glad i'm not a dead head / i like c.c.r." It came out of the sky, Chuck. Go back with it. ✓**INTERNET**→*url* http://cybersight. com/cgi-bin/cs/newsic/news/ .pages.354

Punk Bands Directory A straightforward alphabetical index of most punk bands' home pages on the Internet. It's fun, and it's free—kind of like one-stop shoplifting. ✓**INTERNET**→*url* http:// wchat.on.ca/vic/wwp-band.htm

Punk Junk on the Web The author of this page readily admits that he doesn't like abrasive, cacaphonous punk, and that he prefers the melodic punk of bands like the Descendents and Screaming Weasels. Sometimes called Runk Pock, sometimes called Punk U, this page includes a comprehensive list of bands, labels, distributors, and fanzines. ✓**INTERNET**→*url* http://cssun7.vassar. edu:80/~anschorr/punk.html

Punk Page A huge list of punk links, from Knife in Your Back to the unofficial Lookout Records page. ✓**INTERNET**→*url* http:// astartes.ucsd.edu:8080/punk.html

Punkrock Information on a handful of bands, access to the Gals Panic Webzine, and more. ✓**INTERNET**→*url* http://www.eden. com/punk/

World Wide Punk Music reviews, e-zine reviews, links to punk bands, punk record labels, punk catalogs, and more. The definition of punk is relatively broad—Jello Biafra and Abnegation are included, but so are Billy Bragg and Green Day—and so is the coverage at this site; punk fans will be able to find plenty of information on renowned bands like the Cramps, the Clash, the Dead Milkmen, the Misfits, and the Sex Pistols, as well as newer punk outfits like Tumor Circus and Winona Riders. If you want the lyrics to "Bodies" or information on the Lithuanian e-zine Knk, there's no better site online. ✓**INTERNET**→*url* http://wchat.on.ca/ vic/wwp.htm

Chat

alt.punk (ng) Bob wants to know

how many punk songs treated the delicate topic of masturbation, and other posters on alt.punk are happy to help (although that's hardly the point of masturbation). There's the Buzzcocks' "Orgasm Addict," for one, and "We Jerk Off," an ode to autoerotic exercise recorded by the (possibly fake) Penis Wolves. Talk about the demographics of the genre ("There was a punk scene in any urban environment with do-nothing kids who had enough money to buy a guitar but not enough structure to find another activity"); chat about the Cramps, X-Ray Specs, the Sex Pistols, Stiff Little Fingers, Social Distortion, the Germs, and more; trade news on Oi Polloi events in Scandinavia; and listen to a love-struck fan reminisce about the late, great Johnny Thunders ("Got all the albums, got a Rare Video collection, got his autograph, and got incredible drunk with him once. Without a doubt a legend."). ✓**USENET**→alt.punk

Anarchopunk/Peacepunk List (ml) Do punks like peace?

Bikini Kill's Kathleen Hanna—http:// www.cc.columbia.edu:80/~rli3/

Sure they do, and you can talk about it with them on this mailing list. ✓**INTERNET**→*email* majordomo@well.com ✍ *Type in message body:* subscribe anok4u2-list <your email address>

Live Punk Chat Real-time chat with other punk fans. ✓**PRODIGY**→*jump* chat→Prodigy Chat→Select an Area:→Music Punk

Punk and Hardcore List (ml) Who decides what's punk and what's hardcore? The people who subscribe to this mailing list. No, really. The president of the Punk Nation phones them up one by one, tallies their votes, and then releases a proclamation. Don't be left out. ✓**INTERNET**→*email* punk-list-request@ cpac.washington.edu ✍ *Write a request*

Punk Chat Message-based discussion about mainstream punks (Sonic Youth, Nirvana), pop punks (Rancid, Jawbreaker), and classic punks (the Sex Pistols, the Clash). Good riddance to bad rubbish! ✓**EWORLD**→*go* eaz→Pump Up The Volume→Music Talk →PUNK TALK

Punk List (ml) Talk about punk with other punks. ✓**INTERNET**→ *email* majordomo@cc.gatech.edu

Queercore punks Pansy Division—http://www.city-net.com/~gayboy/pansydiv/

Iggy Pop, punk before his time—from http://sashimi.wwa.com/hammers/pictures/

✍ *Type in message body:* subscribe punk-list <your email address>

Queer Punk (ml) Talk about gay punks on the Net—Team Dresch, Tribe 8, Heavens To Betsy, 7 Year Bitch, Bikini Kill, and Excuse 17. ✓**INTERNET**→*email* muzmorph@ aol.com ✍ *Write a request*

DIY

Deterrent Tour Manual Learn to book a tour on your own, and then do it with the help of the contacts listed here. ✓**INTERNET**→ *url* http://www.islandnet.com/~moron/deterrent/tour_gd.html

Local & regional

Boise Punk Page Want to visit your own private Idaho? Get disaffected with potato-heads like Skidfish, Freak in a Jar, and Malnutrition at this page, which reports on the Boise punk scene. ✓**INTERNET**→ *url* http://www.primenet.com/~hanford

Indiana Punk Shows An admittedly incomplete list of punk concerts in Indiana. ✓**INTERNET**→ *url* http://silver.ucs.indiana.edu:80 /~dorsett/shows.html

Lame Ass Home Page Information on the punk scene surrounding Tucson, Arizona. ✓**INTERNET**→*url* http://radon.gas.uug. arizona.edu/~raulr

Nowhere Sick of looking at that stupid Golden Gate Bridge? Had it up to here with those cute little cable cars? Convinced that Fisherman's Wharf is just mocking you, saying "You're nothing and you'll always be nothing, and there's no future for you"? Bay Area punks rejoice! Finally, there's a page that meets your needs, with a list of radio shows, e-zines, and related Websites. ✓**INTERNET**→ *url* http://radon.gas.uug.arizona. edu/~raulr

Ottawa Punk Rock Concert lists, band home pages, and more.

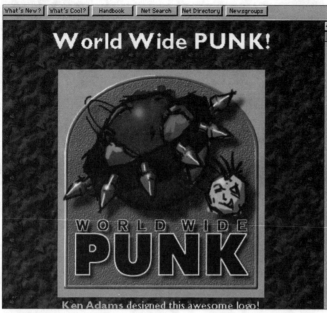

World Wide Punk—from http://wchat.on.ca/vic/wwp.htm

✓**INTERNET**→*url* http://CAPITAL NET.com/~satori/punk/punk.html

Portuguese Punx Recipe for punk: Take a nation, frustrate the expectations of its youth, and add guitars. Skeptical? Just as Inkisi-cao, Sub Caos, or any of the other Portuguese punk bands listed at this site, which collects band bios, e-zine descriptions, images, and more. ✓**INTERNET**→*url* http://metro. turnpike.net/~nofx/index.html

Route 7 Are eyebrows the bull-dozers of the brain? Probably not, but it might make for a good punk lyric. Get the latest on the punk streaming out from our capi-tal city. ✓**INTERNET**→*url* http:// csugrad.cs.vt.edu/~bemmett/

Sonikd Show listings for the vast Midwest, specifically Ohio, Illi-nois, and Wisconsin. ✓**INTERNET** →*url* http://www.infinet.com:80/~ sonikd/

Swedish Punk and Hardcore Archive Lyrics, show listings, and images for angry three-chord Swedes. ✓**INTERNET**→*url* http:// www.csd.uu.se/~d94sma/ archive/

The Texas Punk Directory Is punk bigger in Texas? Find out at this page, which offers show lists, band bios, a list of record stores, and more. ✓**INTERNET**→*url* http:// www.usis.com/~twist/

Skatepunks

Free Cheese In the nineties, punk seems to come from Wash-ington State, so maybe that's why Free Cheese—a Website located at the University of Washington— has such an authoritative feel. With numerous links to punk band pages and lots of skating in-formation, this page patrols the border between skating and punk. ✓**INTERNET**→*url* http://weber.u. washington.edu/~notdead/

"John Lydon's book is a complete joke, and anyone who doens't see right through it is a stupid fucking idiot. I read it and laughted at every page. Lydon's STILL fucking with peopele, but the majority of everyone doesn't even realise it. 'Yes, this is the TRUTH, this is how it REALLY happened…you can trust me' is what he was saying in the interviews but all he wrote was nonsense to see how many people would fall for it. Unfortunately no one seems to have picked up on that fact.

"Punk Diary is good as a reference and nothing else. I don't see how anyone could just sit down and read it, but as a reference book it is indispensable.

"England's Dreaming is quite thorough and extensive, but just one man's view of the scene.

"Deb. Spungeon's book is quite good coming from someone who you would now see show up on Ricky Lake."

—from **alt.punk**

Metal & hard rock

Beavis likes heavy metal (that's Metallica on his never-washed blue t-shirt); Butt-head

likes heavy metal (that's AC/DC on his never-washed black t-shirt)—what other recommendation do you need. Full of dark imagery, dense guitars, and overpowering vocals, heavy metal has long been the music of choice of teenage stoners—not to mention the occasional adult who wants to get in touch with his or her inner teenage stoner. Online metalheads should begin at newsgroups like **alt.rock-n-roll.metal** and **alt.rock-n-roll.metal.heavy**, move on to **Metal Rules!!!** and **Dark Symphonies**, and then explore offshoot genres like industrial music (**NoiseNet**), Japanese Metal (**Japanese Metal**), neoclassical metal (**Rising Force**), and death and black metal (**xKull**).

Black Sabbath—from http://www.cyberspace.com/adrock/bsd/bsabbath.html

On the Net

Across the board

alt.rock-n-roll.metal (ng) Users here favor the Old School, and even indulge in some glam talk—Dokken, Overkill, Saigon Kick, and the Crüe are likely to be on the menu, and Metallica sell-out threads are a permanent feature. Dark Angel and Paradise Lost are rising stars, though, and every once in a while a new band may inspire comparison with classic talent. ✓**USENET**→alt.rock-n-roll. metal

alt.rock-n-roll.metal.heavy (ng) Big name metal bands like Pantera, White Zombie, Metallica, and Megadeth are fodder for discussion. As is the case with many of the other hard music newsgroups, label reps and CD salesmen have moved in *en force* in the last year and are posting product information right and left. ✓**USENET**→alt.rock-n-roll.metal. heavy

Comrades's Music Links Use Comrade's collection of heavy metal links as an easy way to reach the home pages of some of your favorite groups: White Zombie, Primus, Pantera, Faith No More, and Danzig are included in his collection. ✓**INTERNET**→*url* http:// metro.turnpike.net/C/Comrade/ music.html

Heavy Metal Standard heavy metal names—Ozzy! AC-DC! Alice Cooper! Metallica!—get the most airplay on the message board here, but occasionally you'll see discussion of a newer band, like the thread on White Zombie's performance at the MTV Music Awards, which was universally held to be a disaster (Wade comments, "I've played the video four or five times and cringe every time. Rob Zombie was just barely

Metal & Hard Rock Genres

Biohazard, lookin' tough—from http://www1.usa1.com/~ryanwh/biohazard.jpg

hanging on for life on that one. I feel so bad for the guy—ten years of playing hard, and then in front of 300 million people, and bust!!!"). For more heavy metal fun, cruise the library for. GIFs of the Queensrÿche logo, tips on how to best "survive" a Kiss convention, and tons of heavy record reviews by the prolific Bill Vogel III. ✓**COMPUSERVE**→*go* rocknet→Messages *and* Libraries→Heavy Metal

Heavy Metal Chat From Marilyn Manson to Metallica to Megadeth, this message board runs the gamut in heavy metal from M to M, occasionally pausing to let an aspiring death metal guitarist or drummer advertise for band members. ✓**COMPUSERVE**→*go* amgpop→Messages *and* Libraries→Heavy Metal

Metal Dudes Twenty heavy metal dudes have assembled a collection of links to their home pages. Get acquainted with Mooz, Wicewolf, Pest, and their friends and then send them your heavy-metal thoughts with the email addresses listed here. ✓**INTERNET**→*url* http://cc.lut.fi/~mega/dudes.html

Metal List (ml) This list has Bay Area roots, although it now resides in Italy. ✓**INTERNET**→*email* majordomo@inet.it ✍ *Type in message body:* subscribe metal <your email address>

Metal Rules!!! There is heavy metal music being played and loved in Newfoundland. Betrayer, a local band, hosts this site, which offers insightful record reviews (Fear Factory's *Demanufacture* was put on the table recently), a calendar of local heavy metal concerts

and performances, sound samples of tunes like Afterforever's "Get a Grip", and links to big band home pages (you can reach Slayer, Anthrax, and Motley Crüe from here). ✓**INTERNET**→*url* http://europa.cs.mun.ca/~gwaye/metal.html

Death & black metal

alt.rock-n-roll.metal.death (ng) Yea! 'Tis home for thee purists! Fans of Satan, Odin, Thor, and extreme metal congregate here to judge for themselves thee worthiness of this band and that band. 'Tis lucky for us that thee standard tag "brutal" is finally being phased out in favor of richer adjectives. ✓**USENET**→alt.rock-n-roll.metal.death

Dark Symphonies An online record store offering an alphabetical list of black metal and doom recordings from bands like Dark Theater, Immortal, and Necromass. Satan could be a frequent customer of this store. ✓**INTERNET**→*url* http://hamp.hampshire.edu/~cmnF93/dark.html

Death Metal/Black Metal Archive The Granddaddy of all

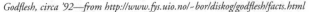

Godflesh, circa '92—from http://www.fys.uio.no/~bor/diskog/godflesh/facts.html

Marilyn Manson—from http://artemis. ess.ucla.edu/~paul/mm/pics/EVB/

extreme metal on the Web. The bulk of the content is discographies, lyric sheets, and band line-up info; there are some reviews from alt.rock-n-roll.metal.death, but the archive is lacking overall in original articles and updated input. ✓**INTERNET**→*url* http:// bigdipper.umd.edu/metal.html

Heavy Metal—Blood Death & Satanic Forces of Evil Highly recommended for those seeking information on underground death and black metal bands. There are original reviews, material culled from alt.rock-n-roll.metal.death, and links to all the other putrid Net chasms of gore, guts, and severe mental anguish. ✓**INTERNET**→*url* http://f_utbserv.cse. hks.se/~lanner/heavymetal.html

xKull A MUD-like complex with information on death and black metal, doom, and some noise. It comes complete with a history of the World according to metalheads, involving spacetime loopholes and a malevolent alien population. ✓**INTERNET**→*url* http:// www.interport.net/~spidr/

Hard rock

Hardrock List (ml) Hard rock only, not thrash, death metal, or speed metal. Parse genres and bang your head here. ✓**INTERNET**→*email* listproc@lists.colorado.edu ✍ *Write a request*

Women of Hard Rock and Heavy Metal (ml) Lita Ford, Pat Benatar, and the Runaways are all fair game. But don't try to talk about speed-classical banshee The Great Kat, because she's just a little bit too annoying for most fans. ✓**INTERNET**→*email* ladykillerz-request@arastar.com ✍ *Type in subject line:* asdf *Type in message body:* subscribe ladykillerz <your full name>

Industrial metal

The Industrial Page Metal Ken explains his personal definition of

industrial music ("All in all, industrial is about discovery. It is about finding the most effective means of conveying the chaos, lies and deception around us"), and then he takes you through a collection of links to industrial record labels, artist home pages, and the newsgroup rec.music.industrial. ✓**INTERNET**→*url* http://bird.taponline. com/industrial/

NoiseNet No reviews. No pictures. No fancy graphics, either. Just sound samples of new releases by industrial bands like Penal Colony, Snog, and X Marks the Pedwalk. ✓**INTERNET**→*url* http:// apollo.gmu.edu/~maz/noisenet/ new.html

rec.music.industrial (ng) Hot and heavy discussion of industrial music. Come to this newsgroup to hear what the Nine Inch Nails pre-concert party in Toronto was

Motorhead's Lemmy—from http://fermi.clas. virginia.edu/~sha3u/motorhead/

Industrial poster boy Trent Reznor—
http://ibms15.scri.fsu.edu/~patters/op.html

really like, or to exchange info on industrial music catalogs. ✓**USENET**→rec.music.industrial

Japanese metal

Japanese Metal No, Japanese metal isn't the "Nipponized bit of the old sixth avenue el" in that old e. e. cummings poem. It's Night Hawks, a band that has released six major-label albums since 1989. ✓**INTERNET**→*url* http://home. netscape.com/home/internet-search.html

Neoclassical metal

Rising Force (ml) Discussion of that subsection of metal music known as neoclassical metal. ✓**IN-TERNET**→*email* Igor_Sinyak@ccm. ch.intel.com ✍ *Write a request*

Progressive metal

alt.rock-n-roll.metal.progres-

sive (ng) An affinity for jazz tim-ings, off-tuning, and non-tradi-tional song structure bind this community of heavy rockers to-gether. Old prog rock operations like Queensrÿche and Pink Floyd vie for attention with newer bands like Dream Theatre, Paradise Lost, and Meshuggah. There's also dis-cussion of the Progressive Metal Page on the Web—while it's not currently being maintained, it still holds various and assorted record reviews, discographies and it offers a succinct exegesis of this thing called "progressive metal." ✓**USENET**→ alt.rock-n-roll.metal.prog ressive

The fringe

A Home Page of a Crook The creator of web page is also a col-lege DJ, a noise freak, and a big fan of militaristic overthrows of society and/or governments. Read about some of the amazing experi-mental bands working today, like Xome, Negativland, Squidlaunch, and the truly legendary Legendary Pink Dots. ✓**INTERNET**→*url* http://hamp.hampshire.edu/ ~cmnF93/ coup.html

MetalWeb The self-proclaimed "home of extreme metal" offers ca-reer bios and tour info for bands like the Disciples of Power, Scape-goat, and Casket, among others. ✓**INTERNET**→*url* http://www.tic. ab.ca/~metalweb/mwebhome. htm

Thee Grievous Page Extreme experimental noise is the topic of choice here, with band news, links, zines (noise From the Spleen of Space), and label information (Charnel House, Rapevine). You can also grab the do-it-yourself sound loop of the week. ✓**INTER-NET**→*url* http://www.fishnet. 80/~grievous/index.html

Lithuanian metal:

"GHOSTORM. You proba-bly understood, about what the speak will go on. I think, it's the most known Lithuanian band in abroad. Ghostorm playing very techni-cal death metal. After very good demo 'The end of all songs,' knowing their potential, GHOSTORM made undoubtedly right decision head-ing out to UNISOUND RECORDINGS, Sweden, in order to record their debut CD mater-ial with Dan Swano at mixing desk. The recording took place in the mid of October '94. BLACK MARK PRO-DUCTION released GHOSTORM debut album Frozen in fire in March '95.

"DISSONANCE. Another really great band in Lithuania is DISSO-NANCE. This band playing very original and the same time technical doom metal. In January' 95 DISSO-NANCE released the first their album (MC) Concealed. This cas-sette consists of nine tracks of doom metal."

-from **xKull**

Soul/R&B/Funk

As any true fan of soul music knows, there's really no other music. Everything else—

blues, rock, jazz, pop—is a sham, a feeble excuse for self-expression, and the only true artistry is the artistry generated by a peerless voice steering a peerless song while a peerless rhythm section moves along in the background. Marvin Gaye? James Brown? Curtis Mayfield? Aretha Franklin? It's like one big epiphany. Online, soul gets the short end of the stick—devotees of Sly and the Family Stone aren't exactly the Internet's primary demographic—but when it comes to finding resources, you can make it if you try. Check out **WRNB—The Web's R&B Source**. Get funked up at **alt.music.funky**. And then get the lowdown on classic soul artists.

TLC, chasing waterfalls—http://www.csua.berkeley.edu/~lingo/music/profiles/tlc.html

On the Net

Across the board

Electronic Urban Report Who's contributing to the soundtrack for the latest Spike Lee movie, *Clockers*? Is it true that the Winans have decided to retire from touring? What's up with TLC? And what possessed Patra to cover Grace Jones' "Pull Up to the Bumper"? While it's not confined to music, this email newsletter furnishes the latest news and gossip on black celebrities. ✓**INTERNET**→*email* majordomo@afrinet.net ✍ *Type in message body:* subscribe electronic-urban-report <your email address> *Type in subject line:* subscribe *Info:* ✓**INTERNET**→*url* http://www.trib.com/bbs/eur.html

I Know You Got Soul A soul bibliography, links to pages for individual artists, lists of record labels, and more. ✓**INTERNET**→*url* http://mosaic.echonyc.com/%7Espingo/Soul/

MP Soul Music Previews Short descriptions of and selected sound clips from the most recent soul, R&B, and funk releases. ✓**INTERNET**→*url* http://www.mpmusic.com/randb/randb.htm

The R&B Article Index Want to read an interview with Prince, who isn't really Prince anymore since he changed his name, but still is sort of Prince because his music sounds like it did when he was Prince? Want to see what *Vibe*'s music critics have to say

about the new Terence Trent D'Arby album? Read features, reviews, and interviews from back issues of *Vibe*. ✓**INTERNET**→*url* http://www.pathfinder.com/vibe/archive/suindex/indexmusic.html#r&b

R&B Page The author of this page is an Italian student, but that doesn't mean that he can't love R&B as much as any red-blooded American teenager. Check out the list of top R&B singles, an archive of producers who have had success fashioning soul and rap singles, a list of upcoming soul releases, and the Samples FAQ, which is a database of bitten songs. ✓**INTERNET**→*url* http://www.dsi.unimi.it/Users/Students/barbieri/music.html

WRNB—The Web's R&B Source R&B doesn't get much coverage on the Web. In fact, if you can't imagine a day without the New Jacks, Jills, and harmonizers (Boyz II Men, TLC, or En Vogue) or their older counterparts (Aretha, Sam Cooke, Sly and the

Soul/R&B/Funk **Genres**

Family Stone, the P-Funk empire, and so on), then you shouldn't spend too much time online. It will only depress you. Good thing, then, that the Web R&B Music Source is doing its job. With the R&B Rap Sheet (a collection of news briefs about today's stars), artist profiles, Billboard's R&B Top 20, and links to other pages, this is a generous resource that should satisfy any and all soul survivors. ✓**INTERNET**→*url* http://www.csua.berkeley. edu/~lingo/music.html

Chart

Top 40 R&B Find out who's on top of the R&B charts this week by downloading the Top 40. ✓**INTERNET**→*url* http://www.dsi. unimi.it/Users/Students/barbieri. top1995.html

Chat

alt.music.soul (ng) Who is the best soul singer of all time? "Aretha—hands down." "How can you argue against Sam Cooke once you've heard 'A Change is Gonna Come'?" "You can say all you want about the weakness of modern singers, but Johnny Gill can really sing, and so can Luther Vandross, and Alexander O'Neal." "Hello— has everyone lost their minds? What about Michael Jackson???" Join the debate, or start your own. ✓**USENET**→alt.music.soul

---

Motown/R&B/Doo-Wop How does the singing of the Five Satins, the Penguins, the Orioles, and other street-corner groups

compare to the silky harmonies of current R&B superstars like Boyz II Men and Shai? Well, Joe thinks that the new generation are pretenders to the throne: "It's all electronic enhancement. If you isolate these singers, they seem like charlatans— nice kids, but nothing special. Then listen to Smokey Robinson. The choice is clear." Discuss the generation gap, soul lyrics, and more (including Paul Simon's new doo-wop music, co-written with Nobel Prize winning poet Derek Walcott) on this message board. ✓**COMPUSERVE**→*go* oldies→ Messages *and* Libraries→Motown/R&B/Doo-Wop

---

rec.music.funky (ng) Funk not only moves; it can remove. Dig? If not, you may want to chase out the Sir Nose inside of your mind by visiting this newsgroup, which covers a broad range of funk artists, from Hendrix to Sly to Clinton to Del the Funkee Homosapien. Which rap artists are sampling Funkadelic these days? Is Michael Jackson really funky, or are songs like "Jam" and "2 Bad" anomalies in a career devoted more to middle-of-the-road pop? And what has happened to Prince? Aaron thinks he knows: "Nothing has happened to him. He's fine. And he's stockpiling his best recordings so that when he's free of his Warner Bros. slavery—oops, I mean contract—he can release a huge album, 50 or 60 songs. I heard he was going to name it Emancipation." ✓**USENET**→rec. music.funky

Soul, R&B, Blues Modern soul sits alongside seventies funk, and seventies funk sits alongside sixties shouters and crooners on this message board. ✓**COMPUSERVE**→*go* rsforum→Messages *and* Libraries→ Soul, R&B, Blues

---

Soul/Motown/Funk With so many great topics to discuss—is Aretha Franklin more closely related to Dinah Washington or Ruth Brown? can Prince play more instruments than Teena Marie? can Philip Bailey sing higher than Al Green?—it's a shame that this soul and funk message board is so empty, with occasional posts on Michael Jackson and little else. ✓**COMPUSERVE**→ *go* amgpop→ Messages *and* Libraries→Soul/ Motown/Funk

Classic soul artists

See also Artist Guide, page 70.

BROWN, JAMES

James Brown It's a man's, man's, man's, man's Web. Get a brief bio and a sound clip on the Web or discuss James Brown on AOL. ✓**INTERNET**→*url* http://www. rockhall.com/induct/browjame. html ✓**AMERICA ONLINE**→*keyword* mmc→Rap/R&B R&B/Soul→James Brown

COOKE, SAM

Sam Cooke Raised in the gospel tradition, Sam Cooke was expelled from the church for singing the devil's music, despite the fact that he sang it like an angel. Get a brief bio and a sound clip. ✓**INTERNET**→*url* http://www.rockhall.com/ induct/cooksam.html

THE FOUR TOPS

The Four Tops Do you remember Levi Stubbs? Get a brief bio of the foursome and a sound clip. ✓**INTERNET**→*url* http://www.rockhall.com/induct/fourtops.html

FRANKLIN, ARETHA

Aretha Franklin Has there ever been a voice like Aretha's? Will there ever be a voice like Aretha's? Can you listen to "Save Me" without weeping tears of joy? Get a sound clip and a brief bio. ✓**INTERNET** →*url* http://www.rockhall.com/induct/franaret.html

GAYE, MARVIN

Marvin Gaye Marvin Gaye has been dead since his father shot him on April 1, 1983, during an argument over an insurance letter, but his music lives on—smoky, seductive, achingly vulnerable. Get a sound clip and a brief bio of the man who changed balladry forever. ✓**INTERNET**→*url* http://www.rockhall.com/induct/gayemarv.html

GREEN, AL

Al Green Al Green seems to be everywhere these days—not just duetting with Aretha at the Rock and Roll Hall of Fame Inaugural Concert, but popping up on the *Tonight Show* to sing "Let's Stay Together," releasing a new album that includes some secular hits along with gospel, and more. Get a sound clip and a brief bio. ✓**INTERNET**→*url* http://www.rockhall.com/induct/greeal.html

MAYFIELD, CURTIS

Curtis Mayfield He's your pusher man, although he's been quiet since a tragic accident paralyzed him during a sound check for a concert. Talk about the undisputed king of smooth soul. ✓**AMERICA ONLINE**→*keyword* mmc→Rap/R&B→R&B/Soul→Curtis Mayfield

PICKETT, WILSON

Wilson Pickett In the midnight hour, the Web will still be there, and you can get wicked with a

brief bio and a sound clip. ✓**INTERNET**→*url* http://www.rockhall.com/induct/pickwils.html

REDDING, OTIS

Otis Redding Try a little cyber-tenderness. Get a bio and a sound clip. ✓**INTERNET**→*url* http://www.rockhall.com/induct/reddotis.html

ROBINSON, SMOKEY

Smokey Robinson In addition to being one of the premier songwriters in Motown's stable, Smokey Robinson was a vocalist without compare, the owner of a piercing erotic falsetto. Learn about Smokey's career and get a sound clip here. ✓**INTERNET**→*url* http://www.rockhall.com/induct/robismok.html

ROSS, DIANA/SUPREMES

Diana Ross/The Supremes You can't hurry love, but you can find out about the classic Motown trio. ✓**AMERICA ONLINE**→*keyword* mmc→Rap/R&B→R&B/Soul→Diana Ross

THE TEMPTATIONS

The Temptations Get a brief bio

of Kendricks, Ruffin, and company and a sound clip. ✓**INTERNET**→ *url* http://www.rockhall.com/induct/temptati.html

TURNER, IKE AND TINA

Ike and Tina Turner Tina met Ike way back in 1956, when she was still Annie Mae Bullock, and after 1961's "A Fool In Love," the hits just kept on coming—both musical and physical. Get a brief bio of the duo and a sound clip here. ✓**INTERNET**→*url* http://www.rockhall.com/induct/turnike.html

WILSON, JACKIE

Jackie Wilson Jackie Wilson could sing anything, and sometimes did. Get a sound clip and a brief bio. ✓**INTERNET**→*url* http://www.rockhall.com/induct/jwilson.html

WONDER, STEVIE

Stevie Wonder First, he was Little Stevie Wonder. Then he was Big Stevie Wonder. Today, he's Superstar Stevie Wonder. Find out all about Steveland Morris, and pick up a sound clip as well. ✓**INTERNET**→*url* http://www.rockhall.com/induct/wondstev.html

George Clinton: the funkiest man alive—from http://www.acpub.duke.edu/~eja/pics/

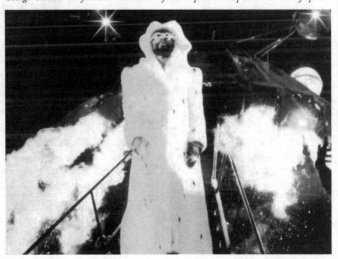

Hip-hop

Ten years ago, rap hadn't broken through into the pop mainstream. Run-DMC's *Raising*

Hell hadn't been released. The Beastie Boys, Public Enemy, and N.W.A. hadn't recorded their debut LPs. No one had heard of Ice-T, or Schoolly D., or even the Wu-Tang Clan. Hard to believe, isn't it? Today, rap is one of the dominant genres of popular music, with dozens of subgenres (from gangsta rap to trip-hop) and more stars than the Hollywood Walk of Fame. And in addition to its economic gains, rap has changed the face of songwriting—the popular poetry of artists like Ice Cube and Chuck D had no real outlet before the dawn of hip-hop. On the Net, rap resources range from **Da House** to **Forty-O-Nine**, from **Lyrix** to **Guillotine**. Word.

On the Net

Across the board

Da House What's in Da House? A rap Top 10, links to other rap sites, and even a home page dedicated to the Sugarhill Gang. ✓**IN-TERNET**→*url* http://www.cs.miami. edu/~ldouglas/house/

Da Penthouse Suite Though the page takes eons to load as a result of large in-line graphics, the Penthouse Suite maintains a large

Ol' Dirty Bastard—from http://www.hooked.net/buzznet/03/beats/4080/oldirty/

collection of music links with a concentration on rap and hip-hop sites. ✓**INTERNET**→*url* http://www4. ncsu.edu/eos/users/t/tfhill/html/nmusic.html

Da SewaSide What's Da Sewa-Side? An online rap 'zine that includes a comprehensive hip-hop artist database, listings of upcoming rap concerts, a radio hit list, and an online bulletin board that treats general issues in music, culture, and politics. ✓**INTERNET**→*url* http://www.pathfinder.com/vibe/dasewaside

Forty-O Nine Seven Penn undergraduates founded 4009 to help promote black life in an unfriendly and preoccupied world ("4009 aint a frat, aint a fellowship, but a family. 7 men all tryin to make it in their world. Strong, intelligent black men that according to statistics should be drug dealers, users, gangsters, in prison, or better yet dead. Livin in West Philly is not the paradise that an Ivy League resembles. Penn and the rest of the Ivy League is not the Blackest of schools but it helps us realize what society feels about us and how far we really must go to be considered equals in their game. So before you count Penn out, realize that we are all in it together and that we all fight our battles in different ways."), and their efforts have produced a wealth of hip-hop resources. With links to most of the major hip-hop magazines, plenty of samples and lyrics, and a growing database of record labels, this is one of the better new rap sites online. ✓**INTERNET**→*url* http://futures.wharton.upenn.edu/~hogan11/html/4009.html

The Hip Hop Hotlist With almost 5,000 hits a month, this busy site offers a Top 10 chart created by Net voters and a huge list of hip-hop links, including pages for dozens of artists (Wu-Tang Clan,

Da Brat, Kris Kross, and even B-Ball's Best Kept Secret, the all-star rap affair featuring the flow of NBA stars). ✓**INTERNET**→*url* http://mmm.mbhs.edu/~cmccoy/

Hip-Hop With resources on break dancing and b-boy culture in general, this site also includes the Top 10 rap singles chart, artist links, and more. ✓**INTERNET**→*url* http://www.interaccess.com/users/bboyb/

Hip-Hop Previews Recent rap releases, with music samples, images, album covers, and more. ✓**INTERNET**→*url* http://www.mpmusic.com/hiphop/hiphop.htm

Nerd World: Hip-Hop Links to newsgroups and Websites. ✓**INTERNET**→*url* http://www.tiac.net/users/dstein/nw222.html

"Join the push toward the future and participate in the interactive, all-Web New Jack Hip-Hop Awards, which lets Netsurfers select their favorites in such categories as Phattest Nasty Group, Phattest Nasty Male Rapper, and Funniest Rap."

Rap Decorated with a vintage picture of the Sugarhill Gang, this page includes a list of all rap chat sites on the Internet, a collection of rap interviews and articles, some record reviews, and dozens of links to related sites online. ✓**INTERNET**→*url* http://www.unix-ag.uni-kl.de/~moritz/rap

Sandbox Distribution Billed as "the largest hip-hop reference library on the World Wide Web," Sandbox includes a wealth of artist links, a record store directory for major metropolitan areas (New York, Los Angeles, and Pittsburgh); radio and television guides for Manhattan; DJ charts; and a generous assortment of sound clips, some from as-yet-unreleased albums. ✓**INTERNET**→*url* http://www.nyu.edu:80/pages/minetta/www/structure/staff/online/mercer/Sandbox.html

Tech 9 The self-named "digital derelicts of the Internet" have one in the chamber and more in the clip when it comes to rap resources, with reviews of new albums, live chat, lists of rap radio stations, images of rap stars, and more. In addition, the Tech 9 staff is conducting an Internet poll to see which rap group fans would most like to see reunited—visit the forum and vote for EPMD, 3rd Bass, Main Source, Brand Nubian, or even N.W.A. (although even if Dre and Cube are willing, it won't be Eazy). ✓**INTERNET**→*url* http://www.seas.upenn.edu/~cswynter/tech9.html

Awards

The New Jack Hip Hop Awards If you're tired of traditional awards, join the push toward the future and participate in the interactive, all-Web New Jack Hip-Hop Awards, which lets Netsurfers select their favorites in such categories as Phattest Nasty Group, Phattest Nasty Male Rapper, and Funniest Rap. The results from the last four years are

Coolio, coolin'—http://www.lollapalooza.com/Bands/Coolio/cooliopict.html

archived at this site, along with short essays about the winners. ✓**INTERNET**→*url* http://www.ai. mit.edu/~isbell/HFh/awards/ njhha-toc.html

Chat

The Attic Do you know the Wu? Maybe you should: "I feel sorry for all the suckas who ain't up on this shit son! I once was ignorant to the ways and teachings of the Clan, but after listenin' to Meth and smoking that Dank, I woke up and heard their message!" Visit this Web chat board, which handles topics on rap, hip-hop, and African-American culture in general. ✓**INTERNET**→*url* http://www. pathfinder.com/vibe/dasewaside/ dbase/docs/rappers.html

Hip Hop List (ml) Talk about hip-hop with other fans. ✓**INTER-NET**→*email* hiphop@maimonedes. lcs.mit.edu ✍ *Write a request*

Live Rap Music Chat Real-time rap chat. ✓**PRODIGY**→*jump* chat→ Prodigy Chat→Select an Area:→ Music→Rap Music

Rap and Hip-Hop Chat Almost

no one on Compuserve's Rap and Hip-Hop message boards seems to be interested in rap. And that's a shame, because there are two entire message boards waiting to be overrun by fans of the Wu-Tang Clan, Mobb Deep, the Roots, the Beastie Boys, and their ilk. If you want to talk rap, come to Compuserve's MusicArts board instead—or book passage for eWorld, where the Let's Talk RAP message board usually has a few interesting discussions in progress. ✓**COMPUSERVE** ...→*go* amgpop→ Messages *and* Libraries→ Rap/Hip-Hop ...→*go* musicarts→ Messages *and* Libraries→Rap/ Hiphop/Techno ✓**EWORLD**→ *go* eaz→Pump Up The Volume→Music Talk→Let's Talk RAP

Rap on IRC Will the Dr. Dre–Ice Cube collaboration ever appear? See what other fans have to say by participating in real-time chat about rap and hip-hop. ✓**INTERNET** ...→*irc* #rap ...→ #hiphop

rec.music.hip-hop/alt.rap (ng) Rap longevity is measured in months rather than years, so don't come to this newsgroup with archival concerns—if you're still

moving to the rhythm of De La Soul or Boogie Down Productions, step off, and step back on for Common Sense, Method Man, and the Notorious B.I.G. International rap and other hip-hop styles (trip-hop, acid jazz, etc.) are discussed as well. ✓**USENET** ...→ rec.music.hip-hop ...→ alt.rap

Consumer

Hip Hop CD Suggestions How can a novice (or a veteran who has been out of the record-buying loop for more than four months) tell the difference between superior product and wack shit. Well, here's one way. Visitors to the Suggestions site (that's you) select their most and least favorite albums from a list and then submit their picks, after which the Suggestion program performs a compatibility match, generating a list of albums with similar tone, style, politics, etc. "Don't trust these suggestions blindly," the site warns. "Listen to the albums before you buy them. In other words, we cannot be held liable for you buying Vanilla Lice by

Ice-T, Original Gangster—from http:// sashimi.wwa.com/hammers/pictures/

The gatefold sleeve of the Beastie Boys' Paul's Boutique *record—http://www.nando.net:80/BeastieBoys/pics/*

mistake." Does CD Suggestions work? Well, a submission that celebrated rock-hard lyrics and P-Funky beats (Ice Cube, Public Enemy) over "alternative" rap (Arrested Development, De La Soul) ran into an error; a simpler version of the same search retrieved albums by Paris and Brand Nubian—but nothing by N.W.A. If nothing else, the list of hundreds of rap albums will help you build your collection. ✓**INTERNET**→*url* http://www.sci.kun.nl/thalia/rapdict/suggest/

Dictionaries

The Totally Unofficial Rap Dictionary What's a 187? It's a murdered policeman, of course, as any good Snoop Doggy Dogg fan knows. Learn more about police codes, Audis, hype, and why punks jump up to get beat down with the help of this rap lexicon. ✓**INTERNET**→*url* http://www.sci.kun.nl/thalia/rapdict/

Images

MSS Photo Music Images Photos of MC Eiht, the Alkaholics, Jam Master Jay, Funkdoobiest, and more. ✓**INTERNET**→*url* http://www.sirius.com/~meatyard/images/music/music.html

Lyrics

Hip-Hop Lyrics Site Is Rakim saying "eternal list" or "eternalist"? Does EPMD make you "wiggle

and jiggle" like Jell-O, or do they name-check the generic "gelatin"? And what exactly is OPP, anyway? Although its detractors may demean it as an artless hemorrhage of ghetto rage, rap was, is, and always will be a powerful poetic form. Not convinced? Consider Ice Cube's eulogistic "Dead Homiez" ("Another homie got murdered on a shakedown / And his mother is at the funeral, havin' a nervous breakdown"), L.L. Cool J's seismic "Mama Said Knock You Out" ("Don't call it a comeback / I've been here for years / Been rockin' my peers / Putting suckers in fear"), the Beastie Boys' loopy, surreal "Egg Man" ("Humpty Dumpty was a big fat egg / He was playing the wall and then he broke his leg / Tossed it out the

window three minutes hot / Hit the Rastaman he said 'bloodclot'"), or Public Enemy's taut slavery narrative "Can't Truss It" ("Cause the wickedness done by Jack / Where everybody at / Divided and sold / For the liquor and the gold / Smacked in the back / For the other man to mack."). Rap lyrics may or may not move language away from formal grammar, away from politesse, but they certainly move it toward something revolutionary. Remember, "Walk with the treble / The rhythm is the rebel." ✓**INTERNET**→ *url* http://www.brad.ac.uk/~ctttaylo/lyrics.html

Lyrix A small collection of rap lyrics, with a heavy concentration of Tribe Called Quest and Jeru the

Method Man, stage-diving—http://www.cldc.howard.edu/%7Eperson/Fever/

Hip-Hop Genres

G. Love & Special Sauce—http://www. sony.com/Music/Images/

Damaja. ✓**INTERNET**→*url* http:// www.unix-ag.uni-kl.de/~moritz/ html/lyrix

Magazines

4080/Hip Hop Online If you're looking for an opinion on the Mobb Deep album, or you need to find out the latest news in street fashion, 4080's got our number. This online version of the popular underground hip-hop magazine offers a sample look at the world of blunts, stunts, and more, from Ol' Dirty Bastard to Common Sense and more. Subscription information is included on the site. ✓**INTERNET**→*url* http://www.hooked. net/buzznet/4080/index.html

Guillotine An excellent online rap 'zine that includes artist profiles, interviews, record reviews, and more. ✓**INTERNET**→*url* http:// www.cipsinc.com/jack/guillotine. html

HardC.O.R.E. HardC.O.R.E. is one of the premier online hip-hop publications, with news, columns, reviews, contests, and more, and

its Website includes full-text versions of both current and archive issues. ✓**INTERNET**→*url* http://www. public.iastate.edu/~krs_one/ homepage.html

The Hitlist A Web 'zine devoted to the hip-hop world that includes record reviews, artist gossip, images, and sound clips. ✓**INTERNET**→ *url* http://www.cldc.howard.edu/ %7Eaja/hitlist/

Pseudonyms

Rap Artists/Groups Database To the uninitiated, rap can be a welter of MCs and Ices, with nary a given name in sight. If this kind of onomastic trickery bothers you, check in here to learn the real names of rap stars. Biz Markie's real name? Marcell Hall. Grandmaster Flash? Joseph Sadler. (MC) Hammer? Stanley Kirk Burrell. Ice Cube? O'Shea Jackson. Surprisingly, John Wayne (real name Marion Morrison) was left off the list—perhaps "Fight the Power" has something to do with it. ✓**INTERNET**→*url* http://www.pathfinder. com/vibe/dasewaside/dbase/ docs/rappers.html

Reviews

Hip-Hop Music Reviews Though new reviews are being added every day, the real value of this site lies in its commitment to filling in the gaps, adding catch-up reviews of classic rap albums like NWA's *Straight Outta Compton*. The reviews themselves provide basic information on albums— number of tracks, producers, and a profanity-content report—along with analysis of the album's distinctness, dopeness, predictions, and political message. ✓**INTERNET**→ *url* http://www.ai.mit.edu/~isbell/ HFh/reviews/000-toc.html

"around the way (n): From the neighbourhood.

blunt (n): Marijuana cigarette, herb stuffed cigar, generally phillies.

buyaka (n): Jamaican, resembles the sound of gunshots.

come correct (v): To represent the real, to do something the way it should be done.

drop science, drop knowledge (v): To demonstrate wisdom or skill.

front (v): Pretend to be that which you are not; act tough.

glock (n): Manufacturer of guns. People usually mean the 9mm glock, which can hold up to 19 rounds. The gun is made of plastic and ceramic, so it has a futuristic `feel' to it.

kangol (n): A brand of hat. LL Cool J used to wear this along with other East Coast rappers."

—from **The Totally Unofficial Rap Dictionary**

Reggae

Reggae music is haunted by Marley's ghost, by the beneficent spirit of Jamaican super-
star Bob Marley, who died of cancer in 1981 after bringing the island genre to the attention of the world and helping launch the career of other reggae artists like Peter Tosh and Bunny Livingston. And reggae is also haunted by the spirit of Jah, the Rastafarian deity whose message of universal peace and brotherhood has made roots music the genre of choice for many twentysomethings in America, Europe, and Asia. Get a taste of the herbal life with the **Afroreggae Home Page** and the **Jammin Reggae Archive**. Branch out with the **Dub Page** and the **Ska FAQ**. And then learn your favorite Lucky Dube or Jimmy Cliff songs with the **Reggae Chordbook**.

The king of reggae, Bob Marley—from ftp://abel.math.uga.edu/reggae/pics/

On the Net

Across the board

Afroreggae Home Page This German-language site contains a wealth of reggae links. ✓**INTERNET**→ *url* http://www.rz.uni-frankfurt.de/ ~tbarth/afroreggae/

The Bush Doktor Straight from the University of Dreadlands comes the Bush Doktor, bringing reggae fans the latest news, sounds, and images about Jah's music. Link to reggae resources in Chicago, Heartbeat Records, a Wailers discography, and more. ✓**INTERNET**→ *url* http://ebhon.jnst. uor.edu:80/Users/doktor/

Cool Runnings Reggae news with a focus on the Chicago area, including lists of record stores, a description of the club scene, and more. ✓**INTERNET**→ *url* http://www. interaccess.com/users/coolcrew/ main1.html

Jammin Reggae Archive This home page features an extensive collection of links to reggae archives including a newsgroup FAQ, a Rasta/Patois dictionary, and a collection of reggae-related directories in such categories as record catalogs, tour schedules, lyrics, discographies, articles, periodicals, pictures, shops, clubs, books, mailing lists, interviews, video clips, and reggae stage names. The page also has links to sound samples of recent releases, other reggae home pages, Bob Marley pages, radio shows' pages, FTP sites, record company sites, newsgroups, and Caribbean culture pages. And if you make it to the bottom of the mile-long list, you'll see a picture of the author of the site, who looks a little bit like Guy Smiley from *Sesame Street*. It's joyful noise, mon. ✓**INTERNET** →*url*

Reggae Genres

Black Uhuru—from ftp://abel.math.uga.edu/reggae/pics/

http://orpheus.ucsd.edu/jammin/

Natty Dread Server Pick through the Natty Dread Server to find links to the University of the West Indies, rec.music.reggae, a Patois dictionary, the Reggae Ambassadors Worldwide home page, the Carribean Connection, African American Haven, and a handful of other reggae servers and fan pages. ✓INTERNET→*url* http://wsogata.cc.u-tokai.ac.jp/

Raggamuffin Reggae Home Page How big is reggae in Germany? Well, it's not exactly the national music. But island rhythms and patois can lift the spirits even in Freiburg, and this page delivers a heavy dose of the Jamaican experience, with links to dozens of Websites and a handful of newsgroups, as well as a very nice .GIF of a map of Jamaica. Sweet. ✓IN-TERNET→*url* http://www.biologie.uni-freiburg.de/data/reggae/reggae.html

Rasta A small collection of links to reggae directories and archives, as well as a link to an article on the history of reggae and a number of reviews written by the author of the home page. ✓INTERNET→*url* http://khartoum.fsl.noaa.gov/LANDIS/rasta.htm

Rasta Rat Home Page The Rasta Rat used to listen to other kinds of music, but his page now proudly proclaims itself a "100% reggae zone." With dozens of reviews, articles, and links, this is one of the richest reggae sites online. One caveat: if you're looking for hard-hitting critical prose, don't ask the rat—he's more interested in paying tribute to Jah. ✓IN-TERNET →*url* http://www.dungeon.com/~rastarat/home.html

Rastaman—The Other Reggae Homepage A collection of reggae links, including an epigraph from Bob Marley ("Open your eyes and look within, are you satisfied with the life you're livin?"). ✓INTERNET→*url* http://www.missouri.edu/~c643267/Rasta.html

Reggae Ambassadors Worldwide What is Reggae Ambassadors Worldwide? It's an international organization designed to boost the popularity of reggae music and spread the positive vibe of Jah across international borders. How did it start? "Frustrated by meager attendance at Reggae concerts and hit-or-miss service by Reggae Labels, Papa Pilgrim of Salt Lake City and Rastaman Nane' formerly of Grand Rapids Michigan formed Reggae Ambassadors Worldwide in the Summer of 1992." What's offered at the RAW home page? A mission statement, newsletters, concert updates, and more. ✓INTERNET→*url* http://www.xmission.com/~turq/RAW/home.html

Reggae Down Babylon Home Page Decked out in grand Jamaican green, this reggae / ska directory offers links to the Jammin Reggae Archive, other

Burning Spear—http://harp.rounder.com/rounder/artists/burning_spear/

Stepping razor Peter Tosh—from ftp://abel.math.uga.edu/reggae/pics/

reggae home pages, a rather short list of artists, some of which are Caribbean artists who have worked in related genres. ✓**INTERNET**→*url* http://nyx10.cs.du.edu:8001/~damjohns/reggae.html

Reggae FAQ in Japanese Learn all about reggae—in Japanese. If you don't speak Japanese, all you'll learn is that the dollar sign gets used a lot by computers without the proper fonts. ✓**INTERNET**→*url* http://www.yamamura.material.tohoku.ac.jp/~shimada/TFJ/music/ReggaeFAQ/home.html

Reggae Home Page With information in both Japanese and English, this page capitalizes on the resurgence of reggae in the Land of the Rising Sun, and provides detailed links for a number of artists, including Alton Ellis and the late Garnet Silk. ✓**INTERNET**→*url* http://www.webcity.co.jp/info/maeda/index.html

Reggae in Your Jeggae! A reggae resource of inestimable value, this page includes links to virtually everything reggae, ragamuffin, Jah, and dreadlocked in Cyberspace. Need to link to an archive of reggae images? It's only a click away. Want to order reggae merchandise? Click. Need information on Ethiopia or Jamaica? Click, click. Get lyrics, lists of 'zines, and even a map of Jamaica. ✓**INTERNET**→*url* http://huizen.dds.nl/~ramone/reggae.html

Reggae SumFest Though it's nominally a promotional site for Summerfest Productions, Ltd.'s reggae festival, this page includes information on new reggae releases, record reviews, and more. ✓**INTERNET**→*url* http://www.access-business.com/reggae/

Ska Reggae Dub "Reggae music is number one for me!" proclaims Joris, the author of this page, and he goes on to prove it,

with links to dozens of sites on artists, labels, and more. Joris also maintains discographies for several artists, including Johnny Baby & the Liberators, Bitty McLean, and Beres Hammond. ✓**INTERNET**→*url* http://www.iaehv.nl/users/bas/srd.html

Chat

rec.music.reggae (ng) Everyt'ing under the sun, from Sunsplash updates to history lessons to lyric sheets. The newsgroup is the best place for regular postings of the reggae FAQ and the Jammin' Reggae Archive. ✓**USENET**→rec.music.reggae

#reggae Chase those crazy baldheads off of IRC, and then talk about Bob, and Peter, and Bunny, and Jimmy, and Eek-A-Mouse, and Lee "Scratch" Perry, and more. ✓**INTERNET**→*irc* #reggae

World/Reggae Almost no traffic here, mon, but now and again a post about Bob Marley, Shabba Ranks, Ini Kamoze, and other popular artists. ✓**COMPUSERVE**→*go* amgpop→Messages *and* Libraries →World/Reggae

Chords & tabs

Reggae Chordbook Learn to play your favorite reggae hits, from "Sitting in Limbo" to "Kaya" to "Satta Amassagana." ✓**INTERNET**→*url* http://www.yamamura.material.tohoku.ac.jp/~endo/index.html

Dub

Beyond Records This home page for the British dub label includes news on new and old releases, a discography, press releases, and an essay on dub by David Toop that tracks the music from its originators (King Tubby) to its nineties innovators (Bandulu). ✓**INTERNET**→*url* http://iuma.south ern.com/beyond/menu.html

Dub Page With a definition of dub, a list of dub artists and labels, reviews of the latest dub releases, links to other dub pages, and a brief history of the genre, this page offers a good starting point for dub enthusiasts. And if you have suggestions or comments, submit them electronically, and they'll be displayed on the dub page forum alongside the remarks of other dubbernaughts. ✓**INTERNET**→*url* http://www.mw3.com/electro/dub -pg.htm

Ska FAQ As Jamaican dance music goes, there are few as infectious as ska. Where did ska come from? What is ska-core? What is skanking? Are there any feature-length ska films? Ask ska and ska will answer. The FAQ also includes a list of dozens of ska artists, from A-Kings to Zwit. ✓**INTERNET**→*url* http://www.cis.ohio-state.edu/hy pertext/faq/usenet/music/ska-faq/ top.html

Zion Train Originally a tiny independent, Zion Records has made a lasting impression on the U.K. dub market, and this page not only includes information on all Zion releases but also connects to an eclectic set of links on topics ranging from reggae to anarchy to lockpicking to Noam Chomsky. ✓**INTERNET**→*url* http://www.city scape.co.uk/users/cs23/ziontrain/ zionrecords.html

Artists

Arturo Tappin This page, which promotes Arturo Tappin's Saxroots—"it's solid reggae, with just a twist of jazz"—includes audio clips in RealAudio format. Listen to the sample, order CDs, and

I jahman Levi—ftp://abel.math.uga.edu/reggae/pics/

send email to Arturo and Saxroots. ✓**INTERNET**→*url* http://www.sax-roots.com

Beres Hammond Beres Hammond's soulful vocals have powered some of the most delectable reggae hits of the nineties, including collaborations with Maxi Priest and Barrington Levy, and this page includes a full discography. ✓**INTERNET**→*url* http://www. iaehv.nl/users/bas/beres.html

Bitty McLean The UB40 collaborator and British reggae star is the subject of a brief career biography and discography. ✓**INTERNET**→*url* http://www.iaehv.nl/users/bas/ bitty.html

Dreadzone Sound clips, Quick-

Time clips, a discography, and more for the British reggae band. ✓**INTERNET**→*url* http://www.vmg. co.uk/dreadzone/sounds/wel come.au

The WWW Electronic Wailers Discography Though Bob Marley is listed elsewhere in *NetMusic* (see his entry in the Artists' Guide), the constellation of reggae voices that surrounded Bob—not only the Wailers (that's Peter and Bunny), but also Judy Mowatt, Marcia Griffiths, and the entire Marley clan—has been vital to the development of the genre. This page lists all the albums recorded by the Wailers and their associates, and links to other reggae sites online. ✓**INTERNET**→*url* http://www. iea.lth.se/~ielbo/wailers.html

Lucky Dube—ftp://abel.math.uga.edu/ reggae/pics/

Garnet Silk Tribute An important figure in nineties reggae, Garnet Silk was only 28 at the time of his death in December 1994. And although the biographical offerings at this page are sketchy, it does provide a complete Silk discography, images, and more. ✓INTERNET→*url* http://www.web city.co.jp/info/maeda/vote_gar nett.html

Inka Inka A biography and discography for this California reggae band. ✓INTERNET→*url* http://sunpath.stanford.edu:3007/ bands/Inka/Inka.html

Irie Time A home page for the Houston-based reggae and soca band, with sound clips, a discography, and a selection of press clippings. ✓INTERNET→*url* http://www. owlnet.rice.edu/~don/irie.html

Johnny Baby This Guyanan / Dutch reggae artist has hit the charts in Europe with "Running Around in Circles," and this page contains a discography that lists his other work. ✓INTERNET→*url* http://www.iaehv.nl/users/bas/ johnny.html

Prince Far I Home Page Who was Prince Far I? The dark prophet of dub, a basso profundo who spooked audiences with his scary stories of spiritual retribution. Subtitled "Voice of Thunder," this page pays tribute to the former Michael James Williams, who was murdered in 1983 in Kingston, with a discography, press clips, and more. ✓INTERNET→ *url* http://www.dungeon.com/ ~rastarat/fari.html

Rock Steady Posse A biography, tour dates, and more information on the California reggae quintet. ✓INTERNET→*url* http:// www.dnai.com/~ridia/posse.html

Strictly Roots Sound clips, images, reviews, and more for the prominent Bay Area reggae band. ✓INTERNET→*url* http://www.crl. com/~haygar/roots.htm

UB40 For more than a decade, UB40 has been one of the most popular reggae bands in the world, a group expert at reupholstering old songs with a reggae beat and topping the charts for months. And for fans of "Red, Red Wine," "I Got You, Babe," "Can't Help Falling In Love," and more, there's no Website better than this one. Need information on Ali Campbell's solo album? Want a translation of the liner notes from the Russian version of *Rat in the Kitchen*? Dying for sound clips of the band's work? Come here. ✓INTERNET→*url* http:// www.cis.ohio-state.edu/hypertext/faq/usenet/ music/ska-faq/top.html

"Best Reggae Covers:

Brain Damage (Pink Floyd)--Bim Skala Bim

Brown-Eyed Girl (Van the Man)--Magadog

Can't Hurry Love (Supremes)--Checkered Cabs

867-5309 (Tommy Tutone)--Less than Jake

I Shall Be Released (Dylan)--Heptones

Let it Be (Beatles)-- Ethiopians

Like a Rolling Stone (Bob Dylan)--Wailers

Lola (the Kinks)--Bad Manners

99 Red Balloons (Nena)--Regatta 69

Sweet Emotion (Aerosmith)-- Bosstones

Tears of a Clown (Miracles)--the Beat

These Boots Are Made For Walkin' (Nancy Sinatra)--Op Ivy

White Wedding (Billy Idol)--Umbrella Bed"

—from **rec.music. reggae**

Blues

What is blues? If it's from the Delta, it's a single instrument—usually a guitar—and a

single performer, singing unadorned tales of hardship, toil, and the equivocal pleasures of drink and sex. If it's from Chicago, there's still a guitar, but it's probably electric, and the lyrics probably have an urban rather than a rural feel. But ultimately, blues is the personality of the performers—the spooky falsetto of Skip James, the unearthly slide guitar of Blind Willie Johnson, the pyrotechnic axework of Buddy Guy, the I'll-swallow-the-Earth vocals of Howlin' Wolf. Online blues enthusiasts should start their day by driving onto the **Blue Highway**, chatting with other fans on **rec.music.bluenote. blues**, and paying tribute at the **Robert Johnson Home Page**.

John Lee Hooker, aka Mr. Lucky—ftp://ftp.teleport.com/pub/users/boydroid/

Across the board

All the Blues That's Fit to Print Adorned with a picture of a Hohner SuperChromonica, this page collects and annotates more than two dozen blues links. ✓ **IN-TERNET**→*url* http://www.charm. net/~turtle/blues.html

Blue Highway Graham Parker once sang, "Get on the blue highway / Follow the blue highway / to

where the real America lies." Parker probably wasn't talking about the Web—though he did once write a song about an escalator—but he might have been referring to this site, which traces the history of the blues, that powerful indigenous art form that absorbs artists as diverse as Memphis Minnie and Son House, Elmore James and Chris Thomas. The site includes bios and pictures of major blues artists, as well as a map of the Mississippi Delta, the fertile stretch of blues history that runs between the Mississppi River and the Natchez Trace. ✓ **INTERNET**→*url* http://www.magicnet.net/~curtis/

The Blues Page While there aren't any fancy graphics on this page, there are plenty of links to help blues fans fight the death of blues info online. Get a list of Grammy winners in the blues category, a list of jazz and blues festivals, and more. ✓ **INTERNET**→*url* http://net.indra.com/~karma/ blues.html

BluesNet "My woman don't love me / poured my Jack down the drain / then my dog got run over / by a green Chevrolet / So I got on the Net man / and I found this Web Page / heard some other guy's problems / and it brightened my day." Link to directories of artists,

The Blue Highway

...winds past the plantation barrelhouses of the Mississippi Delta to the south-side clubs and tenements of postwar Chicago. While it's a somber trip, humbling, even distressing, it's also enchanting and joyful -- and reassuring in its success.

The history of the blues is more than a musical chronology. The blues was born the day the West African shoreline fell from the horizon. It was raised amid the institutionalized savagery of the Deep South and flourished in the dark heart of America's largest cities. We owe the blues to those who bore the pain of enslavement behind the

Learn your history—from http://www.magicnet.net/~curtis/

images, readings and articles, and ways to contact the mentors and masters themselves for questions and maybe some group therapy. ✓**INTERNET**→*url* http://dragon. acadiau.ca/~rob/blues/blues.html

House of Blues Why is there a picture of a skeleton aping Munch's *The Scream* ghosted behind the text on this site? Only Dan Aykroyd knows for sure. Why Dan Aykroyd? Because he has a controlling interest in House of Blues, the newest attempt to commodify artists like Elmore James, Junior Wells, Koko Taylor, John Lee Hooker, and Howlin' Wolf. The site includes a list of blues events (including Blues Brothers events, like a tribute to John Belushi), a place where blues fans canchat, and an advertisement fora recent compilation of classic blues songs. ✓**INTERNET**→*url* http://www.underground.net/HOB /essential/

King Biscuit Time The background is blue, and so is the sub-

ject matter. With chord progressions from Blind Lemon Jefferson's "See That My Grave Is Kept Clean," a link to the online blues 'zine known only as the *Delta Snake Blues News*, and samples from Sonny Boy Williamson, Koko Taylor, Otis Spann, Willie Dixon, Paul Butterfield, and more, this is an excellent site that strikes a balance between scholasticism and fanaticism. ✓**INTERNET**→*url* http://www.island.net/~blues/

rec.music.bluenote.blues FAQ What are Delta blues? What are Chicago blues? Why do barrelhouse players have a quiff, or forelock? What are the essential blues albums for a beginning collector? Is Eric Clapton considered real blues? Get the answers to these and other blues questions at this FAQ. ✓**INTERNET**→*url* ftp://ftp. netcom.com/pub/gi/gilles/rmbb/ rmbbfaq.html

Sonny Boy Blues Society Located in the heart of Helena, Arkansas, the Sonny Boy Society is

dedicated to the preservation and promotion of the Delta blues. Why Helena, Arkansas? Because dozens of artists—including Robert Jr. Lockwood, James Cotton, George "Harmonica" Smith, Elmore James, Little Walter, Robert Nighthawk, Fran Frost, Sam Carr, Willie Love, Pine Top Perkins, Dr. Ross, Roosevelt Sykes, Lewis Jordan, Howlin' Wolf, Muddy Waters, and Houston Stackhouse—have lived or worked there. ✓**INTERNET**→*url* http://www. pccc.cc.ar.us/~durrjr/index.html

Ziggy's Blues Home Page No, this isn't Ziggy, the cartoon character. This is Ziggy, the blues fan, and he's uploaded a set of blues images, as well as interviews with several artists, including Honeyboy Edwards and Charlie Musselwhite. ✓**INTERNET**→*url* http://ivory. lm.com/~davidsr/

Chat

The Blues Compuserve's blues music board isn't terrifically busy, but if you're interested in the chord box, Skip James, or Memphis Minnie, pop over here for blues chat. ✓**COMPUSERVE**→*go* musicarts→Messages *and* Libraries →The Blues

Blues Music List (ml) Discuss various blues topics—from electric to acoustic, from Gus Cannon's Jug Stompers to Robert Cray—on this mailing list. ✓**INTERNET**→*email* listserv@brownvm.brown.edu ✍ *Type in message body:* subscribe blues-l <your full name>

rec.music.bluenote.blues (ng) Discuss Tampa Red's hokum blues, the blues-rock of the Allman Brothers, the fate of Canadian blues, and more on this active and well-informed newsgroup. ✓**USENET**→ rec.music.bluenote.blues

Clubs

Antone's Need the blues? Get on a plane. Go to Austin. Go to Antone's, one of the nation's premier electric blues clubs. Then open your ears, and let them breathe. This page includes a schedule for Antone's, a beautiful picture archive (with images of Buddy Guy, Albert Collins, Pinetop Perkins, and Joe Louis Walker, among others), and a link to Antone's online record store. ✓**INTER-NET**→*url* http://www.quadralay. com/Antones/home.html

Blues guy Buddy Guy—from http://www.webcom.com/~sppg/meanderings/me206/

Delta blues artists

Charlie Patton He wasn't as serious as Blind Willie Johnson, and he doesn't have the mythical pull of Robert Johnson, but Charlie Patton was one of the architects of the Delta blues, with a powerful singing style and expert guitar technique. This page contains a biography and images. ✓**INTER-NET**→*url* http://www.demon.co. uk/london-calling/patton.html

Crossroads "In 1936 a young black man entered a hotel room for the first of two recording ses-

King of the Delta Blues—from http://www.vivanet.com/~blues/tbh1.html

sions. The second was held about seven months later. From these two sessions came 41 recordings of 29 songs (except Kind Hearted Woman, recorded earlier at a music store in Miss.). This would be the entire body of work preserved by Robert Johnson. Fourteen months later, on Aug. 11, 1938, the man who would become known as The King of the Delta Blues Singers was dead at the age of 27. The exact cause of his death is not known but fifty years later his music endures and continues to inspire modern Blues and Rock musicians." With an essay about Johnson, a list of his songs, links to lyrics, and connections to other blues sites, this is a good introduction to the man who supposedly sold his soul to the Devil. ✓**INTER-NET**→*url* http://bytor.chemek. cc.or.us/~ericj/

Robert Johnson One of the seminal Delta blues recording artists and a man whose myth is as powerful as his music, Robert Johnson has risen to the fore of mainstream blues consciousness in the last ten years, with documentaries, a fancy box set, and rumors of feature films (one has Prince starring in a project directed by

Martin Scorsese). This page tells the by-now-familiar Johnson story and inclues one nice image. ✓**IN-TERNET**→*url* http://www.demon. co.uk/london-calling/musrjohn.html

Robert Johnson Home Page A reprint of Johnson's biographical entry in the En*cyclopedia Britannica* and a photo of Robert holding his guitar. ✓**INTERNET**→*url* http://www.ugcs.caltech.edu/ ~godot/bobj.html

Folkways

Smithsonian Folkways Record Order Page Run by the Smithsonian, Folkways is an ambitious blues label that repackages classic artists as well as recording new artists. Get information on releases by Big Bill Broonzy, Elizabeth Cotten, Brownie McGhee, and others, and place your order with a toll-free number. ✓**INTER-NET**→*url* http://www.si.edu/ products/shopmall/records/ blueart1.htm

Hardcore

Blues for the Hard-Core What is hard-core blues? Chicago electric blues, T-Bone Walker, Sonny

Blues gal Marcia Ball—*http://harp.rounder.com:70/0h/rounder/artists/ballmarcia/*

Boy Williamson, Buddy Guy. It's loud. It's powerful. And now it has a page devoted to it. ✓ **INTERNET**→ *url* http://www.charm.net/~turtle/blues2.html

Magazines

Blues Access An online blues magazine that includes CD reviews, a list of new releases, a database of record labels, news articles ("Inner City Blues: A feud between two Chicago businessmen turns deadly"), and interviews with prominent artists. ✓ **INTERNET**→ *url* http://www.interactive.line.com/blues/bluesaccess/

Living Blues There aren't many articles reprinted at the *Living Blues* Website, but blues fans can get tables of contents for past issues and, if they're interested, subscribe to the publication with an email form. ✓ **INTERNET**→ *url* http://imp.cssc.olemiss.edu/blues.html

Regional

Cascade Blues Association Are there blues in Oregon? There sure are, and this site includes information on how Oregonians can enjoy them. ✓ **INTERNET**→ *url* http://www.teleport.com/~boydroid/blues/cba.htm

DC Blues Home Page Get the latest news on blues in the capital city. ✓ **INTERNET**→ *url* http://intelus.com:80/dcblues/

The Toronto Blues Association A list of upcoming events in the Toronto area. ✓ **INTERNET**→ *url* http://www.io.org/~ynot/

NOTES

"Buddy Guy is blues. Phil Guy is blues. Phil Collins is not blues. Albert Collins was blues. Fat Albert is not blues, but could be with a name like that. Big Mama Thornton was blues. Li'l Ed Williams is blues, but Robin Williams is not blues. Charles Brown is blues, but Charlie Brown and James Brown are not blues, which is why there is not a 'Brown' rule like the 'Johnson' and 'King' rules. Rufus Thomas is blues, but Dave Thomas is not blues. Anybody with an album on Arhoolie, Alligator, or Yazoo Records is blues. Some people with an album on Atlantic Records are blues, but they may not be getting royalties for it. Anybody using a stage name with any of the following keywords are blues: 'Blind,' 'Magic,' 'Guitar,' 'Sonny,' 'Junior,' 'Little,' 'Big," 'Screaming,' 'Lightning,' or the name of a city. This makes Detroit Junior doubly-blues and Luther 'Guitar Jr.' Johnson triply-blues."

—from **BluesNet**

Folk

From Woody Guthrie to Pete Seeger, from Phil Ochs to Joni Mitchell, from Tom Rush

to Richard Thompson, folk music has depended on largely acoustic settings that foreground songs, and songs that range from traditional ballads to intimate confessionals to political protests. When Bob Dylan went electric at Newport to shouts of "Judas!," folk shifted somewhat, absorbing elements of mainstream rock just as mainstream rock absorbed elements of it. But the foundation of folk music remained, and today persists in the work of such artists such as John Gorka, Nanci Griffith, Suzanne Vega, and more. Learn about the history of the genre at **Folk Roots**; talk to other folk fans at **rec.music.folk**, and then spend some time with **Dirty Linen**.

Working man's folkie Phil Ochs—http://www.cs.pdx.edu/~trent/ochs/images.html

On the Net

Across the board

The Folk Music Project This organization sponsors folk festivals, workshops, and concerts in the northern New Jersey area. The Project's calendar of events is here, which is handy if you live in New Jersey, but for folk fans nationwide, this site also offers a terrific collection of links to other folk sites. The Project's links will take you to the home pages of more than 50 artists, from Joe Bethancourt to Kate Wolf. If you're looking for news about the All Folks Festival in Ontario or the Philadelphia Folk Festival, you'll find links to these events' pages and others here. There are also connections to articles published about folk music, including a tome on folk music on the Internet. This is a very well-researched site—they sure do know about folk music in northern New Jersey! ✓**INTERNET**→*url* http://www.att.com/community/groups/folkproject/

FolkBook Gather 'round, folks! If it's got to do with folk music, you'll find it here. For a comprehensive list of nationwide folk venues online, complete with concert and artist info, look in at FolkBook, and find such a list. If you're looking for a new place to talk with others about the folk genre, go to the Talking About The Music section, where you'll find a list of mailing lists and newsgroups dedicated to folky chat. For information on just about any folk artist you care to name, Book offers a bio, discography, pictures, tour info, tablature, and sound clips of their work in its Artists section. As far as folk music resources go, it just doesn't get much better than FolkBook. ✓**INTERNET**→*url* http://www.cgrg.ohio-state.edu/folkbook/index.html

Chat

Country/Folk Message-based discussion of folk music, its artists, and its culture. ✓**COMPUSERVE**→*go* musicarts→Messages *and* Libraries →Country/Folk

Folk & Celtic "Can anyone tell me all the words to 'Yankee Doodle,' or where I can find them?" writes Bill. "I am talking about the Revolutionary War song and am using it for my wife's first grade class. I've already checked the encyclopedias with no luck." After almost a week, no one has answered Bill, but the folks on this message board have gone on to discuss other topics, including the musicology of the popular ballad; the overlap between folk, country, and punk; and important female artists of the nineties such as the Indigo Girls, Nanci Griffith, and Shawn Colvin. ✓**COMPUSERVE**→*go* amgpop→Messages *and* Libraries →Folk & Celtic

New American Folk Music

(ml) The term folk music has expanded to include a wide range of artists, from Mary Chapin Carpenter to Christine Lavin to John Gorka to Ellis Paul to Nanci Griffith to Barbara Kessler to Suzanne Vega. All of them and more are discussed here. To check up on messages from up to two weeks ago, head on over to the Folk_ Music archive. ✓**INTERNET**→*email* listserv@nysernet.org ✍ *Type in message body:* subscribe FOLK_ MUSIC <your full name> *Archives:* ✓**INTERNET**→*url* http://www.hidwa ter.com/fmd/archives.html

rec.music.folk (ng) Why is it that an artist like Ani DiFranco is listed as a folk performer until she has some success in the mainstream, and then she's lifted right out and moved over to rock? Why is Joni Mitchell considered folk and Alanis Morissette not considered folk? Not all these issues are covered in the online folk-chat world, but some of them are, along with fan-penned record reviews ("John Renbourne is a folk god"), lyric analyses (what is Joni Mitchell talking about on *The Hissing of Summer Lawns,* anyway?), and equipment news (Luka Bloom plays a Alvarez Yairi DY88 Guitar, in case you were wondering). ✓**USENET**→rec.music.folk

International folk

Canadian Folk Music Gene Wilburn, the author of *Northern*

Journey, a Guide to Canadian Folk Music, has assembled excerpts from his book, Canadian folk music CD reviews, info on Canadian folk festivals, and a collection of links to other Canadian folk sites. ✓**INTERNET**→*url* http://www.io. org/~njo/

Celtic Music on the Net This informative page answers questions about everything you could want to know about Celtic music in Cyberspace. Want to know where to discuss Celtic music on the Net? Answer: rec.music.celtic, which handles about 30 to 80 messages a day. Want to know addresses of lots and lots of Celtic music sites? Come here for info on and links to the Sunsite Gaelic Archive and Lark in the Morning, among others. Also find artist's bios and record-company contact information here. ✓**INTERNET**→*url* http://celtic.stanford.edu/Inter net_Sources.html

Folk Roots English folk music and world music are explored at this online version of the popular English magazine. Get a 1995 folk festival list covering events worldwide as well as album reviews and chart lists. ✓**INTERNET**→*url* http://

www.cityscape.co.uk/froots/edit. html

Irish Folk Songs The lyrics to more than 300 Irish folk songs are here to get your Irish eyes a-smiling. ✓**INTERNET**→*url* http://www. cs.hut.fi/~zaphod/search/

The Rogue Folk List A page presenting folk music concert and dance info for Vancouver, British Columbia. Besides the schedules for local get-togethers and jam sessions, you' ll also find a list of radio stations offering folk in the Vancouver area and a link to a service that furnishes British sports scores. What that has do with folk is anyone's guess. ✓**INTERNET** →*url* http://mindlink.net/Roguefolk/

US/Canadian Maritime Music For seafaring folks, there's Epcom Records, a self-described "maritime recording studio." Epcom's latest project is a musical homage to the *Marco Polo,* known in its time to be the fastest ship in the whole wide world. You can hear sound clips of the songs "We Built This Old Ship" and "The Marco Polo Suite" at this site as well as link to a page promoting the Marco Polo Project, an effort dedicat-

Iris DeMent—from http://www.rahul.net/hrmusic/images/iris300c.jpg

The Three Hits *cover—from http://www.mtp.com/IG/image/*

ed to erecting a full-scale model of the famous ship. Ahoy, ye maties! ✓**INTERNET**→ *url* http://www. cygnus.nb.ca/epcom/index.html

Magazines

Dirty Linen Air someone else's dirty linen for a change by checking out this virtual sampler edition of the magazine of folk, electric folk, traditional, and world music. Who's covered? New artists like Janet Russell and Christine Kidd, legends like Doc Watson, rock crossovers like Maria Muldaur, and more. Each issue also contains record, video , book, and concert reviews, and the Website also contains classifieds, a national radio listing, and a growing gig guide. ✓**INTERNET**→*url* http://www.dirty nelson.com/linen/

Radio

Internet Folk Radio List If you're getting ready for a cross-country drive and you don't want to be caught without any folk music on your radio, come to this site and get a list of every folk-oriented radio station across the country. This hypertext list also offers info on a few folk stations in Canada and abroad. ✓**INTERNET**→*url* http:// web.cgrg.ohio-state.edu/folk book/radio/folkradio.html

Songs

Digital Tradition Folk Songs This database features the full text of hundreds of folk songs. Tunes are written out for about half of the songs. Search the index by title, tune, or keyword. A scan of the Keywords List (which also lists keyword frequency) provides an interesting insight into the folk genre: The keyword "courting" appears 294 times, "death" makes 352 appearances, but "law" comes up only 15 times. ✓**INTERNET**→*url* http://pubweb.parc.xerox.com/ digitrad

Country & western

Often dismissed with a set of stereotypes—the mournful yokel, the tear-stained letter

—country music is in fact one of the richest traditional genres in American culture. From old artists assured a place in the pantheon (Hank Williams, Lefty Frizzell) to the supreme singers of the fifties (George Jones, Patsy Cline), from sixties and seventies stars (Johnny Cash, Willie Nelson, Charley Pride, Dolly Parton) to New Country luminaries of the eighties and nineties (Dwight Yoakam, Lyle Lovett, Rosanne Cash, Garth Brooks), country has endured. Check out **Country Chat.** Play the Music City at **Virtual Nashville.** Study **Cowboy Poetry.** And then write your own "Alone and Forsaken" with the **Do It Yourself Country & Western Song Kit.**

Hank Williams—from http://orathost.cfa.ilstu.edu/public/OratClasses/

On the Net

Across the board

Basket Full Of Country Basket Full of Country? Sounds like a restaurant for the urbanophobe. This site offers an extensive directory for even the pickiest Crook and Chase fan. So sit on the one-step front of your house, admire the way your Mariposa boots look on the dusty wood, try to block out those memories of the South China Sea, and let the songs fill your head. ✓**INTERNET**→*url* http://204.96.208.1/services/staff/dawn/basketc.htm

Country Chart Doug's personal chart of the top 30 country songs of the week. See who rates higher—Collin Raye or Hal Ketchum?—check in on the stars of the past to see if they can resurface in the present, and try to predict who will be the stars of tomorrow. ✓**INTERNET**→*url* http://pages.prodigy.com/FL/doug/chart.html

Country Connection The largest site on the Web for country music is also one of the easiest to use, with a huge artist reference guide, TV and radio listings, and links to fan pages, country 'zines, and record labels. Be careful, though—many of the links are out of date. ✓**INTERNET** ...→*url* http://metro.turnpike.net/C/country/index.html ...→*url* http://uptown.turnpike.net/C/country/

The Country Music Fan Page Links to dozens of resources for the country music faithful, including links to artist pages, reviews of albums, and more. ✓**INTERNET**→*url* http://www.catt.ncsu.edu/users/drmellow/public/www/country.html

Country Music Online You think it's so easy to write a country song, don't you? Mention liquor, your mama, and infidelity and it writes itself. Not true. A true country ballad understands a commitment to artwork, compassion and responsibility. This is a large list of links, including information on magazines, newsgroups, songs, radio stations, concerts, fan clubs, and artist sites (most of which are accompanied by online images). ✓**INTERNET**→*url* http://www.tpoint.

net/Users/wallen//country/coun
try.html

Country Online Links to online
music services generated from the
Country Music Capital of the
World. Find the official site for the
Nashville Music Connection, offering professional information on
recording studios, producers, and
musicians, and even a link to
SESAC, which explains the
labyrinthine process of song licensing and copyrighting. ✓INTER-
NET→*url* http://online.music-city.
com/

Mike's Country Page What's
on Mike's country page? Lots of
Mike, along with pictures of his
favorite country stars. Not neces-
sarily thrilling, unless you want to
see Fan Fair photos of Diamond
Rio and Trisha Yearwood with the
aforementioned wide-eyed fan.
✓INTERNET→*url* http://www.dsu.
edu/~kesslerm/country.html

Name that Country Tune
Whose honeyed tones are those
singing about heartbreak, honesty,
and real-world compromises?—
Alan Jackson's or Joe Diffie's? Test
your musical knowledge with this
online version of Name That
Tune. ✓INTERNET→*url* http://www.
geopages.com/Hollywood/1516/
ntct.html

Nashville Network I'll meet
you Sunday at The Bluebird Cafe.
Try to get a corner table, order me
the baked brie and apples, a
whiskey sour, and maybe we'll see
somebody famous. This site offers
an array of Nashville tidbits from
Music Row to Opryland. Download your favorite artists' bios and
pictures—you can get Mary
Chapin Carpenter harmonizing
earnestly or Clint Black squinting
handsomely. And from this page
you can also reach the major la-

Jimmie Rodgers—http://orathost.cfa.ilstu.edu/public/OratClasses/

bels' home pages—Badcat, Black
Boot, Curb, Justice, Polygram,
and Sony—for some polished
press releases touting the stars you
love. ✓INTERNET→*url* http://club.
eng.cam.ac.uk/~94mab/country

**Nerd World Media: Country
Music** Not the most popular page
on the Web—with only nine vis-
tors since May—this page is something of a building block for other
pages under the supervision of
Nerd World. Still, there are dozens
of country Websites and newsgroups listed, and you can reach
them all with a single click. ✓IN-
TERNET→*url* http://www.tiac.net/
users/dstein/nw223.html

Wayne's Country Music Page
"And the whole town said / That
he should have used red / But it
looked good to Charlene..." If you
don't already know what comes
next, then look it up online. From
this site you can find loads of
lyrics from Dwight Yoakam to
Tanya Tucker, and some classics,
too, like Elvis, Buck Owens, and
Chet Atkins. A definitive source
for your country music needs.
✓INTERNET→*url* http://galaxy.
einet.net/EINet/staff/wayne/count
ry/country.html

What's New In Country Tradi-
tionally, nothing much ever seems
to change in country music. Cow-
boy-lean hips and a gospel-tinged

voice are valued above all else—although NASCAR, pro wrestling, and Jack Daniels should be factored into the mix as well. This page provides enough country links to appease even the most hardened line dancer. From the Vince Gill Golf Challenge to Wynonna gossip (just whose baby is this one?), you can find it here. ✓**INTERNET**→*url* http://204.96. 208.1/services/staff/dawn/whatnewc.htm

Wild Willy's Country Music Page Country music in Cambridge? Line dancing in Provincetown? This country music page focuses on the New England region and includes links to several sites worldwide. ✓**INTERNET**→*url* http://www.ultranet.com/~wmh/msic-page.html

Chat

Country & Bluegrass Virtually no discussion here—only a single message congratulating a convert to country and one short thread worrying about the recorded output of Clarence White. ✓**COM-PUSERVE**→*go* amgpop→Messages *and* Libraries→Country & Bluegrass

Patsy—from http://orathost.cfa.ilstu. edu/public/OratClasses/

Country Chat The big winners on AOL's country music board are the women of modern country—Trisha Yearwood, Kathy Mattea, Mary Chapin Carpenter, Reba McEntire, Wynonna Judd, and Suzy Boggus. Why are they the big winners? Because they have hundreds of messages from adoring fans who pore over the smallest details of their songs. Who are the losers? In fandom, there are no losers. But there are artists who have less active message boards, like Vince Gill, Shania Twain, and Hal Ketchum. Compare notes on the big, the small, the old, the new, and the rest. ✓**AMERICA ON-LINE**→*keyword* mmc→Country/Folk →Country

Country Music List (ml) Is Lyle Lovett really country? What about Mary Chapin Carpenter? And how should Johnny Cash be classified now that he has been discovered by alternative music fans, a la Tony Bennett? Fight over who writes the best songs (Roseanne Cash? Willie Nelson? Hank Williams?), who has the best voice (Kathy? Reba? Suzy?), and which hat act (Garth? Dwight? Billy Ray?) is sexiest. ✓**INTERNET**→*email* maiser@rmgate.pop.indiana.edu ✍ *Type in message body:* subscribe country-l

Country/Folk Is there a song-writing shortage in this fine nation of ours? You'd think so, because the same country that produced such classics as "Alone and Forsaken," "White Lightning," and "I Guess Things Happen That Way," has now been reduced to trolling for songsmiths on Compuserve. Yes, that's right—a full 30 percent of the posts on this Country / Folk message board are from singers looking for songs. Fans are looking for songs, too, although the ones they're seeking are usually

Willie—http://web.msu.edu/mfest94/ willie.html

recorded already. Need a list of country songs related to food, a review of a Billy Joe Shaver concert, or a .GIF of John Denver and his lovely family? Just check out the library. ✓**COMPUSERVE**→*go* musicarts →Messages *and* Libraries→ Country/Folk

Live Country Chat Talk to other country fans live. ✓**PRODIGY**→*jump* chat→Prodigy Chat→Select an Area:→Music Country

rec.music.country* (ng) What's old-time country? Hank Williams, certainly, and Jimmie Rodgers, and Bob Wills, and Roy Acuff. What's not? Anything that has happened in the last twenty years, since new superstars like Garth Brooks, Keith Whitley,, Lorrie Morgan, and Dwight Yoakam (not to mention country rockers like the late, great Gram Parsons) have changed the way that America thinks about its country music. These two newsgroups offer country fans a place to fuss, fight, and then make up. But don't get lost in a thread; before you know it, the sun will be setting and the day will be gone. Ain't it funny how time just slips away? ✓**USENET** …→rec.

The man in black—http://www.catt. ncsu.edu/www_projects/Cash/cash.html

music.country.old-time ... →rec. music.country. western

Cowboys

American Cowboy Jim Morrison was an American poet. William Katt was the Greatest American Hero. And the best cowboy magazine online is *American Cowboy*, the magazine of Western living, culture, art, and fashion. It almost makes sense, doesn't it? ✓**INTERNET**→*url* http://www.csn. net/cowboy/

Canadian Cowboy Net Do you want to know about the materialist philosophy of cowboys? Sure you do. "There's an old saying, Cowboys live poor and die rich. I am more inclined to think it's the Cowboy's definiton of wealth that makes him what he is. I don't suppose you could call Cowboyin' a career. The pay's not great, there are no pension plans, no unions, no benefits and early retirement is out of the question. So why do they do it? Because they love it!" After you have absorbed that, pardner, you can read about cowboy history, cowboy poetry, cowboy gear, rodeos, and more. ✓**INTERNET**→*url* http://www. ccinet.ab.ca/bjj/cowboy.htm

Cowboy Poetry "Well here's what I want ta tell ya / about a wild kinda man / an' one who wears some funny clothes / an' he rarely sports a tan." Every year, cowboys meet in Elko, Nevada, to swap stories, look weatherbeaten, and write poetry; some of their laconic Western verse is collected here. ✓**INTERNET**→*url* http://agri comm.com/agricomm/cp

Cowboy Web Mama, don't let your babies grow up to be cowboys. But don't worry if they grow up to be bespectacled dweebs with a penchant for cowboys, because in that case all that will happen is that they'll spend a lot of time at this Website, reading quotes from Luke Perry from 8 Seconds (that's the movie where he "portrayed" rodeo rider Lane Frost) and staring at pictures of Garth Brooks, Dolly Parton, Tim McGraw, Faith Hill, and more. And those computer-dependent geeks can even download cowboy-themed lyrics like "Billy The Kid" (no, not the Billy Joel song). ✓**INTERNET**→*url* http:// www.hcc.cc.fl.us/services/staff/ dawn/cowboy.htm

Europe

Dutch Country Music The Dutch don't need to listen to our country music. Why? Because they have their own country to worry about. That's right—those tulip-sniffing, wooden-shoe-wearing, coffee-shop-patronizing Europeans sing and twang the same way that we do. This page contains information about Dutch stars such as Dick van Altena, Rowwen Hèze, and West Virginian Railroad. Amster-hot-dam, y'all. ✓**INTERNET**→*url* http://www.stack.urc.tue.nl/~ ericg/country.html

Fan clubs

Fan club info list A master list of fan clubs for a wide range of country artists. Do you need to tell Alabama that you love their sweet harmonies? Send off a letter. Do you want to tell Billy Ray Cyrus that you're sorry he's no longer the flavor of the month? Go ahead. There are more than 150 country artists in all, from Dolly Parton to Kenny Rogers to George Strait to Pam Tillis. ✓**INTERNET**→*url* http:// www.hcc.cc.fl.us/services/staff/ dawn/fanclub.htm

Games

Virtual Nashville So you wanna be a country star. Remember, you need more than boots, a hat, and a cocky smile. You need the savvy and know-how to break through the gridlock of Music City. Do you have what it takes? Find out in this interactive online game, where the winner walks away with a virtual recording contract. Will you be the next Garth Brooks, or will you fail miserably and end up puking out your dream behind the Parthenon? Only Virtual Nashville knows for sure. ✓**INTERNET**→*url* http://virtualnashville.com/

History

The History of Country Music Originally designed to accompany

The essential Parsons—http://www. tyrell.net/~klugl/

a course offered at the College of Fine Arts at Illinois State University, this page traces country music from its beginnings (Jimmie Rodgers and the Carter Family) through the Roy Acuff era and cowboy music, and then demonstrates how the Nashville sound came to dominate country production in the late fifties and early sixties. Along the way, fans of the genre will be treated to some rare multimedia—in addition to samples of Bob Willis, Bill Monroe, and Jim Reeves, there's a Quick-Time movie of Patsy Cline on the Arthur Godfrey show. ✓**INTERNET**→ *url* http://orathost.cfa.ilstu.edu/ public/OratClasses/ORAT389.88 Seminar/Exhibits/JohnWalker/0 home.html

Industry

Nashville Music Connection Designed to assist new country talent with the difficult Nashville market, the Nashville Music Connection links to a variety of publications, production companies, and public relations firms that specialize in country artists. ✓**INTER-NET**→*url* http://online.music-city. com/

Magazines

Absolutely Country You don't normally associate the British with country. Well, one kind of country, of course—fox hunts, polo, kids being blown sideways off cliffs on the Isle of Skye. But at this site, you can trade in your English saddle for a Western setup, and browse back issues of *Absolutely Country*, U.K., the free Internet music magazine that dares to list new releases, review concerts, report gossip, and chart the hottest hits. ✓**INTERNET**→*url* http://http1.brunel.ac.uk:8080/ ~ph93rjh/acuk.html

Folk-country star Tish Hinojosa—from http://www.rahul.net/hrmusic/images/

Cowpie News Published twice a month since November 1993, *Cowpie News* includes lyrics, song transcriptions, and country music news. ✓**INTERNET**→*url* gopher:// gopher.ttu.edu:70/11/Pubs/Mail ing-Lists/Professional/cowpie

News & reviews

Country Music Reviews What's good and what's bad? What's heartfelt and what's corny? Which new singers are working in the fine tradition of Joe Diffie and which are working in the not-so-fine tradition of Billy Ray Cyrus? Get reviews of country releases here. ✓**EWORLD**→*go* eaz→Pump Up The Volume→Country→Country Music Reviews

MP Country Music Previews Get the lowdown on the latest country music releases, along with cover art, sound clips, and a brief

bio of the artists. ✓**INTERNET**→*url* http://www.mpmusic.com/country /country.htm

Nashville News Who is dating Troy Aikman? Who is recording with Kris Kristofferson? And will Keith Whitley ever return from the grave? Get the latest news and gossip from Music City. ✓**EWORLD** →*go* eaz→Pump Up The Volume→ Country→Nashville News

Parody

Do It Yourself Country & Western Song Kit Well, it has to be a song about a woman, and most songs about a woman start with a scene of meeting that woman. Did you meet her in Sheboygan popping uppers, or in a jail cell with Merv Griffin? Piece together your very own tear-jerker with this easy-to-use country music Mad Lib-style-song creation

Ernest Tubb—http://orathost.cfa.ilstu.edu/public/OratClasses/ORAT389.88Seminar/

kit. ✓**INTERNET**→*url* http://www.tpoint.net/Users/wallen//country/song-kit.html

Generic Country Song Generator Operating under the assumption that all country songs are about broken hearts, broken bottles, broken heads, and broken English, this site writes a new country song each and every time. Cry your eyes out, and then cry them out some more when you remember that a computer wrote the song. ✓**INTERNET**→*url* http://www.catt.ncsu.edu/users/drmellow/public/www/generic-country.html

Seattle

Black Boots Records A country music label in the heart of Grungeville, U.S.A.? This Seattle-based record company is more in-terested in Alan Jackson than Eddie Vedder. Black Boots, formerly known as Etiquette Records, caters to musicians of the country-folk scene on both coasts. From this page you can order featured albums like K. J. Corye's *All Hearts Needed* and other hot Black Boots stuff. ✓**INTERNET**→*url* http://www.w2.com/boot.html

Songs

Country Songs Who's here? Alabama, John Anderson, Asleep at the Wheel, Chet Atkins, the Bellamy Brothers, John Berry, Clint Black, Suzy Bogguss, Garth Brooks, Brooks and Dunn, and Glen Campbell, and that's only the first ten. With more than a hundred artists represented, this huge gopher archive offers lyrics, chords, and guitar tabs for country songs galore. ✓**INTERNET**→*url*

gopher://gopher.ttu.edu/11/Pubs/Mailing-Lists/Professional/cowpie-songs

Top 100 Country Songs of All Time Originally published in the October 1992 issue of Country America, this list was generated by combining a readers' poll and a critics' poll. When the smoke cleared, George Jones's "He Stopped Loving Her Today" was the undisputed victor, with Vince Gill's "When I Call Your Name," Garth Brooks's "The Dance," and a pair of Patsy Cline tunes ("Crazy" and "I Fall to Pieces") rounding out the top five. Purists, beware: Hank Williams doesn't even appear on the list until "Your Cheatin' Heart," at #7. ✓**INTERNET** →*url* http://www.tpoint.net/Users/wallen//country/top-songs.html

Tejano

Selena Foundation Oh, Selena! Amor prohibido! This is an informational page for those interested in the Selena Foundation. After the pop singer's death, her family established a Tejano museum and scholarship fund in her memory. Support Selena in Cyberspace by

The late superstar Selena—http://198.3.240.72:1995/selena.pic/pachanga/

paying your respects at this site. ✓**INTERNET**→*url* http://www.neo soft.com/selena/

Tejano Welcome to the La Onda Network, promising to be the site for all your Hispanic needs. From here you can reach several Tejano-related links, like the Largest Belt-buckle in Texas, and some very sad Selena pages. ✓**INTERNET**→*url* http://www.ondanet.com:1995/

Tejano Music Awards These people take their Tejano very seriously. From this page access the Pure Onda Radio Special and the Texas Talent Musicians Association. Also, check out the Tejano Hall of Fame, where Manuel Villafranca and Joey Lopez, Sr. recently won lifetime achievement awards. ✓**INTERNET**→*url* http://www.hispanic.com/TTMA/TMA.html

Artists

Clint Black Clint is starting to get some experience as an actor and director; he's still married to Lisa Hartman; he's touring with corporate sponsorship from Keebler; and he roped both Jay Leno and David Hasselhoff into cameo appearances in his latest video. Get all the latest Black gossip, plus lyrics and a discography. ✓**INTER-NET**→*url* http://andromeda.einet.net/EINet/staff/wayne/country/clint-black.html

Suzy Bogguss Pictures of Susan Kay Bogguss, information on her hobbies (she likes to garden and read), lyrics, a discography, and sound clips. ✓**INTERNET**→*url* http://www.dur.ac.uk/~d3g6cj/suzy.html

Garth Brooks Who couldn't love Garth Brooks? From frat boys to grandmas, we've all got friends in low places. This comprehensive

page offers pictures, album info, and fun stuff about the philanthropic musician. In a cyber-interview, Garth mentions his musical influences were James Taylor, Dan Fogelberg, and George Strait; above all else, however, he thanks his mother and father. What a sweetheart. ✓**INTERNET**→*url* http://www.tecc.co.uk/mparkes/garth brooks/

Garth Brooks Spotlight One of the most successful country performers in the history of the genre (topping Billboard charts several years in a row), Brooks released a collection of his biggest hits in 1994, aptly naming the album *Garth Brooks—The Hits*. Created to promote the release, this site features a Garth biography, pictures of the artist, a fact sheet about his career, and ordering information. ✓**COMPUSERVE**→*go* garth

Alan Jackson Lyrics, tour dates, images, and a link that once allowed fans to order a Visa card adorned with Alan's image but now merely stands as testament that this travesty did indeed exist. ✓**INTERNET**→*url* http://galaxy.einet.net/EINet/staff/wayne/country/alan-jackson.html

Waylon Jennings A biography, a discography, tour dates, and links to other Waylon Websites. ✓**INTERNET**→*url* http://www.catt.ncsu.edu/www_projects/Cash/hmen/waylon.html

Kris Kristofferson Where does Kris Kristofferson fit into the big jigsaw puzzle that is country music? Well, the former Rhodes scholar is one of the genre's premier songwriters, and he's the subject of this page, which opens with an animated summary of Kristofferson's four rules of performance

Roy Acuff—http://orathost.cfa.ilstu.edu/public/OratClasses/ORAT389.88Seminar/

("Tell the truth; sing with passion; work with laughter; love with heart"), and then proceeds to a huge picture. Eventually, the multimedia spectacular gives way to a reference page that includes a Kristofferson discography, a filmography, concert reviews, and more. ✓**INTERNET**→*url* http://www. wu-wien.ac.at/usr/h92/h9225291 /kris/kris.html

Willie Nelson Did you know that before Willie was a recording artist, he was one of the most successful songwriters in the history of country music? It's true—he even wrote Patsy Cline's "Crazy." Get sound clips, a biography, album reviews, and links to other sites about the red-headed stranger here. ✓**INTERNET**→*url* http://www. catt.ncsu.edu/www_projects/Cash /hmen/willie.html#other

Hank Williams Hank's premature death at 29 makes us wonder what talent we missed. Would he have become a parody of himself? Could he have overcome alcoholism? Of his music it was said, "There was rarely a note or word surplus to intention." In a genre where lyrics can sometimes become sodden and overdramatic, Hank Williams's greatest achievement was his brevity. Visit this

The Highwaymen—http://www.catt. ncsu.edu/www_projects/Cash/

page for a tribute to the man and hear some of the classics like "Your Cheatin' Heart." ✓**INTERNET**→*url* http://www.polygram.com/poly gram/mercury_nashville/artists/ williams_hank/Hank.html

Hank Williams, Jr. Hello Bocephus! Lay one on me, baby! Did you know that in Charlotte, North Carolina the entertainer who draws the most fans, the most police, and the most all out hellraising is—not The Dead, not Ice Cube, but none other than—Hank Williams, Jr.? This page provides some Bocephus background, info on the upcoming album, Hog Wild, tour dates, and fan club info for those who dare. ✓**INTERNET**→ *url* http://ucunix.san.uc.edu/ ~roundsda/hankhome.html

Trisha Yearwood "Trisha's like a Cadillac with four-wheel drive—smooth and classy, yet down-home and powerful. She serves up an assertive quality, while also revealing softer colours as she moves effortlessly through this mix of melodic country and pop songs delivered with a great deal of confidence and cool vocals." How do you think she feels about the Cadillac metaphor? Visit this Trishafest and ponder whether or not *you* are in love with the boy. ✓**INTERNET**→ *url* http://irons.king.ac.uk/ty/

Dwight Yoakam Dwight has a new album, a line of high-end country-western clothing (called DY Ranchwear), a movie in the can in which he portrayed outlaw Frank James, and a large fan following. Find out all about the handsome, intelligent, and literate country star at this page, which includes lyrics, a discography, and a review of *Buenos Noches from a Lonely Room.* ✓**INTERNET**→*url* http://www.tpoint.net/Users/wal len//country/dwight-yoakam.html

"Had he lived, perhaps Hank Williams would have become a poor parody of himself; perhaps the violin section insensitively dubbed onto his records after his death would have been added at his own instigation. In terms of forging a legend, there is no doubt that Hank did well to burn out at twenty-nine, before his fire grew dim and the face of country music changed.

"As it stands, his tragically premature death leaves us with a remarkably pure and consistent body of work. There are simply very few Hank Williams records that can be isolated as contrived, hokey, lackluster, or below the remarkable standards that he set for himself.

"The key to Hank Williams is passion. The entire range of human emotions is within these recordings: love, hate, envy, joy guilt, despair, remorse, playfulness, sorrow...and more."

—from **Hank Williams**

Dance music

Call it dance, or trance, or rave, or techno, or ambient, or jungle, but above all, call it

dance music, because that's what it is, an agglomeration of genres, all of which assist in mental and physical transport (aka dancing, clubbing, or plain old rump-shaking). Put your best foot forward at **alt.music.dance, Intelligent Dance Music,** and **Techno Today.** Get ambient at **Epsilon: The Ambient Music Information Archives.** And then rave away at **Hyperreal** and **Virtual Rave Chat.**

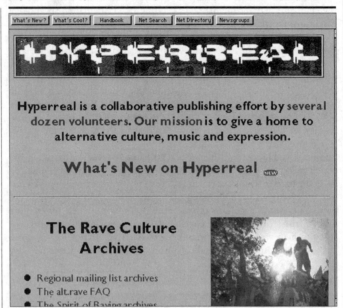

Hyperreal is a collaborative publishing effort by several dozen volunteers. Our mission is to give a home to alternative culture, music and expression.

What's New on Hyperreal NEW

The Rave Culture Archives

- Regional mailing list archives
- The alt.rave FAQ
- The Spirit of Raving archives

The Hyperreal rave culture archive—from http://hyperreal.com/

On the Net

Across the board

alt.music.dance (ng) Delany is upset about the lack of dance music being played on the radio and on MTV. He writes, "I want MTV to play more dance. The same goes for radio. As one person pointed out, the only way to do this would be for someone to start their own station—music video and radio. It is possible, it is logical, and it would bring dance music back to where it belongs—bouncing on our eardrums." That's the kind of talk that will bring the house down on this newsgroup, which is devoted entirely to the throbbing beat of the dance music genre. Fans go here to rant and rave about their favorite songs (Ognen thinks "One More Try" by Kristin W. is fabulous) and to cast their votes for the best clubs in their area. But new discussions emerge all the time—

with the release of the movie *To Wong Foo,* gay-oriented dance CDs became a hot topic. ✓**USENET**→alt.music.dance

alt.music.makers.dj (ng) Put the needle in the groove at this group, which features lots of name-that-track requests ("The song sounds like 'I Got the Music in Me' but with a disco beat and piano chords. What's it called?!?"). Also read about how to become a jockey and the professional code by which all DJs must abide. ✓**USENET**→alt.music.makers.dj

Big Bro Media Europe dances to the beat of Big Bro Media. It features news and articles on the industry, new artists, DJs, and clubs. Learn about the newest dance releases from artists like Unique,

The Jones Girls, and Hi-Gloss, and then shop for their records in the CD Shop section. If you've just gotta dance now, click on the Rave List and find out where you can rave your little heart out (and when). ✓**INTERNET**→ *url* http://www.bigbro.nl/bigbro/

Intelligent Dance Music (ml) Informed techno-babble from dancers doing it all over the world. ✓**INTERNET**→ *email* idm-request@hyperreal.com ✍ *Type in message body:* subscribe idm

Techno/Dance/Disco Don't spend too much time on the message boards here—they're absolutely empty! But the library at this site is chock full of good dance info. Richard Mink, a regular contributor to *Dance Music*

Dance Music Genres

Authority magazine, posts new dance music articles every month. He reviews various house, trance, tribal, and techno releases that are "at least good enough to take to the clubs and play for the masses." These include the work of artists like Dephashe Moog, Caucasian Boy, and Planet Soul, among others. ✓**COMPUSERVE**→*go* amgpop→ Messages *and* Libraries→Techno/ Dance/

UK-Dance Home Page The amount of info here will put you in a trance. Learn how to join the famous UK-Dance mailing list, which delivers up-to-the-minute news on parties, club scenes, and one-off events all over the Kingdom. This home page also offers descriptions of London record stores to help with vinyl shopping in the big city. And before heading off to the record store, consult the record reviews at this site—there are hundreds of them indexed by artist name, label, or album title. The recordings are even rated—a rating of "1" demands an apology from the artist, and a rating of "10" marks the album as an all-time classic. For more dance and techno info, use the links here to jump to other international sites, like the German Techno Online page and the Belgian Rave site. ✓**INTERNET**→*url* http://www. tqmcomms.co.uk/uk-dance/

Yuliana A great big blinking orange is the first thing you see at Yuliana, so you know the site's going to be fun. And it is—especially the Soundbox, which offers clips of Dutch and international dance artists. After listening to some tunes, catch up on dance news in the Benelux Länder by reading Alfred Bro's weekly column, "Postcard from Mokum." And don't forget to consult the weekly calendar of international digital music concerts. ✓**INTERNET**→*url* http:// www.riv.nl/yuliana/

Ambient

Ambience for the Masses For those who still don't quite comprehend the concept of ambient music, the essay at this site, written by ambient fan Lookit, will help illuminate the matter. Lookit explains: "Speaking in the simplest terms, ambient music is meant for sleeping. Good ambient music will make you melt into a puddle of grinning, happy jelly." As British ambient fans might say, jelly good. ✓**INTERNET**→*url* http://under ground.internet.com/lookit/ explain/sleepbot.html

Ambient Music Mailing List Archive The actual mailing list is being reformatted to handle high-volume traffic, so, for the moment, fans will have to go to this site, which is updated daily, for their ambient news, information, and conversation. Messages on a variety of ambient topics are accessible here, like recommendations of good ambient record stores in San Francisco, jokes about ambient master Brian Eno, and queries to identify ambient music samples in film and TV shows ("Was that the *Blade Runner* soundtrack at the end of "The Bomb" on BBC2 last week?"). Yes, it was. ✓**INTERNET** →*url* http://hyperreal.com:70/1/ music/lists/ambient/text

Epsilon: The Ambient Music Information Archive A site dedicated exclusively to the music that gets you in the mood. For those just starting out with ambience, there's a series of essays an-

Ambient pioneer Brian Eno—from http://www.nwu.edu/music/eno/

swering the question "What is ambient music?" including a set of liner notes from Brian Eno's ambient albums. A list of recommended ambient albums gives listening tips to newcomers. The Ambient Artist section here is full of profiles, discographies, images, and sound clips for artists like Biosphere and Voice of Eye (close to 100 artists are covered in all). If you're more interested in ambient record labels, the Label Information section will be more your speed—you'll find discographies and press releases for all the major companies. Those who visit Epsilon are encouraged to send in record reviews—like Gavin, who writes about "Semantic Spaces" by Delerium: "Each track has its own unique style and sound about it, while still having the basic ingredients of merging a sense of atmosphere, and using the right samples at the right time (without just using it for no reason)." A collection of links to other ambient sites makes this one-stop shopping for those with ambience on their minds. ✓**INTERNET**→*url* http://hyperreal.com/ambient/

Homo-Ambiento You'll find this big site divided into three parts. The Mindsets section addresses many philosophical questions facing the dance soundscaper: "Is listening the act of traveling without moving?" "What is the space sound occupies?" "What is the action of sound?" (You'll just have to visit the site to learn the answers to those questions!) In the Discourses part of the site, you can read a top-ten list of required sounds for ambient fans. Links to other ambient sites can be found in the Other Sites section, which takes you to Silent Records, the Reality Society, and Epsilon: The Ambient Archive. ✓**INTERNET**→*url* http://newhamp.hampshire.edu/

Techno-heads Orbital—from ftp://ftp.xmission.com/pub/lists/orbital/images/

~ewsF89/Homo-Ambiento.html

DJs

20Hz "Deep" is a big word in the dance music community, and 20Hz wants to provide you with "the deepest in dance music." With record reviews by hot San Francisco jockeys (like Mark Farina and DJ James) and links to DJ bios and home pages, 20Hz takes you down there. Much anticipated at this site is the new Crackerjack Madness! section, which will feature absurd and funny pictures and articles on the San Fran dance/rave scene. ✓**INTERNET**→*url* http://www.twenty-hz.com/

Dr. Freecloud's Mixing Lab Los Angeles DJs Ron D. Core and Simply Jeff are the Dance Doctor, and they'll give you a musical prescription for what ails ya. They

post a weekly hot list, which will soon be enhanced with sound clips. The site also has an online record store featuring the Doctor's best picks. You can really bug your parents by ordering records from the Doctor's store online! ✓**INTERNET**→*url* http://www.drfreeclouds.com/drfree/

Streetsound's DJ Emporium This is a candy store for DJs. For some good hardcore fantasy, they can read reviews of clubs worldwide and dream about performing in them. Or they can select that perfect outfit for the scene by reading the fashion reviews here (Japanese kimonos will be very hot very soon!). DJs can also catch up on the latest dance music news, reviews, and events by using the links to other dance sites, including Hyperreal and The Industrial Page. ✓**INTERNET**→*url* http://www.

phantom.com:80/~street/

Labels & studios

Cyber Records This Dutch record company is the home of recording artists Cyber House, World Tour, and Sjef and Sjekk. Read about their latest releases here. Also find a calendar for Cyberia, a weekly dance party in Amsterdam sponsored by Cyber Records and *Update Magazine.* ✓**INTERNET**→*url* http://www.dance. nl/cyber/

Energy Moving Masses Promotional page for a studio specializing in recording and mastering dance music. ✓**INTERNET**→*url* http://www.aei.ca/~energy/

Techno and Ambient Labels Considered by many to be the definitive list, this site makes a good stab at listing all techno and ambient labels known to man. Use the links to reach Apollo Records, where they've just updated their discography, or head to Instinct's site to shop their online catalog. Close to 100 companies are online here, so if the techno/ambient label you're looking for isn't here, you might check if they're still in business. ✓**INTERNET**→*url* http://hyperreal.com:70/1/music/labels

Trip N Spin Records Trip N Spin is a group of artists that want to "release booming dance music without interference from corporate record producers, quick-buck promoters or other scene fascists." (They certainly won't have to worry about too much attention from major labels.) The San Francisco bands Island Universe, Mod Squad, Novabass, Jondi & Spesh, and Kellix offer band info, sound clips, and a newsletter (called *Chronicles*) at this site. ✓**INTERNET**→ *url* http://tripNspin. com/TNS/

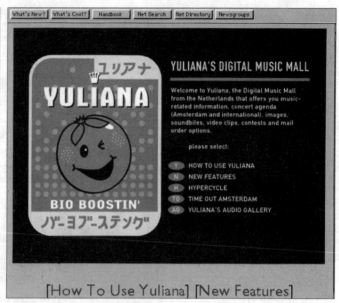

Yuliana's welcoming page—from http:// www.riv.nl/yuliana/

Verb Audio This site asks the provocative question, "How does science feel?" Find the answer by tuning into the music samples of several Atlanta-based artists, like DJ Bobble and Greg White, that are offered here. There's also a Link of the Week section, which highlights related sites like the Virtual Drum Machine. A radio program calendar will let you know when you can catch Verb Audio artists spinning their sonic wares on the airwaves. They're doing more than sitting under peach trees in Atlanta; Verb Audio may even win an Olympic medal for dance music. ✓**INTERNET**→*url* http://www.mindspring.com/ ~brydaguy/verb.html

Zoemagik Records The company that helped launch the careers of Essa 3, the Roman & Winnie Project, and Daisy Glow. Read about their music and shop for their records at this site. ✓**INTERNET**→*url* http://www.cot.com/ Zoemagik.records/index.html

Magazines & reviews

Afterdark Magazine If you speak Dutch, then this magazine promises a wealth of info on dance news, clubs, record releases, and charts. If you don't speak Dutch, you'll be in the dark at *Afterdark*. ✓**INTERNET**→*url* http://www.si.hhs. nl/~v932539/home.html

Mixmag After flipping through *Mixmag*, it's easy to see why it's known as the world's leading dance music and club culture magazine. This is the dance world's version of *Time* magazine. *Mixmag*'s been reporting on techno, house, and hip-hop music, plus clubs, drugs, DJs, and everything to do with the international clubbing life for over 12 years now. A current edition featured articles on Laurent Garnier (a supermodel in the European DJ world) and the results of a test to see whether club kids can drive safely after a night of drugs and dancing (the conclusion: don't try this without a safety net.) Also find a single-of-the-week review and news briefs to keep you in the know. ✓**INTERNET**→*url* http://www.techno.de/mixmag/index.html

Spaced@The Muse Be warned: the psychedelic picture at this site might remind you of the last time you stayed too long at the Pally. Just move on and read reviews of dance clubs, records, and DJs. There are also regular free-ticket giveaways for dance parties in London. ✓**INTERNET**→*url* http://hyperlink.com/muse/music/ambient/dance/techno/music5.htm

Rave

A Rave New World Click on the map here and link to rave and dance resources in the United States, Europe, and Australia. DJs, rave fans, record stores, and clubs have links at this site. ✓**INTERNET**→*url* http://hyperreal.com/~thigpen/rave_map/

alt.rave (ng) Judging from this newsgroup, the undercurrents are strong in the rave scene. The three most-discussed topics here are "Does E cause brain damage?" "Raver chicks are scum!" and "Herbal XTC." They're doing more than just dancing down at the local rave these days! Besides these topics, find hot CD and club tips as well as party listings for events nationwide. ✓**USENET**→ alt.rave

Hyperreal Rave until you drop! This definitive rave site will tell you where and how to rave all night. Hook up with one of the local mailing lists indexed here to find the next rave event near you. The alt.rave FAQ and Spirit of Raving Archive will teach you the finer points of the dance, including an essay on PLUR—the four ideals which make raving a positive, spiritual, and long-lasting experience—peace, love, unity, and respect. If you're inclined to chemically enhance your dance night, Hyperreal provides a very unofficial index (alphabetical by drug name) of raving drug experiences. After the event, you can check the media archive here to see if you made it into the local paper. Wouldn't Mom be proud. ✓**INTER-**

Rave around the World

List of Rave Lists A list of mailing lists that offer rave chat and news. Some of the lists provide direct links to their FAQs. ✓**INTERNET**→*url* http://hyperreal.com/raves/lorl/lorl.html

United States

Boston Raves ✓**INTERNET**→*url* http://hyperreal.com/transeform/boston.html

Kansas Raves ✓**INTERNET**→*url* http://www.cis.ksu.edu/~solder/rave/raves.html

Midwest Raves (ml) ✓**INTERNET**→*email* majordomo@hyperreal.com ✍ *Type in message body:* subscribe mw-raves <your full name> *Info:* ✓**INTERNET**→*url* http://www.physics.purdue.edu/mw-raves/

NE-Raves (ml) ✓**INTERNET**→ *email* listserv@umdd.umd.edu ✍ *Type in message body:* subscribe ne-raves <your full name> *Info:* ✓**INTERNET**→ *url* http://www.ccs.neu.edu/home/thigpen/html/ne-raves.html

San Francisco (ml) ✓**INTERNET**→ *email* sfraves-request@hyperreal.com ✍ *Type in message body:* subscribe

Southeastern Raves (ml) ✓**INTERNET**→*email* listserv@american.edu ✍ *Type in message body:* subscribe seraves <your full name>

Washington D.C. Raves (ml) ✓**INTERNET**→*email* dcraves@american.edu ✍ *Type in message body:* subscribe dcraves <your full name>

International

Belgian Raves ✓**INTERNET**→*url* http://www.dma.be/p/amphion/kamers/music/rave-e1.html

Finnish Raves ✓**INTERNET**→*url* http://nic.funet.fi/~joha/fi-rave-info.html

Oslo ✓**INTERNET**→*url* http://www.ifi.uio.no/~mariuss/techno.html

Rave in France ✓**INTERNET**→*url* http://www.sct.fr/cyber/urave.htm

Sydney Raves ✓**INTERNET**→*url* http://ion.apana.org.au/~mdagn/sydney.html

Toronto Rave Report ✓**INTERNET**→*url* http://ikon.tlug.reptiles.org/trr.html

UK-Dance (ml) ✓**INTERNET**→ *email* uk-dance@orbital.demon.co.uk ✍ *Type in message body:* subscribe uk-dance <your full name>

Dance Music Genres

NET→*url* http://hyperreal.com/

International Rave Scene

They're throwing a big dance party at the Dome in Sydney, Australia next Friday night. And there won't be a quiet spot at the club Atlantis in Toronto next Saturday when its weekly rave event kicks off. If you would rather be raving than anything else, check this calendar of worldwide rave events (organized by country) and never spend a night at home again. ✓**INTERNET**→*url* http://feynman.tlug.reptiles.org/nyquist/rave-index.html

Rave&Techno&Dance

It's very hard to read this list of links—the names of the sites are in gray against a gray background. Use the little smiley faces to find the hypertext, and away you go! Visit Dancemob for hot dance news from Helsinki (in Finnish). Or you can discover the best places for techno trance in France by clicking on the Rave in France link. You can also hook up with TechnoNet from here, which gives you record and club reviews in English and German. A stop at this site is your passport to planet techno. ✓**INTERNET**→*url* http://www.helsinki.fi/~koli/rave.html

Virtual Rave Chat

This site is the home page for Vrave, a forum where ravers worldwide talk about parties, music, and the rave world. The history of Vrave is explained—it had to move several times as its audience escalated to its present count of 900 members. There is a link here to the Vrave FAQ, which lays out the process of establishing and verifying a Vrave account. Get to know your fellow Vravers by clicking through the indexed collection of links to member's home pages. Of course, Vrave can be reached directly at

The Aphex Twin—from http://hyperreal.com/music/artists/aphex_twin/afx.html

Hyperreal with the telnet address listed here, but the home page is a nice place to visit for background information. ✓**INTERNET**→*url* telnet://hyperreal. com:7283 *FAQ:* ✓**INTERNET**→*url* http://hyperreal. com/~laura/vrave.html *Info:* ✓**INTERNET**→*url* http://www.hyperreal. com/raves/vrave/

Record stores

Ellesdesia Record Store

Order dance tracks online and have the option to pay with your Mastercard or Eurocard. The Store's catalog is organized alphabetically by artist name, which is followed by the record title, record label, and the price in pounds. If you're not sure what to buy, you can always consult Ellesdesia's record reviews for some tips. Don't get too excited when you see the Going Deeper section here—it's just a strange little list of record labels that Flippo, the site's creator, thinks are groovy. ✓**INTERNET**→*url* http:// www.ellesdesia.nl/

Kado Records

Kado's store offers a wide variety of music, including techno/dance bins. Currently featured are *Fist Full of Techno* (a collection of ten hot rave hits), *Strictly for the Hardcore* (from New York City's dance scene), and *Gloom and Doom* (tunes from Cafe Soundz). Email, phone, or snail mail your order. ✓**INTERNET**→*url* http://www.nesak. com/kado/

Nashers Records

Bath, England has the real-life Nashers Records to fulfill its dance record needs. The rest of the world can shop there too by clicking through the catalogs at this site. The online catalog features over 10,000 12-inch singles and dance LPs. (The actual store has an even larger inventory!) If you can't find the recording you want in the catalog, then email Nashers, and "they'll do their damnedest to find it for you." Order your selections online or call Nashers with the phone numbers provided here. ✓**INTERNET**→*url* http://www.hub.co.uk/intercafe/nashers/music.html

Techno

alt.music.techno

(ng) Are you dying inside to tell the world that "Happy Clappers" is your favorite techno song? Need to sell your old 12-inch singles to finance buying some new releases for your next dance party? Want to know where the good dance clubs are in New York City? Come to this newsgroup to post and read discussions of all things techno. ✓**USENET**→ alt.music.techno

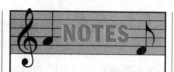

> " Oh God! This disc is orgasm for my ears. I know this isn't directly in the techno vein, but I bought it with several other techno comps and it blows them all away!"

Live Techno Chat Talk techno with other fans in a live chat room. ✓**PRODIGY**→*jump* chat→ Prodigy Chat→Select an Area:→ Music→Techno

Techno Artists and Labels Take a tour of the techno planet with this massive collection of links to dance resources worldwide. Organized into sections like General Techno Info, Some Cool UK Techno Labels, Real Techno Labels Canada/U.K., and Techno Mailing Lists and Archives, this index of links is sure to take you somewhere you want to go. ✓**IN-TERNET**→*url* http://www.mit.edu: 8001/people/trellos/techno.html

Techno Online Thank goodness Teutonic precision has a presence here: the enormous amount of info at this site is neatly organized into five sections: Media Online offers a number of online techno rags, including *Techno Today*, *Mixmag*, and *Sense*; Labels Online lets you read about and listen to clips of new releases from Low Spirit, Suck Me Plasma, and Tunnel Records; check into Parties Online to win free tickets to the Camel Airave and other events; leave a message for your fellow techno dancers on the message board in the Arena section; and play a slot-machine game in the Hot & New topic. A basic knowledge of German—and by basic, we mean more than sauerkraut and Ute Lemper—will help you get the most out of this great dance resource. ✓**INTERNET**→*url* http:// www.techno.de/text.html

Techno Today At least half of your total vocabulary needs to be German to read this magazine. It switches from English to German and back at least twice in every sentence. *Wenn Du Deutsch kannst*, you'll find great party reviews (for events mostly in Germany), record label updates (Dee-Jays Recordings is unleashing a new record next week), and media clippings (pics and articles from the traditional press). ✓**INTERNET**→ *url* http://www.techno.de/techno-today/today.html#personality

XDZebra Techno Review DJ XDZebra is actually a guy named Pete Ashdown, and he's assembled a collection of 31 reviews at this site. Scan the list for record titles that interest you, or view a list of reviews by rating. *Give Peace a Dance, Volume 2: The Ambient Collection* received a 9 out of 10, the highest rating Pete's ever given a record. Here's what he had to say about Peace: "Oh God! This disc is orgasm for my ears. I know this isn't directly in the techno vein, but I bought this comp with several other techno comps and it blows them all away!" ✓**INTERNET**→ *url* http://www.acns.nwu.edu/ xdzebra/

NOTES

"The actual concept of raves is not new - it is as old as time itself. At the base level, raves are very comparable to American Indian religious ceremonies, i.e. pow-wows, and also to the concept of the Shaman in Eskimo and Siberian society - where music is the key towards pulling oneself into a unique emotional and psychological state, a state in which one experiences washes of sensations and visions, not delusions, but visions. Sounds hokey in print, but I'm sure MANY of you know what I'm talking about. The hypnotiz-ing effect of techno music coupled with the seamless transi-tions rave DJ's as the night progresses can be QUITE intoxi-cating, resulting in what could be closely compared to a reli-gious experience. Music in general has always been able to sweep people off their feet, but what distinguishes raves are the concept of the shared experi-ence."

—from **Hyperreal**

World music

The paradox of world music is so conspicuous that it's almost impossible not to remark

upon it—how does the English-speaking world justify dividing its own music into genres (rock, jazz, blues, country) and subgenres (dreampop, hard pop, barrelhouse, bluegrass) while lumping together the musical output of the rest of the world into a single monolithic category? Once you've managed to clear the political hurdles of this taxonomy—or at least to acknowledging their presence with a sheepish shrug—you'll find a wealth of online resources. Want to learn more about King Sunny Ade? Visit **alt.music.africa**. Curious about traditional Celtic sounds? Take some **Irish Music for Your Soul**. And don't stop there. There's a whole planet to explore.

Music of Africa and the Diaspora—from http://matisse.net/~jal/afrcanmx.htm

On the Net

Across the board

alt.music.exotic (ng) "Sound is the same for all the world," said Youssou N'dour in "Eyes Open." International music fans who agree with Youssou converge here to discuss the music, exchange record reviews, and occasionally ask for playing tips; for example, Mike, who writes, "Rednecks of Tennessee want to know: Who's new, bad, and blue in African gui-

tar music? All our Sunny Ade tapes are worn out, and the bootlegger who used to go north and cop for us has crashed his '57 Chevy." It is a small world after all. ✓**USENET**→alt.music.exotic

Asian Contemporary Music List (ml) Join this list to discuss your favorite stars and their music. ✓**INTERNET**→*email* listserv@ubvm. cc.buffalo.edu ✍ *Type in message body:* subscribe actmus-l <your full name>

World & Ethnic Music Brent writes, "I make wood flutes derived from Native American styles. I'm beginning to develop a love of woodwinds from all over the world and would like to begin a collection of them. I really enjoy the sound of both these instruments and would like to trade a custom made wood flute for one. I'm willing to provide a recording

of one of my flutes to verify the quality of my instruments." No one has answered Brent yet, unfortunately, but until he finds someone to swap flutes with, Brent can go to the message boards of this site and meet other international music fans who are just as impassioned as he is. Brent can also enjoy the library at this site, which features some real gems—like a recording of a live gourd dance song and a list of Brazilian music radio stations. Overall this site is not very busy, but the information and discussion that is here is informed and interested. Good luck with your flutes, Brent! ✓**COMPUSERVE**→*go* Music/Arts Forum→ Message *and* Libraries→World/ Ethnic

World Music Where in the world are all the world and international music fans? There is not one message or article at this site, which should be a meeting place for discussion of international music and its culture. ✓**COMPUSERVE**→*go* amg→Message *and* Libraries→ World & Reggae

Africa

alt.music.african (ng) Who is the hottest guitar player in Zaire today? Is it Syran Mbenza, Rigo Star, or Diblo Dibala? If you have an opinion on this issue, or any other topic having to do with African music, then this newsgroup is the place for you. ✓**USENET**→alt.music.african

Music from Africa and the African Diaspora Want to read an article on popular trends in Kenyan music? Or a biography of King Sunny Ade (he was born in Nigeria, the son of a Methodist minister)? Then visit this site, which offers resources and info on the music of every African state. You'll find the site organized alphabetically by country. ✓**INTERNET** →*url* http://matisse.net/~jal/ afrcanmx.htm

Reviews of African Recordings Cliff Furnald, a music writer who has published in *Dirty Linen* and the *CMJ New Music Report*, posts close to 100 reviews of recordings by artists like Najat Atabou, Salif Keita, and Rimitti. ✓**INTERNET**→*url* http://www. rootsworld.com/rw/afrimenu.html

Village Post Outpost Digital recordings of West African drum music. ✓**INTERNET**→*url* http:// www.rootsworld.com/rw/village pulse/outpost.html

China

Chinese Music (ml) A mailing list to keep you updated on CD and laser disc releases in Taiwan, Hong Kong, and China. Some announcements are in Chinese. ✓**INTERNET**→*email* newwave@ rahul.net ✍ *Type in message body:* subscribe whatsnews

The Chinese Music Page A great collection of links exploring different eras in Chinese music. The list begins with links to traditional music sites and ends with links to pages on modern popular music, which is heavily influenced by Western sources. There are also links to sites exploring and explaining traditional Chinese instruments, including the Chinese oboe. ✓**INTERNET**→*url* http://vizlab. rutgers.edu/~jaray/sounds/ chinese_music/chinese_music.html

France

French Music (ml) Two lists, one for male singers (chanteur) and one for female singers (chanteuse). What French singers spring to mind? Well, Francis Cabrel, Daniel Belanger, Patrick Bruel, Celine Dion, Mitsou, and Edith Piaf. Mailing lists are multilingual. Pour yourself some wine, slice yourself some cheese, break off a piece of bread, and then subscribe to these lists for civilized discussion of current French music. ✓**INTERNET** →*email* majordomo@ wimsey.com ✍ *Type in message body:* subscribe chanteur-liste <your email address>

Le Hit Parade A newsletter with the dubious task of bringing contemporary French music to the United States. *Parade* offers English-language record reviews of titles by artists such as Dan Birgras, Robert Charlebois, and Monica Passos. You can even practice your French by singing along to the sound clips offered here! ✓**INTERNET**→*url* http://www.lhp.com/ nsltr/hp_home.htm

NOTES

"Miami diary:

Thursday evening I was at the filming for Los Tres 'Unplugged' at MTV Latino. They are the perfect band for an 'Unplugged' set because they are such incredible musicians and because their material lends itself well to an acoustic set. Roberto Lindl was playing string bass and both his jazz and classical background showed through. Francisco Molina is not only a great drummer to hear, but a creative and interesting drummer to watch as well. Their set included selections from their own material as well as a tribute to the late Roberto Parra. Once I again I have to complain about the fact that we can't get MTV Latino in most of the U.S. If anybody else feels the same way, send me e-mail and I'll forward everything to MTV. Anyway, if you're reading this from a country that has MTV Latino, you can probably pick me out of the crowd."

–from **Latin Music Online**

World Music Genres

Gypsy

The Gipsy Kings The quintessential international band! Often thought of as the Omar Sharifs of the music world, no one is ever really sure where these guys hail from. No one, that is, except Sony Records, and they'll tell you where the Kings started out if you visit their site. You'll also get a discography and preview of *Love and Liberté*, the Gipsys' latest release. ✓**INTERNET**→*url* http://www.music. sony.com/Music/ArtistInfo/Gipsy Kings_LoveAndLiberte.html

India

Indian Classical Music Learn about the basis of classical Indian music, the raga, which is "The combination of several notes woven into a composition in a way which is pleasing to the ear." Then scan the list of Karnatic and Hindustani ragas listed here to find one to play. Also find bios of some great masters of Indian classical music and an online CD catalog where you can shop for and order their music. ✓**INTERNET**→*url* http:// www.vt.edu:10021/org/malhaar/ music.html

Pointers to Indian Music Across the Internet The next time you're in a cab in New York City, impress your Indian cab driver with your knowledge of popular Indian music! This site regularly posts hypertext links to new Internet sites that feature Indian music. ✓**INTERNET**→*url* http://www2. eng.nepean.uws.edu.au/~dbir lase/imusic.html

rec.music.indian.classical (ng) The overwhelming majority of posts to this group advertise or ask for listings of Indian classical music concerts and performances ("Are there any events in the St.

Louis area?" asks Frank). Visitors will also be able to read the occasional CD review, but it's clear that most fans who post here prefer to hear the music live. ✓**USENET** →rec.music.indian.classical

rec.music.indian.misc One post here asserted that Indian singer Lata has sung over 250,000 songs in her career. That statement started a thread of detailed mathematical calculations proving that this was impossible (Lata would have to have sung for 24 hours a day for over 80 years to accomplish the singing of 250,000 songs, and she's only 65!). Although the posts here are not always mathematically correct, they are very rich in discussion of contemporary Indian music and its stars. ✓**USENET**→rec.music.indian. misc.

Ireland

Celtic Music Calendars (ml) Worried that your local paper will neglect Irish sounds? Never miss another Celtic music event in your area again! Celtic Calendars is a family of mailing lists, one for each state in the U.S. and each Canadian province, and each list posts a monthly calendar local Celtic musical events. ✓**INTERNET**→

email majordomo@celtic.stanford. edu ✍ *Type in message body:* subscribe info lists <your email address>

Irish Music for Your Soul RCA Victor sponsors this Irish music site that features in-depth interviews with the Chieftains, who discuss *The Long Black Veil, An Irish Evening,* and *Another Country.* Other albums profiled here are *Irish Night at the Pops* (with Arthur Fiedler), and *Irish Harp Songs,* by Emily Mitchell. ✓**INTERNET**→*url* http://www.irish. com

Irish Music Web Project With the Chieftain's latest album soaring into the Top 20 on the Billboard pop chart, traditional Irish music is no longer for those who look at life through green-colored glasses. This small site offers artist profiles of bands like the Chieftains and Clannad as well as a nice sound clip of the pennywhistle being played. ✓**INTERNET**→*url* http:// orathost.cfa.ilstu.edu/public/ OratClasses/ORAT389.88Seminar/ Exhibits/PeteJuvinall/html/code/ overview. html

Irish Traditional Music (ml) For lads and lassies interested in traditional Irish musical fare.

International faves, The Cheiftains—http://www.irish.com/irish/chieftains.html

Japanese rockers Zenigeva—http://www.twics.com/~yoichi/zenigev.html

✓**INTERNET**→*email* listserv@irlearn. ucd.ie ✍ *Type in message body:* subscribe IRTRAD-L <your full name>

Japan

Bonsai's JPop Page Japanese pop music is alive and well, and Bonsai's site will keep you up to date on the JPop news. In the Idol Biography Database section here, you can read over 150 biographies of the hottest Japanese pop stars (43 percent of the bios also contain pics). Search the data by artist name, and then check out the ranked lists of physiological minutiae, including body mass and height (Mochida Maki is a shade under five feet tall, while Mizuno Miki is a towering 5'7", more than three inches taller than the average height for a Japanese female pop star). You can also read the top-ten pop list, which is updated every week. Bonus: there is an extensive collection of links here, too, which take you to the home pages of Japanese TV shows, karaoke sites, and pop star pages. ✓**INTERNET**→*url* http://www.its.newnham.utas.edu. au/bonsai/jpop/jpop.html

Draggin' The Boot A Japanese site with information on artists, labels, and clubs. ✓**INTERNET**→*url* http://www.st.rim.or.jp/~nagami/

Japanese Rock and Pop (ml) Keep up with that fast-moving Japanese rock and pop market by subscribing to this mailing list. ✓**INTERNET**→*email* majordomo@tcp. com ✍ *Type in message body:* subscribe jpop <your email adress>

Latin America

Brazilian Music Antonio Carlos Jobim. Gilberto Gil. Gal Costas. These are the artists that put Brazilian music on the map and kept it there. This site explores Brazilian music through sound clips, pictures, and bios of its most popular artists. ✓**INTERNET**→*url* http://orathost.cfa.ilstu.edu/ public/OratClasses/ORAT389.88S eminar/Exhibits/GerryMagallan /Artists.html

Latin Music Online A huge resource for Spanish-language music that includes club and concert listings, gossip, album release news, artist biographies, images, sound clips, and reviews of new records.

✓**INTERNET** →*url* http://www. lamusic.com

La Musica Latina A Spanish-language site that features links to Websites dedicated to Latin rock, Brazilian, tango, Caribbean, tejano, and flamenco music. The whole site is in Spanish, but many of the links are in English. ✓**INTERNET**→*url* http://www.bart.nl/~ dtheb/musica.html

rec.music.afro-latin (ng) Topics here cover a lot of ground—from reggae to salsa to Spanish-language rock. Most messages are in English. ✓**USENET**→rec.music.afro-latin

Middle East

Kereshmeh Records Persian music fans need search no further than this site for their classical, folk, and contemporary Persian recordings. Kereshmeh's CD catalog features album covers, sound clips, and ordering information for artists like Alizadeh and Torkaman. There are absolutely no renditions of "Misty" offered here. ✓**INTERNET**→*url* http://www. kereshmeh.com/

Middle Eastern Music (ml) Fans of Middle Eastern music can meet other fans and discuss the genre by joining this Finnish (go figure?) mailing list. ✓**INTERNET**→ *url* middle eastern-music-request@ nic.funet.fi ✍ *Write a request*

Native American

Rainbow Walker Profiles of native artists like the Young Singers of the Puget Sound, two men from the Lummi Nation of Washington State. Also find primers on the flute and whistle tradition in native music as well as pow-wow music and dance traditions (complete with pictures of dance artists

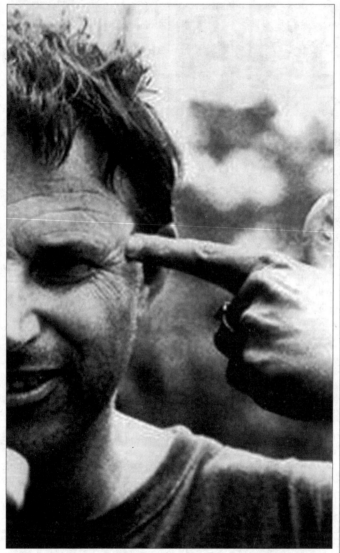

Tall Dwarf Chris Knox—http://www.usyd.edu.au/~mwoodman/knox.html

in the actual act of pow wowing!). ✓**INTERNET**→*url* http://www.tele port.com/~rnbowlkr/

New Zealand

Kiwimusic A page of album reviews (on records like *The Dew Line*, by Gate and *Retraction*, by Omit), band bios (of A Handful of Dust, The Dead C, and Gate, among others), and links to other New Zealand music info sites (including the Many Hands page and UK Guide), most of it culled from the Kiwimusic mailing list. ✓**INTERNET**→*url* http://www.sanger.ac.uk/ ~sd/kiwimusic/HOME

Kiwimusic (New Zealand

Band List) (ml) Discussion of New Zealand bands like the Chills, the Clean, Dimmer, Tall Dwarfs, and more. ✓**INTERNET**→ *email* kiwimusic-request@mit.edu ✍ *Write a request*

Record companies

City of Tribes A very small label that manages to fit the world in its releases. Currently highlighting the band Beast of Paradise, which just released it's five-song debut album, this site offers sound samples, press clippings, and liner notes for its recordings. ✓**INTERNET** →*url* http://www.cot.com/index. html

Lyrichord Records The music of the rain forest Pygmies and the drums of Peruvian mountain dwellers ring through the halls of Lyrichord Records. Its catalog, organized alphabetically by country name, reads like the departures board at JFK—those wishing to visit the music of Australia, Korea, Yugoslavia, or other places can board through the Lyrichord gate. Brief descriptions of the artists and their releases as well as ordering information are available here. ✓**INTERNET**→*url* http://www.Sky Writing.com/Lyrichord/lyrworld. Ohtml

NewTone Records International music has a home at NewTone, which features a catalog of records including Carl Stone's Kamiya Bar (a sampling of Tokyo street noises, voices, and TV programs), Antonio Lara and Efisio Melis playing the dreamy music of the Sardinian Launeddas, and Enzo Favata jamming on Mediterranean acoustic guitar music. Email, phone, or fax your order. ✓**INTERNET**→*url* http://www. inrete.it/musica/robidroli.html

Jazz

It's one of the cruelest ironies of twentieth-century culture that jazz, the great Ameri-

can music, is all but neglected in its homeland. While a few jazz megastars—Louis Armstrong, Miles Davis, Charlie Parker, Wynton Marsalis, Charles Mingus—find their way into the public consciousness, other phenomenal jazz players like Sonny Sharrock, Pharoah Sanders, Sonny Rollins, and Eric Dolphy are consigned to an eternal cult-favorite limbo that sometimes even outlasts life itself. Get jazzed about the United States's single greatest cultural achievement at the **American Music Center Jazz Expansion Project**, **JAZZ Online**, and the **WNUR-FM JazzWeb**. Talk solos at **Improvisation and the Inner Person**. And then read the best jazz lit at **Epistrophy**.

Albert Ayler has sax with himself—from http://ernie.bgsu.edu/~jeffs/

Across the board

American Music Center Jazz Expansion Project Hmm, jazz expansion. Sounds, like, abstract or something. Well, not quite. Best to let the project's mission statement speak for itself: "The American Music Center, with underwriting from the Lila Wallace-Reader's Digest Fund, has created a library of jazz works and information, maintaining a living,

growing record of the music as it evolves. The goal of this project is performances, providing a way for presenters, managers, record companies, orchestras, chamber ensembles, and other performers to find information on jazz composers as well as explore scores and recordings of their music." To date, the collection has acquired more than 300 scores and lead sheets. Play on, collaborators in this living, growing record! ✓**INTERNET**→*url* http://www.amc.net/amc/jazz.htm

Articulate Jazz A large set of artist-specific links, as well as connections to more general jazz re-

sources. One complaint—the blue letters are nearly impossible to read against the grey background, and as a result reading this page is like trying to listen to a McCoy Tyner record while your annoying brother is blasting his Radiohead album in the very next room. ✓**INTERNET**→*url* http://www.wpi.edu/~pj/

Hard Bop Cafe Links collected around jazz and be-bop in Winnipeg and Canada, including festivals/concerts, archives, playlists, and publications, as well as general album and concert reviews and links to other jazz Websites. ✓**INTERNET**→*url* http://www.mbnet.

Anthony Braxton—from http://www. acns. nwu.edu/jazz/gifs/

mb.ca/~mcgonig/hardbop.html

Hogan Jazz Archives This archive is dedicated to the preservation of New Orleans jazz, and includes oral history interviews, music samples, an archive of historical photos and films, sheet music, manuscript materials, and hundreds of articles and books about the form. While the online component of the archive is relatively new, the curatorial staff is in the progress of creating an online catalog of all materials. ✓**INTERNET**→*url* http://www.tulane. edu/~lmiller/JazzHome.html

InterJazz (The Global Internet Jazz Plaza) With a directory of jazz clubs and venues, record labels, booking agencies, and show promoters, as well as individual artist biographies and a link to JazzIRC—a program that allows jazz fans to talk to their favorite artists over IRC—this is one of the most innovative and comprehensive sites on the Web. ✓**INTERNET**→ *url* http://www.webcom.com/~ ijazz/

Jazz Links Annotated links to the major jazz sites online. ✓**INTER-NET**→*url* http://www.ccil.org/~ nmaster/jazzlinks.html

JAZZ Online Full of slick graphics, this page links to general info, a blues room, industry label pages, and news, as well as resources for contemporary, New Age, and world music. ✓**INTERNET**→*url* http://www.jazzonln.com/JAZZ/

JazzNet While it's not really limited to jazz—there's plenty of blues information here, too—this site contains a wealth of resources for jazz fans. Want updates on the Monterey Jazz Festival or the San Francisco Blues Festival? Interested in ordering the U.S. Postal Service's jazz stamps? You can do all those things from this page, and check on labels, artists, newsletters, and academic resources as well. ✓**INTERNET**→*url* http://www. dnai.com/~lmcohen/

WNUR-FM JazzWeb WNUR is only a college radio station, sure, and Northwestern University isn't exactly the first university that springs to mind when you think of jazz. But maybe it should be. Among Internet jazz sites, WNUR's JazzWeb is the rarest of rare birds, a Sonny Rollins among reed hacks. With a large hypertext document ramifying jazz into its styles and substyles, an archive of artist bios, an essay on jazz instruments, a list of jazz venues nationwide, and links to jazz retailers, labels, and more, there's precious little in the jazz world that's not covered here. ✓**INTERNET**→*url* http:// www.nwu.edu/jazz/

Books

Da Capo Press One of the great pleasures available to a jazz fan is listening to the music; another is reading about it. And when it comes to reading about jazz, there's no better place to go than Da Capo. With more than 100 jazz and blues titles on artists ranging from Benny Goodman to Eric Dolphy to Miles Davis—each of which is afforded a dedicated Web page complete with a full table of contents, back cover blurbs, price information, and supplementary multimedia—this catalog takes on the feel of a museum. ✓**INTERNET**→*url* http://www. dnai.com/~lmcohen/dacapo.html

Charts

The Digital Real Book The Digital Real Book project has .GIFs of Real Book charts, suitable for printing. ✓**INTERNET**→*url* http://www.amherst.edu/~ ljnelson/real-book-page.html

Original Jazz Charts Post charts to this area, whether you're a well-known jazz musician or a novice, and then they'll be available for the whole world to see, and maybe the ghost of Miles Davis will be surfing the Net, and

Charlie Parker—http://farcry.neurobio. pitt.edu/Jazz.html

come across your charts, and decide to record your song with a crack band he's assembled in the hereafter—Coltrane, Parker, Armstrong, Dolphy, Rich, Pastorius. You'll be rich. You'll be famous. You'll knock 'em dead. ✓**INTERNET** →*url* http://hokin.physics.wisc.edu/jazz/charts.html

Chat

Jazz & Big Band Though it slants toward modern jazz—that is to say, aesthetically unspectacular improvisation delivered by technically precise musicians—this message board occasionally dips into the past for a consideration of a Miles Davis rerelease or a vintage Sonny Rollins session. ✓**COMPUSERVE**→*go* amgpop→Messages *and* Libraries →Jazz & Big Band

Jazz/Big Bands By far the busier of CompuServe's two jazz message boards (the one in the All-Music Guide Forum has roughly one-tenth of the messages), this board covers everything from Jelly Roll Morton to Miles to two Wyntons, trumpeter Marsalis and pianist Kelly. And as on any jazz message board, soft-fusion saxophonist Kenny G comes in for his share of ribbing— "Heard the latest about Kenny G? He's making his acting debut as an expatriate adult contemporary musician in Paris--the movie's called Round Noon. I know you all will embellish this joke to no end. Go for it." ✓**COMPUSERVE**→*go* musicarts→Messages *and* Libraries →Jazz/Big Bands

Let's Talk JAZZ What's jazz these days? A few new players who become experts on their instrument and then, without even learning the rudiments of improvisation, move into the public eye. What should jazz be? More than

Juan Garcia Esquivel—from http://www.users.interport.net/~joholmes/

just a museum exhibit and a few young turks. Help salvage one of America's most important art forms by putting in your two cents here. ✓**EWORLD**→*go* eaz→Pump Up The Volume→Music Talk→Let's Talk JAZZ

Live Jazz Chat Talk jazz live with other fans. ✓**PRODIGY**→*jump* chat→Prodigy Chat→Select an Area:→Music→Jazz

rec.music.bluenote (ng) What color is jazz? Blue, of course. Blue like the sky. Blue like the Miles Davis record (kind of). Blue like the links on your Web browser. Internet jazz chat is blue, too, mostly because there's so much to talk about and so little time. What are the best CDs of solo drumming? What rock bands have most

successfully integrated jazz signatures into their work? What's the best septet ever? When they're not comparing lists, fans are talking about jazz movies (the Oscar-nominated documentary *A Great Day in Harlem* gets high marks), wishing Louis Armstrong a happy posthumous Fourth of July (and a very happy birthday), and wondering what jazz songs are being used as the soundtracks for network TV shows. ✓**USENET**→rec.music.bluenote→rec.music.bluenote

Clubs

Blue Note Direct from the Blue Note in New York, this site brings you listings and info about one of the nation's premier jazz clubs. ✓**INTERNET**→*url* http://www.webcom.com/~ijazz/bluenote.html

Jazz Genres

Jazz Clubs around the World A directory of jazz clubs, mostly U.S. listings, but also a sprinkling of European clubs and even a few from Israel. The clubs are listed by city, and the info is limited to phone numbers and addresses. There are no reviews, and the list doesn't specify whether the clubs are exclusively jazz venues. Caveat emptor, man. ✓**INTERNET**→*url* http://www.acns.nwu.edu/jazz/lists/clubs.html

Images

The Jazz Photography of James Radke An archive of photos snapped primarily at Yoshi's in Oakland and including such luminaries as Don Cherry, Lester Bowie, Steve Coleman, and Will Nichols. ✓**INTERNET**→*url* http://www.dnai.com/~lmcohen/jr_idex.html

The Jazz Photography of Ray Avery A great resource for jazz fans, musicians, photography mavens, professional photographers, and every combination of the above. Read a short intro about jazz culture in the 1950's, then dive into Avery with a bio, a catalogue of publications and exhibitions, JPEGs of four major exhibitions, merchandise, and more. ✓**INTERNET**→*url* http://bookweb.cwis.uci.edu:8042/Jazz/JPRA1.html

Improvisation

European Free Improvisation What's free improvisation? It's "non-idiomatic improvisation." Not any clearer on the concept? Sorry. Free Improvisation isn't limited to jazz, but includes anyone interested in musical experimentation and creativity. The site includes links to sound clips, concerts, artists pages, indie labels, distributors and retailers, organizations, and a bibliography. ✓**INTERNET**→ *url* http://www.shef.ac.uk/misc/rec/ps/efi/ehome.html

Improvisation and the Inner Person Written by jazzman Gordon Brisker, this work attempts to explore the harmonic and psychological foundations of improvisation. The Website showcases excerpts from the work, including the introduction. ✓**INTERNET**→*url* http://www.dnai.com/~lmcohen/gb_jiip.html

Joan Wildman's World of Jazz Improvisation The online counterpart to a course offered at the University of Wisconsin, Madison, this site addresses the basics of jazz rhythm, melody, and harmony, as well as offering links to other jazz sites online. ✓**INTERNET**→*url* http://www.wisc.edu/jazz/

International

Jazz Facts A complete resource guide for Dutch jazz, including radio programs, club dates, artist bios, venue descriptions, and more. ✓**INTERNET**→*url* http://www.netcetera.nl/jazzfactse.html

Jazz Links of the World A comprehensive list of jazz resources worldwide. ✓**INTERNET**→*url* http://www.pk.edu.pl/~pmj/

Oz-Jazz Worldwide Dedicated to bringing Australian jazz to the Net, Oz-Jazz includes links to the Wangaratta Jazz and Blues Home Page in Australia and a number of other international resources. In addition, the site contains profiles of Aussie musicians, a list of gigs, a radio station database, a list of record stores, and more. ✓**INTERNET**→*url* http://magna.com.au/~georgeh/

Robert's Jazz Corner Articles, links, biographies, discographies, and more for Austrian jazz players and fans. ✓**INTERNET**→*url* http://hgiicm.tu-graz.ac.at:80/F5A72C02/Crojac

Jazz styles

Styles of Jazz A document that traces the evolution of jazz styles, Styles of Jazz shows how the form

Pharoah Sanders—from http://www.hyperreal.com:80/music/labels/axiom/pics/

JazzNow Interactive

The August 1995 issue of **JazzNow Interactive** can be accessed by clicking on the face of the magazine. Any text or image that's bordered or underlined may be accessed by the click of the mouse. Use the "FIND" command in Netscape to search for names within each document, and the "BACK" and "FORWARD" buttons to move within the magazine itself.

And scroll down, there's always more to see!
Volume 5, Number 4 (c) August 1995

JazzNow Interactive Back-Issues!
|FEB95|MAR95|APR95|MAY95|JUN95|JUL95|

A screenshot from JazzNow—from http://www.dnai.com:80/~lmcohen/jazznow.html

arose out of the fusion of blues, European classical, and "world music" (so captioned to question the separation of music into "European" and "Everything Else"), and then proceeds to discuss all the adaptations and innovations that sprang forth from these genres. Derived from Joachim Berendt's *The Jazz Book*, this chart isn't for scanning; if you want to learn about jazz, you'll have to spend some time with it. ✓**INTERNET**→*url* http://www.nwu.edu/WNUR/jazz/styles/

Lectures

What is Jazz? Noted jazz pianist Dr. Billy Taylor gave a series of lectures on "America's classical music," exploring jazz's development from its slave roots through ragtime, swing, bop, and progressive jazz. Sponsored by the John F. Kennedy Center for the Performing Arts, these lectures can be downloaded in a variety of audio formats, and can be searched and sorted by artist, style, chronologi-cal period, or geographical location. ✓**INTERNET**→*url* http://town.hall.org/Archives/radio/Kennedy/Taylor/

Literature

Epistrophy Jazz artists improvise sonically, and sometimes they also improvise verbally, committing their thoughts and fears to paper and contributing to the growing body of work known informally as Jazz Lit. This page contains full-text versions of some of the most famous jazz fiction and poetry, including essays by Amiri Baraka, poetry by Langston Hughes, and autobiographical writings by Charles Mingus. ✓**INTERNET**→*url* http://ie.uwindsor.ca/jazz/

Magazines

All Jazz @ The Muse An online jazz e-zine with artist features, local scene reports, record reviews, and more. ✓**INTERNET**→*url* http://hyperlink.com/muse/jazz/index.htm

Gene Lees' Jazzletter Since 1981, this unique publication has chronicled jazz and the musicians who make it. This page will contain information from and about the *Jazzletter*, articles on various aspects of jazz, and instructions on purchasing the books of Gene Lees, as well as other jazz-related items. ✓**INTERNET**→*url* http://pms.com/pink/jazzlet/

Jazz Now *JazzNow* is one of the premier jazz magazines in the world, and its online edition includes full-text excerpts, regional reports, RealAudio files, an advertisers' directory, and a subscription form. One note: The listed URL connects you to the August 1995 issue, thus the "895" in the address, and if you wish to view magazines from other months, merely replace the month and year. ✓**INTERNET**→*url* http://www.dnai.com/~lmcohen/jn_895.html

Postage

Jazz Stamps Lick Coleman Hawkins, Louis Armstrong, James P. Johnson, Jelly Roll Morton, Charlie Parker, Eubie Blake, Charles Mingus, John Coltrane,

"Eric Dolphy played clarinet and saxophone, played them brilliantly, and then died young."

Thelonious Monk, and Erroll Garner. ✓INTERNET→*url* http://www.dnai.com/~lmcohen/mf_stamp.html

Reviews & previews

Jazz Reviews The latest jazz releases reviewed. ✓EWORLD→*go* eaz→Pump Up The Volume→Jazz & Folk

MP Jazz Music Previews New jazz albums, with brief descriptions of the recordings, album-cover art, and sound clips. ✓INTERNET→*url* http://www.mpmusic.com/jazz/jazz.htm

Artists

Artists of Jazz Index Northwestern University's WNUR has created dozens of profiles for jazz artists, from the major (Louis Armstrong, Miles Davis) to the minor (Shaun Baxter, Tatsu Aoki), and they're all here, along with discographies, biographies, and supplementary links. ✓INTERNET→*url* http://www.acns.nwu.edu/jazz/artists/

Jazz Musician List from UCI An extensive list of jazz artists, along with their most important recordings. ✓INTERNET→*url* http://bookweb.cwis.uci.edu:8042/Jazz/JPRA11.html

Albert Ayler An innovative biography of sax player Albert Ayler in which notes on Ayler's life are interspersed with quotes from the subject himself. Of his move from Cleveland to Stockholm, for example, Ayler says, "I remember one night in Stockholm, I tried to play what was in my soul. The promoter pulled me off the stage. So I went to play for little Swedish kids in the subway. They heard my cry." The page also includes images, sound clips, and a complete discography. ✓INTERNET→*url* http://ernie.bgsu.edu/~jeffs/ayler.html

Charles Mingus A complete discography (both as sideman and bandleader), as well as anecdotes about the brilliant and temperamental bassist and a poll that asks jazz fans to nominate the best Mingus album of all time (the winner? *Mingus Ah Um*, of course.) ✓INTERNET→*url* http://www.siba.fi/~eonttone/mingus/

Don Ellis A fan page devoted to the innovative bandleader, composer, and trumpet player, who died in 1978 at the tragically young age of 44. This page contains a complete discography and links to other Ellis sites. ✓INTERNET→*url* http://www.mbnet.mb.ca/~mcgonig/donellis.html

Eric Dolphy Eric Dolphy played clarinet and saxophone, played them brilliantly, and then died young, the echo of his music still hanging in the air. This page pays tribute to his music, with a complete discography, links to other Dolphy resources, and transcriptions of some of his most famous solos. ✓INTERNET→*url* http://www.cs.berkeley.edu/~jmh/dolphy.html

Eric Dolphy A complete Eric Dolphy discography, along with dozens of sound clips and images. ✓INTERNET→*url* http://farcry.neurobio.pitt.edu/Eric.html

Louis Armstrong His horn sobbed, chuckled, and screamed; his vocals digested the jazz tradition; and his bands proved that nothing beats perfect timing and impeccable taste. It's Satchmo in Cyberspace, with a biography, im-

Eric Dolphy—from http://farcry.neurobio.pitt.edu/GIFs/

Thelonious Monk—from ftp://ftp.njit.edu/pub/images/

ages, sound clips, a bibliography, and more. ✓**INTERNET**→*url* http://www.netspace.org/~haaus/shome.html

Miles Davis Toward the end of his life, he turned increasingly toward soul and funk, working with artists such as Prince and Chaka Khan, but in the four decades before that, Miles Davis was one of the leading innovators in jazz. This page provides a hypertext chronology of Davis's recorded output, with catalog numbers and descriptions of prominent recordings. ✓**INTERNET**→*url* http://www.wam.umd.edu/~losinp/music/md-list.html

Miles Davis List (ml) Talk about early Miles, mid-period Miles, late Miles, and posthumous Miles with other fans. ✓**INTERNET**→*email* miles-request@nic.surfnet.nl ✍ *Type in*

message body: subscribe miles <your full name>

Pat Metheny Spotlight Created to help promote the 1995 release of the innovative jazz guitarist's LP *We Live Here*, the site features a biography of and interview with Metheny, photos, and sound clips from "We Live Here," "Here to Stay," and "Stranger in Town." ✓**COMPUSERVE**→*go* metheny

Sun Ra List (ml) The eccentric jazz pianist and performer helmed his Arkestra, which generated some of the most joyous ensemble sounds in the history of jazz. Now he's dead, but fans can comment on the ongoing legend of Sun Ra on this mailing list. ✓**INTERNET**→*email* listserv@hearn.bitnet ✍ *Type in message body:* subscribe saturn <your full name>

"Fusion developed in the late 1960's and early 1970's as an attempt to merge Rock with Jazz. Miles Davis helped usher in the fusion of jazz and rock in the mid to late 1960's through albums such as Bitches Brew. Jazz/Rock Fusion Bands such as Chick Corea's Return to Forever flourished largely by creating a crossover audience which included many fans of Progressive Rock, and featured players of extremely high technical proficiency.

"Tony Williams formed a rock oriented band called Lifetime with John McLaughlin, who also formed his own high energy group, the Mahavishnu Orchestra. Other groups combined jazz and rock in a more popularly oriented manner, from the crossover Top 40 of Spyro Gyra to the somewhat more esoteric guitarist Pat Metheny. Other popular fusion bands include Weather Report, The Crusaders, and the Yellowjackets."

—from **WNUR-FM JazzWeb**

Classical

If you don't know your Dunstable from your Buxtehude, you're one of the millions of

Americans who are ignorant about the history of classical music. Antique, often foreign, and dauntingly complex, classical music—a generic term that encompasses a number of styles, including Renaissance, Baroque, and Romantic—can seem like an academic task rather than an aesthetic pleasure, although anyone who has ever listened to a Haydn symphony or Bartok violin concert can attest to the beauty, passion, and power of the music. Online, classical resources range from the general (the **All Music Guide Classical Section, BMG Classics World,** and the **Classic CD Beginners Guide**) to the specific (**John Cage, Fredric Chopin,** and **alt.fan.shostakovich**).

On the Net

Across the board

All Music Guide Classical Section This enormous classical music recordings database will help you get your grubby little paws on that hard-to-find recording of Chopin's *Aeolian Harp Etude*. Search the database by any of the following criteria: performance, performers, composer, instrument, period, and rating. Every release is described by listing its composer,

Bach in black—http://www.let.rug.nl/Linguistics/diversen/bach//

title, genre, period, form, instrument, key, date, number, performance quality, performers, and the record company that released it. All in all, this is a great place to start your record shopping or just bone up on your classical music trivia. ✓ **COMPUSERVE**→*go* amg classical

BMG Classics World From

Hildegard von Behrens to Steve Martland, you will find the latest release information, tour dates, artist biographies, and forum discussions for BMG Classics and affiliated labels. ✓ **INTERNET**→*url* http://www.classicalmus.com

Building a Library: A Collector's Guide When you go to the Beethoven bin at your local record store, you'll usually find at least 15 different recordings of each symphony. Which one should you buy? Classical DJ Deryk Barker's definition of what makes a good recording—and his recommendations for the best version of each of Beethoven's symphonies—should be informative to both novice and veteran collectors alike. The article is part of a series intended to educate classical listeners. ✓**INTERNET**→*url* http://www. ncsa.uiuc.edu/SDG/People/ marca/barker-beethoven.html

Classic CD This online magazine is a great resource for any classical music fan. Articles here inform on a variety of topics, like religious music written by atheists, Mozart's piano sonatas, and classical music in the movies. Interviews with famous composers, such as Philip Glass and Georg Solti, are also offered. A list of reviews on top-rated classical-music CDs lets visitors keep up with what's new and hot in classical recording. There's even an archive of back issues for further reading! ✓**INTERNET**→*url* http://www.futurenet.co.uk/music/ classiccd.html

Classic CD Beginners Guide Next time you think you don't know any classical music, check out this beginners' guide, created by the publishers of Classic CD magazine. The Monty Python theme, for example, is actually Sousa's *Liberty Bell March*. You will find this factoid and more in the ID list of classical music in television and the movies. If snotty record-store attendants are getting you down, brush up with Classic CD's list of the top 100 recordings, where you'll find capsule reviews excerpted from the magazine. You'll also find the entire history of classical music broken down by period, in an extremely

Arnold Schoenberg—from http://www.ccnet.com/~drolon/JPEGS/Shoen.JPG

condensed form, by Andrew Stewart. While it may not tell you everything, you'll at least be able to find your way around the record store. ✓**INTERNET**→*url* http://www.futurenet.co.uk/music/ classiccd/Beginners/Beginners.html

Classical MIDI Archives Is it easier to download the entire third movement from Mahler's First Symphony or go out and buy the CD? Who knows? Is it possible to download the entire movement? Sure is. You'll find a wide variety of music here, from Catalan art songs to John Dowland lute songs to an entire page devoted to J. S. Bach. ✓**INTERNET**→*url* http://www. hk.net/~prs/midi.html

Classical Music Classical music fans meet here to discuss their favorite composers and artists (a lot of people here think Mussorgsky is "awesome") and to talk about the instruments of the classical genre (like the lute). To read archived

messages on the merits of various productions of *Madame Butterfly*, turn to the library here. The library also features the *British Harry Partch Society* newsletter, which discusses influences and contemporaries of the American composer, tuning philosopher, and inventor of the theremin. ✓**COMPUSERVE** →*go* amgpop→Messages *and* Libraries→Classical Music

Classical Music A great classical music site for newcomers and old-timers alike. The message boards here are heavily trafficked, with notes on many topics—from what's new at the Boston Symphony to the organization of a dream concert of forbidden songs ("Deutschland über Alles," the Horst Wessel Song, "Marching Through Georgia," "Dixie," etc.). Check out the libraries at this site for the most impressive collection of classical-music cartoons you have ever seen in your life (most of them, unfortunately, are in German). Also in the library are festival, concert, and seminar schedules for classical music events worldwide. ✓**COMPUSERVE**→*go* musicarts→Messages *and* Libraries → Classical Music

Classical Music Home Page

Like a symphony, this is a large site with many important parts, each of which can stand on its own but which make an awe-inspiring noise when considered as a group. A Basic Repertoire List, which is organized by musical period, provides a guide to assembling a well-rounded library of classical recordings. The Buying Guide here lists classical-music recording companies and several magazines and publications that feature classical reviews. For even more suggestions on what to buy and listen to, the Recommended Classical CDs section lists over 1,850 CDs that have been deemed exceptional. Background information about the genre's composers is at the ready in the Composer Data section, which gives info on hundreds of artists. Links to classic-related Websites and newsgroups round out this extensive site. ✓**INTERNET**→*url* http://www.webcom. com/~music/

Igor Stravinsky—from http://www.ccnet.com/-drolon/JPEGS/stravins.JPG

Classical Music Online Although relatively empty at press time, CMO aims to be an online Performing Arts Directory for classical music. Agents and artists can build their own biographies and resumes; starving performers can place an ad in the classified pages; composers can peruse the publisher directory; and fans can read up on the latest news and reviews from the opera and classical world with excerpts from recent issues of *Gramophone, Opera News,* and *CD Review.* ✓**INTERNET** →*url* http://www.crl.com/~virtu alv/cmo/

Classical Reviews Keep up with the current releases by reading these reviews, all of which are reprinted from syndicated Knight-Ridder newspaper columns (like the *Philadelphia Inquirer*). Besides rating newly released recordings, the articles also give background info on the respective artist and his other works. Classical music fans will find these reviews interesting even if they don't have a lot of extra cash to spend on new CDs! ✓**EWORLD**→*go* eaz→Pump Up The Volume→Classical

Conductor's Home Page This collection of links for conductors takes you to Richard Strauss's Ten Golden Rules for Conductors (Rule #2: Never perspire while conducting; only the audience should get warm during a performance), classical music bloopers, and links to other conducting resources (including contact information for joining the American Conductor's Guild). ✓**INTERNET**→ *url* http://hubcap.clemson.edu/ ~alevin/Conductors. html

Early Music Although most of the site is still under construction, early music enthusiasts will still enjoy stopping by for pictures of restored harpsichords, clavichords, and virginals. The early music CD reviews and links to related organizations are two more good reasons to visit this site. ✓**INTERNET**→*url* http://www.virtual.net/jr/earlym. html

Hype!Music Classical Music Reviews A very small collection of reviews excerpted from *Hype!Music. Hype!*'s resident classical expert, Rita Bogna, reports on the sound quality, accompanying booklet, and performance of such pieces as Liszt's *Symphonie Fantastique,* Mozart's Bass Arias, and Wagner's Choruses. ✓**INTERNET** →*url* http://www.hype.com/ music/classic/classic.htm

Chat

rec.music.classical* (ng) Are you a tubist looking for work? Need to sell a cello? Looking for a conductor? Besides basic fiscal queries that will be of interest to any starving musician or composer, this newsgroup serves as the central clearinghouse for classical music chat—from polls inquiring after your favorite sublime musical fragments to debates on using a pedal when playing Scarlatti (purists would say you shouldn't even play it on a piano). Whether you are looking for a favorite Figaro recording, used record stores in Boston, or a Stravinsky biography, you will find ample attention here. Furtwangler fans discuss the latest re-releases while Karajan friends and foes endlessly debate the late conductor's membership in the Nazi party. If you don't want to sort through the general list of messages, check out the rest of the groups in the hierarchy, which focus specifically on classical guitar, performance techniques and announcements, and recordings. √**USENET**→rec.music.classical*

rec.music.classical.performing (ng) Information relating to performance techniques, ensembles, performers for hire, and upcoming concerts around the world. √**USENET**→rec.music.classical.performing

rec.music.classical.recordings (ng) There must be hundreds of recordings of Beethoven's Ninth Symphony available in some shape or form, even 8-track, so if you would like them all, you would do well to consult the record collectors who assemble here. And if you are not lusting for more Ludwig, there's plenty of other composers treated by the group regulars, who offer recommendations, reviews, and feedback on classical recordings past and present. √**USENET**→rec.music.classical.recordings

Composers

A Guide to Composer Data & Works Lists Ever wondered what famous composer was born on your birthday? Or asked yourself which country has sired the most famous composers throughout history? (That would be Germany,

The indeterminate John Cage—http://newalbion.com/artists/cagej/cagej.html

with an awe-inspiring 125 maestros.) Look no further for obscure composer info; this site's database offers enough classic-music trivia to satisfy any buff. √**INTERNET**→*url* http://www.webcom.com/~music/composer/top.html

Classical Composer Biographies Brief informal biographies including birth and death dates, influences, and major works. JPEGs of the composers allow you to stare into Mozart's eyes as you read his history. √**INTERNET**→*url* http://www.cl.cam.ac.uk/users/mn200/music/composers.html

Classical Music An excellent source of pictures and biographies of over 40 composers, from Antonio Allegri to Felix Mendelssohn to Carl Maria Weber. √**INTERNET**→*url* http://weber.u.washington.edu/~sbode/classical.html

The Great Composers All the masters, from Albeniz to Mozart to Wagner, are profiled at this extensive site. In fact, this is one of the few places on the Net to get even a quick sketch of the lives of major composers like Schubert, Stravinsky, Handel, and Hayden. Locate your favorite by searching the index alphabetically by name

Classical **Genres**

or by period. This site is brought to the Net courtesy of the folks at BMG Classics. ✓**INTERNET**→*url* http://classicalmus.com/composer.html

Bach

Bach Home Page Learn about the extraordinary life and works of this classical composer through the essays on his life and the lists of his compositions offered here. ✓**INTERNET**→*url* http://www.web com.com/~music/composer/works /jsbach/jsbindex.html

J.S. Bach Home Page Classical music fan Jan Hanford has assembled a comprehensive Bach page here, including a complete list of his works (organized by BWV number, category, instrument, and title), photographs of the master, a short biography, and a detailed list of recordings. ✓**INTERNET**→*url* http://www.tile.net/bach/index. html

Beethoven

Ludwig van Beethoven Even though Beethoven's father was a heavy drinker, he still realized that his boy had talent and made sure the young lad had some piano lessons. The rest is history! Read about Beethoven's life and scan a list of his compositions at this site. ✓**INTERNET**→*url* http://www.ida.his. se/ida/~a94johal/beet.chtml

Bottesini

Giovanni Bottesini: A Life The International Bottesini Society sponsors this biographical site dedicated to the famous opera and contrabass composer and conductor. ✓**INTERNET**→*url* http://www. webcom.com/~redwards/gbmain. html

Cage

John Cage By reading Cage's autobiographical statement at this site, you'll discover that the world-renowned composer was also a very good storyteller. The story of his life and career is accompanied by an annotated discography. ✓**INTERNET**→*url* http://newalbion.com/ artists/cagej/cagej.html

Chopin

Frederic Chopin A complete an-

notated list of Chopin's piano compositions is the centerpiece of this site. With descriptions of each piece, as well as playing tips and difficulty ratings, the annotations will be especially helpful for players looking for the right piece to match their skills. ✓**INTERNET**→*url* http://www.cs.cmu.edu/afs/cs/ user/pscheng/www/chopin.html

Glass

Philip Glass Explore modern minimalism through the work of

Bela Bartok—from http://www.ccnet.com/~drolon/JPEGS/bartok.JPG

its most representative composer, Philip Glass. A discography, articles on the composer, and sound files of some of his better-known works, including *Knee Play 1*, are here. ✓**INTERNET**→*url* http://www-lsi.upc.es/~jpetit/pg/

Mahler

Gustav Mahler Home Page
This site features informative lists relating to the artist, including annotated notes on his works, a timeline, and more lists of festivals, books, concerts, societies, and organizations. Visit the Mahler picture gallery to see what the visionary looked like. ✓**INTERNET**→ *url* http://www.netaxs.com/~jgr eshes/mahler/

Prokofiev

Sergei Sergeivich Prokofiev
This Russian artist composed primarily for the piano, but he also wrote several all-orchestra pieces and scenarios for a number of ballets. Read a complete list of his works, listen to a recording of *The Love for Three Oranges*, and see JPEGs of Prokofiev at his summer home at this site. ✓**INTERNET**→*url* http://weber.u.washington.edu/~ rikoshae/prokofiev_html/prokofiev. html

Schnitte

Alfred Schnitte Page Considered by many to be the greatest composer living today, Alfred Schnitte is known worldwide for his experimental compositions. This site brings the story of his life and his work to the Net. ✓**INTERNET**→*url* http://ccnet.com/~dro lon/Schnitt.html

Shostakovich

alt.fan.shostakovich (ng) By

Dmitri Shostakovich—from http://cwis.uta.edu/acs/microsys/mac/.HOME/rhudson/

the time of his death in 1975, Dmitri Dmitrievich Shostakovich had composed 15 symphonies, 15 string quartets, 4 operas, and 45 ballet and film scores. Fans of the prolific composer will find discussion of his work (especially those pieces that have appeared on television shows) and about the many books on his life, including the controversial *Testimony*. This newsgroup's FAQ contains wonderful resources including recommended recordings, a bibliography, and a newsletter. ✓**USENET**→ alt.fan.shostakovich *FAQ:* ✓**INTER-**

NET→*url* http://www.uta.edu/ acs/microsys/mac/.HOME/rhud son/faq.html

Rob's Shostakovich Page A devoted fan of DSCH has assembled sound files, a works list, and anecdotes on Shostakovich at this site. ✓**INTERNET**→*url* http://www. futurenet.co.uk/People/RobAins ley/music/shost.html

Shostakovich Recording Register A definitive list of Shostakovich CD releases organized by opus number and title.

Classical **Genres**

✓**INTERNET**→*url* http://www.uta. edu/acs/microsys/mac/.HOME/ rhudson/register

Varese

Edgard Varese Newspaper articles, a discography, and many, many paintings and photographs featuring Varese, a classic modern composer who was idolized by American satirical scatologist Frank Zappa. ✓**INTERNET**→*url* http://www.princeton.edu/~james fei/varese/index_text.html

Vaughan Williams

Ralph Vaughan Williams Page The score of the opera *The Poisoned Kiss* contains a request from the composer asking the audience to talk during the overture, "Or else they will know all the tunes before the opera starts." This and other Vaughan trivia, as well as a discography, bibliography, and a picture of the composer with his cat, Foxy, are accessible here. ✓**IN-TERNET**→*url* http://www.cs.qub.ac. uk/~J.Collis/RVW.html

"Chopin began composing while still a child, and a number of his early works survive. He gave his first public concert in 1818. He studied music theory with Jozef Elsner, director of the Warsaw Conservatory, and, after brilliant debuts in Warsaw and Vienna in 1830, he left Warsaw permanently--the Polish insurrection initially prevented his return--and by 1831 had settled in Paris.

"Chopin was welcomed onto the French cultural scene. Robert Schumann had already acclaimed Chopin's variations on La ci darem (from Mozart's Don Giovanni) with the words 'Hats off, gentlemen! A genius!'

"Schumann later called the composer 'the boldest and proudest poetic spirit of the time.' A concert in 1832 made his name in the fashionable world, and he was soon established as the teacher of a number of wealthy and well-born European pupils."

—from **Classical Music**

Playing the mighty theremin—from http://www.vuse.vanderbilt.edu/~jbbarile/

Orchestras Online

Atlanta Symphony ✓INTER-NET→*url* http://isotropic.com/symphony/asohome.html

Austin Symphony Orchestra ✓INTERNET→*url* http://www.quadralay.com/www/Austin/FineArts/AustinSymphony/aso_home.html

Australian Chamber Orchestra ✓INTERNET→*url* http://www.ibm.com.au/ACO/

Boston Chamber Ensemble ✓INTERNET→*url* http://www.mit.edu:8001/people/jcb/BCE/bce.html

CBC Vancouver Orchestra ✓INTERNET→*url* http://mindlink.net/james_reid/020.html

Colorado Springs Symphony ✓INTERNET→*url* http://www.mothra.com/symphony/index.html

Dallas Symphony ✓INTERNET→*url* http://www.pic.net/dso/

Het Brabants Orkest ✓INTERNET→*url* http://dse.iaehv.nl/cultuur/muziek/muziekcentrum/hbo/indexhbo.html

Imperial College Symphony Orchestra ✓INTERNET→*url* http://www.su.ic.ac.uk/clubs/societies/scab/ICSO/top.html

Indianapolis Symphony Orchestra ✓INTERNET→*url* http://www.in.net/iso/

Keio Orchestra ✓INTERNET→*url* http://www.sfc.keio.ac.jp/~t93414km/eko/katsudou.html

Longwood Symphony Orchestra ✓INTERNET→*url* http:// www.ai.mit.edu/people/lethin/longwood.html

Musica Silvestra Orkest In Dutch. ✓INTERNET→*url* http://snt.student.utwente.nl/campus/MSO/index.html

New England Philharmonic ✓INTERNET→*url* http://www.mit.edu:8001/people/jcb/NEP/nep.html

New Zealand Symphony Orchestra ✓INTERNET→*url* http://www.actrix.gen.nz/users/dgold/nzso.html

Nittany Valley Symphony ✓INTERNET→*url* http://jdb.psu.edu/music/nvs.htm

Orchestra London ✓INTERNET→*url* http://www.icis.on.ca/orchestra/

Oslo Philharmonic ✓INTERNET→*url* http://www.wit.no/wit/OFO.html

Oslo University Symphony ✓INTERNET→*url* http://www.ifi.uio.no/~hph/uso/

pro Arte Chamber Orchestra of Boston ✓INTERNET→*url* http://www.proarte.org/

Prometheus Symphony ✓INTERNET→*url* http://www.best.com/~mallard/prometh.html

Redwood Symphony ✓INTERNET→*url* http://www.globalcenter.net/~redwood/

Salem Chamber Orchestra ✓INTERNET→*url* http://www.teleport.com/~rbobbitt/sco.htm

San Diego Young Artists Symphony ✓INTERNET→*url* http://crayfish.ucsd.edu/home/sinuhe/www/sdyaso.html

San Francisco Symphony ✓INTERNET→*url* http://www.hooked.net/sfsymphony/sfshome.html

San Jose Symphony ✓INTERNET→*url* http://www.webcom.com/~sjsympho/

Saskatoon Symphony ✓INTERNET→*url* http://www.sfn.saskatoon.sk.ca/arts/symphony/index.html

Sinfonia Lahti ✓INTERNET→*url* http://www.php.fi/lahti/eng/sinfonia.html

Stanford Symphony Orchestra ✓INTERNET→*url* http://www-leland.stanford.edu/group/sso/

Symphony Nova Scotia ✓INTERNET→*url* http://www.nstn.ca/kiosks/sns/sns.html

Winnipeg Symphony Orchestra ✓INTERNET→*url* http://www.ee.umanitoba.ca/wpg/WSO.html

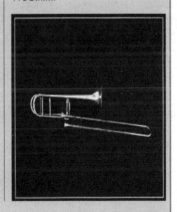

Opera

To opera enthusiasts, the world outside the theater must be a tremendous disappoint-

ment—no high drama, no glass-shattering voices, no spectacular costumes. That's why Verdi and Mozart and Wagner and Puccini decided to commit their fever dreams to music, and why Maria Callas and Joan Sutherland and Bryn Terfel and Placido Domingo and Kathleen Battle decided to lend their magnificent instruments to the cause. If you've ever been transformed by *Rigoletto*, then you know the incredible power coiled up inside an opera. Online, opera resources range from **Current Opera E-Zine** to **Weaver's Opera Field Notes**, from **OPERA-L** to **rec.music. opera**, from **Opera Houses of the Past and Present** to the **Casta Diva, Inc. Home Page**. There's even a **Cyberspace Opera**. Aria ready?

The late diva Maria Callas—from http://sable.ox.ac.uk/~wolf0065/images/

Across the board

Classical Music In Italy An exhaustive list of virtually every opera house, club, theater, and festival in Italy. View the list in either Italian or English. ✓**INTERNET**→*url* http://www.fastnet.it/cultura/music_en.htm

Current Opera E-Zine This e-zine is created by readers who want to share their opinions on opera productions around the world. Whether you want to post your review of Rodion Schendrin's *Lolita* opera or *La Boheme* in Florence, expect feedback. And if you're ready for Battle, you can even comment on diva Kathleen's

designer concert gowns: "By and large, Battle has the most impressive array of gowns in the business. Would that her vocalism more often matched her chicesse." ✓**INTERNET**→*url* http://www.webcom.com/~redwards/

Opera Want to discuss the Japanese production of *La*

Boheme, or argue if there are world-class American opera singers performing today? Would you like to cast your vote for cheesiest baritone on the worldwide opera stage? The message board at this site is the place to post your opinion, vote or other opera topics. The boards aren't just for fans, either; it is very common for singers to meet here to discuss their profession and current productions. In the library, you can read discussions between directors, stage hands, singers, and opera lovers about numerous subjects, including stage direction in different opera houses worldwide. It's not all shop talk here, though—check out the fabulous opera cartoons in the library for a good laugh! ✓**COMPUSERVE**→ *go* musicarts →Messages *and* Libraries→ Opera

Opera-L Server The creators of this site are compiling a database of opera synopses, and they need your help to get the job done. Check their list of operas to be covered and pick up your assignment. While you're there, read biographies of opera stars and check out their pictures (that Bryn Terfel sure is menacing, isn't he?). There is also a collection of links to other opera sites, including the New York City Opera. ✓**INTERNET** →*url* http://www. physics.su.oz.au/~ neilb/operah.html

Weaver's Opera Field Notes If you think opera music is something you only listen to when you are at the dentist's office, these self-proclaimed "field notes of a rookie opera lover" might make you take a more interested look at the genre. A mysterious opera fan identified only as Weaver has collected loving observations of the many, many, many performances he has taken in over the past seven years. ✓**INTERNET**→*url* http://www.

alaska.net/~hweaver/opera-index.html

Chat

OPERA-L (ml) Do you think that attending a performance of Billy Budd at the Metropolitan Opera is better than life and love combined? Would you like to discuss the Anchorage Opera's version of *Die Fledermaus* with others who were in the audience? Or maybe you're looking for others who idolize their autographed photograph of Placido Domingo in *Madame Butterfly*. You'll find good company and great discussion of operatic themes on this mailing list. ✓**INTERNET**→*email* listserv@cunyvm. cuny. edu ✍ *Type in message body:* subscribe OPERA-L <your full name>

rec.music.opera (ng) Put a bunch of opera buffs in the same room and there is bound to be trouble. "Has anyone read a review of Renata Scotto's recent *Der Rosenkavalier* performance?" "Execrable was one comment I read, but I can't remember where." If you're having trouble choosing between a Bartoli or Larmore *Barber of Seville* recording, don't expect any straight answers. You'll most likely be buried in piles of still more recommendations, along with a combination of some on-the-nose and some long-winded reviews. And when the fans leave, the performers remain behind, exchanging performance tips, tipping each other off to potential gigs, and recommending instructors. ✓**USENET**→rec.music.opera

Costumes

Casta Diva, Inc. Home Page Interested in the costuming side of opera? Casta Diva, a major costume supplier, has assembled a

Tenor Placido Domingo—http:// classicalmus.com/artists/images/

JPEG gallery of its famous costumes (most are designed by Lelia Barton). And although the images are presented as thumbnails, you can download a larger version for wall display. ✓**INTERNET**→*url* http:// www.access.digex.net:80/~ castadiv/gallery.html

Schedule

Opera Schedule Search this worldwide opera schedule by artist, location, or time to find out when and where the next performance of your favorite opera is taking place. ✓**INTERNET**→*url* http://www.fsz.bme.hu/opera/ main.html

Venues

Opera Houses of the Past and Present Opera houses were smaller in the seventeenth century—the largest venues seated around 2,000 opera-goers, while today's average house seats between 4,000 and 6,000 people. This interesting study lists the size (in cubic feet) and seating capacity of every opera house worldwide, beginning with the Wiener Staatsoper, built in 1639, and going up through Washington D.C.'s Terrace Theater, completed in 1979. √**INTERNET**→*url* http://www.cc. columbia.edu/~km34/theater.html

Works

Censorship of Verdi Opera To placate censors, Verdi changed various details in his operas, often going to absurd lengths to avoid trouble. In one case, however, he didn't go far enough. Stifellio was written in the late nineteenth century, censored shortly after being composed, languished in obscurity until 1968, and didn't receive its U.S. premiere until 1976. You'll find full details of the story here, plus links to other artworks and artists (from *Ulysses* to Frank Zappa) censored throughout history. √**INTERNET**→ *url* http://fileroom. aaup.uic.edu/ FileRoom/docu-

ments/Cases/307verdi.html

Cyberspace Opera An opera is being composed online, and you can contribute by sending in rhymed couplets based on concepts or quotes from the story line. The couplets will then be set to music and incorporated into a real opera to be performed in Austin, Texas. The opera's working title is *Honoria in Ciberspazio*, and its main characters include Rez, a passionate young writer and philosopher of virtual communities, and Sandy Stone, a Cyberspace goddess who "flips her long black hair before saying something wonderfully brilliant." It's opera for the computer age! √**INTERNET**→ *url* http://www.en.utexas.edu/~ slatin/opera/

John Cage's Europeras 3 & 4 Opera fan John Pritchett wants to tell you what he thinks about Cage's operatic interpretation of nineteenth-century literature, and he wants to tell you in an eight-part essay. √**INTERNET**→*url* http:// www.music.princeton.edu/~jwp/ Europera3n4.html

Synopsis of Wagner's Ring You don't often find Wagner's entire *Ring* summarized in one document. Usually, the opera is broken into quarters, packaged in four box sets, or printed in four programs for consecutive evenings. But once is enough. Find out in 20 minutes what people are willing to sit and watch for 20 hours on the musical stage. √**INTERNET**→*url* gopher:// wiretap.spies.com/00/Library/ Music/Misc/wagner.rng

---

Opera Companies Online

Atlanta Opera √**INTERNET** →*url* http://isotropic.com/atlopera/ ophome.html

Castelward Opera √**INTERNET**→ *url* http://www.gpl.net/ users/millsy/

Chicago Symphony Orchestra √**INTERNET**→*url* http:// student-www.uchicago.edu/users/ achatche/music/concerts.html

Cologne Opera √**INTERNET** →*url* http://www.rrz.uni-koeln. de/koeln/oper/index.html

Colorado Opera √**INTERNET** →*url* http://obenamots.cc. colorado.edu/Operafestival/ opera.html

Dallas Opera √**INTERNET**→ *url* http://www.computek.net/mall/ opera.html

Finnish National Opera √**INTERNET**→*url* http://www.kolumbus. fi/opera/

Huntsville Opera Theater √**INTERNET**→*url* http://fly.hiwaay. net/~mbeutjer/hot.html

National Theater (Munich) √**INTERNET**→*url* http://www. bavaria.com/culture/opera_us. html

New York City Opera √**INTERNET**→*url* http://plaza.interport. net/nycopera/index.html

Pacific Opera Victoria √**INTERNET**→*url* http://www.islandnet. com/~opera/povhome.html

Pittsburgh Opera √**INTERNET**→ *url* http://www.cs.cmu.edu/ afs/andrew/usr/dma4/www/po pera.html

Royal Swedish Opera House √**INTERNET**→*url* http:// soho.ios.com/~gberkson/operan/

Salzburger Festspiele √**INTERNET**→ *url* http://austria-info.at/ kultur/salzfest95/d_oper.html

Santa Fe Opera √**INTERNET**→ *url* http://www.walpole.com/ walpole /Santa_Fe_Opera/

Seattle Opera √**INTERNET**→*url* http://www.webcom.com/ ~redwards/so.html

Western Australian Opera √**INTERNET**→*url* http://www. uwa.edu.au/student/jlchong/ music/waopera.html

Wiener Staatsoper √**INTERNET** →*url* http://www.austria-info. at/kultur/ws-wv/

New Age

Do you feel like your life is full of choas and hostility. Do you feel malignant forces

churning beneath the surface of what should be the tranquil pool of your existence? Then maybe what you need is a heavy dose of New Age music. In the hands of its most renowned practitioners—Yanni, Jean-Michel Jarre, Kitaro, Vangelis—New Age is a largely instrumental music intended to soothe, smooth, and otherwise calm the harried modern. Start with **Music for a New Age**, which not only links to Net resources but also offers a framing philosophy for the genre; then move on to sites like **Maxmillian's Jukebox, Heart of Space Records, Windham Hill Records,** and the **Unofficial Yanni Homepage.** Don't you feel more peaceful already?

New Age heartthrob Yanni—http://www.teleport.com/~celinec/yanni.shtml

On the Net

Across the board

Fractal Music The level of abstraction in fractal music makes it a natural extension of the New Age genre. It's also the perfect music to play while doing your calculus and physics homework! The creators of this site, a group of students at the University of Stuttgart, must have been thinking of just that characteristic of fractal music when they assembled this site, which offers essays about the music and sound clips of some of the students' own compositions. ✓**INTERNET**→*url* http://www-ks. rus.uni-stuttgart.de/people/ schulz/fmusic/

Maxmillian's Jukebox Max has been a busy boy. He's assembled a collection of sound files featuring his favorite New Age tunes. Visit this site and listen to Jean-Michel Jarre's "Calypso I," Earl Klugh's "Dreaming," or Mike Oldfield's "Tubular Bells." Surely your local New Age record store won't be happy to hear that you've discovered Max's great collection of free music! ✓**INTERNET**→*url* http://www.iscs.nus.sg/~yakshuhe/ newage.html

Music for a New Age "Alàs, it's unfortunate that some marketing types coined the term 'New Age' to describe a form of music that, by its very nature, defies definition. After all, when you combine the modern-day sounds of electronic synthesizers with the droning of the ancient Aboriginal didgeridoo, what are you going to call it? Hence the term 'New Age.' The long-term affect of this appellation has been derision and confusion; many people believe that New Age music is meant only to be listened to during meditation, mud baths, or mystic activities. And while any of these activities may be appropriate for this type of music, it is my belief that music should be enjoyed for its value to the listener, whatever that may

Just call him "Vangelis"—from http://bau2.uibk.ac.at/perki/Vangelis.html

be." The author of these words, Fred Puhan, also created this encompassing collection of New Age links. Organized into three sections—record companies, artists, and other New Age resources—the links here will take you into the new age and beyond. ✓**INTERNET**→ *url* http://www.his.com/~fjp/music.html

New Age/Electronic General chat, record reviews, and more for fans of ambient and electronic music. ✓**COMPUSERVE**→*go* amgpop→ Messages *and* Libraries→New Age/Electronic

rec.music.newage (ng) Why bother sending away for the Hearts of Space playlist when you can download it here? These days, "New Age" refers to any type of music with spacey bleeping sounds and a generic synth sound in the background. Ambient music. Meditative music. Sculptural music. Here you'll find records reviewed and sold, from Mike Oldfield's pre–New Age *Exorcist*

soundtrack to Mychael Danna's recent music for *Exotica*. Whether you're looking for the Kitaro Website or upcoming Penguin Cafe Orchestra gigs in your area, you'll find New Age information and camaraderie aplenty here. ✓**USENET**→ rec.music.newage

Record labels

Combs Music Soothing, calming, relaxing. These are the words that come to mind when you play the sound samples of Combs Music New Age recordings found here. Instrumental piano music is the standard—indeed, the only—fare of this independent company, and you can obtain a full list of its nine recordings, as well as hear what they sound like, at this site. ✓**INTERNET**→*url* http://www.infi.net/~combsdm/

Heart of Space Records Stephen Hill started a New Age radio show for the San Francisco Bay area in 1973. The show has evolved into a 58-minute musical

journey that is currently played at more than 300 stations nationwide every week. The success of his show propelled Stephen to found Heart of Space Records, which releases his creations regularly. His mail-order catalog currently boasts more than 70 titles. Shop the catalog, read essays on Stephen and his music, and make requests for his radio show. ✓**INTERNET**→*url* http://www.hos.com/

Higher Octave Records Higher Octave isn't in the record racket just to make money. Octave has a conscience, which becomes apparent at this site's Philosophy section: "We use recycled materials wherever possible for packaging and promoting our products. We donate a percentage of our annual profits to organizations who share our dream of a united world community operating for the common good of all living beings. It is our intent to ensure that our artists, staff, products and procedures together enhance the well-being of our planet." More than 50 New Age artists—from Ariel Kalma to Gambheera to Sirus—are represented at this socially responsible site, which features bios, discographies, and ordering info for the artists. ✓**INTERNET**→*url* http://smartworld.com/hioctave/artists.html

Sonic Images Records Home Page Christopher Franke, a member of the pioneering electronic band Tangerine Dream for more than 18 years, started Sonic to handle the overflow of his sprawling studio, film, and TV soundtrack work. Now Christopher's label is the home of several New Age artists (such as Shadow-Fax), and his site features profiles of new releases, cool album-cover graphics, and sound clips from Sonic's records. ✓**INTERNET**→*url*

Kitaro, looking pensive—from http:// colossus.net/comeback/kitaro/bio.html

http://www.sonicimages.com/

Windham Hill Records Known as the granddaddy of New Age record companies, this label offers the recordings of William Ackerman, Gaia, Ray Lynch, and Torcuato Mariano, among others. Each of Windham's artists is profiled here with a short bio, a discography, tour information, and sound clips. All of the recordings listed here can be ordered online. ✓**INTERNET**→*url* http://www. windham.com/

Artists

Kitaro Everyone has been a living treasure to someone at some point in their lives (to a mother, girlfriend, or family pet), but Kitaro has the awesome honor of being a Living National Treasure of Japan, which is the highest honor the country can bestow on a citizen. Learn interesting facts about his life (for instance, the first synthesizer he ever played was homemade) and get a discography of his work at this site. ✓**INTERNET**→*url* http://colossus.net/comeback/ kitaro/bio.html

Tangerine Dream Tour dates and a very short career bio for this band, which has received six Grammy nominations over the last four years. ✓**INTERNET**→*url*

http://useattle.uspan.com/ miramar/td.html

Vangelis You may think of Vangelis as nothing more than a 1980s film-score composer, but before he ever wrote music for the movies, he almost joined Yes. Here you'll find a biography of Evangelos Papthanassiou's life, both as "Man" and "Artist" (as if the two weren't fused into one New Age demigod). You'll even find out how to pronounce his name by downloading an audio file. And if you can't imagine getting your fill of Vangelis, be sure to check out the video interviews, sound clips, and even excerpts from the films Vangelis scored, which range from *Chariots of Fire* to *Blade Runner.* ✓**INTERNET**→*url* http://bau2.uibk. ac.at/perki/Vangelis.html

Phillip Walker Electronic violinist Phillip Walker brings his strings and bow to the Net. To download sound samples of his songs, including "Agua Marine," "Jungle Healing," and "African Wings," or to see a groovy graphic from Phillip's latest album, *Where Worlds Meet,* just visit this site. ✓**INTERNET**→*url* http://www.teleport.com/~philw/

Unofficial Yanni Homepage "Creativity is an inherent quality of the highest order. When we create, we become more than the sum of our parts." The Master of New Age has spoken; now it's left to the rest of us to figure out what the hell he might be saying. Besides philosophical musings, this home page features a gallery of Yanni pics (including the irresistible "Yanni sitting on some rocks wearing tan clothes"), a list of Yanni fans online, info about LOYOL (the new Yanni fan club on America Online), MIDI files of his songs, and links to other New Age pages. There's also a section called "1995 Tour Dates" that is painfully empty. Yanni, Yanni, Yanni... ✓**INTERNET**→*url* http:// www. teleport.com/~celinec/yanni.shtml

Tangerine Dream—from http://onyx.slu.edu/dylan/tdream/pix.html

Christian & gospel

They say that music is good for the soul; if that's true, then religious music must be

very good for the soul. Once a fringe genre, Contemporary Christian music has become one of the important forces in modern popular culture, responsible for selling millions of records and launching the careers of dozens of new stars each year. At sites like **The CCM Forum** and **Christian Reviews**, fans of singers like Michael W. Smith and and Kathy Troccoli can find out about new album releases, get concert dates, and learn more about the sounds that give praise to the Lord. **LiNeNoIsE** and **The Lighthouse Electronic Magazine** track developments in alternative Christian music. And **The Christian Industrial Info Page** demonstrates that spirituality isn't all soft sounds and sweet smiles.

Michael W. Smith & family—from http://www.ccmcom.com/

On the Net

Across the board

The CCM Forum This is where Christian music fans meet each other and the staff of *Christian Contemporary Magazine* for online company and chat. On the message boards here you can read and exchange messages about Christian music, songs, artists, and the industry. In the libraries you'll find plenty of feature articles and pho-

tos from back issues of CCM, album reviews, and sound clips from various artists. In addition, moderated chats on a variety of topics of interest to Christian music fans are held regularly, including live chats with some of the top artists in the field. ✓**COMPUSERVE→** *go* ccmforum

The Christian Industrial Info Page This site dares to ask the question, "What place, if any at all, does Christianity have in industrial music?" For those who say that Christianity and industrial music are mutually exclusive terms, a visit to the Christian Industrial Info Page is in order. The site features interviews of Christian industrial bands (including Wade Alin from Christ Analogue), Christian industrial news (get the scoop on Argyle Park's breakup), and an impressive index of info and links to over 60 Christian industrial bands (from Aleixa to Fear of Faith to Toxic Church). ✓**INTERNET→***url* http://is.dal.ca/~carson/xii.html

Christian Music Online CMO

informs on the latest in Christian rock. Its profiles of new Christian releases, which are updated weekly, include band biographies, interviews, and sound clips. After they are featured on the weekly list, the reviews are archived in a database that is searchable by artist name or song title. For more reading off-screen, subscription information for two industry bibles, *Release* and *Calendar*, is also provided. ✓**INTERNET→***url* http://www.cmo.com/cmo/

Christian Reviews A database of short reviews featuring new Christian music releases. The database is usefully organized by musical style, including Christian rock, hip-hop, folk, country, instrumental, and gospel releases. If you want an opinion on DOC's *Righteous Funk* album, you'll find it here ("It's a great hip-hop mix with R&B twist that's sure to get you dancing and singing."), complete with song lyrics: "When Jesus died he rose / He did all he could do / So be one of the few / And get up off your pew!" ✓**AMERICA ONLINE→***keyword* chrol Resources→Christian reviews

Christian Rock Collection The mission statement of the CRC makes no bones about its purpose: "To inform, encourage, educate, and promote Christian rock music as a vital form of communicating the gospel of Jesus Christ." To that purpose, this site provides extensive databases of contact info for Christian music publications (*CCM Magazine, Heaven's Metal,* and *Long's Christian Music*), record labels (Alarma, Icehouse, and Word Records), clubs (The New Union and The Coffee House), and radio shows (Audible Light, Convergence, and I Scream Sunday). ✓**INTERNET**→*url* http://uslink. net/kadu/crr/home.html

Contemporary Christian Music Resource List A collection of links to sites like *The Lighthouse Electronic Magazine* and NetCentral. Also at this site is a nifty collection of email addresses for people in the Christian music industry, including radio personalities, record-company executives, artists, and writers. ✓**INTERNET**→*url* http:// www.acs.psu.edu/users/jws/ ccmpage.html

Fish TV MTV meets *Leave It to Beaver!* *Fish TV* is a nationally syndicated music video program that appeals to the fastest growing viewer market in the country—yes, Christian music listeners. *Fish TV* is not just being watched by the Christian community; those who are "tired and frankly scared of typical music TV programming" are also tuning in. The site includes a top-ten video chart, QuickTime video clips, and a map showing viewing areas where *Fish TV* is aired. ✓**INTERNET**→*url* http:// ws1.databank.com/~fishtv/fishtv. html

Grassroots Christian Music Contact List Whether you perform Christian music or just listen to it in your spare time, this is a resource you can use. A comprehensive (5,000-plus) list of Christian music contact info, including phone numbers and addresses for various Christian musicians, clubs, recording studios, radio stations, and many others involved in Christian music, at all levels of the scene, man. You dig? ✓**INTERNET**→ *url* http://www.acs.psu.edu/users/ jws/pulig/index.html

JR Music This is a large collection of links to many and various Christian music resources. For Christian thrashers, the Soae newsletter posts news on the latest releases of bands like Holy Soldier and Ashen Morality. Other links take you to NetCentral, The Fish Page, and 137 Records, among other sites. To catch up on the latest exploits of your favorite Christian rock artists, JR Music has links to both official fan sites, such as those for Brent Bourgeois, Catherine King, and Painted Orange, and unofficial fan pages, including those for Able Cain, One Bad Pig,

Amy Grant—from http://ernie.bgsu. edu/~jmccoy/Jason/MGroups.html/

and Teflon Brain. This site even lists lyrics of popular religious songs, like "Above All Else," "Great and Mighty," and "Father I Adore You." ✓**INTERNET**→*url* http:// music.acu.edu/www/jr/jrmusic. html

Chat

Live Christian Music Chat Discuss God, God's music, and the music of those touched by God's almighty hand. Let the palm of the Lord smooth out the cares of the day. ✓**PRODIGY**→*jump* chat→ Prodigy Cha→Select an Area: →Music→Christian Music

NetCentral Like the name implies, this site is Christian-music central, with links to many major Christian music sites, including the official pages of Charlie Peacock and Brent Bourgeois and big record labels like Word, Gotee, Reunion, Benson, and Sparrow. The NetCentral Digital Underground ("a long-awaited collection of sites created by people just like you") takes you to the home page of artist Jeni V, to the Christian music ezine *LiNeNoIsE,* and to *Fish TV's* site, where you can vote for your favorite Christian rock video. NetCentral is a comprehensive site that covers almost all the major Christian music players. ✓**INTERNET**→*url* http://www. netcentral.net/

rec.music.christian (ng) Conversation about Christians, music for Christians, and Christian interpretations of music. You'll find plenty of friendly chat, although a good knowledge of scripture will be very helpful if you really want to get into the swing of things. ✓**USENET**→rec.music.christian

Religious Music Although the message boards and library here are supposedly for the discussion of all types of religious music, Christian music is discussed almost exclusively. The message board is a place where Christian music fans like Chris can talk to Steven Peters, the keyboard player who played with Steve Taylor during his 1983 tour. It's also a good place to debate topics like whether Bob Bennett is a Christian or folk artist (is it possible he could be both?). Turn to the library if you're interested in directing a church choir, and, if you're looking for a song about forgiveness, you'll find the lyrics to "My Spirit Is Free." No matter what you're looking for, if it's got anything to do with Christian music, this is a good place to start your search. ✓**COMPUSERVE**→*go* musicarts→Messages *and* Libraries →Religious Music

Gospel

Black Gospel Music "To God be the glory for the things HE has done!" proclaims the opening sentence of this site. The Black Gospel Music site promises to be a place to discuss the latest in gospel music—not just the songs, but the stars and concerts also. ✓**INTERNET**→*url* http://pages.prodigy.com/CA/music/BlackGospelMusic.html

Gospel (ml) This is the place to go in Cyberspace to meet others who enjoy praising the Lord through music. ✓**INTERNET**→*email* maiser@rmgate.pop.indiana.edu ✍ *Type in message body:* subscribe gospel-l

Gospel Music Hundreds of files containing lyrics and music for gospel favorites can be found here. ✓**INTERNET**→*url* gopher://sunsite.unc.edu:70/11/sunsite.d/amr.d/topics/Gospel-music-black-and-white

Gospel Music Association This site is a vehicle for reporting the news from the Association's yearly conventions. Daily coverage is provided. ✓**INTERNET**→*url* http://www.netcentral.net/gma/index.html

Magazines

Christian Contemporary Music Online (ml) Christian music's premiere offline magazine, *Christian Contemporary Music*, is now available in Cyberspace. The site offers up-to-the-minute articles on industry news, album and singles reviews, top-ten charts, and concert info. There is also an online store where you can shop for t-shirts, hats, and posters featuring your favorite Christian music stars (but you'll have to call the toll-free numbers listed here to order that Newsboys poster for your wall). Readers can subscribe to the CCM Online mailing list to keep up on announcements and news. ✓**INTERNET**→*email* listserv@netcentral.net. ✍ *Type in message body:* subscribe <your full name> *Info:* ✓**INTERNET**→*url* http://www.ccmcom.com/index.html

The Lighthouse Electronic Magazine (ml) The first Christian music ezine, *Lighthouse* is a comprehensive source of artist and industry information. Its Features section offers in-depth profiles of recording stars like Ashley Cleveland and The Echoing Green, and you can learn about their early influences, their music, and how they got started. The News section offers the full text of press releases from Christian music record companies on subjects like signing new bands and tours. This site even offers live chat with Christian music artists such as Hokus Pokus! You can also subscribe to *Lighthouse*'s mailing list to get previews of up-

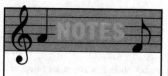

"Could somebody who's up on Christian Rap inform this uninformed lover of music who's hittin in X-ian rap? I've got Gospel Gangstas, but Gang Affiliated is getting tiring.

"Gospel Gangstas is supposed to release a new album in October, and I believe it will be entitled Do or Die.

"If you like Gospel Gangstas (like I do), then you might like:

-LPG, The Earthworm (Mad lyrical skillz!)

—Fred Lynch Give Me The Planet (Beats, beats, beats!!)

—T-Bone, (It's o.k.-- I forgot the title-- but it's the latest release)

—Barry G., Rugged Witness

—SFC, Illumination

"I personally, like the funk, so what I like is based on hard beats and rappers that can flow with the lyrics."

—from **rec.music. christian**

coming editions. Visit this site to get an insider's look at the industry and its artists. √**INTERNET** →*email* listserv@ netcentral.net ✍ *Type in message body:* subscribe Lighthouse-List <your full name> *Info:* √**INTERNET**→ *url* http:// www.netcentral.net/lighthouse/The Lighthouse Electronic Magazine

LiNeNoIsE This publication is the voice of alternative Christian music. The magazine is comprised entirely of articles written by fans. Topics here include reviews of concerts ("The 250-plus people who packed the auditorium / T.V. studio to see Dogbaby for almost four hours had lots of fun while praising Jesus!!") and records ("Karen Peris still stands as one of the best songwriters anywhere. She just must be one of the happiest & most optimistic people on the face of the planet.") This is the hip place to be for alternative Christian rock info. √**INTERNET**→ *url* http://www.catalog.com/ lionsden/linenoise/

Radio stations

American Family Radio In February 1993, American Family Radio consisted of one station. Now there are over 80 ARF stations in 23 states nationwide, from Alabama to Washington. Read about these stations, which promise "100% Christian" programming, and find the station nearest you by visiting this site. √**INTERNET**→*url* http://www.gocin. com/afa/afr1.htm

Audible Light This famous Christian radio show draws big Christian rock stars for interviews. Their site's hottest features are the complete transcripts of some of these interviews, including their visits with The Throes and with Talk of the Curious Fools. You can

> ### "The 250-plus people who packed the auditorium had lots of fun while praising Jesus!!"

also use the links provided here to jump to other Christian music sites, like *LiNeNoIsE* and 137 Records. √**INTERNET**→*url* http:// linus.cs.ohiou.edu:80/~wlhd/ alight/

Christian Radio Pipeline Some Christians in the San Mateo, California area think there isn't enough Christian music on the airwaves today. They have constructed this page to raise spiritual support (and cold hard cash) for their cause: to establish a relay link from a neighboring station so they can broadcast Christian music 24 hours a day! Read about their mission and see a picture of a relay link in action here. √**INTERNET**→*url* http://www.crl.com/~atherton/

KADU Read this Minnesota station's playlist here. √**INTERNET**→*url* http://uslink.net/kadu/home.html

KLTY "America's Number One Christian Radio Station" has recently taken its message to the Net. Their site features programming info (including a "hot-rotation" list) and Christian music news. And by the way, if you're in the Dallas/Ft. Worth Area, you're welcome to visit the station for a tour and a list of other great Christian radio stations! Enjoy your stay. √**INTERNET**→*url* http://

www.webcasting.com/klty/

KTLI The voice of mighty Wichita, Kansas' Christian music community puts up a nice site, featuring sound clips of new Christian releases (Michael W. Smith's *I'll Lead You Home* is currently in the spotlight), news briefs (Rich Mullins will be a guest on America Online's Christian Connection), a Top-20 list ("Cry for Love" by Michael W. Smith is very hot in Wichita), and links to fan clubs (for Steve Taylor and Petra) and record companies (N-Souls Records). √**INTERNET**→*url* http:// www.southwind.net/ktli/

National Religious Broadcast Publications Thinking of starting your own Christian radio station and just don't know where the heck to start? Don't go looking in your Good Book for answers— come on over to this informative site! National Religious Broadcasters is an association of more than 800 religious radio and television stations, program producers, and related organizations worldwide. The articles at their site help you keep up-to-date with industry trends and one step ahead in technology, statistics, finance, sales, and much more. NRB also offers info on Christian broadcasting conventions and workshops. Jump in friend, the water's fine. √**INTERNET**→*url* http://www.mnsinc.com/ nrb/

Positive Alternative Radio Network This station services Christians in southwestern Virginia. Read about their station and music here. √**INTERNET**→*url* http:// www. bev.net/mall/parfm/index. html

Positive Life Radio This noncommercial station is operated by the students and staff of Walla

Walla College. They post their programming schedule and links to other Christian music sites, like Christian Music Online. ✓**INTERNET**→*url* http://www.wwc.edu/staff/depts/plr/

WHJT Before Christian music fans in Missouri call WHJT to request a song, they can go here and search the database of the station's record collection to make sure they have the song. (Oh good, they do have "I'm Not Ashamed" by the Newsboys!) Also here are Christian music concert listings for the local area. ✓**INTERNET**→*url* http://www.mc.edu/~alive935/

Songs

Christian Music MIDI Files MIDI files for all types of Christian music, from hymns to Christmas songs, are located here. Contributions welcome! ✓**INTERNET**→*url* ftp://bach.nevada.edu/pub/midi/

The Contemporary Christian Music Guitar Music Archives This collection of ASCII guitar music, tabulature, and chordsheets lays out the music of popular contemporary Christian artists as interpreted by guitar players worldwide. If you've figured out tunes yourself, the Archive heartily welcomes new contributions. ✓**INTERNET**→*url* http://www.coe.uncc.edu/~cmpilato/music/ccm_guitar.html

Global Access Music According to this site, the thing that music-ministry professionals want and need the most is access to high-quality religious music. Global Access provides just that, offering PDF files of hundreds of songs, from old standards (like "Lord You're Gonna Do It") to new favorites (including "I'll Fly Away").

Amy Grant dances—from http://www.cmo.com/cmo/

✓**AMERICA ONLINE**→*keyword* GAM

Hymns and Praise Songs Find a perfect song for your next church concert or a little tune you can hum at home for inspiration. Each PostScript file here yields sheet music for contemporary songs and classic hymns. All titles are in the public domain. ✓**INTERNET**→*url* ftp://kuyper.cs.pitt.edu/music/

Artists

Abel Cain This California-based band counts The Police, The Choir, and Synergy among their influences. Read profiles of band members, learn how and where you can buy their music, and find out how to contact them by visiting this site. ✓**INTERNET**→*url* http://www.netads.com/netads/arts/music/marathon/ac/

Susan Ashton The "other Amy Grant,", this singer is known for her Christian radio staples like "Down On My Knees," "Wakened By the Wind," "In Amazing Graceland," "Hunger and Thirst," and "Here In My Heart." Read a biography of the artist, flip

through pictures of Susan swinging it onstage, and read the lyrics to her songs line-by-line at this site. ✓**INTERNET**→*url* http://rendall.notis.com/ashton/ashton.html

Margaret Becker Fans of this singer with the fiery-red hair have assembled a discography (complete with pictures and the lyrics to every song), the full text of their fan-club newsletter, *The Wire*, and excerpts of many related articles. ✓**INTERNET**→*url* http://www.cs.iastate.edu/~anderson/mb.html

Brent Bourgeois Formerly half of Bourgeois Tagg, Brent Bourgeois has been reborn as a Christian artist. *Come Join the Living World* is his latest release, and you can preview it through the sound clips here. You can also read a brief biography of Brent and see what he looked like back in 1975 (check out those bell-bottoms!). Bonus: Email your address to the site and get a coupon for $4 off the retail price of *Come Join*. ✓**INTERNET**→*url* http://www.netcentral.net/reunion/brent/e

Bryan Duncan Hear a sound clip of "Things are Gonna Change," read about Bryan's secret to peace ("It starts with confessing your own mistakes"), and scan a brief discography of his work at this site. ✓**INTERNET**→*url* http://www.cmo.com/cmo/cmo/data/bduncan.htm

Twila Paris Twila has won the Gospel Music Association's Dove Award for Best Female Vocalist twice—once in 1993 and again in 1994. Find samples of the music that won her those awards and a biography of her life. ✓**INTERNET**—*url* http://www.cmo.com/cmo/cmo/data/tparis.htm

Charlie Peacock Mr. Peacock is

a busy man. Besides his booming recording career, Charlie finds time to produce other artists' work and build Websites! Read about his latest projects, as well as his past accomplishments, and learn quirky facts about Charlie at this site. (He was once featured in a drinking-and-driving public-service announcement.) ✓INTERNET→*url* http://www.netcentral.net/sparrow/charlie/index.html

Petra Veterans in the Christian music world, Petra has been around since 1974. The illustrated discography, biographies of band members, and tour information listed at this site will catch you up on their activities past, present, and future. ✓INTERNET→*url* http://www.wam.umd.edu/~lbdavies/music/petra/petrapage.html

Point of Grace Denise, Shelley, Heather, and Terry only have two albums out (*Point of Grace* and *The Whole Truth*), so their discography is a little short. But the extensive biographies on these devout ladies will leave fans feeling satisfied. ✓INTERNET→*url* http://www.cmo.com/cmo/cmo/data/pog.htm

Michael W. Smith According to this site, Michael's *I'll Lead You Home* album has sold more copies in ten days than that other Michael's *HIStory* album sold in ten weeks. A discography of his 11 records, info on his book about teenagers and relationships, and pictures of the star are available here. ✓INTERNET→*url* http://www.cs.rose-hulman.edu/~hochstrb/mws/

Kathy Troccoli Find out why Kathy is one of the leading Christian recording artists of today by reading the lyrics of her songs. The compositions transcribed here include "My Life is in Your Hands," "All of My Life," and "I'll Be There for You." And if you kow the songs and want to prove it, there's Kathy trivia online here too! ✓INTERNET→*url* http://www.missouri.edu/~c621412/troccoli/troccoli.html

Whiteheart This site, the most thorough of the six Whiteheart sites on the Web, features a band history, a discography of their ten records, and sound clips of "My Eyes Have Seen" and "Letter of Love." ✓INTERNET→*url* http://www.cmo.com/cmo/cmo/data/wheart/wheart.htm

Indexes

Christian Artists Web Pages
Maintained by the radio show *Audible Light*, this collection of links takes you to home pages for hundreds of Christian artists. The list of bands and singers is organized alphabetically. ✓INTERNET→*url* http://linus.cs.ohiou.edu/~wlhd/alight/cartists.html

The Ultimate Band List
Make that the Ultimate Christian Band List. Updated religiously (no pun intended), this site provides an index of Websites for all major Christian musicians on the Net. The list is organized alphabetically by last name. ✓INTERNET→*url* http://www.vuse.vanderbilt.edu/~greenst/music/artist/

Unofficial Christian Artist Review
Jason McCoy, a student at Bowling Green University, has assembled his personal views on a few artists and records along with links to some major artists' fan pages, including Michael W. Smith, Amy Grant, and Bryan Duncan. ✓INTERNET→*url* http://ernie.bgsu.edu/~jmccoy/Jason/MGroups.html

NOTES

"Christ Whose Glory Fills The Skies:

"Christ, Whose glory fills the skies, Christ, the true, the only Light, Sun of Righteousness, arise, Triumph o'er the shades of night; Dayspring from on high be near; Day-star, in my heart appear.

"Dark and cheerless is the morn, Unaccompanied by Thee; Joyless is the day's return Till Thy mercy's beams I see: Till they inward light impart, Glad my eyes, and warm my heart.

"Visit then this soul of mine; Pierce the gloom of sin and grief; Fill me, radiancy divine, Scatter all my unbelief; More and more Thyself display, Shining to the perfect day."

"Written by Charles Wesley, 1740"

—from **Hymns and Praise Songs**

A cappella & choirs

When they say "lift every voice and sing," they're probably talking about a cappella

groups and choirs, organizations that give otherwise ordinary people a chance to lay down their props—no whammy bars, no amps, no lacquered pianos—and make a joyful noise. Want to sing? Set your pitch at **RARB** and the **A Cappella FAQ**, and then harmonize with other vocal advocates at **rec.music.a-cappella**.

A Capella faves the Bobs—http://www.best.com/~thompson/netfobs/pictures/TheBobs/

On the Net

Across the board

A Cappella FAQ This FAQ provides the curious with Questions from A Cappella Singers, as well as info on a cappella groups and readings, and other a cappella resources on the Net. ✓**INTERNET→** *url* http://yoyo.cc.monash.edu.au/~svlad/MainIndex.html

Primarily A Cappella From Anonymous 4 to Toby Twining, from the Bobs to Vocal Nation, from Black Umfolosi to Zap Mama, get the scoop on every facet of a cappella—Contemporary, Vocal Jazz, Barbershop, R&B, Classical, Gospel, World, Collegiate, Doo-Wop, Folk, and Christmas—at this well produced site. Links to title and group listings, online buyers' clubs, CD reviews, and other a cappella directories. ✓**INTERNET→***url* http://www.accel.com/pac/index.htm

RARB This website, created by the rec.music.a-cappella Album Review Board, gives you a chance both to peruse reviews of a cappella albums, and to get your own album reviewed. So sing out loud and sing out strong—maybe someone will notice. ✓**INTERNET→** *url* http://www.cs.wustl.edu/~seth/a-cappella/RARB/

rec.music.a-cappella (ng) What are the rules for a cappella singers these days? Well, they have to have a voice, preferably a good voice, and then they have to find others who complement their voice in tone, range, and volume. Once that's taken care of, they have to select a repetoire, start performing in venues apprpriateto their demographic (college dining halls, country clubs, churches), and then reap the thin benefits of the practice. What are those benefits? People will love you, but there's not exactly a pot of gold waiting at the end of the rainbow. ✓**USENET→**rec.music.a-cappella

Barbershop

Barbershop Web Server Harmonetters unite! This page acts as a directory for fans, participants, and professionals of the barbershop community. Looking for a copy of "Play That Fussy Rag"? Hoping to get a good spot for the SIA International in New Orleans? Even if you're just casting about for a limerick to tell while the bass fumbles for his pitch pipe, the FAQs from this site will smooth out all your harmonizing glitches. ✓INTERNET→*url* http://timc.pop. upenn.edu/

Singing Buckeyes If buckeyes are lucky, this group will win the lottery. For more than 45 years, this all-male singing group has provided quality entertainment to the Mid-west valley. Hear sound clips of the 70-strong phalanx of singing barbers (although rumor has it that they're not all really barbers), discover the Buckeye Invitational, and investigate the select vocalists known as Joker's Wild. This page also features links to other barbershop sites, along with a little something extra for those who don't sing but cultivate the culture. As they say, "do re mi fa so la ti snip." ✓INTERNET→*url* http://www.infinet.com/~millerwd

Vocals/Barbershop Talk about barbershop quartets, quintets, sextets, septets, octets, nonets, and minyans at this site. ✓COMPUSERVE →*go* musicarts→Messages *and* Libraries→Vocals/Barbershop

Choirs

Akateeminen Laulu—The Academic Choral Society Links to concert info, contacts, FAQs, general information, recordings and training opportunities. A good place to start the day, and also a good place to Finnish (as if you didn't see that joke coming from miles and miles away). ✓INTERNET→*url* gopher:// gopher.helsinki.fi/11/jarjestot/ kuorot/

The Arizona Repertory Singers A Norwegian choir offering info on their concerts and history and some pictures. An English-language version is available

for those not versed in Germanic languages. Curious about a 32-voice mixed ensemble from Southern Arizona? This page provides info about the ARS and a schedule for the upcoming season. ✓INTERNET→*url* http://viking.as.arizona. edu/~taf/ars.html

Ars Nova This Website for Michigan's renowned choir contains links to upcoming concert info, reprints of past concerts, audition information, and a list of Ars Nova personnel. ✓INTERNET→ *url* http://gopher.orsps.wayne. edu/nova/arsnova.html

Austin Handel-Haydn Society The society is not exclusively dedicated to choral music of the classical and baroque periods, but performs works from a wide range of eras and genres. This site features links to a schedule of events, society history, and bios, as well as contact and ticket information. ✓INTERNET→*url* http://www. quadralay.com/www/Austin/Fine Arts/HHS/

The Bach Choir of Pittsburgh Pittsburgh's oldest and largest choral organization. Here you can find a detailed schedule for the group and links to other Bach and classical music sites. ✓INTERNET→

url http://www.lm.com/~lmann/ bach/bach.html

bourb.net The splashy site for the popular Bourbon Tabernacle Choir contains links to tour dates, text files (an FAQ, taping info, etc.), sound clips, graphics, solo projects, and info on booking the band and ordering BTC albums, as well as links to other resources and tech support. ✓INTERNET→*url* http://204.225.233.5/

Cantatille Cantatille is the "first Belgian choir on the Web," but you can bet your bottom dollar it won't be the last! One hopes they will be more interesting than this one, which offers a plea for contact with another small choir and a link to a Belgian resources directory. ✓INTERNET→*url* http://zorro. ruca.ua.ac.be/~windels/cantatille

Con Anima A short bio and links to sound clips from this evangelical choir. ✓INTERNET→*url* http:// www.stud.unit.no/studorg/laget/ arbgrupper/con_animaeng.html

Gyuto Tantric Choir The perfectly synthesized, subtly disturbing music of Buddhist choirs has somehow worked its way into pop culture. These choirs have been sampled by everyone from Enigma

The Austin Handel-Haydn Society—http://www.quadralay.com/www/Austin/

Six monks from the Gyuto Tantric Choir—http://www.well.com/user/gyuto/

to the Beastie Boys, but to hear them in their pure, transcendental state, come to this site and listen to their sound clips. You can also get a schedule of the Tantric Choir's U.S. tour, learn more about Tibetan Cultural Survival, the Endangerd Music Project, and seek enlightenment by linking to other Buddhist resources on the Net. ✓**INTERNET**→*url* http://www. well.com/www/gyuto/

Melbourne University Choral Society This Australian choir offers an informative page with bios of the members and the conductor, rehearsal info, and highlights of the season's performances. ✓**INTERNET**→*url* http://www.cs.mu. oz.au/~winikoff/mucs/mucs.html

MIT Concert Choir Yes, it's true! MIT students do come out of their computer caves to sing! This site features links to ticket and member info, bios, "rave" reviews, dress requirements and more. ✓**INTERNET**→*url* http://www.mit.edu: 8001/afs/athena.mit.edu/course/ 21/21m401/WWW/home.html

Rustavi Choir This choir is part of Georgia's premiere folk-song and dance ensemble, the Rustavi

Company. Learn more in the short bio provided. ✓**INTERNET**→*url* http://www.music.sony.com/ Music/ArtistInfo/ChoirRustavi_ Biography.html

Sacramento Master Singers This accomplished choir of forty singers from the greater Sacramento area maintains a lovely Website, with links to bios, concert and CD info and the choir's most recent repertoire, and dozens of other similar pages. ✓**INTERNET**→*url* http://www.dcn.davis.ca.us/~ jcrowell/sms/

Santa Clara Chorale Links to choir and director bios, as well as information on Santa Clara University and Mission Santa Clara. ✓**INTERNET**→*url* http://www.scc. org/SCC

Sonoma County Bach Choir An earnest mission statement for Bach supporters and links to the Sonoma State University Academic Foundation. ✓**INTERNET**→*url* http://www.sonoma.edu/scbs/

The St. Olaf College Choir For fans of "Beautiful Savior." Find the lyrics and order St. Olaf's rendition on CD. ✓**INTERNET**→*url*

http://www.stolaf.edu/stolaf/ depts/music/stolaf_choir/

Studentkoret Aks A Norwegian choir offering concert info and history and some pictures. An English-language version is available for those not versed in Germanic languages. ✓**INTERNET**→*url* http://www.stud.unit.no/studorg/ aks/index.html

Trondhjems Studentersang-forening This page has Dagens Kor, Undergrupper and Relaterte Linker. Sorry the English language version is not available yet. ✓**INTERNET**→*url* http://www.stud.unit. no/studorg/tss/

TVRC A mammoth home page for those interested in the music of children's choirs. ✓**INTERNET**→*url* http://www.iac.net/~spock/

Unge Akademikeres Kor Home page for an actively touring Danish choir featuring a calendar and musical repertoire. ✓**INTERNET** →*url* http://meyer.fys.ku.dk/~ kerne/uak_us.html

University of Notre Dame Shenanigans Enter the Shenan-archives to dig up photos, reviews, and schedules for University of Notre Dame's singing and dancing ensemble. ✓**INTERNET**→*url* http:// www.nd.edu/~shenana/

Whatcom Chorale Discover the history of the society that has brought 25 years of music to Bellingham and Whatcom counties. ✓**INTERNET**→*url* http://www. pacificrim.net/~arvann/pages/ whatchor.html

Yale University Choir Just a few of the hosts in the Battell Chapel offering heavenly instruction. ✓**INTERNET**→*url* http:// www. cis.yale.edu/uchoir/index.html

University Choirs

AllNighters ✓INTERNET→*url* http://jhuvms.hcf.jhu.edu/~stubert/AllNighters/AllNighters.html

Amazin' Blue ✓INTERNET→*url* http://www-personal.engin.umich.edu/~fizban/ab.html

Bear Necessities (Brown University) ✓INTERNET→*url* http://netspace.students.brown.edu/~howard/bearhome.html

BioRhythms ✓INTERNET→*url* http://138.26.80.156/homepages/plummer/biorh.html

Brown Derbies (Brown University) ✓INTERNET→*url* http://www.brown.edu/Students/Brown_Derbies/Derbies.html

Brown Univ. Higher Keys ✓INTERNET→*url* http://www.brown.edu/Students/Higher_Keys

BYU A Cappella ✓INTERNET→*url* http://students.cs.byu.edu/~glen/home-page.html

Chalmers Choir ✓INTERNET→*url* http://www.dtek.chalmers.se/~d4frodo/ch_sangkor/

Chorallaries ✓INTERNET→*url* http://www.mit.edu:8001/afs/athena.mit.edu/activity/c/choral/Public/WWW/home.html

Columbia University Kingsmen ✓INTERNET→*url* http://www.columbia.edu/~mcf4/

Cross Products ✓INTERNET→*url* http://www.mit.edu:8001/activities/cross-products/home.html

Duke A Cappella Singing Group: The Pitchforks ✓INTER-NET→*url* http://www.acpub.duke.edu/~ntd/index.html

Everyday People (Stanford) ✓INTERNET→*url* http://www-graphics.stanford.edu/~beers/EP/

Harvard-Radcliffe Veritones ✓INTERNET→*url* http://hcs.harvard.edu/~veritone/

Knauskoret—Norway's University of Trondheim ✓INTER-NET→*url* http://www.alkymi.unit.no/~syljua/Knauskoret.eng.html

Mendicants (Stanford University) ✓INTERNET→*url* http://rescomp.stanford.edu/~pweston/mendicants.html

MIT Muses ✓INTERNET→*url* http://www.mit.edu:8001/activities/muses/home.html

MIT/Wellesley Toons ✓INTER-NET→*url* http://web.mit.edu/afs/athena/activity/t/toons/www/home.html

Mixed Company of Stanford University ✓INTERNET→*url* http://www-leland.stanford.edu/group/mixedco/

Mixed Company of Yale University ✓INTERNET→*url* http://minerva.cis.yale.edu/~ericb/gump.html

New Group ✓INTERNET→ *url* http://www.con.wesleyan.edu/~newgroup/newgroup.html

Onomatopoeia Home Page (Wesleyan) ✓INTERNET→*url* http://www.con.wesleyan.edu/~onomatopoeia/onomat.html

Other Guys (University of Illinois) ✓INTERNET→*url* http://lurch.beckman.uiuc.edu/

Pennsylvania Six-5000 ✓IN-TERNET→*url* http://dolphin.upenn.edu/~pennsix/

Perth Undergraduate Choral Society ✓INTERNET→*url* http://www.gu.uwa.edu.au/clubs/pucs/

Pittsburgh Camerata ✓INTER-NET→*url* http://www.ece.cmu.edu/afs/ece/usr/hread/info/Music/camerata.html

Princeton Tigertones ✓INTER-NET →*url* http://www.princeton.edu/~tones/index.html

Princeton University Wildcats ✓INTERNET→*url* http://www.princeton.edu/~wildcats/

Rifrain (Morehouse College) ✓INTERNET→*url* http://drift.winternet.com/~rifrain

Rip Chords (University of Illinois) ✓INTERNET→*url* http://ux4.cso.uiuc.edu/~ecoscoll/ripchords.html

Spizzwinks (Yale) ✓INTERNET→*url* http://www.cis.yale.edu/~keller/winks.html

Testimony A Cappella (Stanford University) ✓INTERNET→*url* http://www-leland.stanford.edu/group/tmony

Xtension Chords A Cappella Singers (University of Illinois) ✓INTERNET→*url* http://echo.phs.uiuc.edu/~kgp/xchords.html

Marching bands

In some ways, a marching band is eerily similar to an Internet newsgroup—a large

group of wacky outsiders—some might even say geeks—who band together to create a productive organization. Fiercely communitarian, relentlessly odd, college marching bands are like armies for the idiosyncratic, football teams for the runts of the litter, and they wear their eccentricities on their epaulets. Online, marching band sites range from general indexes like **Links to Marching Bands** and general discussion sites like the **rec.arts.marching.band*** hierarchy to a host of sites devoted to individual bands. Scramble bands, pep bands, precision marching bands, improvisational comedy troupes disguised as bands—they're all here. Gentlemen, start your tubas.

The pride of UC Davis—from http://seclab.cs.ucdavis.edu/~wetmore/camb/pictures/

On the Net

Across the board

Links to Marching Bands
Want to link to marching band pages? Go ahead—in fact, with this list, linking will be so easy that you'll have enough energy left over to march in lockstep with other tuba-toting football fans. In addition, the page contains links to Usenet newsgroups and instructions on how a drum major or bandleader can set up a Web page

for his or her band. ✓ **INTERNET**→ *url* http://seclab.cs.ucdavis.edu/~wetmore/camb/other_bands.html

rec.arts.marching.band* (ng) What do college marching band members talk about? Choreography. Music. Politics. Football. And sometimes even fashion: "We've decided to go with a new kind of hat, and some of us are in favor of the toboggan, that knit cap that grunge rockers wear. We want our theme to be 'Smells Like Team Spirit,' and we want to smash up our instruments when we are done playing them. What do other drum majors think of this idea?" With newsgroups for college marching bands, high-school bands, drum corps, and color

guards, and a miscellaneous group to collect all the posts that don't belong in those other groups, this is the premier collection of marching band chat online. ✓ **USENET**→ rec.arts.marching.band*

College bands

Auburn University Marching Band What do 330 people in spats and tassles look like? Check out the monster Auburn Falcon Marching Band in action to find out. This site also posts a calendar of more than 30 season performances, so you can be sure to catch the Auburn vs. Western Michigan game. ✓ **INTERNET**→*url* http://www.auburn.edu/~lauband/

Baylor University Golden Wave Band In Texas, they do everything a little bigger and a little louder. Hear sound clips from the best the Lone Star State has to offer. ✓**INTERNET**→*url* http://www.baylor.edu/baylor/Departments/acad/golden_wave_band/bugwb.html

Boston University Marching Band Go BU! Go BU! Why are they so happy, you ask? The candy sale paid off and the archaic polyester uniforms are in the trash. This site lets you take a peek at the new duds for the BUMBs. ✓**INTERNET**→*url* http://www.shore.net/~fang/bumb.html

Brown University "Any officer may be impeached at any time. Any band member may start impeachment proceedings." Ouch! Providence's fiercely democratic marching band posts their Constitution at this site. Did you know this band also takes it to the ice for hockey games? Now that's team spirit. ✓**INTERNET**→ *url* http://www.brown.edu/Students/Brown_Band/

California Aggie Marching Band The pride of UC Davis, supporting the Regents, the Aggies keep going and going and going and going. This page has photos and a performance calendar. ✓**INTERNET**→ *url* http://seclab.cs.ucdavis.edu/~wetmore/camb/

Columbia University Marching Band A characteristically modest page for "The Cleverest Band in the World." The site offers a script archive and band history. ✓**INTERNET**→*url* http://www.cc.columbia.edu/~ct22/cumb.html

Dartmouth College Marching Band The DCMB is the oldest band in the Ivy League, founded in 1889, and band members pride themselves on having a wacky sense of humor. Decide for yourself. ✓**INTERNET**→*url* http://mmm.dartmouth.edu/pages/org/band/index.html

Florida State University Ah, the Florida State Seminoles. Hell of a football team. Bobby Bowden. Charlie Ward. Perennial power. Download some pictures of the band behind the team. ✓**INTERNET**→ *url* http://www.hcs.eng.fsu.edu/~todd/Chiefs.html

Indiana University Department of Bands Gain insight into the bands of Indiana U. ✓**INTERNET**→*url* http://ezinfo.ucs.indiana.edu/~marching/home.html

James Madison University Marching Royal Dukes The Dukes offer a sophisticated Web page that gives you insight into the world of marching bands. ✓**INTERNET**→*url* http://www.jmu.edu/music/mrd/

Leland Stanford Junior University Marching Band "A new low in tasteless behavior"? Some marching bands know no shame. This page has pictures of the troublemakers and a tour schedule.

✓**INTERNET**→*url* http://www-leland.stanford.edu/group/lsjumb/

Louisiana Tech Drumline Access kick-ass drum cadences at this site from the Bayou band. ✓**INTERNET**→*url* http://info.latech.edu/tech/SPA/latechdrumline.html

Michigan State University Spartan Marching Band The Spartan way upholds Tradition, Innovation, and Excellence. From this page they deliver some history, some traditions, and some sights and sounds for your not-so-stoic pleasure. ✓**INTERNET**→*url* http://web.egr.msu.edu/~nolf/band.html

Northwestern University Marching Band What suits a Wildcat best? Photos, highlights, and some purring on the side. ✓**INTERNET**→*url* http://www.nwu.edu/numb/

Notre Dame Band Page The home page of the Fighting Irish Marching Band includes pictures, movies, and a history of the renowned organization, as well as valuable reunion information for alumni. ✓**INTERNET**→*url* http://www.nd.edu/Departments/NDBands/band.html

Ohio State University Marching Band It's a phalanx of Buckeyes! Billions of them. This page offers a performance schedule and pictures of the band that raises the spirits of the largest university in the nation. ✓**INTERNET**→*url* http://www.acs.ohio-state.edu/org/osuband/

Princeton University Band Princetonians believe in "Music, Marching, Mirth, and Merriment." PUB, one of less than a dozen scramble bands in the nation, provides pre-game scripts at this site, as well as some history

The spelling Fighting Irish—from http://www.nd.edu/Departments/NDBands/picts/

and an extensive photo album. √**INTERNET**→*url* http://www. princeton.edu/~puband/

Purdue Marching Band What do Harry S. Truman and Neil Armstrong have in common? They've both signed Purdue's monster drum! Take a look at the percussive goliath on this Website. √**INTERNET**→*url* http://www.cs. purdue.edu/audio/audio.html

Rice University Marching Owl Band A capable home page for the scatter band from Houston that contains pictures of the group and more pictures of its new rehearsal space. √**INTERNET**→*url* http://riceinfo.rice.edu/~lynette/ MOB.html

Riverside Community College Marching Tigers Alias "Hollywood's Band," the Riverside Tigers have a reputation for putting on a show. Get its fall schedule and find out who's who in the RCC. √**IN-TERNET**→*url* http://corsa.ucr. edu/~lisa/rcc.html

Rutgers University Athletic Bands Last seen in the movie *Miracle on 34th Street*—the John Hughes remake, not the Frank Capra original—the Rutgers bands are extremely popular and easy to listen to. Here is an accommodating home page for both the Marching Band and the Pep Band. √**INTERNET**→*url* http://www-caip. rutgers.edu/~tischio/bands/band. html

Syracuse University March-

ing Band A history of the Pride of the Orange, a calendar, and some pictures of the band at work. √**INTERNET**→*url* http://web.syr. edu/~sumb/sumb.html

Texas A&M Sights and Sounds The Fighting Texas Aggies are tough customers when it comes to a tuba and a snare drum. You can find several pictures of college students in fancy hats on this page. √**INTERNET**→*url* http:// tam2000.tamu.edu/~mdm0953/ band/

Texas Tech University Find sounds, pictures, a history, and a newsletter of the 400-member band that specializes in "traditional" and "corps" style routines. √**IN-TERNET**→*url* http://www.crl.com/ ~babovec/gb/techband.html

University of California at Berkeley Pick up some introduc-

tory sound clips here of the one and only Cal band. √**INTERNET**→ *url* http://server.berkeley.edu/ calband/

University of California at San Diego Triton Pep Band Home page for the pep band for San Diego, the backbone of the Fightin' Tritons. Download pictures, sound clips, and a performance schedule. √**INTERNET**→*url* http://sdcc13.ucsd.edu/~ pepband/

University of Connecticut Marching Band The Pride of Connecticut's home page is under construction, but if we're lucky we'll soon be able to hear them, see them, and maybe even smell them. Isn't interactivity glorious? √**INTERNET**→*url* http://www. ucc. uconn.edu/~adr93001/marching. html

University of Illinois Marching Illini Relive the pageantry of the Marching Illini online at this site. Download photos and digital sound clips from an array of CDs arranged by the band hailed by John Phillip Sousa as the "World's Greatest College Band." √**INTERNET**

The Baylor Marching Band—from http://www.baylor.edu/baylor/Departments/acad/

→url http://www.bands.uiuc. edu/Ml/

University of Minnesota Marching Band They've performed with Melissa Etheridge, and they love their Golden Gopher (UM football mascot). The home page for the versatile band offers photos, sound clips, and a history. ✓INTERNET→url http:// www.umn.edu/nlhome/g340/male 0020/ m_band.html

University of Missouri-Rolla UMR has a band to fit all your musical needs—athletic events, concerts, and jazz performances. Download pictures and sound clips from Missouri-Rolla's finest. ✓INTERNET→url http://www.umr. edu/~band/

University of Oregon Marching Band Check out the OMB doing their thing at Disneyland. ✓INTERNET→url http://music1. uoregon.edu/websters/Anna/omb. html

"To audition for this Virginia scramble band, click on 'You Want Me to Do What With That Sheep?'"

University of Southern California A very prestigious home page for the Fighting Trojans. From this page you can access the President's Band, Hollywood's Band, the history of the Invasion of Troy, and even a QuickTime video. ✓INTERNET→url http://www. usc.edu/dept/band/Greetings.html

University of Washington Husky Marching Band Visit the "Cyber-Dawghouse" for still shots, video clips, a schedule, and some background info on the Huskies. ✓INTERNET→url http:// weber.u.washington.edu/~sbode/ husky.html

University of Wisconsin Order your copy now of *Sounds of Thee Wisconsin 2*. From this page, order shorts, shirts, and caps—all emblazoned with the UW insignia. ✓INTERNET→url http://www. wisc.edu/band/

Virginia Pep Band To audition for this Virginia scramble band, click on "You Want Me to Do What With That Sheep?" To get info on the band leaders, click on "Who the Hell's In Charge

High School Marching Bands

Burroughs High School, Ridgecrest, California ✓INTERNET→url ftp://www.ridgecrest.ca. us/pub/users/saustin/bandpage. htm

Chrysler High School Trojan Marching Band, New Castle, Indiana ✓INTERNET→url http:// www.nchcpl.lib.in.us/TMB/TMB. html

Cotter High School Marching Band, Winona, Minnesota ✓INTERNET→url http:// www.mps. org/~chsband/

Homewood High School Marching Patriot Band,

Homewood, Alabama ✓INTERNET→url http://199.88.16.12/ clubs/band.html

Modesto High School Band & Guard, Modesto, California ✓INTERNET→url http://www. moa.com/erik/mhs.html

Monta Vista High School Marching Band, Cupertino, California ✓INTERNET→url http://www.mvhs.edu/music/ marching.html

North Mesquite High School Big Blue, Mesquite, Texas ✓INTERNET→url http://www. metronet.com/~inchrist/NMHS.

html

Oliver Ames High School, North Easton, Massachusetts ✓INTERNET→url http:// www-oit.harvard.edu/wire/ oa.html

Thomas Jefferson Marching Colonials, Alexandria, Virginia ✓INTERNET→url http:// www. tjhsst.edu/people/rstarlin/ tjmc/tjmc.html

Wicomico High School Band, Salisbury, Maryland ✓INTERNET→url http://www.inter-com.net/ user/jmanno/

Princeton's Trash Percussion Unit—
http://www.princeton.edu/~puband/

Around Here, Anyway?" High-steppers with a sense of humor. √**INTERNET**→*url* http://www.virginia.edu/~pepband/

Wisconsin Tubas How many tubas? Many, many tubas, and also football scores from around the country. √**INTERNET**→*url* http://www.engr.wisc.edu/~faessler/tuba/tuba_home_page.html

Yale Precision Marching Band From piccolos to boomerangs, clarinets to tambourines, the YPMB has a little of everything, as does their Web page. √**INTERNET**→*url* http://www.

cis.yale.edu/yaleband/ypmb.html

Pro bands

The One More Time Around Again Marching Band What is the OMTAAMB? It's a Portland, Oregon marching band that describes itself as "simply a bunch of over-the-hill marching band fanatics who aren't smart enough to know any better." Come, come. Don't be so hard on yourselves. It isn't every day that 450 fanatics convene to have fun, drink instruments (or is that play instruments?), and roar through "Louie, Louie" as if it were written this morning. With corporate sponsorship from Miller Genuine Draft, the OMTAAMB is likely to be around for quite some time. Join the fun. √**INTERNET**→*url* http://www.pacifier.com/~akr/omtaamb/omtaamb.html

Reverend Al's Screamin' Hypin' Revival Band Composed mainly of alumni of the U.C. Berkeley Band, the U.C. Davis Aggie Band, and the Stanford Band, Reverend Al's bunch of nutty noise-makers perform up and down California. Get more information about hiring the band, or get the lowdown on its members. √**INTERNET**→*url* http://www.csua.berkeley.edu/~alpetrof/revival/

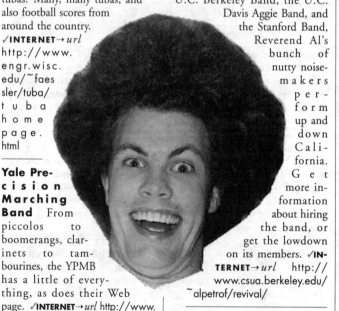

Comfortably NUMB:

"The uniform of the Northwestern University Wildcat Band:
· Black Shined Shoes
· White Spats
· Purple Coat and Pants
· White Overlay
· Black NUMB T-shirt. (Worn under coat)
· White Gloves
· Modified West Point Shako, Beret for Sousaphones
· Purple Warmer with Hood (worn when the weather outside is frightful.)

The Guard uniform:
· White Pants
· White Shoes
· Tuxedo Shirts
· Purple Vest
· Rosette and White Gloves

The Wildcat Marching Band is famous for its flashy high-stepping style. In addition to the traditional Northwestern University chairstep, the band executes the Northwestern University glide-step. With these contrasting marching steps, the Wildcat Band remains unique."

–from **Northwestern University Marching Band**

Soundtracks

In the twentieth century, composers who would have previously written for orchestras

instead turned their talents to the emerging film industry, creating appropriate music to accompany chase scenes, or tense interrogations. Often forced to work under strenuous deadlines, film composers have nevertheless been responsible for some of the most memorable sounds of recent memory—Jerry Goldsmith's chillling *Twilight Zone* theme; Ennio Morricone's stylish spaghetti Western music; John Williams's series of soaring themes for *Star Wars*, *Jaws*, and *Superman*; and virtually the entire oeuvre of Bernard Herrmann. Online, soundtrack enthusiasts can get their fix at **Soundtrack Web, Sony Soundtracks**, and **Shows & Soundtracks** And if you want to suggest that the score of *Avalon* was Randy Newman's finest moment, visit **rec.music.movies** and start campaigning.

On the Net

Across the board

Sony Soundtracks An enormous resource for soundtrack fans, this site gives overviews of hundreds of works—from *A Bronx Tale* to *Frankenstein* to *My Life* to *True Lies*—with information on the artists, song titles, and release date of each recording, and even the plot summary and release date for each movie! All in all, a great way to keep up on new soundtrack releases. ✓**INTERNET**→ *url* http://www.music.sony.com/ Music/ArtistInfo/Soundtrack

Soundtrack Web The home page of the rec.music.movies newsgroup offers a nifty database of soundtrack composers; enter the name of any composer from Ry Cooder to Danny Elfman to Alfred Newman, and a program retrieves a list of their works. There's also an FAQ, fan-written reviews (the *Star Wars* Trilogy set was recently covered), and info on soundtrack-oriented mailing lists. ✓**INTERNET**→ *url* http://www.uib. no/People/midi/soundtrackweb/

Tower Records Soundtracks Sure, this is a catalog for the massive record store, but Tower's album listings are more than mere advertisements—they provide excerpts from record reviews, track lists, and album cover pics. ✓**AMERICA ONLINE**→ *keyword* tower →Other Categories→Soundtracks

Chat

Film Music (ml) Sound out other fans' feelings about various soundtracks. ✓**INTERNET**→ *email* listserv@ iubvm.ucs.indiana.edu ✍ *Type in message body:* subscribe filmus-l <your full name>

rec.music.movies (ng) Soundtracks are unfortunately discussed very rarely here; most of the conversation centers around the movies themselves, and not their musical scores. So if you want to talk soundtracks, come here and start lobbying. And don't worry—it's a righteous cause. ✓**USENET**→ rec.music.movies

Shows & Soundtracks If you spend a lot of time at the movies with your eyes closed and your ears wide open, then this forum is for you. Meet others who share your affliction and chat about favorite composers (Henry Mancini's name surfaces frequently; George S. Clinton's name somewhat less frequently). Entire threads of these messages are archived in the library of this site, so you'll find lengthy back-and-forths about music in motion pictures, on television, and even in animated cartoons (great for Carl Stalling fans!). ✓**COMPUSERVE**→ *go* musicarts→Messages *and* Libraries →Shows & Soundtracks

Reviews

Soundtrack Reviews A big soundtrack fan, Travis Halfman, reviews the music to films such as *Jefferson in Paris, Six Days Six Nights*, and *A Little Princess*. ✓**INTERNET**→ *url* http://web.syr.edu/~ ebedgert/travis.html

Soundtracks on CD 1994 Deep in the halls of the movie site film.com, you'll find this section on soundtracks, with reviews of films like *Searching for Bobby Fischer, Field of Dreams*, and *Glory*. ✓**INTERNET**→ *url* http://www.film. com/film/craft/soundtracks.html

Musicals

When the lights go down, the curtain goes up, and the spotlight follows the dancing

feet, you know you're at a musical. One of the most beloved musical genres in the English-speaking world, the big-budget, gaudy-costume, sentimental-songcraft Broadway musical has been a part of New York and London culture for decades; today, contemporary works like *Les Miserables*, *Miss Saigon*, and *Sunset Boulevard* pack theaters alongside revivals of *Guys and Dolls*, *Damn Yankees!*, and *Showboat*. And there's always *Cats*, the T. S. Eliot-inspired kitty-literature spectacular that answers definitively the question "How long is forever?" Want to go to the show? Start at **Playbill Online**, and then visit the dozens of sites devoted to composers and shows.

On the Net

Across the board

Broadway Musicals In addition to featuring a guide to musical theater in Toronto (get ticket information and a calendar of performances for shows in the Canadian metropolis), this site serves as an index to Websites for Broadway musicals. ✓ **INTERNET**→*url* http://www.undergrad.math.uwaterloo.ca/~mkrishna/musicals.html

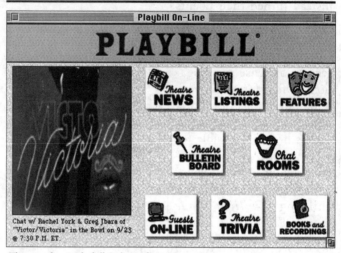

Chat w/ Rachel York & Greg Jbara of "Victor/Victoria" in the Bowl on 9/23 @ 7:30 P.M. ET.

Theatre online is Playbill Online—from America Online

Broadway Show List Read about current Broadway productions, their casts, running times, and histories, and then use the contact information listed here to get tickets. ✓ **INTERNET**→*url* http://eMall.Com/ExploreNY/Broadway/Bway1.html

On Broadway WWW Information Page The Statue of Liberty, the Empire State Building, Central Park, and Broadway plays are all part of the New York experience. But while the first three tourist attractions don't change much from year to year, the scene on Broadway is dynamic (although not so dynamic that *Cats*, *Phantom of the Opera*, or *Miss Saigon* will ever, ever, ever stop playing). Visit the site for a listing of theater performances On and Off Broadway, a year-by-year listing of Tony Award winners and nominees, and links to other musical theater sites. ✓ **INTERNET**→*url* http://artsnet.heinz.cmu.edu:80/OnBroadway/

Playbill Online Playbill Online helps put the Great White Way online, and in spectacular fashion. With the latest news briefs from the busy street; listings for local, regional, national, and international shows; and chat rooms where musical fans can meet and discuss their favorite performers and shows, this is the premier source of information about the musical theater. But it doesn't stop there—Playbill also features online live chat with stars like Rachel York, Gregory Jbara, and even Patrick Stewart! And if that weren't enough, there's also a trivia topic here to test your Broadway knowledge: "Name a musical biography of Tchaikovsky that played at the Adelphi Theater in 1947." It's *Music in My Heart*, of course! ✓ **AMERICA ONLINE**→*keyword* playbill

*Billy Wilder's legacy—http://www.cen.
uiuc.edu/~dd-moore/images/*

Chat

Collab-L (ml) Collaboration of
theatrical and musical talent. ✓**IN-
TERNET**→*email* listserv@psuvm.
psu.edu ✍ *Type in message body:*
subscribe collab-l <your full name>

Musicals (ml) A gateway of the
group rec.arts.theatre.musicals.
✓**INTERNET**→*email* majordomo@
world.std.com ✍ *Type in message
body:* subscribe musicals <your
email address>

rec.arts.theatre.musicals (ng)
A lightly-trafficked newsgroup
with discussion of a variety of topics, including the history of musicals, the latest live chat session at
America Online's Playbill topic,
and the debate of Andrew Lloyd
Webber's status as a modern-day
Mozart (on that subject Margaret
stated, "I don't think even ALW
would put himself in the same category with Mozart!"). ✓**USENET**→
rec.arts.theatre.musicals

Creators

alt.music.lloyd-webber (ng)

Discuss the man and his music
with other Webber fans. ✓**USENET**→
alt.music.lloyd-webber

Gilbert and Sullivan Archive
Sponsored by the Savoy Theatre,
this page offers bios of the famous
collaborators, synopses of their
works, a G&S festivals schedule, a
list of G&S clubs, and links to
other G&S Websites. ✓**INTERNET**→
url http://math.idbsu.edu/gas/
GaS.html

**MIT Gilbert & Sullivan Play-
ers** Get an introduction to the famous pair, a history of the MIT
Players, and links to G&S clubs in
the U.K., U.S., and Canada. ✓**IN-
TERNET**→*url* http://www.mit.edu:
8001/activities/gsp/home.html

**Newcastle Gilbert and Sulli-
van Society** The home page of
the Newcastle University club offers info on its performances, its
Society, lists of theaters in the
U.K., and links to other G&S societies in the U.K. and U.S. ✓**IN-
TERNET**→*url* http://www.ncl.ac.uk/
~n314699/Gilbert.html

**Nova Scotia Gilbert & Sulli-
van Society** They love Gilbert &
Sullivan in Nova Scotia, and this
site proves it by providing a list of
the Society's productions, including a description of their current
show, *The Gondoliers*, and the Society's newsletter. ✓**INTERNET**→*url*
http://www.cfn.cs.dal.ca/cfn/
Culture/GS-Society/GS-Home.html

Steven Sondheim The definitive site on the master. Find an
FAQ on his life and work, current
and back issues of the *Sondheim
Review*, sound clips of his songs,
synopses and info on *Assassins!*,
Follies, and *Into the Woods* (among
other shows), and links to other
Sondheim sites. ✓**INTERNET**→*url*
http://www.innocence.com:80/

sondheim/

Lyrics & synopses

Synopsis Archive Not just Cliff
Notes for popular musicals—like
Guys and Dolls, *Cabaret*, and *West
Side Story*—but also pictures and
reviews of various performances.
✓**INTERNET**→*url* http://www.mit.
edu:8001/activities/mtg/archives/
mtg-archives.html

Tower Lyrics Archive Lyrics
from the world's most famous mu-
sicals, including Andrew Lloyd
Webber's *Cats* and *Phantom of the
Opera*, Boublil and Schoenberg's
Les Miserables and *Miss Saigon*,
Gilbert and Sullivan's *Pirates of
Penzance*, and many more. ✓**INTER-
NET**→*url* http://www.ccs.neu.edu/
home/tower/lyrics.html

Productions

Cats Meow! Meow! Information
about this long-running show.
✓**INTERNET**→*url* http://www2.
msstate.edu/~rdm4/cats.html

**Jesus Christ Superstar: A
Resurrection** A promotional
page for the two-disc CD put out
by Daemon Records. Read reviews
of the recording, scan a track list
(with song lyrics), and read bios of
the performers, who include the
Indigo Girls. ✓**INTERNET**→*url*
http://www.hidwater.com/jcs/jcs.
html

**Hair: The American Tribal
Love-Rock Musical** The age of
Aquarius lives on with a synopsis,
show history, profiles of former
cast members, a photo archive,
and descriptions of current productions. ✓**INTERNET**→*url* http://
www.mit.edu:8001/people/
spwhite/Hair/hair.html

Hallelujah! A plot synopsis of

this musical about two teenagers growing up in religious schools. ✓**INTERNET**→*url* http://www.unt.edu/~cjk0001/hal.html

Jekyll and Hyde Information on the current Broadway production, its cast, the scheduled tour, show-related merchandise, and how to join the *Jekyll and Hyde* mailing list. ✓**INTERNET**→*url* http://reedycreek.stanford.edu/RecArtsJH/

Jesus Christ Superstar Ralf Southard just loves *Jesus Christ Superstar*, so he assembled lists of past and present performers, lyrics to the show's songs, the latest tour dates and productions worldwide, and info about the movie here. ✓**INTERNET**→*url* http://www.webcom.com/~sabata/jcs/welcome.html

Les Miserables Contrast the novel with the musical by reading the essays on both at this site. ✓**INTERNET**→*url* http://www.ot.com/lesmis/

Miss Saigon Dedicated fans of *Miss Saigon* constructed a site with a synopsis of the show, profiles of the actors and actresses, sound bites of the famous songs, and subscription information for the fanzine *Sun and Moon*. A whole section of this site is devoted to the finale—at various times during the show's run, three different songs have been sung at the end of the show, and this page allows you to download bites of each song and vote for which one you prefer. ✓**INTERNET**→*url* http://www.clark.net/pub/rsjdfg/

Miss Saigon A brief plot description. ✓**INTERNET**→*url* http://quercas.santarosa.edu/mainmenu/LeaSalonga/MissSaigon

Have you seen this musical?—from http://eMall.com/exploreny/broadway/cats.html

Nosferatu, The Vampire Cast and show info for this musical rendition of the F. W. Murnau film. What's next, Nosferatu vs. the Phantom? ✓**INTERNET**→*url* http://194.72.60.96/www/phantom/nosfera2.htm

Phantom of the Opera Dodge that falling chandelier and then check into this site to read about the novel on which the show is based, a summary of the musical's plot, a history of 19th-century Parisian opera, and sound clips, images, and locations of current productions worldwide. ✓**INTERNET**→*url* http://www.pinc.com/phantom/

Sunset Boulevard Everything you could want to know about *Sunset*, including news briefs on and reviews of current productions, sound clips, photographs from various renditions, and even a section devoted to the classic 1950 Billy Wilder film. ✓**INTERNET**→*url* http://www.cen.uiuc.edu/~dd-moore/sunset-blvd.html

Tommy Great graphics mark this site, which features a show synopsis, info on the Toronto production, fan mail and reviews, and even a word from Pete Townshend (he wants you to come see the show!). ✓**INTERNET**→*url* http://www.mirvish.com/tommy/

Victor/Victoria It just isn't the same without Robert Preston, but Blake Edwards brings his motion picture to the stage and Cyberspace. This Website includes a production schedule, cast and production credits, biographies of the stars, and ticketing information. ✓**INTERNET**→*url* http://www.fleethouse.com/fhcanada/western/bc/van/entertan/hqe/vrhq-vv1.htm

Wollarbes Winterwens A site about *Sunset Boulevard*, in Dutch. ✓**INTERNET**→*url* http://www.euronet.nl/users/fpwoll/sunset.html

Part 5

The Music Industry

The music biz

In Hollywood, everyone wants to direct. In the music business, everyone wants to be a

star. And the only way to be a star is to negotiate the labyrinth of the industry. Get started at **Backstage Pass**, **The Cyberdog Music Industry Database**, the **Music Industry Forum**, and **On Site Entertainment**. Get your songs polished by **Molly-Ann Leikin, Songwriting Consultant**. Get noticed with the help of **Marketing Music on the Web** and **MusicPro (TM)**. Get promoted with **A&R Associates**. Get on the road with the **Deterrent DIY Tour Guide**. And then, after your debut rockets to the top of the charts— You'll be on Conan! You'll have videos! Maybe you'll even marry a groupie!— check out **Gear Up** to learn where you can record your troubled follow-up LP.

Internet Music World home page—from http://www.mw3.com/imw

On the Net

Across the board

Backstage Pass The offerings here are organized into three categories. The first, Trade Secrets, delivers artist bios, feature articles on industry personalities like Beatle producer George Martin and the "guru of publicity" Lee Solters, record company profiles, release schedules, and tour itineraries. In the Music Notes section, industry professionals and fans discuss mu-

sic copyright legislation, the merits of various unsigned bands, and local radio stations. And there's the Jukebox section, which features photos of unsigned bands, sound files of both indie releases and signed acts, album cover art, and video clips. All in all, a good place to get a handle on the sounds of tomorrow. ✓**EWORLD**→*go* mu→ Backstage Pass

The Cyberdog Music Industry Databases To assist emerging artists, this database lists college radio stations nationwide and links to those with home pages of their own. ✓**INTERNET**→*url* http://www.magicnet.net/rz/three_minute_dog/cyberdog.html

The Music Industry Looking for a live karaoke band in Toronto? Seeking drummers seeking bands? Feel like you just don't know enough about the industry scene in Holland? Stop in at the libraries

here to find the answers to all your music-industry questions. Then go to the message board to discuss hot issues, like what's really going on over at Arista. Activity on the boards is very low-traffic. ✓**COMPUSERVE**→*go* musicarts→Messages and Libraries→The Music Industry

Music Industry Forum Dive into the music industry maelstrom with this library and message board. In the Music News section of the library, there's a comprehensive monthly list of new CD releases (or rereleases), so you'll know exactly when the soundtrack to *Peyton Place* will hit the stores again. Also in the library are the complete texts of the weekly Canadian record review column, "Roch on Music." Big business makes its presence felt here— Peavy Electronics and Gibson Guitars post their company news, info on model renovations, and product specs in their respective sections of the library. (Gibson Guitars also offered the long-awaited transcript of its first virtual guitar clinic, which featured Hot Tuna/Jefferson Airplane founders Jorma Kaukonen and Jack Casady.) There is even a library file where DJs, radio personnel, and roadies can post their resumes. On the message board, professional musicians talk about equipment, including a long thread recalling the glorious look and feel of the 1952 butterscotch Telecaster (the one with the cream-colored pick guard). There are also insiders' discussions of music advertising, music news, and tours. For music professionals and fans who want an intimate look at the industry, this is the definitive forum. ✓**COMPUSERVE**→*go* inmusic

On Site Entertainment A site devoted to the entertainment industry, with dozens of links to music-industry professional services—studios, labels, production companies, bands, radio stations, stores, and more. ✓**INTERNET**→*url* http://www.ose.com/ose/

Pelicore Visionz Home Page Updated daily, this site stays on top of what's going on in the music business. With hundreds of links to industry sites, Pelicore connects to major music networks (Internet Entertainment Network, The Music Industry Contacts List, and the Music Pro Home page), midi resources (MIDILink Musician's Net), and even paralegal services (Trademarking Your Band Name). Keep up with recording artists at work in the Pelicore Visionz Studios (Blyss, Cadmium Orange, and Jason Priebe) with this site's links to band home pages and to the World Wide Weird Newsletter, which promises "Stories from the Edge." ✓**INTERNET**→

url http://walnut.holli.com/~pelicore/

TUMA—Underground Music Archive Not to be confused with IUMA, TUMA is a non-profit organization devoted to distribution, promotion, and exposure of the best new bands worldwide. Divided into dozens of genres—alternative, pop-rock, metal, classical, jazz, gospel, rap, rockabilly, reggae, and more—TUMA doesn't have many bands yet, but it offers home pages for all the bands it lists, and its strong presentation and organization may draw new artists. ✓**INTERNET**→*url* http://www.rust.net/~instacom/TUMA.html

Management

Caught in the Web Get on the Net with the help of this company, which specializes in constructing Web pages for music-related businesses, including Hi-Bias Records and Number Nine Sound Recording Studios. ✓**INTERNET**→*url* http://www.maple.net/citw/

Enigma If flyers aren't getting the word around fast enough, complete the questionnaire included at this site, send Enigma a few pics and album covers, and for a fee (schedule included), the company will assemble your band's very own Website, complete with the option for sound clips. ✓**INTERNET** →*url* http://www.enigma.net/

Gus Swigert Management This site claims that "you don't have to give away creative control and a big percentage in order to enjoy the advantages of financial management, career counseling, distribution, promotion, and marketing." Currently enjoying this beneficial arrangement with Mr. Swigert are the artists Bruce Bec-Var, Nada Shakti, and the Tibetan Monks. ✓**INTERNET**→ *url* http://www.numenet.com/sc/ gsm/

Caught in the Web—from http://www.maple.net/citw/

CAUGHT IN THE WEB

INTERNET INTEGRATION
CONTENT CREATION

THE PROCESS PYRAMID   INTEGRATION & CREATION   INFORMATION DEVICES

Caught in the Web Inc. is a World Wide Web concept, design and development group. A collective of professional graphic artists,

Marketing Music on the Web
According to this site, there are four types of music marketing on the Web today, and they are all explored in detail here. An introduction explains online ordering, catalog services, promotion, and "anarchy" marketing, which is "the next major wave of alternative music distribution, allowing artists to 'self-distribute' to a world-wide audience in a media-less format (virtual distribution)." After describing each form of marketing, the site provides links to hundreds of labels and companies practicing these strategies. ✓**INTERNET**→*url* http://www.numenet.com/sc/gsm/

MusicPro (TM) The advertising agency Neilson/Clyne constructs Web pages for music businesses and makes them accessible through this site. Control Magazine, Kurzweil Pianos and Keyboards, Alchemy Records, the Recording Industry Environmental Task, and Recording Arts Studios in Nashville have joined the site. Use the contact info here to add your business to the offerings. ✓**INTERNET**→*url* http://www.musicpro.com/musicpro/index.html

Steve Shafer Music The guy who co-wrote the McDonald's "What You Want is What You Get" jingle socked some of his royalties away and opened Steve Shafer Music, a Chicago-based company that uses its stable of artists to create custom-made musical services for a number of advertising agencies. Learn all about Steve and his undertakings at this site. ✓**INTERNET**→*url* http://www.ssmusic.com/2sm/index.html

Toby Arnold & Associates "Image music" is a jingle that "moves people to action." TA&A wants to create image music for

your local business that will move customers toward the cash register. Read about and contact the company through its home page at this site. ✓**INTERNET**→*url* http://www.inroads.com/inroads/taa

Ubiquity Representing the groups Galactic, New Legends, Spirit Level, and Sweet Potatoe, this site profiles Ubiquity band members and recordings as well as their upcoming tours and performances. ✓**INTERNET**→*url* http://www.massive.com/ubiquity/

Vision International Vision helped launch the careers of Phish, Widespread Panic, the Samples, and the Dave Matthews Band, and now they're touting new bands such as Aquarium Rescue Unit, Leftover Salmon, and the Winebottles. Get profiles of the bands, their tour schedules for the next few months, and contact info for performance venues here. ✓**INTERNET**→*url* http://www.websys.com/vi/home.html

Musicians networks

Guerrilla Marketing Group A group of 14 independent musicians and music-industry professionals meet offline to discuss topical issues, like the impact of the Net on the music business. Read the minutes of their meetings here. ✓**INTERNET**→*url* http://www.numenet.com/sc/gmg/

Internet Musicians Be the first band on your block to be profiled in Cyberspace! Send your sound files and .GIFs to Internet Musicians and the service will showcase them on the Net (as soon as they construct the site). ✓**INTERNET**→*url* http://jax.jaxnet.com/~dsale/

Musician's Network Join this online club and access advice and

career support from musicians and music-industry people worldwide. Find a list of current Network members here, plus links to those who are online. ✓**INTERNET**→*url* http://www.halcyon.com/spotter/mnet.htm

Musicians Contact Service This musical dating service hooks up Australian musicians looking for others to form bands. Fill in the questionnaire and be entered in the database; the service will find the perfect match for your musical needs. ✓**INTERNET**→ *url* http://gil.ipswichcity.qld.gov.au/~mcontact/contact.html

World Wide Music Post a flyer for all the Net to see! Bands and artists submit descriptions of and contact information for their musical groups. World Wide Music hopes to draw attention for cool bands from Kassel, Germany to Buffalo, New York. ✓**INTERNET**→ *url* http://www.catalog.com/wwmusic/index

Promotion

A&R Associates Want to get signed, get radio play, put CDs into stores, or have your new releases reviewed by indie-friendly music magazines? Read the descriptions of industry-contact lists A&R has put together and then order them online at this site. ✓**INTERNET**→*url* http://www2.connect.net/users/diode/ar.html

Cardinal Productions In addition to representing variety acts, like Penny the Stilt Walker, Cardinal promotes the music of a wide variety of musicians, from Those Darn Accordions (a crazy bunch of 10 fun-loving accordion players) to Madeline Eastman (a jazz vocalist). Cardinal gives a brief history and description of each of

These pages are netscape enhanced, so those without netscape may hate me, whatever.

Indie Front

(as seen in the Canadian Internet Handbook)

*NEW: Malibu Stacey Images

Welcome to Indie Front!—http://charlemagne.uwaterloo.ca/

its artists on this page. ✓**INTERNET**→ *url* http://www.mim.com/cgibin/var/cardinal/cardinal/Cardinal Home.html

CenterStage Productions Whether you need entertainment for the Democratic National Convention or your high-school prom, this organization will select and orchestrate the evening's musical amusement for you. Contact them through this home page. ✓**INTERNET**→*url* http://199.170.0.46/csp/csp.html

Deterrent DIY Tour Guide This guide is essential for any band planning a road trip. Booking agents for clubs all over the U.S. and Canada are listed here, and the accompanying annotations give tips like "Agent is fairly honest," and "Known to pay bands well." If there is a trustworthy mechanic in the area—you never know when the van's going to break down—the Guide includes his info in the annotation. ✓**INTERNET**→*url* http://www.islandnet.com/~moron/deterrent/tour_gd.html

Gary L. Thomas Presents Springfield, Missouri is jumping due to the work of Mr. Thomas, who arranges shows at Springfield clubs like the Western Lights. ✓**INTERNET**→*url* http://www.gltp.com/

Hidden Water Spreading the word about independent musicians like Blue House and David LaMotte, Hidden Water posts information about up-and-coming artists and their music. ✓**INTERNET**→*url* http://www.hidwater.com/

IE MEDIA Advertising for several Toronto-based DJs, including S.O.S. (he'll save your party), and Ryan 7 (whose favorite artists include Funky Gonads and The Eternal Rhythm). ✓**INTERNET**→*url* http://www.interlog.com/~scotta/

NUMUS This not-for-profit organization hosts classical-music concerts in the Waterloo, Canada area. Its site offers a schedule of the season's concerts and profiles of the acts that will perform. ✓**INTERNET**→*url* http://www.worldlinx.com/cdi/numus/numus.html

Varke International Promo- tions Contact any of Varke's artists to perform at an international festival or convention. Varke's acts include Bolt & Nut, a Beatles cover band; singer/songwriter Diane Bond; and the legendary 1960's band The Byrds. ✓**INTERNET**→*url* http://neturl.nl/vip/

Publications

Indie Front Canadian 'zine that addresses the perils and the excitement of independent recording. ✓**INTERNET**→*url* http://charlemagne.uwaterloo.ca/

Internet Music World On-Line A trade magazine about the music industry. ✓**INTERNET**→*url* http://www.mw3.com/imw

Regional

Georgia Tech Musicians Networks Provides band listings, concert schedules, and want ads (for used gear and equipment) for the Georgia Tech community. ✓**INTERNET**→*url* http://www.gatech.edu/std_org/mn/mn.htm

Music Exchange of California Place an advertisement for anything that has to do with music in California, and it will stay up here for 90 days. Ads are organized into three categories: Topic, What's New, and Geographic Location. ✓**INTERNET**→*url* http://www.scsn.net/~musex/exchange/states/California/ca.html

Santa Cruz County Musicians Connection There must be more recording studios than churches in Santa Cruz County—contact information for 15 facilities is listed here. There is also a board for musicians to meet each other, but so far only a lone guitar player has posted his info. ✓**INTERNET**→*url*

http://www.catalog.com/yanomedi/

Texas Music Office A state-funded office for the promotion of the music industry in the Great State. Contact them (email addresses given) for lists of Texas-based music businesses, musical events, radio stations, and a talent register. Yeee-haw! ✓**INTERNET**→*url* http://link.tsl.texas.gov/0/.www/TMO.dir/tmo.html

Songwriting

BMI.com repertoire Songwriters can check out the competition at the BMI database, which houses information on the millions of songs licensed by BMI worldwide. The works of more than 100,000 songwriters and composers and 60,000 music publishers are searchable by title, writer name, or publisher name. ✓**INTERNET**→*url* http://rep.edge.net/

I-Site For over 20 years the National Association of Songwriters has helped aspiring songsters improve their tune-writing and business skills. In addition to membership information, this site offers the full text of SongLine, the NAS newsletter, as well as a schedule of NAS events. ✓**INTERNET**→*url* http://www.i-site.com/

Jeremy Lubbock Spotlight Area Singer, songwriter, and

Molly-Ann Leikin's hit-making house —http://www.earthlink.net/~songmd/

composer Jeremy Lubbock has worked with artists ranging from Barry Manilow to Celine Dion to Michael Jackson, and the site offers a biography, photo, and sound clips from some of his songs. ✓**COMPUSERVE**→*go* jld-1

Molly-Ann Leikin, Songwriting Consultant Have a song in your head? Molly-Ann will work with you until you're singing all the way to the bank. In the past 17 months, one of her clients has netted a Grammy nomination, another has been nominated for an Emmy, and more than 50 have inked deals with music publishers and record labels. Her owns songs have been recorded by artists from Cher to Tina Turner to Karen Carpenter to Placido Domingo, and she's the author of a number of books, audio tapes, and videos to help you get from moon-June-spoon to the Billboard Top 40. She'll work with you by phone, fax, or email, and her fees are relatively reasonable for those seeking stardom ($200 for up to five songs, and $25 for each additional song). So stop chewing down your pencil eraser trying to find a rhyme for "pedophile," and drop Molly-Ann a line. ✓**INTERNET**→*url* http://www.earthlink.net/~songmd/

rec.music.makers.songwriting (ng) Stop by day or night and someone in this newsgroup is likely to be holding forth on the best song ever written (Joe voted for "Beat on the Brat" by the Ramones, since it "conveyed so much power in so few words"). Other popular topics include the impact of songwriting lessons on creativity, and the musical repercussions of copyright legislation as it applies to songs. ✓**USENET**→rec.music.makers.songwriting

songwriter.com (ng) There is strength in numbers, so this group of songwriters have banded together at this site "in the hopes of getting noticed." Songwriters Ritt Henn, Ted Wallace, Andrew Lorand, and Tena Moyer are among the members. ✓**INTERNET**→*url* http://www.songwriter.com/

Songwriter's Corner Setting words to music can be hard, so the Songwriter's Corner provides a wealth of advice on writing lyrics and riffs and putting them together. Post your work-in-progress and receive critiques and encouragement from other musicians and songwriters. The message boards here are frequented by do-it-yourself-type writers who offer practical information on shopping finished songs to record companies and artists. ✓**COMPUSERVE**→*go* Music→Music and Arts→Songwriter's Corner

Studios

Gear Up! Music professionals meet here to discuss the ins and outs of their life's work. In the "Turn On, Tune Up, and Drop In" section, they can scan product reviews written by professional musicians, get music business tips from Bob Baker, and find a comprehensive list of recording studios and rehearsal spaces nationwide. Patch Bay is a forum for musicians and audio pros to exchange info and stories (the "Stories from the Road" topic promises to be especially juicy). Downloadable sound files of people laughing and good music-related graphics in the Multimedia Emporium round out this site. ✓**EWORLD**→*go* mu→Gear Up!

Acoustic Legacy Studios A description of and contact info for this Los Gatos, California studio, overlooking the San Francisco Bay.

✓**INTERNET**→*url* http://www.comet. com/~rick/als/als.html

Bigfoot Recording Studios Rates and booking information for this facility in Fremont, California. ✓**INTERNET**→*url* http://ccnet. com/~crick/bigfoot.html

Bliss Productions Ignorance isn't bliss any longer. But this Boston, Massachusetts studio is, with eight tracks of ADAT sonic control with Vision sequencing. ✓**INTERNET**→*url* http://www.breakfast.com:2500/b reakfast/it/bliss.html

Blue Jay Recording Studio A Boston-area 48-track private recording facility located in Carlisle, MA, 30 minutes west of Boston. ✓**INTERNET**→*url* http:// www.ose.com/ose/studios/blue_ jay/blue_jay_home.html

Chicago Recording Company Look at Lake Michigan while recording your songs in one of the four studios at CRC. ✓**INTERNET**→*url* http://www.interaccess. com/users/coyle/

DDV Studios Specializing in electronically created music, this Tampa Bay area studio will service all your synth recording needs. ✓**INTERNET**→*url* http://under ground.net/Ddv_html/DDV_home. html

Emerald City Studios With 24-plus tracks of digital recording, no task is too formidable for this Boston studio. ✓**INTERNET**→*url* http://www.mw3.com/studio/ studio.htm

Heart Studios Read about this Charleston, South Carolina studio and its new releases at this site. ✓**INTERNET**→*url* http://www.sims. net/organizations/heartstudios/ heartstudios.html

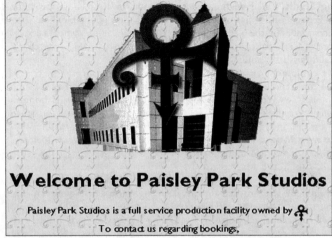

Welcome to Paisley Park Studios

Paisley Park Studios is a full service production facility owned by ♀

To contact us regarding bookings,

That's right,♀'s own studios—http:// www.bitstream.net:80/paisleypark/

MasterTrax Recording This site sports a cool pic of a mermaid and a telephone number for this studio on James Island, South Carolina. ✓**INTERNET**→*url* http:// www.sims.net/organizations/ mastertrax/mastertrax.html

MKB Music Studio Download sound clips, read bios of MKB studio musicians and bands, and see different views of this San Diego, California studio. ✓**INTER-NET**→*url* http://orpheus.ucsd.edu/ mbreen/mkb_music/index.html

Morrisound Studios Tampa, Florida has Morrisound Studios to capture its music. Take a virtual tour of the facilities, learn about this studio's equipment, and get a copy of Morrisound's fee schedule at this site. ✓**INTERNET**→*url* http:// www.digimark.net/Grubbworm/ msound.html

New River Recording Studios Take in a movie at the IMAX theater located right around the corner, while you are waiting to book time at this full-service studio in Fort Lauderdale, Florida. A description of the studio is here.

✓**INTERNET**→*url* http://www.com pass.net/~lance/nrstudio/

Overtom Studio Preview this studio's sound by downloading the sound clips here. The studio, located in Glace Bay, Nova Scotia, has recorded the works of Realworld, Sunfish, and Tom O'Keefe. ✓**INTERNET**→*url* http://137.186.188. 128/overtom/overtom.html

Paisley Park Studios Owned and operated by Prince, this Minnesota studio is one of the top recording facilities in the United States. This page includes specs for all the studios and a contact number for booking time (Studio A will cost you $2,500 for a 12-hour block). ✓**INTERNET**→*url* http:// www.bitstream.net:80/paisley park/

Pan Handler Production A list of equipment, a bio of the house band Sweat Engine, and a schedule of current projects for this La Jolla, California facility are available at this site. ✓**INTERNET**→*url* http://panhand.ucsd.edu/

Perfect Audio Online Record-

ing Studio Carl Franklin, owner of Perfect Audio, has one of the nicest smiles on the Net! See a picture of Carl and learn about his California-based studio by reading the equipment and service lists and contact info here. ✓ **INTERNET**→ *url* http://www.apexsc.com/users/ carlf/paudio.html

Power Music Productions Power has recorded music for Kodak, Fanta, and Mastercard. Its other clients, as well as their equipment, are profiled on this home page. ✓ **INTERNET**→*url* http:// www.hol.gr/business/pmp/

Process Recording Studios, Inc. Fantastic graphics take you through this site, which offers descriptions of the studios, sound clips of sound effects made there, and even a list of equipment Process has for sale. ✓ **INTERNET**→ *url* http://www.theprocess.com/

Q Division Ltd. Take a virtual tour of the studio and read about its equipment. ✓ **INTERNET**→*url* http://www.shore.net/~qdiv/ q.htm

Reel North Recording Studios You'll get just the facts at this Web page for Reel North, a studio in Fredericton, New Brunswick. Read about its staff, some of the artists whor ecord at Real North, and the studio's price schedule. ✓ **INTERNET**→*url* http://www.polaris. net/~chp/reel/home.htm

Sonic Recording Studios Pictures and descriptions of Sonic's studios, located in Philadelphia, Pennsylvania. ✓ **INTERNET**→*url* http://www.netaxs.com/people/ tibet/sonic.html

Soundfarm Recording Studios Dixon, California is alive with the music coming from the Soundfarm. Read about the studio (and its new pool table) here. ✓ **INTERNET**→*url* http://wheel.ucdavis. edu/~eejohnso/sndfarm/ sndfarm.html

Southern Studios Click through indexes of this London studio's artists and labels, and then order their recordings online. ✓ **INTERNET**→*url* http://www.southern. com/

Stonewood Studios These guys make house calls—you can hire them to record your bar mitzvah! The history of this facility in Batavia, Illinois, as well as a list of their services and equipment, are here. ✓ **INTERNET**→*url* http://www. interaccess.com/users/stonewd/ index.htm

Strummers Rehearsal Studios (Best Studio In Brighton) Fee and equipment info for this studio by the sea. And if you are not a musician but are thirsty, take heart—coffee and tea are free if you record at Strummers! ✓ **INTERNET**→*url* http://www.fastnet.co. uk/strummers/

SubPop Music Studios More than just a promo page for the famous Seattle studio and label (SubPop, in case you've been off the planet, released Nirvana's pre-Geffen product), this site offers a monthly column, profiles of various artists, and a link to the Center on Contemporary Arts, which showcases underground alternative artists. Also find info on SubPop's house bands, their discographies, and a link to order their recordings online. ✓ **INTERNET** →*url* http://www.subpop.com/

Synergy Studios A list of services and equipment, sound files of studio artists, tour info for Bill Nork, and a history of this studio located in Harrisburg, Pennsylvania. ✓ **INTERNET**→*url* http://www. paonline.com/synergy

Under the Couch Recording Studio See what this studio at Georgia Tech looked like before $250,000 of renovations, and then learn about the new equipment that the quarter mil bought. ✓ **INTERNET**→*url* http://www.gatech. edu/ std_org/utc/utc.htm

Pavitt & Poneman's cash cow—from http://www.subpop.com/

Labels

The true rock fan knows that the history of artists both surrounds and is surrounded by

the history of labels. Decca. Stax. Mango. Motown. Atlantic. Wax Trax. Chess. Fantasy. Spoon. Shimmy Disc. These are talismanic names, collections of letters that broadcast on both economic and aesthetic frequencies. Who among us hasn't been swept away by the sheer beauty of the sunglassed G-man adorning IRS cassettes? Today's world has more labels than ever; in addition to the massive **Indie Label List**, there are hundreds of names to learn, hundreds of logos, hundreds of otherwise anonymous bands offering sound clips and press releases. Start at **AAA Love Records**. End at **Zo Magik Records**. Absorb an alphabet—nay, a world—in between the two.

On the Net

Across the board

Indie Label List By nature of its religion, an indie label disdains all things megapopular and instead opts to exploit those things original. A double-edged sword for anti-capitalist warriors or a paradox waiting to happen? From Beowulf, to Gritty Kitty to the inestimable Rhino Records, all the last bastions of integrity are represented in this directory for the icono-

Rick Rubin's expanding empire—http://american.recordings.com/

clastic. ✓**INTERNET**→*url* http://www.cs.ucl.ac.uk/~twicks/ill/index.html

By label

137 Records An acoustic folk-rock label whose roster of artists includes Phobic and Portrait of Souls. ✓**INTERNET**→*url* http://www.coe.uncc.edu/~cmpilato/137.records/137.records.html

4AD Records (ml) The estimable independent has a mailing list, which offers fans information on bands like the Breeders, Throwing Muses, Dead Can Dance, and other alternative favorites. ✓**INTERNET**→*email* listserv@jhuvm.hcf.jhu.edu

✍ *Type in message body:* subscribe 4ad-l <your full name>

AAA Love Records AAA's roster includes Astrid Young and Skyfish, and sound clips are available online, along with an order form. ✓**INTERNET**→*url* http://www.goodies.com/biz/alr/newhome0.htm

AArising Records The advocate label for Asian-Pacific-Americans. Based in the Bay Area, AArising Records attempts to unbraid the knots of the Asian-American stereotype and to diversify the musical scene existing within the culture. ✓**INTERNET**→*url* http://www.aarising.com/

Acoustic Disc At Dawgnet, the official Website of Acoustic Disc, acoustic stringed instruments of all kinds get their due—lutes, banjos, guitars, and more. ✓ **INTERNET**→*url* http://www.sfm.com/dawgnet/

AD Music An electronic music label whose artists include David Wright, Robert Fox, Enterphase, Jan Hanford, Bekki Williams, and Chris Harvey. ✓ **INTERNET**→*url* http://tile.net/admusic

Alchemy Records This small, Massachusetts-based independent releases experimental and instrumental records, as well as more traditional recordings. The Website features a recording and includes an online order form. ✓ **INTERNET**→*url* http://www.musicpro.com/alchemy/ *Info:* ✓ **INTERNET**→*email* 74074.1316@compuserve.com. ✍ *Write a request*

Alternative Tentacles What can you say about a label whose URL ends with the word "virus"? Alternative Tentacles was created in 1979 to distribute the Dead Kennedys' single "California Uber Alles," and has grown into one of the most respected punk labels in the world, with releases from Tumor Circus, Eugene Chadbourne, the Butthole Surfers, and the Beatnigs. Get the entire AT catalog, learn about the label, and get information on how to order records. ✓ **INTERNET**→*url* http://iuma.southern.com/VIRUS/

Alternet Sonic Realities This independent cyberlabel specializes in eclecticism, releasing records by the alternative rockers Thanks to Gravity and the ambient outfit Zoar (named for the Edenic sanctuary). ✓ **INTERNET**→*url* http://www.iuma.com/ASR

American Recordings Rick Rubin's label not only includes pages for American artists such as Johnny Cash, Danzig, Julian Cope, and Black Crowes, but houses the Ultimate Band List and a number of other impressive resources for lovers of popular music. ✓ **INTERNET**→*url* http://american.recordings.com/

Andrew Thomas Distribution A distributor with relationships with a variety of punk labels, including Desperate Fight and Victory. Andrew Thomas's Website also includes information on ordering 7-inch records, 12-inch records, and compact discs by artists such as Copper, Enkindel, Glendale, La Gritona, and Neckbrace. ✓ **INTERNET**→*url* http://wilkes1.wilkes.edu/~cslebod/

Angel Angst At the moment, Angel Angest only handles punk writers, but they're looking for bands; interested artists should send cassette or CD demos. ✓ **INTERNET**→*url* http://www2.ari.net/home/siogo/

Angel Thorne Music Order *America the Beautiful,* the Marilyn Monroe rock opera, through Angel Thorne. ✓ **INTERNET**→*url* http://www.e-MediaWeb.com/ATM.html

APB Records Billed as "Chapel Hill's newest record label," APB is home to Regatta Sixty-Nine, Simple Simon, Fat-Free, and other independent rock bands. ✓ **INTERNET**→*url* http://www.cs.unc.edu/~priebe/apb.html

Arista Records Download Area Let the strains of "Moonlight Serenade" or "Sentimental Journey" soothe your weary computer soul. The area offers a few sound and video clips of songs by Arista Records artists. ✓ **COMPUSERVE**→*go* aristpreview

Artist Management Incorporated AMI's Website only has information about a single artist, but when that artist is legendary soul prodigal Ike Turner, it's worth a mention. Get a description of Ike's new single "I'm Blue," and a 30-second excerpt of the song, which features screamer Billy Rogers on vocals. ✓ **INTERNET** ...→*url* http://jax.jaxnet.com/~ejerue/ami.html ...*email* →ami@jaxnet.com ✍ *Email with general correspondence*

Atomic Theory Records A Minneapolis independent that specializes in all types of roots music around the world, including reggae, Cambodian, folk, blues, and country. Subscribe to the Atomic Theory mailing list, learn about the artists, and consult the catalog. ✓ **INTER-**

NET→*url* http://www.tt.net/atomic/ *Info:* ✓ **INTERNET**→*email* myren@ix. netcom.com ✍ *Type in message body:* subscribe

Avalanche Records Gene Loves Jezebel has resurfaced as Edith Grove and released an album on Avalanche; other artists include ex-Asia vocalist John Wetton, British solo star Chris DeBurgh, former Stealer's Wheel vocalist Gerry Rafferty. ✓ **INTERNET**→*url* http://www. bonaire.com/avalanche.html

Bad Habits Order CDs, including Darien Brahms' *Hello! Hello! To the People* and Pluck Theatre's *Five-Finger Disco.* ✓ **INTERNET**→*url* http://www.w2.com/bad.html

Bad Taste A cute pig serves as the mascot of Bad Taste records. Who are some of the artists who follow the way of the cute pig? Bubbleflies, pioneers of hard-hitting, computerized funk rock. The Gothic jesters Ham. Curver, in which "one man abuses his guitar in search of pop and industrial." And super-pixie Björk, who sings a set of standards with Iceland's jazz elite. ✓ **INTER-NET**→*url* http:// www.centrum.is/ badtaste

Bad Vugum An eclectic Finnish label whose artists include Puhelinkoppi, Radiopuuhelimet, Deep Turtle, The Leo Bugariloves, Mieskuoro Huutajat, and Generators. ✓ **INTERNET**→*url* http://www. compart.fi/badvugum/

Badcat Records Download samples from releases by blues artist Jim Norman and country singer Deborah Steel. ✓ **INTERNET**→*url* http://www.opendoor.com/bad

cat/BCR_Home.html

Bar-do Records This Japanese label's Website is organized around the principle of the Bar-do, which "describes the condition which one falls into as the soul transcends into the so-called 'after-life,'" and includes online movies, sound clips, and more about this unique musical experience. ✓ **INTERNET**→*url* http://www.st.rim.or.jp/~soolee/

Beatservice Records A Norwegian label specializing in techno and ambient music. ✓ **INTERNET**→*url* http://www.beatservice.no/ beatservice/

Bedazzled Records Ethereal and ambient pop artists, including Strange Boutique, Siddal, Viola Peacock, and the Curtain Society. Get sound samples and bios here. ✓ **INTERNET**→*url* http://www.iuma. com/Bedazzled

Beyond Records Online Manual What does Beyond specialize in? Well, first of all, it specializes in explaining itself, with a concise essay titled "The Beyond Ethos." "Beyond Records was set up in 1992 to provide a forum for electronic mood music of all descriptions, especially electronic atmospheres of the more relaxed kind." Okay. Fair enough. Learn the Beyond motto, "Underground. Positive. Experimental"; read an essay on dub written by critic David Toop, and get news, a discography, and ordering infor-

mation. ✓ **INTERNET**→*url* http:// iuma.southern.com/beyond/

Big Bro Records Home to European dance musics and a number of subsidiary labels, including Pengo, Jive, Noculan, Mokum, Coolman, and even Chemo. ✓ **INTERNET**→*url* http://www. bigbro.nl/big bro/

Big City Entertainment A wide variety of indie rock bands, including Dave's Big Deluxe, Grimble Wedge, and Cortex Bomb. ✓ **INTERNET**→*url* http://euphoria. org/home/labels/bcae/bce.html

Big Round Records Indie rock, including Myopic Nation's *Get Out of Dodge* and Route 3's *The Folks.* ✓ **INTERNET**→*url* http://www. w2.com/docs2/r/brr.html

BioRhythm / Positive Beat Roots music and reggae/hip-hop hybrids are the staples of this British label. ✓ **INTERNET**→*url* http://www.demon.co.uk/london -calling/posbeat.html

Black Boot Records A Seattle-based country music label. Yes, that's right—the words "country music" and "Seattle" have now appeared together in the same sentence. Don't do anything drastic. Breathe deeply. Say "Soundgarden" to yourself, over and over. You'll be fine. ✓ **INTERNET** →*url* http://www.w2.com/boot.html

Blue Goat Records Have you ever seen a purple cow? How about a green sheep? Complete the hued livestock motif with Blue Goat, a blues and jazz label named after the dyed goatee of the label owner. ✓ **INTERNET**→*url* http:// www.iuma.com/Bluegoat/

Blue Rose Records How do tiny U.S. indies get distributed? They cut deals with slightly larger U.S. independents, of course. Blue Rose serves as an umbrella label for Popllama, Flydaddy, Stickman, and Crunch Melody, among others. ✓**INTERNET**→*url* http://www. ftech.net/~blue rose/

Bogus Records Records by Planet Leo, Bull Moose Jackson and the Flashcats, and other artists. ✓**INTERNET**→*url* http:// www.w2.com/bogus.html

Bomp! Records (ml) Information on new releases from BOMP!, the nation's oldest independent label, and related discussions on surf and garage punk. ✓**INTERNET**→ *email* listserv@netcom.com ✍ *Type in message body:* subscribe bomp-l <your full name>

Boy's Life Records A Los Angeles-based independent that releases music by Southern Californian artists. ✓**INTERNET**→*url* http:// www.iuma.com/Boy's_Life/

Bridger Records An independent label that releases the records of Montana-based guitarist Stuart Weber. ✓**INTERNET**→*url* http:// www.numenet.com/sc/bridger/

Bulb Records Alternative music from Quintron, the Tweezers, Galen, and Mr. Velocity Hopkins. ✓**INTERNET**→*url* http://www.umich. edu/~anfangen/bulb-catalog.html

Burnside Records Blues and jazz from Kelly Joe Phelps, Too Slim and the Taildraggers, the David Friesen Trio, and more.

✓**INTERNET**→*url* http://www.mind. net/burnside/

C/Z Records The Seattle label that was SubPop before SubPop ever existed. Get news and archival releases from Pop Sickle, Alcohol Funnycar, 7 Year Bitch, the Melvins, and the Gits. ✓**INTER-NET**→*url* http:// www.w2.com/ cz.html

Capricorn Download Area Sound and video clips of songs by artists on Capricorn Records, including Lynyrd Skynyrd's "Down South Jukin'" and Vigilantes Of Love's "Last To Know." ✓**COMPUSERVE**→ *go* capriview

Carving Knife Records A colorful Website devoted to the artists signed to this Seattle independent, including Monster Truck Driver, Cat Food, Nothing, Well Hung Over, Monroe's Fur, The Doberman, and Three Blind Mice. ✓**INTER-NET**→*url* http:// www. csos.orst.edu/~flux/ckr.html

Catasonic A California-based independent that releases the records of bands like WebaWorld, Matt Heckert and his Mechanical Sound Orchestra, and Gynomite. ✓**INTERNET**→*url* http://under ground.net/Weba/catasonic.html

Caulfield Records This Nebraska label specializes in American punk and junk, from Sideshow to Christie Front Drive to Giant

Chair. ✓**INTERNET**→*url* http://www. acton.com/bernie/

Changing Tones Records Devoted to "presenting special musical projects embracing all musical styles," this eclectic label has released a solo album by singer/ songwriter Tomas Jones, a funk-flavored outing by New York rocker Simon Walsh, and a solo jazz piano version of the songs of Jimi Hendrix arranged and recorded by Reed Robins. ✓**INTERNET**→*url* http://www.inch.com/~macmusic/ chngtone.html

Chapter Music Chapter releases records by independent bands in Perth, Australia, including Molasses, O!, Squadcar 95, Sulk, and Big Interesting Rifle. ✓**INTER-NET**→*url* http://multiline.com.au/~ langham/chapter/

Chesky Records Jazz, jazz vocals, and modern classical. ✓**INTER-NET**→*url* http://www.chesky.com/ musi

Choke Indie rock bands, including Milkmine, Morsel, Craw, and the Harry Patt Band. The Website contains a catalog, ordering info, band bios, and lyrics. ✓**IN-TERNET**→ *url* http://kzsu.stan ford.edu/uwi/sounds/choke/up date.html

Clean One of the labels associated with Minneapolis's Twin/Tone, Clean releases records by Trip Shakespeare, Polara, the Hang Ups, the Carpetbaggers, and 27 Various. ✓**INTERNET**→*url* http:// www.tt.net/clean/

Cleopatra A Los Angeles label with an eclectic roster of artists that spans punk, ambient, electronic, and more. ✓ **INTERNET**→*url* http://www.hallucinet.com/cleopatra

Cold Meat Industry Dark ambient music from Sweden. ✓ **INTERNET**→*url* http://www.etek.chalmers.se/~e2jovi3/cmi/cmi.html

Compass Records The marquee name here is former Richard Thompson sideman and Any Trouble alumnus Clive Gregson, but Compass has other artists in its stable, including Leslie Tucker, Kate Campbell, and Kalia Flexer and Third Ear. ✓ **INTERNET**→*url* http://www.infi.net/~comprec/index.html

Creation Records Releases from Yma Sumac, Swervedriver, and Ruby, among others. ✓ **INTERNET**→*url* http://www.elmail.co.uk/music/creation/

Curb Records Releases from new and old country stars, including Boy Howdy, Merle Haggard, Hal Ketchum, Tim McGraw, Sawyer Brown, Lyle Lovett, Wynonna, Delbert McClinton, and Ronnie McDowell. ✓ **INTERNET**→*url* http://www.curb.com

Curve of the Earth Press releases, album information, and interactive screen savers for Powerman 5000, Tornado Room, Girl, Roadsaw, and Swank. ✓ **INTERNET**→*url* http://www.mw3.com/curve/cprod.htm

D-Tox The home of Bicycle Face, Drunken Boat, Eugene Chadbourne, Toxic Popsickle, Very Pleasant Neighbor, Well Nigh Forgotten, and more. ✓ **INTERNET**→*url* http://www.binary9.com/~d-tox

Daemon Records Owned by Indigo Girl Amy Ray, this label re-

Creation Records—from http://www.elmail.co.uk/music/creation/

leases records by Atlanta bands, and also includes information on the Indigo Girls' musical vehicle, *Jesus Christ Superstar: A Resurrection.* ✓ **INTERNET**→*url* http://monsterbit.com/daemon/daemon.html

Datolite Records What is Datolite? "Adult Contemporary Acoustic Pop Rock World Music." This label's artists include Lindsay Tomasic. ✓ **INTERNET**→*url* http://www.primenet.com/~dlite/

Decoder Ring Records Split singles, bands named Deep Root, Greensect, and Common Thread... Could this Jacksonville, FL, label be any more independent? ✓ **INTERNET**→*url* http://jax.jaxnet. com/~theidiot/decoder.html

Derailed A roots-rock label that allows online ordering of products, some of which are redistributed versions of records made for other labels. Artists include Dave Alvin,

Blue Nile, the Bad Livers, the Continental Drifters, Alejandro Escovedo, the Jayhawks, Freedy Johnston, Lucinda Williams, and the Charlie Sexton Sextet. ✓ **INTERNET**→*url* http://www.primenet.com/~rthomas/

DMP Records DMP's eclectic roster includes the adult contemporary duo Charles & Friedman, contemporary jazz stars Flim & the BB's, and more. ✓ **INTERNET**→*url* http://www.w2.com/docs2/d/dmp.html

Don't Records Biographies, images, and press releases for a number of pop artists, including Blue in the Face, the Wooldridge Brothers, the Yell Leaders, and Pet Engine. ✓ **INTERNET**→*url* http://www.execpc.com/~dont/

Dr. Strange Records Punk releases from Schleprock, Man Dingo, and the Bollweevils. ✓ **INTERNET**→*url* http://www.cyberg8t.com/drstrange/

E-lan Records A Stanford-based funk and new soul label whose artists include Shaka-Ra, Mister Tone, and the Elders. ✓**INTERNET**→ *url* http://www.-leland.stanford.edu/~olu/

East Side Digital Music Alternative rock artists, including Go to Blazes, Blood Oranges, Bottle Rockets, The Schramms, and the father-son duo Spanic Boys. ✓**INTERNET**→*url* http://www.w2.com/esd.html

Echo Lake Records Who plays out at Echo Lake? Acoustic artists like Ray Chesna, Andy Offutt Irwin, and more. How do they play? Softly and tastefully. ✓**INTERNET**→ *url* http://www.mindspring.com/~echolake

ECM Records ECM has a prestigious roster of avant-garde, jazz, and modern classical artists, including Chick Corea, Keith Jarrett, Carla Bley, Pat Metheny, Meredith Monk, and Steve Tibbetts. ✓**INTERNET**→*url* http://www.ecmrecords.com/

Eggbert Records Modern rock artists, including Melody Fair, Mumps, the Bent Back Tulips, and Action Figures. ✓**INTERNET**→*url* http://www.eggbert.com/home/eggbert/eggbert.html

Elektra Records As major labels go, Elektra is pretty darned major, with a roster that includes AC/DC, Björk, They Might Be Giants, Ween, and dozens more mainstream and alternative artists. The site includes pages for individual artists, as well as information about the label's marketing, publicity, and A&R departments. And unsigned bands can take heart from this encouraging message posted by an A&R intern: "Hi, my name is Ben and I work in the Elektra A&R (Artists & Repertoire, not Angst & Rejection) department. We're the department that discovers new artists, oversees the recording of their albums, helps select singles, and generally helps to guide the creative aspects of their careers. It's my job to find artists across the country that have developed a strong buzz at a local and regional level. Once I hear of a happening band, I bring the music to the rest of the folks in A&R to let them listen and decide whether it's something we want to pursue further. Please don't send us any unsolicited tapes! We just don't have the time to listen to everything. If you have a band that's really good, we'll catch up to you. Thanks." ✓**INTERNET**→*url* http://www.elektra.com/

EMI Records The band made famous by the Sex Pistols' vitriol is now online, with pages for Queensrÿche, Milla, Jethro Tull, Jesus Jones, Roxette, and Butt Trumpet. ✓**INTERNET**→*url* http://www.rockonline.com/emi/

Enemy Records Cutting-edge instrumental music, including Elliott Sharp (with and without Carbon), Gary Lucas, House of Freaks, Jean-Paul Bourelly, Kelvynator, Last Exit, Liquid Hips, and the Sonny Sharrock Band. ✓**INTERNET**→*url* http://www.w2.com/enemy.html

Ex-Voto Records Originally founded to promote the work of The Holy Body Tattoo Society, Ex-Voto is now expanding into records, and the label is looking for artists. ✓**INTERNET**→*url* http://www.vkool.com/exvoto/index.html

Extreme Music Extreme searches out the newest in new, the cutting edge of the avant-garde, and then uploads sound samples and artist bios. From Manhattan composer Elliott Sharp to the pan-European funk band Mo Boma, the acts are continually challenging. ✓**INTERNET**→*url* http://www.xtr.com/extreme/

Factory Records (ml) Discussion of bands from the defunct U.K. label, including Durutti Column, Happy Mondays, Joy Division, Section 25, Quando Quango, and more. ✓**INTERNET**→*email* factory-request@niagara.edu 🖎 *Write a request*

Fish of Death Records What is the Fish of Death? It's an independent record label that includes the noise-rock outfit Tiny Buddy and the pop band Brown Betty. ✓**INTERNET**→*url* http://www.cityscape.co.uk/users/ad69/fod/fodindex.html

Flydaddy Records A pop label that's also a sub-label of SubPop, Seattle's world-famous independent. Confusing, huh? ✓**INTERNET**→*url* http://www.subpop.com/flydaddy/flydaddy.htm

Fresh Fruit A promotional page for Romanovsky and Phillips's *Brave Boys*, a gay-themed LP that includes songs like "Love Is All It Takes (To Make A Family)," "No False Hope," and "What Kind of Self Respecting Faggot/Politically

Correct Lesbian Am I?" ✓**INTERNET** →*url* http://www.gayweb.com/ 404/frshft.html

Funnel Cakes and Guidance Office Records Alternative rock, noise rock, and punk rock, including Wendy and her MCs and the collage experts Giant Testosterone Explosion. ✓**INTERNET**→*url* http:// poe.acc.virginia.edu/~rae4a/ wendy/fcgo.html

Furnace Records With a roster of hardcore and industrial

bands that includes Hellscape, Industrial Heads, Abstinence, ATD Convention, Operation Mindwipe, and Pounce International, Furnace resolves "to drag the present, screaming and kicking, into the future." ✓**INTERNET**→*url* http:// www.cybercom.com/~bsamedi/ furnace.html

Galivant Media Galivant records artists in a variety of cutting-edge genres, including cyberpunk, avant-jazz, New Age, trance, dance, and industrial. As the site explains, "as the word 'Galivant' implies, many Galivant artists are multidisciplinary multimedia artists interested in video, film, painting, sculptures, photography, and the like." ✓**INTERNET**→ *url* http://www.galivant.com/~ tjustman/galivant.htm

Geffen/DGC Records Though Geffen arrived on the Web later than most other majors, the label has made up for lost time, with a nice Website that emphasizes recent releases (including Slash's Snakepit and Elastica), a full artist roster (including Joni Mitchell and Hole), and even links to other music sites. ✓**INTERNET**→*url* http:// geffen.com

Generator "Musclemen, Musclecars, Musclecars, Muscleheads, and most importantly Musclebands." What Musclebands? Polara (also handled by Clean Records), Balloon Guy, Smattering, Mountain Singers, and Ash. ✓**INTERNET**→*url* http:// www.tt.net/ generator/

Global Music Outlet Combining elements of a fanzine, a radio station, and a music store for world music, this site lavishes its attention on artists such as Robert Berry, Johnny Clegg, and Michelle Chappel. ✓**INTERNET**→*url* http:// www.iuma.com/GMO

Globe Records In the Globe Records Sound and Vision Cyberlounge, bands like The Christmas Jug Band, Rhythmtown-Jive, Transistor Rodeo, and even classic San Francisco bands like Dan Hicks (and his Hot Licks), Commander Cody (and His Lost Planet Airmen), the Moonlighters, the Johnny Nocturne Band, and Kathy N. Right get their due. ✓**INTERNET**→*url* http://microweb.com/ globe/

Go! Discs Top British label whose roster includes Paul Weller, The Beautiful South, Trash Can Sinatras, Portishead, and more. ✓**INTERNET**→*url* http://www.godiscs.co. uk/godiscs

Go Kart Records Berserk, Buttsteak, and Sexpod. Doesn't sound like a law firm, does it? The Go Kart artist roster showcases the newest in alternative rock. ✓**INTERNET**→*url* http://www.w2.com/ gokart.html

Goldenrod Records A full roster of alternative bands, including Swivelneck, 4, Nothing Rhymes with Orange, Overwhelming Colorfast, Red Aunts, and Faction. ✓**INTERNET**→*url* http://www. tumyeto.com/tydu/music/labels/ goldenrod/goldenrod.htm

Grand Royal Home of the Beastie Boys, as well as affiliated artists like Lucious Jackson, the Grand Royal Website is also a lesson in how to create a beautiful and functional Web presence. Check your head before you enter—you'll be swept away. ✓**INTERNET**→*url* http://www.nando.net/ music/gm/GrandRoyal

Gravity Records A mainstay of the California punk scene, Gravity supports hardcore bands like Heroin, Second-Story Window, and The Universal Order of Armageddon. ✓**INTERNET**→*url* http:// www.tumyeto.com/tydu/music/ labels/gravity/gravity.htm

Greensleeves Records No, it's not Christmas for this Middlesex record label. Catering to the reggae music industry, Greensleeves currently supports artists like Beenie Man and Bounty Killer, as well as older artists like The Meditations and Wailing Souls. ✓**INTERNET**→*url* http://www.easynet. co.uk/goodvibe/greens.htm

Griffin Music If you've heard of Hawkwind—the U.K.'s quintessential art-rock band—then you're no stranger to the Griffin label. Griffin specializes in hard-to-find rock and roll titles and retro psychedelic bands. ✓ **INTERNET**→*url* http:// www.icom.ca/cgpinc/grif-main.htm

Gut Reaction A British site with info on Right Said Fred, Aswad, and Medicine Hat. ✓ **INTERNET**→*url* http://www.gutreaction.co.uk/gutreact/sounds.html

Halt, Dwarf! What's available from this site? A .GIF of a dwarf impersonating a crossing guard. Bands? Music? Who cares! Didn't you hear? It's a dwarf impersonating a crossing guard! ✓ **INTERNET**→ *url* http://www-leland.stanford.edu/~chabinml/hd/

Harbor Records A happy, smiling gaggle of musicians who's imaginations may or may not be stunted by their perpetual good moods, angelic harmonies, and medication/meditation philosophies. Artists include Gerry Smida, Mary Ann Cota, and William Strickland. ✓ **INTERNET**→*url* http://www.iuma.com/Harbor/

H e y d a y Records San Francisco's premier independent label, with alternative artists such as Barbara Manning, Chris Von Sneidern, Jerry Shelfer, Pat Thomas, and Buck Naked and the Bare Bottom Boys. ("Buck Naked took 'the censorship of Elvis's lower half' and mixed it with his outrageous sense of entertainment to produce a powerful hybrid sound—pornographic lyrics with a rockabilly beat. Buck called it Pornobilly. Buck Naked stood as a true character of rock 'n' roll, wearing no

more than a strategically placed toilet plunger and a pair of pink cowboy boots.") ✓ **INTERNET**→*url* http://www.iuma.com/ heyday

Hibiscus Records This page, in French with no translation, offers the best of Carribean music, featuring bands such as Les Vikings de la Guadeloupe, Kassav and Eugène Mona. Get background on the label, sound clips, images, catalogues, videos, and more. *Trés chaud*! ✓ **INTERNET**→*url* http://www.ina.fr/Music/Labels/Hibiscus/

Higher Octave Music This prestigious label offers one of the largest collections of conemporary instrumental, New Age, and world music from such artists as Craig Chaquico, Prabodhi, and the Soto Koto Band. The site provides artist bios, catalog numbers, and even ordering information. ✓ **INTERNET**→ *url* http://smartworld.com/hioctave/hioct.html

Hiljaiset Levyt An independent guitar rock label from Finland that records bands like Eino-Mies, Roi Soi, Garbagemen, Nightingales, Lowdown Shakin' Chills, Room 100, Wolfmen, and Jalla Jalla. ✓ **INTERNET**→ *url* http://www.sjoki.uta.fi/~latvis/levyyht/hiljais.html *Info:* ✓ **INTERNET**→ ju@prodax.fi ✍ *Write a request*

I Wanna Records You wanna be the coolest kid on your block? Get underground with this Ohio indie label, and find out more about

bands like The Obvious, Cage, and the Highwaymen. ✓ **INTERNET** →*url* http://www.mcs.com/~bliss/IWanna.html

Inspired Music An online label devoted to "interactive music"—mostly soft jazz and New Age. ✓ **INTERNET**→*url* http://www.cts.com/~inspired/musicpg.html

Ionic Entertainment This indie label is small in size but large in funk, with bands like Treble Hum, Mind Groove and Tongue-n-Groove. ✓ **INTERNET**→*url* http://www.iuma.com/Ionic/

Isomorphic Records It looks like other labels, sounds like other labels, even tastes like other labels. Actually, it's as far from isomorphic as they get, producing Dadaesque noize 'n' words releases from groups like Photophobia and GeroGeriGeGeGe. Hey, maybe the label name is ironic! Make friends and influence people at cocktail parties by tossing off the lyrics to "collabodestructivists." Skeptical? Don't be. It works every time. ✓ **INTERNET**→*url* http://weber.u.washington.edu/~isomorph/index.html

Justice Records This socially conscious label "does not begin to make money until the performer does." The label manages a plethora of artists in all genres, from the unknown (Hellhole) to the infamous (Willie Nelson) to the prestigeous (the London Philharmonic). And tree huggers can rejoice; all Justice products are packaged with recycled paper. ✓ **INTERNET**→ *url* http://www.JusticeRecords.com/default.htm

K Records Started in the early 80's by Calvin Johnson of Beat Happening, this Olympia, Washington label has grown into a northwestern indie rock institution boasting such artists as Beck, Lois, Some Velvet Sidewalk, Mecca Normal, and Calvin's new band, the Halo Benders. ✓INTERNET→*url* http://www.wln.com/~kpunk/

LandPhil Records What's in the LandPhil? The dissonant punk of Laquer, the power-pop of Matchbook Shannon, and the comedic pop-punk of Pope Mahone. ✓INTERNET→*url* http://www. novia.net/~landphil/

Last Unicorn This label is the Future of Music. No, really, it says so right on the Website. Last Unicorn wants to help musicians worldwide to sell themselves by giving them Internet exposure, but so far their manifesto is longer than their band roster—the directory contains a number of diverse genre headers, but only a handful of actual artists. Oh, well. If the future was now, what would we have to look forward to? ✓INTERNET→*url* http://www.VirtualAd. com/browse/va/LastUnicorn/

Lipstick & Jazzline A German label layin' out jazz and acid jazz. ✓INTERNET→*url* http://www. berensp.com/amm/

Little Dog Records Little Dog barks at emerging singer-songwriters, including Pete Anderson and Anthony Crawford. ✓INTERNET→*url* http://www.iuma.com/Little_Dog/

Long Play Records Underground pop at its very best—Brotherhood of Lizards, The Cleaners from Venus, and other bands that spent the first six months of their career coming up

with wacky, lovable names for themselves. ✓INTERNET→*url* http://monsterbit.com/longplay/lp.html

Lotuspool Records Cooler than you can ever hope to be, Lotuspool is an underground label representing Bully Pulpit, Zoom, Panel Doctor, and a handful of other strange people. Get the catalog and sound samples from their slick site. ✓INTERNET→*url* http://www.iuma.com/Lotuspool/

Lunch Records Formerly Breakfast Records, this Boston-based independent label was forced to change its name as a result of a conflict with another label. Get information on a variety of New England bands, including Orbit, Institute of Technology, sirensong, and Damn You Peter Pan. ✓INTERNET→*url* http://www.lunch.com:2500/

Mammoth Records Internet Center Mammoth isn't an industry giant, name notwithstanding, but the Carolina label has been the home to such artists as the Blake Babies, the Charlie Hunter Trio, Frente!, Joe Henry, Juliana Hatfield, Machines of Loving Grace, and Victoria Williams. Listen to sound samples, view album covers, and even order the records you think you might like. ✓INTERNET→*url* http://www.mammoth.com/

Manifest Records A Seattle-based Ebm/Industrial Label. ✓INTERNET→*url* http://www.pacifier.com/~coldwave

Marathon Records This group of indie bands say they got together because they "figured there was

strength in numbers..." Support their effort to stand up to the industry bullies who kicked sand in their face and stole their dates, and sample the prog-rock of Animator and the power-pop of The Electric Revival, among others. ✓INTERNET→*url* http://www.netads.com/netads/arts/music/marathon/

MCA Records The home to AMP, MCA's excellent Web e-zine, which reviews music and movies and publishes tour dates for MCA bands ✓INTERNET→*url* http://www.mca.com/mca_records

Megaforce Records All the bands you love and your mama can't stand. In the 1980s Megaforce carried Anthrax and Metallica. Now they're shoving Al Jourgenson's products down your throat—that's Ministry and the Revolting Cocks, plus S.O.D., Sweaty Nipples, Nudeswirl, and Bif Naked. ✓INTERNET→*url* http://www.iuma.com/Megaforce/

MNW Records Group The best of Swedish pop, rock, hardcore, and Nordic world beat. Did you know that they serve McSalmon sandwiches in Scandanavian McDonalds? Explains a lot, doesn't it? ✓INTERNET→*url* http://www.iuma.com/MNW/

Monkeyland Records Underground compilations are this label's specialty, and they serve 'em up pipin' hot and tasty. ✓INTERNET→*url* http://www.primenet.com/~tripmon/

Moonshine Music An L.A. label specializing in dance music. ✓INTERNET→*url* http://underground.net/Moonshine/moon.html

Moosestone Records Moosestone releases compilations and other albums in death metal and techno. Get band bios and sound clips for Fuzz Factor, Sharon Burroughs, and others. ✓ **INTERNET**→*url* http://pasture.ecn.purdue.edu/~stevensb/moose.html

Motown Records The home to hundreds of hours of classic soul records, Motown is considerably less impressive as an on-line entity, with a sparse Website that is composed mostly of rudimentary bios of artists. Mourn the passage of Marvin Gaye, the brittling of Smokey Robinson, and the self-indulgence of Stevie Wonder here. ✓ **INTERNET**→*url* http://www.musicbase.co.uk/music/motown

N-Soul Records House, techno, and soul and all their little baby sub-genres can be found here. Get links to the bios and discographies of LimitX, Gospel Housing Authority, Ambient Theology, and more. ✓ **INTERNET**→*url* http://198.4.164.52/N-Soul/

NESAK Records They ride forth, keeping the peace and rounding up compilations of musical misfits "from techno to jazz to the digeridoos of Australia." We can all sleep a little easier, knowing they're out there. ✓ **INTERNET**→*url* http://www.nesak.com/kado/

Netropolis Records "New World Artists" indeed. Netropolis Records wants you to embrace the multimedia experience in all its glory, and sees the Internet as the next plateau in audience relations. The first to be signed to the label were the "alternative" bands Queve, Eccentrics, and Double Density. The site is snazzy, with great graphics and links to bios and sound clips. One warning: epileptics should avoid the Queve

link at all costs. ✓ **INTERNET**→*url* http://www.rust.net/~instacom/NetropolisRecords.html

Nettwerk Records A Canadian independent label that lists Sarah McLachlan among its artists. ✓ **INTERNET**→*url* http://www.wimsey.com/nettwerk *Info:* ✓ **INTERNET**

email→nettlist-request@nettwerk.wimsey.com ✍ *Write a request*

Nitwit Records An alternative indie with a sizable roster. The bands range from pop-punk to strait rock, and include Helva, Magenta Lip Bomb, R-gie-ooh, and others. The site is more eye-candy than meat, however—material on the bands is usually limited to a sound clip and a pic; bios are sparse and the Live Shows and Merchandise links are often empty. ✓ **INTERNET**→*url* http://soundwave.com/bands/nitwit/nitwit.html

Noteworthy Records This jazz label wishes for an industry where the artist is treated like a person, not a product. Some of the beneficiaries of all those management consultant fees and company retreats are Boy Kantindic, Michael Paulo, and Pauline Wilson; link to bios, images, and sound clips for these artists. ✓ **INTERNET**→*url* http://www.w2.com/docs2/n/noteworthy.html

Oh Boy Records John Prine headlines this label's roster, with The Bisquits, Steve Goodman, Mountain Stage, Arlen Roth, and Heather Eastman playing supporting roles. ✓ **INTERNET**→*url* http://www.nashville.net/ohboy/ohboy.html

Parlophone Decorated with a fruit motif, this is an excellent newsletter for the European EMI imprint, with information on artists such as Radiohead, Everclear, the Beastie Boys, and Heart. ✓ **INTERNET**→*url* http://www.elmail.co.uk/music/parlophone/

Pear Kot This indie-alternative label owns the souls of Daven Port, Hurl, Blunderbuss and the impressive Karl Hendricks Trio, who have released so many albums you couldn't count them on your toes. At Pear Kot, you can link to bios, discographies, images, sound clips, and more. ✓ **INTERNET**→*url* http://www.lm.com/~panzan/peaskor.html

Piece of Mind Links to bios, sound clips, images, and catalogs from the likes of Ethyl Meatplow, Robbie D., Jackass, and Dick Tit (yes, Dick Tit). They also produced a rollicking Rock for Choice compilation, the proceeds from which went to various women's rights organizations. ✓ **INTERNET**→*url* http://www.bouquet.com/pom/

Poor Person Production Album info, sound clips, artwork, band lineups, and other resources for Earcandy, Mynd Muzic, T-H-C Roller, and Dave. ✓ **INTERNET**→*url* http://www.zynet.co.uk/farmer/poor/

Pop Narcotic Records Links to bios and sound clips for The Dambuilders, Bush League All-Stars, Sugar, and Versus, as well as a label history and instructions on how to order a 30-page snail-mail catalog. ✓**INTERNET**→*url* http://www.webcom.com/~popnarc/

Purple Potato Productions You want your Mahler and Mozart transmogrified into synthe-sampler joints? You want garage grunge ska surf punk band Ho-Ho-Homocide to beat the hell out of Perry Como this Chirstmas? You want neo-new wave and no questions asked? Fry yourself up a Purple Potato, and then dream of Idaho doused in red, then blue, then red, then blue. ✓**INTERNET**→*url* http://www.crl.com/~mcdaniel/ppp/

Q Division Records Sound clips and images for Brian Steves, Poundcake, The Gravel Pit, and Expanding Man. ✓**INTERNET**→*url* http://www.shore.net/~qdiv/qrec.htm

Quagmire Quagmire believes in Free Art, and they put no one's money where their mouth is. They offer you, and anyone else, an entire, full-length pop album, online, free. What album? A Western Front's LP *Full Blown Dave*. But forget about that. It doesn't even matter. Did you hear the offer? It's free! ✓**INTERNET**→*url* http://www.iuma.com/Quagmire/

Queenie Records Riot in the street grrrls, this is the label for you. Racecar, Kickstand, Cobalt, Coloring Book, and Sexpod offer up punk and pop, making no apologies and taking no prisoners. Women are on both sides of the vinyl in this gynopunk organization, which is dedicated to Access and Empowerment. ✓**INTERNET**→ *url* http://www.shore.net/nonstop/queenie.html

Radical House Everything you could possibly want to know about the label and the prog-rock they run on. Amy X Neuburg? Here. Big Umbrella? Also here, along with Dennis Phelps, Garden Variety, Splatter Trio, and Wonderboy. The site includes a sound and graphic archive, interviews, album info, label history, submission forms, and more. ✓**INTERNET**→*url* ftp://ftp.netcom.com/pub/cs/cstan/radcat.html

RAS DVA Records Atlanta's acoustic indies come together on this Website, which offers links to discographies, song lyrics, promotional photos, album info, and sound clips for such artists as Queenie Mullinix, Vicky Pratt Keating, Evan & Jaron and CREe. ✓**INTERNET**→*url* http://www.teleport.com/~arcana/ras_dva.html

Rashid Sales Co. A prestegious Arabic label that brings Middle Eastern artists to the West. The band roster furnishes band bios, sound clips, and discographies for hit-makers like Fairouz, Om Kalsoum, and Regheb Alameh. ✓**INTERNET**→*url* http://virtumall.com/Rashid/home.html

Ray's Music Sound clips, album info and bios for Wild Ride, I Travel, C.O.D., Anthony, and My Brother Jake. ✓**INTERNET**→*url* http://www.raysmusic.nl/

RCA Victor Ever since the little dog started doing home theater commercials with Patrick Stewart, sitting next to the Victrola seems like a punishment ("Bad dog! It's inferior technology for you!"). And to make matters worse, all he's got to listen to at this site are cheesy greatest-hits albums like the *Beginners Guide to Classical Music*, the *Idiot's Guide to Classical Music*, and *What is Jazz?* (well, we're not exactly sure, but we're pretty certain it's not limited to whatever back-catalog pulldowns are being rushed out by RCA). Ambitious dogs will dig until they find their buried bones—which in this case are compilation albums featuring Irish music performed by big stars like Willie Nelson, Elvis Costello, and Jackson Browne. ✓**INTERNET**→*url* http://www.rcavictor.com/

Reality Society Records Noize 'n' word sound clips and bios from Hood, Bludgeon Album, Vena Cava and Dead City Radio. ✓**INTERNET**→*url* http://www.iuma.com/Reality_Society/

Red Phraug Modern Medium Graphics and sound clips for bands like Amphibious Maximus and Rythmic Ear Noise. ✓**INTERNET**→*url* http://www.teleport.com/~noise/

Reprise Records A Warner imprint, Reprise is one of the best labels around, with a roster that includes Green Day, Chris Isaak,

Neil Young, Mudhoney, Throwing Muses, Alanis Morissette, Jane Siberry, Belly, Faith No More and Morrisey. The site provides links to sound and video clips, tour info, images, and just about everything else you'd expect from a major. ✓**INTERNET**→*url* http://www. RepriseRec.com/

Restless Records Sounds, images, publicity, videos, and more for artists like Slim Dunlap, Gem, Lori Carson, and Jack Logan and the Liquor Cabinets. ✓**INTERNET**→*url* http://www. numenet.com/sc/ssp/

Revelation Records The fans of these alternative and punk indies, according to the label's own sources, are 14- and 15-year-old straight-edgers. Don't drink, don't smoke, don't have premarital sex...well, what do you do, then? This label lets them release all that tension by moshing to Engine Kid, Gorilla Biscuits, Supertouch, and Orange 9mm, just to name a few. ✓**INTERNET**→*url* http://www. w2.com/revelation.html

Rhino Records An umbrella site for dozens of independent labels, including Bad Habits, Big Round, Bogus, Black Boot. Halcyon, Rage, Propulsion, Silent, Sugo, and Tooth & Nail. ✓**INTERNET**→*url* http://cybertimes.com/Rhino/ Welcome.html

RooArt Records This Finnish label provides links to sound clips and bios for their world music artists, including Afterimage, The Boots, Dave Lindholm, and Plum. ✓**INTERNET**→*url* http://www.rooart. com.au/rooart/

Rpobi Droli Records Barkers of electronic, avant-garde and world music, Rpobi Droli Records gives sound clips, bios, and images for a large collection of artists such as Carl Stone, Mikel Rouse, and Enzo Favata. ✓**INTERNET**→*url* http://www.inrete.it/musi ca/robidroli.html

Rykoverse Everything old is new again here; Ryko has made its make on reissues of great moments in rock history—David Bowie, Elvis Costello, Jimi Hendrix, Frank Zappa, and other legends living and otherwise. But as Rykodisc is quick to point out, they have artists actually working for them in real time, including Sugar, the Roches, Morphine, and Boosty Collins, as well as a host of world music, jazz, and hip-hop acts. This excellent Website includes sound clips, FAQ, catalogs, tour information, and more. ✓**INTERNET**→*url* http://www. shore.net/ rykodisc/

Schoolkids Records Label Links to sound clips and bios from Big Dave and the Ultrasonics, Lunar Octet, and the Tripoli Steel Band. Feel free to eat the paste—it's non-toxic. ✓**INTERNET**→*url* http://www.schoolkids.com/ skr/label/index.html

Septagon Records Yet another alternative indie promoting generosity and honesty, artistic control, open submission policies,

love, peace, and harmony. What's wrong with these people? Record execs should be chompin' on cigars and cheating promising artists. Oh, well. Things aren't like they used to be. Get sound clips, images, and band bios for The Haze, Dark Half, and Audio Savant. ✓**INTERNET**→*url* http://www.net runner.net/~septagon/Records/

Sesha Pres Records Links to bios, sound clips, images, and merchandise for 187 Calm, Drug, Granite Path, River Things, and Broom Cruisers. ✓**INTERNET**→*url* http://www.crl.com/www/users/ rg/rgeimer/seshaHome.html

Shining Star Productions This label produces New Age music and chants from the Tibetan Sacred Temple and Nadar Shakti. ✓**INTERNET**→*url* http://www. numenet.com/sc/ssp/

Silver Girl Records French pop sensation The Drift, plus more indigenous bands like New York rockers Gapeseed and Ruby Falls. Keep sailing on, Silver Girl. ✓**INTERNET**→*url* http://www. tumyeto.com/ tydu/ music/labels/silver/ silver.htm

Sin-Drome Records Wanna feel like a big shot music exec? Enter the screening room of Sin-Drome records for QuickTime clips of Bobby Caldwell, Marc Jordan, and 'Nita Whitaker. Everybody's mooning about love here; maybe you can offer some unsolicited advice in the Mailbox provided. ✓**INTERNET**→*url* http:// kspace.com/ KM/music.sys/Sin-Drome/pages/home.html

Slumberland Records A pop-punk label whose roster includes Henry's Dress, The Ropers, and Belreve. ✓**INTERNET**→*url* http://www.denizen.com/trout/slumberland/

Smithsonian Records The mother of museums records music from all genres worthy of the American flag. Choose from selections in Americana, Children's Music, Classical, Jazz, Old Time Radio, Popular or World divisions, place your order online, and wait for the good stuff to come in. And don't forget—Smithsonian is also the home of Folkways, one of the premier roots and blues albums in the world. ✓**INTERNET**→*url* http://www.si.sgi.com/products/shopmall/records/start.htm

SOB Entertainment What's SOB? Son of Beserkley, a Berkeley-based independent label that releases records by Hobo, Linda Brady, Diamond Head, Repulsa, Greg Kihn, Jonathan Richman and the Modern Lovers, and more. ✓**INTERNET**→ *url* http://www.iuma.com/SOB

Sony Music The giant entertainment company's music division furnishes information for hundreds of artists in rock, pop, folk, jazz, and classical. From Michael Jackson to Sophie B. Hawkins, from Aerosmith to the Allman Brothers Band, this is one of the best places to start browsing for pop music information. Actually, this isn't a recommendation; it's a mandate—Sony is so powerful that if you don't patronize their Website you're likely to disappear in the middle of the night. You are not alone. ✓**INTERNET**→*url* http://www.music.sony.com/Music/MusicIndex.html

Spanish Fly Spanish Fly signs bands with names like Dumpster Juice, Smut, Milk, Queer, Sleep Capsule, Likehell, and Saucer. Cheery, huh? ✓**INTERNET**→ *url* http://www.tt.net/spanishfly/

Squealer Music This Virginia indie rock label thinks locally and acts, well, nationally, with releases by bands like Refrigerator, Geezer Lake, June, and Milk Badger. ✓**INTERNET**→*url* http://www.mal.com/~squealer/

Stubborn Records A commercial page that celebrates Stubborn's All-Star release, featuring four ska bands—The Scofflaws, Skinnerbox NYC, The Insteps, and The Slackers. ✓**INTERNET**→*url* http://www.phantom.com/~giant/hype2/stubborn/stubborn.html

Sub Pop The Nirvanariffic Seattle independent wasn't always so huge, but they always had the good taste to deal with bands like Sebadoh, Six Finger Satellite, Velocity Girl, the Spinanes, and the Friends of Dean Martinez. Get all the latest dope on the hottest indie bands here, along with a lavish electronic 'zine. And don't forget to search for the rare wompus. ✓**INTERNET**→*url* http://www.subpop.com

Tanty Records Finally—a record label for fusion enthusiasts only! This page features a discography for one of their leading bands, The Dub Funk Association, whose influences range from Joe Gibbs to Channel One. ✓**INTERNET**→*url* http://www.easynet.co.uk/goodvibe/tanty.htm

Thunderbird Records The featured artist this month is the long admired Martin Simpson, who has two fantastic fingerstyle guitar albums to his name. From this page you can access Thunderbird's catalog and order official fan stuff like books, instructional videos, and t-shirts. Hey, wouldn't a Tiran Porter (Doobie Brothers) sweatshirt be cool? ✓**INTERNET**→*url* http://www.iuma.com/Thunderbird/

Triloka Records The "tri" stands for three and the "loka" for extra cool. This label is divided into the Living Proof Series, which showcases jazz musicians like the fabulously handsome Chet Baker; the Inheritance Series, which features new artists like Jeff Beal; and Worldy Music, which features a fusion of primitive sounds and world music ethnology. Three's not a crowd here. ✓**INTERNET**→*url* http://www.w2.com/triloka.html

Tunnel Under A label dedicated to the underdog, the little guy, the band that gets beaten silly by corporate bigwigs, Tunnel stands behind bands like Yzark, R.S.D., and Falling Angels. ✓ INTERNET→*url* http://membrane.com/tuntitle.html

Twin/Tone Records TT Net is a gigantic blanket organization for labels like Restless, Twin/Tone, Clean and On-U-Sound. From this site you can reach at least one of your favorite alternative bands, or some old favorites like the Cramps, L7, Soul Asylum, or Zuzu's Petals. ✓INTERNET→*url* http://www.twintone.com/

Underground Resistance This site offers a galaxy of delights for those who are fans of groups like Sonic, Gyroscopic, Nocturbulous Behavior and, of course, The Prince of Techno (no symbols for him!). ✓INTERNET→*url* http://www.cs.vu.nl/~epdouden/ur/

Unity Unity is in the house! And it's still a label for Club music featuring artists like Ellyn Harris and Plush. ✓INTERNET→*url* http://www.webb.com/unity.html

Uprising Records Dog-Swing, The Glenrustles, Resist—just a handful of college bands from the college band capital, Ann Arbor,

Michigan. Check out new releases and sound clips here. ✓INTERNET→*url* http://www.cen.uiuc.edu/~khoury/uprising.html

V.S.O.P. Records Very Special Old Phonography, a label that releases classic jazz and vocal 78s by artists like the Herbie Harper Quintet. ✓INTERNET→*url* http://www.jazznet.com/~lmcohen/vsopidex.html

Victrola Records The Virginia label proudly produces the bands Ugly, Lugnut, and Inertia. Maybe it costs more to have a band name with two words. Go figure. ✓INTERNET→*url* http://dgs.dgsys.com/~dave/vicrecs.html

Virgin Records Smashing Pumpkins, Lenny Kravitz, and Boy George hold court over this branch of the Virgin megalopolis. The page also links to other wings of the Virgin leisure mansion, in-

cluding Virgin Airways. ✓INTERNET→*url* http://www.vmg.co.uk/

Vox Pop An independent Italian label with an upcoming release for the Net by Le Forbici Di Manitu (Manitu's Scissors), the musicians responsible for the scores of the "non movies" by the "non movie" director Luther Blisset. An album in denial. ✓INTERNET→*url* http://www.planet.it/voxpop.html

Wa Nui Records Showcasing the talents of the Pacific rim, Wa Nui gives a big "Aloha" to bands from Hawaii, along with a handful of others like Melodious Thunk and the blues outfit Mojo Hand. ✓INTERNET→*url* http://planet-hawaii.com/wanui/

Warner Bros. Records One of the largest record companies in the world, Warner has been expert at spinning out successful imprints like Slash, Reprise, Luaka Bop, Maverick, Paisley Park, and more. While the AOL site isn't updated as often as it should be, it still remains an impressive source of multimedia press kits and sound clips, and the Website serves as a good entry point for learning more about Warner's roster. ✓INTERNET→*url* http://www.iuma.com/Warner ✓AMERICA ONLINE→*keyword* warner

Warner Brothers Preview Photos of Chris Isaak, sound clips of Elvis Costello, a message from Madonna, and more in this area dedicated to Warner Brothers artists. √**COMPUSERVE**→*go* wbpreview

Warrior Records Started in 1994, Warrior provides financial support for those bands with independent natures but low funds. Recently, Warrior signed Jimmy, Angel South and It's A Beautiful Day. √**INTERNET**→*url* http://www. iuma.com/Warrior/

Waveform Records A label that boasts Sedona, Arizona (otherwise known as UFO country) as its base of operations. This music is not suggested for skeptical listeners. √**INTERNET**→*url* http://iuma. southern.com/beyond/waveform/

Way Over There Way down there would be more accurate. WAT is an independent label based in Melbourne, featuring artists from the alternative Australian music scene like The Ergot Derivative, SickBay, and Breather Hole. √**INTERNET**→*url* http://www. zikzak.net/~woodwire/WayOver There.html

Wiiija Records Here's an arts and crafts project. Put together Kim Gordon (Sonic Youth), Julie Cafritz (Pussy Galore), Mark Ibold (Pavement), and Yoshimi (Boredoms) for an on-and-off indie supergroup called Free Kitten, and then put together a record label called Wiiija to produce them. √**INTERNET**→*url* http://www.state 51.co.uk/state51/wiiija/wiiija.html

Windham Hill Records The Web home of the world's premier instrumental and easy-listening album includes artist biographies, discographies, tour dates, and an open forum for musical discussion, all displayed with state-of-

the-art graphics. Get the latest news on John Gorka and George Winston here. √**INTERNET**→*url* http://www.windham.com

Wingnut Records The foremost producer of hardcore in Southern California, Wingnut deals with lots of bands, which doesn't mean that we have to list their names, or do anything else for that matter. Not in a world so brutal and unfair. √**INTERNET**→*url* http://www -unix.oit.umass.edu/~jona/wing nut.html

Wooden Records From right outside of Atlanta, this idealistic label has survived to sign only quality, sincere musicians. With a bias for the local stuff, Wooden signed Billy Hume and will be releasing a compilation album of Georgia bands featuring Shrunken Head, Pocket, Lenny, and Daisy. √**INTERNET**→*url* http:// www.mind spring.com/~pauld/wooden.html

XDOT25 XDOT25 is involved in any number of dazzling entertainment industry ventures, one of which is music production. The label supports world music and experimental jazz artists like Shaba, Parinaz, and Paul Mousavi, and the Website links to bios, sound clips, and the like. √**INTERNET**→*url* http://xdot25.com/

Zang Tuum Tumb (ml) Trevor Horn's British label ZTT carries a number of high-profile artists, including Art of Noise, Seal, 808 State, and more, and the list serves as a forum for news and discussion. √**INTERNET**→*email* majordomo@xmission.com ✍ *Type in message body:* subscribe ztt <your email address> *Info:* √**INTERNET**→*url* ftp://ftp.xmission.com/pub/ users/lazlo/ztt

ZoeMagik Records ZoeMagik Records, the City of Tribes Communications' tribal trance dance music label, releases 12" discs and CD's for the club and D.J. market. Get hyped and get the beat here. √**INTERNET**→*url* http://www. organic.com/Music/City.o.tribes/ Zoemagik.records/index.html

Name your Band!

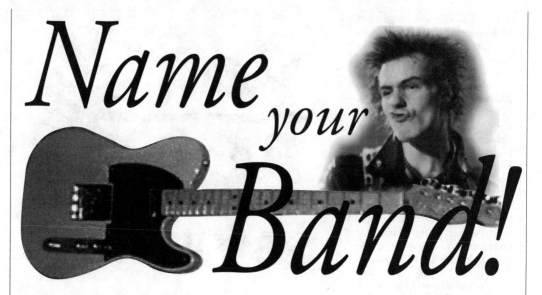

So you want to start a band. Here's the drill. Round up the other guys, or girls; pool your songwriting talents; practice those long hours in the carport or garage; and then pick out an old cover with enough tunefulness, tradition, and underground cachet to launch you into the public eye. Get signed. Get airplay. Practice your interview quotes. "Sky Saxon was what we are, a man whose hands were held by God." Sit back and get rich.

But hold on just a second. You've forgotten the most important thing. What's your band's name? You know, the name—the words that will be on the lips of teens across the nation. "Do you have the new _____ CD?" "Have you heard the new _____ song?" "Are you going to see the _____ concert?" The most famous bands in rock music got that way because they were talented

musicians, sure, but also because they knew that a pop-music career is like an advertising campaign. The Beatles, The Rolling Stones, The Who, The Kinks— these products are as familiar to us as Tide, or Timex. A good band name should have kick, verve, energy. The Sex Pistols had kick. The Cranberries don't. the Afghan Whigs has verve. Verve doesn't. And the best band names—The Breeders, The Pixies, Urge Overkill— can even elevate an inconsistent product. But in recent years, the art of selecting a band name seems to have fallen by the wayside, as willful eclecticism and tin ears have conspired to produce some real clunkers. With a pop landscape cluttered by faceless monosyllables (Blur, Lush, Ride), moronic oxymorons (Smoking Popes, Boxing Gandhis), and nonsensical triads (Ned's Atomic Dustbin, Stone Temple Pilots), nineties pop looks like a paraphrase of Flannery O'Connor's home truth: A good name is hard to find.

That's the rationale behind the **List of Possible Band Names**, which has been on the Web since summer 1995. A Netwide project intended as a clearinghouse for musical monikers, the list compiles a master-list of band names submitted by email. "Up until now," the site designers explain, "bands like yours have had to struggle for years without a name, eventually falling into an alcohol-induced depression and leaving the music business for a life of crime." No more. Are you the proud frontman of a thrashy post-punk outfit that's absolutely stymied on the onomastic front? How about The Leaderless Gambinos, or Shatner, or Alligator Control? Or perhaps your post-modern country band needs a handle that will convince fans that you're capable of complexity, irony, and humor. Try on Preacher Roe, or The Bad Cashiers, or Pitchforked. You're on the cover of *Rolling Stone* already. And if you're not happy with the List of

Name This Band!

We found this band on the Web. It's from Seattle, and it's named Bristle. We've never heard Bristle's music, but Bristle's name is, well, not very good. Granted, it's both a noun and a verb, and that's admirable, but like Sponge (and Bush and Curve and Squeak), it smacks of a five-minute dorm-room bull session. Help this band. Invent a new name, and then email us your suggestions at editors@ypn.com. The best submissions will be judged and posted on our Website (http://www.ypn.com). Maybe Bristle will even pony up a free 7-inch for the winners.

Moniker Archives

The List of Possible Band Names ✓ INTER-NET→http://www-scf.usc.edu/~jdietz/ bandnames. html

Addicted to Sounds Band Names ✓ INTER-NET→http://www.mind spring.com/~labrams/ a2sound.htm

Possible Band Names, visit **Addicted to Sounds Band Names**, which helpfully divides its choices by category. Getting a jump on fame has never been so easy.

It was either Jacques Derrida or Sky Saxon who said, "Names are things, sometimes make things, and the more we deny their power the more we fall under their spell." Hmm…Jacques Saxon. Now there's a name.

Indie industry

Some bands climb right to the top of the heap, bypass the years of struggle, the thou-

sands of nights playing to uninterested drunks in sweaty clubs, the hundreds of promises from agents, managers, and record company executives, the ever-present fear that poverty will force them to lay down their instruments and take up the classified ads. But not most. If you're in a band, and you want audiences to hear your music, the picture is fairly bleak. But not as bleak as it once was. Thanks to the Internet, performers who would have remained entirely remote from the music industry can now connect to the powers that be. Bands on the brink of breakthrough should camp out at **IUMA**, **The Indie Rock Hub**, and **Visual Radio**. You never know.

At the center of the SonicNet experience—from http://www.sonicnet.com/

On the Net

Across the board

Alternative Underground "The greatest alternative music page ever"? Maybe not. But this page does collect many links relevant to the independent music industry. ✓**INTERNET**→*url* http://144.174.145.14/SCHOOL/ALTMUSIC/altmusic.html

The Indie Rock Hub Information on labels, fans, bands, media

contacts, and more. ✓**INTERNET**→*url* http://www.clark.net/pub/rt/indiehub.html

IUMA High-end graphics, cutting-edge sound compression, and a firm sense of purpose are the hallmarks of the Internet Underground Music Archive (IUMA), a huge site with information on every aspect of the independent music industry. Need to know what unsigned bands sound like? Download their sound clips and bios. Want information on the indie industry? Get a list of labels (who can sign your band) and publications (who can promote you). And if you're in a band and want coverage, just upload your own sounds and visuals. ✓**INTERNET**→*url* http://www.iuma.com

MusicNation A grab-bag of resources for independent bands, including links to pages for individual bands, industry pages, and more. ✓**INTERNET**→*url* http://www.actwin.com/MediaNation/music/index.html

Numenet Sound Chamber Roughly two dozen independent artists have pages on this site, including the Eight Lamas from Drepung (who record Tibetan Sacred Temple Music) and Bruce BecVar (who "invites his audience to a banquet where all the subtle senses will be entertained"). Get descriptions of the albums and the artists; and order the music online. ✓**INTERNET**→*url* http://www.numenet.com/sc/

The Internet Underground Music Archive—from http://www.iuma.com

Primordial Shmooze With a front-end image map with dozens of categories (charts, labels, software, comics, gigs, mags, and bands), this Toronto-based page offers a comprehensive resource for independent musicians and bands. Need to learn more about Landslide, J, Slack, Wedge, Bassbag, Positively Stompin', or the Essentials? Come here, and get a critical introduction, cover art, sound clips, and contact numbers. √**INTERNET**→*url* http://www.shmooze.net/pwcasual/

Rich's Music Archive Independent bands from the Northeast, along with sound clips, cover art, and short band bios. √**INTER-NET**→*url* http://deathstar.rutgers.edu/people/bochkay/bands.html

SonicNet After more than a year as one of the leading independent rock bulletin boards, SonicNet has moved onto the Web, and it's a wonderful site that concentrates on alternative music in the New York City area. *The Loser's Guide*

to New York City, Ralph Steadman's *Fouling of America*, vintage rock posters, and lavish festival coverage are all resident on SonicNet, along with live Web chat, and the site's archives continue to grow. All in all, one of the best places on the Web for bands (or convulsively cool fans). √**INTERNET**→*url* http://www.sonicnet.com/

Translatlantic Management TM provides marketing support and guidance for musicians, producers, and songwriters. Investigate sites like the Euphoria World Wibe Music, Inc. for discussions of the fate of independent music on and off the Web. √**INTERNET**→*url* http://euphoria.org/home/labels/transmgt/transmgt.html

Visual Radio With departments for performance art, poetry, dance, and fine art, this stylish site isn't exactly a music-only resource. But Visual Radio does have a wealth of resources devoted to independent rockers, focusing specifically on video clips. One problem: you'll

need to order Visual Radio's CD-ROM to be able to view the rock videos online here. √**INTERNET**→*url* http://www.visualradio.com/

Wood and Wire Many independent bands come from the land down under, and Wood and Wire knows pretty much everything about them—although it doesn't limit itself to Aussie concerns. With a huge list of independent and alternative band pages, a giant list of 'zines, and a repository of industry contacts (band booking information, label addresses, media phone numbers), this is one of the best sites in Cyberspace for bands trying to get a foothold in the confusing, crowded, and cluttered music scene. √**INTERNET**→*url* http://www.magna.com.au/woodwire/

Bands

Indie Front With information relating to "the making and breaking of independent bands," this site collects articles about the new-blood industry, with multiple foci—business, music, distribution, personnel, marketing, and networking. Sponsored by the band Malibu Stacey, this page also collects links to other indie sites online. √**INTERNET**→*url* http://charlemagne.uwaterloo.ca/

Internet Nightclub Arranged like a nightclub, this page collects sound clips of alternative bands and then presents them in an undercard/main event format. If you've never heard 3-D House of Beef, this would be the place to start. √**INTERNET**→*url* http://www.memcore.com/nightclub/

Music et al Archives A large list of links to resources for independent bands in all genres, including rock/pop, folk, avant-garde, reg-

Australia's Wood & Wire—from http://www.magna.com.au/woodwire/

gae, ska, and more. And when you're done perusing genre and industry sites, you can link to dozens of individual band pages for acts like Blogurt, Dirty Job, and Carpet Burn. ✓**INTERNET**→*url* http://www.webjammers.com/projects/bands.html

Unsigned Bands If you have a band you've been talking up for years, bring your enthusiasm to this message board, where fans from across the country tout their favorites, furnish news about indie and major-label signings, and review concerts. ✓**COMPUSERVE**→*go* rocknet→Messages and Libraries →Unsigned Bands

The Virtual Music Spotlight Need your band listed, but worried that your empty pockets and limited talents will keep you down? Worry no more. Blaise Pascal, Bovox Clown, Agent Orange, Apollo Creed, and hundreds of other independent bands get listed

here. And if you don't care for the music, you can at least ransack the listings for a good band name. ✓**INTERNET**→*url* http://www4.ncsu.edu/unity/users/d/decox/WWW/TVMS.html

Cassettes

CassetteNet There are famous cassette-only labels, like ROIR, and then there are the hundreds of other cassette-only labels responsible for promoting unknown musical artists. This Australian page collects news and updates on cassette-only labels around the world. ✓**INTERNET**→*url* http://multiline.com.au/~langham/cassette.html

United Kingdom

The Supersonic Guide A link to British indies that includes a list of more than 150 supersonic artists and labels. ✓**INTERNET**→*url* http://gladstone.uoregon.edu/~nigel/supersonic.html

Artists who have appeared on Sonic-Net's Live Chat:

"Steve Albini
Alice Donut
Lou Barlow
Bush
Exene Cervenka
Cobra Verde
King Coffey
Combustible Edison
D Generation
Thomas Dolby
Echobelly
Elastica
Maggie Estep
Everclear
Faith No More
Marianne Faithfull
Flaming Lips
Giant Sand
The Goats
Michael Ivey
The Jerky Boys
Timothy Leary
Letters to Cleo
Live
Lotion
Madder Rose
Meat Puppets
Morphine
Bob Mould
Pigface
Poster Children
Quicksand
Henry Rollins
Sick Of It All
Jules Shear
Speech
Swans
Squirrel Nut Zipper
Syrup
Triphammer
Voodoo Queens"

—from **SonicNet**

Part 6

Musicians Only

Instruments

What would music be without instruments? Well, singing, and posing, and not much

else. The great virtuosos of musical history—from Miles Davis to McCoy Tyner to Jimi Hendrix to Buddy Rich to Yo-Yo Ma—would be reduced to mimes, and legendary manufacturers like Gibson, Stradivarius, and Baldwin would be failing companies. On the Net, instruments of all shapes and sizes get to share the stage—from **The Accordion Mailing List** to **The Classical Guitar Home Page**, from **Tuba Tunes** to **DOUBLEREED-L**. If you're a harmonica player looking for playing tips, drop by **Cyber Harp World**. If you're a lonely bagpiper, try **rec.music.makers.bagpipe**. And if you want to play an instrument but can't decide which one, check out the prices at the **Big Used Gear List**. You may find a bargain that catapults you to fame.

On the Net

Across the board

Musician's Web With an impressive roster of companies like Sonor and Toca Percussion, Ovation and Takamine guitars, and Gibraltar hardware, this site has a wealth of information for those aspiring musicians interested in

The Les Paul Classic Plus—http://129. 131.19.85/m/lp

learning more about their craft. After previewing pictures of Ovation's celebrity model guitars, visitors can link to the Drummer's Web and read articles and test reports on ride cymbals and other drummer's fare. Musician's Web does occasionally move beyond corporate information—its calendar, for instance, lists events like the Music & Harmony Fair in the Netherlands—but most of this site is content to shake its money maker. ✓**INTERNET**→*url* http://valley. interact.nl/av/musweb/

rec.music.makers (ng) It is possible to play your bass as loud as you want without driving the

neighbors crazy—and you can find out how at this newsgroup, which offers tips on soundproofing your basement. The posts here are informed and intelligent, including discussions of new copyright legislation and its effect on royalties for musicians. And in case you were worried about an absence of clichés, never fear—there are plenty of posts of the looking-for-a-cool-drummer-in-the-Seattle-area variety. ✓**USENET**→ rec.music.makers

rec.music.makers.bands (ng) "I am a bass player in a band called The Haunting. Our singer (ego aside) has an obsession with his hair—he is forever playing with it on stage, pulling it, fluffing, it flipping it—kind of drives you nuts. I thought of putting a guitar in his hands, but he can't play. I keep making threats of Nair in his hair gel…Any other solutions?" This post from Aaron in Ottawa is typical of the obsessions of this newsgroup, which is dedicated to discussion of bands and their members. Advice on Aaron's hairy problem, or any other band-related issue, can be posted to this well-trafficked newsgroup. ✓**USENET**→rec.music.makers.bands

The Big Used Gear List People selling used drums (including cymbals), bass guitars, guitars, amps, effects, and outboard gear (bass compressors, noise gates, and entire studios) can post classified ads here for free. ✓**INTERNET**→*url* http://indyunix.iupui.edu/ ~badrian/ list.html

Instruments Talk tubas, trombones, pianos, guitars, and more. In fact, this site might be the only place in Cyberspace with viola jokes ("How do you keep a violin from being stolen? Keep it in a viola case!"). Messages in the library include a .GIF of a grand piano action (every action has 35 adjustable parts) and an informal history of the glass harmonica. ✓**COMPUSERVE**→ *go* music→ Music and Arts→Instruments

rec.music.makers.marketplace (ng) Get an informal market-value appraisal of your trumpet before heading to the pawnshop, or if you're in the market to pick up some new equipment, shop the classifieds posted here. ✓**USENET**→rec.music.makers.market place

rec.music.makers.synth (ng) Yamaha SY85. Casio VL. Trinity 411. If you aren't into synthesizers, then these probably look like the names of planets, or vitamins. But if you are, you'll love this newsgroup, which is a clearinghouse of comments on makes, models, sound quality, and special features for synthetic drums and pianos. Bonus: one post here will tell you which type of synthetic drum is "very popular in the church setting." ✓**USENET**→rec.music.makers. synth

Tools of the Trade Several companies—including Peavy, Blue Ribbon, and Coda—are online here to showcase their new products. Preview the sound of a new Peavy guitar by checking out the sound clips, then go to the message boards to discuss the products with owners or other interested shoppers. Many of the manufac-

turers post their company histories and newsletters. ✓**AMERICA ONLINE**→*keyword* Music→Music-Tools

Vox-L Vox-L focuses on Vox musical instruments: amplifiers, guitars, effects, and organs for players, collectors. ✓**INTERNET**→*email* listserv@netcom.com ✍ *Type in message body:* subscribe vox-l <your full name>

Accordion

Accordion Mailing List (ml) Sign up here for news on playing and repairing piano and button accordions, concertinas, and all other free reeds (except harmonicas). ✓**INTERNET**→*email* accordion-request @cs.cmu.edu ✍ *Write a request*

Accumulated Accordion Annotations This accordion site has it all—an FAQ, a list of accordion music companies nationwide, a bibliography of accordion books, and even pics of the site creator's trip to Petosa's accordion shop in Seattle. In addition, there are links to concertina sites here too, including a calendar of "squeeze-related" events. ✓**INTERNET**→*url* http://www.cs.cmu.edu/afs/cs/user/phoebe/mosaic/accordion.html

The Big Squeeze Reviews of accordion music from players worldwide (some reviews are in Spanish, Swedish, and Dutch). ✓**INTERNET**→*url* http://www.rootsworld.com/rw/feature/freereed.html

Bagpipe

Bagpipe Mailing List (ml) Discuss the differences between the Great Highland and the Uilleann

bagpipes, and other bagpipe topics, with those who love the reed. ✓**INTERNET**→*email* bagpipe-request @cs.dartmouth.edu ✍ *Write a request*

Bagpipe Music by Ned Smith Mr. Smith and his band, the Northern Border Caledonia, have been bringing the sounds of the Scottish Highlands to the great state of Maine for over 25 years. Now that Ned has put .GIFs and JPEGs of the sheet music for eight of the band's songs online, Netters all over the world can don a virtual kilt and learn some classic pipe tunes by visiting this site. ✓**INTERNET**→*url* http://www.agate.net/~smithr/Bagpipe.html

rec.music.makers.bagpipe (ng) How did bagpipes come to be associated with fire and police departments? Where can urban pipers practice without being hauled away by their bagpiping friends at the police department? Is there a good bagpipe band for hire in Akron, Ohio? Bagpipe fans gather here to discuss these and other issues. ✓**USENET**→rec.music. makers.bagpipe

Banjo

alt.banjo (ng) Pick noise is a constant concern for beginner banjo players. They come here for advice from more experienced pluckers, who advise them. Good, sound advice about buying, playing, and enjoying the banjo is here for the plucking. ✓**USENET**→ alt.banjo

Banjo Tablature Archive Tabs for classical, jazz, bluegrass, and "miscellaneous" banjo compositions. ✓**INTERNET**→*url* http://www.vuw.ac.nz/~gnat/banjo/tab/index.html

Bass guitar

alt.guitar.bass (ng) Discussions of instrument models, music, and culture. ✓USENET→alt.guitar.bass

Bass Resources at Harmony Central Within the depths of the massive musical site known as Harmony Central is this amazing section devoted to the bass. Click on Bass Instruction for the basic tenets of playing the instrument. A link to the rec.music.makers. bass FAQ provides more fundamental playing knowledge. In the Effects section, discover how to get maximum distortion from your bass and how to cheaply concoct original bass effects at home. Info on bass and amp manufacturers will help you build your first (or best) bass rig ever. And if you're feeling scholarly, link to *The Bass Digest* for bass briefs by the experts. Bass newcomers and old-hands alike will find this site helpful. ✓INTERNET→*url* http://harmony-central.mit.edu/Bass/

rec.music.makers.bass (ng) Every bass player thinks he has assembled the ultimate bass rig, and he will discuss it in great technical detail at this newsgroup. Beyond the sound discussions, there are also great debates on why the instrument is pronounced like "base" instead of like the fish. One post answers, "Don't let this spread, but not all things in the world were invented by English-speaking people. Anyway, the word 'bass' derives from Italian 'basso,' a word that refers to low-range instruments and vocals. 'Contra'-prefix is used for instruments that go even lower. Thus, 'contrabass' is called like that because it is the lowest-range bowed instrument used. But this kind of information may be classified in the U.S. So if your teacher says a contrabass is a Nicaraguan fish agree with him. 8-)." This is possibly the only place where bass players won't mind getting feedback. ✓USENET→rec.music.makers.bass

Brass instruments

Brass Mailing List (ml) Although this list is intended mainly for musicians in small brass ensembles, other interested parties are welcome (i.e., wind bands, orchestras, woodwind or percussion players, composers, etc.). Currently the group has around 20 members, and postings are infrequent. ✓INTERNET→*email* brass-request@geomag.gly.fsu.edu ✍ *Write a request*

Drums

DRUM (ml) A loving and informative discussion of all types of drums and their uses. ✓INTERNET→*url* drum-request@brandx.Rain.COM ✍ *Type in message body:* subscribe <your email address>

The Drums and Drumming Page Mike Wilcox, an ordinary guy who just likes drums, has assembled this fun and colorful site complete with a Drummer's Quiz, a list of drumming rudiments, and a collection of drummer-related links. Check out Mike's growing gallery of drum pics to find some graphics for your flyers! ✓INTERNET→*url* http://www.magna.com.au/~mwilcox/drums1.html

The Drummer and Percussion Page Don't be scared off by the bad drummer jokes at this site—there is some good information here, too! Like the events calendar

Now THIS is a drum kit!—from http://www.magna.com.au/~mwilcox/drumpics/

An MC/1 Brian Moore Custom—http://www.teleport.com/~apple/

that covers drum/percussion festivals worldwide. And the link to The Groove Archive, which features .GIFs of 13 standard drum rudiments recommended for beginners (followed closely by a second 13). There's even a directory of drummers and percussionists on the Net that's long enough to be the Drummer's Yellow Pages. Despite the bad jokes, this site is definitely worth a drive-by. ✓**INTERNET**→*url* http://www.cse.ogi.edu/Drum/

rec.music.makers.percussion (ng) Judging from this newsgroup, drums are the only percussion instrument in the world. Read gripping discussions on increasing the power of your weaker hand by changing your stick grip, and the like. ✓**USENET**→rec.music.makers.percussion

Flute

10 Disgusting Things Irish Traditional Flute Players Do Warning: this site, although humorous, is truly repulsive. ✓**INTERNET**→*url* http://celtic.stanford.edu/pmurphy/disgustingflute.html

Flute (ml) Discussions of the instrument and the music made with it. ✓**INTERNET**→*email* flute-m-

request@unixg.ubc.ca ✍ *Write a request*

The Flute Player Home Page The most interesting section of this site is the Master Classes topic, which features interviews of famous flutists like Herbie Mann. Also here are player profiles, model reviews, and supplier and manufacturer directories. ✓**INTERNET**→*url* http://www.windplayer.com/wp/flute.html

French horn

International Horn Society Mailing List (ml) This list is dominated by discussion of the French horn: its repertoire and pedagogy, workshop and festival announcements, alternate fingerings, horn humor and anecdotes, instrumental repair and technology, and scholarly reports. ✓**INTERNET**→*email* majordomo@spock.nlu.edu ✍ *Type in message body:* subscribe horn <your email address> *FAQ:* ✓**INTERNET**→*url* http://www.io.com/~rboerger/IHSFAQ.html/

rec.music.makers.french-horn (ng) Blow your own French horn or someone else's at this newsgroup full of insights (French horn players get performance anxi-

ety like every other musician) and requests (where can someone get busking music that includes the French horn?) about the instrument. ✓**USENET**→rec.music.makers.french-horn

Guitar

Acoustic Guitar Home Page From the folks at rec.music.makers.acoustic comes this page of interesting guitar info, including an intimate guitar lesson with Bo Parker, an explanation of equal-tempered tuning, and a dissecting look at guitar resonances. Also find an extensive list of guitar mail-order companies, reviews of instructional material, and profiles of legendary acoustic guitar players. ✓ **INTERNET**→*url* http://pentagon.io.com:8001/galvis/rmmga/

The Classical Guitar Home Page A set of .GIFs of sheet music for classic guitar works, such as J.S. Bach's "Jesu, Joy of Man's Desiring" and his "Minuet in G." For those seeking classical guitar with a Flamenco twist, there are links here to The Flamenco Guitar Home Page and the Flamenco FAQ for Classical Guitarists. ✓ **INTERNET**→ *url* http://www.teleport.com/~ jdimick/notebook.html

Guitar Archive Musicians worldwide come here to deposit and pick up tabs covering all types of rock-and-roll compositions. Songs are organized alphabetically by title. ✓ **INTERNET**→*url* ftp://ftp.nevada.edu

LUTE (ml) Talk about this precursor to the guitar and its music. ✓ **INTERNET**→*email* lute-request@cs.dartmouth.edu ✍ *Write a request*

rec.music.makers.guitar (ng) Guitar players worldwide discuss a variety of topics, including insuring their instruments, whether Hendrix played with a flanger or not—why not? he played with everything else—and where to meet in London for a good blues jam. Of course, there are also the obligatory guitar-for-sale posts here, too. ✓ **USENET**→rec.music.makers.guitar

rec.music.makers.guitar.acoustic (ng) It's doubtful that there is another newsgroup that discusses fingernails and their preservation with such vigor and intensity as this one does (one favored method involves gluing slices of ping pong balls under each nail!). Beyond the nail issues, discussions cover the gamut from buying recommendations to tributes to favorite acoustic players. ✓ **USENET**→rec.music.makers.guitar.acoustic

rec.music.makers.guitar.tablature (ng)Discover that a tab is more than just a key on your keyboard! Musicians post requests for music they can't work out themselves ("Lightning Crashes" and "Down Under" were among recent requests). Warning: asking for music that is currently getting lots of airplay may result in humiliating flames. ✓ **USENET**→rec.music.makers.guitar.tablature

Vintage Guitar Magazine This site is so popular that its home page sports a McDonald's-style "customers served" notice (they've had over 11,000 visitors in the past five months). While you can't actually read the magazine here, there are plenty of other reasons to stop by. See pictures of coveted classics, like the 1954 Gretsch Round-up, and then click on the pics to read the guitar's vital statistics. Or brush up on your vintage-guitar knowledge in the "Trivia" section. Finally, links to dealers' home pages put you in contact with Gibson USA and Rod and Hank's Vintage Guitars for some vintage and current-model guitar shopping. ✓ **INTERNET** →*url* http://www.vguitar.com/vintageguitar.html

Hammer dulcimers

Hammer Dulcimers Mailing List (ml) Discuss playing the hammer dulcimer, cymbaloms, yanq qin, and related instruments. ✓ **INTERNET**→ *email* hammerd@mcs.com ✍ *Write a request*

Handbells

The American Guild Of English Handbell Ringers For fans of the bells, the AGEHR posts an events calendar for their organization; lists of manufacturers, vendors, and music publishers; and an "Identify the Mystery Bell Ringer" contest every week. ✓ **INTERNET**→ *url* http://www. agehr.org/

Handbell-L (ml) This list discusses the direction and playing of the English handbells. ✓ **INTERNET→** *email* Handbell-L@ringer.jpl.nasa. gov ✍ *Write a request* subscribe

Harmonica

Cyber Harp World Describing itself as the "Home of the Harmonica Heroes of the Future," this site offers a list of events in the harmonica world (festivals, concerts, and seminars), and links to harmonica players' home pages, the Harp-L mailing list archives (including their picture archive), and other harmonica sites, including the *Irish Harmonica News.* ✓ **INTERNET→** *url* http://www.wku. edu/~piercem/harp_home.html

Harp

Harp-L (ml) For discussion of the instrument, those who play it, and the music they make with it. ✓ **INTERNET→** *email* MXserver@WKUVX1. WKU.EDU ✍ *Type in message body:* subscribe HARP-L <your full name>

Keyboards

Hammond Organ (ml) For hardcore users of Hammond organs and their clones. Discussions are low-volume, but also high-density and very technically oriented. Donate your organ expertise. ✓ **INTERNET→** *email* hammond-request@zk3.dec. com

HPSCHD-L (ml) Discuss all kinds of early stringed keyboard instruments—harpsichords, clavichords, fortepianos, virginals—and all similar instruments, except the modern piano. All topics related to these instruments are covered, including theory and principles of their construction, decoration, history, and evolution. The list also includes ads for recordings for sale or wanted and discussions of performances and recordings. ✓ **INTERNET** ...→*email* listserv@albany.edu ✍ *Type in message body:* subscribe HPSCHD-L <your full name> ...→ listserv@albany.bitnet ✍ *Type in message body:* subscribe HPSCHD-L <your full name>

The Piano Page Three cheers for the Piano Technicians Guild for assembling this great collection of links to piano-related sites on the Net. Links to the technicians' archives will teach you how often and how to service your piano. A directory of piano technicians, teachers, and manufacturers in the Industry Guide puts you in touch

with the personnel needed to get your piano up and running well. A collection of piano images includes photos of refurbished vintage pianos as well as paintings with pianos as their subject. For piano conversation on the Net, there are also links to newsgroups and mailing lists here. ✓ **INTERNET→** *url* http://www.prairienet.org/arts/ptg/homepage.html

PIPORG-L (ml) Classical, theater, electronic, reed, tracker, and electropneumatic organs and their history are discussed here. Restoration of classic organs is a big topic. ✓ **INTERNET→***email* listserv@albany. edu ✍ *Type in message body:* subscribe PIPORG-L <your full name>

Playing the Piano—Playing with Fire? The world is a dangerous place, filled with peril. So many things threaten our well-being and safety—drugs, guns, disease...and pianos. In Westerns, piano players are always getting thrown around by gunslingers who want to prove that they are the toughest men in the saloon. But that's only the most obvious problem. According to this site—a thesis by a music medicine major that outlines the risks of tickling the ivories—pianists can be sidelined by loss of dexterity in the hands, stage fright, and other work-related stress disorders. Players who plan to spend a lot of time at the keyboard may want to read the case histories here and ponder what went wrong and how these kinds of mistakes can be avoided. ✓ **INTERNET→** *url* http://rvik. ismennt.is/~jssen/musmed.html

rec.music.makers.piano (ng) Morgan wants to play Beethoven's Fifth Piano Concert for his high-school music camp, but he needs the sheet music for the piano part, minus the orchestra, transcribed into MIDI. And he needs it for less than $50 (he is a high school student, after all). Morgan and others post their unusual piano-related requests here, as well as reviews of recordings and searches for keyboard players for rock-and-roll bands. Paul Shaffer, eat your little bald heart out. ✓**USENET**→rec. music.makers.piano

Saxophone

The International Saxophone Home Page Because there are very few saxophone sites on the Net, enthusiasts will appreciate the well-rounded information available at the International Saxophone Home Page. Visitors can find in-depth reviews of current CD releases that highlight every song's construction and the career history of the album's artist. There is also a nationwide directory of used-instrument dealers and their price lists organized by model. The site's creator has even taken the time to list all the multiphonics fingerings he has been able to come up with. Soon the site will also offer an online beginner's playing manual and interviews with famous sax machines. Stayed tuned! ✓**INTERNET**→ *url* http:// www.teleport.com/~jdumars/

Stringed instruments

The Funny Cello Page Humorous images and quotes regarding the cello. ✓**INTERNET**→*url* http:// pegasus.uthct.edu/ResUTHCT/ Investigators/CZwieb/funnycello. html

The Internet Cello Society Buy and sell used cellos through the classifieds here, or research cello-related topics in the library archive, which houses cello-society newsletters, magazines, and scholarly journals. Also find a presentation on the history of the cello, which discusses its repertoire and its famous artists and teachers. ✓**INTERNET**→*url* http://tahoma.cwu. edu:2000/~michelj/Menu.html

Internet Viola Society *Voila!* A site for the viola including a history of the instrument; a repertoire searchable by publisher or period, lists of CDs, books, magazines and videos pertaining to the viola; and profiles of well-known players like Yuri Bashmet, Nobuko Imai, and Emanuel Vardi. ✓**INTERNET** →*url* http://rucus.ru.ac.za/ ~sean/viola.html

Maestronet A great site for cello, violin, viola, and piano players. Here you can find listings of instruments for sale from dealers worldwide, together with an easy-to-search price-history database. There is also a library of articles and books on maintaining fine stringed instruments. In the Conservatory section of Maestronet, visitors can download files of sheet music. This site will save visitors a trip to the music store! ✓**INTERNET** →*url* http: //www.maestro net.com/w-about. html

rec.music.makers.bowed-strings (ng) An interest in trading, buying, selling, and loving bowed instruments of every kind brings people to this newsgroup. Many posters' obsessions with the bow obviously began at an early age—a query on whether violin lessons for a six-year-old are a good thing or not started a long thread of affirmative responses. ✓**USENET**→rec.music.makers. bowed-strings

rec.music.makers.builders (ng) When Alicia writes, "I am having trouble getting hold of a large diameter pipe section that isn't 12 feet long—plus I worry about hot spot(s) and having to constantly buy propane tanks—I have no clue how many of those are needed for 6-8 hours time?!?" she isn't referring to the assembly of an aircraft carrier. She and the other members of this newsgroup are building their own stringed instruments (Alicia's is a violin), and they come here to swap advice and support. ✓**USENET**→rec.music.makers. builders

Violin Makers: A. Stradivari Located in Cremona, Italy, the Stradivari violin-making school is the only Italian state school of its kind; this page provides information on the school's programs, as well as links to other violin sites. ✓**INTERNET**→*url* http://graffiti.telnet-work.it/stradivari/welcome. html

Trombone

Trombone (ml) An entertaining and informative site about the trombone. Featuring sound files of master trombone player Alain Trudel rendering "Blue Bells," this site also offers a mouthpiece chart for selecting the right piece for different models, a trombone-related bibliography, a discography, record reviews, and an archive of the Trombone-L mailing list. Strangely enough, there is also a picture here of a guy playing his trombone into the Grand Canyon... ✓**INTER-NET**→*url* http://www.missouri. edu/~cceric/index.html

Trombone-L (ml) Forum for trombone players and enthusiasts. ✓**INTERNET**→*email* listproc@

One heck of an echo—http://www. missouri.edu/~cceric/natp.html

showme.missouri.edu ✉ *Type in message body:* subscribe <your full name>

Trumpet

rec.music.makers.trumpet (ng) Continuous breathing is a normal function for all humans. But for trumpet players, it has special meaning: by using the continuous breathing technique, blowers can "literally sustain a note until their horn fills up with saliva," according to one post here. Besides playing techniques, you can also find horns for sale and bands seeking horn players. ✓**USENET**→rec.music.makers.trumpet

Trumpet Mailing List (ml) There's no trumped-up talk about the instrument at this mailing list. Get the facts on trumpet-playing techniques, instrument models, music, and concerts. ✓**INTERNET**→ *email* listserv@acad1.dana.edu ✉ *Type in message body:* subscribe trumpet <your full name>

Trumpet Player's Internation-

al Network Trumpeters at Dana College in Nebraska have assembled an impressive resource at this site. For inspiration, graphics of Dizzy, Cliffors, Arban, and Herseth are here. For shopping, two trumpet music vendors offer their catalogs. For jazz, check out the jazz primer by Marc Sabatella and the selected discographies of Shaw, Byrd, Morgan, and Stamm. For further reading offline, click on the trumpet literature link for an extensive bibliography. ✓**INTERNET** →*url* http://www.dana.edu:80/~trumpet/

Tuba

Tuba Tunes Listen to the tuba section of the University of Wisconsin marching band play "Semper Fidelis," "Beer Barrel Polka," and "On Wisconsin." These songs will make you feel like you are in the stadium at kickoff with a weenie in one hand and a beer in the other. ✓**INTERNET**→*url* http://www.engr.wisc.edu/~faessler/tuba/onwis.au

TUBAEUPH (ml) Don't mistake a euphonium for it's fraternal twin, the tuba. Learn all about these instruments, and the differences between them, at this mailing list. ✓**INTERNET**→ *email* listserv@cms vmb.missouri.edu ✉ *Type in message body:* subscribe <your full name>

Woodwinds

DOUBLEREED-L (ml) Fans of this family of musical instruments, which includes the ever-popular oboe and bassoonDiscuss reedmaking, performances, instruments, cane, clinics, workshops, and festivals. ✓**INTERNET**→ *email* listserv@acc. wuacc.edu ✉ *Type in message body:* subscribe doublereed-l <your full name>

NOTES

"Regarding the Floyd Rose bar problem. I have the exact same bar problem with my Jackson Rhoads EX. If you want the bar to move freely, you can't screw it in too tight but then you get that annoying play in the threads. I brought it to a couple of local music stores with no luck. I was told I would have to live it or replace it. You could try putting some oil in there so you can screw it in a bit tighter.

"Anyone else have suggestions?"

"Teflon tape is a thin, slick tape that is used to seal threads in joints on high pressure gas cylinders and the like.

"Wrap some of this around the threads on the trem bar and it should make the bar fit a lot tighter into the socket, but you will still be able to move it around.

"The tape will fall apart in a couple months."

—from **alt.guitar**

Electronic musicians

In the past, musicians spent years learning their instruments, struggling with the wood

and nylon of the guitar, or the brass of the trumpet. In the present, musicians are just as often concerned with hard drives, modems, and programming languages. Why? Because computers make music, and help composers and musicans refine their art. Curious about how to update your hardware? Anxious to learn about the latest software? From general resources like the **Electronic and Computer Music FAQ** and the **Sound Connections** to specific sites devoted to MIDI music-making (**Harmony Central**, the **World of Audio MIDI Page**, and the **MIDI Software Archive FAQ**), the Net is filled with ways to make your computer sing, and strum, and drum.

On the Net

Across the board

Audio Virtual Library An index of links to newsgroups, utilities, and support for audiophiles. ✓**INTERNET**→*url* http://www.comlab.ox.ac.uk/archive/audio.html

Electronic and Computer Music FAQ A constantly evolving index of frequently asked questions for musicians who want to make

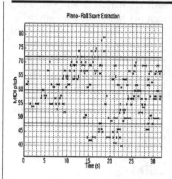

Piano roll from AIFF—from http://sound.media.mit.edu/~mkc/netsound.html

or listen to music on their computers. Arranged by topic. ✓**INTERNET**→*url* http://www.cis.ohio-state.edu/hypertext/faq/usenet/music/netjam-faq/faq.html

Macintosh Music Information Center This is an excellent online primer for Mac users who want to experiment with music composition or playback on their computers. Novices can read several texts introducing issues of computer sound and music, including "Macintosh Sound Basics," "MIDI Basics," "Using Downloaded Files," "All About MOD Files," and "How to Convert Macintosh Sounds into .WAV Files." ✓**AMERICA ONLINE**→*keyword* online→Music Information Center

The Music Studio Linked to the NCT Web magazine, a computer magazine aimed at small business and home office users, The Music Studio reads like a step-by-step overview of PC sound and music technology. Sequencers, notation and printing software, patch editors and librarians, digital record-

ing and editing, and automated composition are all covered in depth. Manufacturer contact information is also provided. ✓**INTERNET**→*url* http://da.awa.com:80/nct/software/musicled.html

Sound Constructors This fledgling e-zine is dedicated to "exposing the artists on and off the Net that use electronic means for the production of their music" through intense study and discussion of their techniques, tips, and musical toys. Check in for an ever-changing array of articles, reviews, columns, and technical babble targeting electronic music in all its manifestations. ✓**INTERNET**→*url* http://isl-garnet.uah.edu/claassen/sc.html

World of Audio Seeking an audio experience? Play that old Yoko Ono album! Or visit the World of Audio, where you can explore MIDI software archives, FAQs on audio and electronic music, a database of audio professionals, and dozens of other music and sound sites on the Net. ✓**INTERNET**→*url* http://www.magicnet.net/rz/world_of_audio/woa.html

MIDI

The Alf MIDI Site Written with the more advanced MIDI enthusiast in mind, this site's focus is on the MIDI Sample Dump Standard (otherwise known as SDS, a method of transferring sound-sample data between MIDI-equipped devices). Extensive technical documentation, samples, and MS-DOS programs related to SDS are available through an FTP link. There is a small amount of general MIDI information added to satisfy newcomers and a fairly large list of links to other popular MIDI and music-related sites. ✓ **INTERNET**→*url* http://www. uib.no/People/midi/midi.html

alt.music.makers.synthesiz-ers (ng) This newsgroup is frequented by MIDI devotees and electronic music lovers alike. Post your questions and chances are a fellow MIDI aficionado will help you with your sequencing problems. ✓ **USENET**→alt.music.makers. synthesizers

alt.music.midi (ng) Need MIDI help? On any given day, the topics here range from heated debates about the best MIDI sequencing software to discussion of the hottest and most functional sound cards, keyboard specs, and FTP and WWW addresses. ✓ **USENET**→ alt.music.midi

Analogue Heaven (ml) The Analogue Heaven discussion list and its companion Website serve music fans interested in playing, collecting, designing, repairing, and modifying analog musical gear. A complete archive of the mailing list is available at the Website, along with spotlight features on various subscribers and their musical accomplishments. ✓ **INTER-NET** ...→*email* majordomo@hyper-real.com ✍ *Type in message body:* subscribe analogue <your email address> ...→*Archive: url* http:// www.hyperreal.com/music/ machines/Analogue-Heaven/

Harmony Central The MIDI section of this enormous music and audio site offers information explaining MIDI, where to get MIDI files, info on building your own MIDI interface, and tools for writing MIDI applications. ✓ **IN-**

TERNET→*url* http://harmony-central. mit.edu/

Mac MIDI Software List A list of software and hardware for all Mac users interested in MIDI programming and playback. Includes price guides and company information. ✓ **INTERNET**→*url* http:// www.interaccess.com/users/ midilink/macsw.html

MIDI Music Forum Let's say you've just developed an interest in MIDI. In this forum, you could head to the message board and ask for a recommendation for a DOS MIDI player, instructions on how to convert a MIDI file to a .WAV file, or advice on how to get started. And if you're more of an old hand at MIDI, you might engage in a discussion about Motown's treatment of strings, computer-controlled sound systems, or composing jazz MIDI. Each of the major computer platforms (Windows, Amiga, Macintosh, etc.) has its own message and library section. In the huge library, the resources include MIDI players and editors for several computer platforms, samples, song files, sound card files, and programming guides. ✓ **COMPUSERVE**→*go* midiform

MIDI Software Archives FAQ A guide to MIDI archives, with addresses for sound utilities and sound clips for several computer platforms. ✓ **INTERNET**→*url* ftp:// rtfm.mit.edu/pub/usenet-by-hierarchy/comp/sys/amiga/audio /Midi_files_software_archives_on_ the_Internet

The Sound Canvas Users Group This group's goal is to compile an archive of original works by a wide variety of composers creating with the Roland SoundCanvas. A detailed FAQ and FTP access to the archive site

are also provided. ✓ **INTERNET**→*url* http://www.eeb.ele.tue.nl/midi/ scgroup/index.html

World of Audio MIDI Page If there were ever a contest for the best MIDI-related Web page, this one would definitely be in the running. For the novice, there's an Introduction to MIDI, a MIDI Overview Chart, the Usenet MIDI Primer, a Bibliography of Electronic Music, and much, much more. Add a comprehensive list of MIDI archive sites, links to Internet MIDI resources, and professional MIDI software vendors, as well as a staggering archive of Mac and PC files. ✓ **INTERNET**→*url* http://www.magicnet.net/rz/ world_of_audio/midi_pg.html

MIDI vendors

MIDI Controllable Analog Synthesizers A nonstop barrage of facts, figures, and specifications, this page is a MIDI technophile's dream come true. Comprehensive stats on every MIDI controllable analog synth from AKAI to Waldorf (and then some) are provided along with subjective interpretations of each synth's strengths and weaknesses, availability, and price ranges. The authors have also included translation options for acronyms. ✓ **INTERNET**→*url* http:// www.me.chalmers.se/~thed/ analog.html

MIDI Vendor Forums Four large forums containing utilities and support for various MIDI-related software and hardware. Companies post press releases and upgrade information here so you can keep abreast of all that is happening in the ever-changing world of MIDI programming and composing. The forums are also a good resource for downloading sound utilities that work with specific products. The site's organization is chaotic, because the four forums are not alphabetized by company. But search and you will find. If you're looking for the Roland Corporation's files, go straight to Library C. The General Library of each vendor forum contains a master index of all the files available within each individual forum. ✓**COMPUSERVE**→*go* midi

Music and Gear This page is your direct link to the major manufacturers of electronic musical instruments and software. A large portion is devoted to all things Roland: an introduction to its sampler owner's group (sgroup) mailing list, sgroup sample libraries and utility archives, FTP sites, an equipment FAQ, and the all-important SoundCanvas Archive. Blend in healthy doses of Ensoniq, Turtle Beach, and Twelve Tone Systems information and you have a data-rife concoction that's very hard to top. ✓**INTERNET**→*url* http://www.halcyon.com/mdf/sound/sound.htm

USA New Gear Price List Maintained by Casey Palowitch, this list is an invaluable resource for anyone in the market for new and used electronic music equipment. The list of items includes keyboards, controllers, MIDI modules, drum machines, MIDI interfaces, patch bays, synchronizers, timecoders, tuners, recording and signal processing devices, sound pickup, computer cards, amplification, music-related internals, and much more. Everything is listed alphabetically by manufacturer for easy retrieval, too. Thanks to Usenet, most of the prices are up-to-the-minute calculations based on national averages; you shouldn't have to resort to guesswork when buying gear. ✓**INTERNET**→*url* http://www.pitt.

Prophet Six-Trak—from http://www.hyperreal.com/music/machines/Analogue-Heaven/

edu/~cjp/newgear.html

MOD

alt.binaries.sounds.mods (ng) This is supposed to be a newsgroup for MOD sound files, but there are also a lot of questions (and answers) about MOD players, programmers, and converters. ✓**USENET**→alt.binaries.sounds.mods

Amiga Music for the PC Everything you need to play or create MOD-format music on the Amiga. The Players and Utilities section includes MOD players (the most popular one here seems to be MODPLAY). There are also hundreds of alphabetized MOD sound files, many of which are original compositions posted by AOL members. ✓**AMERICA ONLINE**→*keyword* pmu→Browse Software Libraries Amiga Music for the PC

AMINet Subdirectory of MODS After you've chosen a sound player for your Amiga computer, visit this huge archive of digital sound modules. Indexed into numerous subcategories—including dreamy and atmospheric music, jazzy and funky music, techno, rock & roll and pop music, and piano music—the site also features subdirectories of MOD composers. So, if you get hooked on somebody's creations, you can access their collected works here.

✓**INTERNET**→*url* http://ftp.wustl.edu/~aminet/dirs/tree_mods.html

MOD FAQ Everything you could possibly want to know about digital music modules (a.k.a. MODs) in one handy little document. The FAQ outlines a brief history of the MOD file, describes similarities and differences between MOD and MIDI files, and lists the best MOD editors and players. ✓**AMERICA ONLINE**→*keyword* pcsoftware→File Search Search by file name: modfag12.zip ✓**COMPUSERVE**→*go* sight→Libraries Search by file name: modfaq.txt ✓**INTERNET**→http://www.cis.ohio-state.edu:80/text/faq/usenet/mod-faq/part1/faq.html

Sound cards/boards

Advanced Gravis Forum A support forum for users of the Gravis UltraSound sound card. Features product lists and updates, a message board for questions and answers, and a software library that houses various utilities that work with Gravis products. ✓**AMERICA ONLINE**→*keyword* gravis

comp.sys.ibm.pc.soundcard.misc (ng) Will it be a Gravis UltraSound or a Turtle Beach sound card? What's the best sound card to convert recorded phone calls into .WAV files? And does anyone out there have a Roland daughterboard they want to get rid of? This newsgroup specializes in questions, answers, and advice for PC users with sound cards. ✓USENET→comp.sys.ibm.pc.soundcard.misc

comp.sys.ibm.pc.soundcard.music (ng) This newsgroup is devoted to sound cards and music composition on PC platform computers. ✓USENET→comp.sys.ibm.pc.soundcard.music

Creative Labs Forum An encompassing resource for owners of Sound Blaster sound cards. Send in your comments and questions to the forum and you'll get professional advice from a representative at Creative. Pick up sound advice from other Blaster owners in the message section, and listen to the original creations of other audio artists in the library. ✓COMPUSERVE→*go* blaster

Soundboards Part of the Music Studio, this introduction to the world of computer audio and sound boards will probably prove invaluable to the burgeoning audiophile. Highlights include a tutorial on understanding audio terminology and specs, tips on choosing the right speakers, and an unflinching critical overview of the many soundboards available. The all-encompassing soundboard reviews include technical specs, installation tips and tricks, performance ratings (if the board is substandard, they'll be sure to let you know), prices, and manufacturer contact information. ✓INTERNET→*url* http://da.awa.com:80/nct/hardware/sondlead.html

Editors & players

alt.binaries.sounds.utilities (ng) Can't figure out how your sound player or MIDI sequencer

works? Post a query in this newsgroup and wait for a cybersound authority to reply with an answer. This is a good place to find out about sound-related software upgrades, too. ✓USENET→alt.binaries.sounds.utilities

Amiga Arts Forum A warehouse of MIDI utilities for the Amiga. Find a host of players, monitors, and samplers here. ✓COMPUSERVE→*go* amigaarts library audio and midi

Amiga Audio Archives Head to the applications subdirectory for sound players, conversion tools, and trackers for the Amiga. Then, pick up some clips. The site carries a fairly large selection of radio broadcasts, MIDI samples, and other sounds. ✓INTERNET→*url* ftp://www.funet.fi/pub/amiga/audio

AMINet Musical Software Archive All the software you'll need to make, play, or edit music on your Amiga computer. Hundreds of downloadable programs indexed by composing software, MIDI software, miscellaneous software, and sound players. ✓INTERNET→*url* http://wuarchive.wustl.edu/~aminet/dirs/tree_mus.html

Apple II Music and Sound Dedicated to music composition and sound on the Apple II computer. Download sound players, editors, and converters from the Applications library and then pay a visit to the sound libraries, where you'll find hundreds of archived sounds. There are also libraries for MIDI and MOD programmers, with original compositions by members of the forum. Have questions about sound digitizing, music education, and MIDI? Post them on the message boards and get feedback from others who make music on the Apple II. ✓AMERICA ONLINE→*keyword* a2→Music and Sound

Atari Music The directory is almost exclusively filled with applications for listening to or manipulating music on the Atari—look elsewhere for sound clips. The range of offerings extends from a MIDI sequencer to a .TUN file player to a MOD player. ✓INTERNET ...→*url* gopher://gopher.archive.umich.edu:7055/00/atari/Music ...→*url* ftp://atari.archive.umich.edu/Music ...→*url* ftp://wuarchive.wustl.edu/systems/atari/umich.edu/Music/

comp.sys.amiga.audio (ng)

Standard MIDI studio—from http://www.magicnet.net/rz/world_of_audio/woa.html

"Does anybody know of a MOD-to-MIDI converter program?" asks Dave. The Doomster, on the other hand, is looking for FTP sites with MOD files. And Chris at the University of Washington-Parkside needs help writing a program that converts sequences of DNA to a MIDI file. It's an informative place to bring your questions about Amiga audio format and conversion. ✓**USENET**→comp.sys.amiga.audio

Mac Shareware 500 This software and sound-file library is based on the *Mac Shareware 500* book from Ventana Press, which reviews and describes the top 500 Mac shareware files. Visit the Sound & Music area and download all the best sound players, editors, and converters for the Mac. (Ventana's editors have tested hundreds of sound players for the Macintosh; SoundMaster 1.7.3 is one of their favorites.) There is also a handy Electronic Music Encyclopedia that will help you when you're stumped on terminology. ✓**AMERICA ONLINE**→*keyword* mac500→Sound & Music

Macintosh Music and Sound Forum Want to make music on the Mac? Go to the Macintosh Software Center's Greatest Hits area in the software libraries to download reliable, easy-to-use sound players like SoundMaster and Now Hear This. Attend a weekly conference or engage in real-time chat with a fellow forum member about the technological and aesthetic issues of digital sound. The software libraries are filled with sound files. Use the America Online sounds to customize your AOL software, or explore the world of pop culture with TV samples, music samples, movie samples, cartoon samples, and science fiction samples. Begin-

ners should head to the message boards for some sound advice: "I can't play MIDI files!" screams one post; "Buy a sequencer program that can play standard MIDI files (SMFs)! All the good ones will play SMFs!" shouts back another. ✓**AMERICA ONLINE**→*keyword* mms

PC Music and Sound Forum "What is the BEST sound card?" (The general consensus on the message board in this huge forum specializing in music composition and playback on most PC platforms is the Roland Rap-10). Want to continue the discussion in a live forum? Attend one of the weekly conferences, where electronic music aficionados can congregate online to swap industry lore or offer tips and tricks to fellow musicians in real time. Pay a visit to the software libraries and download sound players for MIDI, MOD, and other sound-file formats. Get sound samples in MOD, VOC, or .WAV formats from the Digitized Sounds library. ✓**AMERICA ONLINE**→*keyword* pmu

Sound & Music Utilities The Sound & Music Utilities library carries a Windows drum machine, a .WAV converter, a music-composition program, a dual MIDI and .WAV player, sound editors and conversion programs, and other audio utilities. ✓**AMERICA ONLINE**→*keyword* mmw→Library →Sound & Music

Windows Music & Sound For Windows users, this forum contains sound tools and utilities for playback and composing, including WHAM and GoldWave, two highly recommended, easy-to-use sound editors for .WAV files. The .WAV sound clips archive is organized into the following categories: cartoons, comedians, events, games, historical sounds,

interview excerpts, movie and music clips, and radio clips. Scooby Doo fans should head to the cartoons section for dialogue snippets from the old Hanna-Barbera show (catch Casey Kasem, as Shaggy, talking that crazy seventies talk). ✓**AMERICA ONLINE**→ *keyword* winforum→Browse the Software Libraries →More Music & Sound

Windows Shareware 500 The same features as the Macintosh 500 Shareware forum, but for Windows. There are very few sound players to download, but the selection of sound files is impressive (although not primarily music-related). ✓**AMERICA ONLINE** →*keyword* win 500→Windows 500 shareware Library→More... Music & Sound or Utilities

Sound formats

Audio File Formats FAQ This extensive, two-part FAQ is likely to have the answers regardless of your question. Intense, technical dissections of every known audio file format are interspersed with information on hardware, file compression, format conversion, FTP sites, and mailing lists. In short, the most complete and up-to-date guide to computer sound files available on the Net. ✓**AMERICA ONLINE**→*keyword* pcsoftware→ File Search→Search by file name: audiofm.zip ✓**INTERNET**→*url* http://www.cis.ohio-state.edu:80/text/faq/usenet/audio-fmts/top.html

The Music Studio A Web page dedicated to an emerging multimedia data type for WWW audio distribution. The site features sound clips in both .AU format and NetSound format—industrious Netters can compare the quality. ✓**INTERNET**→*url* http://sound.media.mit.edu/~mkc/netsound.html

Education & therapy

It was Mozart, or maybe Johnny Thunders, who said, "Music lovers are born, but musi-

cians are *made.*" And it's true—to really understand the ins and outs of an instrument, or a treble clef, you need training, the counsel of elders, the support of peers. Online music education resources are often folded into more general college curricula; however, there are a few Websites and commercial service forums devoted to composition, harmonics, and syncopation. Begin at **Resources for Music Education**, which collects Internet sites pertaining to music education. Learn about how music can soothe the savaged beast at the **Music Therapy Home Page**. And then consult the dozens of music schools online, from **Keshet Eilon** to **Sibelius Academy**.

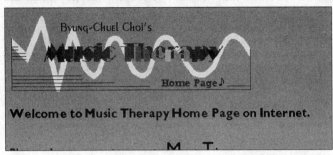

The Music Therapy Home Page—from http://falcon.cc. ukans.edu/~bchoi/mt.html

Music education

Ask The Musical Doctor The Musical Doctor isn't one of those guys who plays old Motown hits during your appendectomy. Rather, he's a music theory instructor who wants you to know everything you can about measures, scales, and hemidemisemiquavers. Pick up publications in the Reading Room; share your opinions and experiences in the

It's Your Turn section; step into the Doctor's Office for some music consultation and tutoring; and speak with the doctor in live-chat sessions. You'll never need musical doctoring again. ✓**EWORLD**→*go* musdoc

Resources for Music Education An extensive list of resources for music teachers collected by Tina Scott, a computer-based music education and choral music methods teacher. Divided into two sections, printed resources and electronic resources, her list includes books and publications on teaching general music, music and early childhood, instrumental music, vocal music, and teaching "special learners." ✓**INTERNET**→*url* http://www.ed.uiuc.edu/EdPsy-387/Tina-Scott/project/home.html

University-Level Music Education Operated by the CTI Centre, a British educational institution devoted to the use of computers in university music instruction, this list addresses a wide variety of topics. ✓**INTERNET**→*email* mail base@mailbase.ac.uk ✍ *Type in message body:* join cti-music <your full name>

Music therapy

Music Theory Principles The fundamental principles of music therapy are explained by E. Thayer Gaston and William Sears, who are both former heads of the Music Therapy Department at the University of Kansas. ✓**INTERNET**→ *url* http://ukanaix.cc.ukans.edu/~ dirkcush/mt.html

Music Therapy Home Page What is music therapy? What types of illnesses are treated with music therapy? Where do music therapists work? Discover how the physically handicapped, mentally ill, emotionally disturbed, and chemically dependent, among others, can benefit from treatment with musical therapy. ✓**INTERNET**→ *url* http://falcon.cc.ukans.edu/ ~bchoi/mt.html

Music Therapy Mailing List (ml) Meet others who are interested in this growing branch of medical science and discuss the issues with them. ✓**INTERNET**→*email* listserv@ ukanvm.cc.ukans.edu ✍ *Type in message body:* subscribe MUSTHP-L <your full name>

Music Schools

Acadia University—School of Music √INTERNET→*url* http://max.acadiau.ca/arts/music/home.html

Batish Institute of Indian Music and Fine Arts √INTERNET→*url* http://hypatia.ucsc.edu:70/1/RELATED/Batish

California Institute of the Arts: School of Music √INTERNET→*url* http://music.calarts.edu/

Canberra School of Music—The Australian National University √INTERNET→*url* http://ausarts.anu.edu.au/www/music/csm.html

Center for Computer Music Research and Composition at UCSB √INTERNET→*url* http://ccmrc.ucsb.edu/

CSU Fresno Department of Music √INTERNET→*url* http://www.csufresno.edu/music/

DePaul University School of Music √INTERNET→*url* http://www.telusys.com/demos/depaul.music1/depaul.music.html

Durham Music Technology √INTERNET→*url* http://capella.dur.ac.uk/doug/dmtg.html

The Esther Boyer College of Music √INTERNET→*url* http://betty.music.temple.edu/EBCM/

Florida State University—Music √INTERNET→*url* http://www.music.fsu.edu/

Furman University—Music √INTERNET→http://www.music.fsu.edu/http://ns9000.furman.edu/~bs

choon/dept/DHome.html

George F. DeVine Music Library (Univ. of Tennessee) √INTERNET→*url* http://www.lib.utk.edu/music/musihome.html

Global Music Centre √INTERNET→*url* http://www.finland.eu.net/gmc/

Indiana University School of Music Library √INTERNET→*url* http://www.music.indiana.edu/

Institut de Recherche et Coordination Acoustique/Musique √INTERNET→*url* http://www.ircam.fr/index-e.html

Keshet Eilon √INTERNET→*url* http://www.actcom.co.il/~eshet/keshet7.htm

Leeds University Department of Music √INTERNET→*url* http://www.leeds.ac.uk/music.html

McGill University √INTERNET→*url* http://lecaine.music.mcgill.ca/

Music at Mizzou √INTERNET→*url* http://www.missouri.edu/~musicwww/

Peabody Conservatory of the Johns Hopkins University √INTERNET→*url* http://www.peabody.jhu.edu

Radford University—Department of Music √INTERNET→*url* http://www.runet.edu/~muscweb/

Sibelius Academy √INTERNET→*url* http://www.siba.fi/welcome-eng.html

University College Salford Music Division √INTERNET→*url* http://www.ucsalf.ac.uk/pa/musdiv/mushome.htm

University of Alabama School of Music √INTERNET→*url* http://stimpy.music.ua.edu/

Univ. of California at Davis—Music and Drama √INTERNET→*url* http://musdra.ucdavis.edu/

University of Edinburgh—Faculty of Music √INTERNET→*url* http://www.music.ed.ac.uk/

University of Louisville—Music Library √INTERNET→*url* http://www.louisville.edu/groups/library-www/music/music.h

University of Michigan—School of Music √INTERNET→*url* http://web-bern.music.umich.edu/

University of Oklahoma—School of Music √INTERNET→*url* http://www.uoknor.edu/music/OUSoM/index.html

University of Richmond—Department of Music √INTERNET→*url* http://www.urich.edu/~music

University of South Florida—School of Music √INTERNET→*url* http://arts.usf.edu/music/music.html

University of Warwick Music Centre √INTERNET→*url* http://www.csv.warwick.ac.uk/~music/

Virginia Tech Music Department √INTERNET→*url* http://server.music.vt.edu/

Appendices

Internet Providers

by region and state

National

America OnLine
800-827-6364 (vox)

CompuServe
800-848-8199 (vox)

Delphi
800-695-4005 (vox)

GEnie
800-638-9636 (vox)

NETCOM On-Line Communications Services
800-501-8649/408-554-8649 (vox)

Prodigy
800-776-3449 (vox)

Regional

Internet Express
800-592-1240 (vox)

Interpath
800-849-6305 (vox)

Alabama

Community Internet Connect, Inc.
205-722-0199 (vox)

db Technology
205-556-9020 (vox)

interQuest
205-464-8280 (vox)

WSNetwork Communications Services, Inc.
800-463-8750/334-263-5505 (vox)

Arkansas

Cloverleaf Technologies
903-832-1367 (vox)

IntelliNet
800-290-7677 (vox)

Arizona

Crossroads Communications
602-813-9040 (vox)

Internet Direct of Utah, Inc.
602-274-0100 (vox)

Opus One
602-324-0494 (vox)

Primenet
800-463-8386/602-870-1010 (vox)

RTD Systems & Networking, Inc.
520-318-0696 (vox)

Systems Solutions Inc.
602-955-5566 (vox)

California

Access InfoSystems
707-422-1034 (vox)

Aimnet Information Services
408-257-0900 (vox)

Beckmeyer Development
510-530-9637 (vox)

CC NET
510-988-0680 (vox)

CineNet
310-399-4421 (vox)

Cloverleaf Communications
714-895-3075 (vox)

CONNECTnet Internet Network Services
619-450-0254 (vox)

CRL
415-837-5300 (vox)

CTS Network Services
619-637-3637 (vox)

Cybergate Information Services
209-486-4283 (vox)

Delta Internet Services
714-778-0370 (vox)

DigiLink Network Services
310-542-7421 (vox)

Direct Net Access Incorporated
510-649-6110 (vox)

Directnet
213-383-3144 (vox)

EarthLink Network, Inc.
213-644-9500 (vox)

Electriciti
619-338-9000 (vox)

HoloNet Information Access
510-704-0160 (vox)

Infoserv Connections
408-335-5600 (vox)

INTERNEX
408-496-5466 (vox)

ISP Networks
408-653-0100 (vox)

KAIWAN Internet
714-638-2139 (vox)

LanMinds, Inc.
510-843-6389 (vox)

Lightside, Inc.
818-858-9261 (vox)

LineX Communications
415-455-1650 (vox)

NetGate Communications
408-565-9601 (vox)

Northcoast Internet
707-443-8696 (vox)

Primenet
800-463-8386/602-395-1010 (vox)

QuakeNet
415-655-6607 (vox)

Regional Alliance for Information Networking
805-967-7246 (vox)

Scruz-Net
800-319-5555/408-457-5050 (vox)

Sierra-Net
702-832-6911 (vox)

South Valley Internet
408-683-4533 (vox)

ViaNet Communications
415-903-2242 (vox)

The WELL
415-332-4335 (vox)

West Coast Online
707-586-3060 (vox)

WombatNet
415-462-8800 (vox)

zNET
619-755-7772 (vox)

Colorado

Colorado SuperNet, Inc.
303-296-8202 (vox)

Community News Service, Inc.
719-592-1240 (vox)

CSDC, Inc.
303-665-8053 (vox)

ENVISIONET, Inc.
303-770-2408 (vox)

Indra's Net, Inc.
303-546-9151 (vox)

Old Colorado City Communications
719-528-5849 (vox)

Rocky Mountain Internet
800-900-7644 (vox)

Stonehenge Internet Communications
800-786-4638 (vox)

Connecticut

CONNIX
203-349-7059 (vox)

Futuris Networks, Inc.
203-359-8868 (vox)

I-2000, Inc.
516-867-6379 (vox)

Paradigm Communications
203-250-7397 (vox)

District of Columbia

CAPCON Library Network
202-331-5771 (vox)

CharmNet
410-558-3900 (vox)

Genuine Computing Resources
703-878-4680 (vox)

Internet Online, Inc.
301-652-4468 (vox)

usNet, Inc.
301-572-5926 (vox)

Delaware

SSNet, Inc.
302-378-1386 (vox)

Florida

Acquired Knowledge Systems Inc.
305-525-2574 (vox)

CocoNet Corporation
813-540-2626 (vox)

CyberGate, Inc.
305-428-4283 (vox)

IDS
401-885-6855/800-IDS-1680 (vox)

The EmiNet Domain
407-731-0222 (vox)

Florida Online
407-635-8888/800-676-2599 (vox)

InternetU
407-952-8487 (vox)

MagicNet, Inc.
407-657-2202 (vox)

MetroLink Internet Services
407-726-6707 (vox)

PacketWorks, Inc.
813-446-8826 (vox)

Polaris Network, Inc.
904-878-9745 (vox)

PSS InterNet Services
800-463-8499 (vox)

SatelNET Communications
305-434-8738 (vox)

SymNet
904-222-8555 (vox)

Georgia

Internet Atlanta
404-410-9000 (vox)

MindSpring
404-888-0725 (vox)

Prometheus Information Network Group, Inc. (PING)
800-746-4835 (vox)

Hawaii

Hawaii OnLine
808-533-6981/800-291-5951 (vox)

LavaNet, Inc.
808-545-5282 (vox)

Pacific Information Exchange, Inc.
808-596-7494 (vox)

Sense Networking
408-335-9400 (vox)

Idaho

Micron Internet Services
208-368-5400 (vox)

Primenet
800-463-8386/602-870-1010 (vox)

Illinois

American Information Systems
708-413-8400/312-255-8500 (vox)

Allied Access, Inc.
800-463-8366 (vox)

InterAccess Co.
800-967-1580 (vox)

Open Business Systems, Inc.
708-250-0260 (vox)

Ripco Communications, Inc.
312-477-6210 (vox)

Tezcatlipoca, Inc.
312-850-0181 (vox)

WorldWide Access
708-367-1870 (vox)

Indiana

Evansville Online
812-479-1700 (vox)

HolliCom Internet Services
317-883-4500 (vox)

IgLou Internet ServiceS
800-436-4456 (vox)

IQuest Network Services
317-259-5050 (vox)

Metropolitan Data Networks Limited
317-449-0539 (vox)

Net Direct
317-251-5252 (vox)

World Connection Services
812-479-1700 (vox)

Kansas

DATABANK, Inc.
913-842-6699 (vox)

Interstate Networking Corporation
816-472-4949 (vox)

Primenet
800-463-8386/602-870-1010 (vox)

SouthWind Internet Access, Inc.
316-263-7963 (vox)

Kentucky

IgLou Internet ServiceS
800-436-4456 (vox)

Lousiana

Communique Inc.
504-527-6200 (vox)

I-Link Ltd
800-454-6599 (vox)

NEOSOFT
800-438-6367/713-968-5800 (vox)

Maine

Agate Internet
207-947-8248 (vox)

Maryland

CAPCON Library Network
202-331-5771 (vox)

CharmNet
410-558-3900 (vox)

FredNet
301-631-5300 (vox)

Genuine Computing Resources
703-878-4680 (vox)

Internet Interstate
301-652-4468 (vox)

jaguNET Access Services
410-931-3157 (vox)

Softaid Internet Services Inc.
410-290-7763 (vox)

usNet, Inc.
301-572-5926 (vox)

Massachusetts
CENTnet, Inc.
617-492-6079 (vox)

FOURnet Information Network
508-291-2900 (vox)

The Internet Access Company
617-276-7200 (vox)

intuitive information, inc.
508-342-1100 (vox)

Mallard Electronics, Inc.
413-732-0214 (vox)

North Shore Access
617-593-3110 (vox)

Pioneer Global
617-375-0200 (vox)

ShaysNet.COM
413-772-2923 (vox)

StarNet Internet Access (Advanced Communication Systems, Inc.)
508-922-8238 (vox)

TerraNet, Inc.
617-450-9000 (vox)

UltraNet Communications, Inc.
800-763-8111/508-229-8400 (vox)

Wilder Systems, Inc.
617-933-8810 (vox)

The World
617-739-0202 (vox)

Michigan
Branch Information Services
313-741-4442 (vox)

ICNET / Innovative Concepts
313-998-0090 (vox)

Isthmus Corporation
313-973-2100 (vox)

Msen, Inc.
313-998-4562 (vox)

RustNet, Inc.
810-650-6812 (vox)

Minnesota
InforMNs
612-638-8786 (vox)

Internet Connections, Inc.
507-625-7320 (vox)

Intrnet.Net
800-254-2818 EXT. 100 (vox)

Red River Net
701-232-2227 (vox)

StarNet Communications, Inc.
612-941-9177 (vox)

Missouri
Allied Access, Inc.
800-463-8366 (vox)

THOUGHTPORT
314-474-6870 (vox)

Montana
Montana Online
406-721-4952 (vox)

North Carolina
Red Barn Data Center
910-750-9809 (vox)

SunBelt.Net
803-328-1500 (vox)

Vnet Internet Access
800-377-3282/704-334-3282 (vox)

North Dakota
Red River Net
701-232-2227 (vox)

Nebraska
Internet Nebraska
402-434-8680 (vox)

New Conclusions, Inc.
800-345-9669 (vox)

New Hampshire
Destek
603-635-7263 (vox)

info@millcomm.com
603-635-3857 (vox)

MV Communications, Inc.
603-429-2223 (vox)

NETIS Public Access Internet
603-437-1811 (vox)

New Jersey
Carroll-Net
201-488-1332 (vox)

Castle Network, Inc.
800-577-9449/908-548-8881 (vox)

The Connection
201-435-4414 (vox)

I-2000, Inc.
516-867-6379 (vox)

INTAC Access Corporation
800-504-6822 (vox)

InterCom Online
212-714-7183 (vox)

Internet For 'U'
800-638-9291 (vox)

Internet Online Services
201-928-1000 EXT.226 (vox)

Internet Providers

K2NE Software
609-893-0673 (vox)

New Jersey Computer Connection
609-896-2799 (vox)

New York Net
718-776-6811 (vox)

NIC - Neighborhood Internet Connection
201-934-1445 (vox)

Planet Access Networks
201-691-4704 (vox)

New Mexico

Computer Systems Consulting
505-984-0085 (vox)

Southwest Cyberport
505-271-0009 (vox)

ZyNet SouthWest
505-343-8846 (vox)

Nevada

Great Basin Internet Services
702-348-7299 (vox)

InterMind
702-878-6111 (vox)

NevadaNet
702-784-4827 (vox)

Sierra-Net
702-831-3353 (vox)

wizard.com
702-871-4461 (vox)

New York

Blythe Systems
212-979-0440 (vox)

Cloud 9 Internet
914-682-0626 (vox)

Computer Solutions by Hawkinson
914-473-0844 (vox)

Creative Data Consultants (SILLY.COM)
718-229-0489 EXT.23 (vox)

E-Znet, Inc.
716-262-2485 (vox)

East Greenwich, Rhode Island
401-885-6855 (vox)

Echo Communications Group
212-255-3839 (vox)

escape.com - Kazan Corp
212-888-8780 (vox)

I-2000, Inc.
516-867-6379 (vox)

Ingress Communications Inc.
212-268-1100 EXT. 105 (vox)

INTAC Access Corporation
800-504-6822 (vox)

InterCom Online
212-714-7183 (vox)

The Internet Channel
212-243-5200 (vox)

Internet For 'U'
800-638-9291 (vox)

Internet Online Services
201-928-1000 EXT.226 (vox)

Interport Communications Corp.
212-989-1128 (vox)

LI Net, Inc.
516-265-0997 (vox)

Maestro
212-240-9600 (vox)

Mnematics, Incorporated
914-359-4546 (vox)

Moran Communications
716-639-1254 (vox)

Network Internet Services
516-543-0234 (vox)

New York Net
718-776-6811 (vox)

NY WEBB, Inc.
800-458-4660 (vox)

NYSERNet
315-453-2912 EXT.294/286 (vox)

Panix
212-741-4400 (vox)

PHANTOM (MindVox)
212-989-2418 (vox)

The Pipeline Network
212-267-3636 (vox)

ServiceTech
716-546-6908 (vox)

TZ-Link
914-353-5443 (vox)

Wizvax Communications
518-273-4325 (vox)

Ohio

APK Net, Ltd
216-481-9428 (vox)

The Dayton Network Access Company
513-237-6868 (vox)

EriNet
513-436-1700 (vox)

Exchange Network Services, Inc.
216-615-9400 (vox)

IgLou Internet ServiceS
800-436-4456 (vox)

Infinite Systems
614-268-9941 (vox)

Internet Access Cincinnati
513-887-8877 (vox)

New Age Consulting Service
216-524-8414 (vox)

Oarnet
800-627-8101 EXT.217/614-728-8100 (vox)

Oklahoma
Questar Network Services
405-848-3228 (vox)

Oregon
Data Research Group, Inc.
503-465-3282 (vox)

Europa
503-222-9508 (vox)

Hevanet Communications
503-228-3520 (vox)

Open Door Networks, Inc.
503-488-4127 (vox)

Structured Network Systems, Inc.
800-881-0962/503-656-3530 (vox)

Teleport, Inc.
503-223-4245 (vox)

Transport Logic
503-243-1940 (vox)

Pennsylvania
City-Net
412-481-5406 (vox)

King of Prussia, PA 19406
610-337-9994 (vox)

Microserve Information Systems
800-380-4638/717-821-5964 (vox)

OASIS
610-439-8560 (vox)

PREPnet
412-268-7870 (vox)

PSCNET
412-268-4960 (vox)

SSNet, Inc.
302-378-1386 (vox)

Telerama Public Access Internet
412-481-3505 (vox)

YOU TOOLS Corporation
610-954-5910 (vox)

Rhode Island
IDS World Network
401-885-6855 (vox)

South Carolina
A World of Difference, Inc.
803-769-4488 (vox)

Global Vision Inc.
803-241-0901 (vox)

SIMS, Inc.
803-762-4956 (vox)

South Carolina SuperNet
803-748-1207 (vox)

SunBelt.Net
803-328-1500 (vox)

Tennessee
The Edge
615-726-8700 (vox)

GoldSword Systems
615-691-6498 (vox)

ISDN-Net Inc.
615-377-7672 (vox)

Magibox Incorporated
901-452-7555 (vox)

Preferred Internet Services
615-323-1142 (vox)

The Telalink Corporation
615-321-9100 (vox)

The Tri-Cities Connection
615-378-5355 (vox)

Texas
The Black Box
713-480-2684 (vox)

Cloverleaf Technologies
903-832-1367 (vox)

Electrotex,Inc.
800-460-1801/713-526-3456 (vox)

I-Link Ltd
800-454-6599 (vox)

Illuminati Online
512-462-0999 (vox)

Internet Access of El Paso
915-533-1525 (vox)

Internet Connect Services
512-572-9987 (vox)

NEOSOFT
800-438-6367 (vox)

Real/Time Communications
512-451-0046 (vox)

Sesquinet
713-527-4988 (vox)

@sig.net
512-306-0700 (vox)

Texas Metronet, Inc.
214-705-2900 (vox)

USiS
713-682-1666 (vox)

Zilker Internet Park, Inc.
512-206-3850 (vox)

Utah

DATABANK, Inc.
913-842-6699 (vox)

XMission
801-539-0852 (vox)

Virginia

CAPCON Library Network
202-331-5771 (vox)

CharmNet
410-558-3900 (vox)

CLARK
410-254-3900 (vox)

DATABANK, Inc.
913-842-6699 (vox)

Genine Computing Resources
703-878-4680 (vox)

Internet Interstate
301-652-4468 (vox)

usNet, Inc.
301-572-5926 (vox)

Widomaker Communication Service
804-253-7621 (vox)

Washington

dBUG
206-932-6369 (vox)

Eskimo North
206-361-1161 (vox)

Halcyon
206-455-3505 (vox)

Internetworks, Inc.
206-576-7147 (vox)

Network Access Services
206-733-9279 (vox)

Northwest NEXUS
206-455-3505 (vox)

Olympus Net
360-385-0464 (vox)

Pacific Rim Network, Inc.
360-650-0442 (vox)

Pacifier Computers
206-254-3886 (vox)

Seanet Online Services
206-343-7828 (vox)

SenseMedia
408-335-9400 (vox)

Skagit On-Line Services
360-755-0190 (vox)

Structured Network Systems, Inc.
800-881-0962/503-656-3530 (vox)

Teleport, Inc.
503-223-4245 (vox)

Transport Logic
503-243-1940 (vox)

WLN
800-342-5956/360-923-4000 (vox)

Wisconsin

Exec-PC, Inc.
800-393-2721/414-789-4200 (vox)

FullFeed Communications
608-246-4239 (vox)

MIX Communications
414-351-1868 (vox)

NetNet, Inc.
414-499-1339 (vox)

WiscNet
608-265-7661 (vox)

West Virginia

WVNET
304-293-5192 (vox)

Wyoming

wyoming.com
800-996-4638/307-332-3030 (vox)

Canada

CCI Networks
403-450-6787 (vox)

Communication Accessibles Montreal
514-288-2581 (vox)

Debug Computer Services
403-248-5798 (vox)

Information Gateway Services
613-592-5619 (vox)

Island Net
604-383-0096 (vox)

HookUp Communications
905-847-8000 (vox)

Okanagan Internet Junction
604-549-1036 (vox)

Sunshine Net, Inc.
604-886-4120 (vox)

@	Separates the **userid** and **domain name** of an Internet address. Pronounced "at."
anonymous FTP	Method of logging in to public file archives over the **Internet**. Enter "anonymous" when prompted for a **userid**. See **FTP**.
Archie	A program that lets you search **Internet FTP** archives worldwide by file name. One variant is called **Veronica**.
ASCII	A basic text format readable by most computers. The acronym stands for American Standard Code for Information Interchange.
bandwidth	The data transmission capacity of a network. Used colloquially to refer to the "size" of the Net; some information transmittals (e.g., multitudes of graphic files) are considered to be a "waste of bandwidth."
baud	The speed at which signals are sent by a **modem**, measured by the number of changes per second in the signals during transmission. A baud rate of 1,200, for example, would indicate 1,200 signal changes in one second. Baud rate is often confused with **bits per second (bps)**.
BBS	"Bulletin-board system." Once referred to stand-alone desktop computers with a single modem that answered the phone, but can now be as complicated and interconnected as a commercial service.
binary transfer	A file transfer between two computers that preserves binary data—used for all non-text files.
bits per second (bps)	The data-transfer rate between two **modems**. The higher the bps, the higher the speed of the transfer.
bounced message	An **email** message "returned to sender," usually because of an address error.
bye	A log-off command, like "quit" and "exit."
carrier signal	The squeaking noise that modems use to maintain a connection. See also **handshake**.
cd	"Change directory." A command used, for example, at an **FTP** site to move from a directory to a subdirectory.
cdup	"Change directory up." Can be used at an **FTP** site to move from a subdirectory to its parent directory. Also **chdirup**.
chdirup	See **cdup**.
client	A computer that connects to a more powerful computer (see **server**) for complex tasks.
commercial service	General term for large online services (e.g., America Online, CompuServe, Prodigy, GEnie).
compression	Shrinkage of computer files to conserve storage space and reduce transfer times. Special utility programs, available for most platforms (including DOS, Mac, and

	Amiga), perform the compression and decompression.
cracker	A person who maliciously breaks into a computer system in order to steal files or disrupt system activities.
dial-up access	Computer connection made over standard telephone lines.
dir	"Directory." A command used to display the contents of the current directory.
domain name	The worded address of an **IP number** on the **Internet**, in the form of domain subsets separated by periods. The full address of an **Internet** user is **userid@domain name**.
email	"Electronic mail."
emoticon	See **smiley**.
FAQ	"Frequently asked questions." A file of questions and answers compiled for **Usenet newsgroups**, **mailing lists**, and games to reduce repeated posts about commonplace subjects.
file transfer	Transfer of a file from one computer to another over a network.
finger	A program that provides information about a user who is logged into your local system or on a remote computer on the Internet. Generally invoked by typing "finger" and the person's **userid**.
flame	A violent and usually *ad hominem* attack against another person in a **newsgroup** or message area.
flame war	A back-and-forth series of **flames**.
Free-Net	A community-based network that provides free access to the **Internet**, usually to local residents, and often includes its own forums and news.
freeware	Free software. Not to be confused with **shareware**.
FTP	"File transfer protocol." The standard used to transfer files between computers.
get	An **FTP** command that transfers single files from the **FTP** site to your local directory. The command is followed by a file name; typing "get file.name" would transfer only that file. Also see **mget**.
GIF	Common file format for pictures first popularized by CompuServe, standing for "graphics interchange format." Pronounced with a hard *g*.
gopher	A menu-based guide to directories on the **Internet**, usually organized by subject.
GUI	"Graphical user interface" with windows and point-and-click capability, as opposed to a command-line interface with typed-out instructions.
hacker	A computer enthusiast who enjoys exploring computer systems and programs, sometimes to the point of obsession. Not to be confused with **cracker**.
handle	The name a user wishes to be known by; a user's handle may differ significantly from his or her real name or **userid**.
handshake	The squawking noise at the beginning of a computer connection when two modems settle on a protocol for exchanging information.
Home Page	The main **World Wide Web** site for a particular group or organization.
hqx	File suffix for a BinHex file, a common format for transmitting Macintosh binary files over the **Internet**.
hypertext	An easy method of retrieving information by choosing highlighted words in a text on the screen. The words link to documents with related subject matter.
IC	"In character." A game player who is IC is acting as his or her **character**'s persona.
Internet	The largest network of computer networks in the world, easily recognizable by the format of Internet **email** addresses: **userid@**host.

Internet provider	Wholesale or retail reseller of access to the **Internet**. YPN is one example.
IP connection	Full-fledged link to the **Internet**. See **SLIP**, **PPP**, and **TCP/IP**.
IP number	The unique number that determines the ultimate **Internet** identity of an **IP connection**.
IRC	"**Internet** relay chat." A service that allows **real-time** conversations between multiple users on a variety of subject-oriented channels.
jpeg	Common compressed format for picture files. Pronounced "jay-peg."
ls	"List." A command that provides simplified directory information at **FTP** sites and other directories. It lists only file names for the directory, not file sizes or dates.
lurkers	Regular readers of messages online who never post.
lynx	A popular text-based **Web browser**.
mailing list	Group discussion distributed through **email**. Many mailing lists are administered through listserv.
mget	An **FTP** command that transfers multiple files from the **FTP** site to your local directory. The command is followed by a list of file names separated by spaces, sometimes in combination with an asterisk used as a wild card. Typing "mget b*" would transfer all files in the directory beginning with the letter *b*. Also see **get**.
Net, the	A colloquial term that is often used to refer to the entirety of Cyberspace: the **Internet**, the **commercial services**, **BBSs**, etc.
netiquette	The rules of Cyberspace civility. Usually applied to the **Internet**, where manners are enforced exclusively by fellow users.
newbie	A newcomer to the **Net**, to a game, or to a discussion. Also called **fluxer**.
newsgroups	The **Usenet** message areas, organized by subject.
newsreader	Software program for reading **Usenet newsgroups** on the **Internet**.
port number	A number that follows a **telnet** address. The number connects a user to a particular application on the telnet site. LambdaMOO, for example, is at port 8888 of lambda.parc.xerox.com (lambda.parc.xerox.com 8888).
posting	The sending of a message to a **newsgroup**, bulletin board, or other public message area. The message itself is called a **post**.
pwd	A command used at an **FTP** site to display the name of the current directory on your screen.
real-time	The **Net** term for "live," as in "live broadcast." Real-time connections include **IRC** and **MUDs**.
remote machine	Any computer on the **Internet** reached with a program such as **FTP** or **telnet**. The machine making the connection is called the home, or local, machine.
RL	"Real life."
server	A software program, or the computer running the program, that allows other computers, called **clients**, to share its resources.
shareware	Free software, distributed over the **Net** with a request from the programmer for voluntary payment.
sig	Short for **signature**.
signature	A file added to the end of **email** messages or **Usenet** posts that contains personal information—usually your name, email address, postal address, and telephone number. **Netiquette** dictates that signatures, or **sigs**, should be no longer than four or five lines.
SLIP and PPP	"Serial line **Internet** protocol" and "point-to-point protocol." Connecting by

	SLIP or PPP actually puts a computer on the Internet, which offers a number of advantages over regular **dial-up**. A SLIP or PPP connection can support a graphical **Web browser** (such as Mosaic), and allows for multiple connections at the same time. Requires special software and a SLIP or PPP service provider.
smiley	Text used to indicate emotion, humor, or irony in electronic messages—best understood if viewed sideways. Also called an **emoticon**. The most common smileys are :-) and :-(
snail mail	The paper mail the U.S. Postal Service delivers. The forerunner of **email**.
spam	The posting of the same article to multiple **newsgroups** (usually every possible one) regardless of the appropriateness of the topic (e.g., "Make Money Fast").
sysop	"System operator." The person who owns and/or manages a **BBS** or other **Net** site.
TCP/IP	The "transmission control protocol" and the "**Internet** protocol." The basis of a full-fledged Internet connection. See **IP Connection**, **PPP**, and **SLIP**. Pronounced "T-C-P-I-P."
telnet	An **Internet** program that allows you to log into other Internet-connected computers.
terminal emulator	A program or utility that allows a computer to communicate in a foreign or non-standard **terminal mode**.
terminal mode	The software standard a computer uses for text communication—for example, ANSI for PCs and **VT-100** for UNIX.
thread	Posted **newsgroup** message with a series of replies. Threaded **newsreaders** organize replies under the original subject.
timeout	The break in communication that occurs when two computers are talking and one takes so long to respond that the other gives up.
URL	"Uniform resource locator." The **World Wide Web** address of a resource on the **Internet**.
Usenet	A collection of networks and computer systems that exchange messages, organized by subject in **newsgroups**.
userid	The unique name (often eight characters or less) given to a user on a system for his or her account. The complete address, which can be used for **email** or **fingering**, is a userid followed by the @ sign and the **domain name** (e.g., Bill Clinton's address is president@whitehouse.gov).
Veronica	See **Archie**.
VT-100 emulation	Widely used terminal protocol for formatting full screens of text over computer connections.
WAIS	"Wide area information server." A system that searches through database indexes around the **Internet**, using keywords.
Web browser	A **client** program designed to interact with **World Wide Web servers** on the **Internet** for the purpose of viewing **Web pages**.
Web page	A **hypertext** document that is part of the **World Wide Web** and that can incorporate graphics, sounds, and links to other **Web pages**, **FTP** sites, **gophers**, and a variety of other **Internet** resources.
World Wide Web	A **hypertext**-based navigation system that lets you browse through a variety of linked **Net** resources, including **Usenet newsgroups** and **FTP**, **telnet**, and **gopher** sites, without typing commands. Also known as WWW and the Web.
zip	File-compression standard in the DOS and Windows worlds.

Index

The *NetMusic* index includes names of every Net site that appears in the book. Some of these sites carry names that are identical to the names of artists. For instance, there is a Website about Alice Cooper named **Alice Cooper**, and a Website about Albert Ayler named **Albert Ayler**. In these cases, we have double-listed items and indexed them both under the site name and the artist name. As a result, a Website named Michael Jackson would be indexed both as **Michael Jackson** and as **Jackson, Michael**.

Index

Index

Index

Index

Index

Index

Index

Index

Index

Index

Index

Uncaptioned images:

Exclaim magazine logo, page 35, from http://www.shmooze.net/pwcasual/exclaim; *Hype* magazine logo, 36, http://www.phantom.com/~giant/hype.html; Spunkzine logo, 36, http://www.usyd.au/~mwoodman/spunk.html; Laurie Anderson, 75, http://www.voyagerco.com/LA/VgerLa.html; Tori Amos, 78, http://watt.seas.virginia.edu/~jds5s/music/tori/tori.html; The Beatles, 87, http://turtle.ncsa.uiuc.edu/alan/beatles/wtb-big.gif; Deborah Harry of Blondie, 88, http://www3.primenet.com/~lab/DHDeborahHarry.html; Jimmy Buffett, 90, http://www.homecom.com/buffett/; Bob Dylan, 97, http://rosa.nbr.no/users/karlerik/gif; Elvis Costello, 100, http://east.isx.com/~schnitzi/elvis.html; Dead Insignia, 104, http://nis-www.lanl.gov/~matt/grateful.html; Jerry Garcia, 106, http://wl.iglou.com/hippie/jgpass.htm; Flower, 107, http://nis-www.lanl.gov/~matt/grateful.html; Michael Jackson with Minnie Mouse, 118, http://www.primenet.com/~listen/photo.html; Julia Fordham, 122, http://www.comp.vuw.ac.nz/~ectophil/jules; Madonna in bath, 126, http://www. buffnet.net/~steve772/picts.html; Slash of Guns N' Roses, 128, http://www.teleport.com/~boerio/slash/images.html; Metallica, 134, http://www.galcit.caltech.edu/~aure/metallica/metallica.html; Nirvana, 143, http://www.deakin.edu.au/~benmo/nirvana1.gif; Kraftwerk, 145, http://www.cs.umu.se/tsdf/KRAFTWERK/; Pearl Jam, 152, http://www.blkbox.com/~clark15/pjimage.htm; Pink Floyd, 160, http://www.smartdocs.com/~migre.v/floyd/floydbs.gif; Elvis, 169, http://www.chron.com/voyager/elvis/gallery/index.html; Prince, 177, ftp://morra.et.tudelft.nl/pub/prince/jpg/portraits/versace5.jpg; R.E.M., 189, http://www.s-gimb.lj.edus.si/peter/rem/pics/rempics1.html; Rolling Stones Tongue, 195, http://www.stones.com/tongues/red-tongue.gif; U2, 206, http://www. med.virginia.edu/~njz7p/; Frank Zappa, 213, http://www.catalog.com/mrm/zappa/html/zimages.html; Sly Stone, 232, http://www.acpub.duke.edu/~eja/pics/sly.jpg; Speakers, 235, http://www.emedia.net/sovtek/CCatDocs/eminence.html; Virginia Pep Band, 305, http://www.virginia.edu/~pepband/; Reverend Al, 306, http://www.csua.berkekey.edu/~alpetrof/revival/; 137 Records logo, 320, http://www.coe.uncc.edu/~cmpilato/137.records/137.records.html; Alternative Tentacles logo, 320, http://iuma.southern.com/VIRUS/; Beatservice Records logo, 321, http://www.beatservice.no/beatservice/; Bedazzled Records logo, 321, http://www.iuma.com/Bedazzled; C/Z Records logo, 322, http://www.w2.com/cz.html; Cold Meat Industry logo, 322, http://www.etek.chalmers.se/~e2jovi3/cmi/cmi.html; Fish of Death Records logo, 324, http://www.cityscape.co.uk/ad69/fod/fodindex/html; Furnace Records logo, 325, http://www.cybercom.com/~bsamedi/furnace.html; Heyday Records logo, 326, http://www.iuma.com/heyday; K Records logo, 327, http://www.wln.com/~kpunk/; Piece of Mind Records logo, 328, http://www.bouquet.com/pom/; Pop Narcotic Records logo, 329, http://www.webcom.com/~popnarc/; Queenie Records logo, 329, http://www.shore.net/nonstop/queenie.html; Restless Records logo, 330, http://www.restless.com/; Silver Girl Records logo, 330, http://www.tumyeto.com/tydu/music/labels/silver/silver.html; Slumberland Records logo, 331, http://www.denizen.com/trout/slumberland/; Spanish Fly Records logo, 331, http://www.tt.net/spanishfly/; Squealer Music logo, 331, http://www.mam.com/~squealer/; Sub Pop Online logo, 332, http://www.subpop.com/; Twin/Tone Records logo, 332, http://www.twintone. com/; Vox Pop logo, 333, http://www.planet.it/voxpop.html; Sid Vicious, 334, http://www.yab.com:80/~stumbras/sex-pistols; Guitar silhouette, 334, http://129.131.19.85/m/52; Bristle, 335, http://www.blarg.com/~turmoil/bristle.jpg; Guitar silhouette, 335, http://129.131.19.85/m/52; Accordion, 341, http://www.mhs.mendocino.k12.ca.us; Guitar silhouette, 343, http://129.131.19.85/m/52; Orange amplifiers, 344, http://www.gibson.com/products/images/orange2.jpg; Steinway piano keyboard, 345, http://www.blackstar.com/stories/steinway/steinway5.html; Hardanger fiddle, 346, http://www.mhs.mendocino.k12.ca.us/MenComNet/Business/Retail/Larknet/BowedInstEurope

Michael Wolff & Company, Inc.

Michael Wolff & Company, Inc. is one of the leading providers of information about the Net and the emerging Net culture. The company's Net Books Series, presently at nine titles—*NetGuide, NetGames, NetChat, NetMoney, NetTrek, NetSports, NetTech, NetMusic*—will expand to more than 25 titles in 1996. This will include *NetTaxes, NetJobs, NetVote, Fodor's NetTravel,* and *NetMarketing.* The entire Net Books Series (to date) is now available on the company's Website YPN—Your Personal Network (http://www.ypn.com). And *Net Guide*—"the *TV Guide*™ to Cyberspace," according to *Wired* magazine editor Louis Rossetto—is now a monthly magazine published by CMP Publications.

Michael Wolff & Company was founded in 1988 by journalist Michael Wolff to bring together writers, editors, and graphic designers to create editorially and visually compelling information products in books, magazines, and new media. Among the company's other recent projects are *Where We Stand—Can America Make It in the Global Race for Wealth, Health, and Happiness?* (Bantam Books), one of the most graphically complex information books ever to be wholly created and produced by means of desktop-publishing technology, and *Made in America?,* a four-part PBS series on global competitiveness, hosted by Labor Secretary Robert B. Reich.

The company frequently acts as a consultant to other information companies, including WGBH, Boston's educational television station; CMP Publication; and Time Warner, which it has advised on the development of Time's online business and the launch of its Website, Pathfinder.

Managing editor Ben Greenman has written cultural criticism for many publications, including *TimeOut, Miami New Times,* the *Chicago Reader,* the *Village Voice,* and *Rolling Stone,* and in 1994 he led a team of intrepid Northwestern University graduate students to victory in the inaugural Rolling Stone Rock and Roll Trivia Bowl.

Websight

THE WORLD WIDE WEB MAGAZINE

Websight Magazine helps you explore the vast, uncharted World Wide Web.

As our title implies, Websight focuses exclusively on the Web. We bring

you feature articles from the foremost authorities on the Web. Think of us

as your travel magazine or "T.V. Guide" to the virtual Web wilderness.

Plus, our WebGuide section
features hundreds of the best
sites on the Web, sorted by subject!

http://websight.com

don't just get wired...

ON OCTOBER 1, 1995

IN CONJUNCTION WITH

Evolution Online Systems

AND

THE LINDEN MEDIA GROUP

Come @live!

@live: The Asian American Connection

DEBUTS...

METRO EAST'S FULL-SERVICE SITE ON THE WORLD WIDE WEB!

- BROWSE THROUGH <u>FULL-TEXT FEATURES</u> FROM THE CURRENT ISSUE OF *A. MAGAZINE*!

- BUY ALL THE ASIAN AND ASIAN AMERICAN GEAR YOU NEED...FROM HONG KONG ACTION FLICKS TO JAPANESE ANIMATION, CDs, BOOKS, MERCHANDISE, AND MORE AT <u>@MALL INTERACTIVE</u>—YOUR ONE-STOP WEB SHOP FOR ASIAN AMERICAN POP CULTURE!

- SEARCH AND DOWNLOAD INFORMATION FROM AN <u>ON-LINE DATABASE</u> OF DIRECTORIES, DEMOGRAPHIC DATA, ARCHIVED ABSTRACTS FROM BACK ISSUES OF *A.*, AND OTHER NEAT STUFF!

- CHECK OUT AN UPDATED <u>CALENDAR OF EVENTS</u>; READ THROUGH <u>CAPSULE REVIEWS</u> OF MUSIC, MOVIES, AND BOOKS...OR ADD YOUR OWN!

- GET YOUR VOICE HEARD, WITH TOPICAL <u>DISCUSSION GROUPS</u> ON HOT NEW ASIAN AMERICAN ISSUES!

- JUMP TO OTHER ASIAN AMERICAN SITES THROUGHOUT THE WEB WITH THE TOUCH OF A BUTTON—FROM THE MOST COMPREHENSIVE AND WELL-ORGANIZED <u>INDEX OF APA INTERNET RESOURCES</u> AROUND!

- AND EVEN GET SPECIAL <u>SNEAK PREVIEWS</u> OF OTHER METRO EAST PUBLICATION PROJECTS—BEFORE THEY HIT THE STANDS!

It's fun, it's informative...and best of all, it's absolutely free! What are you waiting for?

Point your browser at HTTP://WWW.AMAGAZINE.COM/ today!

Who is the world's number one music publisher?

If you guessed Time Warner, you're absolutely right. To find out more about Time Warner and other music moguls go to Hoover's Online, where you'll get free access to the **MasterList Plus database** of over 8,500 public and private U.S. companies.

Use the **MasterList Plus database** to:

- Search on one or more of the MasterList fields, including company name, ticker symbol, metropolitan area, sales, and industry

- Link to stock quotes, stock charts, SEC documents, corporate Web sites, and more

Other free feature areas on Hoover's Online include:

- A weekly featured industry group of companies from the **Hoover's Company Profiles database**

- The week's top business news

- Business bestsellers

- Pointers to corporate Web sites

Hoover's Online also offers a reasonably priced subscription-based service featuring the award-winning **Hoover's Company Profiles database.**

Come explore Hoover's Online at

http://www.hoovers.com

and experience the combination of:

- Valuable free information

- Powerful search and retrieval options

- Dynamic links to related information sources

- Access to the best company profiles anywhere

For more information contact **Matthew Manning** at matmanning@aol.com

Hoover's Business Resources are also available on:

AMERICA ONLINE

CompuServe

*e*World

The Microsoft Network

CompuServe
gives you the Internet.

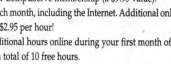